T5-ARD-677

MANAGEMENT INFORMATION SYSTEMS

Managing with Computers

MANAGEMENT INFORMATION SYSTEMS

Managing with Computers

Patrick G. McKeown
University of Georgia

Robert A. Leitch
University of South Carolina

The Dryden Press
Harcourt Brace Jovanovich College Publishers
Fort Worth   Philadelphia   San Diego   New York   Orlando   Austin   San Antonio
Toronto Montreal London Sydney Tokyo

Editor in Chief: Robert A. Pawlik
Acquisitions Editor: Richard Bonacci
Developmental Editor: Ruth Rominger
Project Editor: Sue A. Lister
Assistant Project Editor: Cathy Spitzenberger
Production Manager: Jacqui Parker
Book Designer: Diana Jean Parks
Photo/Permissions Editor: Steve Lunetta

Cover Photo: Copyright © 1992 Dick Patrick

Copyright © 1993 by Harcourt Brace Jovanovich, Inc.

All rights reserved. No part of this publication may be reproduced or transmitted in any form or by any means, electronic or mechanical, including photocopy, recording, or any information storage and retrieval system, without permission in writing from the publisher.

Requests for permission to make copies of any part of the work should be mailed to: Permissions Department, Harcourt Brace Jovanovich College Publishers, Orlando, FL 32887.

Address for Editorial Correspondence
The Dryden Press, 301 Commerce Street, Suite 3700, Fort Worth, TX 76102

Address for Orders
The Dryden Press, 6277 Sea Harbor Drive, Orlando, FL 32887
1-800-782-4479, or 1-800-433-0001 (in Florida)

ISBN: 0-15-500112-4

Library of Congress Catalogue Number: 92-72917

Printed in the United States of America

2 3 4 5 6 7 8 9 0 1   039   9 8 7 6 5 4 3 2 1

The Dryden Press
Harcourt Brace Jovanovich

To my mother, Jane E. McKeown

P.G.M.

To my wife, Paula, and my two sons, Rob and Adam

R.A.L.

The Dryden Press Series in Information Systems

Arthur Andersen & Co./Flaatten, McCubbrey, O'Riordan, and Burgess
Foundations of Business Systems, Second Edition

Arthur Andersen & Co./Boynton and Shank
Foundations of Business Systems: Projects and Cases

Anderson
Structured Programming Using Turbo Pascal: A Brief Introduction, Second Edition

Bradley
Introduction to Data Base Management in Business, Second Edition

Brown and McKeown
Structured Programming with Microsoft BASIC

Carney
Advanced Structured BASIC for the IBM PC

Coburn
Advanced Structured COBOL

Coburn
Beginning Structured COBOL

Dean and Effinger
Common–Sense BASIC: Structured Programming with Microsoft QuickBASIC

Electronic Learning Facilitators, Inc.
The DOS Book

Electronic Learning Facilitators, Inc.
The Lotus 1-2-3 Book

Electronic Learning Facilitators, Inc.
Stepping Through Excel 4.0 for Windows

Electronic Learning Facilitators, Inc.
Stepping Through Harvard Graphics for Windows

Electronic Learning Facilitators, Inc.
Stepping Through Windows 3.1

Electronic Learning Facilitators, Inc.
Stepping Through Word for Windows

Electronic Learning Facilitators, Inc.
Working Smarter with DOS 5.0

Electronic Learning Facilitators, Inc.
Working with WordPerfect 5.0

Electronic Learning Facilitators, Inc.
Working with WordPerfect 5.1

Ellis and Lodi
Structured Programming Using True BASIC

Federico
WordPerfect 5.1 Primer

Goldstein Software, Inc.
Joe Spreadsheet, Macintosh Version

Goldstein Software, Inc.
Joe Spreadsheet, Statistical

Harrington
Making Database Management Work

Harrington
Microsoft Works: A Window to Computing

Harrington
Relational Database Management for Microcomputers: Design and Implementation

Laudon and Laudon
Business Information Systems: A Problem-Solving Approach, Second Edition

Laudon, Laudon, and Weill
The Integrated Solution

Lawlor
Computer Information Systems, Second Edition

Lawlor
Introducing BASIC: A Structured Approach

Liebowitz
The Dynamics of Decision Support Systems and Expert Systems

McKeown
Living with Computers, Fourth Edition

McKeown
Living with Computers with BASIC, Fourth Edition

McKeown
Working with Computers

McKeown
Working with Computers with Software Tutorials

McKeown and Leitch
Management Information Systems: Managing with Computers

Martin and Burstein
Computer Systems Fundamentals

Martin and Parker
Mastering Today's Software with DOS, WordPerfect 5.0/5.1, Lotus 1-2-3, dBASE III PLUS (or dBASE IV)

Martin and Parker
Mastering Today's Software with DOS, WordPerfect 5.0/5.1, Lotus 1-2-3, dBASE III PLUS (or dBASE IV) and BASIC

Mason
Using IBM Microcomputers in Business:
Decision Making with Lotus 1-2-3 and dBASE III PLUS (or dBASE IV)

O'Brien
The Nature of Computers

Parker
A Beginner's Guide to BASIC

Parker
Computers and Their Applications, Third Edition

Parker
Computers and Their Applications with Productivity Software Tools, Third Edition

Parker
Microcomputers: Concepts and Applications

Parker
Productivity Software Guide, Fourth Edition

Parker
Understanding Computers and Information Processing: Today and Tomorrow, Fourth Edition

Parker
Understanding Computers and Information Processing: Today and Tomorrow with BASIC, Fourth Edition

Robertson and Robertson
Microcomputer Applications and Programming: A Complete Computer Course with DOS, WordPerfect 5.1, Lotus 1-2-3, dBASE III PLUS (or dBASE IV) and BASIC

Robertson and Robertson
Using Microcomputer Applications (A Series of Computer Manuals)

Roche
Telecommunications and Business Strategy

Swafford and Haff
dBASE III PLUS

The HBJ College Outline Series

Kreitzberg
Introduction to BASIC

Kreitzberg
Introduction to Fortran

Pierson
Introduction to Business Information Systems

Veklerov and Pekelny
Computer Language C

P R E F A C E

Information-based organizations are becoming increasingly more prevalent in business, industry, and government. This type of organization will continue to grow throughout the 1990s and into the twenty-first century, when power will reside with those who possess the information that will ensure the continued well-being of the organization. To exercise the power of information, employees must know how to use it to manage their respective organizations effectively in a highly competitive economy.

Information-based organizations emerged in the tremendous wake of wide-spread availability of computing power. As recently as ten years ago, only certain persons in the organization benefited from the use of computers. Whereas today, technology exists to provide information to anyone who needs it in the organization. Indeed, it is predicted that the traditional pyramidal structure of the organization will crumble as the computer transforms all employees into managers by providing them with information that will allow them to make individual decisions about their jobs.

Organizations of all sizes are recognizing that they must better manage their information to gain strategic advantages over their competitors. Effectively managing this information usually involves the use of computer-based information systems. Today, most managers understand the importance of information systems and have learned that it is virtually impossible to manage their organizations without some knowledge of information systems.

Approach   Knowledge of information systems is crucial to business and economics students as they prepare to join tomorrow's workforce. The goal of *Management Information Systems: Managing with Computers* is to help students understand the types of information systems organizations actually use today and how the numerous challenges that confront organizations affect the development, implementation, and management of information systems. This textbook is designed for introductory management information systems (MIS) courses at both the undergraduate and MBA levels. It deals not only with the theoretical aspects of these challenging issues but incorporates real-life examples, applications, and cases.

A key pedagogical element of *Management Information Systems* is the ProYacht, Inc., case, which is used throughout the textbook to demonstrate the various concepts discussed in each chapter. ProYacht builds and markets various sizes of sailboats. The first chapters focus on the divisions of ProYacht and how each division uses information systems. As the text advances, we see ProYacht taking over other companies, which requires it to develop, acquire, manage, and control new information systems.

Besides the ProYacht case, the textbook contains over 50 boxed inserts that provide students with insightful examples of how actual organizations use, develop, and control information systems. Finally, there are an average of two major cases (a total of 36) at the end of each chapter. Each case focuses on the chapter material and encourages the student to synthesize, and therefore better understand, the ideas and information presented in the chapter.

Organization

The textbook is divided into five sections. Section I, "The Information Resource," is an introduction. It discusses competitive uses of information, types of information systems, and decision-making concepts. Chapter 1 covers the importance of information as a competitive resource, and Chapter 2 provides the reader with a survey of the types of information systems at work in a modern organization. Chapter 3 discusses various decision-making activities that require information support and includes an introduction to the tools and concepts used in developing information systems.

Section II, "Information System Resources," discusses the various resources critical to the success of any information system. Chapter 4 focuses on computer hardware and software resources that are used in information systems. Chapters 5 and 6 provide complete coverage of file and data base management systems, and Chapter 7 discusses the importance of networks and telecommunications to any successful information system.

Section III, "Managing with Information Systems," details the various information systems surveyed in Chapter 2. Chapter 8 focuses on transaction processing systems (TPSs), which convert raw data into usable form. Chapter 9 discusses management information systems (MISs), which provide many reports to all levels of management. Chapter 10 covers decision support systems (DSSs) and executive information systems (EISs), which are crucial managerial decision-making tools. Finally, Chapter 11 focuses on artificial intelligence (AI) and expert systems (ESs), which further aid managerial decision making.

Section IV, "Developing and Acquiring Information System Resources," discusses the important topic of information system development and acquisition. Chapter 12 covers the feasibility study and structured analysis phases of the process, and Chapter 13 focuses on the structured design and implementation phases. Chapter 14 provides instruction on the acquisition of hardware and software, and Chapter 15 discusses various alternative approaches to systems development.

Section V, "Managing the Information Resource," covers important aspects of managing and controlling information systems. Chapter 16 discusses the management of all elements of the information system—human resources, data, hardware, software, and operations. Chapter 17 discusses control and security of information systems and various aspects of computer crime. Finally, Chapter 18 focuses on the future of information systems.

Pedagogy

Each chapter begins with a chapter outline and introduction and, as we mentioned earlier, contains the ProYacht case, which is used as an example throughout the textbook, and boxed inserts that describe how known organizations use information systems. Each chapter concludes with a summary of the chapter, a list of the key terms discussed in the chapter, 15 review questions, and several discussion questions. Finally, most chapters end with two cases, many of which describe actual situations. The cases require the student to integrate his or her understanding of the chapter material.

Supplemental Material

Several supplemental items are available to adopters of *Management Information Systems: Managing with Computers,* including an instructor's manual, a computer lab manual, and a short introduction to the Pascal computer language appropriate for business and information systems students.

For each chapter in the textbook, the *Instructor's Manual for Management Information Systems* by Patrick G. McKeown and Robert A. Leitch has a corresponding chapter composed of the following teaching aids: teaching objective, learning objective, chapter outline, annotated list of boxed inserts, chapter review, list of teaching suggestions, annotated list of suggested readings, answers to review and discussion questions, suggested solution to the cases, and a glossary of keywords.

A computer lab manual is available for adopters who wish to include in their courses tutorials on the following software packages: MS-DOS, WordPerfect 5.1 for DOS, Lotus 1-2-3 Version 2.2 or above, and dBASE III Plus. The *Computer Lab Manual* by Patrick G. McKeown and Ravija Badarinathi is now available separately or shrink-wrapped with the textbook. The lab manual is divided into Sessions that cover the fundamentals of using each of the four types of software and includes keystroke-by-keystroke instructions, *Try it Yourself* exercises after each section, and exercises at the end of each Session.

Structured Programming Using Turbo Pascal, by Margaret Anderson, provides a short introduction to the Turbo Pascal computer language. It is divided into six chapters and includes *Try it Yourself* exercises after each section and exercises at the end of each chapter.

Acknowledgments

If you are familiar with writing and producing a package such as this, you know that the product is not just the work of the authors, but the result of a team effort. The team for *Management Information Systems: Managing with Computers* included many talented people. We are grateful for their many contributions and hard work.

While writing the text, we received help on numerous technical aspects of the computer from Andrew Seila of the College of Business Administration at the University of

Georgia. Dr. Dennis Calbos of the Administrative Data Processing Department at the University of Georgia aided us greatly in preparing the systems chapters. We are very appreciative to both of them for their help.

We wish to express our appreciation to those who carefully reviewed the manuscript as well as those who participated in our focus group and thank them for their thought-provoking comments. The final text reflects many of their ideas. The reviewers and focus group participants include Gary R. Armstrong, Shippensburg University; Kirk P. Arnett, Mississippi State University; Warren J. Boe, The University of Iowa; Susan I. Brender, Boise State University; Darrell Brown, University of Utah; William E. Burrows, University of Washington; Chandler M. Bush, University of North Carolina at Charlotte; Michael Davis, Lehigh University; Leopoldo A. Gemoets, University of Texas at El Paso; Tom Hilton, Utah State University; John A. Lehman, University of Alaska Fairbanks; M. Khris McAlister, University of Alabama at Birmingham; David J. Nelson, University of San Francisco; Joan K. Pierson, James Madison University; John V. Quigley, East Tennessee State University; Scott H. Rupple, Marquette University; David Scanlon, California State University at Sacramento; and James B. Shannon, New Mexico State University.

We would like to thank those at The Dryden Press who were involved in editing and producing this textbook. First, we express thanks to Peggy Monahan for her outstanding copyedit. Ruth Rominger developed the project and we are appreciative of her efforts. Thanks to our project editor and assistant project editor, Sue Lister and Cathy Spitzenberger; to designer Diana Jean Parks; and to production manager Jacqui Parker. Richard Bonacci has our gratitude for his editorial work in the initial development of this textbook and for being patient with us.

Finally, our acknowledgments would be incomplete without mention of our wives, Carolyn McKeown and Paula Leitch, and families. Without their love and support, we could not have completed this project.

CONTENTS

3 Decision Making and Information Systems   54

SECTION II
Information System Resources

4 Computer Resources   86

5 Data and File Resources

118

6 Data Base Systems

142

SECTION III
Managing with Information Systems

SECTION IV
Developing and Acquiring
Information System Resources

12 Structured Systems Development: Definition and Analysis   354

SECTION V

Managing the Information Resource

16 Management of Information Systems   496

17 Controls in Information Systems   526

18 The Future of Information Systems

Glossary

Index

I

The Information Resource

Section I introduces the information resource and the competitive uses of information in organizations. It provides an
overview of the importance of computers
and information systems to organizations
of all sizes. Chapter 1 introduces the information resource, and Chapter 2 describes
the types of information systems used in
many organizations. Chapter 3 discusses
decision making in the organization and
introduces the process of developing information systems.

The Information Revolution

C H A P T E R

1

Introduction

Over 100 years ago, the industrial revolution changed the way companies were run. Small cottage industries were overshadowed by large companies that could take advantage of economies of scale in mass producing goods. Size and efficiency became the determinants of success that created industrial giants in steel making, transportation, and oil production, for example. Manufacturing enterprises, which constituted approximately one-third of the economy before 1869, accounted for over one-half the economic production by 1899. The U.S. economy showed tremendous gains during this period, with the gross national product increasing sixfold. People were keenly aware that they lived in a new age—an age of factories, machines, and railroads—and that a great potential existed for additional increases in a company's size and efficiency.

During the industrial revolution, the mechanization of industry led to a reduced reliance on human strength to carry out production tasks. Machines run by humans could do the same work with less effort. To take advantage of mechanization, new forms of business organization and methods of modern management were developed. Many of the ideas that were developed during the industrial revolution have been used for the last 100 years.

We are now in an **information revolution.** More and more, an organization's success is a function of its information resources and how effectively it uses these resources to compete in today's dynamic environment. No longer is bigger better. Today, smarter is often better. Today, management can access vast amounts of data and use sophisticated models to make better and more informed decisions. They can process data in a more timely manner to control operations. They can communicate over world-wide networks to manage global enterprises. They can even use the computer to make decisions.

According to management expert Peter Drucker, **information-based organizations** will become more and more prevalent in business, industry, and government. In an information-based organization, power resides with those who have the information. The key to the emerging strength of information-based organizations is the tremendous explosion in the availability of computing power. Today, this computational power is disbursed throughout the organization. This enables managers at all levels to manage with the help of a computer-based information system (CBIS). This widespread availability of computing power means that managers need not depend on manual systems or hand computations based on periodic reports to manage their organizations. Instead, they can easily use a desk-top computer to access a wealth of data and assess various alternatives in arriving at a more informed decision.

These new information-based organizations will look quite different from the traditional pyramidal structure, with layers of middle managers. Many of these managers were essentially information-processing personnel. By providing information directly to operating personnel, via computer systems, they can make informed decisions without the need for many middle managers to disseminate information. Also, with newer systems, top management can have instant access to current information for decision making without the need for middle managers to gather and process it. As a result, new technology has placed information directly in the hands of users and not in the hands of a few computer experts who prepared reports for use in the past. Thus, some predict a much flatter organization structure where the gap between operations and top management is much smaller.

The Role of Computers

A crucial element in the information revolution is the use of computers and other smart machines in our economy. **Computers** are electronic machines that can accept raw facts called **data** and, based on instructions from the user, convert the data into usable **information,** as shown in Figure 1–1. Computers can also store data and information for future reference. Today, over 100 million computers of all sizes are used in our economy, with this number growing every day. Just as the industrial revolution was built on the widespread availability of mechanized tools, the information revolution is built on the computer.

The data used in generating information have many sources. **Internal data** are generated by the daily activities of the organization as it produces its goods and services and interacts with vendors and customers. This type of data is also referred to as **transactional data.** Converting transactional data into information is very important to most organizations because such data provide essential information about an organization's current and past activities. Many older systems concentrated entirely on this aspect of the information system. Now, in addition to the operating statistics normally needed to process a particular transaction, **external data** are gathered via various industry, market, and economic studies and services to which an organization may subscribe. External data may also be generated by surveying customers through market research.

Smart Machines

While we often think of a computer in the form of a personal computer or a computer terminal on a desk, computers are at the heart of many other smart machines that we use every day. A **smart machine** not only carries out operations to reduce human labor, but

FIGURE 1–1

Processing Data into Information

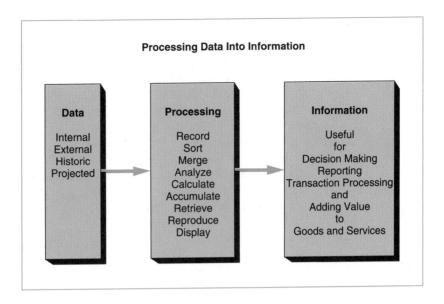

Processing Data Into Information

Data	Processing	Information
Internal External Historic Projected	Record Sort Merge Analyze Calculate Accumulate Retrieve Reproduce Display	Useful for Decision Making Reporting Transaction Processing and Adding Value to Goods and Services

also provides information about these operations. For example, the obvious use of a store checkout scanner is to speed the entry of product code numbers which are linked to prices, allowing the customer to spend less time shopping. These scanners also instantaneously adjust for price changes, record the amount of the sale for future analysis, and reduce product inventory by the number of each item sold. The **transactions** generated from this system can be used to determine the impact of various promotional schemes by collecting data on the products sold, when they are sold, and in what location they are sold. Similarly, an **Automatic Teller Machine (ATM)** can verify checking or savings account balances, supply cash (if the balance is sufficient), accept deposits, and update accounts for a bank hundreds or thousands of miles away.

A decade ago, workers worried about being replaced by robots and computerized manufacturing equipment. In many cases, the exact opposite has occurred—employees not only have *not* been replaced by machines, many have found their jobs made more meaningful by the introduction of smart machines. Many workers today are given more responsibility and authority to deal with problems or make production line decisions that were once reserved for supervisory personnel. They do more than just run machines; they also collect and process data on quality control, inventory, and shipments. The result of this change is an **informated factory,** in which machines not only perform some operation, but they also supply workers with information on the processing operations.

The Information Society

The capability of smart machines to provide information as well as to carry out a user's instructions has made our society dependent on them. This increasing dependence on smart machines was predicted by noted authority John Naisbitt in his books *Megatrends, Reinventing the Corporation,* and *Megatrends 2000.* In these books, Naisbitt discusses the evolution of the U.S. economy from an agricultural society to an industrial society to an **information society,** which he defines as an economy and society built on the transfer

Smart Workers for Smart Machines

As an example of an informated factory, consider the General Electric (G.E.) Salisbury, NC, factory. At this highly automated plant, it was decided in 1984 that factory floor bottlenecks could be reduced by giving workers the information and power to make decisions to keep the manufacturing process running. As a result, workers are largely unsupervised and make their own production and scheduling decisions. A machine operator with a problem can now talk directly to manufacturing engineers about problem solutions or can order machine parts without prior management approval. Employees also serve on committees to hire new workers in the plant. The result of G.E.'s use of smart workers with smart machines has been a 10-fold decrease in customer delivery time, a reduction in employee turnover, a two-thirds reduction in the number of hours per production unit, and an increase in the market share.

SOURCE: Doron P. Levin, "Smart Machines, Smart Workers," *New York Times,* October 17, 1988, pp. 25–29.

of information. He notes that in 1950, only 17 percent of all Americans were involved in information jobs (for example, teachers, programmers, analysts, clerks, bureaucrats, and accountants). In 1983, this number had risen to over 65 percent. In 1985, the information industry made up 3.3 percent of the Gross National Product (GNP). It has also been predicted that the information industry will be the largest in the world by 1995, making up 6 percent of the GNP. Furthermore, the data processing and communications industry, which was a $300 million industry as recently as 1987, may become a $1 *trillion* industry in the 1990s.[1] Figure 1–2 shows how our economy has changed during the last 100 years and how it is predicted to move in the future.

Information Systems

In today's economy, most organizations, whether public or private, profit or nonprofit, have some form of information system that contributes to the efficient management of the organization's resources and achievement of its objectives. An **information system (IS)** is the combination of computers and users that manages the transformation of data into information and the storage of data and information. These information systems and their use in organizations are the subject of this text. This chapter is an introduction to the value of information and how information is used in organizations. Chapter 2 provides an introduction to information systems in organizations.

1.1 The Value of Information

For modern organizations, information is an important asset to be used in the implementation of a firm's strategic initiatives. Of all the assets of an organization—including personnel, financial capital, and plant and equipment—information is by far the most valuable, because it alone describes these physical resources and the world in which they exist. Having physical resources without information about them is of little use, because the organization cannot use the resources effectively to achieve its objectives.

---

[1] William R. Synnott, *The Information Weapon* (New York: John Wiley & Sons, 1987), p. 3.

FIGURE 1–2

***Direction of the
U.S. Economy***

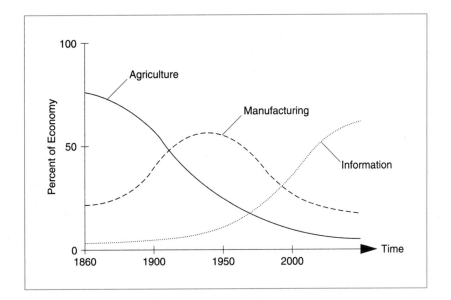

In addition to a description of physical resources, other types of information are essential to any organization. For example, a simple list of clients and customers is the lifeblood of any organization. Without this information, the organization cannot contact those whom it seeks to serve. Similarly, an organization needs information about suppliers and subcontractors so it can order raw materials and parts. External information about its environment is essential to any organization. In today's global economy, successful companies must be aware of the competition's activities, new products on the market, and the availability of needed resources.

Given the value of information, it must be carefully acquired, managed, and utilized like any other organization asset. Furthermore, as the size of the organization increases, management depends more on information rather than on personal observation or contact to manage operations or deal with customers or suppliers.

*The Impact of
Technology*

The past decade has seen a tremendous explosion of **information technology.** This new technology has significantly changed facets of many organizations, including management practices, delivery of goods and services, and information processing for managerial use. Managers can use information in ways not previously considered. First, more data can be processed more rapidly, thus allowing managers access to more information than possible several years ago. Managers can now expect daily inventory reports instead of waiting for weekly or monthly manual counts. Second, managers can track key business indicators in ways that were not feasible several years ago. For example, various stock market indices can be followed on a minute-by-minute basis, facilitating stock trades based on small but important differences between indices. Finally, managers can analyze problems in much more sophisticated ways for more enlightened decision making. For example, financial managers now commonly use computers in decisions on potential mergers and acquisitions.

1.2 Using the Information Resource

Like any other asset, information must be used to have any value for the organization. In addition to the day-to-day use of information for operational purposes, it can also be used to dramatically change the way entire companies and industries do business. In other words, information can be used *strategically.* Information can be used to create competitive advantages, alter the competitive balance between companies, change the nature of industries, and spawn new business for many organizations.[2]

The potential for using information strategically is great; at the same time, the result of not using it can be catastrophic. An organization's survival may depend on its strategic use of information.

ProYacht, Inc.

As an example of a company that may need to use information strategically, consider a hypothetical firm, ProYacht, Inc. ProYacht manufactures small- to medium-sized (up to 30 feet long) sailboats for the growing market of young professionals interested in sailing as a leisure activity. The sailboats are sold through dealers located primarily on the Atlantic and Gulf Coasts, around the Great Lakes, and in major cities in the eastern half of the United States. Located in Annapolis, MD, ProYacht currently employs approximately 400 workers who are involved in design and engineering, production, marketing and sales, and administration. Currently, ProYacht produces an 18-foot day sailer and sloops in five lengths—22, 25, 27, 28, and 30 feet—at the rate of over 23 boats per day in two production shifts. Sails are purchased from another company also located in Annapolis.

Business for ProYacht has been good, with gross revenues in excess of $50 million last year and an annual payroll of $10 million. Table 1–1 shows ProYacht's production, revenue, and cost figures for last year. ProYacht's management realizes that the company must find new markets and improve its production process if it is to remain prosperous.

The organization of ProYacht, Inc. is shown in Figure 1–3. Note that the company currently has four divisions—sailboat operations, parts, service, and ProYacht Acceptance. The corporate office includes the executive offices as well as the finance, personnel, and payroll departments. The sailboat operations division handles the actual manufacturing and marketing of ProYacht's primary product—sailboats. The parts division handles the distribution of marine components and parts for sailboats produced by ProYacht as well as for various types of boats produced by other manufacturers. The service division provides technical support for dealers who carry ProYacht boats and for customers who buy them. Finally, the ProYacht Acceptance division finances both dealers who carry ProYacht boats in inventory and customers who purchase these boats.

The types of information systems currently in place at ProYacht are discussed in Chapter 2, and the computer hardware and software used in ProYacht's information systems are discussed in Chapter 4. In subsequent chapters, we discuss ProYacht's use of information and the changes in ProYacht's information systems as it expands its business and seeks to improve existing operations.

---

[2] See Ives, B. and G.P. Learmonth, "Information as a Competitive Weapon," *Communication of ACM,* December, 1984, pp. 1193–1201 and Michael E. Porter, *Competitive Advantage* (New York: Free Press, 1985) for a complete discussion of these uses of information.

TABLE 1–1

***ProYacht, Inc.
Production,
Revenue, and Cost
Figures for Last
Year***

Sail Boat Length	Wholesale Price	Annual Sales	Wholesale Sales Dollars	Average Daily Production	Payroll Costs (20.00%)*
18	$ 3472	2000	$ 6,944,000	10	$ 1,388,800
22	8000	1000	8,000,000	5	1,600,000
25	16000	750	12,000,000	3.75	2,400,000
27	22800	500	11,400,000	2.5	2,280,000
28	28000	250	7,000,000	1.25	1,400,000
30	33600	150	5,040,000	0.75	1,008,000
Total		4650	$50,384,000	23.25	$10,076,800

Average Wholesale Price $10,835

Average Salary ($10,076,800/400 employees) $25,192

---

* Hourly = 15% and Adminstrative = 5%

*Managing
Day-to-Day
Operations*

Management needs to make good use of information on a daily basis to manage its operations successfully. Management has only a limited set of personnel and financial and physical resources at its disposal to achieve the organization's objectives in terms of delivering products or services to its customers or clients. To compete in today's economy, these resources must be used effectively and efficiently to accomplish these objec-

FIGURE 1–3

***Organization
Chart for
ProYacht, Inc.***

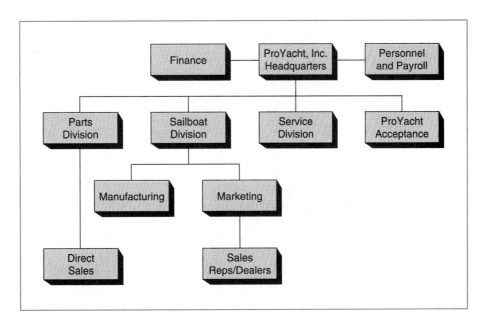

tives. Thus, sound planning is required to ensure the proper utilization of these resources. For example, production orders must be carefully scheduled to deliver products on a timely basis. Preparing such a schedule requires information on material and machine availability, knowledge of production orders in process, operations lists, and required materials. Moreover, appropriate feedback information on daily operations is essential to ensure the efficient use of these resources.

In the ProYacht sailboat division, information on the current status of orders, actual time and material used, actual number of boats produced, and actual costs is needed to monitor the progress of production orders. If the production process deviates significantly from the plan, management must determine if the problems are due to an inefficient production process or whether some other type of problem has occurred.

Creating
Competitive
Advantage

In the past, the major competitive weapons used by organizations were usually related to product characteristics or market savvy. With the increase in computer processing power available to organizations, we can expect information to be used more as an aggressive competitive weapon.

Information can be used to create a **competitive advantage** for a company in several ways, including reducing costs, differentiating products, linking the customer with the company's information system, adding value to the company's product, or some combination of these tactics. In many cases, information that is already available to the company as a result of information processing can be used as a competitive weapon. It usually requires only a manager with vision to see how the information can be used.

Cost reduction is an important objective because it enables a company to provide its product or service at a lower, more competitive price. A key cost component for most nonservice industries is inventory—that is, raw materials, work-in-process, and finished goods that are held by the company. Because inventory ties up cash and storage space, reducing inventory is often a way of reducing costs. One way in which information is used to reduce inventory is a **Just-in-Time (JIT) system.** A JIT system informs vendors when supplies are needed so that they are shipped and arrive ''just in time'' for utilization in the production process. Consequently, inventory costs are greatly reduced and flexibility is increased because only those parts and components actually needed for current production are in the supply channel. For example, a large warehouse is not kept full of raw materials and various components that might be needed for future production.

To continue our example, ProYacht has developed a JIT system that links the company to its suppliers and its dealers. On the supply side, ProYacht does not take delivery of sails from a vendor until just before a boat is test-sailed. Similarly, the diesel engines that are installed for auxiliary power are not delivered until this same time. On the dealer side, since ProYacht has restricted itself to the eastern half of the country, it can promise three-day delivery of boats to dealers when orders are received. This allows the company to have fewer production runs for larger boats and to produce them when they have already been sold, rather than building up an inventory of larger boats. Because the 18-foot day sailer and the 22-foot sloop are in high demand, these two sailboats are produced for inventory on a regular basis.

A company can obtain a competitive advantage by differentiating its products from those of its competitors in such a way that they are more useful to customers. An important component of any decision on how to differentiate a product is information about customer needs. For example, a large computer systems firm can use an information system to select the most appropriate configuration of computer components to meet its customers' needs. As a result, their product is differentiated from those of its competitors because it is customized to meet the precise requirements of its customers.

An organization can create a competitive advantage by tying its information system to its customers' product life cycle. This entails helping the customer with physical and support systems, including such activities as determination of the appropriate market in which to compete, product development, component and raw materials ordering, manufacturing of a product or the delivery of a service, management of inventory, material and product testing, and product marketing and distribution. For example, a company can provide the use of a computerized design service to help a customer add value to a generic product. By tying the use of the design service to the purchase of raw materials, the customer is locked into using the company providing the service.

Increasing the information component of a product or service is also a use of information for competitive advantage. For example, a pharmacy can provide its customers with itemized records of yearly drug purchases to assist them with income tax preparation. Another example would be the establishment of a toll-free telephone line to assist customers in using a company's computer hardware or software products.

In general, any way in which an organization's information system helps customers can provide a competitive advantage. For example, ProYacht might gain a competitive advantage in the sailboat market by providing a video instruction tape to buyers on the finer points of sailing a ProYacht sailboat. This type of service might build customer loyalty and increase the probability of a repeat sale. However, as with any product or service, efforts to build a competitive advantage will never overcome a lack of quality in the product. For this reason, ProYacht has also sought to develop a tradition of building easy-to-sail, high quality sailboats that have a high resale value.

Altering the Competitive Balance

According to B. Ives and G.P. Learmonth,[3] information can be used to alter the competitive balance among companies in three areas — customer services, supplier relations, and product development. In customer services, information can be used to provide a unique service. For example, daily delivery of parts to an organization using a JIT system is a customer service that can favor one company over another. Information can be used in supplier relations to communicate directly with suppliers on the quality and quantity of components needed for manufacturing so that only the amount of product components needed arrive at the factory. Similarly, for product development, a survey of customers can reveal their desires for product modifications, information that can give a company an advantage over the competition.

[3] Ives, B. and G.P. Learmonth, "Information as a Competitive Weapon," *Communications in ACM,* December 1984, pp. 1193–1201.

Examples of Information as a Competitive Weapon

Successful uses of information for a competitive advantage include a large toy manufacturer, two national airlines, a health products provider, and a software developer. Coleco Industries, which marketed the Cabbage Patch Doll series, maintained a list of information on each doll that was sold. With this information, the company sent each purchaser a birthday card for the doll, a strategy that inspired customer loyalty and spurred additional sales.

Both American and United Airlines established computerized reservation systems that gave priority listings to their flights whenever travel agents requested information. By 1984, these two carriers had locked up 80 percent of the computerized travel business and had effectively raised their competitors' costs because they charged other carriers to be included on either reservation system.

Baxter Hospital Supply Corporation now dominates the hospital supply business thanks to an information system it implemented in hospitals across the country. Terminals installed in each hospital provide direct access to a computerized order-entry system through which hospital staff can order any Baxter's product.

WordPerfect Corporation has maintained the loyalty of its many customers by providing an extensive system of toll-free telephone numbers. These telephone lines are monitored by knowledgeable employees who can help solve users' problems with any WordPerfect word processing product.

Changing Industry Structure

Michael Porter[4] identifies the five major **competitive forces** in an industry as shown in Figure 1–4. Information can significantly alter each of these components—rivalry among existing competitors, threat of new entrants into the market, pressure from substitute products, bargaining power of suppliers, and bargaining power of customers.

Information systems that provide for automated order processing and billing make companies more efficient in those areas. Rivalry among competitors increases because when one company implements such a system, others need it as well to compete effectively and to process orders in a timely manner.

Some banks provide their customers with ready access to account information and automated checking via home computers. Because the computer programs required to run these systems are expensive, they tend to pose a tremendous barrier for new entrants into the banking business in the metropolitan areas where these systems exist.

Computer-Aided Design (CAD) in manufacturing industries facilitates the quick entry of substitute products into the market. CAD enables engineers, managers, and industrial sales personnel to interact with various design features to develop the best product at the lowest cost. As a result, a company no longer has time on its side before new competing

---

[4] Porter, Michael E., *Competitive Advantage* (New York, Free Press, 1985).

FIGURE 1–4

*Competitive
Forces*

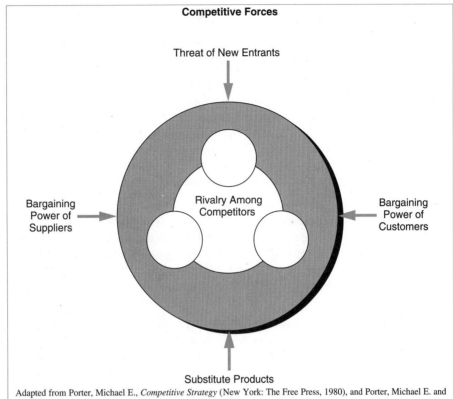

Competitive Forces

Threat of New Entrants

Bargaining Power of Suppliers

Rivalry Among Competitors

Bargaining Power of Customers

Substitute Products

Adapted from Porter, Michael E., *Competitive Strategy* (New York: The Free Press, 1980), and Porter, Michael E. and Victor E. Millar, "How Information Gives You Competitive Advantage," *Harvard Business Review,* July–August 1985, p. 153.

products are designed and introduced. In other words, product life cycles have been reduced significantly via CAD. For example, ProYacht's early use of CAD in sailboat design has contributed to overall customer satisfaction and reduced the lead time to develop new products.

Computerized vendor files for even the smallest companies have made the search for the most reasonable price and delivery schedule easier. This, in turn, gives companies a better bargaining position with suppliers and reduces their overall operating costs.

Computerized customer lists enable a company to target customers with promotional material and to customize products for particular customer tastes. As an example, the structure of the life insurance industry has been modified through the expanded availability of information to agents. To compete successfully today, a company's agents must access client information contained on a large corporate computer system and then analyze a customer's policy needs using a personal computer.

In general, because of information availability, the competitive boundaries now include the entire value chain (the supplier, the organization itself, the distribution channels, and the customer). Changes in this chain can profoundly affect the balance of power in supplier–purchaser relationships.

Spawning New Business

An organization can utilize the power of the computer and the information it produces to create a new business or a spin-off division from its existing business. Only a highly creative management can transform otherwise unused information into competitive advantage for the organization. For example, assume ProYacht decides to enter a new area of the expanding aquatics recreational industry (say, by producing and marketing windsurfers). The company could make current sailboat customers aware of the new products by using the information customers supply on the warranty cards they return.

As another example of the use of information for new purposes, consider the automated checkout lanes at a grocery store. Not only do these lanes speed the purchase process, but the tapes produced generate detailed information on the items purchased. This information can be used by consumer testing companies, which pay customers for the privilege of analyzing their checkout tapes. As a result of such an analysis, a company may change its product mix.

1.3 The Role of Management in the Organization

According to Henri Fayol,[5] the role of management is to plan, organize, staff, direct, and control the activities of an organization. To accomplish these tasks in a modern organization, information is essential. Management may use such quantitative techniques as accounting and marketing research to measure current activities and to plan for the future. Whether the techniques involve the use of statistical analysis or other mathematical methods to develop better forecasts, all make extensive use of information. Managers also need vast amounts of information on production, sales, and finances to control the organization's daily activities. The information system management develops must fit the company's organizational and strategic needs.

Managers must be cognizant of human and organizational behavior to accomplish their role. For example, to better control an organization, management may develop and implement a new computerized accounting system. As part of the process, management must ensure that the employees who implement the new system are not threatened by it and that end users are adequately trained to interpret the information generated by the new accounting system.

In addition to these activities, managers actually do a wide variety of other things. In many cases, managers act as organization leaders, information centers (users and providers of information), and decision makers. According to a well-known study of managerial roles by Henry Mintzberg,[6] every day a manager faces many different tasks, often requiring frequent switching from one activity to another. Mintzberg's managerial model also involves a network of contacts and the constant use of verbal communication.

---

[5] Fayol, Henri, *Administration industrielle et generale* (Paris: Dunods, 1950) (first published 1916).

[6] Mintzberg, Henry, ''Managerial Work: Analysis from Observation,'' *Management Science,* Vol. 18, October 1971.

TABLE 1–2

*Management
Activities and
Types of
Information*

Activity Level	Management Level	Type of Information
Strategic	Top	Less detailed approximations and predictions based on external and historical data for strategic planning
Tactical	Middle	Summarized and timely information involving compliance with plans and policies
Operational	Lower	Very timely detailed, accurate, and internally generated information on day-to-day activities

Managers need many different types and kinds of information to perform these tasks. As a result, information systems are extremely important to the efficient management of any organization.

*Levels of
Management*

To fully understand the various information systems within an organization and how they meet management's information requirements, it is necessary to look at an organization's levels of management. According to R.N. Anthony,[7] a company's **managerial levels** can be classified as strategic, tactical (managerial), and operational, as shown in Table 1–2 and Figure 1–5. These levels involve different types of activity and as a result require different types of information.

*Operational
Activities*

At the lowest, or **operational management,** level supervisors need detailed information on the day-to-day operation of a company's production process. Control of operational activities involves determining the most effective and efficient way to implement the tasks set forth by management and evaluating the results. This decision-making process requires information on the tasks to be implemented, the resources available, the coordination required with other operations in the organization, the standards and budgets requiring compliance, and feedback for evaluating the results.

Operational managers must make decisions on records to be kept, job assignment, and shipment checking on the basis of the policies and rules set forth by tactical managers. Information for these activities must be very detailed, accurate, and provided on a routine basis. It also consists of a vast amount of day-to-day transactions that describe daily production, sales, and finances. At ProYacht, the managers who oversee the actual production of boat hulls and decks would be considered operational managers.

*Tactical
Activities*

Tactical managerial control involves the effective and efficient acquisition and use of resources to carry out the policies and objectives of top management. Managers at this level plan the activities of the operational units such as sales and manufacturing work centers to carry out the organization's objectives. Middle-level managers need summary reports on the firm's operations to make **tactical decisions** to implement the policy decisions made at the top, or strategic, level of the company. For operational and some

---

[7] For a complete description of these managerial levels see Anthony, R.N., *Planning and Control Systems: A Framework for Analysis* (Harvard University Graduate School of Business Administration, 1965, pp. 24, 25, and 67.)

FIGURE 1–5

Managerial Levels

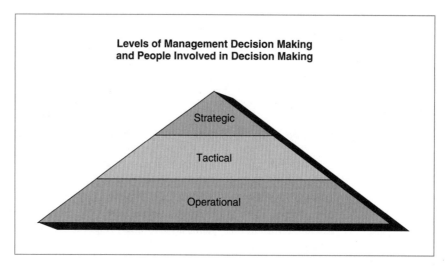

tactical managers, timely reports are very important in their decision making. For tactical and strategic managers, more long-term information about the firm's financial health is needed to make forecasts about the future.

Strategic Activities

Strategic management involves the determination of the organization's objectives, the strategy required to accomplish these objectives, and the organizational structure needed to implement the strategy. Strategic managers set policy and determine the financial, personnel, information, and capital resources needed to accomplish the organization's objectives. Decisions are made about the future direction of the organization, including new products, markets, and manufacturing technology.

Information at this level is generally less formal, less detailed, and often composed of approximations and projections. Managers at this level need information on demand and in specialized form. It tends to include more external data and less internal data than information required for lower levels of managerial control. Moreover, this information must be presented in an understandable and useful form to top management, who may not be well-schooled in information technology.

In summary, the pyramid in Figure 1–5 demonstrates the relative number of people in an organization that make each type of decision and the relationships among the three levels of decision making. Every company has a broad base of nondecision makers who simply carry out management's decisions. Above nondecision making employees are a large number of day-to-day operational decision makers, fewer tactical decision makers, and only a few strategic decision makers. The flow of decision making is from the top down, each level depending on the level above for the policy, plan, or set of parameters needed to make its decisions. On the other hand, the flow of transaction and summary information on which decisions are made is from the bottom up.

For example, at ProYacht the strategic decision-making level is made up of the chairman of the board and chief executive officer (CEO); the president; and vice presidents of finance and operations. The tactical level is composed of various division heads—parts, services, sailboat, and ProYacht Acceptance—as well as department heads—payroll and personnel, sailboat manufacturing, sailboat marketing, and so on. This level also includes numerous individuals who perform so-called ''staff'' roles, providing many important information gathering and processing activities. The operational level includes the production supervisors who manage the employees who actually build the sailboats, the sales representatives, and the clerical employees who support the tactical level managers.

1.4 Managerial Use of Information

Management uses information for planning and control activities as well as those related to the production of goods and services. These activities involve decision making, reporting, and the incorporation of information into the product or service. However, before information can be used for these activities, data must be processed into information.

In many companies, this process involves the transactions that take place at all levels of the organization. This type of processing, referred to as **transaction processing,** generates much of the information that is internal to the company. Ongoing transactions involving suppliers, the production of goods and services, the distribution and storage of finished products, and the sale of these goods and services must be recorded on a day-to-day basis. Sales must be recorded, cash receipts must be posted, costs must be allocated to goods as they are produced, and employees must be paid for their services. This sample indicates the types of transactions that must be processed into information.

Planning and Control

Planning must precede any other activity in the organization. In the planning process objectives must be defined, actions to accomplish the objectives are selected, and the resources necessary to implement the actions are determined. Success does not just happen; it comes about through the creation of a **strategic plan** that meets the objectives defined by the organization's executives. Managerial planning also takes place at the tactical and operational levels of management. These plans are based on the strategic plan. Often these plans are in the form of budgets.

Control activities direct actions through the planning process. This is often accomplished through budgets, standards, and other performance criteria. The control process also includes feedback that compares the results of the action with the planned outcome. Many reports and other modes of information dissemination are used in the planning and control process. These are discussed throughout this text.

Decision Making

In general, information is vital to the decision-making process, whether the decisions are made at the operational, tactical, or the strategic level. Management relies on its information systems to provide accurate, relevant, and timely information to assist in decision making. The nature of the information depends on the type of decision and the organization level at which the decision is made. The decision may require the use of many reports generated by the organization's information system. The nature of decision making is detailed in Chapter 3.

Reporting

In addition to reports generated by the information system for planning, control, and managerial decision making, outside parties may require reports from an information system. For example, regulatory agencies require reports on the number of accidents or the emissions produced by a manufacturing process, tax authorities require payroll tax information, and stockholders require annual reports. The information system must be able to generate these reports. Failure to report to outside agencies or parties may result in severe penalties, even complete shutdown of the company.

Product and Service Information

Information may be an integral component of the product or service an organization provides to its customers. For example, brokerage houses may offer extensive financial planning services which are linked with its clients' investments to better serve their financial and planning needs. These services may range from a simple status report to an analysis of a client's investment posture. As another example, banks that provide their customers the convenience of ATMs for deposits and withdrawals may now provide account statements on demand at the ATM terminals. As a final example, many software vendors maintain a customer file so that they can inform customers of modifications and upgrades. Some firms even send out regular newsletters to keep customers abreast of new developments and help them use the software by relating other users' experiences.

Assessing the Value of Information Systems

The monetary savings offered by an automated transaction processing function should not be the only criterion used in the evaluation of an information system. Better decision making due to the availability of needed information and the value that is added to the product due to the information system are more difficult to measure, but they must be considered to appreciate the full impact of information technology on the organization. These other benefits are often the primary justification for a new or revised information system. Therefore, a strictly financial analysis of an information system may provide only a shortsighted view of the results of managerial information use.

In general, knowledge of the effective use of information and of the computer-based information systems available is essential for a company to compete effectively in today's rapidly changing economy. The information resource must be managed with as much care as is any other strategic resource in the organization. Failure to incorporate information technology into all levels of managerial planning, control, and decision making can bring an early demise to an otherwise successful organization.

1.5 Looking Ahead

Using this text, future managers will understand the nature of computerized business information systems and how they may be used to compete in a dynamic business world. The various types of information systems are summarized in Chapter 2, so that future managers see the great competitive potential inherent in information systems. In Chapter 3, decision making concepts and information systems theory will lay the foundation for examining how the information system supports management in its various activities.

Citibank Gets
Control of Its
Information
Overload

At one time, having unlimited amounts of information was considered an unqualified boon to an organization. However, as many companies found during the 1980s, uncontrolled information can frequently be nothing more than a burden to employees. One such company that realized that it had to do something about this information overload was Citibank, one of the nation's largest banks. When Citibank executives looked at how information was disseminated within the firm, they saw that information did not flow, it hemorrhaged. Information had to be controlled for the bank to remain competitive. As one Citibank executive put it, "The financial industry demands speed, but a big company moves slowly, partly because it is paralyzed by not knowing what to do with the reams of information it has access to."

Internal reports were being read only by a small circle of people around the writer of the report. For example, when a study was done on the teller service time for customers, no structured means existed for distributing the findings. Similarly, external information from trade journals and other sources was delivered in an uncoordinated fashion.

To improve the control of information at Citibank, an outside firm was hired to create a huge data base of information stored on the bank's main computer. This information was culled, filtered, and delivered to every corporate personal computer in the form of financial industry news summaries, news analyses, and abstracts from trade journals. The results of this new information system have been dramatic. For less than $100,000 a year, over 1,000 employees use the data base. Executives estimate that the benefits of the system are as much as 20 times the costs.

SOURCE: Jeffrey Rothfeder, "A Tale of Two Companies Coping with Information Overload," *PC Week*, June 21, 1988, pp. 61–62.

Chapters 4–7 discuss the nature of computerized information resources available to managers. Chapter 4 considers the hardware and software parts of an information system, and Chapters 5 and 6 discuss the data storage and structure methodology needed to produce useful information from data. The methods available for communicating among managers and resources needed for communication are explained in Chapter 7. Chapters 8–11 illustrate how various types of information systems can be used to support management activities. These systems include transaction processing systems, management information systems, decision support and executive information systems, and systems which can be taught to follow specific patterns to make decisions.

Chapters 12–15 concentrate on analyzing managerial problems so that information resources can be brought to bear on the problems. These chapters also describe how to use these resources to solve an informational problem or to take advantage of a competitive opportunity, and how to solve the problem or build a more competitive organization by adding value through information. This discussion includes methods of acquiring the elements of a computerized information system as well as procedures for individual managers (called end users) to design and implement their own information systems. Finally, the effective management and control of these resources and the future of information systems are discussed in Chapters 16–18.

1.6 Summary

Information technology has had a tremendous impact on business organizations. Computers pervade almost every aspect of society, and the smart machines based on these computers can significantly affect the way we do business. As a result, a wide spectrum of information is available to help users manage their organizations. The information revolution is a reality, and organizations that do not take advantage of the opportunities afforded by the information available may not be able to compete effectively in tomorrow's market. An organization's information is a vital resource that should be managed as carefully as any other important asset. Many organizations now use chief information officers to manage the information system resource.

In addition to the improvements in the day-to-day management due to the rapid growth in information technology, many organizations now use information resources in ways never considered before, including many strategic initiatives. Information value—such as better supplier or customer relations or an improved product—can be added to a product or service. The competitive balance within an industry can shift as a result of this added value, thus giving the firm that uses information wisely a competitive advantage. Moreover, the whole structure of an industry can be changed by the introduction of new ways to add information value to a product or service. Effective use of information can alter relations between suppliers and customers, erect barriers to entry by new businesses, and heat up competition.

Management uses information for the processing of day-to-day transactions, the planning and control activities at all levels in the organization, the addition of value to products and services, and reporting and decision making at all levels of management. As a result, an organization's information is a very important asset and key to its success in accomplishing its objectives.

Key Terms

Automatic Teller Machine (ATM)	information-based organization
competitive advantage	internal data
competitive forces	Just-in-Time (JIT) system
Computer-Aided Design (CAD)	managerial levels
computers	operational management
data	smart machine
external data	strategic management
informated factory	strategic planning
information	tactical decisions
information revolution	transaction processing
information society	transactional data
information system (IS)	transactions
information technology	

Review Questions

1. According to Peter Drucker, what type of organization will become more and more prevalent in business?

2. Describe the role of computers in the information revolution.

3. How do smart machines relate to computers?

4. What is an informated factory? How does John Naisbitt define the information society?

5. List some types of processing and sources of data that can be processed into information.

6. Why must information be considered a resource like money and inventory in a modern organization?

7. How has information technology affected organizations?

8. Name some ways in which the information resource can be used in an organization.

9. How can information be used to manage day-to-day operations?

10. Give an example of using information to create a competitive advantage.

11. Describe how information can be used to alter the competitive balance.

12. List the five major competitive forces given by Michael Porter.

13. According to Henri Fayol, what is the role of management? How can a manager's daily activities be characterized?

14. Discuss R.N. Anthony's levels of management.

15. In what ways does management use information? Why is it difficult to assess the value of information systems?

Discussion Questions

1. For the following industrial situations, give an example of how information technology can have or has already had an impact on transaction processing and tactical decision making. Indicate an area in which information technology can be used by the organization to achieve a competitive advantage over other companies.
   a. A regional bank
   b. A large department store chain with its own credit card operations
   c. A small manufacturing firm that makes new and replacement auto parts
   d. A local dentist
   e. A regional architectural and construction firm

2. In the current information revolution, information is the key to an organization's success. What does this statement mean in terms of day-to-day

transaction processing, planning and control, decision making, reporting, and product or service delivery activities?

3. In what ways has information given an organization a competitive advantage, altered the competitive balance in an industry, changed an industry's structure, and created new business opportunities?

4. As a clothing manufacturer, how can you use information technology and your information system to compete effectively with foreign companies even though these foreign competitors have lower labor costs?

Case 1-1
Southwestern
Mutual Life

For many years, Southwestern Mutual Life maintained a low profile while consistently topping the industry's annual ranking of highest dividends paid to policyholders. Today, the San Antonio, TX, life and disability insurer, boasting assets of $22 billion, is receiving quite a bit of attention. The company has given each agent a portable personal computer that can be linked to the home office in San Antonio via the Life Information Network (LINK). Bundled with the personal computers are about 25 different ledger and proposal software programs that illustrate various life insurance and investment options for policyholders. The personal computers also give agents quick access to all their clients' insurance records via telephone connections to the large home office computer.

Southwestern Mutual's PC acquisitions reflect the fact that competitive forces and the changing nature of the life insurance business now make it impossible to sell life insurance without personal computers. "An agent can't do business without a PC," said Al Johnson, LINK's technical planning officer. "Without one, he or she has no access to sales-illustration charts, which are impossible to calculate manually." Life insurance is no longer just a safety net that pays death benefits to a policyholder's beneficiaries. For example, Flexlife, Southwestern Mutual's most successful new product, combines term and whole life insurance with investment options that allow policyholders to select their annual premiums, defer income, or build retirement funds.

"Because our rates, dividend schedules, and products are unique, we have to write all of our own computer programs (software)," Frederick Baker explains. "We listen very closely to our agents, then try to tailor the software to aid in the sales process." The personal computers help in both selling new policies and servicing existing ones. When selling a new policy, the agent can create a needs analysis tailored to the policyholder's specific financial situation. For example, the customer may want to use the policy to defer income, pay for a college education, or plan for retirement. The agent then produces various documents illustrating premium payments over time, as well as the guaranteed and projected cash value of the proposed policy. Using this information, the agent can run many "what if" scenarios showing how the figures might change if the policyholder chooses to pay a higher or lower premium or if the person borrows money against the policy.

For servicing existing policies, the agent is linked via a telecommunication system to the large corporate mainframe, which stores all insurance records for Southwestern Mutual's more than two million policyholders. If a policyholder wants to increase insurance coverage, needs to know the cash value of his or her policies, or wants to change premium payments from monthly to quarterly, the agent can send a request to San Antonio and make the changes or have the answers by the next day. As agents and actuaries use more sophisticated computer systems, marketing people at Southwestern Mutual will surely follow with more innovative life insurance products.

SOURCE: Adapted from Graig Zarley, ''PCs an Essential Tool For Insurance Sales,'' *PC Week,* March 15, 1988, pp. 47 and 53. Copyright ©1988, Ziff Communications Company.

Case Questions

1. How has information technology changed the competitive nature of the insurance industry?

2. Can agents provide better service to customers? How?

3. How could Southwestern Mutual Life use its policyholder information to develop better products and improve service?

Introduction to Information Systems

2

Introduction

Chapter 1 explained that an organization's information is an extremely important resource or asset, similar to its capital and personnel assets. Without an information resource, most companies would cease to exist very quickly. Because information is such an important resource to the organization, it must be managed effectively to yield the maximum benefit. As noted in Chapter 1, managing information is handled by the organization's **information system,** defined as the combination of computers and human users that manage data collection, storage, and the transformation of this data into useful information.

The information system must serve the managerial decision making that ultimately determines the well-being of an organization. Moreover, it can help the organization compete more effectively in changing economic environments. To do this, the information system must be flexible enough to meet the different needs of users at various levels within the organization. For example, the information needs of first-line supervisors are radically different from those of the Chief Executive Officer (CEO). Facilitating the input, processing, storage, retrieval, and flow of information throughout the organization may require the use of several types of information systems. One information system processes raw data into information for normal day-to-day operations, and a different one may provide reports to first-line managers. Another type of information system may be used to help top-level managers make their decisions. In this chapter, we discuss the evolution of information systems and introduce the various types of information systems at work concurrently in complex organizations. We also discuss the relationship of information systems to managerial levels within the organization, as well as consider how these information systems work together to facilitate the flow of information throughout the organization.

Background of
Information
Systems

At one time, information systems consisted solely of the manual processing of raw data into information, which was then used by managers in making decisions. Such systems included typewritten or handwritten reports, word-of-mouth, and the infamous "grapevine." However, since the first commercial computer was developed in 1951, the computer has assumed increasing amounts of this manual data processing. Now, the **Computer-Based Information System (CBIS)** is synonymous with the concept of the information system in general, and conducting business in today's world without computers is virtually impossible. Surveys of different companies have determined how long any type of company thought it could continue operations without computers. Insurance companies could last as long as six days; other types of companies — including banks and distribution and manufacturing companies — could continue operations for shorter periods.

Computer-based information systems were developed in the 1950s with the advent of the computer to process transactions. Initially, CBIS handled the processing of raw data into long lists and tables that were stored in an electronic form called **data files.** The term **Data Processing (DP)** was coined to describe this process. Data processing systems were effective in processing customer account and inventory data and in producing periodic reports to help management cope with the organization's daily activities. Data processing was a major improvement over manual processing, but it still had its shortcomings. Managers had to pore over several pages of lists and tables for the information they needed. This time-consuming process often overwhelmed managers with too much data.

In the 1960s, the speed and the power of the computer increased, enabling managers to process more operational data and to use the resulting information more effectively in the decision-making process. During the same time, Management Information Systems (MIS) were developed. An MIS solved the manager's problem of searching for information because it produced reports that selected data relevant to decisions and summarized this information in a tabular form. Once MIS became a key source of information for managers, the objective of data processing (now often referred to as the Transaction Processing System [TPS]) evolved into the conversion of data to information for MIS and other information systems. **Data Base Management Systems (DBMS)** were also developed at this time to manage the large amounts of data stored in a data base. Before the electronic data base, this data was stored on paper or on tape and card data files.

Although the development of MIS was an important step in providing managers with the information needed to make better decisions, they could not ask questions of an MIS or find solutions to analytical problems. These actions required the reporting function of MIS, graphic displays, and the problem-solving capabilities of management science. This combination, first discussed in the early 1970s, is called a Decision Support System (DSS) due to its emphasis on supporting decision makers rather than just providing reports on past events.

FIGURE 2–1

Evolution of Information Systems

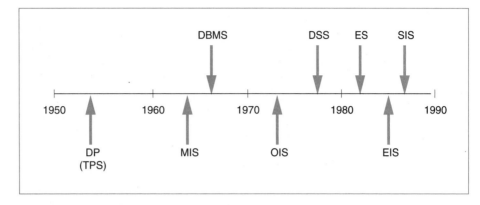

With the proliferation of personal computers in the middle 1980s came the realization that something besides DSS was needed for top-level executives. Executive decision makers who found that the DSS did not always provide the needed information required an Executive Information System (EIS). The personal computer-based EIS is linked to the company's primary computer and uses graphics extensively to display the information needed for executive decisions.

While the four information systems—TPS, MIS, DSS, and EIS—were developed from the original data processing function, the office was also changing. Through the process known as **office automation,** the jobs of clerks, typists, secretaries, and other professionals were irrevocably altered. This process began with the introduction of electric typewriters in the late 1950s and continued with word processors in the late 1970s. The most dramatic changes occurred in the early 1980s, when the arrival of the personal computer coincided with the rapid development of telephone and communication technology. The personal computer and its related systems join network software and communication devices like the fax machine to yield an Office Information System (OIS) that supports all other information systems.

Two other information systems are becoming important in organizations—Strategic Information Systems (SIS) and Expert Systems (ES). An SIS enables an organization to use strategic information for a competitive advantage, as suggested in Chapter 1, and an ES provides workers at all levels with the knowledge and expertise needed to do their jobs better.

The evolution of information systems is shown in Figure 2–1, which contains a time line of the approximate dates of the recognition of each type of information system. These time placements are not exact, and in fact, an information system might be in existence some years before it is recognized as a separate and distinct type.

Advances in Information Technology

The technology underlying information systems, or **information technology,** has made seemingly unbelievable advances in the past. Even so, the rate of these technological advances is expected to accelerate during the current decade. Recent innovations in computer technology have resulted in dramatic increases in power and corresponding reductions in size and cost of processing capability. With these advances in technology, many more users can access the power of the computer. Most business managers today use personal computers for a wide variety of productivity tasks, from manipulating budget figures to preparing reports with graphic analysis of their key points. Managers are using DSS for decision making and corporate planning. The implementation of expert systems for solving problems is also becoming more widespread.

High-powered personal computers enable users to manipulate large amounts of data for making decisions that may result in a competitive advantage and even add information value to their products or services. Significant technological advances and cost reductions in data storage also allow management to store and access large amounts of information for decision making.

Due to advances in communication equipment and software, managers in widely dispersed global locations can communicate effectively enough to integrate their operations. For example, they can transmit data and document facsimiles through their computer systems to react quickly to changing markets. Furthermore, with the development of local area networks, employees in an office can share data, information, and equipment to enhance their productivity.

A Conceptual View of Information Systems

Different information systems interact to facilitate the processing, storage, and flow of information within an organization. As an example of this interaction, a conceptual information system is shown in Figure 2–2.

In Figure 2–2, the TPS, MIS, DSS, EIS, OIS, and a data base interact to form a complete information system that supports managerial decision making. Data from internal and external sources are input through the TPS before being stored in a data base. Next, a DBMS is used to find needed data for processing in the MIS, DSS, or EIS. For example, MIS is used to create various periodic reports for management, or the DSS is used to answer a manager's question.

The data in the internal data base can also be combined with external data bases for use in models and for presentations to top-level executives through the EIS. The same data base can be used as a source of information for the SIS or as a part of the knowledge used in an ES.

Throughout this process, the OIS supports the decision-making process at all stages by facilitating the preparation of text and sending information and filing results electronically. The actual movement of information is handled by a computer network in which computers are tied together using communication links.

Information Systems at ProYacht, Inc.

As an example of the use of information systems, consider again ProYacht, Inc., the hypothetical company introduced in Chapter 1. As discussed there, ProYacht specializes in manufacturing sailboats for the growing market of young professionals who like to sail. ProYacht sells boats to independent dealers, which in turn sell to the customer. As part of its marketing effort, ProYacht employs a group of sales representatives who visit current ProYacht dealers to discuss new and existing products and who work to sign up new dealers to carry the ProYacht sailboat line.

FIGURE 2–2 *Conceptual View of Information Systems*

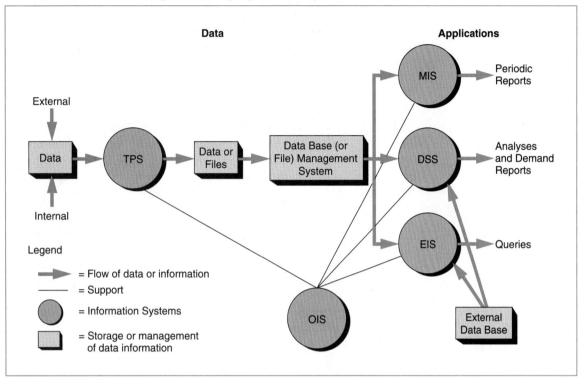

Assume that ProYacht's management wishes to determine which dealers are purchasing the largest total dollar volume from the company and which sales representatives are generating the most business. Unfortunately, ProYacht's sales transaction data are maintained by individual transaction only, without totals or summaries. Before this transactional data can be used to answer management's questions, this data must first be processed and stored in a data base.

At this point, these transactions are only in electronic rather than paper form. The next step is to use the DBMS to retrieve the necessary information for the reports that can answer management's questions. In this case, the reports should include the total sales for each dealer and the total sales for each sales representative arranged in descending order by dollar volume. The MIS is used to devise the needed reports, and the OIS is used to forward them to operational management and, if needed, to higher levels of management.

At the same time, the data base may be queried by the DSS for specific information that can be used to generate sales forecasts using a mathematical model. These forecasts are sent to ProYacht's tactical managers for use in preparing next year's budget. The EIS can also use the data base to create a graphical presentation for upper management, which

Information Systems at Wal-Mart

One reason that Wal-Mart is the fastest growing retailer in the United States is its emphasis on the use of information systems to support retail operations. Wal-Mart, which grew from 276 stores to more than 1,400 by 1990, has always viewed information technology as a key part of its strategic thrust. As one industry analyst put it, Wal-Mart stands out in the use of information technology because it was the first to realize that information systems were "integral to their success. They've been pursuing this for the last ten years." Wal-Mart has invested an estimated $500 million in information technology in the last five years.

Wal-Mart has the industry's first private satellite network, which links almost 1,600 computers at stores, distribution centers, and central management in Arkansas. With this satellite network, Wal-Mart can quickly collect and distribute ordering and sales information. It also allows the constant flow of information among the operations, merchandising, and distribution functions. Wal-Mart also has information systems that monitor each store's daily sales and inventory and send this data to Wal-Mart's 17 distribution centers around the country. As a result, Wal-Mart can provide a "quick response" to sales trends without carrying large in-store inventories — the retail industry's equivalent to the Just-in-Time (JIT) systems in the manufacturing industry.

Online storage capacity is growing at the rate of 100 percent per year. About 5,000 terminals are added each year, including point-of-sale devices, personal computers, and handheld radio units. Wal-Mart's office information system supports over 4,000 users.

SOURCE: Ellis Booker, "IS Trailblazing Puts Retailer on Top," *Computerworld*, February 12, 1990, pp. 69–70.

uses this information to make long-range marketing and distribution plans as well as manufacturing plans. This process is shown in Figure 2–3.

2.1 Elements of the Information System

Although not all information systems are computerized and many processing activities can be performed manually, this text focuses on the CBIS. A CBIS is composed of the following elements:

1. Computer hardware

2. Computer software that process data into information

3. Data and information stored in data bases

4. Procedures that are used to direct information system activities

5. Personnel who operate the computers

The hardware, software, data, procedures, and personnel of a CBIS are shown in Figure 2–4. The information system integrates these elements to convert data into information useful for management decision making and reporting.

FIGURE 2–3

Information Systems at ProYacht, Inc.

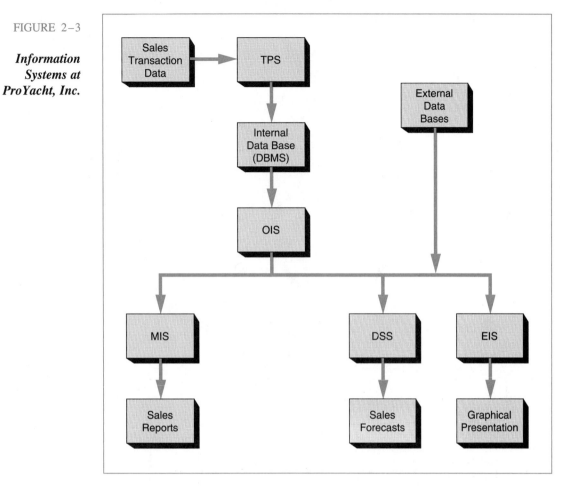

Hardware

Computer hardware is the physical equipment used in the gathering, entering, and storing of data; the processing of data into information; and the output of the resulting information. Hardware is classified generally according to its use in the processing operation—input, processing/internal memory, secondary storage, and output. **Input hardware** includes any device that is used to enter data or instructions into the computer. Commonly used input devices include the keyboard and bar code reader. The **processing/internal memory unit** handles the actual processing of data into information, as well as the necessary internal storage of data and information. To handle permanent storage of data and information, **secondary storage units**—like disk and tape drives—are used. **Output** is achieved via display terminals or printers or by communication to remote computers or display terminals. Figure 2–5 shows the primary hardware elements of a computer.

FIGURE 2–4

Elements of
Computer-Based
Information
Systems

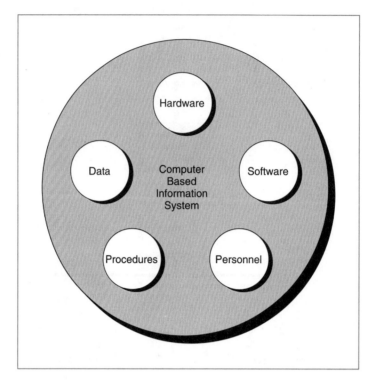

Software   **Computer software** comprises the set of programs used to operate the hardware and to process data into information. Without software, the hardware would be totally useless, because it requires instructions to work. Figure 2–6 shows the process whereby software is combined with hardware to process data into information.

Most software can be divided into two categories—applications software and systems software. **Applications software** consists of a particular set of software used for a specific activity, such as payroll processing or the statistical analysis of marketing data. On the other hand, **systems software** is used to manage the operations of the computer, controlling input, processing, and output activities, as well as accessing data from storage media. The key component of systems software is the **operating system.**

Hardware and software elements of the information system are discussed in Chapter 4.

Data   The third component of a computer system is data and information stored in data bases. As discussed in Chapter 1, **data** consist of all the facts that are processed to supply management with the information needed to engage in its various activities. Obviously, without data and processed information, the entire information system would collapse.

FIGURE 2–5

*Computer
Hardware
Elements*

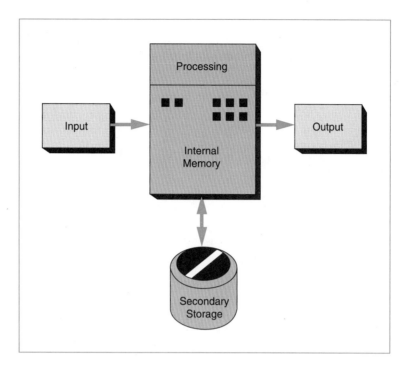

Another key concept regarding data is that processed information for one level of the organization may be only raw data for another level. For example, individuals' time cards processed into a payroll might be considered information by the first-line supervisor. However, the personnel manager might consider the same payroll information as data to be processed into departmental payroll summaries. At an even higher level, the production vice president would consider the payroll summaries as data to be processed into overall company production costs. For this reason, the distinction between data and

FIGURE 2–6

*Combination of
Hardware and
Software*

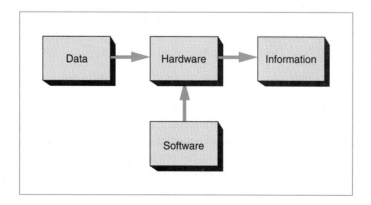

FIGURE 2–7

*Various Levels of
Data and
Information*

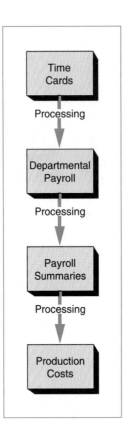

information is always relative to the needs of the user. This process is demonstrated in
Figure 2–7.

Procedures   **Procedures** are the set of instructions or rules that guide the operation of the computers in
an information system. Procedures are necessary to instruct operators as to which hardware, software, and data are used to obtain needed information. Procedures are also
needed to control access to the computer; to outline backup computer information
activities (that is, to create second or third copies of information stored on secondary
storage); and to handle problems when they arise.

For example, a computer operator would use a set of procedures to decide which payroll
data, hardware, and software to use in processing payroll checks. Another example of a
procedure would be the matching of documents related to a purchase — the requisition
authorizing the purchase of a product, the purchase order telling the vendor the nature and
the amount of the product needed, the receiving report indicating that the product has
actually been received, and the vendor invoice, or bill, indicating the charge for the
products that were purchased. This control procedure ensures that only the goods needed
are ordered, that those orders are received, and that the invoice is only for those goods
ordered and received. The purchase requisition, purchase order, receiving report, and

vendor invoice are all stored in the data base. A program is written to compare this stored information and to indicate to management any exceptions that need investigating before a check is printed.

Personnel

The final important component of the CBIS is the **personnel** who use and operate the information system. Without well-qualified personnel to run a system, it cannot function up to its potential and, in fact, may fail to function. Users must be trained to use the system and to use the output generated by the system for the information to be effective in decision making, reporting, and other managerial activities.

2.2 Transaction Processing Systems

The type of information system used to convert raw data from operations into a machine readable form, store the transaction details, process the transactions, and if needed, print out the details of the transactions is called the **Transaction Processing System (TPS).** Data input, processing, and output functions are included in a TPS. A TPS is often dedicated to processing accounting, sales, or inventory data, because such data are needed by other information systems throughout the organization. Figure 2–8 shows a conceptual TPS.

In the transaction processing operation, data are input into the information system's computers using a keyboard, bar code reader, or various other input devices. The information is stored in the computer until it is ready to be processed, which can be immediately or later, depending on the application. After the data are input, processing activities transform the data into information useful to management. The information generated by the processing component of the information system can be in a multitude of forms, such as reports, tables, graphs, video and audio, and so on. The form of the information must match the needs of the person who will be using it.

Many sources of data are used to generate the information. Some are **internal data,** which are generated by the daily activities of the organization as it produces its goods and services and interacts with vendors and customers. Processing internal data is very important to most organizations, because it provides essential information about current and past activities of the organization. Many older systems concentrated entirely on this aspect of the information system. Now, in addition to collecting the operating statistics normally needed to process a particular transaction, other information, **external data,** are gathered from various industry, market, and economic studies and from services to which the organization subscribes. External data may also be generated by surveying customers through market research.

FIGURE 2–8

Conceptual View of the Transaction Processing System

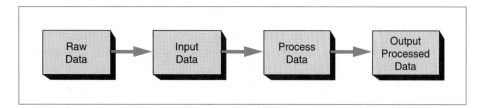

An example of transaction input would be sales data keyed into an electronic cash register as sales occur. Transaction processing might involve the posting of these sales to a sales journal, to the accounts receivable file, and to the inventory records. Output of a TPS would be a printed list of detailed monthly statements for customers or a personal computer screen display of inventory items in stock.

A TPS should process raw data and ensure those data are stored in the correct file for further processing or retrieval. **Files** are collections of information (programs, documents, data, and so on) to which the user or software can assign a name.

Transaction Processing System Input, Processing, and Output

Transaction input at one time was handled by keypunch operators who transcribed data onto punched cards, which were then fed into the computer for further processing, storage, and reporting. Keypunching may still be performed, but the current trend is toward entering data directly from a computer terminal into the computer or to some form of secondary storage (usually a magnetic disk). Although the skills needed to perform this method of input are similar to those with keypunching, the results are stored in a different form that can more easily be accessed by a variety of computer applications. As an example, direct data input is important for telemarketers who take orders over the telephone. Another trend in transaction input is toward the use of Optical Character Recognition (OCR) devices and bar code readers.

A TPS can be classified according to how the data are processed—either batch or online. In a **batch processing system,** the data from multiple transactions, users, or periods are combined, input, and processed as a group, or batch. All the data or transactions are batched according to some common criterion, such as the type of transaction. Daily sales returns that are all processed at one time would be an example of batch processing. This system is used when up-to-date data are not needed and when a great deal of similar data must be processed at the same time.

In an **online processing system,** transactions are processed as they occur. The two types of online processing are transactional and real-time. In **transactional processing,** the data are processed at the time of entry rather than held for later processing. Grocery store bar code checkout systems are examples of transactional processing systems. This type of system generates an itemized receipt immediately after the items are processed.

In **real-time processing,** a control or feedback system is used in such processes as regulating the temperature of a shopping mall and refining crude oil into various petroleum products. In real-time processing, the action of processing can actually affect the transaction itself if several users are competing for the same resources, such as seats on an airplane or in a college class.

Once data are input and processed, they are usually stored in files, displayed on a screen, printed, or most often, all three. Recall that processing of data at this step is often just the beginning; the resulting information may be processed several more times through summarization or combination with other data to provide useful information to decision makers in an organization.

FIGURE 2–9

*ProYacht, Inc.
Transaction
Processing System
for Sailboat Orders*

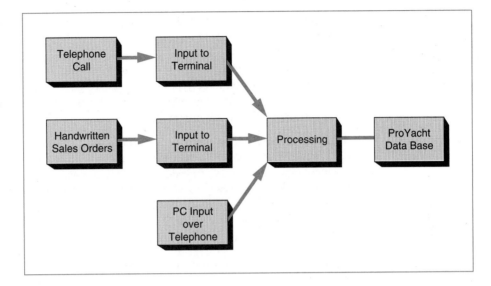

*Transaction
Processing
System at the
ProYacht, Inc.
Sailboat
Division*

As an example of the use of a TPS, we return to ProYacht, Inc. Recall that ProYacht has sales order data for all of its sales transactions for the past month. These sales orders are in three forms—handwritten orders from dealers, customer telephone orders entered at ProYacht via a computer terminal, and sales representative orders entered in a personal computer and telecommunicated to the company. ProYacht's management wants to determine which dealers are purchasing the largest total dollar volume from the company and which sales representatives are responsible for the most business. The sales order data must first be processed by the TPS and stored on a file in a data base. Figure 2–9 shows this process, beginning with the three forms of sales order data. Handwritten data are keyed into the computer and combined with the data entered into a terminal or telecommunicated from a sales representative. The combined data are then processed into a form acceptable by ProYacht's data base system. In this case, the ProYacht Sailboat Division is using an online transaction processing system.

**2.3
Management
Information
Systems**

When information systems were introduced to relieve the information overload caused by the use of data processing, one of the first objectives was to generate meaningful reports for managerial use. With reports, managers did not have to search reams of computer output to find the information they needed to make decisions. This led to the development of management information systems. A **Management Information System (MIS)** can be defined as ''an integrated user–machine system for providing information to support operations, management, and decision-making functions in an organization.'' [1] This definition emphasizes support, because the purpose of

---

[1] Gordon B. Davis and Margaret H. Olson, *Management Information Systems,* 2nd. ed. (New York: McGraw Hill, 1985), p. 6.

MIS is to generate needed reports to provide support for operational, tactical, and strategic decision making.

Reports can be in as many forms as required by the different management levels in an organization. Basically, three types of reports are generated by the MIS—scheduled reports, exception reports, and demand reports. Each one serves a different purpose for the organization, but all are important.

Scheduled reports reflect the periodic and historical information on the organization's operations. They are much like the original information produced by the data processing function with the addition of needed categorization and summarization. These reports help the lowest level manager make operational decisions to meet the objectives set by the higher level managers. For example, a production manager may want to see a daily report on the number of defective items coming off the production line and a weekly report on the number of overtime hours needed for that week.

Exception reports are generated only if some condition, often abnormal, has signaled the need for a report. The exception report is useful to the manager in detecting problems. Because a manager is a problem solver, early detection is essential to good management. At the same time, the exception report does not overwhelm the manager with unnecessary information. For example, an MIS might be used to generate an exception report when overtime for a payroll period is greater than 10 percent of total time worked. When such a report comes to the production manager, he or she can investigate the reasons for the excessive overtime, whether due to a big production job or to poor planning. In the latter case, the exception report may be the first evidence of a problem.

Demand reports are requested by a manager on a particular subject. Such reports may be predetermined but not normally distributed or they may be the result of an unexpected event in another MIS report or from external information. For example, if the production manager sees excessive overtime in an exception report, as previously discussed, he or she may request a report on the possible causes of the excessive overtime. This report would include all production jobs in process, the number of hours required for each job, and the amount of overtime associated with each job. A data base must be available so the staff of the MIS department can gather the needed data and produce the manager's report.

As discussed earlier, ProYacht, Inc. is processing sales orders into a form that can be used by managers to make decisions. In this case, the sales order data has already been processed and stored in ProYacht's data base. The next step is for the MIS to use the information in the data base to create reports. One such report may be a scheduled monthly report showing a list of the sales representatives from highest to lowest sales and a list of dealers in order of sales volume. Another report might be an exception report showing the sales representatives whose sales are significantly less than their monthly quotas. The sales manager may need to meet with these people to determine the reason for the low sales. Because of increased competition, the sales manager may also request a demand report showing the dealers that purchased less this month than the same month last year. Figure 2–10 shows the production of these reports by the MIS.

FIGURE 2–10

Sales Reports Produced by the Management Information System at ProYacht, Inc.

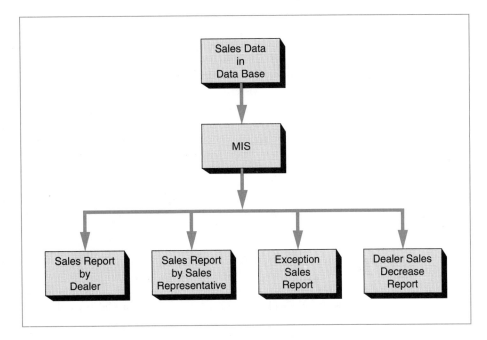

2.4 Decision Support Systems

Eventually, managers discovered that the preparation of various types of reports was not the complete answer to their problems with decision making. The lack of timely information and the inability of the manager to test the effect of a decision using MIS led to the development of decision support systems. The objective of this information system is to allow the manager to find answers to questions and to make better decisions with quantitative and graphical models. Ralph H. Sprague and Eric D. Carlson have defined **Decision Support Systems (DSS)** as ''computer-based systems that help decision makers confront ill-structured problems through direct interaction with data and analysis models.'' [2] These problems tend to be more prevalent at the tactical and strategic levels than at the operational level in an organization.

The DSS is made up of a data base, a model base, and a user interface (dialogue base). The **data base** provides the data used in the models that are contained in the **model base,** and the **user interface** handles the interaction between the system and the user. This interaction among the components of the DSS is shown as Figure 2–11 on the following page.

A DSS has been used for such diverse activities as designing a ski resort, financial planning, and police patrol analysis. The system can be as simple as an electronic spreadsheet on a personal computer or as powerful as specially designed software on a mainframe. Although a DSS is most often implemented on a large, mainframe computer because of the additional processing power, storage capabilities, and advanced graphics,

---

[2] Ralph H. Sprague and Eric D. Carlson, *Building Effective Decision Support Systems* (Englewood Cliffs, NJ: Prentice-Hall, 1982).

FIGURE 2–11

**Components of
the Decision
Support System**

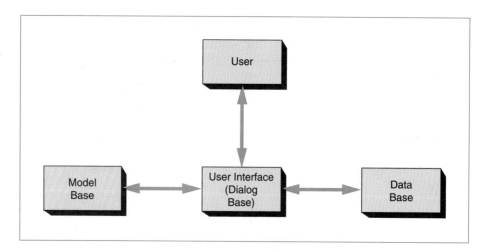

many personal computer DSS packages are also available. In addition, combination spreadsheet–graphics packages such as Lotus 1-2-3 or Excel can be used to help a manager make decisions.

*Using Models
in a Decision
Support System*

The decision maker who handles hard-to-solve problems needs a system that allows him or her (or his or her staff) online interaction with the computer. In addition to obtaining information from a data base or external source, the decision maker must be able to "simulate" the effect of changes in information or the effect of new information. The model must represent the physical, economic, or financial situation being studied. A **model** is a simplified version of reality that describes the interrelationships between important variables in a particular environment. Types of models include optimization, forecasting, and simulation models. Optimization models seek to find the "best" solution to a problem, forecasting models try to predict the future based on current data, and simulation models replicate many years' results in just a few seconds of processing. These models are discussed in more detail in Chapter 10.

*Decision
Support System
at ProYacht*

At ProYacht, Inc., decision support systems are used for a wide variety of purposes including scheduling sailboat production, financial analyses, forecasting future demand for various types of sailboats, and simulating the effect of various promotional activities on demand. While many of these DSS are run on the ProYacht corporate mainframe, powerful PCs are also used to run other DSS. For example, spreadsheets are used to retrieve, analyze, and graph sales data once they have been processed by the TPS. In addition, a forecasting model is used in the spreadsheet to predict sales for the remainder of the year. The results of this forecasting model are then displayed as a line graph. Figure 2–12 shows this forecasting process in a spreadsheet along with the graph showing the predicted sales levels.

FIGURE 2–12   *Decision Support System Forecasting Model at ProYacht, Inc.*

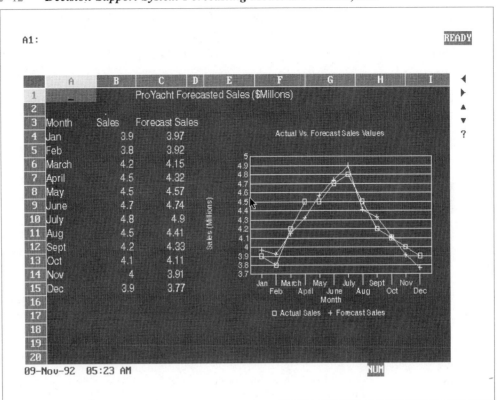

2.5 Executive Information Systems

The DSS is aimed at solving problems and answering "what if," goal seeking, and risk analysis questions about specific problems for decision makers in an organization. Often, middle-level managers who tend to be most concerned with the specific problems involving their unit of the organization are the major users of DSS. DSS does not always provide top-level executives—Chief Operating Officers (COOs) and CEOs—with the type of information they need.

Top-level executives must take a global view of the organization. Because the one commodity that such executives are always short of is time, their information system should be very easy to use. They also want the needed information provided in a form that is easy to understand. The sources of information often include external data as well as internal data from the TPS or MIS. Their information system should enable them to find the underlying causes for various results. This **Executive Information System (EIS)** then, as James Martin has expressed it, becomes an executive's "presentation system" [3] which helps him or her in making decisions for competing effectively.

---

[3] James Martin, "EIS Helps Managers Gain Insight into Factors for Success," *PC Week,* April 24, 1989, p. 54.

A problem facing virtually every police department is how to create patrol officer schedules—that is, assigning police officers to patrol certain geographic areas during various times during a 24-hour period. The goal of this scheduling is to keep the number of assigned officers to a minimum while achieving the desired level of protection as defined by local government. Most police departments perform this scheduling operation using manual methods, for example, with an experienced scheduler who uses a "hit or miss" approach. However, with manual methods, it is difficult to determine how well the schedules are meeting defined objectives and to evaluate alternative scheduling policies.

In an attempt to improve previous manual patrol scheduling methods, the city of San Francisco has created a DSS to handle this task. San Francisco has a population of 700,000 people and approximately 850 officers are normally assigned to patrol duties. Patrol coverage costs approximately $79 million per year. The new DSS was created to improve patrol coverage while also reducing costs. This system forecasts hourly patrol needs and then uses a mathematical model to create patrol schedules that maximize coverage. This DSS also allows for "fine tuning" of patrol schedules to meet the human needs not accounted for by the mathematical model. This fine tuning mode also allows police supervisors to evaluate schedule changes and then suggests alternative schedules.

The San Francisco Police Department DSS has generated schedules that make 25 percent more patrol units available when they are needed. This is equivalent to adding 200 officers to the force using previous scheduling methods and results in a savings of $11 million per year. At the same time, response times have improved by 20 percent.

SOURCE: Phillip E. Taylor and Stephen J. Huxley, "A Break from Tradition for the San Francisco Police: Patrol Officer Scheduling Using an Optimization-Based Decision Support System," *Interfaces*, Jan.–Feb. 1989, pp. 4–24.

The EIS combines the power and storage capability of the mainframe with the ease of use and graphics capability of the personal computer. Information is transferred to the personal computer from the mainframe or from external data bases. The executive then uses some type of pointing device such as a mouse to select from a menu of results and presentation modes. The keyboard is seldom used in an EIS, because the executive is usually searching for information and answers to questions rather than entering data. Output on the personal computer monitor is often in graphics form or in a combination of graphics and tables. The success of any EIS is measured by the degree to which output is personalized for the needs and style of the executive. If the system does not present information the way the executive thinks about the problem, he or she will be uncomfort-

FIGURE 2–13   *Executive Information System at ProYacht, Inc.*

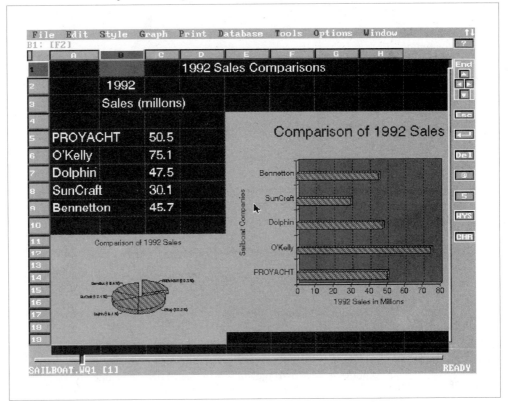

able with the EIS and probably not use it. Today, state-of-the-art systems provide such strategic information using the company's data base and other sources. These new systems support graphic as well as tabular presentations that can be made an integral part of a report.

Executive Information System at ProYacht

Assume the CEO of ProYacht, Inc. wants to compare his company's last year's sales with those of various competitors. To do this, he uses his EIS to access the reports to the stockholders of the publicly held companies, which are available from the financial data bases to which ProYacht subscribes. The EIS is designed to access these data bases with several very simple instructions from the CEO. The EIS can also access the yearly sales figures for ProYacht. The competitors' sales are graphically compared with ProYacht's sales as shown in Figure 2–13. Using this combination of internal and external information, the CEO can make the decisions that enable his company to compete more effectively in the marketplace.

FIGURE 2–14

*Linking
Information
Systems to
Managerial Level*

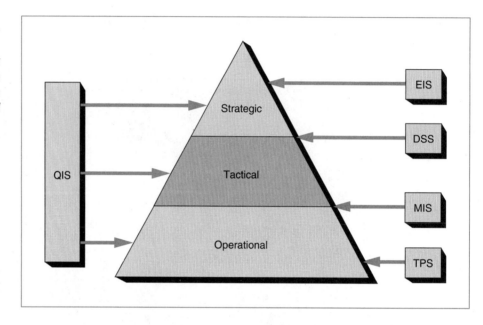

*Comparison of
Executive
Information
Systems to
Decision
Support
Systems and
Management
Information
Systems*

A great deal of discussion concerns the relationship among MIS, DSS, and EIS, because all three "support" managerial decision making. Where does one stop and the others begin? One way of looking at this differentiation is to consider the report generation emphasis of MIS, the modelling emphasis of DSS, and the presentation emphasis of EIS. Another way of distinguishing EIS from MIS is presented by Effraim Turban and Donna M. Schaeffer, who note that MIS is directed toward control through exception reporting, and EIS concentrates on problems and opportunities.[4]

MIS, DSS, and EIS can each be linked to a different level of management, as shown in Figure 2–14. For example, MIS is used by all levels of management, especially lower and middle management, to make operational and tactical decisions. These decisions by lower and middle management implement the decisions made by top management. On the other hand, DSS is often used by middle and upper management to solve problems. Finally, EIS is usually used only by a small group of executives and must be personalized to executive needs. MIS and DSS tend to use internal data, whereas EIS uses both internal and external data.

MIS, DSS, and EIS may also be differentiated by the type of decisions that each information system supports. Decisions may be structured or unstructured. **Structured decisions** are well defined, routine, and have set procedures for selecting the best course of action. MIS is most useful in providing information in the form of reports or tables to a manager making structured decisions. DSS and EIS are generally used to help make unstructured decisions in such areas as project management, budget preparation, and

[4] Effraim Turban and Donna M. Schaeffer, "A Comparison of Executive Information Systems, DSS, and Management Information Systems," in *Decision Support Systems: Putting Theory into Practice,* 2nd. ed., Ralph H. Sprague, Jr. and Hugh J. Watson, eds. (Englewood Cliffs, NJ: Prentice Hall, 1986), p. 296.

Hardware	Software
Mainframe terminals	Word processing
Personal computers and peripherals	DBMS
LAN cabling and personal computer adapters	LAN management software
Scanners	OCR software
Telephones	Telecommunications software
Reproduction and facsimile machines	

TABLE 2–1

***OIS Hardware
and Software
Resources***

research and development. **Unstructured decisions** require judgment and insight, are nonroutine, and have no agreed upon procedure for making the decision.

Making the differentiation among MIS, DSS, and EIS is not always possible from a single point of view. A more general way of thinking about these information systems is to combine the three approaches discussed. MIS is a report-oriented system used primarily by lower and middle management for well-structured decisions. DSS is a model-oriented system used primarily by middle and upper management for semistructured and unstructured decisions. EIS is a presentation-oriented system used by top-level executives to make highly unstructured decisions based on information gleaned from a wide range of sources.

2.6 Office Information Systems

The presence of computerized office information systems in the workplace has been one of the most dramatic changes brought about by the use of the computer. An **Office Information System (OIS)** — often called office automation — supports all other information systems by providing for the free flow of data and information throughout the organization, not just in the office. The first OIS included electric typewriters, dictaphones, and telephones. Today's OIS comprises a variety of electronic and computerized office equipment often connected via a special type of computer network called a **Local Area Network (LAN).** The hardware and software components of an OIS are listed in Table 2–1.

*Office
Information
System
Functions*

The OIS performs many different functions, depending on the type of office. The following six functions tend to be part of any OIS:

1. Text preparation

2. Voice and electronic mail

3. Facsimile transmission

4. Electronic Data Interchange (EDI)

5. Electronic filing

6. Access to internal and external data bases

The most widely used operation in an OIS is **text preparation.** This function is accomplished through word processing on a personal computer or by using an electronic typewriter. However, the use of scanners and optical character reader (OCR) software is growing as a method of text preparation.

Communications have always been the lifeblood of an office and, for well over 100 years, the telephone has played an important role in the office. Today, **voice mail** has extended the use of the telephone by allowing the sending, receiving, storage, and relaying of spoken messages. The messages are stored in a ''mailbox,'' which the recipient can access at his or her discretion. Another form of electronic communication is **electronic mail,** with which workers send messages and files back and forth between their mainframe terminal or personal computers. Electronic mail has reduced the ''down-time'' for participants who are communicating on pressing issues.

One of the fastest growing office communications systems is **Electronic Data Interchange (EDI).** In EDI, companies use computers and communication links to electronically transmit and receive data. These data can include customer inquiries, purchase orders, invoices, and other purchase and shipping information. EDI can give a company a distinct advantage over its competitors by reducing shipping errors and the amount of time between an order and the subsequent shipment. Another rapidly growing form of communication is through the **facsimile machine,** which can send almost instantaneously any written or electronic document anywhere in the world.

In an effort to manage the ever-growing mass of paper that offices generate, many organizations use **electronic filing** on magnetic or optical disks. Items on file may be word processing documents, electronic mail documents, or paper documents that are scanned and converted into an electronic form. Finally, the OIS is involved in making both **internal** and **external data bases** available to decision makers through the various types of information systems.

Figure 2–15 shows one possible arrangement of the hardware resources in an OIS. OIS is discussed in more detail in Chapter 7.

2.7 Expert and Strategic Information Systems

Two types of information systems that are becoming more important to companies of all sizes are expert systems and strategic information systems. An **Expert System (ES)** attempts to incorporate the knowledge and rules from several experts on a given subject and store this information in the computer. The ''computer'' software then becomes an ''expert'' on the subject by combining this information to aid decision makers in tasks which require a fair amount of expertise, yet are fairly routine in occurrence.

In the traditional view of information systems, basic operations like payroll are automated and managerial decision making is supported. Today, some forward-thinking companies are beginning to use their information systems as strategic weapons in the constant battle for a higher market share, as noted in Chapter 1. A **Strategic Information System (SIS)** is typically used to support or develop a company's competitive strategy. Examples of the ways that an SIS can be used include increasing product differentiation, creating or distributing an innovative product, and reducing costs in order to increase the company's market penetration.

FIGURE 2–15   *Hardware Resources in an Office Information System*

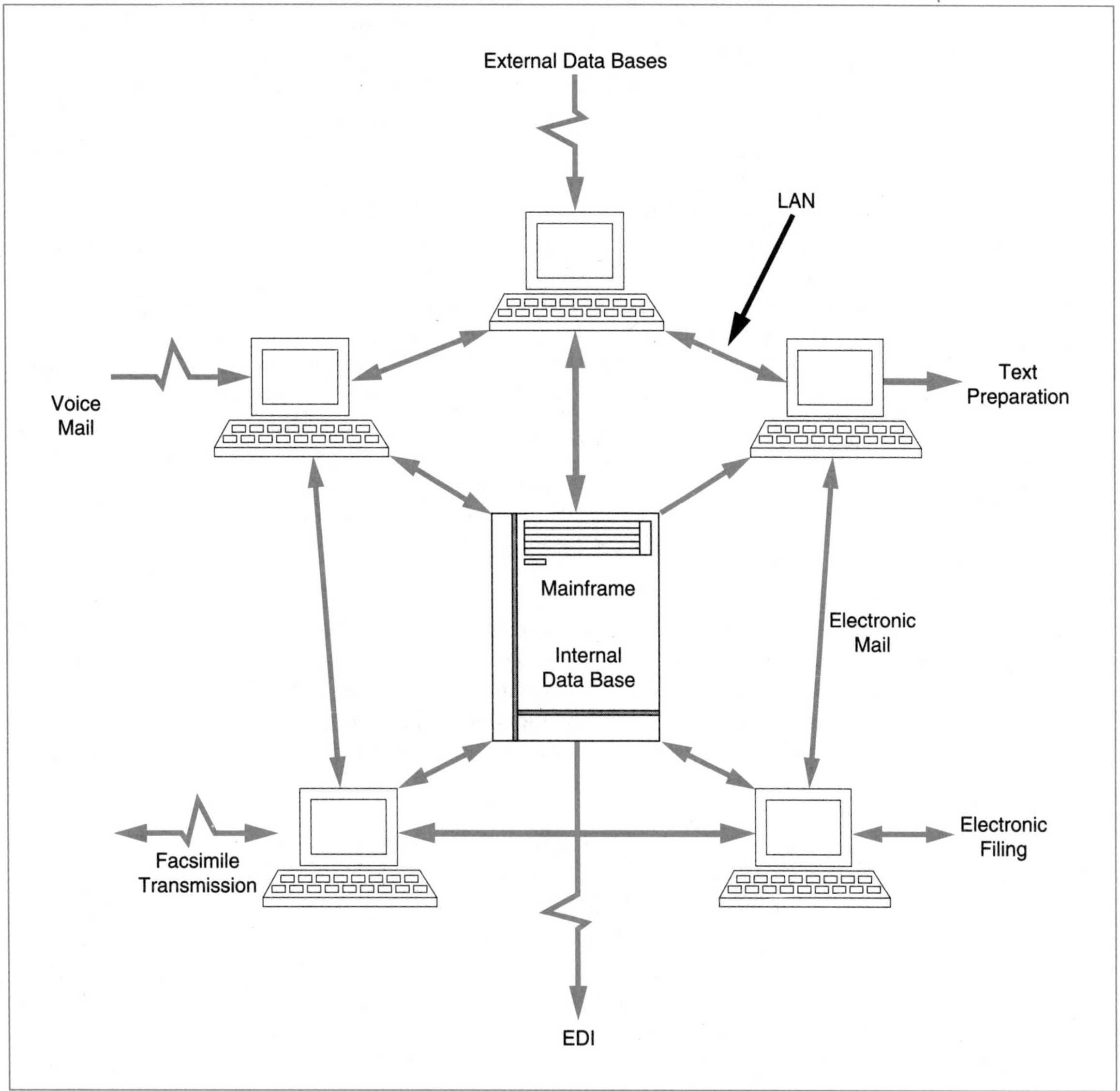

Expert Systems   Almost every organization has at least one individual whose knowledge is key to the successful operation of the organization. These people are experts in their field and, without them, very little would be accomplished. Experts can cut through superfluous, unimportant details and get to the heart of any problem. Whether their expertise is used to decide when a commercial soup is ready to be canned or to diagnose a pulmonary disease, experts use a body of knowledge and some ''rules of thumb'' to make decisions or recommendations to other decision makers. Such experts are obviously important to any

Scrapping Paper at USAA

One of the country's largest insurance companies, USAA, is in the process of converting paper mail into an electronic form. With over 5 million policies in force, USAA could not answer policy holders' queries in a reasonable amount of time. If a policy holder called to follow up a letter, a USAA agent would have to track the letter down and call the customer back. To reduce this problem in the office, the company instituted the "Image Project," in which all incoming letters are scanned and converted into electronic copies. The electronic version of the letter is then "attached" to the customer's file in the policy holder data base.

Now when a customer has a query, USAA can cut the reply time from over 10 days to a very low number. Customers do not need to call, and the problem is not handled twice. However, if a customer does call, the file and letter can be accessed and displayed together on a terminal screen by a USAA service representative while the customer is still on the phone. USAA never expects to have a "paper-less" office, but John Crisci, Vice President of Property and Casualty Systems, believes that "What we're trying for is a less-paper office."

SOURCE: David Coursey, "Erasing the Office Paperwork," *USA Today,* June 6, 1988, p. 6e.

organization; they are few in number, can be very expensive, and can be very difficult to replace. Thus, many organizations want to use the expertise of some key decision makers to solve recurring problems. These experts are still needed for their creativity in solving infrequent, nonroutine problems for which it is not economical to construct a system. Expert systems are one very practical facet of the rapidly growing field known as **Artificial Intelligence (AI).**

Expert System at ProYacht

As an example of the use of an ES at ProYacht, Inc., assume that a production supervisor has spent many years on the process of positioning the fiberglass sheets for the sailboat hulls. This tricky process must be carefully supervised to avoid defects in the hulls. Because this employee is preparing to retire, ProYacht is creating an ES to replace him. This ES will incorporate the knowledge and rules of thumb that this production supervisor has been using to provide advice on solving the problems that often arise during the fiberglass laying process.

Strategic Information Systems

A company that uses information systems to gain an advantage over its competitors, as suggested in Chapter 1, is using a strategic information system. Numerous companies have gone out of business because they lacked what James Martin calls "strategic vision" [5] to see the result of changing technologies. **Strategic information** can be used in many ways to help a company obtain an advantage over its competition, including using available information for new purposes, providing an early warning system against

[5] James Martin, "Strategic-Information Systems: A Formula for Success," *PC Week,* November 28, 1988, p. 36.

a decline in market share, finding new markets for existing products, and even redefining the mission of the organization.

As an example of the use of strategic information, consider a large department store in the United Kingdom. As with all retail establishments in that country, this store must collect a Value-Added Tax (VAT) on products sold. This tax is refunded to noncitizens if they fill out a request form as they leave the store. The department store viewed this onerous task as a nuisance and discarded the names of U.S. customers to whom it had refunded the VAT. However, at the suggestion of AT&T, the store now uses this information to create a mailing list for its new mail-order business. Without an information system, this information is worthless; with an information system to manage the names and addresses, the store can capitalize on the strategic information and start an entirely new business.

2.8 Summary

A CBIS ensures that the appropriate information is available to managers for better decision making. Information systems consist of the computer hardware, the software necessary to use the hardware, the data needed by the software to supply information to management and for transaction processing, the personnel needed to operate the system, and the procedures necessary to control and operate the information system. Important types of information systems are TPS, MIS, DSS, EIS, and OIS. The TPS converts raw data into either processed information or data for use in other processing operations.

An MIS provides managers with various types of reports, including scheduled reports, exception reports, and demand reports. DSS uses models to assist decision makers by providing a software environment in which managers can experiment with various alternatives. In general, the DSS helps by interactively answering queries. A spreadsheet is a simple version of a DSS. An EIS presents information to executives in more graphic terms so they can easily picture the nature of the problem and the alternative courses of action at their disposal.

An OIS expedites all these systems via text preparation, electronic and voice mail, facsimile transmission, EDI, electronic filing, and access to internal and external data bases. Many functions are carried out over a LAN.

An ES tries to incorporate a human's expertise into an information system using factual knowledge and rules. An SIS helps the company remain healthy by providing it with a competitive advantage in the marketplace. All these systems combined help an organization to take advantage of information technology to compete more effectively.

Key Terms

applications software
Artificial Intelligence (AI)
batch processing system

Computer-Based Information System
 (CBIS)
computer hardware

computer software
data
data base
Data Base Management Systems (DBMS)
data files
Data Processing (DP)
Decision Support System (DSS)
demand reports
Electronic Data Interchange (EDI)
electronic filing
electronic mail
exception reports
Executive Information System (EIS)
Expert System (ES)
external data base
facsimile machine
files
information system
information technology
input hardware
internal data base
Local Area Network (LAN)
Management Information System (MIS)

model
model base
office automation
Office Information System (OIS)
online processing system
operating system
output
personnel
procedures
processing/internal memory
real-time processing
scheduled reports
secondary storage units
strategic information
Strategic Information System (SIS)
structured decisions
systems software
text preparation
Transaction Processing System (TPS)
transactional processing
unstructured decisions
user interface
voice mail

Review Questions

1. Discuss the evolution of information systems.

2. List the types of information systems that are used to help managers in organizations.

3. What are the elements of an information system?

4. What are the components of computer hardware? Name the two types of computer software.

5. Which element of the information system gives instructions on the processing of data into information? What other purposes does this element serve?

6. What part does a TPS play in an information system? Name the various modes used in transaction processing.

7. Name the three types of reports generated by an MIS, and explain the purpose of each.

8. What is the role of a model in a DSS? What types of models are commonly used in a DSS?

9. What are the three parts of a DSS? With which one does the user interact?

10. What is the purpose of an EIS? How is it different from a DSS?

11. Explain the differences between an MIS, a DSS, and an EIS. Use two approaches to differentiate between the types of information systems.

12. What are the commonly used hardware and software elements of an OIS? What is the relationship between a LAN and an OIS?

13. List the most common functions of an OIS.

14. Why is ES included in our discussion of information systems?

15. How does an SIS relate to the future health of an organization? How can it be used to make the organization more competitive?

Discussion Questions

1. How have advances in information technology led to the evolution of the various types of information systems that were outlined briefly in this chapter?

2. For each information system outlined in the chapter, describe the following:
   a. Its objective
   b. The level of management activity it is designed to support
   c. A major shortcoming
   d. An example of its use

3. What do you believe are the future uses of EDI with respect to transaction processing systems? How could EDI be used to support a manufacturer's wish to reduce inventory?

Case 2–1
Campbell Soup Company

Quality products alone do not guarantee success in the competitive grocery foods industry. The products must be made efficiently, marketed creatively, and distributed cost effectively. Campbell Soup Company relies on the effective gathering, dissemination, and use of information for its success. Campbell is implementing an information strategy designed to make the company considerably more competitive. This strategy involves the development of an overall information system that links the core elements of the $4 billion company's marketing, distribution, and manufacturing.

With an organized network of personal computers and larger computers, Campbell Soup has identified savings and improved earnings in the tens of millions of dollars per year. The most significant benefits have come from analysts and planners using mainframe production and sales data to discern trends, uncover opportunities for new products, identify untapped markets, and determine where advertising and promotion money can expand sales of established product lines. For example, a model of inventories and shipments by a logistics department analyst resulted in interplant transport cost savings of more than $1 million. In another example, PC-monitored field tests of freezing equipment led to the purchase of less expensive freezers for Le Menu dinners, yielding a $5 million savings. Product inventories have been reduced as a result of analyzing operations, saving $13 million per year.

Another successful experience with new technology came with the development of an expert system to troubleshoot hydrostatic cookers in the soup manufacturing process. The PC-based system, which includes the expertise of cooker maintenance technicians, is now in use at eight Campbell Soup plants in the United States, Canada, and England. The company now has a manager to coordinate artificial intelligence work, and new expert systems are under development to maintain other production machinery and to monitor Campbell's mushroom farming operations.

Company management sees these kinds of applications as just the beginning. They believe computers and telecommunications should be implemented as "a total system," tying together all company operations from the fields (where Campbell grows its vegetables and contracts for its meat), through the grocery store chains and brokers, to consumers with varied regional and ethnic tastes. The key is reducing the cost of supplying products to the consumer. Someday, the computers of large supermarkets and major broker distributors may be linked to Campbell systems. With sales and manufacturing connected by computer, warehousing needs are reduced and fresher products are delivered to the customer.

Ultimately, this scheme could be extended to the point where the company actually makes products according to customer order. Ingredients and supplies would go to manufacturing plants only when needed—reducing the time that carrots and tomato paste are stored and that inventories of steel plate for cans are maintained. Using small computers, the sales force would transmit sales data back to regional sales offices. Outside market-research reports would not be needed, because Campbell's sales representatives could instantly know how Campbell products are selling in individual stores. The rep might tell a chain store buyer, "Le Menu is selling very well in this store, but you aren't supplying it properly. It's not being brought into the store quickly enough."

Clearly, grocery foods manufacturers are facing ever increasing competition as the market stops expanding. Campbell Soup hopes that its aggressive use of automation keeps it at the top of the industry.

SOURCE: Adapted from Henry and Elizabeth Urrows, "Campbell Soup Company," *PC Week,* May 6, 1986, pp. 57–59, 62. Copyright © 1986, Ziff Communications Company.

Case Questions

1. Describe how Campbell Soup saved money or expected to save money with MIS, DSS, and ES.

2. What does company management believe is the key to success in the grocery foods industry? How do they plan to use EDI to accomplish this?

3. How do you think Campbell Soup can use marketing, distribution, purchasing, and inventory data to aid in transaction processing and management decision making?

Decision Making and Information Systems

3

Introduction

All organizations have a physical system that is used to produce and market products and services. They also have information systems to support this physical system as well as to add value to their products and services. As we saw in the previous chapters, an information system is an integrated collection of hardware, software, data, personnel, and procedures that provides management with the necessary information to support its activities. These managerial activities are a function of an organization's objectives, strategy, and structure.

One of the most important managerial activities is **decision making**—that is, recognizing problems, generating alternative solutions to the problem, choosing among the alternatives, and implementing the chosen alternative. Because decision making is such a crucial managerial activity, the designer of an information system that supports decision making must consider many aspects of this activity. These aspects include various decision-making models, the decision maker's style, the organizational structure within which decisions are made, and the level and structural arrangement of the decision itself. Several types of information systems have been developed to accommodate the different types of decisions.

In this chapter, we concentrate on decision making and organizational structure, which are very important to the design of an effective information system. In addition, we outline a procedure for analyzing users' needs and designing an information system that can supply the necessary transaction processing, decision making, reporting, and value-added information required by the organization.

3.1 Decision-Making Theory

Because decision making is such a complex activity, many theories try to explain how individuals and organizations make decisions. Some decision-making theories are descriptive in nature, some are behavioral models, and others are founded on organizational theory. Because information systems are used to support all levels of managerial decision making, these theories are important in the design and implementation of an information system. All are dependent on the objectives and strategies of the organization.

Objectives and Strategies

In general, management typically sets **organizational objectives,** determines a **strategy** to accomplish the objectives, and organizes its resources to carry out its strategy. An organization may have a single objective, such as the maximization of market share, or it may have more than one objective, such as the maximization of market share while maintaining a respectable profit.

Once objectives are determined, the organization can adopt one of many different strategies to accomplish these objectives. For example, one building contractor may use subcontractors to handle the tasks involved in the construction of homes. Another building contractor may employ directly the necessary carpenters, masons, plumbers, and other skilled personnel on a full-time basis. Their mission is the same, yet their strategies are different. The different strategies lead to different organization structures and different information system requirements. In the first case, the information system needs to evaluate subcontractor bids and track their work progress. In the second case, an extensive cost accounting system records the costs associated with the contractor's employees.

Organizations make decisions within this set of objectives. They are constrained by their objectives and directed by their strategy as they plan and make decisions. These objectives often serve as the criteria for evaluating various alternatives in the decision-making process.

For example, at ProYacht, the CEO and the president have developed a strategic plan for the company that has the following two major objectives:

1. To expand the company into other marine recreational product lines
2. To improve the company's information systems

For the first objective, the planners have decided that because the market for marine recreational products is forecast to grow, they can use their boat-building expertise and dealer network to expand into this market. The second objective derives from the fact that only the information systems in the sailboat operations are up-to-date. A variety of hardware and software systems are used in different divisions, and the CEO feels strongly that they should all be updated. These two objectives are the focus of several chapters in this book, as ProYacht moves to expand into new marine recreational areas and to build more effective information systems.

Decision-Making Process

According to H.A. Simon,[1] the **decision-making process** consists of several stages. These are generally defined as the seven steps shown in Figure 3–1. The decision-mak-

---

[1] Herbert A. Simon, *Administrative Behavior,* 3rd ed. (New York: Free Press, a division of Macmillan, Inc., 1976) and H.A. Simon, *The New Science of Management Decision,* revised edition (Englewood Cliffs, NJ: Prentice-Hall, 1977).

FIGURE 3–1

Decision-Making Process

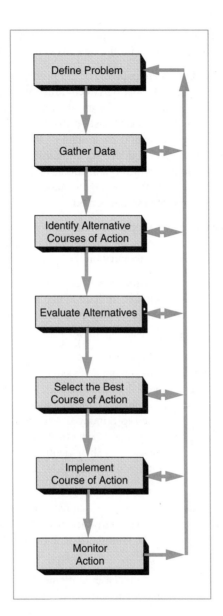

ing process begins with the definition of the problem. The decision maker must be careful to define the actual **problem,** not just the symptoms of the problem. Problems are not inherently bad; they may actually be opportunities to gain a competitive advantage. To determine the existence and nature of the problem or opportunity, managers need an information system that monitors internal activities and the business environment. Note that the decision-making process does not occur in a vacuum—environmental constraints limit the process as well as strategic resources and organizational objectives and strategies. These constraints ensure that the final decision can actually be used to solve the problem and that it will coincide with the objectives of the organization.

Once the problem is defined, **data** are gathered on the problem or competitive opportunity; this activity is an important information system function. In the next step, **alternatives** must be identified for a resolution of the problem or for exercising a competitive initiative. An effective information system must be able to generate an array of feasible alternatives. These alternatives are evaluated in light of the criteria established by the organization. This criteria is usually founded on organizational objectives. Sometimes this evaluation is not so simple, given the organizational and political constraints as well as possible conflicting objectives within the organization. Eventually, the most appropriate alternative is selected and then implemented.

Finally, the results of the implementation are monitored to provide **feedback** to management for review of the selection criteria, the alternatives, and the decision. An effective information system is also necessary to carry on these monitoring activities.

In each step of this process, the decision maker needs different types of information. Generating this variety of information is difficult. This basic decision-making model shown in Figure 3–1 is used to illustrate management's use of information at ProYacht, Inc.

Decision Making at ProYacht, Inc.

To demonstrate the decision-making process, we again consider ProYacht, Inc., which manufactures small sailboats. Assume that an analysis of sales statistics by ProYacht's marketing department has determined that sales of the 18-foot day sailer have fallen dramatically over the last six months. This trend implies some sort of problem, and some action by management may be needed to remedy the situation. After gathering more detailed data on the sales of the day sailer, on other models, and on competitors, alternative solutions to the decline in sales are then identified. ProYacht may reduce the price of the day sailer, improve the quality of the day sailer, or take both actions together.

Once identified, the alternatives must be evaluated in light of various criteria defined by ProYacht's management. One alternative is chosen using a selection process based on these criteria. If ProYacht's management determines that their customers consider product quality more important than cost, then the alternative to improve product quality may be selected.

Next, the decision is implemented. In this case, implementation may require new production techniques and greater employee training in equipment use so that defects are minimized in the production process. Finally, the sales of the higher quality day sailers should be monitored to determine if sales increase. If they do not, then ProYacht must go through the decision-making process again. The effective use of information technology in each step is essential for an organization to compete successfully in today's market.

Decision-Making Concepts

In an attempt to describe decision making in a firm, R.M. Cyert and J.G. March[2] proposed four major decision-making concepts that firms use to bring order to this process. These

[2] R.M. Cyert and J.G. March, *A Behavioral Theory of the Firm* (Englewood Cliffs, NJ: Prentice-Hall, 1967).

A Bad Decision
in California

In California, an important function of the Secretary of State's office is to check whether property used as collateral for a bank loan is already pledged for another loan. Banks use this information to decide whether or not to make a loan. In the mid-1980s, state officials determined that the semiautomated mainframe information system in use at that time was inadequate and that a new system was needed. Of the various alternatives considered, an optical disk-based system was selected.

The design and development of the new system went well until it was time to install it. At this point, officials had to decide between two alternative installation procedures—run the new system in parallel with the old system or simply convert directly to the new system. The company supplying the new system recommended that both systems be run concurrently for at least 30 days so that problems in the new system could be fixed without delaying processing. On the other hand, by converting directly to the new system before any testing was carried out, the state would save money. In this case, state budget officials selected what they thought would be the less expensive alternative—switch to the new system directly.

As would be expected with a new optical disk system as large as the one installed in the Secretary of State's office (up to 204 disks and 50 personal computer workstations), numerous problems resulted with the direct conversion alternative. Problems included failures of online laser printers, bugs in the software, and the lengthy training period required to teach employees to use the new system. As a result, the system ran at only 30 percent of capacity, resulting in a backlog of over 50,000 property checks. Commercial banking at 470 banks tied into the system came to a virtual halt. At that point, the state was forced to bring the old system back up at a cost to taxpayers of $500,000. The cost to banks was estimated to be in the millions of dollars.

SOURCE: J.B. Miles, ''System Collapse Stymies Borrowers in Golden State,'' *PC Week,* June 19, 1989, pp. 1, 8.

four concepts are quasi-resolution of conflict, avoidance of uncertainty, problematic search, and organizational learning.

Conflict naturally occurs among the various segments and individuals in any organization. According to the concept of **quasi-resolution of conflict,** this conflict may be resolved by allowing the organizational segments or individuals to pursue their own goals and make their own decisions within specified bounds, such as a budget. Conflict is also resolved sequentially, so that the decision process proceeds in an orderly manner and is not overloaded with multiple, conflicting decisions.

Second, **avoidance of uncertainty** is accomplished by shortening the time horizons of the decision-making process. For example, an organization can require faster turnaround or feedback of information related to the consequences of an action. Management may also enter into long-term arrangements (linkages) with such third parties as suppliers or customers to avoid uncertainty by reducing the risk of changes in supplier relations or customer demand.

Third, a **problematic search** implies that the search for alternative solutions to a problem starts with the problem itself and then moves to the next most likely problem location. In other words, a definite sequence exists in the search process for a problem solution and in the selection of the best alternative. Thus, an information system should provide the necessary information to support this sequential search process.

Finally, the concept of **organizational learning** states that organizations learn and adapt with time and changes in the environment. These changes may be driven by market factors (such as foreign competition), technological factors (such as the advent of micro-computers and communication technology), and organizational changes (such as a merger with another organization). An information system can help measure these changes and monitor an organization's reaction to these changes. For example, an organization might use an information system to track the productivity increase resulting from the use of personal computers.

The designer of an information system that meets the decision-making needs of an organization must be aware of these decision-making concepts. Without these concepts, the information system may not support the organization's managerial decision making adequately. As a result, management may dismiss the information system as an expensive failure.

Application to ProYacht

As an example of the application of these decision-making concepts, consider the decision facing top management at ProYacht, Inc. To meet an objective of the strategic plan discussed earlier (that is, to expand further into the recreational marine products market), management is considering adding a line of windsurfers to ProYacht's successful line of sailboats.

ProYacht management uses the concepts outlined earlier throughout its decision-making process. First, management at ProYacht avoids conflict by taking into account the concerns of the managers of the existing product line about the affect the windsurfer line might have on their budgets. Second, ProYacht avoids uncertainty by working with its dealers to add this windsurfer line to the existing sloop line and by staying with a familiar type of product—that is, sailboats. Moving into the jet ski product line, for example, would involve a great deal more uncertainty, because jet skis are dramatically different from sailboats. Third, ProYacht management considers this decision by looking at the potential problems associated with adding the windsurfer line—that is, design considerations, production capacity concerns, marketing, and distribution. The decision process is sequential; only after management feels that a successful windsurfer can be designed will they then tackle production problems. Similarly, only after the production problems are solved will the marketing concerns be addressed.

This sequential process continues until all problems are solved. If any problem cannot be resolved in an acceptable manner, then ProYacht will decide not to enter the windsurfer market. Finally, management learns by moving into a new market area to meet the growing demand for windsurfers.

An essential part of this decision, ProYacht's information system must provide management with answers to questions regarding design considerations, production and distribution capacity, and marketing linkages. Otherwise, the decision is made with inadequate information, which could lead to unfortunate results for ProYacht.

Structured and Unstructured Decisions

In general, decisions can be classified as either structured or unstructured.[3] They may also be called **programmed** or **unprogrammed,** according to Simon. **Structured decisions** can be made by following a set of rules, are usually made frequently, and are especially amenable to solution by computerized techniques. For example, ProYacht management can make a structured decision on ordering raw materials based on the current level of inventory.

On the other hand, **unstructured decisions** are more complex decisions that are usually made on an ad hoc basis using whatever information is available. These decisions are much harder to make, because rules or procedures do not exist for making these decisions. For example, the decision by ProYacht on whether to add a windsurfer line is a once-only decision having no prior experience or rule.

Somewhere between unstructured decisions and structured decisions are **semistructured decisions,** for which both human intuition and mathematical methods might be used. This type of decision may be made on a repetitive basis under changing or uncertain conditions. For ProYacht, the decision on how much to spend in advertising for their line of sailboats is an example of a semistructured decision that is made each year under varying market conditions.

Regardless of the type of decision to be made—structured, unstructured, or semistructured—decision makers must have the right information at the right time to have even a small chance at making a good decision. Without appropriate and timely information, decision making is too often a game of chance. Providing this information is the role of the information system. Several examples of structured, unstructured, and semistructured decisions at the three levels of managerial activity are presented in Table 3–1 on the following page.

Decision-Making Styles

Information systems must comply with the cognitive style of the decision maker. **Cognitive style** is how an individual assesses information and evaluates various alternatives. Some managers are systematic and use formal procedures for gathering information about a problem and searching for the best or the most satisfactory solution. On the other hand, some decision makers are much more intuitive, using a wider range of information without formal search procedures for selecting a solution. They like to get a "feel" for the problem and rely on their intuition, judgment, and experience to find the most appropriate solution.

Individuals who make decisions may be classified in other ways. For example, some decision makers are **problem avoiders** who seek every method to avoid any sort of problem. Others are **problem seekers** who relish the challenge of tackling interesting problems. Still others are simply **problem solvers** who deal with problems as they arise.

---

[3] G.A. Gorry and M.S. Scott-Morton, "A Framework for Management Information Systems," *Sloan Management Review,* Vol. 13, No. 1, 1971, p. 59.

TABLE 3–1

*Examples of
Decision Making
and Managerial
Activity*

Managerial Activity Levels	*Types of Decisions*		
	Unstructured	*Semistructured*	*Structured*
Strategic	Policies and Objectives	Takeovers and Mergers	Acquisition of Resources
Tactical	Organization of Division	Product Mix	Product Mix to Maximize Profit
Operational	Personnel Hiring and Firing	Assignment of Personnel	Production Schedule and Sequence of Tasks

Adapted with permission from G.A. Gorry and M.S. Scott-Morton, ''A Framework for Management Information Systems,'' *Sloan Management Review,* Vol 13, No. 1 (Fall 1971), p. 59.

Another way of looking at decision makers has to do with their preferences for the nature of the information they use in decision making. Some decision makers are very perceptive and prefer to see only the information relevant to a particular problem. The information provided in an exception report would probably satisfy this type of decision maker. Other decision makers are more receptive and prefer to look at everything available on a problem and then sort through the information themselves. A manager's individual style is important to consider when developing an information system (especially Decision Support Systems [DSS] and Executive Information Systems [EIS]) to support managerial activities. This presentation of information to decision makers is discussed at length in Chapter 11. If a decision maker's style is not considered, that manager will likely not use the information system much.

3.2 Decision-Making Models

Several **decision-making models** may be used to handle the decision-making process shown in Figure 3–1. Because they are mathematical and behavioral in nature, more than one model may be used in any given circumstance. The models discussed in the following paragraphs are examples of models that are highly structured (rational model), moderately structured (satisficing and bounded rationality model), and unstructured (incremental model).

Rational Model

The **rational model** assumes that the decision maker has a set goal; the criteria for ranking or evaluating this goal; a weighing or ordering procedure, in the case of multiple objectives; and a finite set of alternative courses of action, each with known outcomes. Unfortunately, the decision process is generally more complex than this model allows. Often, multiple goals must be considered, as indicated in the descriptive theory. Not all alternatives are known, and in an optimization model, they probably cannot all be considered at once. Most likely, the search process is sequential, as described earlier. The selection criteria may also be difficult to define in many cases. However, in some very structured situations, primarily in manufacturing, rational optimization

The Cuban Missile Crisis: Who Made the Decisions?

In October 1962, the world stood on the brink of a nuclear war between the United States and the former Soviet Union. Soviet missiles were discovered in Cuba and President John F. Kennedy demanded their removal. When he ordered a naval blockade of Cuba, a confrontation between U.S. and Soviet ships seemed imminent, but Soviet Premier Nikita Khruschev relented and agreed to remove the missiles. A potential holocaust was avoided. The outcome seemed to result from a series of decisions by the two countries; however, in an excellent discussion of the crisis, Graham Allison discloses the parties that actually made the decisions that controlled the outcome.

Allison identifies three decision-making forces: country versus country; leader versus leader; and bureaucracy versus bureaucracy. The opposing countries in the crisis were the United States and the Soviet Union—superpower faced superpower. Although the "country" element was the most obvious of the decision-making forces, it was probably the least important, because countries are represented by human leaders but run by bureaucracies. In the case of leader versus leader, the decisions made by Kennedy and Khruschev were the most publicized given the personalities involved—young American president up against Bolshevik leader. However, the manner in which each country's military bureaucracy responded to its leader's decisions may have actually played a greater role in the crisis than any other element.

For example, once Khruschev decided to place missiles in Cuba, the Soviet military bureaucracy built the installations in Cuba exactly like they built them in the Soviet Union. Presumably, Khruschev did not want the missile sites found; however, the military bureacracy made no effort to camouflage them. As a result, U.S. surveillance planes easily detected the missile sites. On the U.S. side, Kennedy asked the air force to carry out a "surgical strike" against the missile sites. However, the military bureaucracy informed Kennedy that it was not prepared to implement this type of operation and proposed, instead, to begin a massive bombing strike on Cuba. In both cases, decisions made by the leaders of each country were not supported by the military bureaucracy.

SOURCE: Graham T. Allison, *Essence of Decision: Explaining the Cuban Missile Crisis.* Boston, MA: Little, Brown, 1971.

models can be used effectively. These models require specific information from the information system.

ProYacht's use of a rational model might include linear integer programming to determine the mix of different sizes of sailboats to build to maximize profits. This programming requires specific information about market demand, resource availabilities, and labor costs.

Satisficing and
Bounded
Rationality

To overcome the limitations of the rational model, J.G. March and H.A. Simon[4] proposed that individuals and organizations really search for the most satisfactory rather than optimal solution using a sequential process. All alternatives are not considered in this sequential process, and only one goal is generally considered at one time. In other words, management solves one problem based on one objective in a satisfactory way and then moves on to the next problem, goal, or competitive opportunity. The bounds on the search process and the satisfactory, rather than optimal, selection criteria led to the common use of the terms **bounded rationality** and **satisficing** in reference to this model. An information system must track this process so management has the necessary information at the appropriate time in the decision process.

As an example of bounded rationality, consider ProYacht's windsurfer decision, which is restricted to two possible alternatives—begin production of a line of windsurfers or do not begin production. Management has made a conscious decision not to consider the production of all possible recreational aquatic alternatives, that is, jet skis, knee boards, power boats, and so on.

In the satisficing aspect of the windsurfer decision, ProYacht is not attempting to maximize its profit by expanding its product line in multiple directions. Instead, the company is simply trying to decide if it should expand in one new direction to take advantage of existing expertise and capacity. ProYacht would be satisfied with the profitable addition of a line of windsurfers.

Incremental
Model

Another approach often used involves not setting forth any selection criteria or a set of alternatives. Instead, management just muddles through its decisions. According to C.E. Lindblom[5] these decision makers adopt an **incremental model** of decision making and select the alternative which appears only marginally different from the current mode of operation. This process leads to an evolutionary sequence of small changes in an organization's activities. For example, instead of making major price or quality changes to improve sales, an organization using the incremental decision-making process makes a minor price change and sees how it works; then the organization would make another minor price change until the problem is resolved. An information system must collect and process the appropriate data for management to assess these marginal effects in the decision-making process.

All of these Models use a search process to find a solution. According to contemporary literature,[6] decision makers use a compensatory search process when the problem is small enough to consider all factors and alternatives. A weighting scheme often helps to find the best alternative when the number of factors and alternatives is

---

[4] J.G. March and H.A. Simon, *Organizations,* (New York: John Wiley, 1958); Herbert A. Simon, *Administrative Behavior,* 3rd ed. (New York: Free Press, a division of Macmillan, Inc., 1976); and H.A. Simon, *New Science of Management Decision,* revised edition (Englewood Cliffs, NJ: Prentice-Hall, 1977).

[5] C.E. Lindblom, "The Science of Muddling Through," *Public Administration Review,* Vol. 19, 1959, pp. 79–88.

[6] E.R. Iselin, "The Effects of Information Diversity on Decision Quality in a Structured Decision Task," *Accounting Organizations and Society,* Vol. 13, 1988, pp. 107–64; A. Tversky, "Elimination by Aspects: A Theory of Choice," *Psychological Review,* Vol. 79, 1972, pp. 281–99.

small. Only some highly structured models may be classified as compensatory. On the other hand, decision makers use a noncompensatory search process when the number of factors or alternatives is large. In a noncompensatory search process, factors must either be prioritized or some alternatives eliminated.

3.3 Organizational Decision-Making Environments

A discussion of decision making by organizations must consider the structure of the organization. Many different types of **organization structure** can be used by management to implement its strategy. In a **centralized organization structure,** all the control and decision-making authority are vested in a few individuals at the home office. A **decentralized organization structure** gives functional or product managers more control and responsibility to make decisions. These two organization structures are contrasted in Figure 3–2 on the following page.

Combinations of these structures may be more appropriate for certain management strategies. In particular, in a **matrix organization,** employees are organized both by function and by project. For example, an engineering firm may be organized according to an employee's function as an electrical or civil engineer or programmer, with each functional group having its own manager. These same employees may also be organized by the projects to which each is assigned, with a project manager in charge of each project. Table 3–2, on page 67, shows an example of such a matrix organization.

Organizational Constraints

In addition to the procedures, models, and styles for decision making and organizational structure, many **organizational constraints** must be considered. These constraints affect the speed of decision making and the boundaries within which individuals and organizations may search for solutions. In large bureaucracies, specific rules and regulations— often referred to as **Standard Operating Procedures (SOP)**—specify how decisions are to be made, what policies must be followed, and what resources are at the disposal of the decision maker. Often a course of action must be approved at many levels in an organization, particularly if the resources required to seize an opportunity or to solve a problem are substantial. Long lead times may be needed for an organization to react. As a result, opportunities can be lost or problems can grow because of the time required to gain approval. To minimize this problem through quasi-resolution of conflict, lower level managers are often given authority over specific types and sizes of decisions.

Because SOPs are often not easily changed, an organization may find it difficult to adapt to changing environmental conditions and to pursue competitive opportunities. In most cases, SOPs are institutionalized as part of the data processing and information system of the organization.

In addition to bureaucratic problems, politics plays a role in decision-making activity in most organizations. Rather than making decisions using rational or even satisficing criteria, management may base its decisions on political grounds. Actions are negotiated between an organization's power brokers, bounded by such political constraints as job security, and founded on a compromise among many sets of organizational goals and individual agendas.

FIGURE 3–2   *Examples of Centralized and Decentralized Organization Structures*

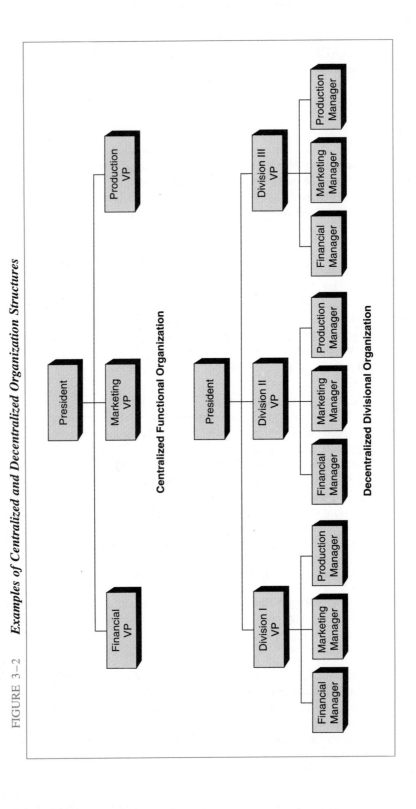

66

TABLE 3–2

Example of a
Matrix
Organization

	Function		
Project	Engineering	Computer Programming	Staff Support
Project A	LeBeau and Jones	Johnson	Fernandez and Edwards
Project B		Johnson and Strong	Edwards
Project C	LeBeau		Edwards
Project D	Jones	Strong and Chen	Edwards and Fernandez

Sometimes these SOPs hinder the rapid decision making necessary for a firm to compete effectively. Thus, an organization must be careful not to let the information system and its related paperwork inhibit the flexibility needed to be competitive. For example, ProYacht management needs a complete market study of the demand for a new windsurfer product line, the projected production costs for that line, and the windsurfer engineering specifications. In the past, this type of study for a new sailboat had taken a year to complete. However, ProYacht can accomplish this quickly using a new Computer-Aided Design (CAD) package, which also assists in the engineering and production planning, as discussed in Chapter 9.

In other organizations, no association exists among decisions, resource constraints, and goals or criteria. Decisions are made without a careful study of alternatives, the use of prescribed rules, or a political compromise involving several objectives. Needless to say, because the decision makers in this type of organization often cannot clearly state what information they need, information systems are seldom useful. Not surprisingly, many organizations that use such a decision-making ''process'' do not survive for long.

Organizational
Changes

Many behavioral issues are involved in the organization and control of information systems. First, changes in information systems can affect an organization's structure, as well as the way it conducts its business. This can cause major shakeups in individual employees' jobs and career paths. For example, a clerk who once manually processed data on the receipt of merchandise may now be required to enter the information on a computer terminal. Without adequate training, the clerk may be terrified of the computer and feel threatened.

As another example of the organizational changes resulting from a new information system, consider the middle-level manager who has routinely reviewed purchase orders and made vendor decisions. The firm installs an automated purchase system with predetermined purchase decision rules tied to a Just-in-Time (JIT) inventory system and direct communication to vendors. The manager now negotiates with new vendors over product quality and delivery arrangements and reports to a higher level manager in the organization. In this case, the nature of the manager's job is vastly different with greatly increased decision-making responsibilities.

In both illustrations, the **job social structure** has changed. Because employee resistance to these changes is often great, care must be exercised in the analysis, design, implementation, and use of information systems. In general, an organization can minimize the effects of these changes via good communication on the need for change and adequate training in new tasks, including the new decisions to be made.

3.4 General Systems Model of an Organization

System Definition

Throughout this text, we have discussed the information system. However, to this point we have not actually defined what a system is and how the information system relates to other systems in an organization. The following paragraphs consider systems in general and then systems in an organization.

A **system** is a set of elements or components organized and integrated to accomplish an objective. The components include data input, processing, storage, information output, and feedback. **Input** includes any data that is entered into the system. **Processing** is the transformation of the input into some form of **output** information. **Storage** is a repository of data for future processing and output. **Feedback** is a form of output which is sent back to the system's input or processing function and enables the system to change its operation if necessary. Feedback can originate within the system or in the environment. In a sense, feedback monitors the system to ensure that the system meets its goal.

To accomplish the required feedback, reports are generated by the information system. In advanced information systems, managers may even obtain needed information from an **online system,** which shows the current status of the physical transformation process, input, or output. An example of a report that provides feedback at ProYacht would be a production report showing the stage of completion of each order placed in production. With this report, management can track the progress of each boat to see if delivery schedules can be met. If production falls behind schedule, management can act to remedy the problem because of this feedback knowledge.

Systems do not exist in a vacuum but function in an environment. This **environment** constrains the activities of the system from an organizational perspective, provides input into the system in the form of resources and information, and monitors the output from the system in terms of products, services, and information. The various factors and constraints present in a business environment include customers, vendors, stockholders and owners, employees, organizational structure, government regulators, competitors and their actions, the financial community, and the community in which the organization operates. The system is separated from its environment by a **boundary.** Figure 3–3 shows the relationships among the input, processing, storage, output, feedback, environment, and boundary for an information system.

Subsystems

Most systems have at least one **subsystem,** which works as a system on its own to handle some detailed task for the larger system. The information system we have discussed has various subsystems, which include the components of the information system. The information system itself is a subsystem of the larger organizational system.

For example, a business may be subdivided along functional lines into financial, marketing, and production subsystems. Each of these management subsystems and correspond-

FIGURE 3–3   *Elements of an Information System*

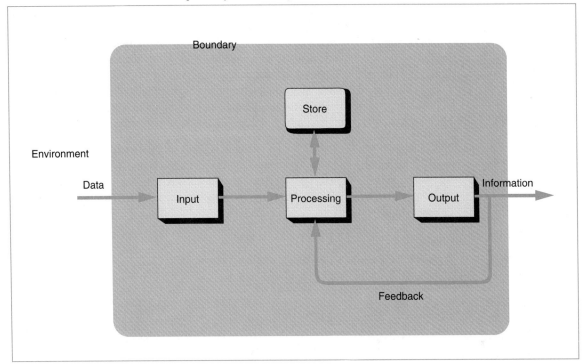

ing information subsystems can then be analyzed in terms of inputs, transformation process, and outputs to ensure that the systems support management's decision-making needs. Moreover, each system affects the other organizational units in the larger system.

3.5 Physical, Management, and Information Systems

In general, an organizational system comprises a physical system, a management system, and an information system. The **physical system** transforms such input resources as personnel, financial capital, raw materials or components, equipment, and information into products and services. This physical system is monitored and controlled by a **management system,** which makes decisions regarding the input, transformation process, and the nature of the output. Information is received from these three physical stages and transmitted to those responsible for each stage by the **information system.** How these three organizational subsystems are related in a typical organization is shown in Figure 3–4.

For ProYacht, Inc., the physical system is the actual manufacturing, distribution, and sale of boats. The management system includes the organization described earlier. The information system includes all the various ProYacht systems discussed in earlier chapters.

As an example, external data on the recreational and economic environment and internal data on ProYacht's production and distribution system are input into the information system. The information system then transforms this data into information, which is stored or output to support managerial decision making. From this, ProYacht managers make decisions on which boats to manufacture. The information system monitors the progress of the physical manufacturing process and, through a feedback loop, reports to management any deviations from planned production. Feedback of this type is necessary for ProYacht to respond to market-driven changes by modifying which boats they manufacture, manufacturing schedules, and distribution channels.

Integrating Major Organizational Systems

The objectives of the information system and its subsystems are to provide management with the information needed to process day-to-day transactions, make decisions, and to add value to its products and services. The decisions involve daily operations, the management of vital resources, and the accomplishment of the organization's objectives through strategic decisions.

FIGURE 3–4   ***Physical, Management, and Information Systems***

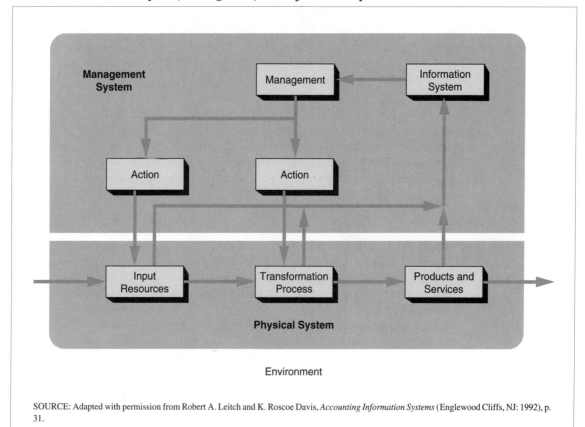

SOURCE: Adapted with permission from Robert A. Leitch and K. Roscoe Davis, *Accounting Information Systems* (Englewood Cliffs, NJ: 1992), p. 31.

For an organization to be effective, the inputs, transformation processes, outputs, feedback controls, and environmental constraints illustrated in Figure 3–4 must be coordinated so that they work together as a composite system. If each component (input, transformation, and output) is allowed to operate separately, a problem of **suboptimization** can occur. For example if ProYacht's sales and marketing departments do not communicate with the production department as to the number of boats to build, inventory may not match demand. Likewise, if production does not communicate with procurement about production components, production might grind to a halt for lack of parts. Thus, the physical system's value chain must operate as an **integrated system,** with all its activities coordinated through effective management and information systems. All the components of the value chain or its supporting systems need not be located in one place. If the components are spread over a wide area, the system is termed a **distributed system.**

Formal and Informal Information Systems

A **formal information system** represents a set of responsibilities and procedures for data input, processing, output, and utilization of information. This formal system is emphasized in this text. However, most organizations also have an **informal information system** that is not as well organized as a formal system. Every office has a ''grapevine'' that informally passes information around an organization. Knowledge of the informal information system can be important in understanding an organization and its lines of authority, power, and communication.

Information Systems Role

In general, the information system should assist management in its various activities by providing timely, accurate, clear, and relevant information so that it can manage the physical activities of the organization as well as make tactical and strategic decisions. As shown in Figure 3–4, data are gathered from the environment, and the resources are used in the physical transformation process. The transformation process yields the products and services sent on to customers and the feedback data that are sent to the information system. All the data are organized and disseminated by the information system to managers who make the decisions that affect the organization's actions regarding the input and transformation process. Moreover, as discussed in Chapter 1, the information may be used aggressively to enhance the value of the organization's products and services and to compete more effectively in the marketplace.

All the major elements (components) of the information system—hardware, software, data, personnel, and procedures—must be organized to support the management and physical systems. A computer system is not an information system in itself, but a subsystem composed of some of the elements of the overall information system. As with the physical system, the information system elements must form an integrated system for effective and efficient delivery of information.

3.6 Developing Information Systems

In today's dynamic environment, objectives, strategies, and organizations are constantly changing. Management must always be aware of new and varying information needs and the potential for increased information usage due to improvements in technology. As a result, information systems also change, and this process must be well managed so that new organizational objectives are achieved. The **systems development** process must be as well planned as the process of acquiring, developing, and monitoring any key organization resource. Information needs are analyzed; new systems are designed or old ones are modified to meet these needs; the most appropriate design is selected and implemented; and the system is operated and monitored until it must be changed again. Then the whole process starts over. This systems life cycle is shown in Figure 3–5.

An organization may use any one of several approaches for managing the development of new systems or modifying old systems in this life cycle. Each approach contains the basic elements of what is commonly called the **structured analysis and design** approach that is described in the next section and detailed in Chapters 12, 13, and 14.

The Structured Systems Development Process

Figure 3–5 illustrates the flow of the **structured systems development process,** often called the **system development life cycle.** It is popularly called **structured analysis and design;** we call the process by all these names in this text. **Project definition** may involve isolating a new information need or defining an opportunity in the marketplace. A **feasibility study** is then undertaken to determine the existence of a practical solution to the problem, given the organization's existing constraints. A detailed **requirements analysis** of information needs is performed. These indicate *what* must be done to solve the problem. Following this analysis, the **general systems design** is developed, outlining *how* the problem should be solved; stated from a different perspective, the general design describes feasible alternatives for solving the problem.

Next, the most appropriate alternative is selected and a **detailed systems design** is developed. At this time, specifications are spelled out for the development of computer software or purchase of various elements of the proposed information system. The **implementation** step involves solving the problem via the acquisition, software development, installation of the information system, and the training of personnel on the new elements of the system. In some cases, software must be written, while in other cases, software can be purchased from a vendor. Finally, during **evaluation operation and maintenance,** the system is monitored for continued compliance with management needs and maintained for efficient operation. When it fails to meet management's needs, the cycle is started again.

Other versions of this approach have a shorter development cycle—for example, the prototyping and end user development discussed in Chapter 15. Nevertheless, the structured analysis and design concept underlies these other approaches and is fundamental to the effective use of an organization's resources and its information technology.

Describing an Information System

The basic elements of an information system are described in several ways by analysts and others who communicate with users and system designers. These descriptive methods include system flowcharting and data-flow diagraming, which are presented here and used throughout the text to illustrate various types of systems. **System flowcharting** is a standardized graphical method of presentation that demonstrates the interrelationships among the elements of an information system. The symbols shown in Figure 3–6, on page 74, are universally understood and, as a result, minimize the verbal explanation needed to describe an information system. These symbols are used throughout this text.

FIGURE 3-5

*System
Development Life
Cycle*

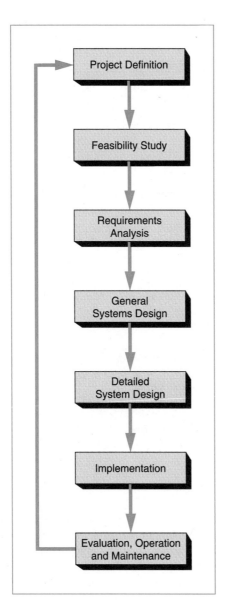

In Figure 3-6, the rectangle represents computer processing, and the trapezoid represents manual processing. In a computer system design, the latter usually is used to illustrate the preparation of input documents and the review and distribution of output. The document symbol is used to represent computerized reports and input documents such as sales invoices or customer orders. In contemporary computerized system design flowcharts, data entry is represented by the terminal or manual key input symbol, and output is often shown as an online terminal display symbol. In many batch processing

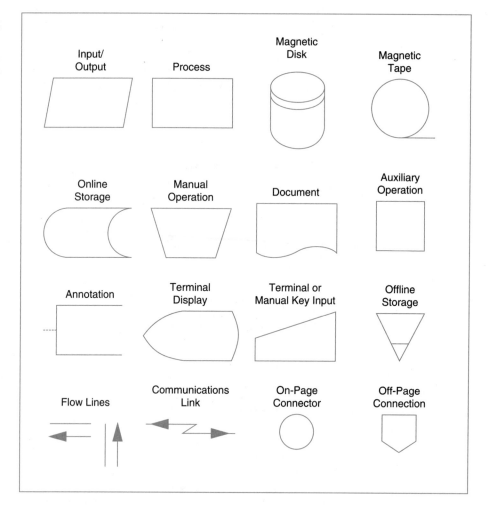

FIGURE 3–6

System Flowcharting Symbols

systems, large quantities of information are stored on magnetic tape, so the flowchart contains the magnetic tape symbol. In online system designs, either the online storage symbol or the magnetic disk symbol is used to indicate that data is stored on a magnetic disk; the first symbol indicates the mode of storage and the latter indicates the medium. When disks are used in a batch processing system, the disk symbol is shown. An auxiliary operation is used to process data that is not under the control of the computer. Offline storage usually is representative of manual files.

Communication between input devices and processing steps, between processing steps and storage media, and between processing steps and output is shown by directional flow lines. These lines, shown in Figure 3–6, are assumed to flow from top to bottom and left to right; an arrow on the end indicates a different direction of flow. In addition, communication links with remote input devices, other computers, and output devices are indicated by the communication link symbol.

Software from
J. P. Morgan

Very few people would think of software development when they hear the name "J. P. Morgan." Instead, they usually think of money. This is not surprising given that J. P. Morgan & Co. is the fifth largest bank in the United States and is possibly the most widely respected financial institution in the country. However, a reason for J. P. Morgan being associated with software development and design is a unique product called MPI/PC Report that the institution introduced in 1986. MPI/PC Report seeks to exploit a niche in the issuing and paying agency services market that allows Morgan to offer reporting services that are superior to those of the competition, but at radically reduced prices. Specifically, companies use the product to generate sophisticated financial and analytical reports on their commercial paper programs.

Commercial paper is one of the largest financial debt securities in use by institutions today, with a total market size of over $500 billion. Commercial paper is short-term promissory notes that are sold by issuers to investors to handle cash flow needs. To monitor the amount of commercial paper outstanding, and to generate detailed analytical reports, issuers rely on issuing and paying agents (that is, the banks responsible for creating the debt security) to provide them with a reporting service. Most bank systems, however, limit issuers to relying on expensive mainframe computer resources to generate reports. These expenses can exceed $100,000 per year. With MPI/PC Report, however, issuers use a PC-based software package that allows issuers to generate reports using the processing powers of their own PCs. The Commercial Paper Management Group at Morgan made the decision to develop and write a PC-based product in 1985 to lower issuer costs and to enable their clients to use PCs, which were becoming more commonplace in the business environment. The system design, analysis, and programming effort was completed within nine months, and the product was launched in August 1986.

MPI/PC Report does two basic operations. First, it retrieves the commercial paper issuance data from Morgan's mainframe computer and downloads it to the issuer's PC. Second, it uses this downloaded information to generate reports offline. Selling for $2,500 with a $250 per month usage fee for the basic system, this package is substantially cheaper than the mainframe alternative. Currently, the product is used by over 100 "Fortune 500" clients, some sovereign governments (for example, Canada and New Zealand), and numerous foreign issuers. Since the product was introduced it has generated over $1 million in revenues for the Commercial Paper management Group, while offering flexibility to Morgan's clients.

Morgan has not rested on its laurels, however. In the first quarter of 1990, the bank introduced the second release of MPI/PC Report, which was totally redesigned. The new version is written entirely in the "C" programming language and has several added features to enable issuers to take advantage of hardware and software developments (for example, local area networks and pop-up window screens). Additionally, Morgan is already looking into expanding the product to include other debt securities, such as certificates of deposit and medium-term notes.

SOURCE: Jeffrey Rothfeder, "Bank-Developed Software Transforms Lackluster Service into a Profit Leader," *PC Week,* No. 24, 1987, pp. 66, 70; and Morgan Guaranty Trust Company of New York, a subsidiary of J. P. Morgan & Co., Incorporated, 1990.

FIGURE 3–7   *ProYacht, Inc. Information System*

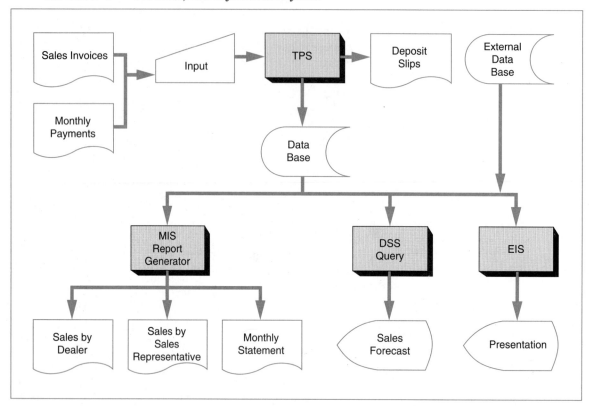

These symbols may also include a brief description of the process, the type of report or input, the nature and kind of the data stored in the storage device, or the individual or department that processes the information. When the symbol is not large enough to note some important information about a process or a file, the annotation symbol shown in Figure 3–6 may be used. In addition, on-page and off-page connectors may be used to clarify the flow of information on the same page or to other pages of the flowchart.

These symbols provide the basis for describing an information system and its fundamental input, processing, and output activities. Consider the generalized information system for ProYacht shown in Figure 3–7, which uses the flowchart symbols in Figure 3–6. Sales orders for sailboats entered into the system are stored in an online data base, which is used to produce reports for management on dealer and sales representative sales. In addition, transaction data relating to the terms of the sale are used to generate the statements mailed to dealers and customers every month. Upon receipt of these statements, dealers send ProYacht their monthly payments, which are keyed into the data

FIGURE 3–8

Data Flow Diagram Symbols

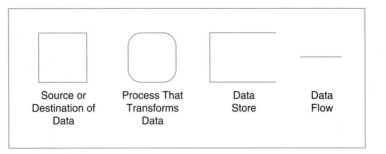

| Source or Destination of Data | Process That Transforms Data | Data Store | Data Flow |

base. A Transaction Processing System (TPS) takes this input, posts a cash receipts journal which is also stored in the data base, and prepares a deposit slip from the total of these receipts. The cash receipts are then attached to this deposit slip and forwarded to the bank for deposit. A Mangement Information System (MIS) uses the output from TPS to develop various reports. A Decision Support System (DSS) and an Executive Information System (EIS) may be used to query different combinations of data to help management make decisions. For example, management may decide to borrow money because the sales order and cash receipt history stored in the data base indicate an inadequate cash receipts pattern. An Executive Information System uses TPS and external data to create presentations.

Data flow diagraming shows the processing, flows, and storage of data and information within the information system. This method is often utilized in the general systems design step to determine alternatives for the new system design. The symbols used in data flow diagrams are shown in Figure 3–8, and the data flows in ProYacht's generalized information system are illustrated in Figure 3–9 on following page.

3.7 Management and Control of Information Systems

The information system needs to be well managed and controlled to be effective in supporting management's needs. A **strategic plan** should exist for the traditional as well as the strategic use of information to assist management in the delivery of the organization's products and services. The organization must know how it expects to use and control its information resource, and all analysis and design decisions regarding the information system should fit this plan.

Some organizations employ a manager of information systems who coordinates all the information activities and implements policies with regard to the development and use of information systems. This person often reports directly to the president or other senior officer in the firm. In general, someone must have the responsibility to manage and control the information resources available to the organization. This person should also have significant authority within the organization, considering the strategic nature of information today.

FIGURE 3–9

Data Flows in
ProYacht's
Information
System

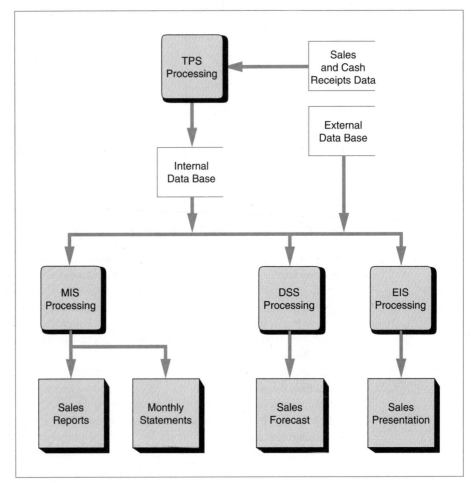

3.8 Summary

An organization has objectives, it determines a strategy for carrying out these objectives, and it structures itself to implement this strategy. Throughout this process, management continually makes decisions; the information system must provide management with the necessary information to make day-to-day decisions as well as tactical and strategic decisions when necessary. As a result, the characteristics of the organization and its decision-making process are vitally important to the designer of an information system.

Decision making is a multi-step process that includes problem definition, data gathering, alternative identification and evaluation, and alternative selection and implementation. Finally, feedback is used to monitor the results of the decision. An effective information system is necessary for these monitoring activities. Four concepts that describe decision making are quasi-resolution of conflict, avoidance of uncertainty, problematic search, and organizational learning. In designing an information system, these decision-making concepts should be considered.

Several decision-making models are used in organizations, including the rational model, satisficing and bounded rationality model, and the incremental model. Decisions may be structured, unstructured, or semistructured. The various decision-making cognitive styles include systematic and intuitive styles. Decision makers can be problem avoiders, problem seekers, or problem solvers. Organizational structures include centralized, decentralized, and matrix organizations. Organizational constraints must also be taken into account in making decisions.

Organizations can be described as systems that have data input, processing, information output, feedback, a boundary, and an environment. Most systems also have subsystems. Organizations have a physical system that produces and markets products and services. Organizations also have a management system to manage the physical system and an information system that supports the physical system and management system and adds value to products and services. An information system monitors the activities of the physical system and helps managers make decisions.

Information systems have a certain life cycle. When problems and opportunities arise, new information systems are designed and implemented using the structured systems development process. Analysts and designers describe information systems through the use of data flow diagrams and systems flowcharts. New information systems must meet managerial and decision-making needs.

Key Terms

alternatives
avoidance of uncertainty
boundary
bounded rationality
centralized organization structure
cognitive style
data
data flow diagraming
decentralized organization structure
decision making
decision-making models
decision-making process
detailed systems design
distributed system
environment
evaluation operation and maintenance
feasibility study
feedback
formal information system
general systems design
implementation
incremental model
informal information system

information system
input
integrated system
job social structure
management system
matrix organization
online system
organization structure
organizational constraints
organizational learning
organizational objectives
output
physical system
problem
problem avoiders
problem seekers
problem solvers
problematic search
processing
programmed decision
project definition
quasi-resolution of conflict
rational model

requirements analysis	structured systems development
satisficing	suboptimization
semistructured decisions	subsystem
Standard Operating Procedures (SOP)	system
storage	system flowcharting
strategic plan	system development life cycle
strategy	systems development
structured analysis and design	unprogrammed decision
structured decisions	unstructured decisions

Review Questions

1. List the steps in the decision-making process.

2. Discuss briefly the four concepts used in classical decision-making theory. Using one of these concepts, discuss how you might decide what to do when you graduate.

3. Name the three decision-making models described in this chapter and give an example of each.

4. What is meant by the term cognitive style? How does it apply to decision making?

5. List the three cognitive styles of decision makers described in the chapter. Which style do you think describes you?

6. What does organizational structure have to do with decision making? What is a matrix organization?

7. What is an SOP? How does it relate to organizational constraints?

8. How are lower-level managers allowed to make decisions without going to higher levels for approval?

9. How does resistance to change affect decision making within an organization? Give an example of how change in job social structure can affect employees.

10. What is a system? What are the components of a system? Give an example of a system with which you are familiar and identify these components.

11. Name three systems that exist simultaneously within an organization.

12. What role does feedback play in the operation of the organizational system?

13. What is the difference between formal and informal information systems?

14. What is the rationale for stating that the organization is itself an information system?

15. Name the process of designing, creating, and implementing a new information system. What are the seven phases (steps) in this process?

Discussion Questions

1. Give an example of how information technology and an information system can support each step in the decision-making process.

2. How can an information system and its related information technology be used to support the physical system of an organization that manufactures and distributes lawn mowers and other small-engine home and recreation vehicles? How can the information system be used to support a decentralized management system that gives each plant, warehouse, and marketing region the authority to make its own business decisions?

3. Bob Smith needs to computerize his hardware store so that he can better manage his buying, inventory, sales and collection activities. After discussing his problem with friends, he purchased a SUPER X microcomputer from Fast Freddy's Discount Computer Store. Fast Freddy also sold him the least expensive business management and accounting software. Discuss the appropriateness of Bob Smith's choice, and the likelihood of his new system satisfying his information needs.

4. Identify the steps you went through or are going through now to select a major in college, and link these steps to the decision-making process outlined in the chapter. Identify your decision-making model and style.

5. As a systems analyst, you are assigned the responsibility for developing a new decision support system for a real estate and development firm's financial planning. What organizational and decision-making factors should you consider?

6. A salesperson at a microcomputer store tells you that most of her customers use Business Management II as their computer system. She claims all types of businesses can use it, based on her experience at the training classes for the software. Comment on the salesperson's contention that Business Management II is universally applicable.

Case 3–1
Citizens' Gas Company

Citizens' Gas Company, a medium-sized gas distribution company, provides natural gas service to approximately 200,000 customers. The customer base is divided into three revenue classes. Data by customer class are as follows:

Class	Customers	Sales in Cubic Feet	Revenue
Residential	160,000	180 billion	$160 million
Commercial	38,000	15 billion	25 million
Industrial	2,000	50 billion	65 million
		245 billion	$250 million

Because residential customer gas usage is primarily for residence heating purposes, it is highly correlated to the weather. Commercial and industrial customers, on the other hand, may or may not use gas for heating purposes, so consumption is not necessarily correlated to the weather.

The largest 25 industrial customers account for $30 million of revenues. Each of these 25 customers uses gas for heating and industrial purposes in a consumption pattern that is governed almost entirely by business factors.

The company obtains its gas supply from 10 major pipeline companies. The pipeline companies provide gas in amounts specified in contracts that extend over periods ranging from 5–15 years. For some contracts, the supply is in equal monthly increments, but for others, the supply varies in accordance with the heating season. Supply above the contract amounts is not available, and some contracts contain a take-or-pay clause — that is, the company must pay for the volumes specified in the contract, whether or not it can take the gas.

To assist in matching customer demand with supply, the company maintains a gas storage field. Gas can be pumped into the storage field when supply exceeds customer demand, and gas can also be obtained quickly when demand exceeds supply. No restrictions exist on the use of the gas storage field, except that the field must be filled to capacity at the beginning of each fiscal year (September 1). Consequently, when the contractual supply of gas for the remainder of the fiscal year is less than that required to satisfy projected demand and replenish the storage field, the company must reduce service to its industrial customers (except for quantities that are used for heating). The curtailments must be carefully controlled so that an oversupply does not occur at year-end. Similarly, the curtailments must adequately protect against the need to reduce commercial or residential customers in order to replenish the storage field at year-end.

In recent years, the company's planning efforts have not provided a firm basis for the establishment of long-term contracts, and the current year is no different. Planning efforts are not adequate to control the supply during the current year. Customer demand is projected only as a function of the total number of customers. Commercial and industrial customers' demands for gas has been curtailed excessively, resulting in lost sales and an excess of supply at year-end.

In an attempt to correct these problems, the president of Citizens' Gas has hired a new director of corporate planning to develop a logical concept and several design alternatives for a system that can be used to analyze the supply and demand of natural gas. The system should provide a monthly gas plan for each year for the next five years, with particular emphasis on the first year. The plan should also provide a set of reports that assist in the decision-making process and contain all necessary supporting schedules. The system must provide for the use of actual data during the course of the first year to project demand for the rest of the year and the year in total. The director knows that the president will base his decisions on the effect of alternative plans on operating income.

Case Questions

1. What decisions must Citizens' Gas make?

2. What are the alternatives for each decision?

3. What information (reports and data) is needed for each decision?

(CMA adapted)

Case 3–2
T&F Network Services

Teresa Cook, who worked for a well-known communication hardware manufacturer as an engineer, rapidly advanced as the microcomputer industry mushroomed in the last two decades. As her career leveled off, Cook considered several opportunities to branch out on her own using her considerable investment in company stock as capital. Over lunch with Barbara Fuentes, an old college roommate and an accountant with a large bank which had recently merged with another large bank, Cook determined that Fuentes' career was also in the doldrums. They decided to go into business together in a firm that would develop and install computer networks for companies. With Fuentes' banking connections and Cook's engineering expertise, they were immediately successful. They named their firm T&F Network Services.

T&F Network Services' clients were small banks and savings and loans in the Rocky Mountain states. The company grew to employ around 100 staff personnel, mostly management information system professionals, computer engineers, and accountants. The company had been using an antiquated accounting system on some dated personal computers for its sole source of routine information on business activities. For appearance reasons and for their own operational efficiency Cook and Fuentes decided to purchase the latest network and communication technology and the latest accounting and office information system.

Business decreased as the company approached the saturation level of the financial institutions that needed their assistance. Large banks could do their own work, and many small financial institutions were merging with larger ones. Cook and Fuentes decided to branch into the real estate and development market, in which they had only limited success. They wondered what to do next.

Case Questions

1. A business associate suggested that Cook and Fuentes take a systems approach to their business. Did they do this at the outset and as they developed their business? How would they take a systems approach now?

2. Did they develop their own information system to support their business activities (management and physical systems)? What is their physical system? What can you determine from the case about their management system? What should they do to develop a more effective information system?

3. Did Cook and Fuentes use information to add value to their product or service? Suggest some ways they could have done this and how these ways may have improved their competitive position.

II

Information System Resources

Section II discusses the information resources that are critical to the success of information systems in organizations. Chapter 4 describes computer hardware and software resources. Chapter 5 discusses data entry and file management systems and introduces data base management systems. Chapter 6 follows up with a full discussion of data base management systems, emphasizing the relational data base model. Finally, Chapter 7 focuses on network sharing of information resources and includes discussions on local and wide area computer networks and telecommunications applications.

Computer Resources

4

Introduction

Two of the key elements of an information system introduced in Chapter 2—computer hardware and software—are discussed in detail in this chapter. Coverage of hardware includes a look at computer components and how they work together, but does not give a detailed description of the individual devices that actually carry out the operations.

This chapter also introduces the software that directs the actions of the hardware. The discussion covers the importance of software for the successful use of the computer, the two major types of software (systems software and applications software), and some important software package terminology. The chapter summarizes software for both mainframes and personal computers (PCs). Five types of personal productivity software—word processing, spreadsheet, data base management, graphics, and telecommunications—are also introduced in this chapter.

**4.1
Information
System
Computer
Resources**

The preceding chapters described the computer as a crucial part of the Computer-Based Information System (CBIS) that manages an organization's most important resource—its information. Manual information systems have always existed, but a CBIS obviously cannot exist without a computer. The computer is the key resource in an information system that facilitates the efficient storage of large amounts of data and the high-speed processing of data into information. To understand a CBIS requires basic knowledge of computer operation and the elements that make up the computer.

A **computer** is a machine that stores and processes data into information based on a series of instructions. The ability to execute a list of instructions differentiates the computer from a calculator or other office machine. Two important computer characteristics are its speed and accuracy. The speed of a computer's operations is measured in nanoseconds—billionths of a second—and the computer always does exactly what it is instructed to do. These two characteristics can also lead to problems when the computer is given wrong instructions. Instead of processing data into usable information, the computer quickly performs incorrect operations resulting in the output of useless garbage.

The two main parts of a computer are the machinery and the human-provided logic. The computer's machinery, or **hardware,** is made up of electronic devices and circuits. The human-provided logic is also called the computer's **software,** without which the computer can do nothing. The software is composed of a series of instructions called **programs.** Hardware and software together make up the computer resource that is necessary for a CBIS.

Classifying
Computers

Now that we know what a computer is, we can consider the types of computers in today's information systems. The most common classification of computers is based on size. In terms of size, computers can be classified into three types—mainframes, minicomputers, and microcomputers (or personal computers).

A **mainframe** is a large, expensive computer (often costing over well over $1 million) that requires a special support staff and physical environment. Mainframes are usually housed in a computer center and used in large businesses, government, or academic situations where they support multiple functions and users (usually in excess of 100 at one time). A subset of mainframes are **supercomputers,** which are the fastest computers in use today. These very large computers are used by universities, businesses, and government agencies for processing applications that require extremely high speed and large storage capacities.

At the other extreme in terms of size are **personal computers,** which are small, single-user computers that are relatively inexpensive ($500–$10,000) and do not require a special environment or special knowledge to use them. Personal computers can be used in a manner very similar to a mainframe, but they are generally much slower and cannot store nearly as much data as a mainframe.

The computer size between a mainframe and a personal computer is the **minicomputer** (also called a **midsize computer**), which is used by many organizations that need more processing power than that available with personal computers, but less than that available with mainframes. A minicomputer can support multiple users and often requires a special environment and some support staff, but not on the same level as a mainframe. Currently, the size line between personal computers and minicomputers is getting hazy as personal computers become more powerful and can support multiple users. Generally, a computer that serves a single user is a personal computer; if it serves multiple users, it is a minicomputer or mainframe. In the remainder of this text, when we refer to mainframes and personal computers, we include minicomputers under the label of mainframe.

Types of
Personal
Computers

With all of the emphasis given to personal computers in the popular media, a little information about the various types of personal computers used in business, education, and the home is useful. Today's personal computer is one of four major types—the IBM PC-XT class of computers that works like the original IBM PC-XT; the IBM PC-AT class of computers that works like the original IBM PC-AT (including the Compaq Deskpro, IBM PS/1, and various other work-a-likes); the IBM PS/2 series; and the Apple Macintosh series.

The first two categories of personal computers are referred to as **IBM compatible PCs,** because they work just like the original IBM models. Other than the IBM PS/1 computer, IBM does not sell computers in either of these categories. Instead, IBM has developed a second generation of personal computers—its **PS/2 series.** These computers run the same software as the IBM compatible PCs, but their internal hardware differs dramatically from those computers and cannot be copied by other manufacturers. This precludes the development of PS/2 work-a-likes without a license from IBM.

The fourth category of personal computer is the Apple **Macintosh,** or Mac, first available in 1985. The Mac is an extremely innovative personal computer that easily combines text and pictures on the display screen. The Mac is without peer for tasks involving pictures, but more important is its increasing acceptance as a business machine that can compete with the IBM compatible PCs and the PS/2 series. The entire field of desktop publishing has developed because of the Mac's unique capabilities. Now, as more software is developed for this machine, the Mac is used in many new situations that once were reserved for IBM compatible PCs or the PS/2 series.

Computer Hardware at ProYacht

Like many companies, ProYacht, Inc. does not have an overall plan for acquiring computers. Instead, each division makes its own decisions regarding the purchase and installation of computer hardware. As a result, a good deal of computer incompatibility exists among the various divisions. In this section, we consider the types of computers used in each division of the company. Figure 4–1 is the ProYacht organizational chart again, but this time, it includes the type of computer hardware used in several divisions.

Figure 4–1 shows that the headquarters office has a mainframe computer that is used by the finance and personnel departments as well as the Service and ProYacht Acceptance Divisions to maintain their records and to handle their data processing needs. The mainframe is also used to supply information to executives on the current status of company operations. Most executives and managers at headquarters have terminals tied to this mainframe. At the Parts Division, a large minicomputer is used to keep up with the large inventory of marine parts that ProYacht stocks. Unfortunately, this minicomputer is not compatible with the headquarters mainframe, so only minimal sharing of information occurs between the two computers.

As with most operations at ProYacht, the manufacturing and marketing departments of the sailboat division have tended to be the most advanced in their use of computers. The sailboat division has a small mainframe that is used to handle such data processing needs as tracking the production schedule for each sailboat, handling the Computer-Aided Design (CAD) and Computer-Aided Manufacturing (CAM) operations, and managing Electronic Data Interchange (EDI) activities. A Local Area Network (LAN) composed of personal computers is used by the clerical staff for word processing and electronic filing. The division managers also have personal computers that are tied to the LAN so

FIGURE 4-1

ProYacht, Inc.
Hardware
Organizational
Chart

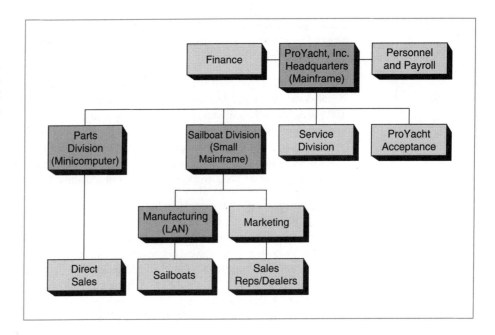

they can access electronic mail as well as obtain information from the mainframe over a
"bridge."

4.2 Hardware Resources

Now that the various computer sizes have been explained, this section describes the
elements of computer hardware. In this discussion, we use a conceptual computer that
demonstrates the major functions of a computer without involving the operational details
of the machine. The conceptual computer shown in Figure 4-2 has the five major
elements introduced in Chapter 2—processing unit, internal memory, secondary storage, input, and output. It also shows the flow of information into, within, and out of the
computer.

In Figure 4-2, note that the data and the instructions for processing that data flow into the
computer through the input unit or from secondary storage. Once the data and instructions are input, the computer stores them in its internal memory. After the data and
instructions are stored internally, the computer processes the data into information by
carrying out the instructions in the processing unit. The combination of the internal
memory and processing unit is comparable to a human brain, which also stores and
processes data into usable information. In addition to the computer's internal memory, a
computer has a secondary storage unit outside of internal memory. This secondary
storage unit is needed because a computer's internal memory is not unlimited and
because anything in internal memory can be erased when the computer loses power for
any reason. The data or instructions can be transferred back to internal memory as
needed. The fifth unit of the computer is the output unit, which provides a means for
displaying processing results to the user. A special type of input and output is

*Mainframe
Tracks
Hazardous
Materials for
LG&E*

In the mid-1980s, the federal government cracked down on the way industry accounted for the handling of hazardous materials. As a result of this move, Louisville Gas and Electric (LG&E) realized that its manual tracking system would be inadequate to meet the reporting requirements of the Environmental Protection Agency (EPA) and the Occupational Safety and Health Administration (OSHA). The manual tracking system required that files be kept at each facility and updated on a regular basis on the thousands of materials used by LG&E.

To solve its problem, LG&E decided to develop the Hazardous Materials System (Hazmat) that would run on an IBM 3090 mainframe. The purpose of Hazmat was to let employees at any LG&E site determine information on any hazardous material used by the company. A mainframe would be used for this system because LG&E wanted hazardous materials tracked throughout its 17 different sites and because LG&E has a huge amount of materials that are considered hazardous.

Users work directly with Hazmat to determine the hazardous nature of a material. Any employee working with LG&E's inventory system is also linked to Hazmat. This link automatically alerts the user if the material accessed on the inventory system is considered hazardous. When Hazmat detects a product that includes at least one hazardous material, it generates a report on a special government form about that material. Hazmat can also generate annual and daily activity reports on the amount of hazardous materials used.

After two years of Hazmat's use on the IBM 3090, LG&E is very happy. Although the results are difficult to quantify, LG&E feels the elimination of outside contract work and the smoothing of the federal inspection process has saved several hundred thousand dollars per year.

SOURCE: Maura J. Harrington, ''Computer Watchdog Tracks Hazards,'' *Computerworld*, March 25, 1991, p. 31.

telecommunications—that is, the transfer of data and information between computers over various types of communication links. Telecommunications hardware is discussed later in this chapter.

Having discussed the parts of a computer in general terms, we can now consider how these five parts are built into an actual computer. This discussion includes coverage of telecommunications hardware. Although personal computers and mainframes are different sizes, the principles of computing are very much the same for all types of computers.

*The Processing
Unit*

To manipulate and store symbols, the computer must have a ''brain'' that can perform certain predetermined operations and ''remember'' information. This ''brain'' is composed of the processing and internal memory units of the computer. The processing unit, or **Central Processing Unit (CPU),** uses computer chips—tiny pieces of silicon that pack thousands of electronic elements in a very small area. These elements, called **transistors,** actually carry on the control and logic operations at over 1 million opera-

FIGURE 4–2

*The Conceptual
Computer*

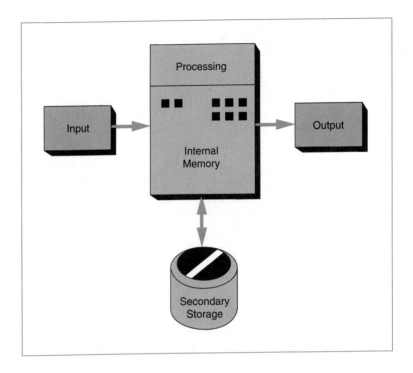

tions per second. Because the transistors are on/off switches, the computer uses the **binary number system** (0 and 1) to perform all of its processing. A combination of transistors and circuits on a chip is an **integrated circuit,** which is the key to the power and speed of all computers. Because the chip is so small, it must be attached to a carrier device that plugs into the main circuit board. The circuit board contains other chips for the internal memory and the control of input, output, and secondary storage devices. Mainframe computers have several CPU chips, but a personal computer usually has only one CPU chip. With multiple CPU chips, the mainframe can run faster and handle a large volume of processing.

*Internal
Memory*

Internal memory, which is also made up of computer chips, is divided into two major types—random access memory and read only memory. **Random Access Memory (RAM)** is the section of memory that is available for storing the instructions to the computer and the symbols that are to be manipulated. RAM is accessible to the user and is so named because any area of the memory can be accessed with equal ease regardless of the location of a piece of information. Unfortunately, RAM is volatile—it exists only while the computer is turned on. A mainframe computer is almost never turned off, but one user's information stored in RAM is replaced by other users' information when the first user disconnects from the computer. This volatility and the limited availability of internal memory requires that secondary storage be used to save information when the computer is turned off or the user disconnects from the mainframe.

Read Only Memory (ROM) is the section of nonvolatile memory that is placed in the computer during the manufacturing process. This permanent memory contains the startup instructions, or **booting process,** which occurs before the user gives the computer any instructions. During startup, instructions stored in ROM tell the computer to read instructions from secondary storage into RAM that allow the computer to process data into information. ROM also manages many computer operations, such as providing the characters on the screen when a key is pressed or results are displayed.

Representing and Storing Symbols

It is useful to understand how a computer in an information system stores information in internal memory or secondary storage. The binary number system is used for handling numbers, but because the computer manipulates letters and symbols as well as numbers, a system that uses bits and bytes has been developed for representing them. A **bit** is the basic unit of measure, corresponding to one switch within the computer. The term is a contraction of BInary digiT. The actual number of bits that are manipulated and transferred depends on the type of CPU used in the computer. However, a standard procedure involves using groups of 8 bits. By working with a group of 8 bits, called a **byte,** the computer can store, manipulate, and transfer information. The number of bytes with which a computer works is called a **computer word.** The number of bytes in a computer word depends on the type of computer. Supercomputers use 8 bytes (64 bits), many mainframes use a 4-byte (32-bit) word, and personal computers use words of 2 or 4 bytes in length.

To represent a given symbol in a computer, the user simply chooses a pattern of bits. Several standard patterns of bits exist, but the two most commonly used codes are the EBCDIC (pronounced eb-c-dick), which is an acronym for Extended Binary Coded Decimal Interchange Code, and ASCII (pronounced as-key), which is an acronym for American Standard Code for Information Interchange. EBCDIC, which uses 8 bits to represent symbols, was developed by IBM for use on their mainframe computers. ASCII, also an 8-bit code, is the standard code for personal computers. Both RAM and ROM use memory chips to store symbols in binary form. The amounts of RAM and ROM available in a particular computer are measured in **Kbytes** (1 Kbyte = 1,024 bytes). The letter K stands for kilo, which is Greek for 1,000. Even though 1,024 (which is 2^{10}) does not equal 1,000, the term Kbyte or simply the letter ''K'' is still used. For example, 640K of memory means $640 \times 1024 = 655,360$ bytes of memory. The next measure of memory after a Kbyte is an **Mbyte** (megabyte) which is 1,024 Kbytes (2^{20} bytes), or approximately 1 million bytes, of storage. For computers with more storage, the **Gbyte** (gigabyte)—approximately one billion bytes (2^{30} bytes)—is a common measure of storage. Mainframe computers may have 64 Mbytes of RAM and personal computers often have well over 1 Mbyte RAM. Table 4–1, on following page, shows the relationships among the bit, byte, Kbyte, Mbyte, and Gbyte.

Secondary Storage

Because of the limited amount of internal storage and the volatility of RAM, external or **secondary storage** is necessary. Data and programs for complex operations are stored in a form that does not disappear when the power to the computer is turned off or the user disconnects from the mainframe. This secondary storage is usually available in one of two forms—disk or tape. With either the disk or tape, stored information is accessed by

TABLE 4–1

Memory Size
Relationships

1 bit	=	1 on/off switch
1 byte	=	8 bits
1 Kbyte	=	1,024 bytes (2^{10} bytes)
1 Mbyte	=	1,024 Kbytes (2^{20} bytes)
1 Gbyte	=	1,024 Mbytes (2^{30} bytes)

internal memory when the control unit decides that this information is needed by the processing unit. Because the secondary storage unit must locate the information, read it from the disk or tape, and then transfer the information to internal memory, secondary storage is a much slower form of memory than internal memory. However, this slow transfer of information is balanced by the virtually unlimited storage capacity.

Disk secondary storage uses a thin, record-like piece of metal or plastic that is covered with an iron oxide whose magnetic direction can be arranged to represent symbols. This magnetic arrangement is accomplished by a **disk drive,** which spins the disk while the **read/write head** reads or writes information onto the disk. The read/write head rides on or immediately above the disk, depending on the type of disk. In a sense, a disk is like a compact disk that is "played" by the disk drive. However, two crucial differences exist between a computer disk and a compact disk. First, signals on the computer disk are recorded magnetically rather than by a laser beam burning pits in the surface of the compact disk. Second, the computer can record data on a disk in addition to just playing it. The two types of disk are alike in that signals are recorded on concentric **tracks.** Figure 4–3 shows the storage of the letters U, G, and A on a magnetic disk.

Mainframe computers have large **disk packs** made up of several disks, each about the size of an LP record. These disk packs usually remain in the disk drive except when a special need requires a transfer. Because disk packs can hold so much information, many users can store data on a single disk pack. When a user connects to the mainframe, his or her user number tells the computer where to look on the disk pack for the user's data. Figure 4–4 shows a schematic diagram of a disk pack.

For a disk pack, all tracks with the same track number on all sides of the disks are precisely aligned, one above the other. A series of tracks in the same vertical plane with the same track number is called a **cylinder.** Information that requires more than one track (a common occurrence) is written on other tracks in the *same cylinder* rather than on the same disk. The disk pack's read/write heads move together, so they are automatically all on the same cylinder at any time. Thus, as one head finishes transferring information to a track, another head transfers information to another track in the same cylinder without moving the heads. When all tracks in this cylinder are full, the read/write heads are moved to a new cylinder. The cylinder concept of disk storage is shown in Figure 4–5.

Personal computers use plastic disks, called **floppy disks,** and metal, or hard, disks to store information. Floppy disks are made of Mylar plastic and covered with an iron oxide. They are easily moved, but hold only a fraction of the data stored on a hard disk or a

FIGURE 4–3

Storage on a Disk

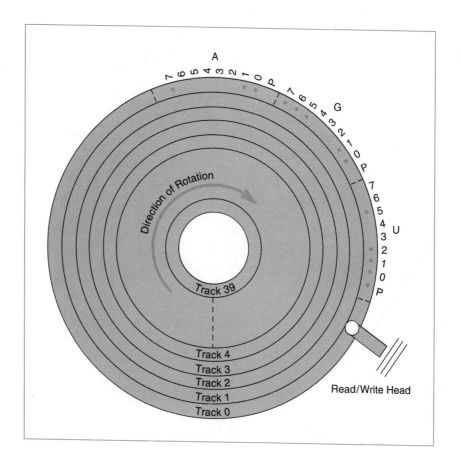

FIGURE 4–4

Mainframe Disk Pack

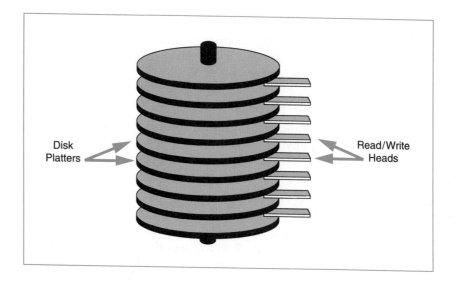

FIGURE 4–5

*Cylinder Concept
of Disk Storage*

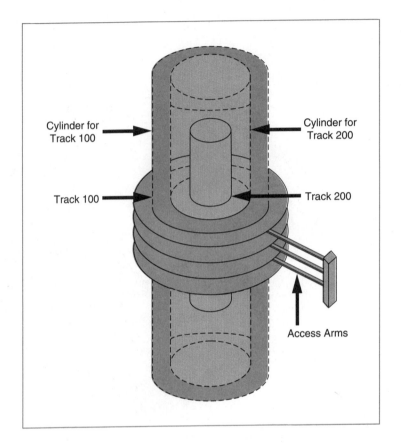

mainframe disk pack. For this reason, a user may need many floppies, one for each type of data stored. Today, floppies are either 5.25 inches or 3.5 inches in diameter, with the smaller disk also called a **microfloppy.** Figure 4–6 shows the parts of both the 5.25-inch and 3.5-inch floppy disks. A PC **hard disk** is a scaled-down version of a mainframe disk pack that until recently was not removable from the personal computer. The hard disk rotates at a much faster speed than the floppy and stores a great deal more information.

With mainframe disk packs or PC floppy or hard disks, each character can be accessed and read by the disk drive with equal ease. This capability of going directly to any character on a disk is known as **direct access storage.** Disk packs are often referred to as **DASD** for **Direct Access Storage Devices.**

Tape used for secondary storage can be either reel-to-reel or cassette. Like disk, tape is covered with an iron oxide that is arranged magnetically to store symbols. A tape can easily store millions of characters. However, it is much slower than a disk because the tape must be ''played'' by the tape drive to transfer data. Another drawback with tape is that information is accessed in the same order or sequence in which it was placed on the

FIGURE 4-6   *PC Floppy Disks*

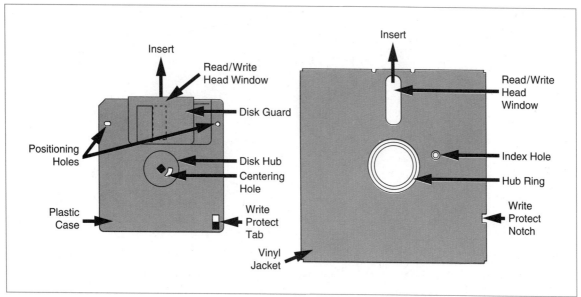

tape, a process known as **sequential access.** Figure 4–7 shows a magnetic tape section storing the letters U, G, and A.

Mainframe computers depend on reel-to-reel tapes to store large amounts of information not needed immediately. Such information as financial statistics, payroll records, and student academic records are usually stored on tape. When needed, the tape is mounted on a **tape drive,** where a read/write mechanism similar to that used on a disk drive transfers information to and from the tape. Tape is also used as a disk drive **backup,** which stores all of the information contained on the disk in case the information on the disk is lost. Figure 4–8 shows a schematic of a reel-to-reel tape drive.

The **optical** or **video disk,** the newest form of secondary storage, can hold *billions* of characters. Optical disks are similar to compact disks, but optical disks are larger and can hold more information. Like audio compact disks, most optical disks are *read only* storage devices, but some read and write optical disk systems are now being manufactured.

Secondary storage is measured in the same units as internal memory, because similar information is stored in both internal memory and secondary storage. Tape and disk pack storage for mainframes is measured in Mbytes, and PC hard disks commonly store 50 to over 100 Mbytes. Most personal computers in use today can store either 360 Kbytes or

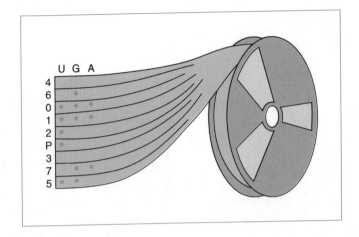

FIGURE 4–7

Tape Storage

1.2 Mbytes of information on each floppy disk and either 720 Kbytes or 1.44 Mbytes on each microfloppy. Read only video disk storage is measured in Gbytes.

Input/Output   As noted earlier, the computer must have some type of input so that data and instructions can be processed. Similarly, the computer must generate output so that the results of the processing can be provided to the user. Input converts data or instructions into a binary form so the computer can work with them. Output reverses this process by converting the binary form of information into a displayed or printed form. In this section, we consider various methods of input and output.

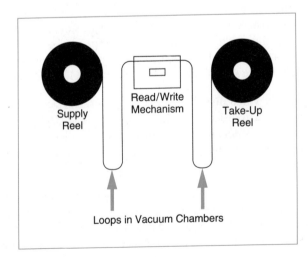

FIGURE 4–8

Reel-to-Reel Tape Drive

FIGURE 4–9   *PC Keyboard*

The methods of input to a computer range from grocery checkout bar code readers to keyboards to a mouse to voice input. Currently, the most popular input device is the typewriter-like **keyboard,** which sends the appropriate electrical signal to the computer when a key is pressed. The symbol corresponding to this key is stored in internal memory and is usually simultaneously shown on the screen. Figure 4–9 shows a popular PC keyboard.

Another method of input used with personal computers is a device that fits in the palm of the hand. This device, a **mouse,** controls the **cursor,** a blinking rectangle or underline on the screen that denotes the location where data are input. The mouse gets its name from its small size and the ''tail'' that connects it to the computer. Using one, two, or three buttons on the mouse and rolling it over a flat surface, the user can perform various operations when the cursor is located in the desired position.

The two most popular output devices are the printer and the video screen, or monitor. Other names for a monitor are Cathode Ray Tube (CRT) and Video Display Terminal (VDT). The **monitor** is useful for any computer system for two reasons. First, it shows the user the data or instructions input from the keyboard or other input device. The cursor moves on the screen while the data or instructions are input. Second, the monitor is an almost instantaneous outlet for results.

Several varieties of monitors are available, but the primary distinction between monitors is that its display may be either monochrome or in color. **Monochrome monitors** display single-color light symbols on a contrasting background, and **color monitors** can display

Reasons to Buy a Mini

Contrary to popular opinion, the minicomputer is far from dead—in fact, many corporate users still favor it over both mainframes and PC networks for the following 10 reasons:

1. Lower cost—the raw processing cost of a minicomputer measured in dollars per million instructions per second (MIPS) at $50,000 is less than that for a mainframe ($200,000), but more than that for a personal computer ($5,000). However, in terms of software cost, the mini is considered to be competitive with the PC network.

2. More flexible input/output—a definite shortcoming of a personal computer is in the area of input/output; personal computers cannot handle ''industrial strength'' input/output.

3. Better multiuser functionality—minis are built for multiple users and have multiuser operating systems; personal computers do not.

4. Easier expandability—a user may easily run out of processing capability on a personal computer; even several personal computers linked together may not have the required processing power. A mini can be added for around $150,000, compared with $10 million for a mainframe.

5. Better networking—minicomputers are easily networked together on an equal footing, so called ''peer-to-peer'' networks that neither mainframes nor personal computers have.

6. Local processing power—minis can be installed locally to give individual sites the needed processing capability.

7. Integrated applications—a multiuser mini system's strength is that users can share frequently accessed common applications.

8. Centralized system control—security is easier to implement for a central facility. Users need not worry about backup or physical processor security.

9. Less user skill required—compared with PC networks, for which knowledge of the disk operating system (DOS) is often required.

10. Common interface—all minicomputer applications have the same interface. Mainframes and personal computers are working toward this.

SOURCE: Paul E. Schindler, ''For Many, the Mini Is Far from Dead,'' *PC Week,* March 6, 1989, pp. 41–42.

multiple colors on the screen. The question of which monitor—monochrome or color—depends on the user's task and budget.

Output to a printer usually yields a printed page that is useful because the output to the monitor disappears when additional output appears, when the computer is turned off, or when the user disconnects from a mainframe. For mainframe users, output on the monitor is easily diverted to a page printer at a computer center. A **page printer** is a high-speed printer that can print an entire page in one motion. For PC users, a tremendous variety of printers is available today in all speeds, qualities of print, and price ranges.

Secondary storage can also be used for input and output if the user sends results to a disk or tape for storage or reads data or instructions from disk or tape. Read only secondary storage such as cartridges or video disks are designed to be used as an input to the computer.

Input/Output Telecommunication

A device that facilitates both input and output is the **modem,** which sends and receives information over telephone lines from another computer. The modem converts the electrical signals from RAM in the computer into the type of electrical signals that can travel over telephone lines. In other words, in most cases today the digital output from the sending computer must be modulated into an analog form before it can be sent over a telephone line, and the analog input received over the telephone line must be demodulated into digital form before it can be used for input into the receiving computer. New systems are currently being implemented that will transmit voice and data over telephone lines in a digital form.

The term modem is derived because the device MOdulates/DEModulates signals. With a modem, a computer terminal or personal computer can be used to communicate with a mainframe or another personal computer. In either case, the modem acts as both an input and output device so the computer can send and receive information over telephone lines. The modem is useful for persons who wish to work at home, access a computerized information service to research some topic, or simply communicate with other computer users.

4.3 Software Resources

The hardware advances of the recent decade have been mind-boggling, but a computer without software would be nothing more than a well-constructed combination of silicon chips and electronic circuitry. Recall that software is the general term for all of the instructions given the computer by the user or the manufacturer. The idea of a computer without software has been described as a car without a driver or a camera without film. Whatever the analogy, the hardware elements of a computer must have software to direct them.

Computer Programs and Languages

Earlier in this chapter, we discussed the idea that a computer manipulates and stores symbols. For the computer to perform this manipulation and storage, it must be given a very specific set of rules called a **program.** All software—whether built into the machine by the manufacturer, purchased by the user, or developed by the user—is the result of a person who creates the program for the computer.

Because the computer knows only what the program tells it, the program must tell the computer everything about the desired process. The program must be developed by a programmer using a step-by-step approach, so that no steps are assumed to be known by

TABLE 4–2

Commonly Used
Computer
Languages

Language	Full Name	Common Use
BASIC	Beginners All-purpose Symbolic Instruction Code	Teaching programming; writing software on PCs
COBOL	COmmon Business Oriented Language	Writing business software
FORTRAN	FORmula TRANslator	Writing scientific software
Pascal		Teaching programming; writing software on PCs
C		Writing software on minicomputers or PCs

the computer. These steps are then written in a computer language. Many (well over 100) computer languages can be used to communicate with a computer. Some commonly used languages are listed in Table 4–2, along with their full names (if different from the popular name) and common uses. Each computer language, like a human language, has its own vocabulary and grammatical rules, but most share a similar logical approach to communication with the computer.

Although the cost of hardware has decreased dramatically over the last decade, the cost of software has remained the same or increased. The reason for this is that hardware can be mass produced, but each software program must be individually developed by one or more people.

Types of
Software

The two major categories of software—systems software and applications software—are usually at work in the computer at the same time, each serving a different purpose. **Systems software** controls all internal computer operations. These operations include managing the input and output devices and the secondary storage units as well as overseeing the operation of the applications software. **Applications software,** on the other hand, performs all the computer's processing and problem-solving tasks.

Systems
Software

The primary component of systems software is the **operating system,** which manages the many tasks that occur concurrently within a computer. In mainframes and minicomputers, the operating system manages the allocation of memory and processing time to each of the multiple users. In this environment, the operating system must also handle all users' requests for different types of operations, for example, disk storage or printer access.

The personal computer operating system must manage the almost constant transfer of information between internal memory and mass storage. Because today's personal computers use a disk secondary storage system, the operating system is called a **Disk Operating System** (**DOS**—rhymes with floss). Many different types of computers can use DOS, so some degree of standardization exists among personal computers through the operating systems. MS-DOS (MicroSoft DOS), UNIX from AT&T, and OS/2 (Operating System/2) from IBM are the three most widely used operating systems for the

PS/2 computers and IBM compatible PCs. The operating system for the Macintosh computer is a proprietary system that is easier to use than the other three operating systems.

In addition to managing the various hardware devices used by the computer and overseeing the operation of the applications software, the operating system must enable the user to handle the many housekeeping tasks that keep a user's information organized on the disk. All information on a disk (or tape) is organized into units called **files,** each of which is named by the user or program that placed them on the disk. Some files may be written by the developer of the operating system and others by the user of the computer. The operating system's housekeeping operations include listing a directory of these files or copying a file to another disk or to tape.

Applications Software

By far the largest amount of software available to the computer user is applications software. Available applications software covers such wide ranging topics as religion, astronomy, marriage counseling, contract bridge, horse racing, genealogy, accounting, word processing, and ham radio operation. In fact, it would be safe to say that software exists (or will soon exist) for any topic you can imagine.

For many years, computers were only used in business and government, so it is no surprise that a large amount of applications software is available for businesses. Numerous business uses of computers affect our everyday lives—for example, computerized billing systems—but many other business uses of the computer are not always so evident. For example, many ''junk mail'' letters you receive are the result of computerized mailing list systems. Data processing is also important in many companies for computing payrolls with many different pay scales and deductions. A not-so-hidden business use of the computer is the Point-of-Sale (POS) system in retailing, which is used to speed the check out process and automate inventory control. Airlines and hotel chains depend on large mainframe computers to handle reservations. Very few offices today are without either a personal computer or a terminal hooked into a mainframe. The personal computer is often used for business analyses and for such clerical operations as word processing. In every case, the business use of the computer is possible because one or more applications software programs direct the computer to carry out the desired action.

Computer Packages

When one or more programs are combined with a set of directions known as a **user's manual,** the result is a **software package.** Some packages may also include telephone user support, consulting or training provisions, and upgrade agreements in which new versions of the package are automatically sent to the user.

The use of computer packages has spawned a unique terminology. One of the most overused terms in reference to computer packages and to computers in general is **user friendly.** If a package is described as user friendly, then the implication is that the package is easy to use. Unfortunately, quite a few packages that are advertised as ''user friendly'' are really complex and quite difficult to use. In some cases, sophisticated business packages cannot be totally user friendly because they are designed to solve complicated problems. The number of advertisements for classes that explain some

FIGURE 4–10   *Pull-Down Menu Interface*

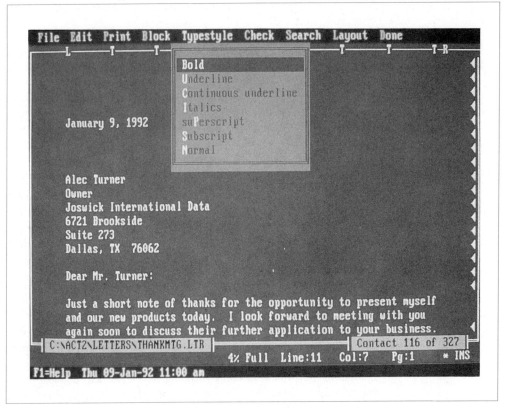

advanced software packages demonstrates the need for more than a few hours of personal study or classroom instruction.

Various packages have a different type of **user interface,** which determines how data and commands are entered. The three most common types of user interface are menu-driven, command-driven, and graphical. In a **menu-driven package,** the user is presented a **menu,** which shows a list of commands from which to choose or requests that data in a particular form be entered. Menu selection may involve entering a letter or number or moving the cursor to an option. In many cases, the user not only selects from a menu but is also asked to enter a file name or other specific data. For example, in an accounting package, a menu may request the user to enter amounts budgeted for various categories. A widely used type of menu system is referred to as a **pull-down menu,** because making a selection from one menu results in the appearance of a sub-menu from which a choice can be made. Figure 4–10 shows a pull-down menu in a popular word processing system, in which the user is requested to enter a selection from several options.

FIGURE 4–11 *Graphical User Interface on Apple Macintosh*

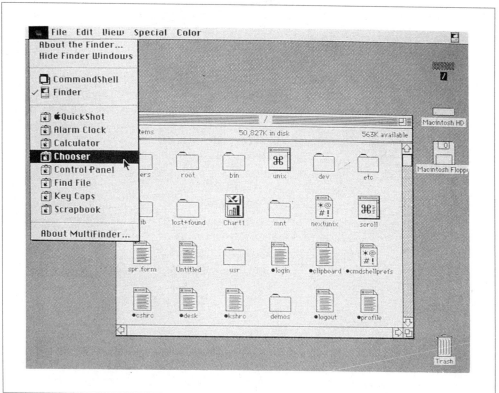

A second method for entering data or commands is called a command-driven package. A **command-driven package** does not request a command or data, but simply waits for the user to input the appropriate command or data. The user must learn the necessary commands by reading the package documentation. Many operating systems are command-driven; the software expects the user to know the next command to be entered at any point in the execution of the package.

The type of user interface that is gaining in popularity is the **Graphical User Interface (GUI).** In a GUI, **icons** (pictures) represent the functions to be performed, and a mouse is used to position the cursor over the desired function. Once the cursor is positioned over an icon, a button on the mouse is pressed and the function is carried out. With a little practice, commands can be entered quickly. The use of GUI was pioneered on the Apple Macintosh, but many packages for IBM compatible computers and the OS/2 operating system use icons. In fact, the popular Windows operating environment was developed to provide MS-DOS users with this type of interface. Figure 4–11 shows the use of a GUI on the Apple Macintosh.

Computers Write Computer Industry Contracts

An expensive element of doing business in the computer industry is having lawyers draw up contracts to handle software licensing agreements, system integration contracts, confidentiality agreements, and agreements with vendors bidding on computer contracts. However, one computer package—Quickform Contracts—can dramatically reduce the time and expense involved with this process. With this package, a business manager can draft a near-custom contract by answering questions about the proposed agreement. Then, based on the manager's answers, the package creates the contract by pulling together appropriate elements from a library of hundreds of contract clauses.

For example, a high-technology company uses Quickform to create software and teaming contracts for air-traffic control systems. The company's lawyer then reviews the document, but instead of reading all 20 pages, the lawyer only checks the Quickform summary to determine how the contract handles the standard issues. The lawyer then focuses his or her expertise on any unique issues that are handled by Quickform. The package is designed to ensure that the contract contains key clauses (such as warranty agreements) and to warn the user about tricky areas of the law.

SOURCE: Mitch Betts, "Software Aids Contract Writing," *Computerworld,* September 2, 1991, p. 82.

All three types of interfaces have advantages and disadvantages, and what appears to be an advantage for one is a disadvantage for the other. For packages with a menu-driven interface or GUI, the user does not have to learn a series of commands before using the package. The user only has to select from a menu or choose the appropriate icon. However, once the user has learned the commands for the package, it can be bothersome to wait for the next menu or set of icons before making a selection. On the other hand, for a novice user or a user of many packages, a command-driven interface can be difficult, because both the proper command and the appropriate spot on the screen to enter it must be learned. However, once the data format and list of commands for the package is learned, data or commands can be very quickly entered.

Mainframe Versus PC Packages

Over the last few years, all forms of popular media have published many discussions of computer use, particularly, the use of various software packages for personal computers. The emphasis on PC software occurs because only large organizations buy mainframe software, and PC software is also sold to individuals. This leads to a great deal of advertising for PC software and relatively little for mainframe software. Lack of advertising does not mean that the use of mainframe software is declining. On the contrary, the dollar volume of mainframe software sold each year continues to grow right along with PC software.

In addition to the difference in the type of consumer for mainframe and PC software, mainframe software is not usually transferable from one computer to another, as most PC software is. The only generic software packages for mainframes are some scientific packages and language compilers that allow the same language to be used on different computers. In other words, packages written for one machine may or may not run on a different brand of computer. Hardware and emulation software have been developed to make an Apple personal computer work like an IBM and vice versa, but little work in this area has occurred for mainframes. As a result, only machine-specific software is developed.

Software at
ProYacht

ProYacht, Inc. uses a wide variety of software on its computer systems, including operating systems and utility software specific to each type of computer and many different applications software programs. Much of the software used to process personnel and financial records on the headquarters mainframe is written in COBOL specifically for ProYacht operations. The same is true of the software used to manage the inventory on the minicomputer in the Parts Division. On the other hand, the technical software used for CAD/CAM and EDI are mainframe computer packages purchased from the mainframe vendor or from software houses. The software used on the personal computers in the LAN was purchased rather than developed. This software includes the electronic mail and word processing software as well as several personal productivity software packages of the type to be discussed in the next section.

4.4 Personal Productivity Software

Although most business applications software is used on mainframe computers to handle an organization's many large-scale processing tasks, PC-oriented business software is also important. Where mainframes are used for large-scale data processing applications, personal computers are often used for performing various types of business analyses; handling many data base management chores; and accomplishing such office operations as word processing, slide preparation, and electronic mail. **Personal productivity software** includes word processing, spreadsheet, data base management, graphics, and telecommunications software. The advent of personal productivity software has meant an entirely new group of computer users—end users. An **end user** is a worker involved either in developing programs for personal use or in using existing software to its fullest extent to do a job better. End users are usually not information systems professionals or computer scientists; they are people who use the computer to solve problems. In doing this, they often become quite knowledgeable in the use of personal productivity software packages.

Word
Processing

One of the most useful functions of a personal computer is the ability to manipulate letters, digits, and punctuation marks to compose correspondence, papers, and documents using **word processing software.** Word processing on a personal computer means composing and editing text on the video screen and then printing the final result. If text entry and editing were the only capabilities of word processing, it might not be worth the expense of buying a personal computer and the necessary software. However, word processing software also allows easy setting of margins, line spacing, and tabs to arrive at a desired page format. When text is entered from the keyboard, lines ''wrap around'' the

John Deere Runs 1-2-3

For a Fortune 500 company, estimating the amount of computer hardware and software that will be in use at year-end can be an arduous task. However, the $7.2 billion John Deere Company uses PC-based spreadsheets that greatly reduce the difficulty in monitoring its investment in information technology equipment. Prior to using spreadsheets, Deere spent large amounts of time and effort consolidating data on a mainframe for a master status report of its large number of hardware and software investments. For example, just to plan enhancements to its $89 million worth of computer equipment took 21 weeks. Now, with Lotus 1-2-3 Release 3.0 on a Local Area Network (LAN), the MIS department can generate a more robust and flexible report on the company's seven IBM mainframe computers, over 100 personal computers, and literally hundreds of disk and tape drives, printers, and other peripherals.

The new spreadsheet-based system, developed by two members of the Deere MIS department, is composed of at least 20 spreadsheets that are linked together to provide a status report that contains all data and information on the computer equipment investment. Using the spreadsheets and the LAN, Deere employees can track spending without worrying about incomplete or outdated information, different data formats, or incompatible reports. It all appears in a spreadsheet format familiar to managers.

SOURCE: Richard Cranford, "Nothing Runs Like 1-2-3," *Lotus,* October 1990, pp. 44–47.

margins by automatically continuing to the next line. This frees the user from having to monitor the margins and "return" the cursor at the appropriate time.

Other useful functions of word processing software are text insertions, deletions, and strikeovers on the screen; document search for a particular sequence of characters; easy centering of material; automatic pagination; and, on most packages, the ability to underline, boldface, or italicize text. Word processing software allows a user to electronically "cut" a block of material from a document and "paste" it somewhere else in the current document or in a completely different document. Most word processing software also has spell checker and mail merge features to enhance office productivity. Figure 4–12 shows a document in a popular word processing package.

Spreadsheets

This software consists of a table of values called a **spreadsheet.** The user defines various relationships between the table values using formulas. The intersection of each row and column is a cell which can hold a value; a label that describes a row, column, or cell; or a formula that determines the value in that cell depending on a mathematical relationship involving other cells. When the user changes a value, the package uses the formulas to recompute all other values that depend on the changed value. This sort of analysis allows the user to ask "What if?" questions about the values in the spreadsheet. This function is extremely important to the manager who must plan ahead for next year's possible

FIGURE 4–12 **_Document in a Word Processing Package_**

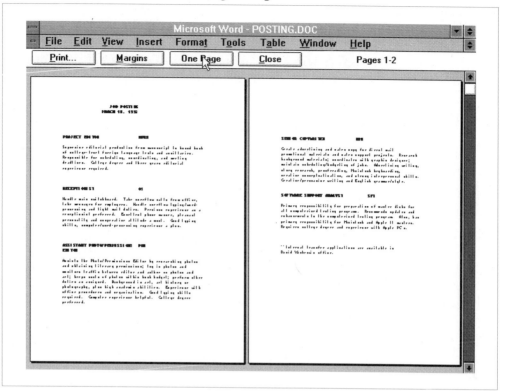

budgetary situations. Figure 4–13, on page 110, shows a financial analysis spreadsheet on a popular spreadsheet package.

Data Base Management Software

A common operation at both work and home is that of storing information. This storage may be as simple as a 3 × 5 index card box of customers for a small business or as complex as rows of filing cabinets containing personnel records. The storage process often entails arranging this information in some order based on a particular element or criterion. With **data base management software,** a user can electronically perform the same operations on a computer. In a sense, this type of package is an electronic filing clerk. A **data base** is a collection of information that is arranged for easy manipulation and retrieval. Data base management packages are important to an individual or firm that must manage large volumes of data so that information for decision making is easily found. Many PC data base software packages also have provisions for users to write their own application programs.

Common operations on data base management packages include sorting (rearranging) the data base, finding information that matches specific criteria, or creating a report.

FIGURE 4–13   *Financial Analysis Spreadsheet*

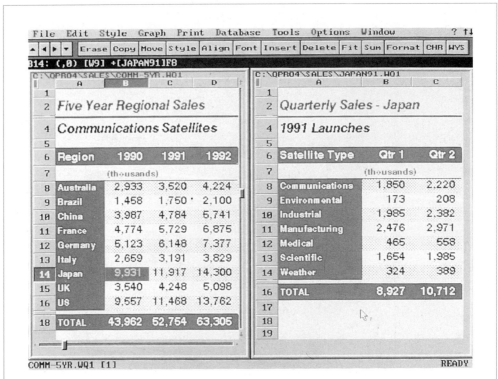

Figure 4–14 shows the use of a popular data base management package to rearrange a mailing list.

Graphics Software

The old saying that "a picture is worth a thousand words" is certainly true when applied to the graphic portrayal of computer results. Showing the information generated by data analysis in a bar or pie chart adds meaning to the results. Businesses often use **graphics software** for data analysis or to make a dramatic presentation. Graphics can also speed up the laborious job of designing anything from a computer chip to an airliner.

Business analysis and presentations utilize the following commonly used graphics:

1. A line chart, which simply connects a series of points

2. A pie chart, which assigns a section of a round pie proportional to the amount of data

3. A bar chart, which draws a series of either horizontal or vertical bars depicting the data

FIGURE 4-14   *Use of Data Base Management Package*

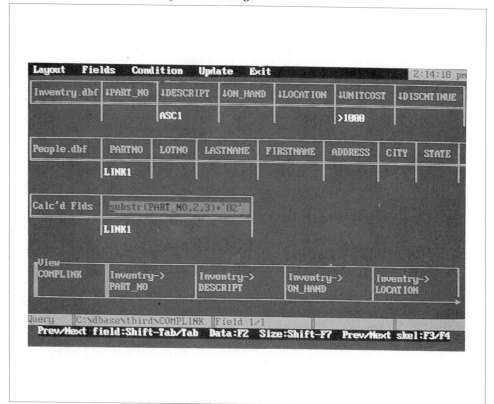

4. A histogram, which is a bar chart with a line connecting the top point of each bar, as in a line chart

Figure 4-15, on the following page, shows a graph created with a popular presentation graphics package.

Communications Software

The earlier discussion of computer hardware included the types of hardware that could be used for communication. **Communications software** is needed to instruct the hardware to actually carry out the transfer of data and information between computers. This software is combined with a modem to allow the PC user to communicate with mainframe computers or with other personal computers. National networks, such as Prodigy and Compuserve, can be used via the communication package/modem combination to send electronic mail, post messages on an electronic bulletin board, or to access national general purpose or special interest data bases.

Communications software can be used in the personal computer for many tasks, including dialing telephone numbers, answering phone calls, sending and receiving data and information over the telephone line, and accessing other computers. Communications

FIGURE 4–15   *Presentation Graph*

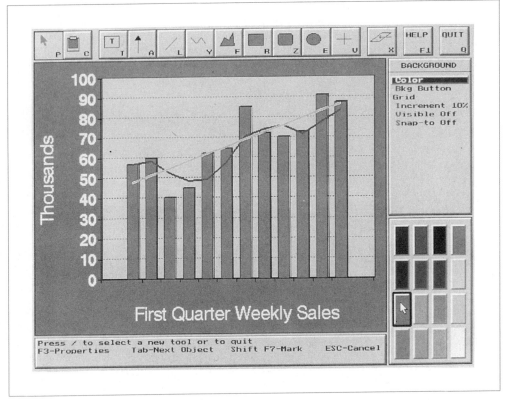

software such as Procomm, White Knight, and CrossTalk allow the PC user to communicate with other computers.

4.5 Summary

In developing a CBIS, the key resource is the computer, which is a machine that stores and processes data into information based on a series of instructions. The computer is divided into two parts—the machinery portion called hardware and the instructions called software. Computer sizes range from small personal computers that sit on a desktop to huge mainframes that occupy an entire room.

Computer hardware is composed of input, internal memory, processing, secondary storage, and output units. The processing unit is usually referred to as the CPU. Data and instructions are stored in internal memory before being processed into information by the processing unit. Internal memory is made up of RAM and ROM. RAM is accessible to the user for storage of data, programs, and processed information. ROM is built into the computer by the manufacturer and is needed to start up the computer and handle certain operations within the computer. Both the CPU and internal memory are built onto silicon chips, which can contain more than 1 million transistors to handle memory and logic operations.

The binary number system is used in computers because the computer uses on/off switches to handle logic and memory. The EBCDIC or ASCII codes can be used to represent letters, digits, and symbols in eight bits (1 byte); one character corresponds to one byte. Memory is measured in Kbytes (1,024 bytes), Mbytes (1,024 Kbytes), or Gbytes (1,024 Mbytes).

Secondary storage is needed because RAM is both limited and volatile; tape and disk are common secondary storage devices. Mainframe computers use disk packs, and personal computers use floppy disks and hard disks. The input unit sends data and instructions to the computer; the keyboard and the mouse are common input devices for personal computers. The output unit transmits the results from the computer to the user; the monitor and printer are common output devices. Communication with another computer is accomplished with a modem that translates computer data into a form that can be transmitted over the telephone line.

The computer hardware must have software to control its actions. A software package is made up of one or more computer programs that are written in computer languages. Of the two major types of software—systems and applications software—systems software manages the computer's operations. The key part of systems software is the operating system that manages the operations of all other parts of the computer. Applications software performs tasks as directed by the user.

Software packages allow nonprogrammers to use the computer to achieve a desired objective. The three types of user interface are menu, command, and graphical user interface. Pull-down menus are a special type of menu system.

The five most commonly used personal productivity software packages are word processing, spreadsheet, data base management, graphics, and telecommunications. Word processing allows a user to compose, edit, and print documents from the computer keyboard. Spreadsheet software enables a user to create budgets or forecasts from a table (called a spreadsheet) of values, labels, and formulas. With a data base management package, a user can manipulate large files of data to find desired information. Graphics packages are useful in analyses of data, presentations, or for creation of art forms using the computer. Communications software combines the computer with a modem and telephone line to link it to other computers.

End users are individuals who use the computer to solve their own problems either by writing programs or using personal productivity software.

Key Terms

applications software
backup
binary number system
bit
booting process

byte
Central Processing Unit (CPU)
color monitor
command-driven package
communications software

computer
computer word
cursor
cylinder
data base
data base management software
direct access storage
disk drive
Disk Operating System (DOS)
disk packs
end user
file
floppy disks
Gbyte
Graphical User Interface (GUI)
graphics software
hard disk
hardware
IBM compatible PCs
icons
integrated circuit
internal memory
Kbytes
keyboard
Macintosh
mainframe
Mbytes
menu
menu-driven package
microfloppy
midsize computer
minicomputer

modem
monitor
monochrome monitor
mouse
operating system
optical disk
page printer
personal computers
personal productivity software
programs
PS/2 series
pull-down menu
Random Access Memory (RAM)
Read Only Memory (ROM)
read/write head
secondary storage
sequential access
software
software package
spreadsheet
supercomputers
systems software
tape
tape drive
tracks
transistors
user friendly
user interface
user's manual
video disk
word processing software

Review Questions

1. Explain the analogy between the parts of the computer and the way humans think, act, and keep records.

2. Discuss the various sizes of computers used in business, industry, and government. Give examples of where each type of computer might be used.

3. Why does the computer need the CPU? What device contains the CPU of a personal computer?

4. Differentiate between RAM and ROM. Which is accessible to the user for storage of data, programs, and information?

5. Differentiate between direct access and sequential access secondary storage devices.

6. Explain why bytes are important in a computer system.

7. List two commonly used input devices for a computer. List two commonly used output devices.

8. Explain the meaning of the term modem in computer communications. What is the purpose of a modem?

9. Discuss the importance of software to the use of a computer.

10. List three commonly used computer languages.

11. Name the two major categories of software that work concurrently in a computer. Discuss the purpose of each type of software.

12. What is a DOS? What role does it play in the use of a personal computer?

13. What are the three types of user interfaces? Discuss the advantages and disadvantages of each.

14. List the five personal productivity software packages discussed in the text. What is an end user?

15. Discuss a situation from your home, school, club, fraternity, or sorority in which a spreadsheet or data base package would be useful to you.

Discussion Questions

1. A wholesale warehouse must store its book inventory, vendor, customer, and invoice records. For its 20,000 items in inventory, the following number of characters (bytes) of information are needed: Name (15), ISBN Number (10), Location (4), Cost (6), Selling Price (6), and Vendor (6). The following items must be stored for each of 20 vendors: Name (15), Address (25), Number (6), Credit Terms (4), and Delivery Time (2). For each of 2000 customers the following is needed: Number (4), Name (15), Address (25), Credit Code (1), and Outstanding Invoice Numbers (20*6). For each of 5000 possible invoices, the following must be stored: Invoice Number (6), Customer Number (4), Date (6), Books Ordered (25*(ISBN(10), Quantity (4), and Selling Price (6))).

   How much storage capacity does warehouse management need? What storage medium do you recommend and why?

2. Recommend a hardware configuration for each of the following situations:
   a. A utility company with thousands of customers must process large volumes of data periodically to update customer files and bill customers.
   b. A regional realty firm with branch offices throughout the state must match customer needs with residential and commercial property. The company has hundreds of property listings and must show customers pictures, surveys, and floor plans. The company must store this data so that agents can easily access the information for use with clients.

c. A tool manufacturer must control its manufacturing activities, including its materials, in-process, and finished goods inventories.

3. You are a systems consultant for a microcomputer vendor. An architect comes in your store. She is considering purchasing some hardware and software to be used for accounting, bid preparation, cost estimation and accumulation, drafting, design, and communication with vendors. She has little computer experience and wants the easiest system to use. Discuss the types of software and hardware that might satisfy her needs.

Case 4–1

Unisource Corporation

Formed by the merger of Carpenter/Offutt and Blake, Moffit, & Towne in 1985, San Francisco-based Unisource Corporation distributes paper products—from rolls of printing paper to shopping bags—to 45 West Coast distribution centers. Carpenter/Offutt brought a Hewlett-Packard (HP) minicomputer to the new corporation, and Blake brought a mainframe. In 1990, Unisource purchased three large HP minicomputers—two HP 3000 Model 960s and one 980. These machines were rated at 15 million instructions per second for up to 600 users to go with the Bull DBP 8000/40 mainframe. The HP machines are used for online orders, routing, and inventory, and the mainframe is used for analysis in the batch mode. Richard Hrapczynski, Jr., vice president of MIS at Unisource states "We took the best of both worlds. Bull at that time had no online capability."

At the main computer site in San Francisco, the day's sales data are fed into the Bull mainframe and processed each night to develop recommendations for the next day's buying schedule for Unisource's three divisions (San Francisco, Seattle, and Los Angeles). Hrapczynski states, "If everything goes right, when the staff arrives in the morning, [the buying schedule] should be sitting on their printers." The online capability of the HP minis is critical to the company, because most orders are called in between 3 and 5 in the afternoon, and the firm promises next-day delivery.

A problem that faces Unisource as a growing company is that much of the software written by independent vendors for the minicomputers is suited for smaller companies. For instance, an application that handles millions of dollars should handle hundreds of millions of dollars for Unisource. As Hrapczynski notes, "These products were built for smaller companies. A general ledger system will have two location fields, which should handle 99 locations. But, bigger companies have many more sites than that." While trying to persuade software vendors to convert the software to faster machines serving larger sites, Unisource is getting around the bottlenecks by using its own programmers to write short-term fixes for the existing software.

Unisource is automating its last division in Alaska. When installation of terminals and printers connected to the HP computers is completed, the company will decide whether to acquire a new mainframe or some other configuration as a host. A decision on this issue is expected by mid-1994.

SOURCE: J.A. Savage, "HP Minis Unsnarl Unisource Tangles," *Computerworld,* July 29, 1991, p. 29.

Case Questions

1. Why does Unisource need a mainframe and several minicomputers?

2. Why is the software supplied with the minicomputers causing problems for Unisource?

3. Do you think that either the mainframe or the minicomputers could be replaced by a network of personal computers? Why or why not?

Case 4–2
Atlantic
Container Line

How much does it cost to send a shipment overseas? If you are sending a birthday present to a friend in Germany, the question may not be a major concern to you. However, for Atlantic Container Line (ACL), a large transatlantic shipping company located in South Plainfield, NJ, the answer to this question is crucial to the company's financial health. Thanks to a huge (215 Kbytes) PC-based contribution analysis spreadsheet model developed by ACL employee Tom Kaminski, the company's pricing analysts can answer that question while on the phone with customers. Salespeople simply respond to a series of prompts about a proposed shipment's revenue and cost factors, such as its origin and destination, land connections needed, and size and weight. Users can type in their answers or select them from a menu of choices. The model then computes the associated costs to determine how profitable the shipment is for ACL.

According to Corporate Marketing Manager Lon Grasso, the spreadsheet model is used every day. She states, "The model gives ACL a better understanding of its business. We know the profitability before the billing process. That helps ensure that all deals are profitable and pushes decision making down to a lower level, because the answers are right in front of people." In terms of competitiveness, Kaminski states, "I think it's helped us become very competitive. Our response time has improved dramatically. [Now], when a customer calls in to get a rate, the analyst knows instantly whether [the job will] make money or not. Another company might have to call back a couple of hours later and tell the customer that it can't do it at that rate."

Kaminski developed his model using Lotus 1-2-3 while working as a marketing analyst for ACL. The original development took four months, and the model is frequently modified to account for changes in company policy and environmental conditions. Even though he is now ACL's manager for Canadian trades, Kaminski still suggests modifications to the spreadsheet model, which is maintained and updated on a quarterly basis by the ACL marketing department.

SOURCE: Fredric Paul, "Cost Container," *Lotus,* December 1991, p. 25.

Case Questions

1. Why was a PC-based spreadsheet used for the ACL contribution analysis rather than a special program written in a mainframe-based computer language?

2. What factors did the developer decide were important in doing the rating analysis?

3. How does this spreadsheet model contribute to the overall competitiveness of ACL?

Data and File Resources

C H A P T E R

5

Introduction   Throughout this text, we emphasize the importance of information to any organization. Information is crucial to the success of an organization, involving its transaction processing, decision making, and competitive strategy. Most businesses could not function for more than a few days without information.

Information results from processing raw facts, or data, about an event (such as a sale) or an entity (such as an employee). This processing may be manual or computerized. Data are stored manually in many different ways—handwritten scraps of paper in a desk drawer or file folder; Rolodexes of customers' names, addresses, and telephone numbers; and inventory lists. Most modern organizations have fairly sophisticated filing systems consisting of folders stored in file cabinets and arranged by name, subject, or number. These data are an extremely valuable resource because they can be processed into the information that the organization uses to make decisions.

Working with data that are filed manually is usually tedious, involving a great deal of paper or card shuffling to derive any summary information or reports. Because the computer can store and manipulate data electronically, it can provide the same information much more quickly and with less effort. With specially designed software, a user may find needed data, manipulate data into another form, or isolate portions of data for special attention. The data may also be processed into information in whatever form is useful for decision making, including a summary report or graph. The computer software that works with data stored in an electronic form can usually perform the following three basic operations:

1. Inputting and storing data

2. Rearranging data

3. Retrieving data that meet some criteria

We discuss these operations in some detail in this chapter.

Storing Data

To be processed by a computer into needed information, data must be input and stored in a form that facilitates easy retrieval. If data are unavailable or in a form inconsistent with the input needs of the software used, then the necessary information cannot be generated. Recall from Chapter 4 that most data are input from a keyboard and are stored on magnetic disk or tape in a single file. These files are essentially collections of data to which a name is assigned; they are roughly analogous to the file folders used in many manual storage systems. When multiple files are used together to process information, the aggregate of these single files is referred to as a data base. This chapter discusses the processing of individual files and briefly introduces the use of multiple files and data bases. The next chapter builds on this discussion, covering the many uses of data bases in an organization.

The Data Hierarchy

To fully understand data resource storage, we need to consider the **data hierarchy.** As noted in Chapter 4, the smallest element of data is the **bit,** which corresponds to a single on–off switch in the computer or a single magnetic spot on a tape or disk. Groups of eight bits are called **bytes,** which correspond to alphabetic characters, digits, and special symbols. One or more bytes that form a single fact or data item are a **field.** A field may be a name, customer number, or sales amount. For some sophisticated computer software packages, fields may also contain graphic images. Fields are usually identified within a file by a unique **field name.** A collection of fields that pertain to a single person or thing is a **record.** A **file** is then a collection of related records all having the same fields. Finally, multiple files that are accessed together to generate needed information constitute a **data base.** The data hierarchy from bit to data base is shown in Figure 5–1 on following page.

The Data Hierarchy at ProYacht

As an example of the data hierarchy, we return to ProYacht, Inc. ProYacht sells its sailboats through dealers that sell only the ProYacht line and through a network of independent dealers and marinas. The ProYacht dealers communicate directly with the factory, and the independent dealers work through ProYacht's sales representatives. For each independent dealer, ProYacht had maintained a transaction file containing sales records with fields for transaction number, dealer name, date sold, product number, sales amount, and sales representative code. A new record was created in the file when these fields were filled with data related to a sale. (ProYacht has replaced this system with a new data base system that is illustrated in Chapter 6. The old system is shown in this chapter.) The ProYacht transaction file containing 10 such transactions is shown in Figure 5–2 on page 122.

In addition to the transaction file, ProYacht maintained an accounts receivable file, an inventory file, and a dealer file. The accounts receivable file contained the name, address, code number, and outstanding balance due for each dealer. The inventory file contained

FIGURE 5-1

Data Hierarchy for ProYacht, Inc.

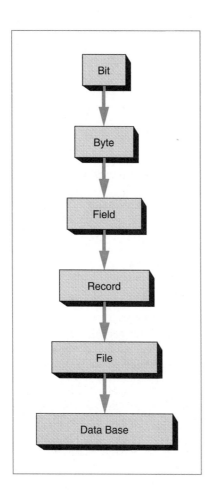

the product number, current price, and amount in stock of each type of sailboat. The dealer file contained each dealer's name, code number, and location (state); the number of each type of sailboat sold this year by that dealer; and the dealer's total sales in dollars for the current year. By accessing these combined files, ProYacht management could generate various reports, including one which showed the products being sold by each dealer in each state. This information could be helpful in deciding whether a dealership should be added and, if so, where it should be located. Figure 5-3 is a schematic representation of ProYacht's old data base files.

5.1 Data Input

Without the input process, the computer could not receive data or the instructions necessary for processing data. The following paragraphs discuss the data input process and the difficulties associated with it.

The Data Entry Process

Because the input process usually requires human interaction, it is the slowest part of the computer compared with the blinding speed of the Central Processing Unit (CPU) and

FIGURE 5–2

Transaction File for ProYacht, Inc.

Transaction Number	Dealer Name	Date	Product Number	Sales Amount	Sales Rep
3271	Bowman Yachts	05/10/92	SB2200	9,985	NY100
3272	Lakewood Boats	05/12/92	SB2800	35,000	VA200
3273	Baxter Marine	05/12/92	DS1800	4,340	MD250
3274	James River Marina	05/13/92	DS1800	4,340	NY100
3275	Lakewood Boats	05/17/92	DS1800	4,340	VA200
3276	Williams Outdoors	05/18/92	SB3000	42,000	PA100
3277	Baxter Marine	05/20/92	SB2800	35,000	MD250
3278	Miller Boats	05/22/92	SB2500	19,500	VA200
3279	Pointer Sailing	05/25/92	SB2200	9,985	PA100
3280	Smith Lake Marine	05/26/92	SB2700	28,500	MD250

internal memory or even the slow transfer of information to and from secondary storage. For example, a proficient typist working at a keyboard can input instructions and data at a rate of 8 characters per second (75 words per minute), but the CPU can process millions of characters per second. Unless some method of separating the input and processing operations is used, the processing of data into information is restricted by the slow rate at which input occurs.

This problem is part of the **data entry problem.** In this case, instructions are considered part of the data because the same problems occur when they are input. The data entry problem is especially troublesome on mainframes and minicomputers because of the relatively greater quantities of data that are processed on the larger computers. However, the increasing use of personal computers is compounding the data entry problem.

One solution to the slow data input rate is to store data temporarily in a **keyboard buffer,** a storage area within the computer. The keyboard buffer frees the CPU from waiting for data by sending the data to the CPU when needed. A second approach is to uncouple the

FIGURE 5–3

ProYacht, Inc. Data Base Files

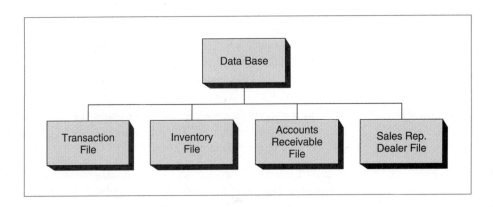

Filtering Data to Make Better Decisions

For many companies, the problem in decision making is not a lack of data but the ability to filter through the blizzard of raw data at their disposal. Many companies find that information systems can help them discover hidden opportunities among the facts and figures that are routinely collected about both new and existing products.

Ocean Spray Cranberries, Inc., almost decided not to introduce its Mauna La'i guava drink based on initial test market results. However, Information Resources, Inc. (IRI) rechecked the test results and discovered that brand loyalty would generate sufficient repeat purchases to make up for the lack of initial sales volume.

Cadbury Beverages, Inc., maker of Canada Dry and Hires drinks as well as Mott's Applesauce, used IRI and A.C. Nielson's Scantrack services to filter a huge amount of grocery store scanner data. Based on an analysis of this data, market researchers at Cadbury discovered an untapped market for cooking wines at the national level. This led to the addition of Cadbury's Holland House cooking wines.

SOURCE: Barbara Francett, "Marketers Dig for Openings in a Blizzard of Raw Data," *Computerworld*, October 15, 1990, pp. 93–97.

data entry process from the computer by going offline for data entry. In this process, the data are first placed onto a secondary storage medium using a machine that is not tied into a computer. The data are then transferred to the computer from secondary storage as needed. As a result, the computer is not delayed by a slow data input rate, because the data can be quickly transferred from secondary storage directly to the computer. Punched cards and magnetic tape have been used for this purpose in the past, but currently the most popular medium is the magnetic disk. Data are input using a **key-to-disk machine** and stored on a magnetic disk from a keyboard like that used on a computer.

Verification and Editing

The second part of the data entry problem involves the errors introduced during the keying process. This problem is solved to a large extent through two processes—verification and editing. In **verification,** the data entry process is repeated, and the information being entered is compared with the information already on the disk. If the data input from the keyboard on the second pass are the same as the data already on disk, then the data are assumed to be correct. If a difference occurs, the operator can check the value on the disk and correct it if necessary.

In addition to the verification process, data that have been input are usually edited using a series of checks. Such **editing** can include a reasonableness check, a range check, a value check, and the use of check digits. The reasonableness check tries to determine if the data are appropriate, and a range check determines if a data value falls in the applicable range. The value check tries to ensure that the value being input is among acceptable entries, and an extra check digit at the end of the code is used to ensure that digits are not transposed or missing. A validity check may also be used to reference a master file to see if a data item (for example, a customer or part number) is indeed valid.

*Betting on Bar
Code at Kmart*

In the early 1980s, Kmart management decided to provide its merchandise buyers with up-to-date sales information by installing a bar-coded point-of-sale system. This system, which cost nearly $1 billion, was finally completed in 1990 and now tracks the more than 100,000 items carried in each of the chain's 2,250 stores. At least 20 point-of-sale cash registers in each store are linked into a Local Area Network (LAN) with personal computers. The daily sales data are collected by the personal computers and then fed via satellite into the mainframe computers at the retailer's headquarters. This satellite link is also used to send revised price information from headquarters to each store.

The results of this huge investment are difficult to quantify, but Kmart profits were up 7 percent the year after system installation was completed. Kmart management also felt that the system helped reduce markdowns in the 1990 Christmas season by $87 million from the year before, when only one-half the stores were on the system. An example of how the system facilitated this process involved the pricing strategy for a certain doll. When the doll was priced at $29.88, the sales data showed slow sales. Based on this data, the price was cut to $24.88, and sales rose so much that the price was increased to the original level. When subsequent sales data indicated a slowing in sales, the price was cut a second time, which resulted in an almost complete sell-out. Without the bar code system, management could not have tracked sales and fine tuned the pricing strategy so quickly.

SOURCE: Mel Mandell, ''Kmart's $1 Billion Bar-code Bet,'' *Computerworld*, August 12, 1991, pp. 53, 55.

For example, a reasonableness check for a transaction entered into the ProYacht, Inc. transaction file would determine if the sale amount entered is a series of digits with no letters or other symbols. For the same entry, a range check might determine if the value is between upper and lower numeric limits for the size of sailboat (the length is part of the sailboat product number). A value check would determine if a dealer code is acceptable, and a check digit would ensure that the code digits are not transposed.

Although verification and editing cannot guarantee accurate data entry, these procedures are a major step toward that goal. Data that are input, verified, and edited, may then be input to the computer with a minimum of delay and a minimum of errors.

5.2 File Secondary Storage

Data are entered, checked, and then saved in secondary storage. As discussed in the previous chapter, the two primary forms of secondary storage are magnetic tape and disk. Tape is a **sequential access storage device,** so records are accessed in the same order that they are physically stored. Records stored sequentially must be accessed one after the other; the user or software cannot easily skip around among the records. Disk is a **Direct Access Storage Device (DASD),** on which any record may be accessed at any time. As a result, either random access or sequential access of records is possible on disk.

Three methods of organizing and accessing data files on secondary storage devices are commonly used—sequential access, direct access, and indexed sequential access organization. In **direct** (or **random**) **access,** any record on the disk may be accessed directly without going through any previous records, as long as the user or the software knows the address of that record. In **sequential access,** the records are accessed in a linear fashion, one right after the other. **Indexed sequential access method (ISAM)** is a combination of random and sequential access. The type of file organization directly affects how records are modified or updated by the user. We discuss the three types of file organization.

Sequential File Organization

Whether on tape or disk, a **sequential file organization** is used when records are accessed in the same order in which they are physically stored. This order sequence is usually based on the contents of some field. For example, the transaction file shown earlier might be stored sequentially in the order of the sales invoice number. Because of its inflexibility, sequential access storage is seldom used when files must be accessed frequently for data retrieval. On the other hand, it is often used to produce reports when a large proportion of the total number of records must be processed or when a large proportion of records are updated. In general, sequential files are processed in a batch mode on a periodic basis. It is also useful in situations with a high **activity ratio**—that is, the number of records updated compared with the total number of records in the file.

Direct Access File Organization

In **direct access file organization,** a magnetic disk is used to store the information, because all information on a disk can be accessed directly. However, to find a record, the computer must have its address on the disk. One method of finding a record's address involves the use of a primary key. The **primary key** is one field (or combination of fields) that uniquely distinguishes one record from all other records. In the transaction file shown in Figure 5–2, the transaction number is a primary key. The other fields cannot be used as primary keys because they are not unique to each record. In most files involving people, the social security number is used as a primary key. Nonunique fields, however, can be used as **secondary keys.** For example, the product number on the transaction file can be used as a secondary key if a list of all sales by a certain product number is desired.

Once a primary key is identified, the next step is to find the corresponding record's location, or **address,** on the disk. Two types of addresses are used—absolute address and relative address. A record's **relative address** gives its position relative to other records. The computer's operating system converts this relative address to an **absolute address,** which is used to find the record on the disk. The difference between the relative address and the absolute address is similar to the difference between a description of where someone lives and his or her address. ''The fourth house on the right from the end of the street'' is a relative address, and 130 Pinehill Road is an absolute address.

In computer terms, a relative address is expressed in terms of the position of the record from the beginning of the group of records being processed. This position is also known as the **record number.** On the other hand, an absolute address is expressed as the cylinder and track (which specifies the surface) on which the record is located. For addressing purposes, the tracks must be subdivided into **blocks,** which are the smallest addressable units on the disk. For example, a record's absolute address might be expressed as Cylinder 10, Track 5, Block 2.

Most software uses the relative address of the record and the operating system to actually find a record's absolute address. To find a record's relative address on disk, software may use **hashing,** in which the primary key is converted by a formula to a relative address for the record. A popular hashing scheme for a numeric primary key is the **division/remainder procedure.** In this procedure, the primary key number is divided by the prime number closest to but less than the number of storage positions on the disk, and the remainder is used as the relative address. For example, assume that 1000 storage locations are on the disk containing ProYacht's transaction file. The prime number closest to 1000 is 997. If the record with transaction number 3275 is divided by 997, we obtain a remainder of 284, so this record is stored in relative address position number 284.

When two records have the same calculated relative address, the second record is placed in the next storage location. In this case, when the primary key is hashed and the desired record is not found in that storage location, it can be found in the next relative location. Because of the possibility of such collisions, a hashed data file can only be 70–80 percent full. Other hashing schemes handle key fields made up of letters and symbols.

Because records in direct access storage can be accessed in any order, updating a direct access file is relatively easy. Records to be changed are found via their primary key and a hashing procedure, read into internal memory, modified as necessary, and then written back onto the direct access file, overwriting the previous version of the record. Records to be deleted are identified so that the operating system can use the space occupied by this record for a new record. Records are either added at the end of the list of records or in an available space.

Indexed Sequential Access Organization

The final method of storing and retrieving records on secondary storage is the **Indexed Sequential Access Method (ISAM).** This method combines direct and sequential access methods using disk storage in a way similar to the method used in telephone books for storing names, addresses, and phone numbers. In a telephone book, a primary key may be a person's full name and address, because this information is usually unique. Because the names of the first and last persons on each page are shown at the top of the page, a user can go directly to the page that contains the desired name and then begin a sequential search. The same procedure is used with ISAM on a computer disk, except that the primary key field is used to locate the area on the disk where the sequential search begins.

ISAM works well as long as a large number of additions and deletions are not made. Deletions are not actually removed from the disk, but are marked for removal when the disk is rewritten. Additions to the file are placed at the end of the records already present in the appropriate area. When this area is filled, an **overflow area** is used. If a record cannot be retrieved from the appropriate search area, the user must perform a sequential search of the overflow area. Table 5–1 compares sequential access, direct access, and ISAM in terms of ease of making additions, changes, deletions, inquiries and the type of storage device used.

Master File Update

In the **master file update** process, an existing file (called the **master file**) is updated with the additions or deletions of records from the file or with changes to records on the file.

TABLE 5–1

Comparison of
File Storage
Methods

Operation	Filing Method		
	Sequential	*Direct Access*	*ISAM*
Additions	Easy	Hard	Hardest
Changes	Hard	Easiest	Easy
Deletions	Hard	Easiest	Easy
Inquiries	Hard	Easiest	Easy
Activity Level	High	Low	Moderate
Storage Device	Tape/Disk	Disk	Disk

Whether on tape or disk, the master file update process is used when a file is updated periodically. Examples include weekly, biweekly, or monthly payroll file updating, periodic changes to accounts receivable files, and modification of grade files at the end of the quarter or semester.

The process is sequential for sequentially organized files. The changes are usually stored on an update file that is sorted in the same order as the master file, and the old master file and the update file are merged into a new master file. Updates are easy for a file stored on a direct access storage device, because each record is read into memory, updated, and then written back to disk. This direct access update process is destructive; the old copy of the record on the disk is written over with updated data. If the file is stored on tape, changes are made to a new copy of the tape.

In the sequential update (merge) process, records on the master file and the update file are compared. If a record on the master file is not on the update file, it is automatically written to the new master file without change. If a record on the update file is not on the master file, the update file record is written to a special error file. Finally, if a record on the update file matches a record on the master file, the revised record in the update file is written to the new master file in place of the existing record on the new file.

As an example of the master file update process, assume that ProYacht, Inc. has the transaction and master commissions payable files for independent dealers stored on magnetic tape. The transaction file has a record for each sailboat sale which contains the transaction number, dealer name, date of sale, product number, sales amount, and the sales representative code. The master commissions payable file contains one record for each sales representative with fields for the representative name, address, code number, and current sales balance. In order for this file to be processed sequentially, the records must be physically rearranged alphabetically by sales representative code before being input on tape. This file is modified on a weekly basis using the transaction file. In this case, the transaction file is arranged in the same order as the master file, that is, by sales representative code. The sales representative code on the transaction record is compared with the sales representative code on the master commissions payable file. If a match exists, then the sales amount on the transaction record is added to the sales balance on the master commissions payable file, and the new commissions record is written to the new master file. If no match occurs, then either this sales representative has no sales this week or no master record exists for this representative. In the first case, the current master record is written directly to the master file. In the second case, the record is written to an error file.

5.3 File Processing Systems

Data files are an important component in the processing of information for decision-making purposes, and not surprisingly, a great deal of software is available to work with them. This software is usually known as a **file processing system** or a **file processor.** Regardless of size, most organizations have some form of record keeping that requires single-file processing, usually straightforward accounting and inventory systems. In some cases, these files merely list the members or employees of the organization. In large organizations, the files could contain much detail about the people and products or services provided by the organization. Prior to computers, these files were kept on cards, on paper lists, or in folders in filing cabinets. Collecting the information management needed for its decision making required a manual search of the cards, lists, or folders.

Today's file processors are essentially electronic forms of these single-file record-keeping systems that allow the user to quickly and easily scan a file. These software packages work with information organized as one file made up of many records to generate needed reports. File processors are often used on personal computers when list management operations can be restricted to one file. Such PC file processing packages commonly cost less than $500.

Elements of a Single-File Processing System

File processing systems have three elements in common—the file, the file manager, and the report generator. Data are stored in the file, which is controlled by the **file manager.** The file manager controls the creation of the file, including giving it a name, setting up the field structure, and entering data into the file. The file manager also handles such manipulation tasks as rearranging the file according to a particular field and searching for records that meet some criterion.

The **report generator** outputs the information with appropriate headings in the order it was input or in some other order. It can also output only the records that match a desired characteristic. For example, the report generator can be used to output the first three fields of a file for all records that meet a specified criterion. Finally, the report generator can output information to an appropriate business form or create a report with headings and labels in a desired format.

Although sequential access storage can be useful for a file processing system, direct access storage is usually used because of its flexibility and speed. In this text, we assume that direct access storage is used.

Flat Files

The types of files used in file processing systems are often referred to as **flat files,** because they can be represented in the form of a two-dimensional table. The transaction file shown in Figure 5–2 is an example of a flat file. Flat files are important for two reasons. First, many applications can use data stored in a single flat file which can then be manipulated or rearranged as needed. Several PC-based data base management software packages are really flat file management systems that only work with one file at a time. In many situations, only a single file is needed to handle an organization's information needs. The second reason flat files are so important involves their use as parts of multifile data bases on personal computers and mainframes. This second use of flat files is discussed in more detail in Chapter 6.

File Manager Operations

Operations within the file manager may include the following:

- Creating the file
- Defining the field structure of the file
- Setting up a data entry screen for entering information into the file
- Sorting and listing information in some specified order
- Searching for a particular record or listing all records on the file with a special characteristic

With file processing software, creating a file is usually easy, often requiring only that a unique, meaningful name be assigned to the file. To work with a file, the type of information needed for each field—or the **file structure**—must be determined by defining field names, widths, and types. The field name is unique—usually a combination of letters, digits, and underscores—and given to each field in a file. **Field width** is the number of positions needed in each field. The **field type** is the type of information stored in a field. The allowable field types depend on the package used, but four common field types are character, numeric, date, and logical.

A **data entry screen** prompts the user for data through one or more monitor screens. Different data base packages may have different types of data entry screens, and sometimes the user can develop data entry screens to fit specific needs. With a data entry screen, a user can simply answer questions to enter the needed data. Often once a user enters some of the information, the software can supply the remaining information by referencing data files. For example, the entry of a part number could result in the display of the description and the price for the part. An appropriate user command or menu option could then generate reports containing desired information. Figure 5–4 shows a data entry screen for a popular PC-based file processing system.

Sorting Flat Files

An important concept often used in reference to a flat file is **sorting**—that is, arranging information in a file in some specific order. The resulting list can be in ascending or descending order, alphabetically or numerically, depending on the field used to decide the sort order. For example, if the flat file shown in Figure 5–2 is sorted on the Sales Amount field in ascending order, then it would appear as shown in Figure 5–5.

A flat file can be sorted by physically moving records around, but this process can be slow and require large amounts of disk storage space. Sorting records can be made easier with record numbers, which are usually associated with the order in which records are entered. With record numbers, files can be sorted using a **linked list** that "ties" records together through a **pointer system.** In this system, a pointer value "points" to the next

FIGURE 5–4   *Data Entry Screen*

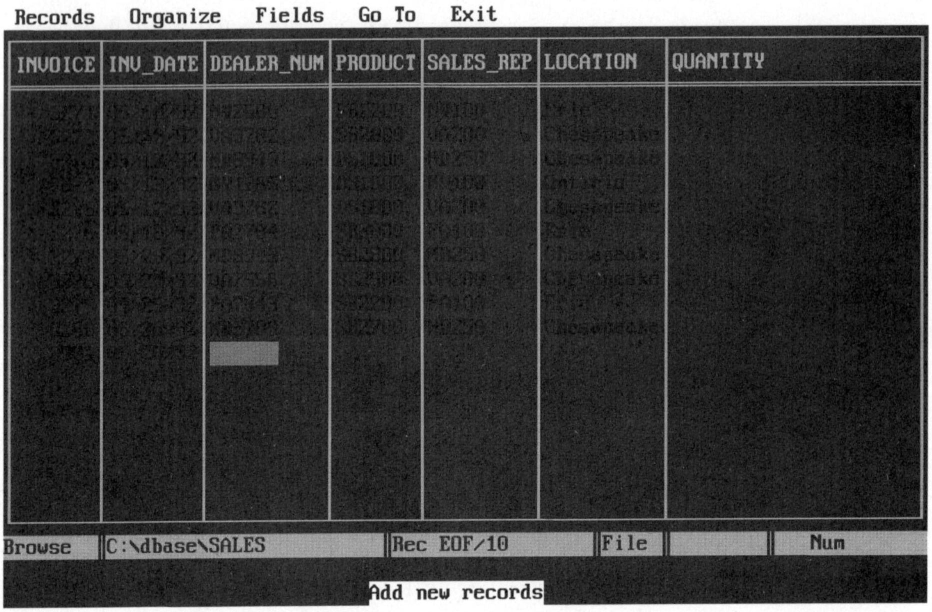

```
   Records   Organize   Fields   Go To   Exit
 ┌────────┬──────────┬────────────┬─────────┬──────────┬──────────┬──────────────┐
 │INVOICE │ INV_DATE │ DEALER_NUM │ PRODUCT │ SALES_REP│ LOCATION │   QUANTITY   │
 ├────────┴──────────┴────────────┴─────────┴──────────┴──────────┴──────────────┤
 │                                                                                │
 │                                                                                │
 │                                                                                │
 │                                                                                │
 │                                                                                │
 │                                                                                │
 ├────────────────────────────────────────────────────────────────────────────── │
 │ Browse    C:\dbase\SALES           Rec EOF/10        File            Num        │
 │                                   Add new records                               │
 └────────────────────────────────────────────────────────────────────────────── ┘
```

FIGURE 5–5

Sorted Flat File

Transaction Number	Dealer Name	Date	Product Number	Sales Amount	Sales Rep
3273	Baxter Marine	05/12/92	DS1800	4,340	MD250
3274	James River Marina	05/13/92	DS1800	4,340	NY100
3275	Lakewood Boats	05/17/92	DS1800	4,340	VA200
3271	Bowman Yachts	05/10/92	SB2200	9,985	NY100
3279	Pointer Sailing	05/25/92	SB2200	9,985	PA100
3278	Miller Boats	05/22/92	SB2500	19,500	VA200
3280	Smith Lake Marine	05/26/92	SB2700	28,500	MD250
3272	Lakewood Boats	05/12/92	SB2800	35,000	VA200
3277	Baxter Marine	05/20/92	SB2800	35,000	MD250
3276	Williams Outdoors	05/18/92	SB3000	42,000	PA100

*Data Base
Saves the
Salvation Army*

Using kettles to collect coins at Christmas may be about as "low-tech" as you can get, but the Salvation Army's Greater Chicago divisional headquarters uses a PC-based data base system to improve the operation. Keeping track of the 650 kettle sites in the Chicago area that are manned by volunteers was too much for a paper-and-pencil system. Instead, the PC-based Microsoft Works data base system now manages the collection process more effectively.

Because many sites are not manned continually, an important concern is having a volunteer at a site for the greatest collection opportunity. The data base system has proved to be very effective in doing

this, as well as ensuring that each site is not over-manned.

The system is useful for trouble-shooting during the hectic Christmas season. If a problem is reported, a supervisor can quickly determine the officer responsible for the site and dispatch immediate assistance. The data base system can also track the amount of money collected at each site. By combining this information with the number of hours each site is manned, an hourly intake figure can be computed for use in future planning.

SOURCE: Carol Hilderbrand, "Data Base Helps Keep Bells Ringing," *Computerworld*, December 17, 1990, p. 6.

record in the sorted ordering. A pointer system that indicates the location of the next record is much faster than a system that physically moves records.

As an example of using a linked list and pointer system, consider again the transaction file shown in Figure 5–2. First, we assign record numbers corresponding to the order in which each record is entered. Showing the order by sales amount as a linked list requires the addition of a second list of values, or pointers, as shown in Figure 5–6 on the following page.

In Figure 5–6, the initial pointer is at record 3, which has a pointer value of 4+. The + in the pointer field indicates that it is the first record in the linked list. This means that record 4 is next in the sorted ordering. Similarly, record 4 has a pointer value of 5. The resulting ordering of record numbers is 3, 4, 5, 1, 9, 8, 10, 2, 7, and 6. Note that no record points to record 3 because it is the first record in the ordering, and that record 6 has an * in the pointer field because it is the last record.

If a record is added to or deleted from the file, the pointer system can be changed quickly and easily to reflect the addition or deletion. For example, assume the following record 11 is added to the transaction file:

Record Number	Transaction Number	Dealer Name	Date	Product Number	Sales Amount	Sales Rep
11	3281	High & Dry Marina	05/27/92	SB3000	42,000	GA150

FIGURE 5–6 *Transaction File with Pointer System*

Record Number	Transaction Number	Dealer Name	Date	Product Number	Sales Amount	Sales Rep	Amount Pointer
1	3271	Bowman Yachts	05/10/92	SB2200	9,985	NY100	9
2	3272	Lakewood Boats	05/12/92	SB2800	35,000	VA200	7
3	3273	Baxter Marine	05/12/92	DS1800	4,340	MD250	4 +
4	3274	James River Marina	05/13/92	DS1800	4,340	NY100	5
5	3275	Lakewood Boats	05/17/92	DS1800	4,340	VA200	1
6	3276	Williams Outdoors	05/18/92	SB3000	42,000	PA100	*
7	3277	Baxter Marine	05/20/92	SB2800	35,000	MD250	6
8	3278	Miller Boats	05/22/92	SB2500	19,500	VA200	10
9	3279	Pointer Sailing	05/25/92	SB2200	9,985	PA100	8
10	3280	Smith Lake Marine	05/26/92	SB2700	28,500	MD250	2

To account for this new record, we need only add a pointer value of 11 to the pointer field of record 6, because record 11 is now the last record with an * in the pointer field. As a result, the new record number order is 3, 4, 5, 1, 9, 8, 10, 2, 7, 6, and 11. For deleting a record, the record number of the deleted record is simply removed from the pointer system, and the record pointing to the deleted record now points to the next record in order.

Another useful feature of pointer systems is that multiple pointers can be associated with the same flat file. This allows the file to be sorted on multiple fields without physically changing the record order. For our example, in addition to the pointer system for the sales amount, other pointer systems could be associated with the product number, dealer code, or transaction number.

Retrieving Data from Files

In addition to sorting flat files, a user may want to retrieve records that meet some criterion. For example, in the transaction flat file in Figure 5–2, we might want to find all records with a given sales representative number or a certain product number. As with sorting, physically searching through records can be time consuming. However, with pointer systems, records that have a pointer value for a specific key can be quickly found.

A second method of finding records in a flat file is to use an **inverted,** or **indexed, file,** which is a second file containing one or more fields from the original flat file arranged in order of some value (the **index**) which points to the appropriate records in the file. For example, using the product number as an index, we can create an inverted file containing the dates on which each type of product was sold, as shown in Figure 5–7.

Although more efficient than physically sorting long files, linked lists and inverted files have shortcomings. Linked lists require the creation and maintenance of a separate pointer system, and inverted files require the creation of an entirely new file for each

FIGURE 5-7

Inverted File by
Product Number

Product Number	Date
DS1800	05/12/92
DS1800	05/13/92
DS1800	05/17/92
SB2200	05/10/92
SB2200	05/25/92
SB2500	05/22/92
SB2700	05/26/92
SB2800	05/12/92
SB2800	05/20/92
SB3000	05/18/92

index used. Because inverted files can quickly use up a great deal of secondary storage space, linked lists are more commonly used for searching flat files.

The Report
Generator

A simple list of records may meet an organization's needs, but some situations may require more formal reports. Most file processing packages have a built-in report generation function that includes special formats or headings, the summing or averaging of fields, and the creation of new columns by combining existing columns. The report created by this function can be essentially a template for the output of some or all of the data.

Problems with
File Processing
Systems

As discussed in the previous section, file processing systems are useful for working with lists of information contained on a single file. They are often easy to use and quite inexpensive. However, working with only one file at a time is severely restrictive in many situations. Information that exists on two separate files may be needed to answer various questions or aid in decision making. For example, a college could have one file containing a student's application and admissions data, another file with housing information, and still another file with information concerning scholarships and loans.

Accessing information on separate files is not an easy task. One approach is to use a **sort/merge operation,** similar to that used for the master file update, to combine information from two files into one. Unfortunately, the use of separate files raises fundamental questions regarding data redundancy, data integrity, and data dependence.

Data redundancy is the repetition of the same data on different files. Different offices in a college may have separate files containing much of the same information—for example, name, social security number, and address. Such redundancy is costly in terms of money required to collect, process, and update the data for computer storage and in terms of computer storage itself.

The second problem, **data integrity,** is closely related to data redundancy. When the same information is stored in multiple files throughout an organization, any change in one file must be changed in *all* files. For example, a student's change of address must be entered in all related files at the college. Incorrect data in only one file could lead to severe problems for the users of the data or the student.

The third problem occurs when different departments in an organization collect, process, and store information using different software. One department might use a computer language like COBOL to create files on a mainframe computer, and another department may use a commercial file processing package for the same operation on a personal computer. Another department might use Pascal on a minicomputer to process and store information. To compound the dependency problem, each software application is written based on specific file organization, and files and record contents are designed for specific software applications. This situation produces a problem with **data dependence** between the software and the files. When one department's files are incompatible with another department's files, combining the information from the two files is extremely difficult. Moreover, adding new software applications is often difficult because applications must conform to existing files, existing files must be modified (for example, have more pointers), or new files must be created.

Taken together, the problems of data redundancy, data integrity, and data dependence can cause serious problems. For example, assume that a college administrator wished to write a report on the number of accepted applicants who also requested financial aid and on-campus housing. The process of collecting the necessary data from three different departments' files could be quite slow and awkward.

5.4 The Data Base Solution

To avoid the problems encountered when each department in an organization creates its own files, an organization can use an integrated data base managed by a **data base management system (DBMS)**. With an integrated data base, data are entered into all files at the same time. This common data base is then used by all units and computer applications. A single-file management system that can only handle one file at a time is not acceptable for the demands of a multiple-file integrated data base. The organization needs a DBMS that can link all applications with its many data files.

The Logical View

Problems of data redundancy, data dependency, and data integrity can be avoided if the logical relationships among all parts of a data base are carefully planned. System designers use a **schema,** which is a logical plan for determining the data elements in a data base and the relationships among these elements. A **subschema** is a reduced view of the data base for a particular application.

A schema can show *what* should be done to make data available to users. The next question is *how* the data should be organized. This logical view of the data base involves the use of **data models** to represent the data base. Currently, three data models are commonly used for a DBMS—the hierarchical data model, network data model, and relational data model. In a **hierarchical data model,** data elements are related to one another from top to bottom, with each lower level element linked to only one upper level element. A **network data model** also has a hierarchy, but a lower level element may be linked to multiple upper level elements. In a **relational data model,** a series of tables is

FIGURE 5–8

Schematic of Various Data Models

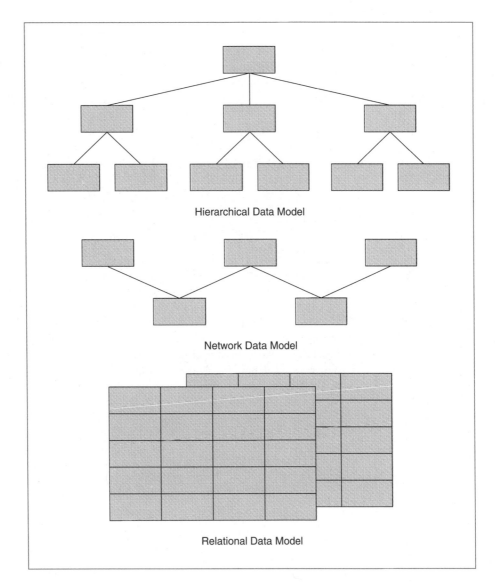

Hierarchical Data Model

Network Data Model

Relational Data Model

used to show the relationship among the data elements. Figure 5–8 shows each data model schematically.

Each data model has been implemented in various commercial DBMSs, and each has its strong and weak points. These data models are covered in more detail in Chapter 6.

In a hierarchical data model, each data element can only have one root, some other data element, often called the **parent.** However, because each root element can have many branches, a hierarchical model is also called a **one-to-many data model** or a tree

It seems that ordering a pizza for home delivery is as familiar to college students as buying textbooks and studying for exams, and now Domino's Pizza has a data base system called OASIS that makes it even easier for students and other pizzaphiles to indulge. The next time you call Domino's to place an order, an employee may request your telephone number and then simply ask if you want the "usual." This is possible because OASIS, which is installed on each store's UNIX-based personal computer, gathers information about the store's customers. Types of information the data base stores include the customer's address, favorite toppings, number of pizzas usually ordered, method of payment, and special requests, such as delivering the pizza to a dorm room. The data base also knows if the caller is telephoning from a number that has been used by a prankster, who, for example, requests pizza delivery to a nonexistent address, or by someone who refuses to pay for the pizza.

When the employee enters the caller's telephone number in the store's computer, the caller's buying habits are displayed on the screen and the Domino's employee can ask "Do you want the same toppings as last time?" or "Do you want it delivered to your dorm room?" Drivers have all this information before leaving the store. If a customer does not want to provide his or telephone number, the system allows the employee to key in the order rather than pull up the information from the customer data base.

In addition to speeding the order process for both the customer and the Domino's employee, the OASIS system automates order preparation and delivery by creating a "door slip" when an order is taken. The slip tells the pie maker exactly what the customer ordered and the driver exactly where to deliver the pizza. Further, OASIS provides Domino's management with the demographic characteristics of each store.

SOURCE: "New Domino's Computer System Could Help the Company Avoid Those Noids," *The Atlanta Journal-Constitution,* September 11, 1989, p. C14; and interview with Domino's on December 12, 1991.

structure. For example, a company may have several product lines (parents) consisting of several models, and each model has several versions or characteristics. Model data are accessed only through the parent nodes and not from model characteristics.

A network data model is a **many-to-many model,** because each data element can have numerous roots or parents. For example, a student may take many different courses, and each course is taken by many different students. Both the course number and the student number can serve as the root node used to access information on a particular student's courses or all the students in a particular course. In a network, data can be accessed from many directions.

A relational data model consists of tabular information on many topics, such as product model characteristics. **Relational operators** combine this information in a number of ways (not necessarily predetermined) to provide management with a variety of information. This data model is very flexible in that the associations among data items via hierarchies or networks are not predetermined.

5.5 Summary

Because the most important resource in any organization is information and information results from the processing of data, data make up an equally important asset. The computer has enhanced management's ability to access and use this resource because of its ability to store and quickly process data in the form of files. The data hierarchy, which describes data type, goes from the bit up to the data base.

Data entry is a problem because of the time necessary to enter large amounts of data into the computer and because this process can generate errors. One solution to the data entry problem is to decouple the function from computer processing. The data must be validated and edited to detect and correct as many errors as possible before the processing function occurs.

Files are physically organized in three forms—sequential access, direct access, or indexed sequential access method. A common operation on a large sequential access file is the master file update of information through a merge process. In direct access storage, every record has an address. Hashing on the primary key is used to determine a record's relative address, from which the operating system determines the absolute address. The indexed sequential access method combines direct and sequential access principles using disk storage.

Today, file processing software works with data by performing three important operations:

1. Storing and retrieving data

2. Manipulating and rearranging data

3. Generating reports

A single file is a collection of records all having the same fields. The field width is the number of positions taken up by a field, and field names are used to identify fields on a record.

Single data files are commonly stored as flat files organized as lists of records. A common operation on flat files is sorting, or rearranging the records in some specific order. Another common operation is searching for records that meet a specific criterion, often using linked lists or inverted files. Sorting direct access files via indexing and pointer systems eliminates the need to physically move records.

File processing systems, or file processors, work with single files using a file manager and a report generator. The file manager controls the actual creation of the file, sets up the structure of the file, and manages data entry. A data entry screen is used for input to a data base. The file manager also handles file manipulation tasks. The report generator controls output of the information in the file. Common operations using a file processor include sorting records, searching for a given record, listing a group of records, and generating a report on the information.

A DBMS is needed when multiple files contain the data needed for management information. A DBMS has an integrated data base that helps avoid problems of data redundancy, data integrity, and data dependence on software applications. A schema is used to plan the logical organization of a data base. Data models help to implement the logic developed in the data base schema. Three common data models—hierarchical, network, and relational—are discussed in the next chapter.

Key Terms

absolute address
activity ratio
address
bit
blocks
bytes
data base
data base management system (DBMP)
data dependence
data entry problem
data entry screen
data hierarchy
data integrity
data models
data redundancy
direct access
direct access file organization
direct access storage device (DASD)
division/remainder procedure
editing
field
field name
field type
field width
file manager
file processing system
file processor
file structure
flat files
hashing
hierarchical data model
index

indexed file
indexed sequential access method
   (ISAM)
inverted file
key-to-disk machine
keyboard buffer
linked list
many-to-many model
master file
master file update
network data model
one-to-many model
overflow area
parent
pointer system
primary key
random access
record
record number
relational data model
relational operators
relative address
report generator
schema
secondary keys
sequential access
sequential access storage device
sequential file organization
sort
sort/merge operation
subschema
verification

Review Questions

1. Why are data important in an information system? What are the various types of data?

2. Describe the data entry problem. Explain how decoupling can work to solve part of this problem.

3. What role does verification and editing play in solving the data entry problem?

4. What are the elements of a file and how are they ordered? What are the field width and field name?

5. What is the data hierarchy? List the elements of the data hierarchy.

6. What are the three forms of file organization? Which form is associated with tape storage? Why?

7. Why is the master file update procedure an important operation? Explain how it might be used on a payroll system.

8. What is hashing used for? What is the difference between the absolute and relative addresses?

9. Explain the use of ISAM. Why is an overflow area needed for ISAM?

10. Name the three operations that are commonly performed on data files.

11. What is a flat file? What happens to a flat file when it is sorted?

12. How are linked lists or inverted files used with a flat file?

13. How does a pointer system speed up the sorting process in a direct access file organization?

14. What problems can occur when separate files exist within the same organization? How can a DBMS help avoid these problems?

15. List the three data models used in DBMS.

Discussion Questions

1. Computer processing circles use an expression called garbage in, garbage out (GIGO), which means that erroneous input causes inaccurate output. How can data input routines reduce this phenomenon?

2. In file management systems, linked lists and inverted files (indexed files) can be used to organize and retrieve data for specific applications. What problems arise when new records are added and when new applications, which require different views of the data on the files, are needed? How can a data base system solve this problem?

3. For each situation below, describe the preferred file organization and file access method:
   a. A payroll system that generates weekly payroll checks for thousands of employees in a large manufacturing firm.

b. A customer file system for a retail department store that needs up-to-date sales records for buyers and inventory management and credit granting decisions.

c. An insurance company policy file system that is used to process changes in policies, send out premium notices periodically, and respond to occasional queries about a policy.

Case 5–1

Metro Realty

The property management division of Metro Realty leases thousands of residential and commercial properties in the metropolitan area. The division's new file management system stores records randomly on a magnetic disk. Listed below are some of the records, along with corresponding disk addresses and key fields used to organize data for various reports:

Disk Address	Renter Number	Renter Name	Property Location	Amount	Due Date
7	0010	Lawn and Garden	Northside	$ 2000	10
5	0015	Greens Gifts	Lakeside	8000	20
9	0020	B & B Auto	Lakeside	5000	01
3	0025	AAA Bakery	Midlands	10000	01

Case Questions

1. Prepare a six-column matrix with columns for renter number, renter name pointer, location pointer, amount pointer, and due date pointer. List the disk address to the left of these columns. Then in the row under each column, enter the pointers needed to create a linked list for retrieving values in the following sequences:

a. Renter number from highest to lowest
b. Renter name alphabetically
c. Property location alphabetically
d. Amount from lowest to highest
e. Due date chronologically

The pointers that form the renter number list would appear as follows (where + is the beginning of the linked list, and * is the end of the linked list):

Disk Address	Renter Number Pointer	Renter Name Pointer	Location Pointer	Amount Pointer	Due Date Pointer
7	5 +				
5	9				
9	3				
3	*				

2. Explain how the linked list can be employed to determine the payments due by the first of each month.

Case 5–2
Quick Tax
Company

Quick Tax Company uses hundreds of tax preparation personnel during a three-month period leading up to April 15. Most employees are part-time and paid on an hourly basis, with overtime paid for extra hours on the weekends. The company maintains minimal records on these employees, including social security number, name, address, phone number, tax preparation experience code, years of education, hours worked per week, and cumulative hours worked for the tax season. The company also keeps minimal records on its customers, including fields for name, customer number, federal and state form reference numbers, list of forms used, address, preparation date, filing date, hours needed to prepare the return, fee charged, date of fee payment, and tax form code for accessing a copy of the forms filed.

Case Questions

1. How could a flat file management system be used to pay employees, process their tax information, and contact them for next season's work?

2. How could a flat file management system be used to bill customers and keep track of payments for services, contact them for next season's services, inform them of tax law changes, tell them what records to bring to the preparer, and assess the demographics of each customer to provide better service next year.

3. How can the information in the flat file be used to schedule employees for next tax season?

4. Name some shortcomings of the use of flat files in this case. How could a DBMS improve the management of personnel and customer information?

Data Base Systems

6

Introduction   The previous chapter described data files and several ways of organizing data and retrieving information from single files. Chapter 5 also introduced data bases and the advantages of data base processing over single-file processing. In this chapter, that discussion of data bases is continued, including a presentation of the nature and the various components of data base processing, a description of various data models or structures, and an outline of the managerial uses of information from data bases.

A **data base** is a collection of data that is organized for easy utilization. For example, a data base may be a logical collection of integrated data files like the ones mentioned in Chapter 5, or an integrated collection of data used by all applications. The logical integration of data is the basis of the **data base concept,** as compared with a **file processing system,** in which each application uses a separate file. The data base system reduces some shortcomings of traditional file-oriented systems. A **Data Base Management System (DBMS)** is the software interface between the data base and the user. Data may be stored in flat files, in tables, or as records, as with file-oriented systems. The DBMS links these data items[1] and records through a series of pointers and linking mechanisms.

The difference between file-oriented systems and data base systems is shown in Figure 6–1. In Figure 6–1(a), each application in a file-oriented system uses only a single file. On the other hand, in Figure 6–1(b), the data base is independent of the applications

---

[1] A data item is made up of bits and bytes; however, data are only significant to a data base user at the data item level. The relationships between bits, bytes, characters, and a data item are discussed in Chapter 5.

FIGURE 6-1

*File and Data
Base Concepts*

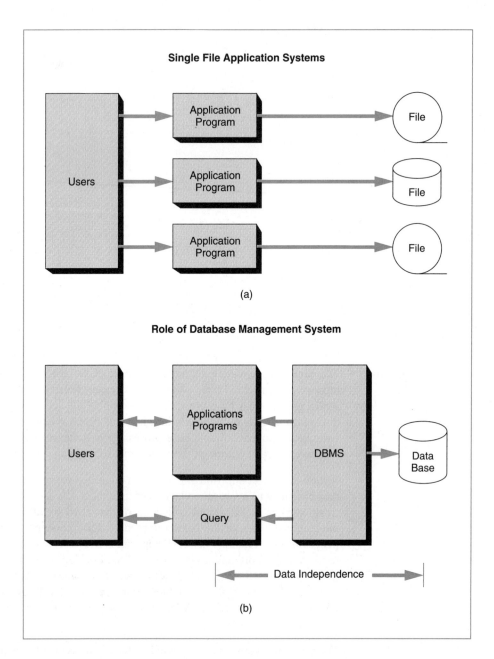

Single File Application Systems

(a)

Role of Database Management System

(b)

programs, and a DBMS is used to combine the necessary data elements for each application.

Two key concepts in a data base system are data integration and data independence. **Data integration** means that individual data items from traditional files are integrated to form the data base, and a DBMS separates the data from the applications programs. The applications programs still perform their original functions, but the DBMS retrieves the necessary data from the data base when all the data are integrated for easy access. For example, a report listing sales commissions for a particular line of merchandise could, in most cases, be generated without changing the data base. An application program simply accesses the data base via the DBMS, which extracts and processes the data in the form desired by the user or application program. Many DBMS's even provide a query language with which reports can be generated on-line without using a special application program. This separation of applications and data—**data independence**—allows a significant degree of flexibility and accessibility that does not exist in single-file systems.

6.1 Components of Data Base Processing

A data base processing system has four components—users' applications programs, the data base administrator, the data base itself, and the DBMS. These components are shown in Figure 6–2. Note that the host computer operating system is also an important aspect of the data processing system.

A multitude of **data base users** may place many demands on the data base for transaction processing (TPS), management information (MIS), decision support (DSS), and executive information (EIS) requirements. These needs will often span the marketing, production, and financial functions of the organization. The user is generally a manager,

FIGURE 6–2

Data Base Processing System Components

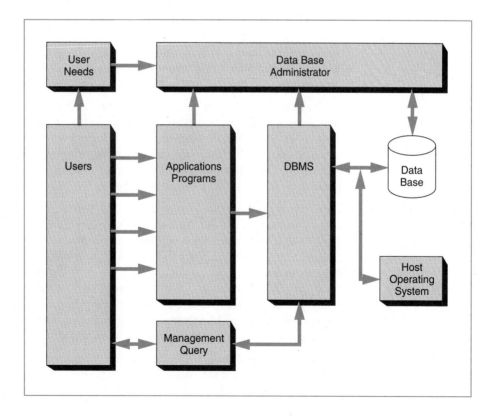

operations supervisor, employee, or staff member who interacts directly with the information stored in the data base. The **data base administrator** controls the overall operations of the data base and, as such, is the data base custodian. The administrator's duties involve creating, adding, and deleting records as well as data security and recovery. He or she ultimately decides on the organization of the physical data and the various logical relationships needed to satisfy user requests. The data base is the repository of data available for various users and their applications. Finally, the DBMS is the interface between users and their applications and the host computer's operating system and its repository of data.

Data Base Users

In most organizations today, the number of data base users is expanding rapidly, because of the flexibility and accessibility of data in a data base compared with single-file systems. Contemporary organizations have many different types of data base users — clerks who process transactions on the sales floor, production personnel who assemble products to meet a computerized schedule, product designers who design better products to satisfy customer needs, market research personnel who study consumer trends, tactical managers who prepare budgets and plans with the assistance of data patterns, and executives who chart the organization's future using business and economic data. As noted in the early chapters, these data are increasingly used to compete aggressively in the marketplace through customer services and interfaces with suppliers and customers.

These users have applications programs for routine information requirements, and the query languages provided by most DBMSs can handle nonroutine inquiries about various aspects of the organization. This query provision is shown in Figure 6-2. Often, users can write their own applications using a report generator or a PC programming language. The number of these **end users** is growing rapidly because many new data base systems have user friendly interfaces.

Users can interface with the data base using three methods — direct interaction, applications programs, and end user programs. Direct interaction with the data base is feasible using either a command language or a menu-driven system that requires users to respond to questions or fill in blanks on a monitor. Applications programs written by programmers can also be used to generate needed reports. Finally, end users can write their own applications for managing information or processing daily transactions.

The Data Base Administrator

The data base administrator — either an individual or a department — controls the logical and physical structure of the data base. He or she is responsible for the overall configuration of the DBMS and all the hardware and software that support the system. The administrator sets policies and standards for the user-system interface, the applications, and the method of data input. For example, a department or individual user wishing to modify a record format must receive the approval of the data base administrator. Changes of this type are only made when they are in the best interests of the organization. In other words, the data base is the property of the organization, and the data base administrator must consider all the organization's needs when administering the data base.

The data base administrator provides a number of basic services. He or she plans the file addressing schemes for the data base, the logical structure, the physical data layout, security procedures, and a means for recovery after failures occur. He or she also selects the data management software that allows end users to utilize the data base. End users often need the data base administrator's support to understand what data are available and the procedures (query language) for accessing that data. The data base administrator also assists applications programmers with data definitions and the data base structure.

In general, the data base administrator is responsible for the overall data base configuration. He or she must encourage standardization of data items and specify the data structures and layouts that are best for users as a group. A data base administrator must also settle differences between groups or individuals who request that data be defined, represented, and/or stored differently from the standard.

For a large organization with a complex data base system, a single individual would probably not have the technical expertise, knowledge of the corporation's data, and communication skills to handle all these tasks. A large data base may require an administrative unit made up of several individuals, including an overall data base administrator, a data base design analyst, a definition analyst, a data operations supervisor, and a security officer.

6.2 The Data Base

The third component of the data base system is the data base itself. To better understand the data base structure (often called the architecture of the data base), we need to examine some basic concepts. Data can be considered from three viewpoints—the user's view, the logical view, and the physical view. The **user's view** is the report, output display, and input menu, for example. It is what the user sees as he or she interfaces with the computer to use information for decision making, reporting, or carrying out day-to-day transactions. The user wants a data base that is easy to access and use and secure from errors and mischief. Users seldom care about the other two views, which are concerned with how the data for problem solving and decision making are stored. However, these other two views of data can have a major impact on the user.

The **physical view** of the data describes how they are physically stored on some type of magnetic media. The physical view involves maximizing storage efficiency, minimizing duplication, and providing easy access. On the other hand, the **logical view** of the data defines how data are organized and accessed for applications and the end user interface. Note that the logical view is usually quite different from the physical view. In a sequential-access single-file management system that uses magnetic tape the physical and the logical are the same.

In general, applications are *independent* of the physical arrangement. This independence concept requires that applications and queries not be tied to the data base other than through the DBMS as shown in Figure 6–2. The data base design does not depend on a particular application. Thus, the data base administrator organizes the logical view of the data to fit the varied needs of management.

Schemas and Subschemas

Two important concepts in the logical definition of the data base are schemas and subschemas. A **schema** describes how the data base is organized from a logical view. A **subschema** is that portion of the schema that is of interest to a particular user or application. A schema is analogous to a map of a city, and the subschema is the portion of

FIGURE 6–3

*Schema and
Subschema*

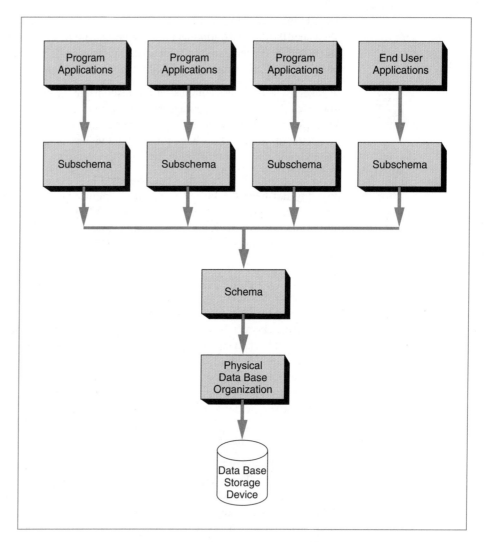

the map that includes a given individual's subdivision. Figure 6–3 illustrates the relationship between schema, subschemas, data, and applications/end user programs.

The schema and subschema concept separates the descriptions of the entire data base from the descriptions of those portions employed by individual users. This concept is important for the following reasons:

1. The data base probably contains data that are shared by many applications. With subschemas, individual users can focus only on the portion of the data base that is relevant to their information needs, making programming and data base use more efficient.

2. The employment of subschemas ensures a certain amount of privacy and integrity of the data base, because individual programs access only the data base portion identified by the subschema.

3. Data independence is enhanced, because changes to the schema and the data base do not affect individual programs.

4. The schema uses a common language to define the entire data base. Based on the needs of the individual user, a variety of languages may be used to describe a subset of the data via the subschema.

The schema can be expressed in the data structure or model. A data dictionary lists all the data items in the data base, as well as their associated definitions, sources, and uses. This list may be used to describe the model to users and applications programmers.

Data Structure

The **data structure (data base structure),** or logical organization of the data base, is a function of an organization's needs for decision making, reporting, and transaction processing. This structure, in turn, is used to specify the processing modes and the equipment needed to process information. Described briefly in Chapter 5, three popular logical **data base models** — relational, hierarchical, and network data models — are used to structure data in a DBMS.

Logical associations among data base elements enable data to be retrieved from multiple files. Data in one file can be linked to data in another file so that management may generate reports and make decisions from data stored in several files at once. The **logical integration** of data files can be either established *explicitly* using a structural model like the hierarchy or the network data models or *implicitly* using the relational data model. An explicit model establishes predetermined relationships between logically related data items using indexes and pointers to link fields. These indexes and pointers point to different files as well as the records within a single file. These indexes and pointers are part of individual records and must be maintained by the DBMS. An implicit model defines these relationships differently as will be shown in the discussion of relational data bases.

6.3 Data Models

Three types of data models — hierarchical, network, and relational — are currently in wide use. Because each data model is the basis of several commercial DBMSs, a user commonly refers to the DBMS by the data model on which it is based. For example, a DBMS based on the hierarchical data model is often called a hierarchical DBMS.

Hierarchical Data Model

A **hierarchical data model** is also referred to as a **tree data model,** because it resembles the structure of a tree.[2] The model's ''trunk'' (a parent) has several large ''branches'' (descendants), and from each branch emerge other small branches (the next generation of descendants). Thus, the data elements have hierarchical relationships, with each succeeding element linked to only one leading element. This is called a **one-to-many**

---

[2] One of the first widely used hierarchical data base systems on the mainframe was the IBM Information Management System (IMS), released in 1968.

FIGURE 6–4

*Hierarchical Data
Model*

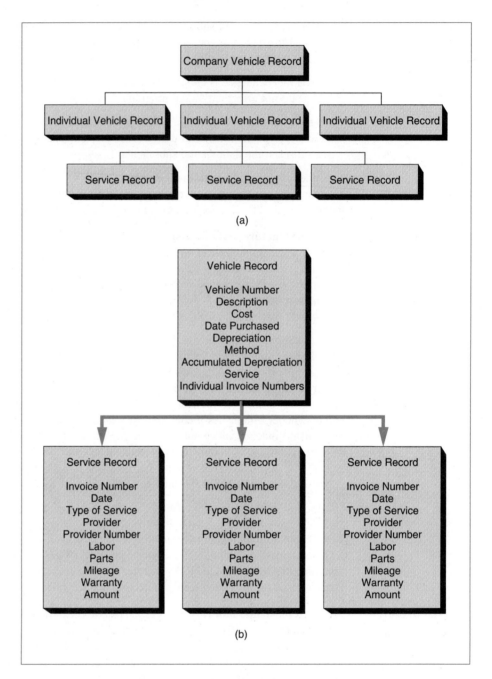

(a)

(b)

relationship. For example, consider the simple situation involving a small business which owns several vehicles, as shown in Figure 6–4. Each vehicle has its own maintenance history. In Figure 6–4(a), the top-level is the company vehicle record. Second-level elements are the individual vehicle records, and third-level elements are the various service records for each vehicle. The company record may include fields for each vehicle owned by the company, as well as a pointer to the vehicle records. As shown in Figure 6–4(b), the vehicle records indicates general information on each vehicle as well as pointers that reference the appropriate invoice numbers and corresponding service records in the service file. The file of service records contains data on the exact type of service provided with corresponding dates, service providers, and amounts.

As shown in Figure 6–4, a manager using the hierarchical data base first enters the data base via the company vehicle record, or the **parent** or **root node.** A pointer then directs the user to a **descendant node** such as an individual vehicle record. The vehicle record in turn has the necessary pointers to direct the user or the applications program to the next level, which contains detailed records of the actual service carried out, including parts and labor, mileage, and warranty conditions. The hierarchical data model allows management to access information in a hierarchical format.

As another example, assume that a retail store's monthly statement for merchandise purchased can be accessed via a hierarchical structure. The manager assembles the sales invoices (descendant records) for each customer in the customer file (root) to compile a sales history report by customer, even though each customer has numerous purchases and the customer file and the sales invoice file reside in different segments of the data base. The DBMS manages the pointers, which link the data for this report.

Hierarchical structures, common in data bases, are effective as long as data base maintenance and access sequence follow the tree structure. In other words, the root nodes clearly dominate the data contained in the descendant records.

Because the hierarchical data model explicitly accommodates a particular set of applications, the model may not be flexible enough for an organization's various needs. For example, management of the small business referred to in Figure 6–4 may need to determine which vehicles require transmission work. In this situation, the data base must be accessed via the type of service (in the service record). The structure (including the pointers) shown in Figure 6–4 obviously would not accommodate such an application or management query. Each new information need requires a new set of pointers, which must be maintained by the DBMS discussed earlier. These links are necessary, because the data may not be accessed without the pointers. In other words, a hierarchical data model may include more than one tree structure that is explicitly defined by its schema. Such a data model is generally called the network data model.

Network Data Model

Networks[3] are widely used in business to organize data for a variety of managerial needs. In a **network data model,** the data base can be entered via different parent nodes. Like a

[3] One of the best known mainframe network data base systems is the Integrated Data Base Management System (IDMS) developed by Cullinet Software and based on the Conference on Data Systems Languages (CODASYL) system.

FIGURE 6–5

*Network Data
Model*

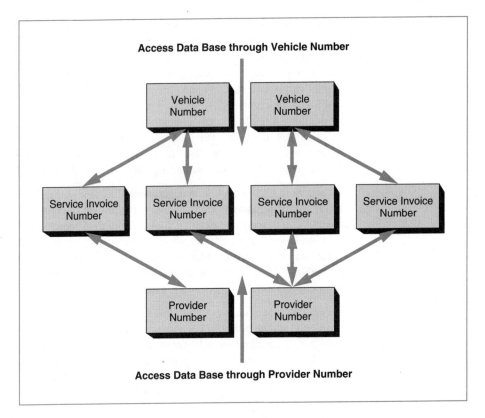

hierarchical or tree structure, a network structure is composed of nodes and branches. However, a network can have multiple parents. The relationship from child to parent and from parent to child in a network can be many-to-many, as shown in Figure 6–5. In that figure, both vehicle and service records contain pointers to other records. For example, assume management suspects that a substitution of parts occurs at a particular repair shop. Accessing the service record through the network allows the service department to determine which vehicles may have been repaired by that shop or provider. Management could access all service records for the suspected service provider and trace the service to particular vehicles through individual invoice numbers. The appropriate pointer to each invoice record would provide vehicle identification numbers. Furthermore, with this network of pointers, management can use different elements of the service information without always needing to access the information through vehicle records, as in the hierarchical model in Figure 6–4.

Many other forms of networks can be derived and maintained via the DBMS. Logical relationships can be represented in the form of networks, regardless of the complexity involved. The data structure is explicitly specified, and the links between data items are *essential* to the functioning of the network. Unfortunately, a network's increasing complexity can make it more difficult to maintain and operate.

Saving Money on Ulcers

The overprescription of a popular and costly class of ulcer medication to Medicaid clients cost the state of Texas over $18 million per year. In 1989, after spending 8 percent of its entire Medicaid drug budget on this class of drugs, Department of Human Resources investigators found that physicians were prescribing maximum levels of the drug beyond the 8 weeks recommended by the drug manufacturer. Over one-half of the patients receiving the drug had exceeded this maximum. To stop this practice, the department installed a combination mainframe–personal computer voice-response information system that checks each prescription before it is written or filled.

With this system, a data base of Medicaid clients is stored on the department's mainframe. This data base is searched on a weekly basis to identify clients that have reached the 8-week limit. The records on these individuals—over 15,000 per week—are downloaded to the personal computer, which is linked to the voice-response system. Participating physicians and pharmacies call this system prior to writing or filling a prescription for one of the ulcer drugs and enter an access code and patient information. The personal computer checks its data base of clients to determine if the patient has exceeded the dosage limit. If the limit is reached, a message alerts the caller; otherwise, the caller is given the go-ahead to write or fill the prescription. Each response takes between 30 and 45 seconds.

In addition to responding to calls, the system can track information on callers, patients, and responses. Initial estimates on cost savings with this system, which cost approximately $10,000 to install and $25,000 per year to run, are almost unbelievable—over $11,000 *per day*. If the system is transferred to other states, the national savings could be over $100 million per year for this class of drugs alone.

SOURCE: Richard Pastore, "Voice System Reins in Agency's Costs," *Computerworld,* September 17, 1990, p. 67.

Although the hierarchical and network data models are an improvement over single-file systems, they still fall short of accomplishing complete data independence. The explicitly defined links among data items do not allow the flexibility needed for many organizations in which information requirements are numerous and not easily specified in advance. Furthermore, the required links may become so complex that loss of these essential links and corresponding access to data may become a real concern.

Relational Data Base Model

In response to the disadvantages of hierarchical and network data models, data base researchers E.F. Codd and C.J. Date developed an *implicit* approach to establishing associations between data items. Today, this approach is known as the **relational data model.** Many new DBMSs use the relational data model because it minimizes the numerous problems that are inherent with such file-oriented systems as those discussed in the previous chapter. This model offers the most flexibility, achieves the maximum

FIGURE 6–6

ProYacht, Inc.
Sales Relation

Sales Invoice No.	*Date*	*Dealer Number*	*Product Number*	*Sales Representative*	*Location Lake/Bay*	*Quantity*
3271	5/10/92	NY2509	SB2200	NY100	Erie	1
3272	5/12/92	VA3782	SB2800	VA200	Chesapeake	1
3273	5/12/92	MD8943	DS1800	MD250	Chesapeake	1
3274	5/13/92	NY1765	DS1800	NY100	Ontario	1
3275	5/17/92	VA3782	DS1800	VA200	Chesapeake	1
3276	5/18/92	PA2784	SB3000	PA100	Erie	1
3277	5/20/92	MD8943	SB2800	MD250	Chesapeake	1
3278	5/22/92	VA2556	SB2500	VA200	Chesapeake	1
3279	5/25/92	PA7843	SB2200	PA100	Erie	1
3280	5/26/92	MD3789	SB2700	MS250	Chesapeake	1

data independence, reduces redundancy, and achieves the most data integration of all the data models commonly used in organizations. In this model, data relationships are implicitly determined from data which are stored in logically independent flat files to meet information needs as they occur. As mentioned earlier, the data structure is not explicitly defined in advance. Therefore, only the data items are essential to the data base; the linkages are not.

A relational data base using the relational data model is composed of **tables of attributes.** These tables, or **relations,** are simply flat files in which the rows correspond to records and the columns are fields (data items or **attributes**). As an example of a table of attributes, consider ProYacht, Inc., which uses a relational data base for its sailboat division. ProYacht's sales relation is shown in Figure 6–6. This sales relation is composed of a unique sales invoice number as well as six other sales attributes—date, dealer number, product number, sales representative number, sales location, and quantity sold. The unique sale invoice number represents the **primary key** used to access the data in the table.

Relational Operations

To generate information like that found in a single large transaction file using a relation, data in relational tables must be associated through **relational operations** to other tables. For implementing these relational operations, the tables which are to be combined must have a common **primary key,** such as a product number, invoice number, dealer number, or sales representative number. For ProYacht, Inc., additional relations might involve the ones shown in Figure 6–7, including a dealer relation, an inventory relation, and a sales representative relation.

Three relational operations are needed to combine the information from individual tables—projection, join, and selection operations. **Projection operations** reduce the number of columns in the relations to those needed by the user or report, thereby reducing the amount of data to those relevant fields. The **join operation** combines all the data from

FIGURE 6–7

Dealer, Inventory, and Sales Representative Relations

Dealer Relation

Dealer Number	Dealer Name	Dealer Address	Credit Rating
MD3789	Smith Lake Marine	200 Old Washington Rd., Smith Lake, MD	A
MD8943	Baxter Marine	100 Pine Ave., Bayside, MD	A
NY1765	James River Marina	100 James River Pike, Jamestown, NY	A
NY2509	Bowman Yachts	256 Lakeshore Ln., Ripley, NY	A
PA2784	Williams Outdoors	65 N. Elm, Erie, PA	A
PA7843	Pointer Sailing	250 Lee Street, Northeast, PA	A
VA2556	Miller Boats	750 Duke St, Williamsburg, VA	C
VA3782	Lakewood Boats	320 Black Creek Rd., Richmond, VA	A

Inventory Relation

Product Number	Product Name	Suggested Price	Wholesale Price	Production Cost	Location	Quantity	Reorder Point	Reorder Quantity
DS1800	18′ Day Sailer	4340	3472	1736	Madison	200	100	200
SB2200	22′ Sail Boat	9985	8000	4000	Annapolis	50	40	60
SB2500	25′ Sail Boat	19500	16000	8000	Annapolis	20	25	25
SB2700	27′ Sail Boat	28500	22800	11400	Annapolis	10	20	20
SB2800	28′ Sail Boat	35000	28000	14000	Ocala	7	5	10
SB3000	30′ Sail Boat	42000	33600	16800	Ocala	3	5	10

Sales Representative Relation

Sales Rep	Social Security Number	Name	Address
NY100	576-64-4704	Watson, Jim	100 Washington Rd., Buffalo, NY
MD250	395-07-8364	Peake, Walter	45 Elm, Fredricksburg, MD
PA100	152-43-3570	Mason, Linda	50 Lake Ave., Erie, PA
VA200	678-22-5866	Jackson, Jason	700 Petersberg Rd., Richmond, VA

two or more relations using the primary keys of each relation to create one large combined relation. Finally, the **selection operation** is used to identify the records (rows) that satisfy the user or the report criteria. Usually, two or more operations are combined to produce the needed information.

As an example of relational operations, assume that ProYacht, Inc. uses the relations in Figures 6–6 and 6–7 to create a new table showing sales to Baxter Marine. This table

FIGURE 6–8   *Use of Projection Operation*

Sales Projection		
Dealer Number	Product Number	Quantity
NY2509	SB2200	1
VA3782	SB2800	1
MD8943	DS1800	1
NY1765	DS1800	1
VA3782	DS1800	1
PA2784	SB3000	1
MD8943	SB2800	1
VA2556	SB2500	1
PA7843	SB2200	1
MD3789	SB2700	1

Dealer Projection	
Dealer Number	Dealer Name
MD3789	Smith Lake Marine
MD8943	Baxter Marine
NY1765	James River Marina
NY2509	Bowman Yachts
PA2784	Williams Outdoors
PA7843	Pointer Sailing
VA2556	Miller Boats
VA3782	Lakewood Boats

Stock Projection	
Product Number	Suggested Price
DS1800	4340
SB2200	9985
SB2500	19500
SB2700	28500
SB2800	35000
SB3000	42000

should include the product number, quantity, and amount sold by this dealer. ProYacht management wants to use this sales analysis report for marketing research. The series of operations used to generate this report are shown in Figures 6–8, 6–9, and 6–10.

In Figure 6–8, columns (fields, data items, or attributes) corresponding to the desired data items are projected into new relations. These new relations retain all of the information needed in the analysis. All other columns shown in the original relations are not included. Note that this operation is repeated for each relation to find all desired columns.

In Figure 6–9, two new relations are created using the join operation. In Figure 6–9(a), the sales projection and dealer projection are joined using the dealer number as a primary key. Then, in Figure 6–9(b), the result of the first join operation, the dealer/sales relation, is joined with the inventory projection to form the dollar sales relation. This second join operation uses product number as a key.

Finally, only those records with the dealer number for Baxter Marine (MD8943) are selected by eliminating irrelevant rows from the dollar sales projection shown in Figure 6–9. The result of this final operation in Figure 6–10 contains only the desired information on Baxter Marine. The series of relational operations used to arrive at the desired information is summarized in Figure 6–11.

Data Integrity Rules

Relational data bases follow certain **data integrity,** or **normalization rules,** which provide a more fundamental degree of data integrity than other data base structures, including single-file systems. These rules ensure valid data references, so that the data actually exist, all relationships are logical, and data are not duplicated. Using these rules, data can be decomposed into simple basic relations (tables) to achieve a logically coherent data base with minimal redundancy.

FIGURE 6–9

Use of Join
Operation

Dealer Number	Dealer Name	Product Number	Quantity
NY2509	Bowman Yachts	SB2200	1
VA3782	Lakewood Boats	SB2800	1
MD8943	Baxter Marine	DS1800	1
NY1765	James River Marina	DS1800	1
VA3782	Lakewood Boats	DS1800	1
PA2784	Williams Outdoors	SB3000	1
MD8943	Baxter Marine	SB2800	1
VA2556	Miller Boats	SB2500	1
PA7843	Pointer Sailing	SB2200	1
MD3789	Smith Lake Marine	SB2700	1

(a)

Dollar Sales Relation				
Dealer Number	Dealer Name	Product Number	Quantity	Sales Amount
NY2509	Bowman Yachts	SB2200	1	9985
VA3782	Lakewood Boats	SB2800	1	35000
MD8943	Baxter Marine	DS1800	1	4340
NY1765	James River Marina	DS1800	1	4340
VA3782	Lakewood Boats	DS1800	1	4340
PA2784	Williams Outdoors	SB3000	1	42000
MD8943	Baxter Marine	SB2800	1	35000
VA2556	Miller Boats	SB2500	1	19500
PA7843	Pointer Sailing	SB2200	1	9985
MD3789	Smith Lake Marine	SB2700	1	28500

(b)

Applications or end user inquiries are not restricted to a predetermined path through the data, such as the pointers which characterize the hierarchical and network structures. Instead, relational data bases utilize implicit relationships derived from needs as they arise. As a result, relational data bases are more logically independent of applications than other data base structures because they are not dependent on explicit linkages. The relational structure also provides a conceptually simple view of the data. In other words, a series of simple tables may be combined in a variety of ways for management's use in processing transactions, managing the organization, and reporting on the results of the organization's operations.

FIGURE 6–10

Use of Selection Operation

Baxter Marine Dollar Sales				
Dealer Number	Dealer Name	Product Number	Quantity	Sales Amount
MD8943	Baxter Marine	DS1800	1	4340
MD8943	Baxter Marine	SB2800	1	35000

Semantic Data Modeling

Semantic data modeling carries the relational model concept one step further. Rather than designing the tables and relations to maximize logical independence, management may want its data base to reflect the organization's natural business transactions and entities. The net result is a relational data base that may not comply totally with all the normalization rules. However, it reflects the business environment more accurately. As a result the semantic data model may be more robust over time as data and information requirements are added to the information system.

Comparison of Data Models

In comparing the three data models, in general, hierarchical and network models tend to be more efficient in processing large volumes of transactions, and relational models are more effective in processing specific inquiries. Relational models do not need to maintain the pointers required in hierarchical and network models. On the other hand, relational models that do not comply completely with normalization rules can duplicate data

FIGURE 6–11

Summary of Relational Operations

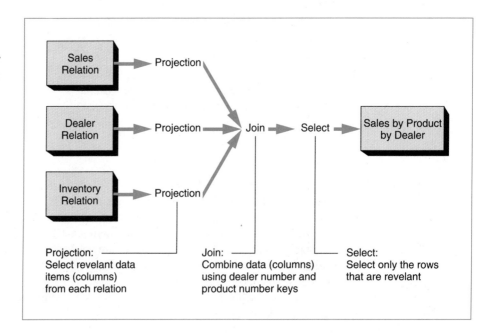

Projection:
Select relevant data items (columns) from each relation

Join:
Combine data (columns) using dealer number and product number keys

Select:
Select only the rows that are relevant

Security
Pacific Goes
Relational

At Security Pacific Corporation, one of the 10 largest U.S. bank holding companies (over $80 billion in assets), the trading day begins in Sydney, Australia, and ends 17 hours later in Los Angeles. Trading involves about $20 billion per day in 40 different currencies. To keep up with the data involved in these trades, Security Pacific decided to use a relational data base system that can be accessed by hundreds of users working on DOS-based workstations.

Management concluded that centralizing all its data in a relational data base that could be accessed through a world-wide network would give Security Pacific a competitive advantage over other banks in this same market. A relational data base allows transaction data to be accessed for pattern analysis and ad hoc queries. This accessibility and flexibility is not easily achieved with their current system, in which much of the data are stored in hierarchical, indexed, or flat-file data base and file processing systems.

SOURCE: Jean S. Bozman, "Security Pacific's New Strategy," *Computerworld,* June 18, 1990, p. 29.

on various tables. In fact, in order to process data more efficiently, many relational models (like those determined semantically) do not comply completely with normalization rules. In many cases, an organization's data base may reflect a compromise between semantic reality and processing efficiency and data independence. Figure 6–12 summarizes the advantages and disadvantages of these data models.

6.4 Data Base Management System (DBMS)

As shown in Figure 6–2, the fourth component of the data base processing environment is the DBMS. Although a variety of DBMSs exist, most systems have at least the following three common components:

FIGURE 6–12

*Advantages (+)
and
Disadvantages (−)
of Data Models*

Issues	Data Models			
	Hierarchical	Network	Relational	Semantic
Processing Large Volumes	+	+	−	−
Processing Specific Inquiries	−	−	+	+
Processing Efficiency	+	+	−	−
Data Independence and Ease of Adding New Applications	−	−	+	+
Representation of Real Events and Entities			+	+
Maintenance of Pointers	−	−	n/a	n/a

*Fidelity Turns
to Hypertext*

At Fidelity Investments, over 1,000 telephone representatives must quickly and correctly answer many seemingly unrelated questions from busy customers about both current and future investments. Until recently, these representatives relied on binders of reference information, daily bulletins, and a file of customer information. Today, these same representatives are using a hypertext system running under Windows on personal computers.

Hypertext can be described as a software system that allows the user to navigate a data base largely free of the constrictions or conventions dictated by traditional data base software. In hypertext, information is stored in discrete nodes or groups that can be accessed from any other node. A hypertext author creates links in the system that can be keyed off anything in the document—a particular word, phrase, or character string. Movement within the data base is motivated by the user's own mental connections. For example, Fidelity's telephone representatives can access an index of topics, use a mouse to choose a topic, and immediately see a list of answers to frequently asked questions about that topic. From there, they can select a particular question and move to more detailed information on that topic.

Since hypertext was installed at Fidelity, 96 percent of the representatives feel that their interaction with customers has improved. By pointing and clicking with a mouse, they can call up anything from a customer's phone number to the latest changes in Fidelity's line of mutual funds.

SOURCE: Robert L. Scheier, "Hypertext Breaks Fidelity's Paper-Laden Tradition," *PC Week*, July 30, 1990, p. 113.

1. A data base manager

2. A data definition language

3. A data manipulation language

Some systems also contain an interactive inquiry facility built around a query language. The **query language** employs a variety of commands for searching the data base to satisfy the management's data needs. Figure 6–13 shows these DBMS components in more detail as they interact with the remainder of the data base system.

*Data Base
Manager*

A **Data Base Manager (DBM)** in a DBMS actually controls the data base access and monitors storage. Because of this operation, the DBM is sometimes called the **control function.** Note that the DBM is not the data base administrator; it is a DBMS software component. The DBM controls the data base organization, formats storage devices, and provides storage and retrieval access to the data base. The DBM also supplies management with operational statistics to assist it in monitoring data base activity.

FIGURE 6–13　　**Data Base Managment System Components**

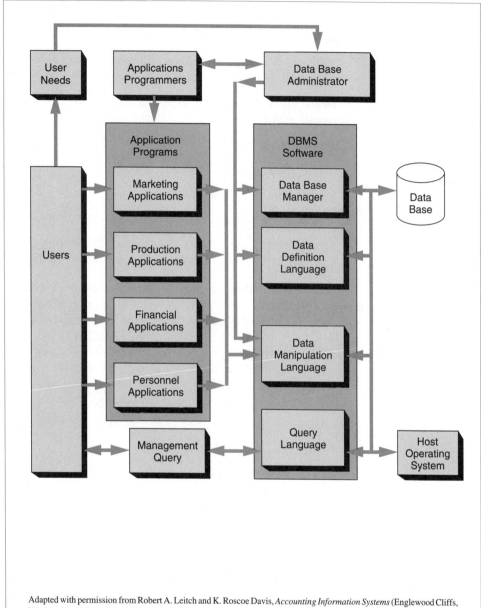

Adapted with permission from Robert A. Leitch and K. Roscoe Davis, *Accounting Information Systems* (Englewood Cliffs, NJ: Prentice-Hall, 1992), p. 257.

Data Definition Language

The **Data Definition Language (DDL)** links the logical and the physical representations of data and helps describe the logical structure of the data base. Even though applications and even the physical structure of data may change, the DDL remains constant. This enhances the independence between applications and the data base.

The DDL provides a number of specific functions which help describe the logical structure of the data base, including the following:

1. Define the characteristics of each data base record, such as the name and data type of each field

2. Describe the schema and subschemas for the data base

3. Specify the grouping of fields into records

4. Identify primary and secondary keys

5. Provide a means to specify the relationships among data tables or records

6. Specify security and integrity features, such as requiring that each record have a primary key or that dependencies be minimized in relational data bases

Data Manipulation Language

The **Data Manipulation Language (DML)** describes how applications and end users may process data. The DML provides the ability to carry out a variety of actions through manipulation verbs and associated operands. Some examples of these verbs and operands are FORMAT, SAVE, FILE, PRINT, LIST, DISPLAY, DO, SELECT, READ, and COPY. By employing the manipulation verbs and the associated operands of the DML, a user or applications programmer can easily work with the data base. The DML also relieves the user from making such structural data base changes as the addition and deletion of pointers. The user simply issues the appropriate command.

In summary, the DML is designed to do the following:

1. Provide data manipulation techniques

2. Provide a means to work with the data base at a high level in easily understandable terms

3. Make the user independent of physical data structures

Data Base Operation at ProYacht, Inc.

To enhance our understanding of a DBMS, we trace the steps involved in reading an inventory record from ProYacht's data base. The sequence of events is as follows:

1. The user instructs the DBMS to display an inventory record for a particular boat model using the DISPLAY command, along with appropriate descriptive information about the record. This information might include the model number and the boat name.

2. The DBMS examines the inventory query application subschema to determine which inventory and purchase order records should be read for the necessary information.

3. The DBMS examines the schema to determine which files (or tables) contain the required records (data).

4. The DBMS passes control to the operating system after requesting the appropriate records, files, or tables.

5. The operating system interacts with the storage device on which the data base resides.

6. The data on the boat model in question are transferred from the data base to a buffer for temporary storage.

7. Using the subschema and the schema, the DBMS extracts the data required by the inventory program.

8. The DBMS transfers the data to the inventory query application program.

9. The query program, in turn, displays the inventory status (such as the number in stock and in production) of the particular boat model for ProYacht's management to review.

Data Dictionaries

A data dictionary provided with most DBMS packages can assist in the development and management of the data base. A repository of information about data, the **data dictionary** contains the definition of data, the structure of the data base, and other important information about each data element, often including the following:

1. Data name (field)

2. Data classification or type

3. Subschema associated with the data item (such as the record name which contains the data item for each application), indicating the use (outputs and programs) of that data item

4. Schema associated with the data item (such as the record and file, if appropriate, which contains the data item), indicating the logical location of that data item

5. Source of data (data input)

The data dictionary can be used by the data base administrator, data processing personnel, and users (managers). It can be accessed by the DBMS when a user needs information about the data contained in the data base.

6.5 Distributed Data Bases

The increased power and reduced price of personal computers and the increased processing capability of larger computers have led to the rapid growth of distributed processing systems. **Distributed data bases** offer increased economies with the use of smaller computers, reduced vulnerability to failure of a centralized data base, and increased responsiveness to management's needs. In many cases, these benefits outweigh the added costs of more complex and more reliable communication systems that are needed and the erosion of data and processing standards and control that result from the distribution of data.

FIGURE 6–14

*Distributed Data
Bases*

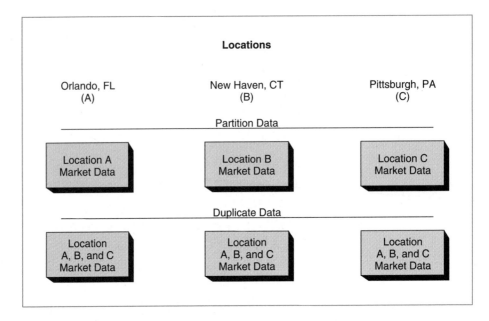

Several methods can be used to distribute data, as shown in Figure 6–14. Data may be *partitioned* into various subsets, which are usually based on region or product line. For example, a firm's market data for the southeastern United States may be housed in the Orlando, FL office, whereas data for the northeast may be housed in the New Haven, CT office. Most of the data are used and located regionally, but each office has access to the other's data. Another way to distribute the data is to maintain duplicate data at each location. For example, the Orlando and New Haven offices may have a duplicate of the market data that is stored at the home office in Pittsburgh. Duplicate files in such a distributed system have a potential for inconsistency.

The partitioning of data at remote locations calls for a method of locating the relevant data for managerial decision making or for processing of day-to-day transactions. This may be accomplished by searching each location for the needed data or by using a centralized index at the home office that indicates the location of the data. Regardless of the method used, the information system must have an effective and efficient communication system to transfer any volume of data in a reliable manner.

*Structured
Query
Language*

A **Structured Query Language (SQL)** that is designed to work with Codd's relational data model is a high level, well planned method of accessing data. SQL commands are concise and work well across a variety of computer platforms. As shown in Figure 6–15, SQL commands can be used for personal computers, minicomputers, and mainframes. Furthermore, it is well suited for new multiuser environments often found in distributed processing systems. It has built-in commands that resolve user conflicts and provide security in multiuser environments.

FIGURE 6–15

Structured Query Language in a Multiuser Distributed Data Base Environment

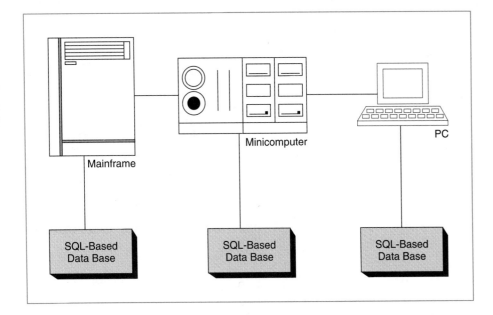

SQL uses a set of terse commands to accomplish the same task that requires many commands in several popular data base programs. Quick data retrieval is easily achieved through catalog features, which contain the structure of the data base, and an optimizer feature, which determines the best way to access the data. The optimizer feature also allows SQL data base systems to easily access data from multiple files in widely distributed data bases.

The basic SQL language consists of 12 commands. Data manipulation commands are used to insert, delete, select, and update the contents of the data base. Data definition commands are used to create data bases, indexes, and views of data. Data control statements enhance the integrity and security of the data by restricting access to data. These 12 commands have been extended by many vendors to cover other situations.

An example of SQL is shown in Figure 6–16, which shows a list of all sales, followed by a list of sales by Chesapeake dealers ordered by sales amount. The language is not particularly user friendly because of the mathematical logic needed to write SQL programs. As a result, many vendors are developing menu-driven English language front-end processors to translate user requests into SQL commands for data base operations.

6.6 Advantages and Disadvantages of Data Base Processing

The materials surveyed throughout this chapter and the discussion at the end of the last chapter may lead to the mistaken conclusion that a data base is the only rational choice for all data processing requirements. In fact, single-file systems may be more appropriate in some situations. This section considers the advantages as well as the disadvantages of data base systems when compared with single-file processing systems.

Advantages of data base systems include reduced data redundancy, resulting in greater data integrity, data integration, data independence, reduced cost of program development

FIGURE 6–16   *Structured Query Language Example*

```
R>SELECT * FROM SALES
  INVOICE     INV_DATE DEALER_N PRODUCT  SALES_RE LOCATION    QUANTITY
  ----------- -------- -------- -------- -------- ----------- -----------
         3271 05/10/92 NY2509   SB2200   NY100    Erie               1
         3272 05/12/92 VA3782   SB2800   VA200    Chesapeake         1
         3273 05/12/92 MD8943   DS1800   MD250    Chesapeake         1
         3274 05/13/92 NY1765   DS1800   NY100    Ontario            1
         3275 05/17/92 VA3782   DS1800   VA200    Chesapeake         1
         3276 05/18/92 PA2784   SB3000   PA100    Erie               1
         3277 05/20/92 MD8943   SB2800   MD250    Chesapeake         1
         3278 05/22/92 VA2556   SB2500   VA200    Chesapeake         1
         3279 05/25/92 PA7843   SB2200   PA100    Erie               1
         3280 05/26/92 MD3789   SB2700   MD250    Chesapeake         1
R>
R>SELECT DEALER_N,PRODUCT,SALES_RE FROM SALES WHERE LOCATION = 'Chesapeake' O+
+>RDER BY SALES_RE
  DEALER_N PRODUCT  SALES_RE
  -------- -------- --------
  MD8943   DS1800   MD250
  MD8943   SB2800   MD250
  MD3789   SB2700   MD250
  VA3782   SB2800   VA200
  VA3782   DS1800   VA200
  VA2556   SB2500   VA200
R>
```

and maintenance, better data management, faster retrieval of information, and better security. Disadvantages of data base systems include greater complexity, higher processing expenses, backup and recovery problems, more vulnerability to intrusion, and implementation problems. We now consider these advantages and disadvantages in more detail.

Reduction in Data Redundancy

In a DBMS, duplicate data that often exist in single-file processing systems due to the multiplicity of files can be reduced significantly. In a data base system, the data need only be recorded once rather than input and stored on a separate file for each application. This reduction in data duplication results in lower storage costs and, more importantly, a higher level of data consistency and integrity. Because the same data item may exist in more than one file, a file processing system, changes in the data in one place may not be reflected elsewhere. Moreover, data that are input more than once may not be consistent in value or in definition at all locations.

Data Integration

With a DBMS, a user can more easily integrate data from several files or from within the data base than with a file processing system. This increased integration allows for more rapid processing of unanticipated requests via a query language or the use of end user applications programs.

Data Independence

Because the DBMS acts as the interface between the data base and the user or application, physical storage and logical data structures are separated. As a result, the data and application programs are independent of the physical storage structure. This situation is particularly true for relational data base systems in which flat files are created to be independent of any application. Programs can be changed without altering data files, and data files can be changed without altering programs. Programs need only be concerned with the logical symbolic names of the data, not physical storage. As a result, a data base system is more flexible and data is more accessible than with a single file.

Reduced Cost of Program Development and Maintenance

Data independence greatly reduces the cost of program development and maintenance. New programs can be written more easily because they do not affect data files, new files need not be created, and the old programs that interact with these files do not require change. Unlike a single-file processing system, the data base can be expanded without having to be reorganized. For example, data fields can readily be added or deleted.

Better Data Management

When the data are centralized (not necessarily physically, but by responsibility), data base processing can lead to better data management. A data base administrator can manage and control the activities of the data base for the benefit of all users. He or she (or, in a large organization, a department) can specify data standards and ensure compliance with those standards, reducing the data definition confusion often present in single-file systems, in which one data item can have different meanings in different applications.

More Rapid Retrieval of Information

Because DBMS users can access data directly via a query language or develop their own applications programs, they can easily retrieve needed data not contained in routine, often untimely, reports. The development of user friendly data base software for personal computers has also made data base systems easier for PC users. A greater amount of information is at the disposal of small business management.

Security

In one sense, a data base system is more secure than a single-file system because the centralized data are more tightly controlled. For example, better access controls can be implemented to enhance the security of the system.

Complexity

Data base processing is more complex than working with a single file. The software must bridge the gaps among numerous requests with a wide range of formats and a common set of standardized data items. Sophisticated design and programming skills are required in developing a DBMS. Likewise, because of the complexity of the overall process, applications programs (with the exception of end user applications) may take highly qualified programming personnel a long time to develop.

Expense

A major disadvantage of a data base processing system can be the expense involved in developing or purchasing a large system. Depending on the quantity of data to be organized and the number and needs of users, the software cost of a mainframe DBMS could be more than $100,000. The software alone may not be the total expense. Additional memory (hardware) may be required along with a larger computer. With a new computer, an organization may incur conversion expenses in changing from the old to the new system. Systems that must support multiple users who access the data at the same time must be more complex. More skilled personnel are also needed to operate and administer the DBMS.

Backup and Recovery

Because several users may be using the DBMS concurrently, and because of the complexity of the entire system, backup and recovery processes can be difficult. The following three general problems exist:

1. The status of the data base must be determined after equipment failure or a data error

2. A method of fixing any errors in the data must be determined

3. The necessary transaction records and periodic copies of the data base must be maintained to reconstruct the data base should something happen

Vulnerability

Because the DBMS is the center of data base processing, a malfunction in any system component can have a major impact on the data base and its users. Without backup procedures, the failure of a data base system could bring a company's operations to a halt. Moreover, because several users may access the data base for different applications, an error in one application may create problems in others. For example, assume user A attempts to modify several data base records, but an error occurs in the application program, placing invalid data in the data base. If user B reads the same records immediately after user A's modifications, that invalid data is accessed by user B.

Implementation Problems

In many organizations, the implementation process may be difficult because various departments may not want to relinquish control of confidential or sensitive files. In other cases, management's loss of control of ''their'' files may not be palatable.

Summary of Advantages and Disadvantages

A summary of the advantages and disadvantages of data bases compared with file processing systems is shown in Figure 6–17. Many advantages of data base processing systems are intangible and long term, whereas the costs involved in these types of systems are immediate and real. Management may not be willing to make the necessary investment if the current single-file system is adequate. In other words, the implementation of a DBMS is an immediate cash outlay, but the benefits have a long-term payoff, which may need to be heavily discounted. The key to overcoming this last disadvantage is to assess management's information requirements adequately and to consider a DBMS as part of the overall system analysis and design. These advantages and disadvantages are also present in PC data base systems. Many advantages of PC DBMS are not as significant, and the disadvantages are not as severe.

FIGURE 6–17

Advantages and Disadvantages of Data Bases

Advantages	Disadvantages
Reduction of Duplicate Data	Complexity
Data Integration	Expense
Data Independence	Backup and Recovery
Reduced Cost of Program Development	Vulnerability
Better Data Management	Implementation
More Rapid Retrieval	
Security	

6.7 Summary

Data base processing is quite different from the traditional single-file approach to data processing, and this chapter has highlighted these differences. Essentially, the data base system uses multiple files or an integrated repository of data. In addition, application programs, queries, and end user programs are independent of the physical structure of the data base. In a single-file system, each application is tied directly to a specific file. A DBMS bridges the gap between applications and the data. This independence gives the data base system a tremendous amount of flexibility in providing management with needed information.

Data can be viewed from three perspectives—the user's view, a physical view of how data are stored, and a logical view of how data are organized and structured. This logical organization may be quite different from the physical storage of data. The logical view of the data structure is described by a schema. A schema may be divided into subschemas for a logical view that pertains to individual applications.

Three basic data structures or models are used in data base systems. A hierarchical (tree) model structures logical relationships among data in a simple hierarchy with a single access path. A network model permits multiple access to data via a number of paths using several sets of pointers. A relational model consists of simple sets of tables, called relations, which can be combined via the project, join, and select relational operations. A relational model has no predetermined access path. As a result, it is the most flexible of the three models.

The components that make up a DBMS include the user, the data base administrator, the DBMS, and the data base. We have attempted to illustrate the essential differences in various data base structures. Finally, there are advantages and disadvantages to using a DBMS and management must select that system which best suits its information requirements and budget.

Key Terms

attributes	join operation
control function	logical integration
data base	logical view
data base administrator	network data model
data base concept	normalization rules
Data Base Management System (DBMS)	one-to-many relationship
	parent node
Data Base Manager (DBM)	physical view
data base models	primary key
data base structure	projection operation
data base users	query language
Data Definition Language (DDL)	relational data model
data dictionary	relational operations
data independence	relations
data integration	root node
data integrity rules	schema
Data Manipulation Language (DML)	selection operation
data structure	semantic data modeling
descendant node	Structured Query Language (SQL)
distributed data bases	subschema
end users	tables of attributes
file processing system	tree data model
hierarchical data model	user's view

Review Questions

1. What is a DBMS and what are its components?

2. How is a data base different from a file-oriented system? What are the key concepts of a data base system?

3. What is the difference between a data base administrator and a data base manager? What is the role of each?

4. Why is the independence concept important for data base users?

5. What is the difference between the hierarchical and network data models?

6. What is the major shortcoming of the network data model?

7. How can a relational data model overcome the major shortcoming of hierarchical and network data models?

8. What is the advantage of using a semantically determined relational model compared with one that is determined via strict adherence to normalization rules?

9. Contrast the hierarchical, network, and relational data models in terms of data independence and the type of transactions for which they are best suited.

10. What is the difference between a Data Definition Language (DDL) and a Data Manipulation Language (DML)?

11. What is a distributed data base? How can a distributed data base be implemented?

12. What are the advantages of data base processing and file management systems? Can single-file management systems still play a major role in today's computerized information systems?

13. What are the disadvantages of converting from a single-file processing system to a large DBMS?

14. What data and information are needed to recover from a data base failure?

15. What type of data base environment is advantageous for the user of SQL? Why? Are there any difficulties associated with its use in such an environment?

Discussion Questions

1. Contrast the three data models in terms of how managers would do the following:
   a. Access data from different files
   b. Develop a new application
   c. Manage data resources

2. Explain how the various components of a DBMS make it easier to do the following:
   a. Manage data resources
   b. Develop new transaction processing, management reporting, and decision support applications
   c. Query data
   d. Develop new reports
   e. Add new data elements or fields

3. Why is data independence an important concept? Give an example.

4. How does a DBMS make (a) data more accessible, (b) use of data more flexible, (c) data more consistent, (d) redundant data less likely, and (e) integrated applications which use many files less costly and easier to develop and implement?

Case 6–1
*Mariposa
Products*

Mariposa Products, a textile and apparel manufacturer, acquired its own computer in 1978. The first application developed and implemented was production and inventory control, followed by payroll, accounts receivable, and accounts payable applications. The applications were not integrated due to the piecemeal manner in which they were developed and implemented. Nevertheless, the system proved satisfactory for several years.

A combination of increased operating costs and industry competition adversely affected profit margins and operating profits. Ed Wilde, Mariposa's president, authorized the preparation of reports that would help management improve operations. Unfortunately, the data were not consistent among the reports, and data by product line or by department were not available. The problems were attributable to Mariposa's piecemeal applications implementation, which resulted in inconsistent duplicate data stored on Mariposa's computer system.

Wilde was concerned because Mariposa's computer system could not generate the information his managers needed to make decisions. He called a meeting of his top managers and certain data processing personnel to discuss potential solutions to Mariposa's problems. The consensus of the meeting was that a new information system integrating Mariposa's applications was needed. Mariposa's controller suggested that the company consider a data base system for all departments to use. As a first step, the controller proposed hiring a data base administrator on a consulting basis to determine the feasibility of converting to a data base system.

SOURCE: Adapted from CMA.

Case Questions

1. Identify the components of a data base system.

2. Discuss the advantages and disadvantages of a data base system for Mariposa Products.

3. Describe the duties of a data base administrator.

Case 6–2
ProYacht, Inc.

Consider ProYacht's relational data base presented in the chapter. The basic sales relation was presented in Figure 6–6, and other relations pertaining to dealers, inventory, and sales representatives were presented in Figure 6–7.

Case Questions

Using the relational operations illustrated in the chapter, construct a relational table that can be used to determine the following:

1. The sales invoice numbers for the boats sold by Walter Peake

2. The product numbers and names of the boats purchased by Smith Lake Marine

3. The boats sold by Linda Mason

4. The names and addresses of the dealers who bought 18-foot Day Sailers, who will be sent promotional material on a new product line

5. The sales representative with the greatest gross margin (Suggested Price less Production Cost) for the boats sold—set up the table from which the data can be analyzed to provide the mathematical solution

Network Sharing of Information Resources

$$C \quad H \quad A \quad P \quad T \quad E \quad R$$

7

Introduction

The use of **telecommunications** to transmit data and information between computers is one of the most exciting topics in information systems today. According to Martin,[1] "telecommunications refers to the transmission of any electronic information including telephone calls, television signals, data, electronic mail, facsimile, and telemetry from space craft."

Voice transmissions have been with us since Alexander Graham Bell invented the telephone well over 100 years ago, and radio and television transmissions have become common occurrences over the last 50 years. However, the electronic transmission of data, mail, and pictures between computers is a new use of telecommunications dating only from the 1960s.

Today, telecommunications enables computer users to be involved in such activities as teleconferencing, voice and electronic mail, electronic bulletin boards, videotex, downloading software, and so forth. In fact, computers and communications have become so intertwined that communication of any kind, other than face-to-face conversations, usually involves the use of computers in some manner. In this chapter, we will discuss the importance of telecommunications to an organization's information system.

Using Shared Information for a Competitive Advantage

Throughout this text, we have emphasized repeatedly that an organization can use information to achieve an advantage over its competitors, especially when that information is shared throughout the organization. Information that may not be useful to one unit of the organization can become a competitive tool when shared with other units. Whereas

---

[1] James Martin, *Principles of Data Communication,* (Englewood Cliffs, NJ: Prentice-Hall, 1988), p. 3.

paper and voice channels have carried information for many years, the ability to transfer large amounts of information between computers has vastly enhanced the potential for competitive use of that information.

Methods of sharing information for a competitive edge can be as simple as providing wide area pagers to traveling salespeople, or as complex as creating an electronic payment system that provides information on frequent customers. In the first case, an MCI national account representative found that the SkyPager he carried to alert him when his wife went into labor also kept him in close touch with a major account. As a result, he saved a large sale that was in trouble due to software problems. Even though he was in a different part of the country, through SkyPager, the sales representative had the problem solved by a technical representative. In the second case, full-service supermarket supplier Associated Grocers achieved a competitive edge by being the first to provide its stores with a retail electronic payment system that also included marketing information about customers.

Data Communication and Teleprocessing

In addition to defining telecommunications, Martin also defines two other concepts that are often identified with telecommunications—data communication and teleprocessing. According to Martin, **data communication** ''refers to the electronic transmission of data [and] . . . encompasses telegraphy, telemetry, and similar forms of data transmission.'' **Teleprocessing** ''. . . refers to the accessing of computing power and computerized data files from a distance, generally using terminals and telecommunications facilities.'' Telecommunications can refer to voice and TV transmissions, but data communications and teleprocessing refer precisely to communications between computers. In this text, we use the term *telecommunications* to refer to all three cases—voice and TV transmissions, data communications, and teleprocessing.

7.1 Networks in Organizations

At one time, a Computer-Based Information System (CBIS) needed only a very simple form of telecommunications that involved direct linkages between a mainframe computer and an array of ''dumb'' terminals. Users could send instructions and data to the mainframe over these terminals. A **dumb terminal** looks like a personal computer in that both have a keyboard and monitor. However, the dumb terminal has no Central Processing Unit (CPU) or secondary storage. It functions only as an input/output device for the mainframe.

As information systems have grown, so too has the need for more sophisticated telecommunications systems. Today, in addition to terminals or PCs linked to mainframes, information systems need **computer networks,** which use telecommunications to link two or more computers together. In networks, computers can share data, spread out processing chores, or serve as huge repositories of information for users. Examples of computer networks include the following:

- Banking networks that allow one bank card to be used at many automatic teller machines over a widespread area

- Message networks that allow users to send and receive mail electronically

- U.S. Department of Defense networks that allow users in universities and research centers to exchange results and data

- Airline, rental car, and hotel reservations networks that enable travelers to make reservations from anywhere in the country

- Corporate networks that transfer the results of data processing operations among corporate locations

- Commercial information networks—like CompuServe or Prodigy—that provide different types of information for individual users and function as a mail drop and an electronic bulletin board

- PC-based networks that allow student and office users to share peripherals and information as well as communicate with one another

Computer networks can be local area networks or wide area networks. **Local Area Networks (LANs)** are usually defined as a network of personal computers or workstations that serves multiple users in a confined geographical area. On the other hand, a **wide area network** connects distant geographical regions such as cities, states, or even countries. Wide area networks often involve computers of all sizes, from supercomputers down to personal computers. We discuss each type of network in more detail in later sections.

Computer Networks and Distributed Data Processing

Networks are an important element in **Distributed Data Processing (DDP).** DDP places computing power as close to the point of actual information processing as possible, compared with centralized computer resources. DDP networks can connect mainframes, minicomputers, and personal computers using evolving telecommunications technology. Using DDP allows systems analysts to design a CBIS that matches organizational structure, supports unique business strategies, and provides a more natural use of information systems.

A common architecture for DDP includes one or more central computers with numerous smaller computers scattered throughout the area covered by the organization. The central computer(s) handle the processing that affects the entire organization. The smaller computers are linked to the central computer (usually a mainframe or large minicomputer) via some form of communications link. The remote computers can obtain needed information from the central processing site and transfer the results of local processing back to the central computer. The central computer stores the company's primary data base, and the smaller computers have local **distributed data bases,** separate from the primary data base.

Using DDP has certain obvious advantages. The users of the smaller computers do not compete for access to the mainframe and, at the same time, the mainframe's processing load is reduced. With DDP, local users can customize software and individual CBISs and still interface with the central computer. These advantages often result in lower costs for the whole organization.

FIGURE 7–1   *Use of Distributed Data Processing at ProYacht, Inc.*

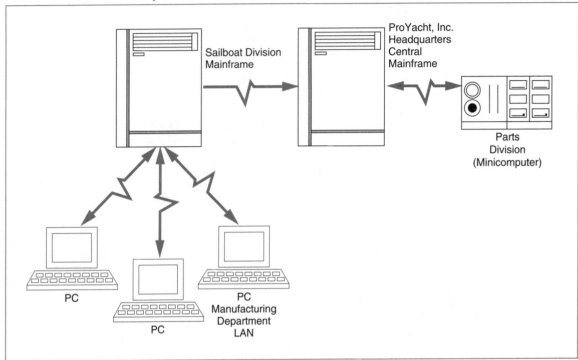

Problems with DDP include data security leaks on the communications links, incompatibility of remote software and hardware with that at the central computer, and possibly less technical support at local sites than at the central site. The hardware inconsistency is aggravated when users find they cannot interface their personal computers with the mainframe or local minicomputers. Often, the personal computers cannot ''talk'' to the mainframe or transfer data without additional hardware or software.

Distributed Data Processing at ProYacht, Inc.

ProYacht, Inc. uses DDP to handle its many processing needs. As discussed in Chapter 4, ProYacht has a central mainframe computer that services the corporate office as well as the financial, personnel, and service divisions. The parts division has a minicomputer, and the sailboat manufacturing division headquarters uses a small mainframe. Both of the smaller computers communicate directly with the central mainframe and share information. The small manufacturing division mainframe is tied to a ''super'' personal computer located at each manufacturing plant. As the central computer in a secondary DDP system, the small mainframe controls local processing at those plants. Figure 7–1 shows the use of DDP at ProYacht.

Electronic Data Interchange

A growing use of computer networks is in the area of **Electronic Data Interchange (EDI),** which involves the electronic transmission and receipt of data and information between computers. The system automates much of the routine business that occurs among retail stores, distributers, and manufacturers. Instead of sending such paper documents as purchase orders, invoices, bills of lading, and packing slips back and forth through traditional communication channels, EDI allows companies to transmit the same information electronically.

By combining EDI with point-of-sale inventory systems, a computer at a retail store can automatically order goods from a supplier based on sales information. The supplier can then automatically ship the goods to the retail store, along with an electronic verification of the shipment. EDI greatly reduces human involvement in the ordering and shipping processes, thereby reducing costs and speeding service. Figure 7–2 shows the difference between EDI and the traditional method of ordering inventory using paper documents.

EDI can also link retailers and distributers to banks or other financial institutions to allow **Electronic Funds Transfer (EFT),** with which a retailer can arrange automatic payments for orders received from suppliers. On the other side of the process, a manufacturer can use EDI to automatically reorder raw materials based on retailers' orders and pay for the raw materials using EFT. With EDI, the consumer purchase, retail store reorder, production, and raw materials order can be considered a single chain of events.

From a competitive viewpoint, EDI offers numerous advantages over traditional methods of sending information. These advantages include reducing the time required to order goods from a manufacturer, eliminating human errors, and reducing inventory due to the shorter time required to order and receive goods.

A problem with EDI is that a single company cannot implement it alone—companies that are involved in both the ordering and shipping must agree to use EDI before it works. At one time, standards for selecting a telecommunications methodology for EDI did not exist. However, several years ago, the American National Standards Institute (ANSI) and several industry groups have started to cooperate to create a standard methodology for use in EDI.

The future of EDI appears promising, with many experts believing that by the end of the century all business will be conducted using EDI. The next major industry to adopt EDI may be the transportation and shipping industry, which currently has a large paper-based system that can be significantly streamlined through the use of EDI.[2]

Office Information Systems

As discussed in Chapter 3, Office Information Systems (OIS) are crucial to the success of an organization's overall information system, as well as the various individual information systems—TPS, MIS, DSS, and EIS. Although we do not discuss OISs any further in this chapter, be aware that the effectiveness of an OIS depends on the use of telecommunications and various types of networks to faciliate communications between people and machines in an office.

7.2 Local Area Networks

As mentioned above, computer networks are common in organizations of all sizes. Although communications between large computers either within an organization or between organizations are essential for DDP and EDI, PC-to-PC communications—

---

[2] Bart Ziegler, "Linkups Seen as Next Phase in Computing," *The Charleston Post-Courier,* May 6, 1990, pp. E1, E8.

FIGURE 7–2

*Use of Electronic
Data Interchange*

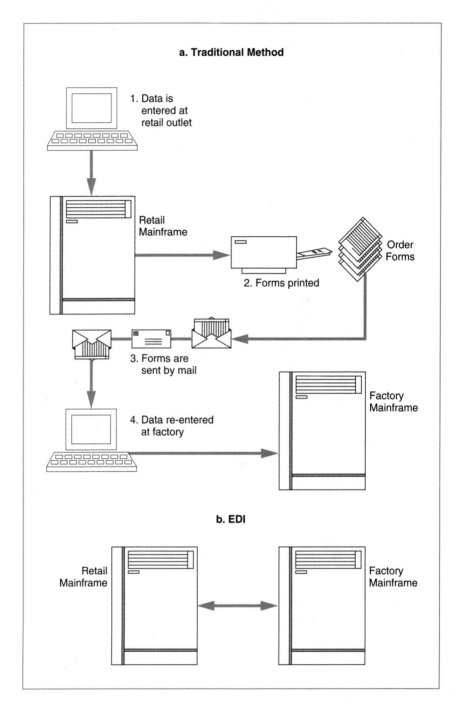

a. Traditional Method

1. Data is entered at retail outlet

Retail Mainframe

2. Forms printed

Order Forms

3. Forms are sent by mail

Factory Mainframe

4. Data re-entered at factory

b. EDI

Retail Mainframe

Factory Mainframe

Using EDI at Levi Strauss

A leader in the implementation of EDI is apparel maker Levi Strauss. Best known for making Levi's jeans, Levi Strauss has automated much of its distribution system, using the following steps:

- Clothes produced by Levi Strauss are preticketed with bar-coded tags that identify each item.

- When an item is sold at the retail store, the point-of-sale scanner identifies it by reading the bar code and sends the information to the store's computer, which subtracts this sale from the in-store inventory.

- When the in-store inventory reaches a predetermined reorder level, the store's computer automatically reorders that item.

- Levi Strauss's computer responds to this order by electronically sending packing slips to alert the store about the incoming order.

- The preticketed Levi's apparel is received in bar-coded boxes. The bar code on the box is cross-referenced against the electronic packing slip, so that when the bar code is scanned, the store immediately knows how many items are in the box. This eliminates the need to count items by hand before they are placed on the store's shelves.

- At the manufacturing end, Levi Strauss's computers automatically order denim and other supplies to produce the jeans being shipped.

- Large retailers—like Sears, Roebuck and Co.—use EFT to pay for orders from Levi Strauss by having their computers automatically credit a Levi Strauss bank account.

SOURCE: Bart Ziegler, ''Linkups Seen as Next Phase in Computing,'' and ''Data Interchange System Working for Levi Strauss,'' *The Charleston Post-Courier*, May 6, 1990, pp. E1, E8.

---

usually in a LAN—are important for individual users in an organization. In the near future, all personal computers in an organization may be linked together through LANs, making stand-alone personal computers obsolete. Mainframes may be replaced with one or more LANs due to the LAN's increased flexibility and reduced processing cost.

In a LAN, personal computers are linked together via some type of communications media and to a central personal computer that allows users to access files on a single large hard disk. This central personal computer, usually called a **file server,** contains data files or software packages that all users may access. The user can usually work with these files as if they were stored on a local hard disk. For example, the user can retrieve a software package to his or her machine, load it into Random Access Memory (RAM), and then execute it.

LANs composed of personal computers allow users to communicate among themselves as well as share information, secondary storage, peripheral devices, or a data base. Users with an **electronic mail** capability can communicate over the network. Most electronic

FIGURE 7–3

Sharing Information, Secondary Storage, Peripherals, and Data Bases in a Local Area Network

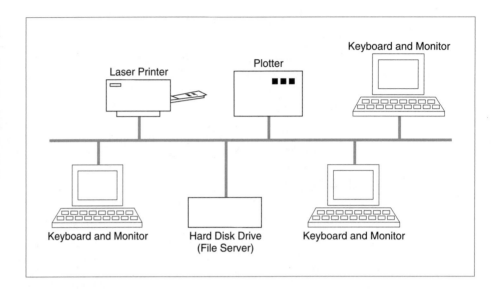

mail systems on LANs can send and receive messages, data, or program files; send the same message or file to a group of users; and access another user's calender to schedule a meeting at a mutually agreeable time. If the user is not at his or her machine when the message arrives, a ''Mail is waiting'' message appears when the computer is turned on. When a user wants to make a document, graph, or analysis available to another user, electronic mail is very useful. Without it, the only way to share information is by physically delivering a floppy disk. Using the network to send and receive such information is much faster.

Sharing secondary storage, peripherals, or a data base are other ways that a LAN can be useful. By having a single shared hard disk drive, each local computer need not have a hard disk. Disk access would depend on the file server. These **diskless workstations** more easily control access to software and data, thus improving the system's security.

Networks often have at least one high-speed laser printer. Rather than using individual printers or carrying a floppy disk to the personal computer that is linked to the printer, users can simply send print jobs to the print queue to be printed in their turn. Similarly, having a single shared data base means that all users can access data base information. In many cases, users can access, but cannot change, the data base, thereby ensuring the security of the information. However, many new TPSs for LANs have multiuser capabilities that allow many users to access, update, and use the same data. Figure 7–3 shows how information, secondary storage, peripherals, and data bases can be shared on a LAN.

Classification of Local Area Networks

LANs can be classified in three ways—the transmission medium used, the network configuration, and the network's overall function. The transmission mediums used most often are **coaxial cable,** which is shielded so that electrical fields do not adversely affect the signal, and the less expensive **twisted pair wiring**, like that used in telephone lines.

LANs have basically three configurations—star, bus, and ring. In the **star network,** a host computer has multiple "slave" computers connected to it. Because the host controls all data communications, any communications between any two computers must be routed through the host computer. If the host computer fails, then the entire system goes down.

A **bus network** has computers that tie into a main cable, or **bus,** with no one central computer. The failure of any one computer does not affect the overall network performance. To send a message to another computer only requires software that can signal the correct computer to receive the message.

In a **ring network,** the computers are connected in a loop, or ring, and communications between two computers goes around the ring. Most ring networks are set up so that if one computer goes down, the system does not also go down. Figure 7–4 shows the diagrams of the star, bus, and ring networks.

Because a user may not know when another user is sending information over the network, some access control is needed. Two procedures are often used to control the sending of information from computer to computer—token sharing and multiple access. In a **token sharing network,** a special bit pattern, called a **token,** is sent to each computer sequentially around the network. Only the computer that has the token can transmit. In the **multiple access network,** all computers are free to transmit at any time, but collision-detecting software is needed in case two or more computers try to transmit simultaneously. Figure 7–5 shows the operation of a token sharing ring LAN.

In terms of overall function, LANs can be designated as file server, client server, and peer-to-peer. With a **file server** network, files are stored on a central hard disk, but local personal computers do most of the processing. For the **client server** network, the processing burden is on the central computer. The server computer is often dedicated to a single purpose, such as a data base engine or communications. In this approach to networking, users do not just share files or periperals, they share the processing device as well.

Finally, in small **peer-to-peer** networks, users primarily share files. The network has no single dedicated file server, so every computer functions as both a server and a workstation. This network is significantly less expensive than either the file server or client server, but it is not well suited for heavy-duty transaction processing.

Network Operating Systems
The file server LAN—easily the most popular type in use—must have a **network operating system** to manage the interaction between various local personal computers and the central file server. The network operating system has many features in common with single PC operating systems, which manage disk access, file storage, and memory use. The network operating system must also control who can log onto the server and access its files. This security issue grows more important as increasing amounts of the organization's data and information reside on the file server. The network operating system must protect this information without excluding authorized individuals. The most popular network operating system in use today is NetWare from Novell.

FIGURE 7–4   *Star, Bus, and Ring Computer Networks*

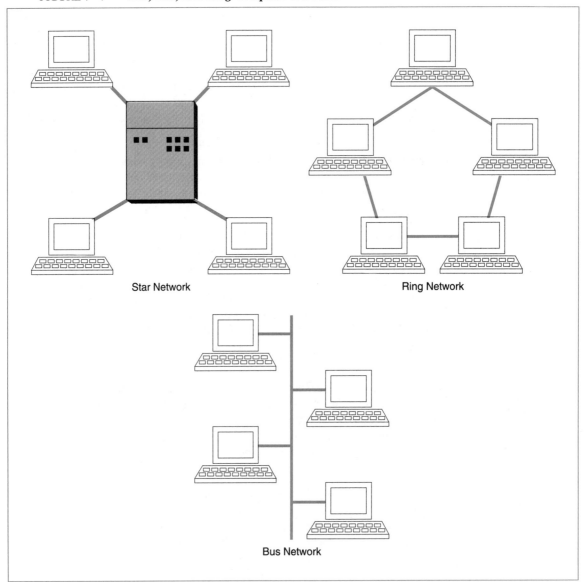

The network operating system must enable the individual who manages the network—the **network administrator**—to control which users have access to the various software programs and data files. For example, the network administrator can restrict access to certain programs and files to managers, while allowing staff personnel to access other programs and files.

FIGURE 7–5   *Operation of Token Sharing Ring Local Area Network*

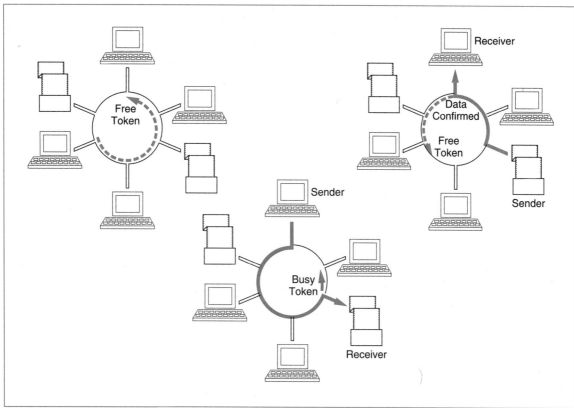

Promises and
Problems with
Local Area
Networks

The future of LANs appears to be very bright, as a great deal of attention is paid to them and to computer networks in general. As more personal computers are appearing in the office, the advantages of tying them together are being realized. The OIS depends heavily on LANs, and many organizations have upgraded from a minicomputer to a network rather than to a more expensive mainframe. Combining the advantages of the personal computer with the power of multiple processors can achieve the processing capability equivalent to a mainframe at a lower cost.

Definite problems must be surmounted before LANs become commonplace equipment. The incompatibility of different types of computers and operating systems is probably the biggest problem. Managers are quickly finding that tying an IBM PC, an Apple Macintosh, and the office minicomputer together is not as easy as a sales representative's claim. The lack of an industry standard for either data transmittal or access control is another outstanding problem.

7.3 Wide Area Networks

Although LANs are becoming increasingly popular for office use, wide area networks have been used for many years in the form of long distance telephone networks. Today, as the need for transferring data and information between computers over long distances

Saving Money with a LAN

After trying to manage Chicago's $40 billion yearly cash flow with manual accounting methods, City Treasurer Miriam Santos knew that something had to change. She considered having the MIS Department create an accounting system on the city's mainframe, but decided that the MIS Department lacked the required experience and sensitivity to Treasury's needs. Instead, she obtained $300,000 from the City Council to install a 16-PC LAN and the necessary software.

In addition to managing the city's budget, the city treasurer is treasurer of the Board of Education and responsible for investing the proceeds from Chicago's bonds, managing escrow funds, and being a trustee for $2 billion in pension funds. To manage this money efficiently and make the correct investment decisions, Santos needed information from a LAN. With the LAN, Santos now knows exactly how much is available for investing on any given day and, as a result, can obtain better rates. The LAN has also made it possible to reduce banking fees, improve returns on short-term investments, and add investment flexibility.

Treasury has identified other, less quantifiable results from installing the LAN. Santos feels that the availability of better information over the LAN saves staff members several hours of extra research per day. The LAN is also credited with stopping a check-kiting scam.

SOURCE: Michael Fitzgerald, "LAN Benefits Chicago Treasury," *Computerworld,* May 6, 1991, p. 62.

grows, wide area networks are also becoming important tools for business, industry, and government. Three basic types of wide area networks are used—academic and research networks, private networks, and value-added networks.

These wide area networks use a special form of telecommunication called **packet switching,** in which terminals are linked to a host computer through interface computers. The host computer breaks long messages into data units, called **packets,** which are then given to the interface computers for transmission through the network. The destination terminal receives the packets and reassembles them into a copy of the original message. Such packet-switching networks usually transmit data at rates of at least 56,000 bits per second (bps). Figure 7–6 shows a schematic of a typical packet-switching network.

Academic and Research Networks

To facilitate interaction between universities and other research institutions involved in defense-oriented research, the U.S. Department of Defense established the first packet-switching network, called ARPANet (for Advanced Research Projects Agency Network). Spanning the entire United States, this network has been so successful that it has spawned several related networks, including Internet, which links many subnetworks. One such subnetwork is BITNET, which is a subscription electronic mail system serving over 1,500 colleges, universities, and other academic and research institutions. On BITNET, a user at a subscribing institution, or **node** in the network, can access the main system from a terminal and send mail to any other user on the network, as long as the

FIGURE 7–6   *Packet-Switching Network*

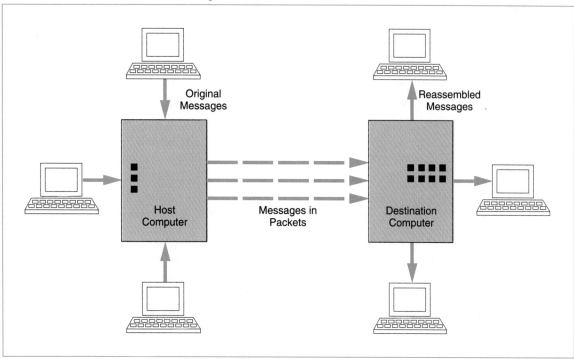

other user's address is known. With this network, a professor or researcher can send messages, letters, or even papers to colleagues in the United States, Europe, and the Middle East. Finally, MCI Mail is a commercial electronic mail system that allows subscribers to send messages electronically across the country.

Private Networks

A private company that decides to set up a wide area network to link its own or outside terminals into its mainframes must determine the type of telecommunications medium to use. The choices include using a standard or wide area telephone service (WATS), leasing a dedicated private line or **leased line,** from the telephone company, or using satellite communications. This decision depends on the number of transmissions to be made and the quality and speed of the required transmissions. Computer networks that require high-quality, high-speed lines on a frequent basis would make the use of leased lines or satellite transmissions economical. Another network may find the use of standard, low-speed, voice quality lines to be adequate as well as economical.

A company using a private network must either manage the telecommunications function itself or hire an outside company to perform this role. This management role includes deciding on the speed of transmissions, the protocol, the method for routing of transmissions, and the error-checking mechanisms.

The third alternative wide area network is the **value-added network (VAN).** These long distance computer networks are public networks that are available by subscription, providing clients with data communication facilities. The company that runs the VAN assumes complete responsibility for managing the network, including providing protocol and conversion between different systems. VANs may also offer other services, including multiple terminal sessions, electronic mail, and network data base access. In a sense, a VAN adds value to information by ensuring that it reaches its destination with little effort by the subscriber.

VANs may also be used by smaller EDI customers and suppliers who need to communicate periodically and translate this communication between different computer environments. Many VANs provide ''mailboxes'' where organizations can deposit or access EDI communications.

A VAN provides its subscribers with connections, or **ports,** to its wide area network through a local telephone call. Once the subscriber accesses the network, data are routed between the local terminal and a distant host computer that is connected to the network via a leased line. By using wideband communications channels that are shared among many users, these public data networks take advantage of economies of scale to supply services at an acceptable cost. In some cases, data can be forwarded from one VAN to another to reach a destination computer that is not linked to the user's VAN. Figure 7–7 depicts a VAN.

FIGURE 7–7   ***Value-Added Network***

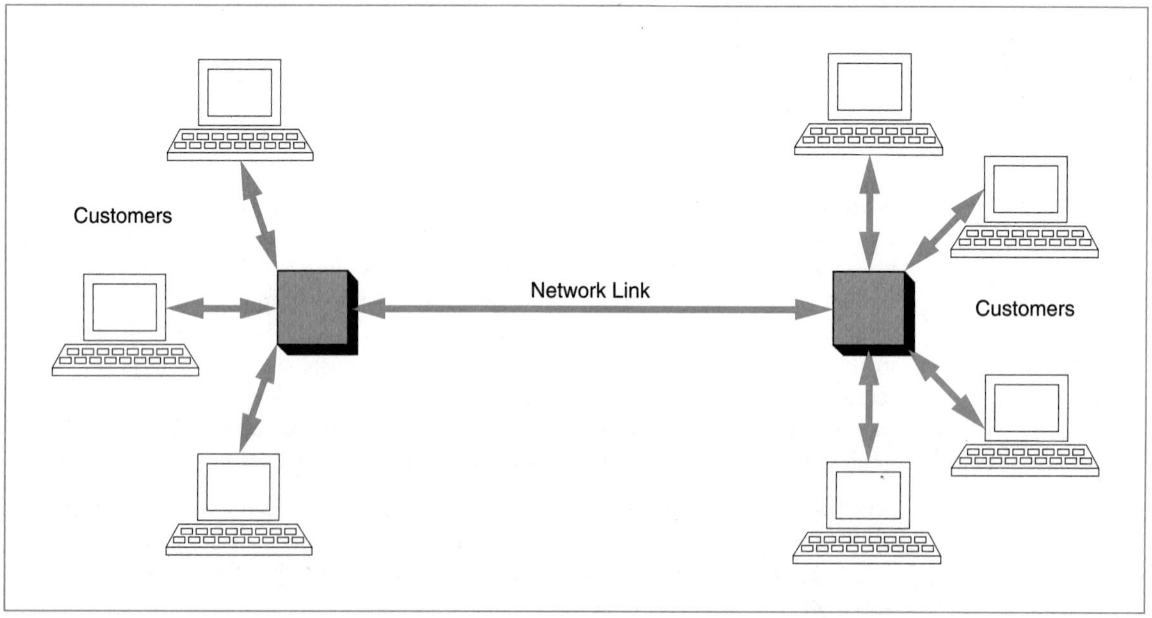

Examples of VANs include Infonet, Tymnet, GTE Telenet, and ATT Information Services NET. A company may subscribe to multiple VANs to take advantage of lower rates in different markets and to ensure that its clients always have a network available to them through a local telephone call.

7.4 PC Telecommunications Concepts and Terminology

A popular use of the personal computer is for communicating with a mainframe or other PC users. This telecommunications operation is usually accomplished through a modem connected to an ordinary telephone line in combination with communications software.

To understand how a computer sends and receives data and information, recall that the information in a computer is stored and manipulated in the form of bits. A **bit** is either an electronic pulse (one) or the absence of a pulse (zero). Usually, the electronic form of information must be translated into a different form before transmission. Currently, this translation process has two steps—conversion of data from parallel to serial form and conversion of the data in digital form to an analog form. The future trend is toward transmitting the digital form over telephone lines rather than using the analog form.

Data Conversions

Data are stored and processed in the computer in a **parallel form**— 16, 32, or 64 bits at a time, depending on the type of computer. On the other hand, data must be transmitted one bit at a time, in **serial form.** To understand the difference, think of parallel form as bits marching through the computer 16, 32, or 64 abreast, and serial form as the same bits moving in single file. In the first conversion step, the computer's **serial port** converts the data from parallel to serial form for transmission, and converts data from serial back to parallel form.

The second step of the translation process involves converting the data from binary, serial form into an analog equivalent that can be transmitted over telephone lines. The word *analog* refers to a physical relationship that represents data. This physical relationship is an electrical wave form that the communication link can carry. For example, information sent over an ordinary telephone line must be converted to an audio form—that is, a one-bit is translated into one tone and a zero-bit into another tone. The translation of data from binary to analog form is executed by a device known as a modem. As mentioned in Chapter 4, the name **modem** comes from the process of converting digital data into analog data by MOdulation and the reverse process of DEModulation.

A bit that is modulated is converted into a particular wave form. One frequency represents the digit zero and a second represents the digit one. When these frequencies are demodulated, they are converted back into a zero or one. Figure 7–8 demonstrates the process of sending information from one computer to another over telephone lines.

Asynchronous Communications

Data can be sent between computers in one of two modes—synchronous or asynchronous. In **synchronous communication,** large numbers of characters are sent as a block, and in **asynchronous communication** the characters are sent one at a time. Synchronous communications are much faster but also require more expensive equipment. Most communication between two personal computers or between a personal computer and a larger computer are asynchronous and involve only the purchase of an inexpensive modem and appropriate software. The speed at which modems can send and receive

FIGURE 7–8   ***Communication between Computers***

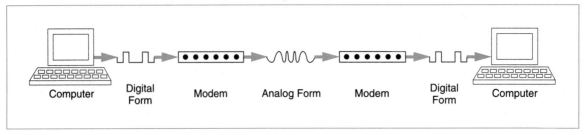

information is measured in terms of bits per second (bps). For modems used with personal computers, rates of 1,200 bps, 2,400 bps, and 9,600 bps are now standard. A modem can be either internal or external, depending on whether it is installed inside the computer or connected to the serial port outside the computer. Most modems can now dial or answer the phone, hang up the phone if a busy signal is reached, and even dial a second number if the first one is busy.

The final consideration for a communication is the protocol. This is a particular problem for modems. The **protocol** is the set of rules that the two computers must follow in sending and receiving information. Mainframes, minicomputers, and personal computers often have different protocols. A **gateway** is a communication device used to link networks using different protocols. If two networks use the same protocol, they can be linked by a communication device called a **bridge**. A LAN might be linked to a mainframe network via a gateway, but two similar LANs might be linked via a bridge. The continuing standardization of communications and modems has reduced the significance of this problem.

Telecommuni-
cations
Software

The communications software for telecommunications using a personal computer is personal productivity software that allows the personal computer to perform many tasks, including dialing telephone numbers; answering phone calls; sending and receiving software, files, data, and information over the telephone line; and accessing other computers.

7.5 Using the Personal Computer for Telecommunications

Accessing
Information
Sources

As mentioned earlier, the personal computer is a great communications device for individuals and organizations alike. PC telecommunications fall into five categories—accessing information sources, interacting with other users, sending electronic mail, telecommuting, and using videotex, all of which are important to managers.

One of the oldest functions of telecommunications is obtaining information from commercial data bases, which have been available since the early seventies. The early data bases were accessed via terminals available only at academic institutions and large corporations. With a personal computer equipped with a modem and communications software, anyone can access these information sources. Four types of information sources are available to users via telecommunications—information utilities, news and business information services, encyclopedic data bases, and specialized networks. In every case, the host computer is either a mainframe or a large minicomputer, because of the storage area needed for the information and speed necessary to search the data bases for a particular piece of information.

Two of the most widely used information utilities for subscribers are CompuServe and Prodigy. Currently, CompuServe has nearly 900,000 subscribers, and Prodigy has over 1.1 million subscribers. Both offer a wide range of information to their subscribers, including general information of the type found in an encyclopedia, news services, newspaper articles, business and financial information, stock market quotes, magazine articles, airline schedules, and medical information. These services can provide a wealth of general knowledge to researchers.

CompuServe and Prodigy offer news and business information services. In fact, both operations offer commodity reports, newsletters, reports on various subjects, and miscellaneous information. In addition to these two operations, the Dow Jones News/Retrieval Service (DJNS) specializes in news and business information. The DJNS offers comprehensive services, including news and general and financial information. A subscriber can also use a key word to search for articles in either *The Wall Street Journal* or *Barrons.* These services are invaluable to an organization interested in the status of the economy in general, its market, or its competitors. This information can be very useful to the managements of companies as they chart their future business strategies. For example, it can help a company determine the true condition of potential merger partners or takeover targets.

With encyclopedic data bases, a PC user can specify a subject such as ''computer'' and then receive a list of all available bibliographic references to that subject. The information is the result of a search through many data bases that are stored in each service. Choosing from these bibliographic listings, the subscriber can then obtain summaries of articles. Based on these summaries, a user may either order a photocopy of an article or find the articles in the library. This service can help managers keep up with the latest trends in their business.

Approximately 5,500 encyclopedic data bases are available to the public through 600 providers, including such companies as DIALOG, BRS (Bibliographic Reference Services), CompuServe, and CORIS (Company Research and Information Service). Some overlap of information exists among the services because they do not actually create their data bases. Information is purchased from outside companies who collect and compile the information that makes up the data bases.

The cost of using an encyclopedic data base service ranges from a low of $25 per hour up to $300 per hour. These amounts may sound expensive, but the results may well be worth the cost. A data base user's search for all the references to a particular topic may last only 15 minutes. Compare that time with a search in the library that could take days to complete.

The number of specialized data bases that are available to a user through telecommunications seems to increase every day. These data bases are available to special groups of users, who might find it difficult to obtain specialized information through their own resources. Examples include The Information Bank, for abstracts from newspapers and magazines; NEXIS, for the full text of articles from newspapers, magazines, and wire services; Medline, for articles in medical journals; and Lexis, for the full text of legal decisions and statutes. As with the encyclopedic data bases, a data base search can be performed quickly by use of a key word.

Interacting with Other Users

As the personal computer allows users to obtain information from mainframe computer data banks and information services, it may also be used to communicate directly with other users. This interaction can take place through a bulletin board service or a teleconference.

For a **bulletin board service,** a user, club, or corporation combines a computer with one or more telephone lines, a modem, and communications software that allows users to call in and ''post'' messages for other users. Both Prodigy and CompuServe have national bulletin board facilities, and thousands of local bulletin boards are located throughout the United States. A personal computer is adequate for local bulletin boards, but national bulletin boards require the speed and storage capabilities available only on mainframes.

One of the most popular uses of a bulletin board—national or local—is exchanging public domain software. This software is not copyrighted and therefore can be copied without breaking copyright laws. Exchanging software (or other information) involves downloading and saving the software. Software sent from a user's PC disk to the host computer is uploaded.

Because national services like CompuServe and Prodigy can serve multiple users simultaneously with their mainframe host computers, these services support conferences or other types of multiple-user sessions. These sessions can be informal ''gab'' sessions or formal, long-term conferences on a particular topic. Formal teleconferencing can occur on a real-time or a delayed basis. In a **real-time conference,** all participants are actually logged onto the system at the same time. With a **delayed conference,** the comments of the participants are stored sequentially as they are entered. A delayed conference can last for months, with participants taking whatever time they need to formulate replies to other participants' comments. Normally, a real-time conference is used for a pressing topic that requires a quick resolution, and the delayed conference deals with philosophical or policy questions that do not require immediate decisions. Teleconferencing is also popular for training a company's employees in widely separated locations around the country.

Sending Electronic Mail

As discussed in Chapter 2, electronic mail is very useful within an organization's LAN. Electronic mail can also be useful in wide area networks using mainframe terminals. PC users can often access the same wide area network mail services that are available to mainframe users. PC users can also use the electronic mail services of such operations as CompuServe and Prodigy. These network services offer users the facility to communicate with any other subscriber through electronic mail services. A subscriber can send a ''letter'' to another subscriber by using the recipient's account number. This electronic mail service enables managers to communicate within an organization or to communicate quickly with customers and suppliers.

Using Electronic Mail for Strategic Purposes

Electronic mail is widely used in business, industry, and government, and now it is also used by many companies to gain a competitive advantage. For example, a company can transform the work process by improving response time, cutting costs, and creating closer ties with customers. The following three companies currently use electronic mail for competitive purposes:

- Westcon Associates, Inc., of Eastchester, NY, a distributer of PC network products, has greatly reduced its dependency on conventional paper mail and telephone calls to contact outside representatives, customers, and vendors. Instead, Westcon uses an electronic mail product on its 40-node LAN that allows salespeople to dial in through portable personal computers. Vendors can also hook in through gateways provided by Westcon. Installed at a cost of $100,000, Westcon's electronic mail system should pay for itself in one year through increased sales and a 10 percent productivity increase in the sales department.

- American Sterilizer of Erie, PA, a producer of commercial sterilization equipment, uses an electronic mail system to inform a network of 65 Just-in-Time (JIT) vendors when to ship their products or what future needs may be.

- Royal Bank of Canada of Toronto is developing PC applications that its employees can run through its electronic mail system. One planned application will allow a bank officer to call up a loan request and then run a bank-developed application with which the officer can analyze the potential loan and route a decision to other officers. The bank has already developed systems that allow personal computers to exchange information with the bank's mainframe.

SOURCE: Robert L. Scheier, "LAN Managers Harness E-Mail for Strategic Uses," *PC Week,* September 4, 1989, p. 64.

Telecommuting

One of the first forms of telecommunications involved a worker using a portable terminal, modem, and telephone to contact a mainframe to work on some project. The introduction of the personal computer only made this task easier by not always requiring the access to a mainframe. Now, a user can work on a personal computer at some location other than the office, store the results on disk, and then download the information to the office computer. In 1988, an estimated 27 million employees worked at home, either full or part time. A recent study showed that almost 15 million home-based businesses exist, and this number is expected to grow to almost 21 million by 1995.

Generally, three groups of people are **telecommuting**—individuals who use their personal computers to access a mainframe to avoid making a trip to the office; individuals who use their personal computers at home to continue work begun at the office; and individuals who work on a personal computer at home the majority of the time and visit the office only occasionally to review their work with a supervisor. For the first two types of telecommuter, having a computer at home is a convenience that allows them to complete their work more quickly and easily. For the third type of telecommuter, work at home is a way of life.

Problems exist with any type of telecommuting. For the mainframe user, problems involve reaching a free line into the computer and using the telephone line for long periods of time. The PC user who tries to complete work begun at the office faces problems with accessing the data bases on the office mainframe. These mainframes may not be set up for outside access. Solving this problem requires cooperation from the company's Management Information System (MIS) department to change its policies toward outside access.

For the telecommuter who works primarily at home, what may be perceived as the perfect work situation has its own set of problems. These problems can include time management and lack of interactions with office co-workers and superiors.

Using Videotex

When a new avenue of communication opens up, businesses are always quick to use it for advertising and sale purposes. The same is true of telecommunications applications. Today, with a computer, telephone, modem, and appropriate software, users can view and purchase various services and products. **Videotex** is currently a small industry that many people feel has potential for enormous growth over the coming years, especially after the introduction of Prodigy by IBM and Sears. Although all prior attempts to implement videotex in the United States have failed for lack of interest, Prodigy may be successful. By mid-1991, over 1 million users signed up for Prodigy. Initially available only for IBM compatible computers and only in some cities, Prodigy is now available for Apple computers in many U.S. cities.

Nearly 500 services are offered by Prodigy—ordering clothing, sporting goods, and other items; buying airline tickets; viewing current news stories and weather reports; banking at home; using electronic mail; and playing games. Prodigy is similar to CompuServe, except that it uses a colorful graphics menu system that makes it more popular with first-time computer users. It is expected that Videotex will change the way customers shop. The impact on retailing and mail order business may be substantial.

**7.6
Managerial
Considerations**

For the manager, sharing information resources through telecommunications and computer networks offers tremendous possibilities and equally large problems. A manager can achieve competitive advantages through various uses of telecommunications and computer networks. Employees can share data, information, hardware, and software in the office; external data bases can be accessed; text and graphics can be sent long distances; and workers can telecommunicate using personal computers, performing their jobs more efficiently.

A manager must also consider the various telecommunications and computer network alternatives and develop a plan that accommodates current information system needs without locking the organization out of future technological advances. Developing this telecommunications plan involves examining the organization's current telecommunications capabilities and needs both for voice and data. This examination must consider how the OIS and long distance communications help meet the objectives of the organization. Only by comparing the current status of the telecommunications system with the organization's objectives can rational decisions be made. The following questions must be addressed and answered:

- Is a LAN needed, or can we use our existing telephone system to share data and information within the office?

- If a LAN is needed, what configuration and vendor would best suit the needs of the organization?

- What kind of voice mail, electronic mail, or facsimile system is needed for both internal and external communications?

- Should the organization subscribe to an enclyopedic data base, or should a series of specialized data bases be used?

- Should the organization create a private wide area network, or should it subscribe to a VAN?

- How should personal computers be used for telecommunications within the office? Will telecommuting be encouraged or discouraged?

Once these and other related questions are answered, the manager can create the telecommunications plan that best matches the needs of the organization. After the plan is developed, reviewed by the appropriate individuals, and modified for any problems, bids are obtained from various vendors. Finally, the actual hardware and software needed to implement the plan can be installed and tested.

Future Considerations

Even as this textbook is being written, telecommunications technology is rapidly evolving. In fact, this area may be changing even faster than computer technology. In addition to the increasing use of fiber optics and satellites as communications media, the use of digital (binary) voice transmissions rather than analog is the technology of the future. The transition to the Integrated Services Digital Network (ISDN) will standardize transmissions of all types of signal—voice, video, and data. Many experts expect that as ISDN becomes a standard, EDI and other electronic business communications will expand rapidly. Moreover, the use of home-related information services will increase tremendously. Users will have better access to the data bases discussed earlier in this chapter, and businesses will be able to communicate directly with their customers.

7.7 Summary

One of the most exciting aspects of computer use today is telecommunications via computer networks, which can be used in many ways to achieve a competitive advantage. Telecommunications refers to the electronic transmission of information, including data communications and teleprocessing. This transmission may occur mainframe to mainframe, personal computer to mainframe, and personal computer to personal computer.

Telecommunications also includes DDP, in which small computers handle local processing, relieving the central mainframe of many local processing tasks. Computer networks can be either wide area or local area (restricted to one geographical location) networks. LANs can be configured as ring, star, or bus networks.

When computer communications are required over long distances, wide area networks are used. Three types of wide area networks exist—academic and research networks, private networks, and value-added networks (also called VANs). In most cases, the method of moving data over the network is called packet switching.

A very popular use of the personal computer is for telecommunications using a modem, telephone line, and communications software. Common applications include accessing information sources, interacting with other users via teleconferencing or electronic bulletin boards, sending electronic mail, and telecommuting. Managers must carefully consider the potential advantages and problems involved with the various uses of telecommunications. Before installation of telecommunications equipment, a plan must be developed that will satisfy current needs, but not lock the user out of new technological advances.

Key Terms

asynchronous communication	network administrator
bit	network operating system
bridge	node
bulletin board service	packet switching
bus	packets
bus network	parallel form
client server	peer-to-peer
coaxial cable	ports
computer networks	protocol
data communication	real-time conference
delayed conference	ring network
diskless workstations	serial form
distributed data bases	serial port
Distributed Data Processing (DDP)	star network
dumb terminal	synchronous communication
Electronic Data Interchange (EDI)	telecommunications
Electronic Funds Transfer (EFT)	telecommuting
electronic mail	teleprocessing
file server	token
gateway	token sharing network
leased line	twisted pair wiring
Local Area Networks (LANs)	value-added network
modem	videotex
multiple access network	wide area network
multiplexing	

**Review
Questions**

1. Define telecommunications. What is the difference between data communications and teleprocessing?

2. Discuss the competitive use of shared information by organizations.

3. What is DDP? List its advantages and disadvantages.

4. What is EDI? How is it used by a company to increase its efficiency?

5. List and discuss the different types of networks. Discuss one use of networks with which you are familiar.

6. Discuss the three ways used to differentiate LANs.

7. Describe the three physical configurations commonly used for LANs.

8. Describe three functional types of LANs. Which is in widest use?

9. Why is a network operating system necessary for a LAN?

10. Discuss the promises and problems associated with LANs.

11. Describe the three types of wide area networks. Why is packet switching used in these networks?

12. Discuss one type of wide area network in some detail.

13. List the five main categories of telecommunications for PC use.

14. Discuss one category of PC telecommunications in more detail.

15. Discuss the important elements that a manager must consider in creating a telecommunications plan.

**Discussion
Questions**

1. You have a part-time position in a local computer store. A partner in a local engineering contracting firm tells you that he has a variety of personal computers that are used for everything from accounting, to cost estimation, to drafting, to Computer-Aided Design (CAD). He has just returned from a mechanical contractors convention, where he was impressed with some of the LAN applications for mechanical engineering contracting companies like his. He particularly liked the way cost data could be linked with cost estimation and CAD via a network of shared data. He wants you to explain to him the potential benefit he may receive from networking his personal computers. He also wants to know what problems may result from using a LAN.

2. Today the large automotive companies require virtually all vendors to use EDI. Discuss what EDI is and why you think this requirement is necessary. Some small organizations cannot link their computers to a large automotive firm's computer on a continual basis. Describe the role of third party value-added networks in EDI communications.

3. Many individuals need assistance in planning and managing their financial affairs. As a financial planner who serves these clients, explain how you would use your personal computer and its telecommunications capability to manage investment portfolios, tax planning, and retirement planning.

4. Describe several ways you believe Levi Strauss benefits from its EDI system.

Case 7–1
Green Spring
Mental Health
Services

A network of off-the-shelf software recently solved a system crisis for Green Spring Mental Health Services (GSMHS), a provider of mental health care review and case management for insurers such as Blue Cross and Blue Shield (BCBS) of Maryland. The company's insured base jumped from one-half million people in August 1990 to 2 million today, with several more million expected soon. The Green Spring staff also multiplied, from 30 people in the beginning of 1990 to more than 130. GSMHS management was uncertain about its ability to develop a secure computer system that could track care and benefits for millions of insured and hundreds of thousands of patients in several states. The company's new computer system would have to handle rapid growth. The new system also would have to communicate with insurers, using dissimilar systems that communicate differently.

In the search for a solution to its data and communication needs, GSMHS management looked at systems and proposals from a variety of consulting firms and vendors. Many required a large investment in purchasing or leasing mainframe or minicomputer hardware and software.

In August of 1990, Green Spring hired Janice Beldon and Ed Grant to build its data processing system. Both realized GSMHS did not need to replicate its clients' data bases. Beldon and Grant saw the LAN as a single communications bus linking workstations around the network to a host of data and communications services. "Instead of building a data processing system replicating the systems of our clients, the insurers, what we really had to do was design a system that could flexibly communicate with a wide variety of existing systems while providing relatively simple data base services," said Beldon. GSMHS not only had to communicate with its clients' mainframes, but it needed to make basic information available on a 24-hour basis to care managers, psychiatrists, and psychiatric nurses who advise care providers on acceptable treatment plans.

With these objectives, Grant and Beldon designed and implemented a system by the end of 1990, only four months after they had started their jobs. They made a LAN the center of a communications-oriented system. The LAN uses a single server running on a popular network system. All communications to the 100 LAN workstations move over an Ethernet network, which uses network interface cards and hubs for users in the three-floor building that houses GSMHS. The file server provides storage on six drives and maintains common executable software such as WordPerfect and Microsoft Excel and other office automation software and files. Most workstations are diskless, to maintain security and reliability within the system. Windows is used to manage the user interface, as well as to multitask the applications.

The primary data base functions on the LAN are handled by a Client Utilization Review Expediter (CURE) system developed by Crealock Data Systems, Inc. of Paoli, PA. The CURE system is updated by periodic tapes received from insurers listing eligible insured clients and providers. These data are augmented by an arsenal of wide area network links to the insurer's systems that give the GSMHS network its greatest versatility, as shown in Figure 7–9. LAN users share two Attachmate Systems Network Architecture (SNA) gateways. Each gateway can support as many as 99 concurrent users. GSMHS ties into the Blues Net, which is a collaborative nationwide network among BCBS providers.

Three personal computers equipped with a Network Products Asynchronous Communications Server provide outgoing asynchronous gateway capability to several diverse systems like those used at the Medigroup Health Maintenance Organization (HMO) in New Jersey and the Columbia Free State HMO in Maryland. Asynchronous servers provide incoming access for care managers working in other states. These remote users can also use asynchronous and SNA gateways to link to the various state systems to query data.

The mental health data handled by GSMHS is confidential, and security is a paramount concern. Remote users are connected only when the system calls them back at the predetermined phone number assigned to their password. Logging in to the file server requires a password, and retries and hours of use are limited. Gateways can be accessed only by users specifically authorized by the system administrators, and remote hosts require additional passwords and identification codes.

This wide array of communications capabilities allows GSMHS to adapt quickly to the diverse communications requirements of different insurers and data systems. However, the implementation was not smooth. It took several months to get all the applications running smoothly. Overall, the majority of hardware and applications have worked as promised by the vendors, and GSMHS personnel have been able to focus on getting their jobs done rather than tinkering with recalcitrant software and hardware. "We were able to bring the systems in New Jersey on-line within 30 days after we were awarded the contract," Grant said. "We have insurers who can't even get their own systems at different sites to communicate with each other, but for us, it's no problem. The LAN is our front end into any system."

SOURCE: Adapted with permission from Chet Schuyler, "Off the Shelf Network Offers Solution to Rapid Growth," *PC Week,* June 24, 1991, p. S-8. Copyright © 1991, Ziff Communications Company.

Case Questions

1. Why did Green Spring Mental Health Services select a LAN?

2. How does it use a wide area network and telecommunications to support its LAN?

3. How does it protect the confidentiality of mental health data?

FIGURE 7–9 **Green Spring Mental Health Services' Off-the-Shelf Network**

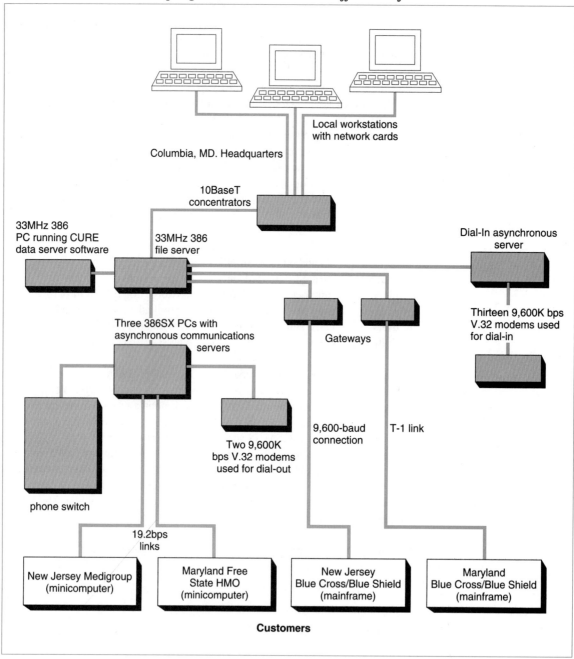

Case 7–2
*Pittsburgh
Plate Glass and
Electronic Data
Interchange*

PPG Industries Inc., a $4 billion glass, coatings, and chemicals company based in Pittsburgh, has realized a dramatic increase in the speed with which it receives payments from General Motors (GM), the company's largest customer, since it linked into GM's EDI system in 1987. PPG does $500 million in domestic business each year with eight different GM divisions, selling the automaker window glass, points, adhesives, fiberglass, and body parts. According to company officials, PPG has received considerable benefits since going online with the GM EDI network, both in terms of the overall increased speed of the GM payments and the easy-to-process electronic form of the payments. "We've gone from 50 or 60 percent past-due [unprocessed payments from GM] down to 4 percent," said Roger Bailey, PPG's manager of bank relations.

The benefits of electronic linkages are not new to PPG. Early in the electronic age, PPG saw the advantage of moving product orders and invoices quickly over phone lines instead of through the conventional mail system. "Our roots in EDI go back a long way," said Sally Wellinger, PPG's director of corporate MIS. "PPG and GM were involved in EDI-like applications such as the electronic confirmation of shipments as far back as the 1960s," Wellinger said. In the mid-1970s, PPG established a direct connection between the company and its bank. Financial executives at PPG convinced the bank to link its mainframe to theirs and send daily updates on the PPG account's status and transactions directly into the PPG accounts receivable system. The bank accommodated PPG with an innovative link that employed the standard Bank Administration Institute (BAI) funds-transfer format, which until then had been used almost exclusively for interbank transactions. In 1986, when GM wanted to pay all of its suppliers electronically instead of through the mail, PPG was ready for the technology. GM's proposed EFT system, in fact, provided the missing link in what is now a complete order-billing-payment system for PPG with some GM divisions.

Today, for example, PPG's computers can accept an electronic order for windshields from GM's Buick-Olds-Cadillac (BOC) division, automatically transmit an acknowledgement and an invoice for the windshields to BOC, and have BOC's bank transfer the payment directly to PPG's bank. The bank updates PPG's accounts receivable system with information about the payment. Remittance data that describe the payment are attached to the payment. "The speed at which the information flows through the cycle has been sped up by 8 to 10 days," Bailey said.

Aside from the decreased turnaround time, Bailey stated that there were many unanticipated benefits from PPG's electronic linkage with GM. For one, disputed PPG bills are now paid immediately on resolution, rather than at the next bimonthly payment period. PPG has picked up millions of dollars in such interim payments, according to Bailey.

Perhaps more significant are the "cleaner" accounts that PPG now has in its dealings with GM. "Today we're taking in 1,200 to 1,500 invoices in a single [electronic] check," he said. "We're able to apply virtually all of them electronically to our A/R [accounts receivable] system. There's no human and no human error."

Business with GM, however, is not the full extent of PPG's electronic dealings. Increasingly, the company is getting its own suppliers online with EDI invoicing and is setting up electronic payment plans with other business partners, particularly in the chemical industry. PPG set up a two-way funds-transfer link with Dow Chemical, which is both a PPG customer and supplier.

The company also established a corporatewide EDI ''clearinghouse'' that lets its independent divisions do business electronically with suppliers through a standard system. The clearinghouse lets any division send files to a mainframe, where the software converts the files into the American National Standards Institute (ANSI) $\times$ 12 format and sends data to the suppliers' EDI mailboxes. Dave Rose, PPG's director of distribution systems and the mastermind of the EDI clearinghouse, said the centralized system was needed because in the past, the divisions made separate EDI links with their business partners.

Beyond EDI, PPG is piloting a system that allows its glass customers to browse electronically through what was once an internal data base for glass inventory and production. Customers access PPG's Glass Track data base and check PPG inventories to plan orders and production. With a nationwide undercapacity in glass, the current goal of this system is not so much to win customers but to help keep production costs down. ''The idea behind an electronic-order system is to lower inventory-carry costs,'' he explained.

''We're not blindly devoted to EDI,'' said MIS director Wellinger. ''Rather than going into it lock, stock, and barrel, we're approaching it as we do any other systems project. We're doing pilots, standardizing to minimize our investment, and working with our business partners to see where EDI can be applied as a sensible business value.''

''It doesn't surprise me at all that PPG, as a user of EDI, is one of the outstanding competitive companies in the country,'' said the president of an EDI consulting firm. ''Quite clearly, their use of EDI is an effective strategic business tool.''

SOURCE: Adapted with permission from Don Steinberg, ''Link to GM's EFT Net Speeds Payment Processing at PPG,'' *PC Week,* October 6, 1987, pp. C-1, C-6, and C-43.

Case Questions

1. What is EDI used for?

2. What are the objectives of PPG's use of EDI and how do these objectives fit into its competitive strategy?

III

Managing with Information Systems

Section III describes how each type of information system discussed in Section I is strategically used to effectively manage an organization. Chapter 8 discusses transaction processing systems (TPSs). Basic merchandising and manufacturing transactions are illustrated. Chapter 9 explores management information systems (MISs) and includes examples of marketing, production management, financial decision-making activities, and supporting data and information systems. Chapter 10 discusses decision support systems (DSSs) and executive information systems (EISs), and Chapter 11 focuses on artificial intelligence (AI) and expert systems (ESs).

Transaction Processing Systems

8

Introduction

As discussed in Chapter 2, **Transaction Processing Systems (TPS)** convert raw data from operations and external sources and the results of various decisions into information that is useful to management. Figure 8–1 shows how a TPS supports structured and operational decision-making activities. A TPS also provides data which is stored to support other decision-making activities.

The objective of transaction processing is to compile a current, accurate record of an organization's activities. Some records are required by state and federal law, financial institutions, generally accepted accounting principles (GAAP), and industry regulations. Others are required for operational control, tactical decision making, and strategic planning. Several transaction processing activities must take place before raw data can be used effectively to accommodate these regulations and requirements. These transaction processing activities include input (data gathering, entry, and transmission), processing (manipulation), storage, and output (reporting). Processing may be accomplished via a batch, on-line, or real-time mode, depending on the organization's information needs.

Transaction Process Steps

Transaction processing involves the following steps:

1. Gathering, entering, and transmitting the data that describe the organization's activities

2. Processing (arranging and manipulating) the data into a form that is usable for a variety of potential managerial and operational uses

FIGURE 8–1

*Information
Systems and
Decision Making*

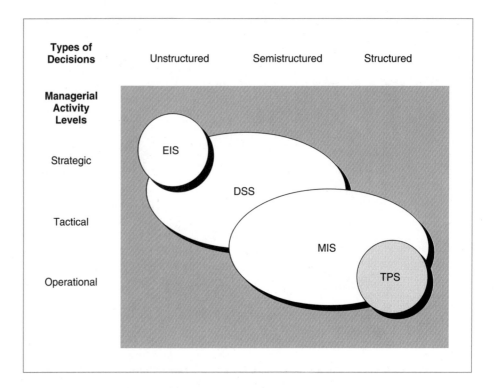

3. Storing data for easy retrieval when needed by organizational units

4. Processing stored data into a form that is usable

5. Reporting output information to a large variety of users

The basic transaction process for an online computer system is summarized in Figure 8–2. Data that are gathered and collected from operations (feedback) and from the external environment of the organization are entered into the TPS. Sometimes, data must be transmitted via telecommunications equipment to the data processing center, where the information is processed and stored for future use. Management Information Systems (MIS), Decision Support Systems (DSS), and Executive Information Systems (EIS), which are discussed in Chapters 9 and 10, use these processed data. Next, the data are retrieved from storage and further processed for operational reports, tactical reports, financial statements, and managerial inquiry. This output, in turn, is used to control operations and make decisions. The results of operations and decisions are monitored and become part of the data that must be collected and stored for future use.

Management uses this information to monitor the ongoing operations of the business and engage in tactical decision making and strategic planning. Generally, transactional data consist of operational statistics that describe the nature of the transaction, for example, number of units sold, price, name and address of customer, and date. Because the

FIGURE 8-2

Transaction Process

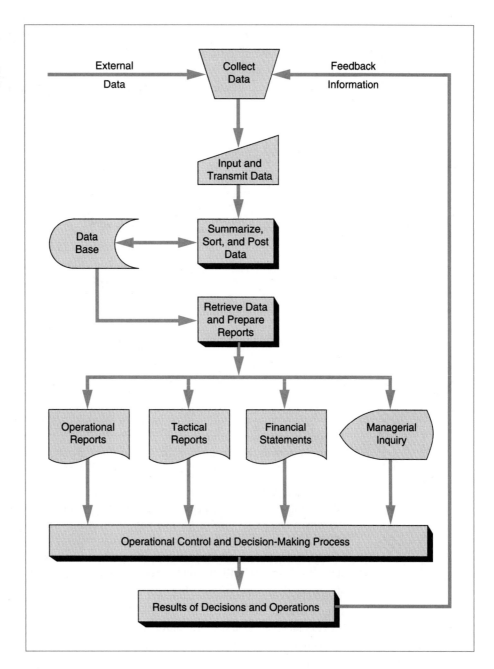

FIGURE 8–3   *Use of Transaction Data to Support Management Information Systems, Decision Support Systems, and Executive Information Systems*

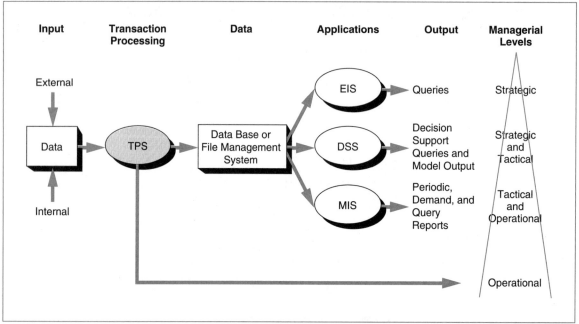

financial accounting information system is a primary user of such information, data may be used to post accounting records. The primary objective of the financial accounting information system is to monitor the organization's financial operations and to report the results in terms of account balances, revenue and expenses, and cash flow.

Transaction data can also be used to assist operations and general management in controlling operations and in managing the organization. For example, operating or sales personnel should be aware of changes in inventory via the TPS in order to make decisions. In general, these data must be stored in order to satisfy the organization's many informational requirements. Figure 8–3 illustrates the use of transaction data in supporting MIS, DSS, and EIS and their respective management levels.

When computers were first introduced, transaction processing was called **data processing,** and most applications involved only accounting data. Obviously, today's TPSs process far more than just accounting information. They produce data used to monitor and control all the operations of an organization.

Transaction Processing Cycles

Transaction processing comprises several cycles. In the revenue cycle, a sale is made, goods are shipped, invoices are sent to the customer, and cash is collected. Major transactions in the revenue cycle are order entry, shipping, billing and accounts receivable, and cash receipts. Other cycles in an organization include the expenditure cycle, the administrative cycle, and the conversion cycle. The major transactions in the expenditure cycle include purchasing, receiving, and cash disbursements. Transactions in the conversion cycle include work order preparation, material requisition, manufacturing and cost allocation, payroll, and inventory. The transactions in each processing cycle have the same essential input, processing, storage, and output characteristics illustrated in Figure 8–2. However, the importance of each cycle varies for each organization depending on the industry. Some organizations have very sophisticated point-of-sale data input systems. Others concentrate on manufacturing data input or Electronic Data Interchange (EDI) systems. These transaction processing cycles are discussed in more detail later in the chapter.

Transaction Processing Modes

Transactions may be processed in a batch or online mode, as discussed in Chapter 2. In a **batch mode,** similar transactions are accumulated in a batch and periodically processed. For example, the time each employee works during a week may be input to payroll records at the end of each day as a batch. At the end of the week, payroll checks are written in a batch for all employees who worked that week. In contrast, with an **online mode,** a system processes transactions as they occur. In this situation, employees would be paid as they completed each work order. Another example of an online mode is the processing of a grocery sale at a checkout counter. As the sale occurs, the item sold is entered, the price is checked, inventory is reduced by the sale, and various sales statistics are gathered for marketing and buying decisions. Over the last two decades, batch processing and report generation have given way to online transaction processing and decision support through queries.

Real-time processing is another type of online processing, except that the processing actually controls the operation. For example, as a guest registers for a motel room at a national chain, room availability information is immediately updated before the next reservation is processed. Thus, not only is the processing of reservations online (as they occur), the processing controls the availability of rooms.

8.1 Transaction Processing Activities

Data Gathering, Transmission, and Entry

As mentioned earlier, transaction processing can be considered a series of steps—from data gathering, entry, and transmission to processing, to storage, to final output of information to users. In this section, we consider these activities in more detail.

All data from an organization's physical operations must be gathered, including the input of resources, transformation of these resources into products and sales, and distribution of goods and services. These activities involve a number of transactions with external parties as well as the organization's internal units. Transactions include sales, inventory reduction, shipping, billing, cash receipts or collections, purchasing, inventory receiving, payment, and conversion of labor and materials into finished goods and services. Data may be gathered for future processing in a batch mode or processed as transactions occur using online processing.

Data may be entered into the computer system using many different input devices—keyboard, mouse, Optical Character Recognition (OCR) device, magnetic ink reader, light pen, and holographic bar code reader. All data entry requires editing and verification

Using Pen and Voice to Enter Data

Although bar code readers and keyboards are by far the most widely used methods of data entry, two new forms of input— voice and pen—are gaining wider acceptance. Being able to talk to a computer has long been an objective of computer science researchers, but only recently has that objective been within reach. Because the ability to enter handwritten data on a computer screen is more natural than using a keyboard for many people, this form of input is coming into widespread use.

With voice recognition systems, the medical profession can speed the compilation of reports as well as guard against errors that might cause malpractice suits. For example, 22 physicians and other health care workers at one hospital can use four computers hooked into a local area network equipped with a voice recognition system. Emergency room physicians who see 30–50 patients per day must write a report on each one. Using a verbal shorthand made up of "trigger phrases," the physician can create and print a standard one-page report in about two minutes. A less detailed handwritten

report can take longer than five minutes, and a dictated and transcribed report is not ready for five days. The system saves the hospital up to $200,000 in transcription and insurance costs per year. Each doctor saves about $4,000 per year in malpractice insurance costs because the system's documentation is better than previous reports.

Handwritten input using computer "notebooks" is improving companies' operations. For example, Best Foods' decision to give pen-based personal computers to a group of independent distributors has saved the delivery-truck drivers an average of $1\frac{1}{2}$ hours per day. Rather than using hand-held calculators to calculate sales and paper forms to send delivery summaries to company headquarters, drivers now use the pen-based personal computers. The results for Best Foods are fewer errors and quicker feedback on marketing data at the end of each day.

SOURCES: Michael Alexander, "Doctors Save Time Writing without Pens," *Computerworld*, January 28, 1991, p. 20; Christopher O'Malley, "Is the Pen Mightier Than the Keyboard?," *Lotus*, August, 1990, pp. 10–11.

as discussed in Chapter 5 to ensure that input is accurate and complete. The data are often transmitted from remote sites to be processed and stored for future use.

Processing and Data Manipulation

The processing of data into a useful form involves several activities, including classification and coding, organizing, calculating, and summarizing. A **classification system** must be developed to store data for effective use by managers.

Data should be coded for logical organization and easy retrieval. Several coding schemes can be used, including sequential, block, group, and mnemonic coding. In a **sequential code,** every record is given a sequential numeric code—a useful method for controlling and referencing transactions by number. For example, checks are numbered sequentially for control over cash disbursements. A **block code** classifies transactions via blocks that have some meaning. The blocks can be characterized by either numbers or letters. For example, all the assets in an accounting system may begin with a block code, 100. A Zip Code is a good example of a block code in which the first two numbers represent a region and the subsequent numbers represent a particular postal district. A **group code** is similar to a block code, except that every number or letter in the code represents something different. For example, an expense item may have a group code that includes division, department, employee, and expense account numbers or letters. Finally, a **mnemonic code** is similar to a group code, except that each aspect of the code has a readily identifiable meaning. For example, a man's shirt code may be 16-34-B-O for a 16-inch neck, 34-inch sleeve, blue color, and oxford cloth material. All these classification schemes are designed to make data use easier for operational control, tactical decision making, and strategic planning. In general, the choice of a specific classification and coding scheme is determined by the intended future use of the data, as well as the file management and data base structures in use.

An organization's information needs may require that data manipulation and analysis be performed. Data must often be manipulated before they are stored for management's use. This process may involve combining data to arrive at subtotals or totals, such as number of units in stock, total amount of an invoice, or amount payable by a customer. On the other hand, all data need not be stored; sometimes, a simple summarization is sufficient. For example, sales summary data may be more useful to a sales manager than the details of each sale for a period of time. Sales patterns that are obvious when summary data are reviewed might not be evident in detailed data. Sophisticated analysis may be necessary before data are useful for management activities. For example, sales trends may need to be analyzed and combined with economic indicators to prepare a sales forecast.

Data Storage

Chapters 5 and 6 presented numerous ways of storing data for future use. The number of data elements that need to be stored may be quite large for some types of transactions. In general, a transaction must be identified by number, the persons who make the transaction (by customer number and salesperson number), what was transacted (by stock number and amount of merchandise sold), the date of the transaction, the department where the transaction took place, and the authorization (such as a supervisor's "OK" for necessary overtime hours). In summary, the who, what, when, where, and authorization of each transaction must be gathered, classified, and stored. The actual physical and logical structure used to store this data for further use should be determined by the current and future user requirements.

Output and Reporting

The product of a TPS is the output of information. This output may be printed periodic reports such as labor variance reports for the plant supervisors or online queries such as a request for the amount of components on hand for marketing personnel. These reports may be internal documents or messages displayed on a computer monitor, or they may be formal financial statements for outside parties. The output may be periodic or on demand, depending on the needs of operational personnel in marketing, production, or financial services.

8.2
Transaction
Cycles

Transactions in a typical business do not generally involve the simple input, processing, and output of information. As illustrated earlier, data are often stored for future output. Many transactions also lead to output that, in turn, prompts some new action and involves more data input, processing, and possible storage. In other words, transactions are often linked to other transactions via output documents, which become input for another set of transactions, or via storage of data for the next operational or tactical activity. A series of tactical and operational activities, each requiring a transaction, is called a **transaction cycle.** As mentioned earlier, businesses have a revenue cycle, an expenditure cycle, and an administrative or financial cycle. Organizations that convert materials and labor into goods and services also have a conversion cycle. These transaction cycles are detailed in this section, along with the documents typically associated with the transactions. Many of these documents (or similar reports) are common in batch processing systems. Many, however, do not physically exist in an on-line environment. In an advanced on-line computer system the substance of these documents is either stored in computer files or can be extracted from the transaction elements that are stored in a data base. For purposes of exposition, these basic transaction processing documents are illustrated in Figure 8–4 and subsequent figures to graphically describe the flow of transactions.

In Figure 8–4, note that the transaction cycle has internal and external input, a series of data processing steps, and output. Data may be stored in this cycle for further processing as more information is gathered. Output from one process may be input into a second processing step in the cycle. The final result of the cycle is an output.

Basic
Merchandising
Transaction
Flows at
ProYacht, Inc.

The basic transaction cycles found in most merchandising organizations are revenue, expenditure, and administrative (or financial) cycles. We illustrate these cycles using as an example the procurement and sales of parts through the ProYacht, Inc. parts division. ProYacht's organizational setup is shown again in Figure 8–5 with the parts division highlighted. ProYacht's parts division currently uses minicomputers and a batch processing system.

ProYacht's parts division buys various sailboat parts, such as sails, engines, and rigging, from manufacturers and sells them to ProYacht dealers and other marine retailers. The majority of such sales are on credit. The basic accounting and data gathering for the expenditure cycle are shown in Figure 8–6. The cycle flows clockwise, with the key documents and the major processes numbered and shown in the appropriate place with respect to timing and information flow. Each transaction process involves data input, processing, and an output document or storage.

The basic system illustrated in Figure 8–6 is typical of those used to manage the day-to-day operations of buying and selling in a merchandising operation. It also may be used to describe the operations in a manufacturing operation in which components are purchased and products are sold to customers. In manufacturing, merchandising inventory is replaced by components and raw materials. This illustration includes all the documents found in batch processing systems. In an online computerized environment, many documents and processes are stored and carried out electronically, as noted in the

FIGURE 8–4   *Transaction Cycle*

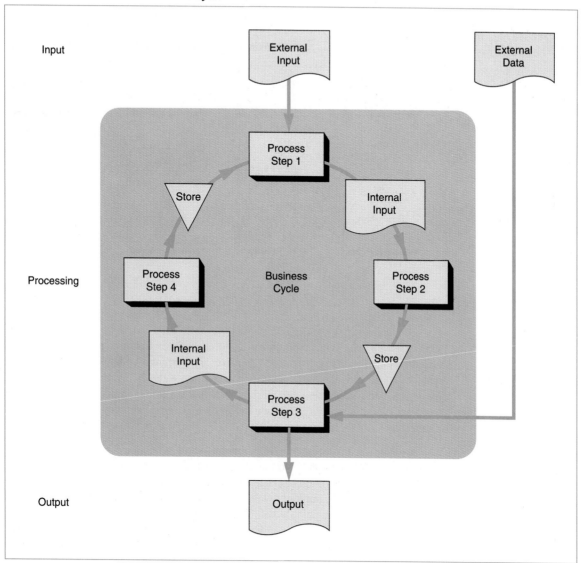

following discussion of the transaction cycles. The basic transaction cycle illustrated here provides the essential operational data for an organization. In many cases, the amount of transaction data is far greater, to satisfy management information needs.

Each transaction cycle is discussed below, along with data flow diagrams for the important processing activities and documents in each cycle. Data flow diagrams describe the essential inputs, processes, data storage, and output for each processing step.

FIGURE 8–5

*ProYacht, Inc.
Parts Division*

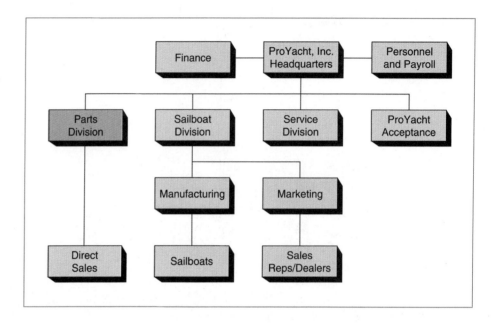

Expenditure Cycle

In the **expenditure cycle,** an organization purchases merchandise (parts for ProYacht's parts division) for inventory, receives these components, updates accounts payable, disburses cash, adds the merchandise to inventory, reduces inventory due to sales or production, and issues a new purchase order when stock gets low. These processes and their associated documents are shown in Figure 8–6, with each key process, document, or stored data numbered sequentially.

Purchasing: Sales forecasts (1) help plan the acquisition of merchandise for resale or the manufacture of a company's products. Often a **purchase order** (PO) is prepared from a sales forecast. The inventory system also generates a message that more merchandise (parts in this example) is needed when stock falls below a predetermined reorder point (2). Usually this reorder point is sufficiently high to allow time for shipment from the vendor. With this input from the inventory system, a **purchase requisition** (PR) (3) is sent to the purchasing department, which prepares a PO (4) for the needed merchandise.

Purchasing must determine the appropriate vendor to supply the merchandise. A formal purchase requisition may not be issued. In some cases, the generation of a purchase order is automated. The purchase order can be viewed as the original source document that initiates the expenditure cycle. A copy of ProYacht's purchase order is illustrated in Figure 8–7. In this figure, the part number, part description, quantity, price, discount, date, and vendor name and address are essential data for this purchase transaction. These data are contained in the inventory or vendor files. One copy of the purchase order is held in purchasing, and the original is sent to the vendor (5). A data flow diagram illustrating this transaction is illustrated in Figure 8–8.

FIGURE 8-6   *Expenditure Cycle*

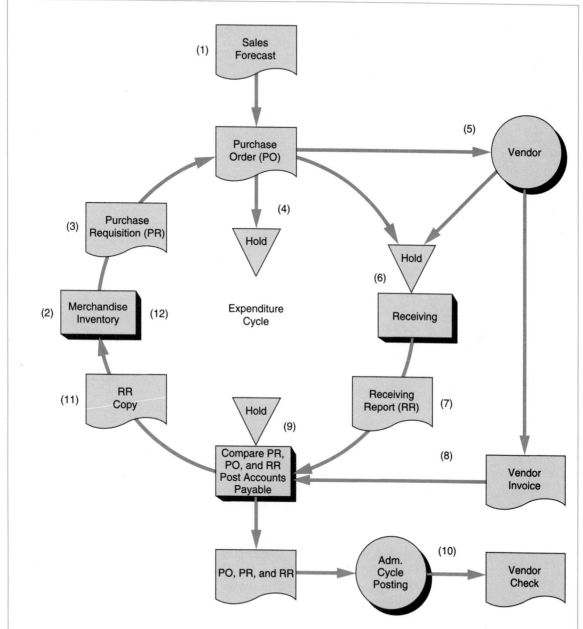

SOURCE: Adapted with permission from J. Davis, W. Alderman, and L. Robinson, *Accounting Information Systems: A Cycle Approach* (New York: Wiley & Sons, 1990), p. 26.

FIGURE 8–7

ProYacht, Inc.
Purchase Order

ProYacht, Inc.			Purchase Order	
100 Bay Street			Number _____	
Annapolis, MD 21404			Date _____	

Vendor Name _____

Address _____

Shipping Instructions _____

Part Number	Quantity	Description	Unit Price	Total Price

Subtotal _____

Discount / Terms _____

Total _____

Approval _____

Receiving: In the receiving transaction, the vendor sends the merchandise to ProYacht's parts division (6). When the goods are received at the warehouse, a clerk prepares a **receiving report** (RR) (7), which indicates the items received, how many were received, and the date. In systems similar to ProYacht's, the original receiving report (11) and the merchandise are forwarded to inventory to replenish stock (12). This transaction may also be accomplished via a computer terminal located in the receiving department, so that inventory balances are updated as soon as possible. In a manual system, a copy is retained in the accounts payable department, where it is compared with the requisition (3), purchase order (4), and vendor invoice (8). At ProYacht, many of these transaction activities are processed using a computer as a batch once a day. A data flow diagram illustrating this transaction is illustrated in Figure 8–9.

Cash Disbursement and Accounts Payable: If all the paperwork (or records in a computer system)—including the purchase requisition, purchase order, receiving report, and

FIGURE 8–8

*Purchase
Processing and
Data Flow*

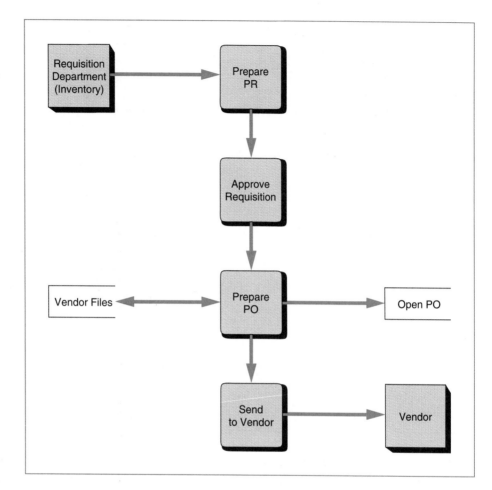

vendor invoice — is in agreement (9), accounts payable is posted, a cash disbursement is authorized, and a check (10) is written to the vendor for payment of the invoice. The data flow for this transaction is also shown in Figure 8–9. The actual processing of this cash disbursement is part of the administrative cycle, which is described later in this chapter. If only partial shipments are received, then partial payments are made. The purchase requisition, purchase order, and receiving report copies are then filed.

In summary, the expenditures cycle starts with either a forecasted need or an existing inventory need and ends with an addition to inventory and an expenditure. Inventory is discussed later in this chapter.

Revenue Cycle   A typical **revenue cycle** consists of an order entry process (a sales order is entered), a shipping and inventory process (goods are picked from stock and shipped), a billing process (an invoice is sent to the customer), an accounts receivable process (records the

FIGURE 8–9

Receiving and Invoice Processing Data Flow

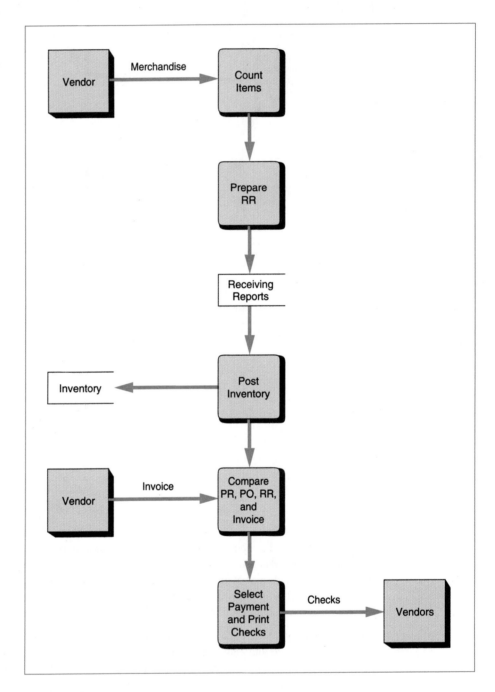

invoice amount), and a collections process. The sequence of these transaction processing activities and their linkage with associated documents is shown in Figure 8–10.

Order Entry: The initial transaction processing activity on the revenue cycle is the sale of merchandise (13), also referred to as an **order entry.** ProYacht's parts division collects only the minimal data for each sale, consisting of name and address of dealer, dealer number, component number and description, number of units sold, selling price, and credit or discount terms. For a more comprehensive MIS, this data set may be vastly increased in size to assist marketing management. Point-of-sale systems used by retail organizations can capture a large amount of data very quickly.

From the order entry, a sales order is prepared (14). The sales order is the original source document that starts the chain of events in the revenue cycle. In general, sales orders may originate from phone calls, purchase orders from customers, sales orders completed by salespersons at customer locations, or sales orders that are communicated via **Electronic Data Interchange (EDI),** in which the customer's computer "talks" to the supplier's computer. The received order is then edited as discussed in Chapter 5 for missing or incorrect data. Often, this editing is done electronically as the order is entered into the organization's computer system. Orders that fail the editing test are returned to the customer for completion or correction of data. A credit check is often made next, before credit is granted for the order. ProYacht, for example, references its accounts receivable history file to see a customer's account balance, payment history, and credit limit prior to authorization of a sale for credit. The sales order is then filed in an **open order file** (15) until it is completed and shipped. The open order file used to keep track of the order is especially useful when orders may be in process for a long time. This file is also useful when partial shipments are made because some components are out of stock and back ordered. A data flow diagram illustrating this transaction is illustrated in Figure 8–11.

Shipping and Inventory: Once an order is edited and approved, the stock on hand is checked through the inventory system. In many organizations, this process involves simply checking the data base via an online terminal. If the order cannot be filled, a back order is recorded in the open order file or on a copy of the sales order. A **back order** is a note to the customer and to the vendor indicating that the order will be shipped as soon as the merchandise is received in inventory.

A copy of the sales order is then sent to the warehouse where merchandise (parts in this example) is picked from stock. Inventory (16) is reduced by the number of parts that are picked. This process is often keyed into the inventory system from the warehouse. From the data on the sales order and the record of the actual number of parts picked, a **packing list** (17) is prepared for shipping the merchandise. Many organizations also use a computer for this activity. Merchandise is then shipped (18) to the customer. A **bill of lading** (19) accompanies this shipment, so that the carrier is aware of the nature and destination of the shipment and who will compensate the carrier. The data flow diagram 8–11 also shows these activities.

Invoicing (Customer Billing):   After the merchandise is shipped, a customer invoice (20) is prepared for the parts actually shipped. An **invoice** is a bill sent to a customer for

FIGURE 8–10 *Merchandising Revenue Cycle*

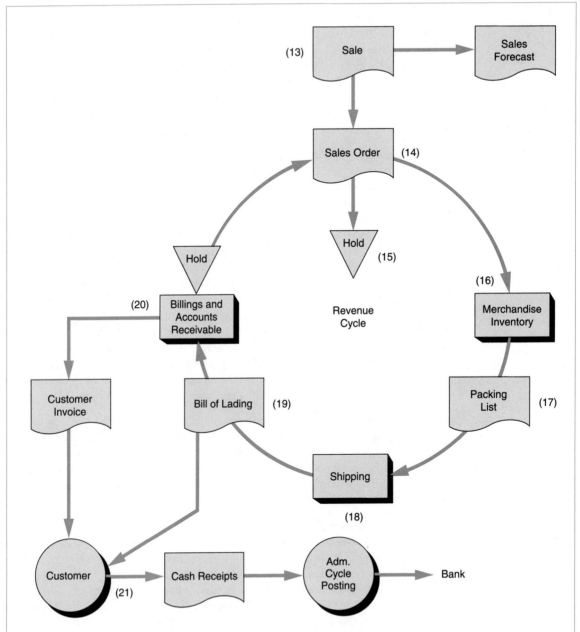

SOURCE: Adapted with permission from J. Davis, W. Alderman, and L. Robinson, *Accounting Information Systems: A Cycle Approach* (New York: Wiley & Sons, 1990), p. 26.

FIGURE 8–11

Sales and Order Entry Processing and Data Flow

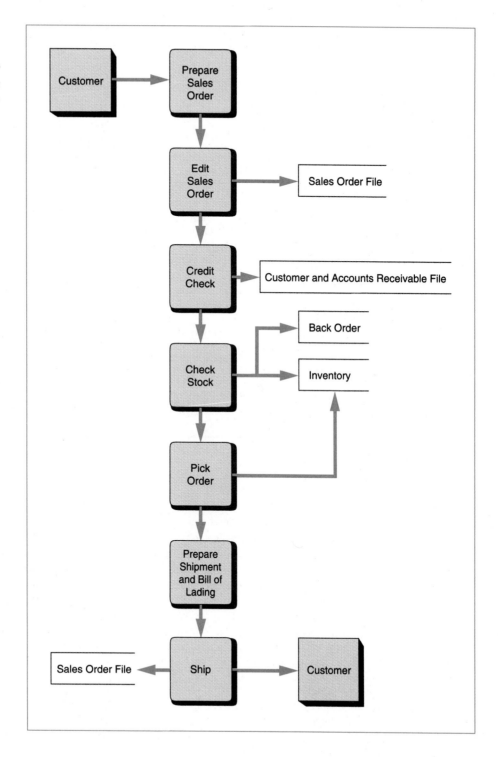

FIGURE 8–12   *ProYacht, Inc. Invoice*

ProYacht, Inc.
100 Bay Street
Annapolis, MD 21404

Sales Invoice
Number _____
Date _____

Customer Name _____
Address _____
_____
_____

Due Date _____
Terms _____

Product Number	Quantity		Date Shipped	Back Ordered	Description	Unit Price	Total Price
	Ordered	Shipped					

Subtotal

Discount

Total

services rendered or merchandise purchased. ProYacht's customer invoice is shown in Figure 8–12. This invoice indicates an invoice number, the name and address of the customer, the name and number of the products (parts) that were ordered, the number actually shipped, the shipping date, the billing terms, and the description and number of units that were back ordered. The number shipped is then multiplied by the selling price to get a total for each product; these amounts are added to obtain a total due on the invoice. All the data on the invoice are obtained from the customer file, the sales order, and the inventory records, which contain such details as the product price and description. The billing and cash collection transaction process is shown in the data flow diagram in Figure 8–13.

Accounts Receivable: A customer's **accounts receivable,** the accumulation of unpaid invoices, is increased by the amount of the billing transaction. Generally, a customer receives a monthly statement (invoice), which lists the details of all unpaid invoices. Past due amounts and finance charges are also noted. Usually a past due account has been

FIGURE 8–13

*Invoicing and
Accounts
Receivable
Processing and
Data Flow*

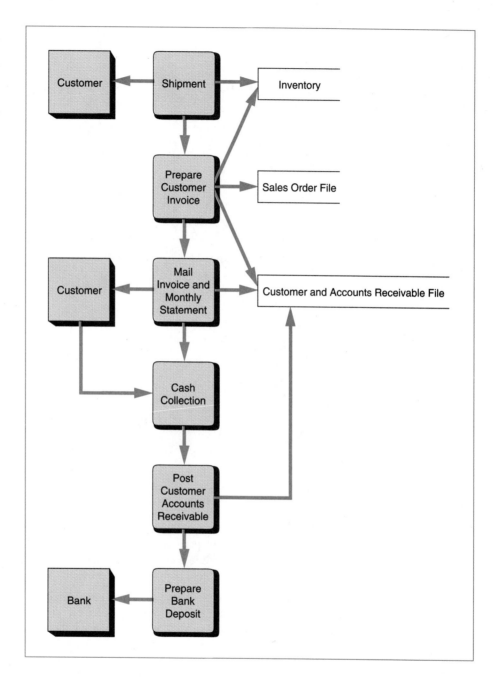

FIGURE 8–14

*Administrative or
Financial Cycle*

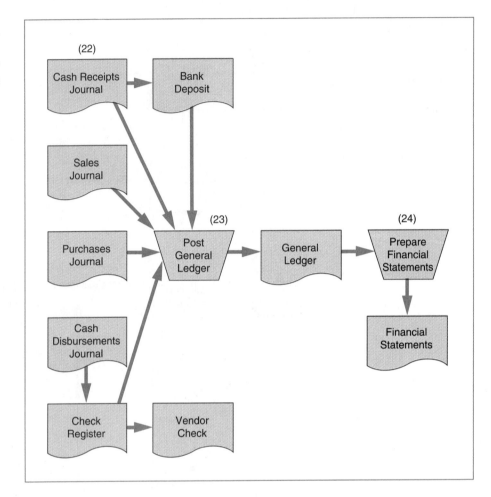

outstanding for at least 30 days. Management generally receives a list of receivables for all customers indicating the portion of each customer's account that is past due and by how long. This **aging schedule** is useful for managing collection activities and determining which unpaid invoices to write off as bad debts.

Cash Receipts (Collections): The revenue cycle is completed when the customer remits (21) cash or a check for the goods or services received. This cash is applied either to the individual invoice or to the overall customer balance, thereby reducing that customer's receivable balance. A **deposit slip** is then prepared, and the cash is deposited in the bank, as shown in the administrative cycle. This billing and collection process can be automated with EDI, using the bank as a clearinghouse.

*Administrative
and General
Ledger Cycle*

The **administrative cycle** is shown in Figure 8–14. All of the documents used in the transaction processing steps are numbered for control and reference purposes. Though called a cycle, it is more of a summarization and posting process. In this process the general ledger accounts for sales, expenses related to sales, inventory, accounts payable, accounts receivable, cash, payroll, and fixed assets are posted in batch from various journals where they are recorded.

The core of this administrative cycle is the **general ledger system,** which summarizes the organization's activities in financial terms. The general ledger is the major data source for financial statements and for financial planning in MIS. When a transaction occurs in the expenditure, revenue, or conversion cycle, a record of the transaction is entered (22) in a journal. A **journal** is simply a list of the financial aspects of each transaction. For example, the sales journal indicates the dollar amount of a sale and the general ledger accounts to which that amount is posted. After a sale, these postings reflect an increase in the sales and accounts receivable accounts, an increase in cost of goods sold, and a decrease in inventory. Sometimes, registers are used instead of a journal; for example, a check register is a list of all cash disbursements by check. A general journal is used for infrequent transactions, such as the purchase of equipment. In a computer system these journals are equivalent to transaction files.

The general ledger is the running balance of all the postings (23) from the various journals and registers. For example, the total of the sales recorded in the sales journal for one day is posted to the general ledger sales account. These postings, which update the balances in an organization's financial accounts, are generally made from journal summary data. However, they may occur concurrently with transaction processing and journal posting, in online computer systems. In summary, the general ledger represents the balances of an organization's financial accounts (such as the dollar amount in inventory or the accounts receivable), and journals represent logs of transaction activities in dollar amounts.

Financial statements are prepared on a periodic basis (24) from these general ledger accounts. These are used by such outside parties as bankers and regulatory authorities as well as by owners (stockholders) to assess the financial well-being of the organization.

Conversion Cycle

The TPS for a manufacturing organization is like that of a merchandising organization, except that a **conversion cycle** is added to record the transactions associated with the production of goods. This conversion cycle is shown in Figure 8–15. Two key differences distinguish the expenditure and revenue cycles for the manufacture of boats from the same cycles for the acquisition and sale of merchandise (parts). In the expenditure cycle, components and raw material are purchased for production rather than for sale as merchandise. The purchasing, receiving, and cash disbursement transactions are basically the same. In the revenue cycle, finished goods are sold rather than merchandise (parts) inventory; otherwise the sales, shipping, billing, and cash receipts transactions are the same.

The basic processing activities in a conversion cycle include the preparation of work orders from sales or a production plan, the requisition of materials, the allocation of costs to goods as they are produced, the accumulation of labor hours charged to production, and the addition to inventory of finished goods. For illustrative purposes, we discuss the conversion cycle for ProYacht's sailboat division, which manufactures ProYacht's

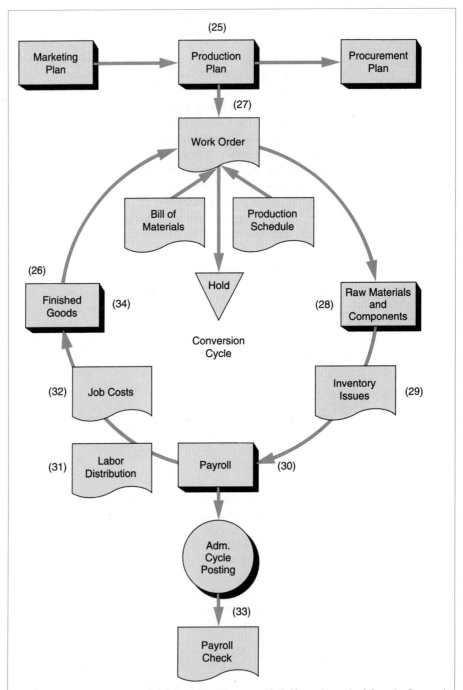

SOURCE: Adapted with permission from J. Davis, W. Alderman, and L. Robinson, *Accounting Information Systems: A Cycle Approach* (New York: Wiley & Sons, 1990), p. 28.

*Using
@Factory to
Blend Spirits*

Productivity improvements have been essential to the survival of Corby Distilleries, Ltd., a Canadian producer of over 100 different types of distilled spirits. In a declining market, Corby has found that blending one more batch of a particular whiskey per day can be the key to making a profit. Management wanted to improve productivity and cut costs by creating a real-time link between the factory floor and the spreadsheets management uses to make blending decisions.

Traditional methods had the blender locating a recipe for the desired whiskey in a spreadsheet, multiplying the ingredient proportions by the desired size of the batch, printing out the quantities for the recipe, and then punching in the data at the blending pump using pressure sensitive keys. This laborious task had great potential for error and wasted precious time during the production day. To solve this problem, Corby turned to a package called @Factory, which provides live connections between the cells within a spreadsheet and controllers on the factory floor. For Corby's, this eliminated the manual data transfer between the spreadsheets and the blending controller. This, in turn, eliminated data input errors and often saved enough time to actually generate an additional blending batch each day—all for a total investment of less than $8,000. As the plant manager said, "@Factory allows us to cycle more product through here without increasing the size of the plant."

SOURCE: Kelly R. Conatser, "The Spirit of @Factory," *Lotus,* November, 1990, pp. 56–60

sailboats. Currently, the sailboat division uses an online revenue system as well as an online expenditure system. The sailboat division develops a marketing plan indicating the number of boats it expects to sell. This plan and inventory information are input to the production plan (25). In turn, this production plan and component inventory data lead to a raw material and component procurement plan.

Work (Production) Order: In the beginning of the conversion cycle, **work orders** (or production orders) (27) are generated to replenish finished goods inventory (26) when stock gets below a certain point and such action is in compliance with the production plan. For example, if ProYacht is low on its inventory of 18-foot day sailers and the marketing plan indicates an increasing demand for these products, the company issues a work order for more. Since ProYacht carries a low inventory of larger boats, a single sale may trigger a work order because there may be no large boats in inventory. ProYacht uses a work order for each job like the one shown in Figure 8–16. It contains a work order number, date, product number, product name, the quantity to be manufactured, the materials (components) required, component part numbers, the work sequence (assembly instructions), the expected labor requirements, and the time schedule (or completion date) for the order. The data come from the **bill of materials,** which describes the components needed for each boat, the manufacturing sequence (plan) for each boat, and the **production schedule.** This work order, stored in the computer, provides ProYacht's

FIGURE 8–16   *ProYacht, Inc. Work Order*

ProYacht, Inc.
Work Order

Work Order Number   121
Date   11/15/92
Customer/Marina
(Optional)   _ _ _ _ _ _ _

Model (Product) Number	DS1800	Work Sequence		Labor Hours
Name	18' Day Sailer	Hull	1	360
		Fiber Glass & Gelcoat	2	240
Quantity to be Manufactured	20	Deck	3	80
Components Required		Join Hull & Deck	4	80
Bill of Material #	18	Cabin Millwork	n/a	
		Mast	5	80
Expected Starting Date	1/1/93	Rigging	6	80
Expected Completion Date	1/5/93	Total		920

FIGURE 8–17

*Conversion
Processing and
Data Flow*

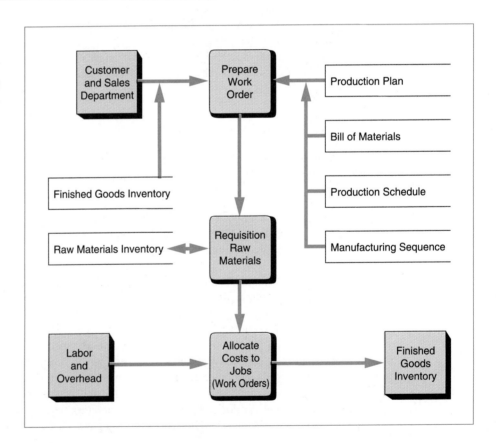

FIGURE 8–18   *Job Cost Sheet*

Date Job Started _____						Job / Work Order		
Date Job Completed _____						Number _____		
Scheduled Completion Date _____						Date _____		
Customer Number _____ Name _____								

| Dept No. | Material | | Direct Labor | | | Overhead | | |
	Requisition Number	Amount	Employee	Time	Amount	Hours	Rate	Total
Cost Summary								
Total Cost							_____	

production operations with the basic information it needs to assemble its boats. A data flow diagram detailing this transaction is presented in Figure 8–17.

Material Requisition: The second transaction required to produce the sailboats is the **requisition** (28) of raw materials or components. The components required by the work order are issued (29) to the production department. Requisition may be accomplished automatically if the production system is automated with **Computer-Aided Manufacturing (CAM)** or **Material Requirement Planning (MRP)** systems, which are described briefly in the next chapter.

Manufacturing Cost Allocation: In the next step, the factory workers assemble the sailboats, and the hours worked on each job are distributed (30 and 31) to each work order. Traditionally, these costs are detailed and summarized (32) on a **job cost sheet.** An appropriate labor rate is then used to assign a dollar amount to each work order (or job). At the same time, requisitioned materials and components and associated costs are posted (32) to these job cost sheets. Overhead is also allocated to each work order and posted (32) to the job cost sheet. **Overhead** is the total of all the costs associated with plant assets and administration. An example of a job cost sheet is shown in Figure 8–18. This sheet is used to accumulate all costs, including an amount for overhead, to a work order. At ProYacht, the data on this job cost sheet are stored in a computer file.

Labor distribution (31) is a record of the time spent on various work orders and other plant activities. Each employee's time is recorded (often on a **clock card**) in order to charge the appropriate amount to each work order. This time is often keyed in as the employee completes one work order and begins a new work order or another task such as setting up for a new order or maintaining the equipment.

Payroll: The clock cards generated in the previous step are usually compared with **time cards,** which record the times an employee enters or leaves the plant. In theory, the total time an employee spends in the plant should match the time the employee spends on various tasks, including work orders. The time recorded on time cards is used to prepare the payroll (check) register and issue a payroll check (33).

Inventory: When the conversion process is complete at ProYacht, the assembled sailboats, along with their job costs and work order, are transferred to finished goods (34) for sale. Finished goods inventory is increased by the number of completed sailboats.

8.3 Summary and Operational Use of Transaction Data

All the documents and processing activities for the transaction cycles of a manufacturing company are summarized in Figure 8–19; the administrative portion is abbreviated.

In the revenue cycle, a sales order is used to initiate a sale and the reduction of inventory. This sales order is often prompted by a dealer's purchase order. Once the manufacturing firm or the warehouse receives the sales order, it is authorized to assemble the merchandise for shipment. Sometimes the shipment differs from the order; in some companies, a packing list is prepared of those goods that are to be shipped. The difference is a back order to be shipped when the rest of the merchandise is finished. Sometimes a copy of the sales order is used as a packing list. If the goods are shipped by common carrier, then shipping instructions, an identification of the contents, and the terms by which the carrier will be paid are specified in a bill of lading. After the merchandise is shipped, an invoice (bill) is sent to the customer specifying what was sold and shipped and the amount due. The customer in turn uses this invoice to pay the amount due on receipt of the merchandise. In this manner, a firm maintains tight control over sales, inventory, and collections. Again, many PC software houses offer excellent microcomputer **sales order processing systems,** which automate this whole transaction process for small organizations.

In the conversion cycle, a production plan and the shortage of finished goods trigger the generation of a work order. These work orders explain to production personnel what, how, when, and how much to make. Work orders are used to schedule production facilities and personnel and to request raw material and components for production. They may be referenced at any time by operating personnel to monitor the progress of an order. For example, if a customer inquires about an order, the production manager can look at the work orders, usually on a computer terminal, and tell the customer the order's current status or projected completion date. Inventory issues (sometimes called materials requisitions) document the reduction of inventory and the charge of inventory to a particular work order. This transaction process helps maintain control over inventory. Job cost sheets—one for each work order—are the basic document in a production process. In many cases, these documents are stored electronically. All productive labor hours and

FIGURE 8–19 *Revenue, Disbursement, and Conversion Transaction Cycles for a Manufacturing Organization*

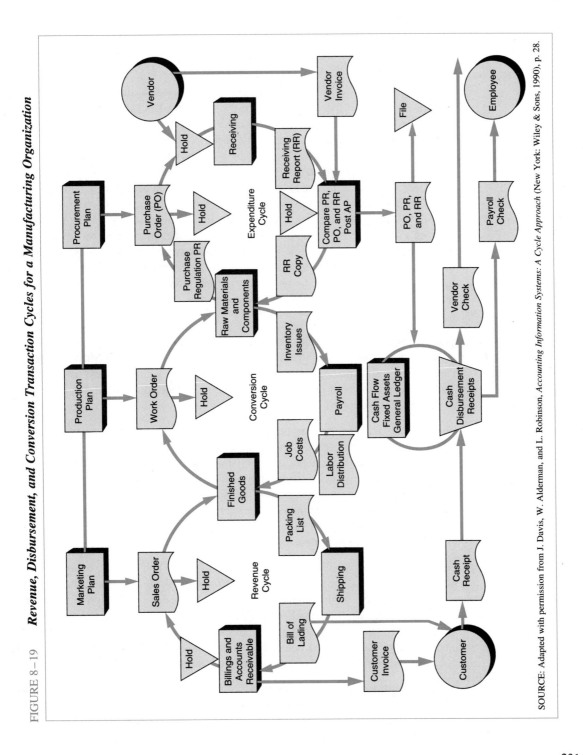

SOURCE: Adapted with permission from J. Davis, W. Alderman, and L. Robinson, *Accounting Information Systems: A Cycle Approach* (New York: Wiley & Sons, 1990), p. 28.

their costs, materials and their costs, and manufacturing overhead charged to a job are noted on these sheets or their computerized counterpart. The total of these costs constitutes the cost of a job (or work order). This cost can then be used to help determine the profitability of a product.

In the expenditure cycle, purchase requisitions are used to authorize the purchasing department to obtain more inventory. Purchasing considers sales trends, approves the request, and sends a purchase order to a vendor. This act constitutes a binding contract to purchase certain merchandise under some specified terms. The vendor then ships merchandise to the purchasing company, where a receiving clerk counts the items. The clerk's receiving report is then compared with the requisition, the purchase order, and ultimately, the vendor invoice to be sure that they all match before any payment is made to the vendor. Meanwhile, the components (if that is what was ordered) are added to inventory. Management keeps a running record of inventory by adding component receipts and subtracting component requisitions so that production personnel always know what is in stock. In such a **perpetual inventory system,** clerical personnel need only enter a stock number at a display screen to determine the current status of an inventory item. Many PC software vendors offer systems that can automate this entire transaction process for even the smallest companies.

8.4 Electronic Transaction Processing Input and Output

Point-of-Sale (POS) Systems

Many organizations have such a high volume of transactions and a large amount of detail about each transaction that specialized systems must be devised. Such systems are required in sales, in manufacturing operations, and in transacting business with suppliers, vendors, banks, and other divisions. These systems include Point-of-Sale (POS) systems, CAM, and EDI systems.

The volume of transactions in some organizations is so high that the formal preparation of sales orders would be impractical. On the other hand, these organizations still need to reduce inventory by the amount of merchandise sold and charge customers. The data requirements of many organizations may also dictate that a tremendous amount of data must be collected about the nature of the sale and the customer. Department stores, discount merchants, and supermarkets are examples of organizations with this data input transaction processing problem. To help alleviate this problem, special **Point-of-Sale (POS) systems** have been developed to process sales transactions.

For example, many retail companies use an **electronic cash register** equipped with a holographic light (or light pen) that reads the bar code—the **Universal Product Code**—present on every product. The light passes over the bar code, and the product number is read into the register's internal memory and matched with price, sale, and discount information to generate the current price of the item. Prices of all items are then totaled electronically. The sales clerk enters the amount tendered, and the register automatically computes the correct tax and change and reduces the store's inventory by the units sold.

In large department stores, a salesperson may be led by a sequence of data entry steps to key the customer number, the stock number, and the quantity of units sold. The register communicates via a local area network to a larger store computer, which references the

FIGURE 8–20

*Holographic Data
Input*

customer information to check credit and inventory information for prices. The system then posts the amount of the sale to receivables and reduces inventory by the amount purchased.

In large supermarkets, a holographic light shines up through the checkout counter; as merchandise is passed over the light, the Universal Product Code is read, as illustrated in Figure 8–20. This code is matched with prices, sales are recorded, taxes are calculated, totals are generated, inventory is reduced, and change is computed. In each illustration, a great volume of accurate data can be collected quickly with minimal human intervention.

Saving Money and Time at Denny's with POS

By their own admission, managers at the over 1,000 company-owned Denny's restaurants in 46 states spent too much time each week manually entering data into a paper-based payroll and sales system. This process turned them into bookkeepers who were bogged down in paperwork and, as a result, not spending adequate time training employees, overseeing pricing of entrees, and handling customer relations.

To remedy this problem, Denny's has installed a Point-of-Sale (POS) system in each restaurant that consists of three to five terminals for data input by servers, another terminal for a cash register, a personal computer in the back office, and a printer in the kitchen. Servers enter data into a terminal, and information from each restaurant is summarized and sent to company headquarters on a daily basis.

Benefits from the POS system were immediately measurable—a revenue increase in excess of 1 percent resulting from sales previously not reported (for example, free cups of coffee or food given to friends). This saving represents an additional $10 million per year for the 1,000 stores. Additional benefits include the time saved in administrative activities—about 14 hours per week per store, which translates into about $25 million annually. This time is now directed toward customer service and other managerial activities. Other benefits from the POS system include more efficient information gathering on new employees and the identification of problems that hinder restaurant operations.

SOURCE: Charlotte A. Krause, "Denny's POS Effort," *Computerworld*, May 27, 1991, pp. 81, 84.

Manufacturing Transaction Data Input

The amount of units produced, the time needed to produce them, and the components used in them need to be entered in an expeditious way on the factory floor. Company employees cannot waste precious time filling out forms when they should be assembling products. Companies need information on production activities to post costs to job cost sheets, to track the status of work orders, to respond to customer status inquiries, and to reschedule work orders if necessary. To record these transactions efficiently, some companies use **turn-around documents,** or cards on which a worker enters only the time worked and the number of units processed. All other data concerning the job are already precoded or prepunched for the employee. As a result, the data are quickly "turned around" (sent back) with a minimum amount of new information—the number of units produced and the number of hours worked. If this process is automated, the employee may simply fill in the blanks on a terminal at each workstation. Bar codes (like the Universal Product Code) can also be used to track the assembly and the stocking of components and products. The terminals can be linked to a larger system via a LAN if data on assembly and job status are needed.

Any combination of computer assistance in terms of input and control is called Computer-Aided Manufacturing (CAM); the whole conversion operation can be computerized via a **Computer-Integrated Manufacturing (CIM)** system. In these situations, all transactions are not only performed electronically, they automatically trigger the next transaction step. CAM and CIM systems are reviewed in detail in Chapter 9.

With the advent of the telecommunication systems and computer networks (presented in Chapter 7), an organization can easily carry on business operations with another company located a continent away. The figures illustrating the transaction cycles show such documents as invoices, purchase orders, remittances, and checks that are used to communicate with customers and suppliers. Just as internal company documents can be handled electronically, these external documents can be transmitted electronically using Electronic Data Interchange (EDI), described in chapter 7. Universal Product Codes can now accommodate data input, and newly developed standards can enable one company to communicate electronically with another.

Because ProYacht, Inc. conducts business with a large number of customers and suppliers, it has instituted EDI for its sailboat manufacturing operation. As shown in Figure 8–21, EDI with other companies expedites ProYacht's purchasing, merchandise receipt, and cash disbursement transactions. In the ProYacht Sail Boat Division's EDI system, the production scheduling process alerts the purchasing department to electronically send a purchase order to its vendors' sales departments. The receipt of the purchase order is then electronically acknowledged by the vendor. Prior to the shipment of the needed components from the vendor, an advanced shipment notice is sent electronically from the vendor. Similarly, when the shipment is received, an acknowledgement of delivery is sent electronically from ProYacht back to the vendor. Finally, the shipment is paid for through the use of Electronic Funds Transfer (EFT) from ProYacht's bank to the vendor's bank.

8.5 Transaction Processing Packages

General Accounting Packages

A wide assortment of transaction processing packages are available for large mainframes as well as personal computers. These packages range from basic accounting packages to highly specialized transaction processing packages for specific industry needs.

Accounting packages may be designed to process specific types of transactions—for example, payroll, inventory, accounts receivable, accounts payable, client billing, check writing, sales orders, job cost systems, and general ledger systems. The most common accounting package is a general ledger system, because all organizations have a general ledger. These **separate application packages** are independent of one another and automate only one or two areas of an organization. When applications are independent, a sales order transaction does not automatically update inventory and accounts receivable. These subsequent transactions must be processed as separate steps, called runs. These systems—particularly older packages that are run on large mainframes—tend to process large volumes of transactions in batch mode for efficiency and speed. Data are often stored on magnetic tape.

For an organization that needs to automate and interrelate its transaction processing, an integrated accounting system may be better. In an **integrated accounting system,** an entry in one part of the system automatically updates all other applications in the system. These packages are usually based on an integrated database. For example, the entry of a

FIGURE 8–21   *Electronic Data Interchange at ProYacht, Inc.*

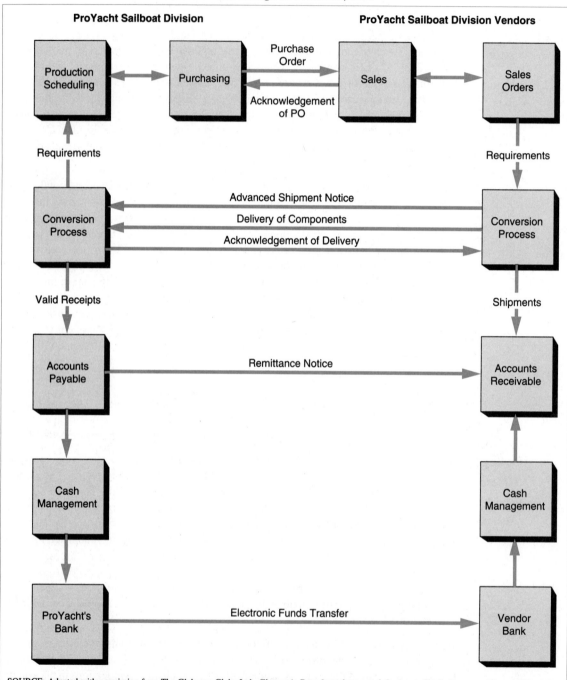

SOURCE: Adapted with permission from The Globecon Globe Ltd., *Electronic Data Interchange and Corporate Trade Payments,* Financial Executive Research Foundation (FERF), Morristown, NJ, 1988, p. 64, and Corporate Controller, Navistar International Corporation.

sales order automatically reduces inventory and increases accounts receivable. Online systems tend to be integrated because they can often update or access data pertaining to several transaction cycles. For example, a salesperson may inquire about the status of a sales order for a boat that is being manufactured by ProYacht.

The types of transactions that can be handled by these separate and integrated packages are actually quite varied. Figure 8–22 shows the types of transactions processed, the data that are stored, and the reports that are available on a number of PC packages. More integrated and more expensive packages have more features available. In other words, mainframe packages tend to be much more complex and able to process much larger volumes of transactions.

The most expensive package may not always be the best for a company's particular circumstances. Expensive packages may require too much data and provide more reports than are needed and, as a result, strangle the firm's operations. In these cases, small, simple packages may be far easier to use, require less data, and still generate the necessary reports.

Special Industry Packages

For some firms, a general accounting package is more than adequate. However, in some industries, transactions are very specialized. With sufficient demand, specialized transaction processing software is developed to meet these data processing requirements. Because pharmacists have special needs for inventory and insurance reimbursements, many specialized reports and careful control are needed in these two areas. The job cost system used for a typical manufacturing firm does not work for a dairy farmer who must track the productivity of livestock. Similarly, a physician has special needs for patient care, billing, and insurance claim filing, and a car dealership has special financing, inventory, and commission needs.

With these few examples, it is easy to see that neither separate application software nor integrated accounting software is suitable for many businesses. Specialized packages are the only way to accommodate these needs.

8.6 Summary

A TPS is used to convert raw data from operations into information that is useful to management. The system can be batch or online. Data collected from operations and from the external environment of the organization are input into the TPS. Data must sometimes be transmitted to a transaction processing center via telecommunications equipment to be processed and stored for future use. Data retrieved from storage are processed into information for many operational, tactical, and strategic uses. These include formal reports or monitor displays of operations control information, managerial information, financial statements, and managerial inquiry.

All the transaction processing activities in an organization's processing cycle have these essential input, processing, storage, and output characteristics. Transaction cycles include the expenditure cycle, the revenue cycle, the administrative cycle, and the conversion cycle. The major transactions in the expenditure cycle are purchasing, receiving, and cash disbursements; for the revenue cycle, major transactions are order entry, shipping, billing and accounts receivable, and cash receipts. The major transactions in the

FIGURE 8–22

Personal Computer Package Transactions, Data, and Reports

Typical Transaction Processing Characteristics	
Accounts Payable	*Accounts Receivable*
Processes Transactions by:	Processes Transactions by:
Single Invoices	Sales Invoice
Multiple Invoices	Credit Memos
Credit Memos	Applies Cash Receipts to:
Debit Memos	Specific Items
Recurring Invoices	Multiple Open Items
Handwritten Checks	Handles Cash Sales
Stores Data by Vendor	Stores Data by Customer
Calculates Discount by Due Date	Computes Discounts
Supports Partial Payment	Supports Partial Payment
Captures Job Code	Allows Manual Override of Terms
Selects Invoices to Be Paid	Permits Write-offs for Uncollectibles
Combines Multiple Invoices for Payments	Processes Bank Deposits
Provides Batch Control	Provides Batch Control
Writes Checks Automatically	Calculates Finance Charges Automatically
Data Typically Stored for Each Transaction	
Accounts Payable	*Accounts Receivable*
Maintains and Recalls Data Fields	Maintains and Recalls Data Fields on
on Screen for Each Vendor:	Screen for Each Customer:
Vendor Number	Customer Number
Vendor Name	Customer Name
Vendor Address	Customer Address
Purchase History	Sales History
Data and Amount of Last Purchase	Finance Charges
General Distribution of	Date and Amount of Last Sale
Expenses, Payables, or Assets	Tax Codes
Terms	Terms
Contract Identification	Credit Limit
Phone Number	Salesperson Code
Tax Information	Contract Identification
Payment Data	Phone Number
	Collection Data
Common Reports	
Accounts Payable	*Accounts Receivable*
Purchasing Data by:	Sales Data by:
Vendor	Customer
Product	Product
Department	Salesperson
Check Register and Check	Department
Cash Requirements	Cash Receipts Journal
Payables (Aging—Details and	Receivables (Aging—Details and
Balance) by:	Balance) by:
Vendor	Customer
Due Date	Due Date

conversion cycle are work order preparation, materials requisition, manufacturing and cost allocation, payroll, and inventory.

Organizations that have a large volume of transactions need such special systems as POS, CIM, and EDI to cope with the amount and detail of transactions. Moreover, many software houses have written specialized software for organizations with special information requirements.

In general, transaction processing activities are at the core of a business information system. They aid in the ongoing operations of the organization as well as collect and store data for the management decision-making activities that are discussed at length in the next few chapters.

Key Terms

accounts receivable
administrative cycle
aging schedule
back order
batch mode
bill of lading
bill of materials
block code
classification system
clock card
Computer-Aided Manufacturing (CAM)
Computer Integrated Manufacturing (CIM)
conversion cycle
data processing
deposit slip
electronic cash registers
Electronic Data Interchange (EDI)
expenditure cycle
financial statements
general ledger system
group code
integrated accounting system
invoice
job cost sheet
journal

labor distribution
Material Requirement Planning (MRP)
mnemonic code
online mode
open order file
order entry
overhead
packing slip
perpetual inventory system
Point-of-Sale (POS) systems
production schedule
purchase order
purchase requisition
real-time processing
receiving report
requisition
revenue cycle
sales order processing systems
separate application packages
sequential code
time cards
transaction cycle
Transaction Processing Systems (TPS)
turn-around documents
Universal Product Code
work orders

Review Questions

1. Beginning with the sale of an item, list in order the basic activities in a revenue cycle, noting the appropriate input, output, files, and documents for each activity.

2. Beginning with the purchase requisition, list in sequence the basic activities in an expenditure cycle, noting the appropriate input, output, files, and documents.

3. What transaction processing activities are common to any transaction cycle?

4. How does the TPS support MIS, DSS, and EIS?

5. Name the fundamental transaction processing cycles in most organizations.

6. Contrast batch, online, and real-time processing.

7. Name several ways of capturing and entering data into a transaction processing cycle.

8. Compare a sequential, block, group, and mnemonic code.

9. Describe what happens if insufficient stock is available for a customer order for (a) a retail store and (b) a manufacturing firm.

10. When is an invoice sent to the customer? What is included on an invoice?

11. What files, documents, and reports are used in cash collection activities?

12. What is a journal? What is a work order and what function does it provide?

13. Describe the function of a job cost sheet. How are labor hours charged to a job? How can this be done electronically?

14. What is a perpetual inventory system and how do the revenue and expenditure cycles affect it? What is an integrated accounting system?

15. How can the Universal Product Code aid in transaction processing?

Discussion Questions

1. Consider the conversion cycle with its data input, files, processing activities, and output, as well as its interface with the revenue and expenditure cycles. Propose a way to automate this process and link it to a CIM system.

2. Consider the expenditure cycle with its input, processing, output, files, and links with the revenue and conversion cycles. Explain how EDI can be used to make this process more efficient and reduce inventory.

3. Data gathered during the processing of day-to-day transactions can be used to assist management with decision making. Select any type of retail merchant and describe the data that can be gathered via a POS system to assist marketing management with its decisions.

4. Develop a group code for a sales transaction at a department store in which salespersons are paid on a commission basis and sales are linked to an inventory system that automatically purchases more merchandise when stock is low.

5. Mountain Brook Manufacturing, which manufactures light gage steel products, has decided to convert from an antiquated file management system to a

contemporary DSS and EIS to aid in management decision making. Rather than develop an online transaction processing system at the same time, the company is keeping the old batch transaction processing system with its periodic weekly reports, and developing only a state-of-the-art DSS and EIS, because "that is where the real payoff is." Comment on the company's systems development strategy.

Case 8–1
Pinta Company

Pinta Company is a regional discount chain in the southeastern United States selling general merchandise. The company may acquire a POS system for use in its stores. Three types of firms typically use POS systems—large retailers, grocery stores, and fast food chains. Pinta would probably employ cash registers that use holographic bar code readers to read the Universal Product Code that is printed on packages. Because the equipment is very expensive, Pinta's president wants a report on POS systems, including a survey as to what companies are employing POS systems and why they have adopted them.

(SOURCE: CMA adapted.)

Case Questions

1. Explain how a POS system operates.

2. What are the advantages of a POS system with respect to the quality of data and management's use of data?

3. How would such a system interface with other TPSs?

4. What data would you suggest Pinta capture via a POS system?

5. What other POS options should the company consider?

Case 8–2
Weekender Corporation

Weekender Corporation owns and operates 15 large departmentalized retail hardware stores in major metropolitan areas of the southwestern United States. The stores carry a wide variety of merchandise, but the major thrust is toward the weekend "do-it-yourselfer." The company's business has almost doubled since 1980.

Each retail store acquires its merchandise from the company's centrally located warehouse. Consequently, the warehouse must maintain an up-to-date and well-stocked inventory ready to meet the demands of the individual stores.

If Weekender Corporation wishes to maintain its competitive position with other companies' stores in its marketing area, it must improve purchasing and inventory procedures. The company's stores must have the proper goods to meet customer demand, and the warehouse, in turn, must have the goods available. The number of company stores, the number of inventory items carried, the volume of business—all are providing pressures to change from basically manual data processing routines to automated data processing procedures. Recently the company has investigated two different approaches to automation—computer batch processing and computer online processing. No decision has been reached on the approach to be followed. Top management has determined that the following items should have high priority in the new system procedures:

1. Rapid ordering to replenish warehouse inventory stocks with as little delay as possible

2. Quick filling and shipping of merchandise to the stores (this involves determining whether sufficient stock exists)

3. Some indication of inventory activity

4. Perpetual records in order to determine inventory level quickly by item number

In the warehouse, stock is stored in bins and is located by an inventory number. The numbers should be listed sequentially on the bins to facilitate locating items for shipment. However, this system is not always followed, making some items difficult to locate. When a retail store needs merchandise, a three-part merchandise request form is completed — one copy is kept by the store and two copies are mailed to the warehouse the next day. If the merchandise requested is on hand, the goods are delivered to the store accompanied by the third copy of the request. The second copy is filed at the warehouse. If the quantity of goods on hand is not sufficient to fill the order, the warehouse sends the quantity available and notes the quantity shipped by the warehouse. At the end of each day, back order memos are sent to the purchasing department. When the ordered goods are received, they are checked at the receiving area, and a receiving report is prepared. One copy of the receiving report is retained at the receiving area, one is forwarded to the accounts payable department, and one is filed at the warehouse with the purchase memorandum.

In the purchasing department, purchase orders are prepared when purchase memoranda are received from the warehouse. Vendor catalogs are used to select the best source for the requested goods, and the purchase order is prepared and mailed. Copies of the order are sent to the accounts payable department and the receiving area; one copy is retained in the purchasing department. When the receiving report arrives in the purchasing department, it is compared with the purchase order on file and the invoice before forwarding the invoice to the accounts payable department for payment. The purchasing department strives periodically to evaluate vendors for financial soundness, reliability, and trade relationships. However, because of the tremendous volume of requests received from the warehouse, this activity currently does not have a high priority. Each week, a report of open purchase orders is prepared to determine if any action should be taken on overdue deliveries. This report is prepared manually from scanning the field of outstanding purchase orders.

(SOURCE: CMA adapted)

Case Questions

1. Weekender Corporation is considering two possible automated data processing systems — a batch processing system, and an online computer system.
   (a) Which system would best meet the needs of Weekender Corporation? Explain your answer.
   (b) Briefly describe the basic equipment configuration that Weekender would need for the system recommended in (a).
   (c) (optional) Using a system flowchart describe your suggested solution.

2. Regardless of the type of system selected by Weekender Corporation, data files must be established.
   (a) Identify the data files that would be necessary.
   (b) Briefly indicate the type of data that would be contained in each file.

Management
Information Systems

9

Introduction

A Management Information Systems (MIS) is defined in Chapter 2 as "an integrated user–machine system for providing information to support operations, management, and decision-making functions in an organization." [1] An MIS is designed to provide reports for managers so that they can make decisions and manage their segments of the organization. MIS reports use information stored in a data base by the Transaction Processing System (TPS) to provide information via specific application programs for operational and tactical decision making. As shown schematically in Figure 9–1, MIS reports provide information for structured as well as semistructured decisions.

They include:

1. Reports scheduled on a periodic basis, such as a monthly sales analysis by product line

2. Exception reports, such as the variance from production standards

3. Demand reports, such as the status of a particular sales order in the production process

These reports may be in printed form, displayed on a monitor, or used by another program to actually make a decision for management based on predetermined criteria. The automatic processing of a purchase order when stock is low is an example of this last type of output.

---

[1] Gordon B. Davis and Margaret H. Olson, *Management Information Systems,* 2nd ed. (New York: McGraw Hill, 1985), p. 6.

FIGURE 9–1

*Information
Systems and
Decision Making*

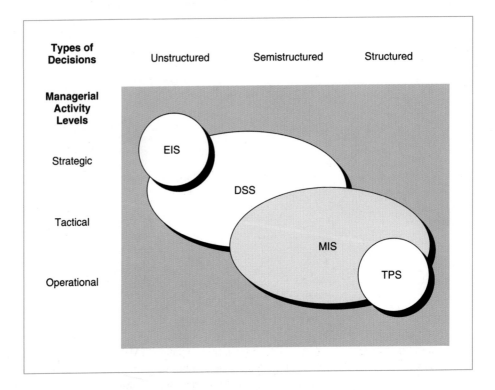

These MIS reports aid management's decision making in many of the ways outlined in Chapter 3. For example, an MIS report can help identify an opportunity to expand in an existing market. Once the market is identified, the relationships set forth in the reports among such key variables as prices, sales, and product costs can be used to suggest several possible courses of action with regard to a pricing strategy. Next, using the data in these reports, a Decision Support System (DSS) can evaluate many options and suggest the best course of action. Finally, the MIS can be used to monitor various activities to ensure compliance with the course of action selected by management. For example, productivity can be monitored in terms of labor hours, machine hours, and the throughput.

In general, the basic MIS model for supporting tactical decision making and operational control is shown in Figure 9–2. Managers use MIS information to make strategic and, to a much larger degree, tactical and operational decisions, which direct the organization's course of action. These decisions control the physical activities of the organization—the input of resources, the conversion of these resources into products and services, and the sale and distribution of the products and services to customers. The operations are controlled and monitored by the TPS, which collects data for the data base. Data are also collected from the external environment. The management information system then uses these data to provide management with information for its managerial control and decision-making activities.

FIGURE 9–2   *Decision Making, Information Systems, and the Physical Transformation Process of an Organization*

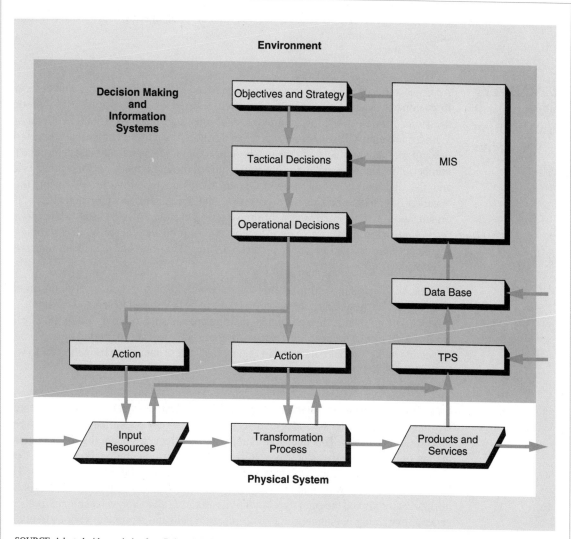

SOURCE: Adapted with permission from Robert A. Leitch and K. Roscoe Davis, *Accounting Information Systems*, (Englewood Cliffs, NJ: Prentice-Hall, 1992), p. 31.

To further explore the nature of Management Information Systems, their use, and the value they can add to an organization, we look at each major functional area of an organization—marketing, production, and finance. We consider them in this order because this general order is used in managerial decision making in progressive, market-oriented organizations.

9.1 Marketing Management Information Systems

An organization's marketing management needs an MIS to deliver its product or service to customers. Marketing activities are often referred to as the "four Ps"—product decisions, pricing decisions, promotion decisions, and place (distribution) decisions. With a marketing MIS, an organization can develop products that fit market characteristics and get these products into the hands of customers. Management must determine the number of products to make, the characteristics of these products, an appropriate price, and the distribution of these products. In today's competitive environment, these "market-oriented" decisions are critical to the success of most organizations. The organization with a superior system for assessing customer needs, establishing prices, promoting its product effectively, distributing its product efficiently, and serving its customers has a decided advantage. These activities, decisions, and data requirements are noted in Figure 9–3.

These activities begin with market research, which leads to product development and planning. From these plans, a marketing plan can be developed to sell and distribute the product. The product is then promoted, distributed, and sold, often on credit. Finally, an organization must service its customers. All these activities are supported by a data base consisting of the various data noted in Figure 9–3. These data come from the TPS as well as from other MISs and external sources.

Market Research

Product development and planning begins with an effective system of market research. Given its overall business strategy, management must first determine the products that meet customer needs. This decision requires an intelligence system that tracks current market trends and forecasts new developments and their potential market impact. Consider again ProYacht, Inc., which manufactures and markets sailboats of all sizes. The market research department at ProYacht collects data on current sales and studies existing market trends and the economic conditions affecting all major water sport markets. In general, marketing personnel use market research data and reports on various trends to develop a market strategy. For example, assume ProYacht determines that sales of smaller sailboats are increasing throughout its markets. On a general economic note, market research finds that disposable income is rising, and that young people have a significant impact on the purchase of recreational equipment, especially windsurfers. From these studies, ProYacht management decides to enter the windsurfer market by manufacturing these smaller boats using excess factory capacity. These boats will be marketed through ProYacht's existing distribution networks. Figure 9–4 shows the revised ProYacht, Inc. organizational chart with the new windsurfer manufacturing department added to the sailboat division.

FIGURE 9–3

Marketing
Management
Information
Systems Data Flow

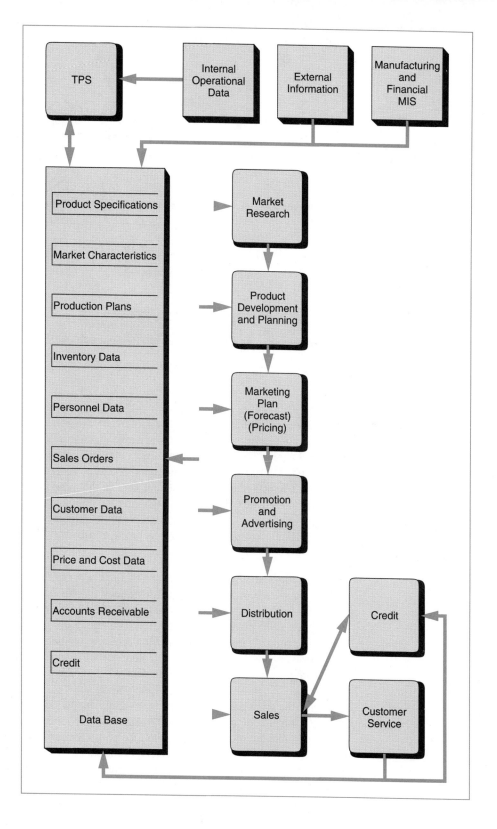

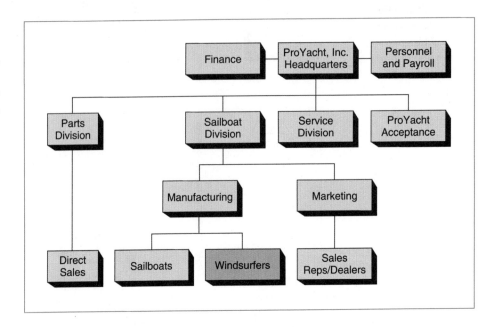

FIGURE 9–4

Revised
ProYacht, Inc.
Organizational
Chart

Product
Development

To enter the windsurfer market, ProYacht must develop a windsurfer model that can be manufactured in its current facilities at a cost that allows the company to compete on a price and quality basis with manufacturers already in the market. The Computer-Aided Design (CAD) and Computer-Integrated Manufacturing (CIM) techniques discussed briefly in Chapter 8 and in more detail later in this chapter can help develop this new product. CAD and CIM use the computer as a tool to manipulate design features, assembly sequences, components, and costs to attain the best design in terms of customer needs, financial resources and manufacturing constraints.

Marketing Plan

Based on the design for a new windsurfer, ProYacht can develop a marketing plan that includes a sales forecast and a pricing strategy for this new product. A **sales forecast** usually requires input from field sales personnel who have firsthand information about trends such as the potential demand for windsurfers. Sales management adds their global view of a product's market potential from economic and industry MIS reports to develop the forecasting model. Regression and other statistical models are often used to incorporate these relevant factors into the model.

Input into the pricing strategy for the new windsurfer includes an estimate of demand, the pricing structure of competitors, an analysis of economic conditions, the projected disposable income of the target market, the cost structure of the product, and the company's portfolio of existing products. Data should be readily available on competitors' prices, overall market demand (historical sales volume), and general economic indicators (inflation and interest rate levels).

Promotion and Advertising

Following the development of a marketing plan, a specific plan for advertising and promotion must be formulated. Information on the effectiveness of previous marketing campaigns can help management coordinate its promotional efforts. Most large organizations relate promotional expenditures and the media used to sales results. Advertising and sales management receive regular MIS reports on these relations, including some statistical analyses linking recent promotional efforts to changes in sales.

Sales

The **sales strategy** devised depends on the product involved and the company's overall goals. For ProYacht, the starting point is to identify selling location opportunities. One obvious place is the retailers (boat dealers and marinas) that carry ProYacht's other products. Other possibilities may be retailers that carry competitors' products but not windsurfers. A good market research and intelligence data base should enable sales management to identify good prospects. ProYacht may offer dealers that carry the windsurfers the opportunity to link into its service, inventory, and distribution system, thereby accessing ProYacht's repair and inventory information.

Salespersons must be trained on various aspects of the product and on the best way to personally promote the product. Computers can be used to assist sales personnel at the customer (dealer) site. ProYacht, for example, can provide each salesperson with a portable personal computer that can access the company's data base for inventory status on products; special order status; service and repair information; product characteristics, costs, warranties, and financing; and electronic mail messages from customers. By making the access to product information easy and fast, salespersons can react more quickly to customers' needs.

All this available information significantly increases sales productivity and ties the customer to ProYacht's distribution system for its boating supplies. The result creates a competitive advantage for ProYacht, making it more difficult for other companies to do business with the marinas and boat dealers that sell ProYacht's products.

Once the sales strategy is adopted, ProYacht management must monitor sales activities, usually through sales reports that are prepared with output data from the TPS. These reports help management identify new opportunities, compliance with plans, deviations from expected demand, sales activity by product and region, and various trends. As an example, the sales report shown in Figure 9–5 summarizes ProYacht sales to dealers by type of product and region.

Distribution

A sale is complete when the product is delivered to the customer. A company's **distribution system** places the product in the most advantageous location for a sale. Assuming that ProYacht plans to market windsurfers, the company must outline a distribution strategy.

After the windsurfers are produced, they are sold and distributed to independent retailers (customers) throughout the marketing area. Some are also sold through ProYacht distributors directly to the final customer. This distribution decision requires statistical data on sales, promotion, and retail outlet inventories. Moreover, inventory information for ProYacht's own inventory of boats and boating supplies must be available. Management

FIGURE 9–5   *ProYacht, Inc. Sales Report*

ProYacht, Inc.
Sales Report by Region and Product
First Quarter

Region/Product

Product	Number Sold	Wholesale Price/Boat	Production Cost/Boat	Gross Margin/Boat	Quarterly Sales Total	Total Gross Margin
Great Lakes						
18′ Day Sailer	180	$ 3,472	$ 1,736	$ 1,736	$ 624,960	$ 312,480
22′ Sailboat	150	8,000	4,000	4,000	1,200,000	600,000
25′ Sailboat	75	16,000	8,000	8,000	1,200,000	600,000
27′ Sailboat	60	22,800	11,400	11,400	1,368,000	684,000
28′ Sailboat	25	28,000	14,000	14,000	700,000	350,000
30′ Sailboat	20	33,600	16,800	16,800	672,000	336,000
Total					**$5,754,960**	**$2,882,480**
Chesapeake						
18′ Day Sailer	150	$ 3,472	$ 1,736	$ 1,736	$ 520,800	$ 260,400
22′ Sailboat	45	8,000	4,000	4,000	360,000	180,000
25′ Sailboat	40	16,000	8,000	8,000	640,000	320,000
27′ Sailboat	25	22,800	11,400	11,400	570,000	285,000
28′ Sailboat	20	28,000	14,000	14,000	560,000	280,000
30′ Sailboat	15	33,600	16,800	16,800	504,000	252,000
Total					**$3,154,800**	**$1,577,400**
Florida						
18′ Day Sailer	175	$ 3,472	$ 1,736	$ 1,736	$ 607,600	$ 303,800
22′ Sailboat	60	8,000	4,000	4,000	480,000	240,000
25′ Sailboat	60	16,000	8,000	8,000	960,000	480,000
27′ Sailboat	15	22,500	11,400	11,400	342,000	171,000
28′ Sailboat	10	28,000	14,000	14,000	280,000	140,000
30′ Sailboat	2	33,600	16,800	16,800	67,200	33,600
Total					**$2,736,800**	**$1,368,400**

uses these inventory and sales reports to help ship the appropriate number of windsurfers and other products to the locations with the greatest potential demand and to make sure that inventories in other areas do not exceed a specified amount. An example of an inventory status report that a salesperson might generate on a portable PC screen is shown in Figure 9–6.

FIGURE 9–6 ***Inventory Status Report from Portable Personal Computer***

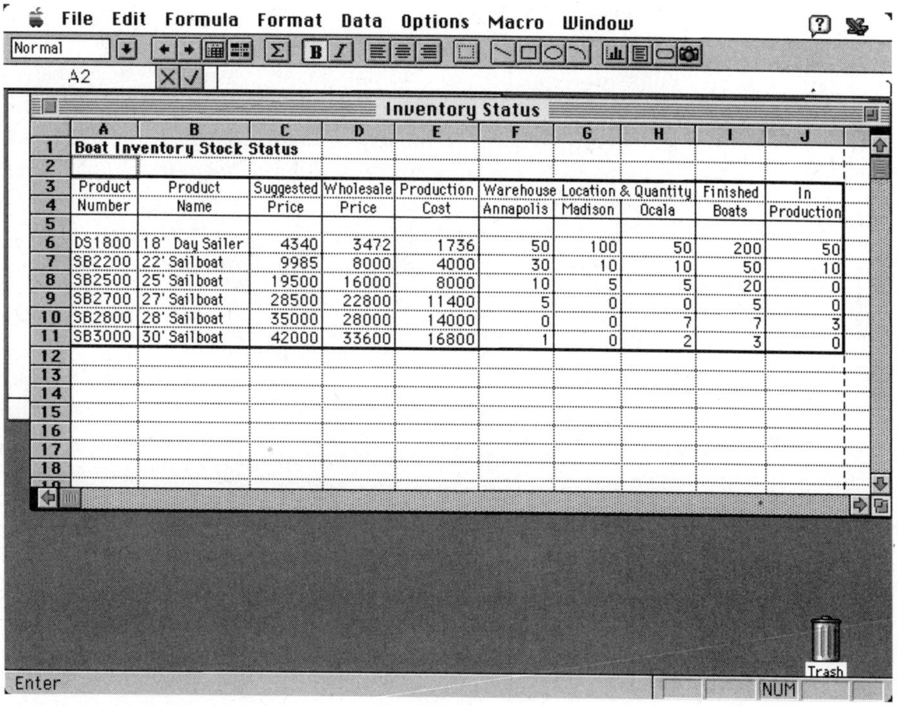

Boat Inventory Stock Status

Product Number	Product Name	Suggested Price	Wholesale Price	Production Cost	Warehouse Location & Quantity Annapolis	Madison	Ocala	Finished Boats	In Production
DS1800	18' Day Sailer	4340	3472	1736	50	100	50	200	50
SB2200	22' Sailboat	9985	8000	4000	30	10	10	50	10
SB2500	25' Sailboat	19500	16000	8000	10	5	5	20	0
SB2700	27' Sailboat	28500	22800	11400	5	0	0	5	0
SB2800	28' Sailboat	35000	28000	14000	0	0	7	7	3
SB3000	30' Sailboat	42000	33600	16800	1	0	2	3	0

Credit As part of the sales strategy, credit policies must be established for the retailers who agree to sell ProYacht's windsurfers to consumers. These terms are a function of past history for ProYacht in dealing with its current retailers. Statistics, which detail a retailer's purchase and payment history, are quite useful in establishing credit for individual retailers who sell to the public. An aging schedule is a commonly used report which shows the amount that is past due for each customer. These credit history reports and aging schedules derived from accounts receivable data are routine in organizations. They are used to continually revise credit status of customers (ProYacht's retailers). This process is often automatic, with a computer using an algorithm to establish credit status. For example, some ProYacht retailers may be given blanket credit for a certain size of purchase, but others may require management approval prior to the shipment of merchandise. Management can monitor credit and cash collections via these MIS-generated reports. Independent retailers and ProYacht distributors then sell boats to customers who may likewise be granted credit through ProYacht's acceptance division.

Providing "Down Home" Service at General Electric

In its advertising, General Electric (GE) promotes an image that its customers can relate to with its slogan, "We bring good things to life." To back up this image, GE has one of the most ambitious customer support systems in the country. Through advanced information technology, customers can feel that GE is not only highly accessible, but actually cares about them. A custom-built mainframe text retrieval system allows its 250 employees to handle over 6,500 calls each week relating to 8,500 GE products. When a call comes into one of the 150 GE operators, the operator enters one or more keywords relating to the caller's question via a terminal keyboard. The text retrieval system searches for a match to the keywords and, if one is found, displays a paragraph of text that is read to the caller.

If no match is found (an event that occurs about 20% of the time), the call and a summary of the question are transferred to one of 50 technical specialists who are more familiar with the GE product data base. These specialists use more sophisticated query techniques to answer another 15% of all calls. Finally, the remaining 5% of questions that cannot be answered by the text retrieval system or by technical specialists are researched further.

In addition to answering questions about products, front-line operators can also have literature sent to the caller or provide the caller with the name of a local service center. At the same time, the customer's name and address are forwarded to the service center via a telecommunications network.

SOURCE: Larry Stevens, "How GE Uses Technology to Turn Back the Clock," *Computerworld,* November 6, 1989, pp. 103, 106.

Service

After merchandise is delivered, a company usually has follow-up service for its customers. An MIS should provide data concerning who needs service and what type of service is required. Statistics on the types of repairs, repair manuals (possibly electronic), and a parts inventory system are essential to providing this service. Much of this activity can be expedited by using computers. Field engineers, for example, could use portable personal computers for immediate access to product specifications, repair instructions, parts availability, and repair requests. Moreover, feedback MIS reports on service frequency are useful for future product development and quality control.

Data and Transaction Input

As shown in Figure 9–3, much of the information needed by the marketing MIS is processed through the TPS, which converts raw data into useful information. The major source for much of an organization's market data is the sales order. Even the smallest organization can extract useful sales statistics and trends from sales data involving pricing, picking, shipping, invoicing, and cash receipts. These data may reside in a data base or in a number of files, such as accounts receivable, customer, and inventory files. Much of these data are used by production and financial management for decision making and reporting requirements.

TABLE 9–1

Type of Data	Origin	Examples
Customer Characteristics	Warranty Reply Card	Location, age, income, purchase habits, type of purchase
Retailer Characteristics	Retailer Staff	Number of units sold, type sold, sales history, competitor's products carried, pricing and discounting policies
Product Data	Production	Current production plan, cost, inventory levels
Market Characteristics	Outside Sources	Industry statistics on prices and sales volumes, promotion exposure information, "shelf space" presence, general economic information, regional demographic trends
Competitor's Actions	Observation	Price changes, special promotions, changes in discounting policies
Credit	Internal	Credit policies, collections, customer payment characteristics

Along with the data collected during the sales transaction, other marketing information can be collected to assist management in making decisions. Table 9–1 shows some of these data types, the possible origin of the data, and examples of the data. The data collection activity is classified as **market intelligence** when it involves competitors' information and **market research** when it involves consumers and retailers.

A marketing MIS can be a great assistance to management. Sales and inventory information can be made available to sales personnel in the field as well as sales management. Sales management can receive up-to-date reports on sales, promotional activities, and customer order status via a telecommunications network that contains a data base of sales and inventory transaction data, market research and intelligence data, product information, and customer information. Reports can often be downloaded to a personal computer, allowing managers to manipulate the data any way they deem necessary. Moreover, management can query any sales transaction, inventory record, or customer record to process a sale or follow up on a customer request. Follow-up service is also accomplished by accessing the production files to assess the status of a customer order or the availability of a product in the production process. In summary, a well-designed marketing MIS is invaluable to marketing management and sales personnel in promoting, selling, distributing, and servicing an organization's products.

A production MIS can supply product development and manufacturing management with information that helps them make informed decisions. These decisions entail product design and development, facilities design, production planning and scheduling, production operations, quality control, and inventory. The data flow diagram in Figure 9–7 shows the basic sequence in which these decisions are performed; the data they reference; and their interrelationships with transaction data, external data, and other functional areas.

FIGURE 9–7

Manufacturing Management Information System Data Flow

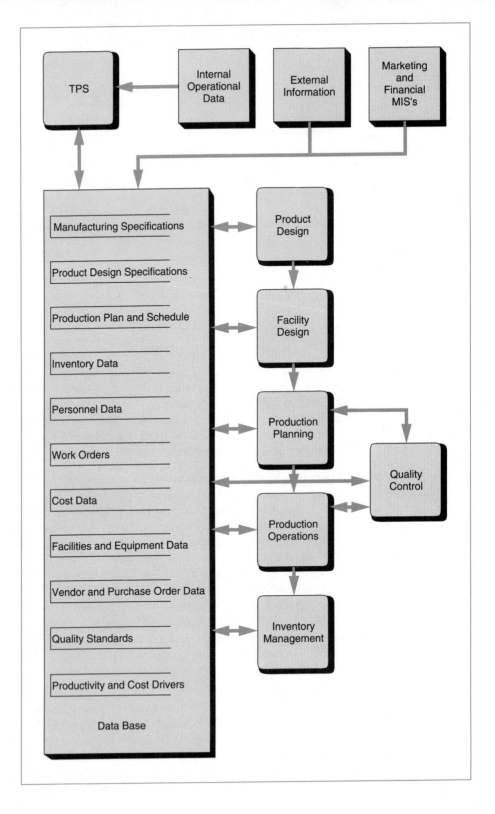

As seen in Figure 9–7, the general production management sequence begins with a product design. Next, a new production facility may need to be designed, or management may need to determine how to modify existing facilities. Management must then plan the manufacturing of the product, including labor, material, facility, and utilization. An MIS is needed to coordinate this plan with the manufacture of other products that use the same labor pool and facilities. Acceptable quality levels are an important component of this plan. Once the planning is done, operations can commence to manufacture the product or, in the case of a service industry, deliver the product. Finally, the company must manage its inventory to supply the appropriate products for distribution and sales. All these activities draw on a data base that consists of the data sets noted in Figure 9–7. These data are obtained in the TPS, in other MISs, and from external sources.

Numerous periodic reports can be prepared to assist production management in its responsibilities. The MIS can also be designed to provide management with production activities information on demand via online terminals. Managers can monitor production operations closely and respond quickly to any change needed due to problems or shifting requirements for various products. With such a capability, a well-designed production MIS can give an organization a competitive edge. For example, a shift in demand for a particular line of sailboats at ProYacht, Inc. can be readily incorporated into a revised production schedule with little effort using an integrated manufacturing system controlled by the computer.

Product Design

All manufacturing begins with product design. During this stage, product specifications are developed, manufacturing procedures and standards are specified, materials and components to be used are determined, costs are estimated, and the level of quality is specified. A common objective is to design a high-quality product that is easily produced using standard components and that meets customer standards. This process is not easy to accomplish, particularly if the development time is short. For example, if ProYacht wants to fill its distribution channels with a sufficient supply of windsurfers for the next sailing season, the company has less than two months to design the windsurfer.

Traditionally, an engineering and design staff consists of product engineers, production management personnel, and management accountants. Product design is a critical process. It determines the success and profitability of the product. As much as 90 percent of production costs are determined during the design stage.

Computer-Aided Design (CAD) is a computer application that assists in this design process. Using CAD, an engineer, architect, or draftsperson can greatly reduce the time necessary to develop a blueprint for an electronic or structural design. A product design engineer can input a rough sketch, a scanned copy of a drawing, or a photograph of a similar product. CAD can also reference the most recent design for a similar product. For example, a designer can work with the ProYacht windsurfer design right on the screen, and the computer automatically generates equations that represent the modified design, a bill of materials for the new design, and, using artificial intelligence, a production sequence given the equipment configuration available in the factory. The cost of the product and even its durability can be ascertained for decision makers. The **bill of materials** generated by the CAD package specifies the materials and components needed

FIGURE 9–8

*ProYacht, Inc.
Windsurfer
Division,
Bill of Materials*

Assembly Mast Base System		
Part	Part Number	Quantity
Mast Extension Cap	PA527538	1
Mast Extension Offset Ring	PA530499	1
Aluminum Locking Ring	PA530599	1
Extension Tube	PA500030	1
Triple Pulley Downhaul	PA017588	1
Quick Release Spring	PA420749	1
Locking Nut	PA022229	1
Small Washer	PA420759	1
Quick Release Cup	PA420369	1
Large Washer	PA400020	1
Dual Joint with Plate	PA420069	1

to manufacture a product. For the windsurfer mast base system, the bill of materials is shown in Figure 9–8.

In this area of product planning, tremendous value can be added to a product via design features that improve the product or reduce costs, thereby adding to the product's margin or giving it a distinct cost advantage. Product planning is important to ProYacht managers as they seek to penetrate an existing windsurfer market. Quality can also be built into the design and into the manufacturing process via the product design. Pro Yacht is trying to obtain a competitive edge using CAD procedures. Figure 9–9 is an example of a CAD drawing for the wiring on the yacht Intrepid. Manufacturing requirements for a product can be developed from CAD drawings such as the one shown in Figure 9–9.

Facility Design   Facilities must be designed, and specific operations must be outlined in order to manufacture a product efficiently and effectively. These operations are usually performed at workstations in the plant. Computer software can assist engineers and production management personnel in the layout of a facility. Simple drawing packages can indicate the location of various workstations and material flows, and complex simulation models enable management to determine the facility configurations that works best for the particular manufacturing environment.

Flexible Manufacturing Systems (FMS) are a recent development in facilities utilization and scheduling. In these systems, production workstations and machinery can be switched from one operation to another or from one product to another, with a minimum of interruption due to setup time. Many operations are directed by computers or numerical controls (an elementary form of a computer), and a product switch simply involves a program change for the equipment. For example, a painting facility at ProYacht can easily be adjusted to paint various sizes of boats, from small windsurfers to large yachts.

FIGURE 9-9   *CAD of Yacht Intrepid Electronic System*

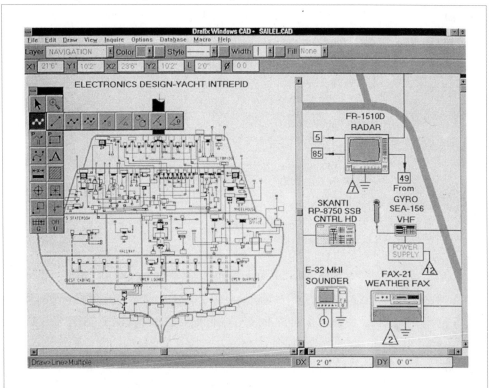

These flexible systems minimize down time due to setup and enable numerous products to use the same facilities. As a result, the overall cost of all products is reduced, throughput is enhanced, and the organization's ability to react to shifting product demand is improved. From a strategic perspective, the ability to seize an opportunity — to bring a product, such as a windsurfer, to the market fast—has tremendous benefits. ProYacht may then be able to capture a significant market share, even with a large profit margin, until competitors bring a product to the market with a similar cost structure. As a result, FMS can be a tremendous competitive weapon.

Production
Planning

Production planning is the determination of what to make, how much to make, and when to make it. Production planning requires MIS information on manufacturing specifications, product specifications, and quality standards. This information is the result of the product design procedures noted earlier. The following data are also required:

1. The amount of finished product available for determining the amount to be produced

FIGURE 9–10

Production Schedule for ProYacht, Inc.

Model Number	DS1800	SB2200	SB2500
Name	18′ Day Sailer	22′ Sailboat	25′ Sailboat
Bill of Material #	18	22	25
Production Run	50	10	10
Begin Production	1/1/93	1/5/93	1/15/93
Work Sequence			
Hull	1	1	1
Fiber Glass & Gelcoat	2	2	2
Deck	3	3	3
Join Hull & Deck	4	4	4
Cabin Millwork	n/a	5	5
Mast	5	6	6
Rigging	6	7	7
Work Order (#)	120 (25)	123 (10)	124 (5)
	121 (20)		125 (5)
	122 (5)		

2. The materials and components in stock and on order from vendors

3. Work orders and a marketing plan, which specify how much is needed

4. Personnel and equipment data, which specify the resources available to make the products

5. Vendor data, for expediting needed materials

6. The current schedule, for ascertaining the availability of personnel and equipment, given what has already been planned

ProYacht's production schedule in Figure 9–10 indicates production run size, work sequence (which often includes equipment needed), work order numbers, and references to bills of materials. Some of this information can be obtained from the data base shown in Figure 9–7. Use of a relational data base, such as those illustrated in Chapter 6, makes production schedule preparation easy because it ties together product specifications, production sequences (facilities needed), and bills of materials.

As indicated in the previous chapter, a vast amount of data on inventory, work orders, costs, vendors, and purchase orders are obtained from the data base via the TPS. Much information is contained in periodic MIS reports that are used by management in the planning process. Additional data may be obtained from the financial and marketing MIS. Data on manufacturing, product design, and quality specifications are determined internally.

Production Operations

The actual production of goods or services are contingent on the availability of facilities and personnel, the requirements of the production plan and schedule, and the product design. Before production operations begin, all components and materials and sufficient resources (facilities and personnel) must be on hand to produce the product.

Estimating with a Computer

Ask any contractor to describe his or her toughest job and the response will probably be estimating the cost of a building project. The estimating process involves determining the cost of all raw materials as well as the labor and overhead costs to turn those raw materials into a finished building. The contractor must also figure an adequate profit. Manually estimating the cost of a project is a time-consuming task—a skilled person must carefully review blueprints, accounting for every element of a project—and the estimate must be accurate. Estimate too high and the project is lost to a competitor; estimate too low and the contractor loses money on the project. Fortunately, new hardware and software systems can make the job of estimating faster and more accurate.

One such estimating system developed by Quantum Technology of Raleigh, NC,

uses a digitizer with a mouse-like device that converts information about a blueprint into data the computer can use to calculate a project's cost. For example, an electrical contractor might use this system to determine the amount of copper wire needed as well as the number of junction boxes and switches. The contractor moves the cursor over the blueprint's wiring diagram and presses a button each time a junction box or switch is encountered. A data base for the electrical devices is then accessed to compute the actual cost of each component. System users have found their estimating time reduced by a factor of 10 and their accuracy improved significantly.

SOURCE: Michael Walker, President of Quantum Technology, January 21, 1990.

In general, the production sequence shown in Figure 9–11 involves the following steps:

1. Initiate a work order
2. Order necessary materials or components
3. Receive necessary materials or components
4. Schedule the production run
5. Carry out production run by requisitioning materials and adding labor (or machine time) as the job (work order) moves from one work station to the next
6. Inspect for quality
7. Complete production and transfer job to finished goods

To determine if sufficient materials are available to manufacture a product, manufacturing and product specifications must be referenced and a bill of materials must be explored. The bill of materials details all the parts, components, and materials needed to manufacture a single product. These figures are then multiplied by the production run size to determine the total number of each part required. Manufacturing specifications also detail the manufacturing sequence, so the schedule can determine the order that

FIGURE 9–11 *Production Flow and Communication Network*

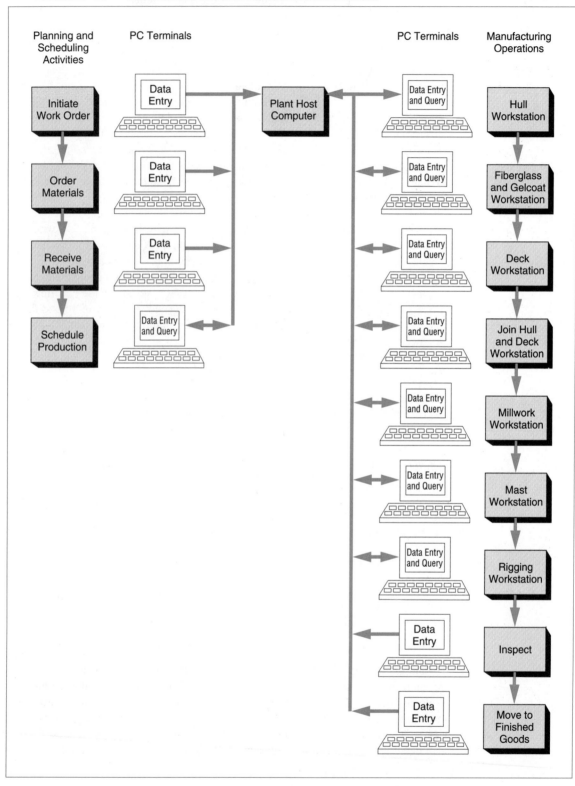

resources are needed. Purchase orders must be prepared and sent to vendors if necessary; production may be held up until missing components are received. Once all resources are available, production resumes. Usually, this information is presented to management as a daily report indicating which work orders can be scheduled for actual production. Production is then scheduled and each workstation is notified of the revised production schedule, which tells machine operators what to make, how to make them, how many to make, when to make them, and what parts to requisition.

An organization needs an efficient method for keeping production schedules up-to-date, tracking the progress of work orders, and allocating time and resources to products as they proceed through the plant. Often, individual products are batched by job or work order. As shown in Figure 9–11, these functions may be accomplished via a PC workstation terminal, where operators enter a job or work order number, number of units in a batch or volume of units processed, materials requisitioned, and the times that a job is started and completed. With a bar code reader, a bar code on the work order that accompanies the job through the plant or on an employee's badge is read, indicating the beginning and the end of a job. Nonproductive idle and setup times are also entered via these terminals. Computer software usually can compute the time spent on a batch by comparing time at the end of a job with the time the job was initiated.

Material Requirements Planning Systems

One of the procedures designed to accomplish the scheduling and material requisition task is **Material Requirements Planning (MRP).** MRP software is used to prepare the production schedule given what is under production; new work orders that require scheduling; bills of materials and issuance of purchase orders for missing parts; consideration of facilities and personnel to accomplish production activities; and ultimate compliance with customer demands in terms of delivery timing, quantity, and quality. MRP is a totally integrated approach to traditional product scheduling that automates many decision-making activities and eliminates some reports found in a traditional MIS.

In traditional product scheduling, all production is initiated by work orders based on sales forecasts and a production plan. With such a system, each workstation begins work on products as they arrive from the previous workstation. In general, products are pushed through the system. The MRP system is used to track each job (work order or batch) through the entire production process, from the initiation of the work order, the ordering of materials to begin manufacturing, and the scheduling of production, to the completion of the production process and the transfer of the job to finished goods. The entire process is monitored at each step and rescheduled as needed. MRP systems require a tremendous amount of feedback information from each step in the production process.

Just-in-Time

In contrast to the MRP and the traditional scheduling algorithm is a relatively new approach to scheduling—**Just-in-Time (JIT) manufacturing** system. A JIT system pulls a product through the manufacturing system as it is needed by the next workstation, sales, or the distribution system, as is the case for ProYacht. The JIT works as follows:

1. As soon as a sale is consummated, the system asks for a new unit or units to make up the number sold.

FIGURE 9–12

Kanban Ticket

ProYacht, Inc.

From: Product No. SB2200   Kanban No. 2
Hull Assembly   Lot No. 34
                         Name 22' Day Sailer
To: Workstation
Deck Assembly   Quantity 10   Fiberglass and
                                                       Gelcoat

2. This request triggers the need to finish a job or a specific number of units.

3. The jobs or units in the next to last workstation in the production process must be completed.

4. This process continues in sequence until the demands reach the beginning of the production process, where new components are ordered for the start of the production process.

In the ideal case, no excess finished goods, work in process, or materials inventory exists, because the materials, components, or goods in one processing stage are not ordered or made until they are needed by a customer or by the next step in the process. A move ticket is generally used to signal the need for a workstation to provide needed components for the next one in sequence. A move ticket, or **Kanban ticket,** for ProYacht is illustrated in Figure 9–12. Kanban is the Japanese name given to this process.

JIT systems are so tightly integrated that any glitch in the process has immediate consequences throughout the production process. An entire assembly line may shut down after a single workstation malfunctions, either because the workstation cannot keep up with demand for products by the next workstations in line or it cannot create any demand for new components from workstations that precede it in the production sequence. Scheduling information is far simpler for a JIT system compared with an MRP system, because an order to produce simply comes from the next step in the production process or from a customer. The need for complex monitoring and feedback information is minimized.

Production Operations Reports

The nature of the reports generated by each production control operation differs. Some reports are scheduled routine reports; others are exception reports that monitor a number of production variables, called cost drivers when they affect the cost of a product. The essential items on most product cost reports reflect the information on job cost sheets, including summary information by job (work order) on labor costs, materials costs, and overhead that is applied to the job. Information may also be summarized by workstation. Information that is reported as an exception is compared with actual standards, and the difference is called a **variance.** An example of a variance report for a production run for

FIGURE 9-13 *Variance Report*

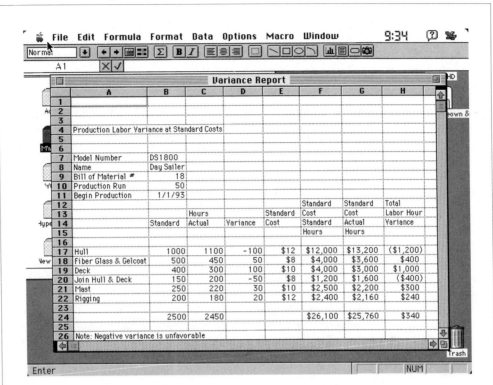

ProYacht's Day Sailer is shown in Figure 9-13. Reports that monitor quality and other key cost drivers, which are discussed next, are also very important in managing production operations.

Quality Control Systems In today's manufacturing environment, the quality of input, processing, and output must be closely monitored to meet customers' demands. Traditionally, output has been tested and defective units returned to the production process for modification or sold as irregulars or seconds. Variances from cost and standards have been monitored via variance reports such as that shown in Figure 9-14. Because this practice has proven costly for many organizations, much more effort is given to inspecting input such as materials and ensuring the quality of labor through training so that defects and variances are reduced. Coupling quality control systems with JIT or MRP systems helps monitor production quality in an expanded MIS production reporting system.

Other Cost Drivers In addition to the costs that are allocated to products in the TPS and costs associated with quality control, many other factors are key indicators of product costs. Management needs information on these key indicators also, including the number of setups, the time required to transport products from one part of the manufacturing facility to another, the time needed to revise a design, the time it takes an order to be shipped from the time it is received (called throughput), storage of work-in-process and other inventory, idle time, the number of designs, and the number of different components used. Reports on any measure of productivity or activities that affect productivity can be stored in the data base and reported to management, which assesses the effectiveness of the manufacturing system.

Linkage with Inventory and Purchasing Transaction Processing Systems

All these production activities are closely linked to an organization's inventory and purchasing TPS. Each time a product moves from one workstation to the next, materials are ordered, or products are completed and sold, an entry is made to the inventory transaction system. Moreover, each time the planning and control software is used for scheduling, the inventory of work in process, materials, finished goods, and materials on order is referenced. As a result, significant interaction exists among production, inventory, and purchasing data.

Interface with Cost Data

Costs are applied to a job as it moves through a series of workstations. These costs may be compared with expected standard costs and variances reported to management for control purposes. Management's production planning involves a necessary interface with a cost accounting system to estimate the costs of producing products and to determine the impact of productive activities on the financial plan. This is especially true for new ventures, such as ProYacht's production of windsurfers. Today, new **Activity-Based Cost (ABC) systems** include many of the cost drivers noted earlier and, as a result, contribute to more accurate product costing and cost estimation.

Computer-Aided Manufacturing and Computer-Integrated Manufacturing

Computer-Aided Manufacturing (CAM) is the use of a computer to control various aspects of the production process. This system includes the computerized scheduling of production activities such as the use of a JIT system, the computerized monitoring of those activities, and the computerized control of individual workstations. Scheduling and controlling production activities by computer can add tremendous control and flexibility to a production system. Not only can management monitor each activity in the process, it can react quickly to any malfunction or to any shift in plans prompted by the market. This ability can reduce costs significantly and enable management to take advantage of opportunities as they occur—gaining a significant advantage over the competition. For example, ProYacht can use CAM in some its facilities to change its product mix and JIT to ensure that the correct mix of components is available to produce a revised product mix of boats.

Computers can also control the activities at individual workstations via numerical control or robotics. Many machine tools can be programmed to do different kinds of tasks via numerical controls. For example, these programs can specify part size and where to drill holes in the part. Modern robots can also be programmed to perform a variety of activities that may be considered too strenuous or even dangerous for a human operator. These computer-controlled workstations can significantly improve the flexibility of a manufacturing system.

*Systems Save
the Sensor*

In July 1988, Gillette Company's management decided to create an entirely new Sensor razor that would be introduced during the 1990 Super Bowl. The decision meant that engineers and product designers had to cut the normal three-year razor design time in half. Not only did Gillette's engineers face a huge design task, the product designers had to rethink their production information system. The new razor involved 157 raw materials, 39 finished components, and 34 assembly processes, all of which had to be managed differently from Gillette's previous razor designs.

To complete the razor design in the limited time, the designers turned to three-dimensional CAD. This software en-

abled designers to modify drawings on the screen and to share them with other designers. With CAD, designers could also send designs to their Canadian counterparts over the telephone, thereby avoiding delays at U.S. Customs associated with mailing drawings or tapes.

To produce the new razor, the production system was completely revamped and placed under the control of an IBM mainframe. The system included factory-floor data collection with programmable logic controllers that sent data to a computer that compared product information with quality control parameters.

SOURCE: Clinton Wilder, "Systems Give Gillette the Razor's Edge," *Computerworld,* November 27, 1989, pp. 1, 113.

Computer-Integrated Manufacturing (CIM) is the complete integration of all the production process steps outlined in Figure 9 – 7. Computer-integrated design, CAM, and other computerized control activities such as MRP are linked together to control the entire process from design through the final output. This system enables management to enter customer requests, modify product design, change manufacturing and material specifications, reschedule production activities, modify programs for robotic workstations, adjust quality standards, and monitor the entire process. ProYacht uses a CIM system to integrate one of its small sailboat facilities so that the company can immediately comply with the changing demand mix reflected in the orders received from retailers around the country. The system is an important competitive advantage, because it can help ProYacht supply the necessary number of small sailing craft to meet a seasonal demand pattern. Even a small delay could mean a loss for a season.

Computer integration can also be modeled in a what-if scenario so that an organization can bid more intelligently on a new product. These concepts are reviewed in depth in Chapter 10 on Decision Support Systems (DSS). CIM allows management to bring a new product to the market very rapidly, which is a tremendous advantage. In today's market, the turnaround time from a new idea to the actual delivery of the product is often critical to an organization's success.

*Data and
Reports*

For management to effectively operate a productive facility, a great deal of information is required. A number of reports for various activities have already been described. The nature of the information contained in these reports is a function of the activity itself and the method used to carry out the activity. For example, an MRP scheduling procedure requires a different set of information than a JIT Kanban system. The output from an MIS may be a periodic report that aids management decision making and subsequent action. Stored MIS data may also be used as input into a decision model in which the computer takes action based on a prescribed set of criteria. Management-directed activities may be performed automatically using rules programmed into a computer. Examples would be a CIM or the automatic ordering of inventory when stock falls below a reorder point. Communication networks linking the terminals in a plant with management's personal computers can help management access needed information via periodic reports or a query. For example, ProYacht can immediately query labor hours used, machine hours used, and maintenance activities to assess the reason and possible solutions for a work flow stoppage.

Data such as those shown in Figure 9–7 are needed to support these reporting activities. The degree of detail stored in the computer depends on an organization's information needs. Much of it can be obtained from internal transaction sources. Some examples of these data and their sources are described below.

- Product design specifications include blueprints that detail a product's exact dimensions, the nature of the raw materials to be used, the product's colors, and its performance criteria. This information comes from customers, the sales department, and the engineering department.

- Manufacturing specifications detail the sequence of activities needed to produce the product. They also detail the materials, machine operations, type of labor needed, time requirements, and necessary tolerances. The industrial engineering and production planning departments compile these data.

- The production plan and schedule specifies the plan for manufacturing a number of products. Information may include the sequence of production, the workstations to be used, the size of production runs, the work order numbers for each planned production run, and the materials needed to manufacture the products. This production plan is prepared by production management, usually with the help of MRP or CIM computer software.

- Inventory data include details on the raw material and component parts in stock and on order, the status of work-in-process and its accumulated costs to date, and finished goods inventory that is awaiting sale and shipment. These data are output from the TPS.

- Personnel data summarize the skills and pay rates of personnel who are used in the production process and may also include hours worked. The personnel department develops these data.

- Work orders are the basis for production runs. They contain the essential data on the number of units in the production run, the customer, the work order number, the required shipment date, and any product modifications required by the customer. Work orders originate in the sales transaction.

- Cost data are maintained on each product so that bids can be prepared and costs can be applied to products as they are manufactured. Actual costs are also accumulated and compared with standard or expected costs to determine if the process is proceeding as planned. The data are also important in costing products from an accounting perspective. Sources of these data include engineering, the history of past manufacturing activities, and current activities.

- Facilities and equipment data detail the capability of each workstation or piece of equipment. This information is necessary to prepare the production plan and schedule and bids on new jobs. Moreover, information on equipment repairs can help determine when a machine has reached the end of its useful life. This information comes from equipment manufacturers, the engineering department, and firm maintenance.

- Purchase order data and vendor data are required for the issuance of purchase orders for materials as they are needed. Purchase order data show what materials are on order and when these materials should arrive for scheduling. The data are output from the purchasing TPS.

- Quality standards outline the standards or tolerances required for the manufacture of a product. This information comes from engineering, sales returns, and warranty repairs statistics.

Productivity and other cost drivers are statistical measures of the basic activities that determine the cost of a product or product line. For example, a product's cost may be a function of the number of setups for a new production run, the materials used in the product, the labor and machine hours used, the productive capacity needed to comply with customer demand, the storage costs of inventory, the capital investment in equipment, the design modifications, and the amount of defective products that are produced. The data are collected as part of the transaction processing cycles, as well as during the manufacturing process.

Summary of Production Management Information Systems

The ability to use the information contained in these reports effectively to manage manufacturing activities can add significant value to an organization. For example, ProYacht can quickly change product design, specifications, and schedules to comply with dynamic changes in the market. The company can expedite the production of a sailboat needed by a valued customer by automatically changing the schedule. Management can also modify the schedule quickly if certain materials are not delivered on time, thus reducing potential equipment down time. Moreover, the computerized monitoring of production activities—either electronically or via periodic reports—gives management valuable feedback information for controlling production activities and delivering products to customers at the lowest possible cost.

9.3 Financial Management Information Systems

Financial planning and the raising of capital to meet an organization's objectives is the role of financial management. A financial MIS must be designed to support the following financial management activities (also shown in Figure 9–14):

1. Financial planning and budgeting

2. Cash management

3. Capital acquisition and funds management

4. Capital budgeting

5. Auditing

Developed from marketing and production plans, financial plans usually take the form of a budget that guides financial decision making. Cash must be managed to support these plans, and more must be obtained if insufficient cash is available. Sometimes more financial resources (including credit) are needed to acquire capital resources to implement marketing and production plans. Capital acquisition decisions usually require capital budgeting. Finally, the financial affairs of the organization are audited to ensure that the financial statements fairly represent the financial position of the firm and that various segments of the organization have followed management's plans.

A summary of the financial data from the marketing and production information systems can be tied into the financial MIS. The previous chapter on TPS illustrated how financial and managerial accounting data are used to control and report on marketing and production operations and to prepare financial reports. In addition to this financial accounting data, management needs a financial MIS to provide sufficient information to manage the financial affairs of the organization.

In most organizations, the persons responsible for financial activities are the controller and the treasurer. The controller is responsible for the processing of financial transactions, planning activities, and the auditing of these activities. The treasurer is responsible for the acquisition of capital, cash management, and capital budgeting.

Financial Planning and Budgeting

Financial management's major activities are planning and budgeting, specifically, merging the marketing and production plans into a financial plan. All resource and market constraints must be considered. Resource constraints include production, warehouse, and distribution facilities; manpower skills and availability; and financial resource limits. Market constraints include competitors' actions, product demand, pricing policies, promotional funds, and outside agency regulations.

The first step in the preparation of a financial plan is the development of a forecast. This process involves input from marketing and production, often including marketing's sales forecast and production's constraints. Mathematical and statistical models may be used to prepare this forecast. These models—for example, regression, exponential smoothing, and simple moving averages—attempt to capture key patterns and provide management with the best estimate of future revenues and costs. Given the set of plans developed by marketing and production and the various constraints on market resources, a budget is prepared that each unit can use as a guide for its operations. The decision support systems

FIGURE 9–14

Financial Management Information System Data Flow

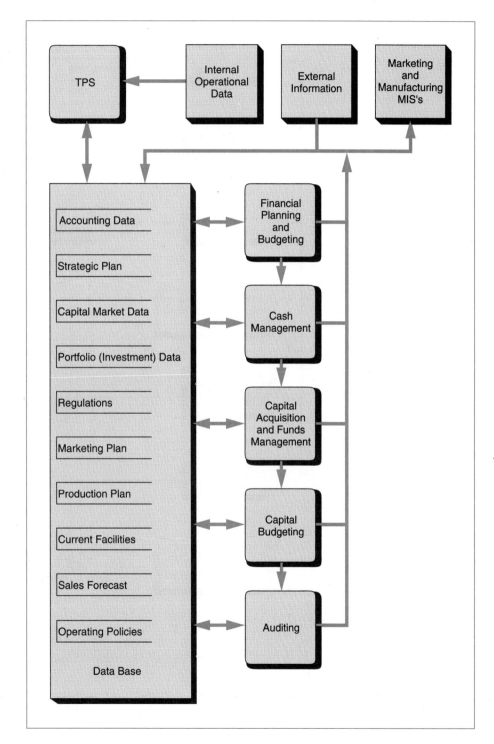

FIGURE 9–15

Budget Process at ProYacht, Inc.

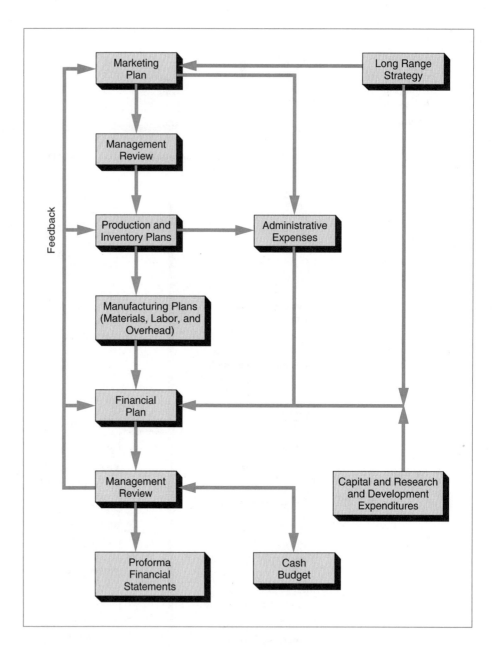

presented in the next chapter are useful in helping financial management develop and integrate all these plans.

The budget process, illustrated in Figure 9–15 for ProYacht, is often iterative. First, a marketing plan is forwarded to management, which prepares a set of guidelines for production. This marketing plan includes elements from the organization's long-range

Making
Deals with
Spreadsheets

Because today's mergers, acquisitions, and leveraged buyouts can involve billions of dollars, the spreadsheet has become an essential tool for performing the required analyses. It is hard to say which came first—the spreadsheet or the growing complexity of corporate deals. However, without spreadsheets, many of these deals would not be possible. In fact, the spreadsheet has changed the way many financial organizations do business.

To analyze an acquisition, a financial analyst first creates a ''deal'' spreadsheet, into which the key data on the company being considered for acquisition are entered. These data may include figures from the company's balance sheets and income statements, as well as data on capital expenditures and growth projections. The spreadsheet is used to analyze the data to determine if the company should be acquired. This decision is based on various ratios that indicate the current and future financial health of the company. If the results are promising, then the analyst fine-tunes the spreadsheet for a closer look at the candidate company.

If a deal involves many investors, the analyst uses a spreadsheet to assign portions of the proposed investment to the various ''players.'' Because the spreadsheet is flexible, it can quickly be restructured to accommodate new investors, change priorities, or revise economic assumptions. With a spreadsheet, the entire analysis of the company being acquired, including the apportionment for investors, can take less than 24 hours.

SOURCE: Chris Brown, ''Where 1-2-3 Makes Deals in a Hurry,'' *Lotus,* June 1989, pp. 52–55.

strategy and sales forecast. Given these guidelines, production prepares manufacturing plans to meet the needs of marketing. If it complies with marketing's plan, the budget is then forwarded to finance for the final step in the planning process. If the marketing and production activities can be financed, then the budget is reviewed to make sure it complies with the overall strategy of the organization. If, for some reason, production cannot produce all the products at the cost specified by marketing or the finance department cannot raise the necessary funds, then the plans are returned to the production and marketing managers for revision. Revised plans are sent through the same channels until all levels of management can reasonably comply with the budget. These plans may take the form of either an MIS report or an on-line display.

Often, plans must be revised due to to unforeseen events. If the plans are online in the computer, they can be quickly revised to adjust operations. Even the smallest business can develop an online budget using a simple spreadsheet with the basic economic, financial, and accounting relationships built into it. This capability ensures that the organization can react to an unforeseen event in a coordinated and efficient way.

FIGURE 9–16   *ProYacht, Inc. Sailboat Division Cash Budget Report*

	January	February	March
Monthly Cash Budget – ProYacht, Inc. Small Sailboat Division			
18- and 22-Foot Boats			
Beginning Cash Balance	$500,000	$751,680	$4,480
Cash Receipts	298,880	1,494,400	3,094,400
Bank Loan	1,500,000		
Total Cash Available	$2,298,880	$2,246,080	$3,098,880
Cash Disbursements			
Manufacturing Wages	$232,080	$336,240	$336,240
Material Purchases	154,720	224,160	224,160
Equipment Purchases	10,000	2,000,000	35,000
Product Development	185,664	268,992	268,992
Administrative Expenses	309,440	448,320	448,320
Selling Expenses	309,440	448,320	448,320
Total Disbursements	$1,547,200	$2,241,600	$2,241,600
Cash Available – Disbursements	$751,680	$4,480	$857,280

Cash Management

A key component of the budget is the cash management plan. Expected cash receipts and disbursements can be projected from past transaction history and adjusted to accommodate new marketing and production plans. Figure 9–16 is an example of a cash budget report for a portion of ProYacht's sailboat division. If cash is not sufficient, either the budget must be revised or additional funds must be raised. Again, a simple spreadsheet can be used to determine the cash flow and the need for more capital, for example, during fall and early winter months when the cash flow from ProYacht's boat sales is slow. Decision support models, illustrated in the next chapter, play a large role in the development of a cash management plan.

Capital Acquisition and Funds Management

To engage in the production of windsurfers, ProYacht's management must raise additional capital. The company has to finance a large inventory of finished windsurfers, a greater variety of components, more work-in-process inventory, and added materials and labor needed to manufacture and sell the new product. The amount of necessary funds is usually determined through a series of reports internally generated by the controller with regard to the financial implications of the new venture.

Capital may be obtained either internally, via a loan from the bank, or by issuing more stock. A plan to support a request for additional capital outlines the future revenues and expenses for the new venture. This **business plan** is founded on marketing plans (such as sales forecasts and market research data) and production plans, which include costs and resources required to produce the new product. The business plan must be meshed with a company's strategic plan. A significant amount of this information is derived from transaction data; the rest is obtained from external sources.

ProYacht can also use information from a news retrieval service to monitor stock and other investment prices. The service tracks prices and flags potential buy and sell situations—not only for individual securities but for ProYacht's entire investment portfolio. Such reporting and monitoring software is invaluable to financial managers who are responsible for monitoring a firm's investments.

Capital Budgeting

Management needs financial information to make capital budgeting decisions. Suppose ProYacht needs to add production equipment to produce enough windsurfers to make the new venture worthwhile. The company needs sufficient information to make this capital budgeting decision, including the cost of the equipment, interest rates and the cost of raising capital and other funds, expected useful life of the equipment, operating and maintenance costs of the equipment, and, most important, the savings or increase in cash flow due to the presence of the new equipment. Management must also consider this potential addition along with other capital projects (investments) and assess the company's overall investment portfolio. In other words, ProYacht must assess the impact of this investment on other company activities, such as the inability to pursue another project which may result in a significant cost savings for the company. This activity must be closely tied to the marketing and manufacturing plans, investment data, capital market data (such as availability of funds and interest rates), operating policies, and the capabilities of other fixed assets. An MIS can provide much of the information management needs to do its capital budgeting.

Auditing

Basically, two types of audits are performed—an **operational audit,** which monitors a company's compliance with plans, policies, and budgets, and a **financial audit,** which attests to the fairness of financial statements. Internal auditors usually perform operational audits. In operational audits, variations are reported to management for review and possible action. Sometimes a change in plan or budget is made in order for the company to conduct business in an organized fashion. Internal auditors also monitor the measurement system and the TPS to ensure that information is accurately gathered and classified. For example, sales for ProYacht must be classified properly to ensure that the inventory amount is accurate and that any plans based on inventory and sales are based on solid data. To the extent that financial data are measured in this process, internal auditors also perform a financial audit.

Most organizations are required to have an external financial audit of their financial statements to ensure that they fairly present the organization's financial status to investors, bankers, and other interested parties. In the typical financial audit, an independent CPA firm attests to the fairness of the organization's financial statements, including the fact that they were prepared according to generally accepted accounting principles. As a result, the investment community can trust the information in the financial statements.

In both types of audits, many reports cited in the marketing, production, and financial MISs and the reports generated by the TPS are reviewed and checked for accuracy. Moreover, other reports are required to test compliance with management's plans or the accurate recording of transactions. For example, data for a randomly selected project are monitored closely as the product is sold, work orders are prepared, materials are requisitioned, the product is manufactured, the product is shipped, the customer is billed, and payment is received from the customer. In this way, auditors and managers can trace transactions through the accounting system. These data are displayed in a report in which management can see if the accounting system is functioning correctly.

Financial Data

Sources of financial data shown in Figure 9–14 are explained below. The data are generated in other MISs, TPSs, and external sources.

- Accounting data from the TPS form the basis of an organization's financial data. This data set is also the basis for financial statements. The transaction data come from marketing, production, and finance activities.

- The strategic plan is also a key data input that serves as the basis for all planning activities. The plan is developed by top-level managers, who formulate a strategy to accomplish the objectives of the organization.

- Capital market data, an externally generated market-based figure, is essential for all facilities management and capital budgeting decisions. The data are also used in financial planning and cash management, because the cost of capital is an important factor in investment analysis and capital budgeting.

- Portfolio data are important in capital budgeting and funds management decisions, because all decisions regarding investments and the acquisition of capital involve the consideration of other investments in an organization. For example, a company that wants to diversify probably does not invest all its resources in one type of investment.

- Management also needs information on tax, labor, and marketing regulations, so that the company operates within the law and the restrictions often imposed via regulations. All company plans should abide by these restrictions.

- Both the marketing and production plans, which originate in their respective functional areas, form the basis for the organization's financial plan. A key component of these plans is the sales forecast.

- Capital investment decision makers need to know the characteristics of all current facilities. This information is generated by facilities management and industrial engineering personnel.

- Finally, operating and managerial policies must be known for management to develop a financial plan. This important set of guidelines acts as a constraint for planning.

*Summary of
Financial
Management
Information
Systems*

Financial management information can help managers obtain a competitive edge by connecting the marketing, production, and financial operations of an organization. The organization's activities are better coordinated and directed toward the ultimate objective of the organization. Financial data should help focus managers as they implement their plans, minimizing waste due to conflicting activities. The financial MIS should provide the information management needs to maximize the efficient delivery of products and services to customers.

9.4 Summary

MISs provide reports and online inquiry to managers responsible for different areas in an organization. These areas include marketing, production, and finance. Each area has a set of decisions supported by an MIS, and each requires data from TPSs and other MISs.

In general, marketing plans are made first; manufacturing then decides how to make the product, and finance must find the resources to implement the marketing and production plans. An MIS facilitates this process with periodic reports on compliance with these plans, as well as online inquiry to help managers make decisions regarding the plans. As a result, a good MIS can be of significant value to an organization in helping managers coordinate all the company's activities.

A marketing MIS assists management in the development, distribution, and sale of its goods and services. It provides needed market research information which in turn helps management decide what products to sell. Likewise, market characteristics can be used to aid in the development of new products that will meet consumer demands. An MIS can supply the necessary reports to help marketing management plan its promotional, sale, and distribution strategies. A sales forecast is one of the key reports in this planning process. An MIS provides useful sales statistics to monitor sales and respond to changing customer demands. Product data can be used by the sales force to market the product. Distribution and inventory data can be used to serve customer demand and keep sales persons informed on content and location of stock. Sales and collection information from the TPS helps to grant credit and manage cash collections. Finally, customer and product data can be used to service its products.

A production MIS assists management in the design of products and facilities. Computer-aided design makes sure the product meets the characteristics desired by the market and that the product is manufactured efficiently and at a low cost. An MIS helps managers plan the production process; schedules, bills of materials, production sequences, facility characteristics, material inventories, work orders, and personnel data can all be reported to management for use in the production planning process. Simple reports may be used to report production progress, or advanced computerized systems may control the whole process. Material requirement planning, just-in-time, computer-aided manufacturing, and computer integrated manufacturing systems are some of the systems that help an organization manage its production process.

A financial MIS helps an organization finance its day-to-day operations as well as its long-term capital needs. It assists in the financial planning process to make sure sufficient funds are available to produce, distribute, and market the organization's products or services. This is primarily a budget process. The MIS makes this process much more effective by providing needed information and reports for communication purposes. Spreadsheets have been used extensively in this process. Moreover, the MIS aids capital budgeting by providing needed information on capital markets and the characteristics of proposed investments.

Key Terms

Activity-Based Cost (ABC) systems
bill of materials
business plan
Computer-Aided Design (CAD)
Computer-Aided Manufacturing (CAM)
Computer-Integrated Manufacturing (CIM)
distribution system
financial audit
Flexible Manufacturing Systems (FMS)

Just-in-Time (JIT) manufacturing
Kanban ticket
market intelligence
market research
Material Requirements Planning (MRP)
operational audit
sales forecast
sales strategy
variance

Review Questions

1. How does an MIS support managerial decision making?

2. List the activities of marketing management in sequence.

3. What is the basis for a marketing plan and what information is required for such a plan?

4. How can an information system aid sales management and sales activities?

5. What data are needed for sales management to assess market conditions?

6. Suggest the type of customer data needed by a merchandise retailer.

7. List the basic activities of production management in sequence.

8. Why is product design so important to production efficiency and effectiveness? How can computer software aid in this activity?

9. What is a bill of materials and why is it important to the production schedule?

10. What is an FMS? How does an effective information system facilitate an FMS?

11. Contrast JIT and MRP systems in how they work and in what information is needed to operate each.

12. What data are needed to plan production?

13. What general steps are used to produce an item? How can an information system track these steps?

14. How can MRP be used to schedule production and materials requisitions?

15. How does a JIT system work and what information is needed to operate it? How does it interface with materials requisitions and sales?

16. List the various cost drivers that affect the ultimate cost of sailboats at ProYacht.

17. What is the difference between CAM and CIM?

18. What data are typically needed to control the production or the delivery of goods and services?

19. Name the various financial management activities of an organization.

20. What information is needed prior to the development of a financial plan?

21. What sequence of activities is involved in the development of a financial plan and how can an information system assist each activity?

Discussion Questions

1. Discuss several ways a personal computer can be used to gather sales transactions for sales management activities.

2. Why does a JIT inventory system require less data than an MRP system? How can each be integrated into a CIM system?

3. A printer who produces college T-shirts, sweatshirts, mugs, pennants, and a variety of paper products needs to schedule production. What information does the printer need to schedule and commence a printing run? How can the printer use an MIS to monitor the status of a printing order?

4. A home builder must manage cash resources. What information is needed to accomplish this? Assume the builder's own equipment and skilled employees are used to build homes.

5. A manufacturer of special purpose computer chips for missile guidance systems must maintain a competitive edge. Explain how CAD, CAM, and CIM can help the company maintain its competitive edge via the information generated and used to control the manufacturing process.

Case 9–1

USAir

In today's turbulent airline industry, carriers are either swallowing their competitors or being swallowed themselves. In spite of recent financial difficulties in the airline industry, USAir has managed to continue flying.

USAir has carefully proceeded on two major fronts to better connect the airline's activities—the implementation of a PC-based Local Area Network (LAN) and the development of applications for PC-to-mainframe communication. With ticketing offices in many major U.S. cities and administrative offices in two states, connectivity is essential for the airline's continued survival and profitability.

The airline has three large mainframes located in a data center in Fairfax, VA. Numerous personal computers and IBM 3270 personal computers are located in the corporate administrative offices at Pittsburgh International and Washington National airports and at other suburban Virginia offices.

Pittsburgh International Airport serves as an operational hub for the airline's many passengers and for data. Many USAir passengers catch their connecting flights at Pittsburgh. The airline's system control center is also located at the airport. The control center keeps track of aircraft status and national weather conditions. Each plane is in constant communication with the system control center staff via a special radio network called Aeronautical Radio Communications Addressing and Reporting System (ACARS).

This large geographic dispersal of equipment made the companywide adoption of computing standards as well as a uniformly high quality of support essential to keep USAir's planes flying and its passengers happy. USAir support is complicated by the heavy connectivity needs of the PC workstations. Early PC purchases by the airline were mostly used as stand-alone devices, but MIS planners quickly realized the benefits of connecting personal computers to the mainframe and to one another.

USAir has two connectivity projects under way—the 3270 PC's High-Level Language Application Program Interface (HLLAPI), and a PC LAN. The 3270 PC HLLAPI applications were developed to manage the massive amount of information flowing through the Pittsburgh system control center. The center monitors the position of each plane via a mechanical time-line type slot on an enormous wall chart. The dispatchers at the center also track the maintenance milestones needed at a plane's next stopover and other flight status information. Dispatchers at the center use 30 IBM 3270 personal computers connected to the corporate mainframes in Fairfax.

The airline has online maintenance and crew-management systems, as well as a separate reservations system, each of which runs on a separate mainframe. The PACER reservations system receives current flight information in several ways. Most late-model aircraft have special computer consoles in the cockpit, so pilots can update PACER directly. The consoles can also be used to send messages to other terminal-equipped USAir planes, for example, about rough weather conditions. Planes not equipped with the special terminals must communicate with dispatchers via radio. PACER displays are installed at each gate and at the main reservation desks in each airport handling USAir passengers. Information from the displays is extracted and keyed in separately for passenger viewing. Gate agents also enter information into the reservations systems, such as the time a plane leaves a gate. These communications are extremely time-sensitive, and dispatchers must monitor many flights simultaneously and get information out quickly in case of trouble. To help increase the productivity of the dispatching staff as well as provide more computing power, the corporate applications programmers wrote their own customized HLLAPI programs for the dispatcher's 3270 personal computers.

One application automatically copies messages from one PACER system to another. This capability is useful when a dispatcher is communicating with two different aircraft, or with an aircraft and an agent waiting at the arrival gate for the plane. In this case, the dispatcher can copy information directly from the gate agent to the pilot. Information can also be transferred from the reservations system to the maintenance system without having to rekey the data. The applications, which run in the PC window of the 3270 personal computer, present simple menus to the dispatchers for choices, such as copying messages or updating records across mainframe systems. Data entered in response to the menus are sent automatically by the HLLAPI application through the 3270 control program and directly to the mainframe, freeing the dispatcher for tasks other than data entry.

USAir programmers developed a second HLLAPI application for the airline's revenue accounting department. This department receives all collected passenger ticket coupons. The department must reconcile funds collected by the airline and determine how to split the fare on a ticket coupon that includes non-USAir flights. The process of dividing fares is complicated. Airfares change almost continuously and have a confusing array of conditions, as most air travelers know. Information used to be available in printed form from the Airline Tariff Publishing (ATP) Co., located at Dulles International Airport in Herndon, VA. Currently, ATP only provides this information electronically. USAir employees access the ATP data base and are connected via an SNA high-speed link.

USAir must account for the funds collected each day from each city reservation office, as well as fares collected at each airport gate. Programmers wrote an HLLAPI program, which takes the fare information from the PACER reservations system and brings it automatically into an ASCII file that is read by Lotus 1-2-3. Prewritten spreadsheet macros and "shells" massage this information mass into meaningful accounts, performing the cross totals and other mind-numbing detail work. The combination of HLLAPI programs with the spreadsheet macros makes the fare accounting process easier, faster, and more accurate.

USAir's second area for increased productivity has been with the installation of the airline's first LAN. Users on the network include airline executives in marketing, sales, and consumer affairs. Currently, 60 users share 30 workstations connected to the network, which runs over the IBM broadband network adapters and PC LAN program software. One department heavily involved with the network is consumer affairs, which handles passengers with service complaints, such as lost luggage or missed flights. With the network, consumer affairs personnel can talk to passengers on the phone and resolve their problems during the call. Online reservations and tariff systems are displayed through the LAN for quick problem-solving. Moreover, agents can use electronic mail to respond to complaints from the same flight in a consistent manner.

SOURCE: Adapted with permission from David Strom, ''LAN and PC-to-Mainframe Links Keep Airline Flying High,'' *PC Week,* March 24, 1987, pp. C-1, C-9, C-10. Copyright © 1987, Ziff Communications Company.

Case Questions

1. How does USAir use its TPS and MIS to keep up with and account for changes in fares?

2. How does USAir use its MIS to manage reservations and flight schedules?

3. How does USAir use its MIS to enhance its competitive position via customer service?

Case 9–2
Thunderbird Sportswear

Thunderbird Sportswear has over 1,000 high-fashion sportswear outlets throughout the United States, Europe, Australia, and New Zealand. Many outlets are in upscale malls and in resort areas. The company does not make any of its merchandise; items are purchased from numerous small manufacturing firms throughout the world.

The vice president of marketing must forecast fashion trend accurately for hundreds of products for several countries. These forecasts must be translated into production work orders for vendors. Company policy is to react quickly to market changes to avoid costly writedowns. As a result, vendors must be informed of changes to work orders in terms of quantity and style as soon as the marketing staff detects any change in the market.

Orders are placed by individual retail outlets to regional warehouses, which in turn forward the order to the home office, which contacts the preferred vendor. The vendor is sent a purchase order, and the vendor manufactures the product and ships it to the regional warehouse for transfer to retail merchants or to another regional warehouse. Each day, vendors report on the status of each work order, and each retail store reports on sales via the same communication network.

To effectively implement the sales and purchase order MISs, sales must be tracked for each item at each location. The marketing staff must also know the status of each work order and the status of each order in the distribution system. Marketing can then determine what is selling and what is in the manufacturing and distribution pipelines.

Thunderbird Sportswear uses a large mainframe at its home office in Denver and small minicomputers at six distribution warehouses located around the world. Each vendor uses a microcomputer or a minicomputer (depending on the vendor's size) to tie into the regional minicomputers. Each retail outlet uses a microcomputer to tie into the regional minicomputers.

Case Questions

1. What information should Thunderbird transmit to and from retail outlets and manufacturing vendors via its communication network to support management decision making at the home office? At each retail location? At each warehouse? At each vendor's location?

2. How does the communication network facilitate the distribution system and the manufacturing system?

3. What management reports do you think would help the marketing staff manage the sales and distribution system of Thunderbird Sportswear?

4. Using this system, can Thunderbird react quickly to changing trends? How? How can the marketing staff detect trends and how can the production and distribution of obsolete merchandise be minimized?

Decision Support and Executive Information Systems

10

Introduction

The initial chapters of this text stressed the importance of decision making to the management of an organization. Although the summaries generated by the Transaction Processing System (TPS) and the reports generated by the Management Information System (MIS) are very important in the decision-making process, many decisions require different information than that provided by these information systems. When decisions tend to be unstructured, sophisticated information systems must provide the required information and answer managers' questions. Depending on the managerial level of the decision makers involved and the type of queries, either **Decision Support Systems (DSS)** or **Executive Information Systems (EIS)** are needed.

Review of Decision-Making Concepts

Recall from Chapter 3 that decision making is a key managerial activity. **Decision making** involves recognizing a problem, generating alternative solutions to the problem, choosing among alternatives, and implementing the chosen alternative. Figure 10–1 shows the decision-making process.

Decisions can be structured or unstructured (or programmed or unprogrammed). **Structured** or **programmed decisions** are usually made on a repetitive basis by following a set of rules. Problems requiring this type of decision are especially amenable to solutions by computerized mathematical models developed by management science researchers. Examples of structured decisions include ordering raw materials based on the current level of inventory, scheduling checkers in a grocery store based on the time of day and day of the week, or determining the least-cost feed mix for poultry to obtain the desired rate of growth.

FIGURE 10–1

Decision-Making
Process

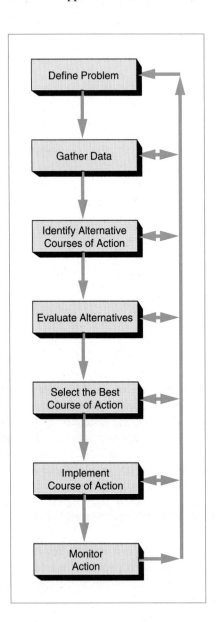

On the other hand, **unstructured decisions** (also known as **unprogrammed,** or **ad hoc, decisions**) involve complex situations and are made on a "once only" basis using all available information. Because no clear-cut solution methodologies exist for these tough decisions, human intuition and judgment are necessary. Table 10–1 compares the model and data characteristics of structured and unstructured decisions. Middle- and top-level managers must have the support necessary to make unstructured decisions to ensure the continued existence of the organization. Examples of unstructured decisions include

TABLE 10–1

Type of Decision	Model	Data
Structured	Well defined	Well defined
Unstructured	Not well defined	Not well defined

planning new services to be offered; hiring, firing, and assigning personnel; and investigating takeovers and mergers.

Somewhere between unstructured decisions and structured decisions are *semistructured* decisions, for which both human intuition and management science solution methods can be used. This type of decision may be made on repetitive basis under changing or uncertain conditions. As a result, the solution from a mathematical model often cannot be implemented without considering nonlinear side effects. That is, changing one value or assumption in the model causes a change in the solution that is not proportional to the change in the value or assumption. For P.G.W. Keen and M.S. Scott Morton,[1] examples of semistructured decisions include trading bonds, setting marketing budgets for consumer goods, and performing capital acquisition analysis. To make semistructured decisions, managers need to choose among alternative solutions using their judgment. Managers may need a ''worst case'' analysis that indicates what would happen if all assumptions are wrong.

Having enough information to make unstructured and semistructured decisions is important, but even more important is having the right kind of information at the right time. In addition, managers also need to know how sensitive the results are to the assumptions used in making the decision. In other words, if an assumption changes, how much do the results change? This sensitivity is the reason for the volume of information needed by many decision-making models. Providing this information is the job of the information system—particularly, DSS and EIS.

Role of
Information
Systems in
Decision
Making

Because decision making is crucial to the well-being of any organization, information systems must facilitate good decision making. We now consider how information systems are used in the various steps of the decision-making process shown in Figure 10–1.

To define a problem, the decision maker must first be aware that a problem exists. A decision maker may receive information either that current results do not match past results or that a new opportunity exists. Recall that problems are not inherently bad—they may simply be new situations that must be considered in the decision-making process. This information may be contained in summaries from the TPS, but more likely it is found in MIS-generated reports or terminal displays or in a review of external data. We have already discussed MIS reports in Chapter 9, but a manager may review external data by reading newspapers, news magazines, or industry periodicals. External data may also be found by scanning electronic data bases such as those discussed in Chapter 7 or

[1] P.G.W. Keen and M.S. Scott Morton, *Decision Support Systems: An Organizational Perspective* (Reading, MA: Addison-Wesley, 1978).

through a special information system for top-level managers—the EIS. An EIS is the executive's ''personal presentation system,'' which provides needed information in any form required. We discuss EIS in more detail later in this chapter.

Once the problem is recognized and defined, data must be gathered. Once again, the information system must provide this information through demand reports from the MIS or direct queries to the organization's data base. Top-level executives may also perform data gathering through the EIS.

The next three decision-making steps—identifying alternatives, evaluating alternatives, and selecting the best course of action—require information that may not be provided by the TPS or MIS. The development of DSS was a direct result of this inadequacy of TPS and MIS for helping managers with these activities. Recall that DSSs are ''computer-based systems that help decision makers confront ill-structured problems through direct interaction with data and analysis models.'' [2] Based on this definition, the DSS can be used with the organization's data base and one or more models to identify and evaluate alternatives and then select the best alternative.

Information systems must supply the decision maker with appropriate information on implementing the selected course of action. Such information includes internal MIS reports on potential implementation problems as well as DSS-generated scenarios that could cause implementation problems. The EIS can also be used to search external data sources for possible implementation problems.

After the selected alternative is implemented, results are monitored through feedback provided by MIS reports and the EIS. If problems are detected, then the whole decision-making process starts again.

At the upper levels of the organization, the DSS and EIS provide information to the decision maker throughout the decision-making process. The DSS also helps the decision maker identify, evaluate, and choose among alternatives. Because these information systems can be so useful to a decision maker, we consider them in detail in this chapter.

Comparing Decision Support Systems and Executive Information Systems

DSS and EIS support managerial decision making at different managerial levels and in different ways. In terms of managerial level, a DSS is used at both the tactical and strategic levels of management, and an EIS is used by strategic managers and other personnel designated to find answers to questions (for example, executive or administrative assistants). In terms of how they are used, DSS helps solve semistructured and unstructured problems, and EIS is used almost exclusively for unstructured problems. The use of DSS and EIS relative to TPS and MIS is shown in Figure 10–2.

A DSS is usually designed to help search for alternative solutions to problems and then explore the ramifications of selecting one alternative. Groups of middle managers or analysts interact with the DSS to enter data and assumptions, develop models, test the effects of changes in the data and assumptions, and report to the top-level executives who

[2] Ralph H. Sprague and Eric D. Carlson, *Building Effective Decision Support Systems* (Englewood Cliffs, NJ: Prentice-Hall, 1982).

FIGURE 10–2

Use of Decision Support Systems and Executive Information Systems Relative to Transaction Processing Systems and Management Information Systems

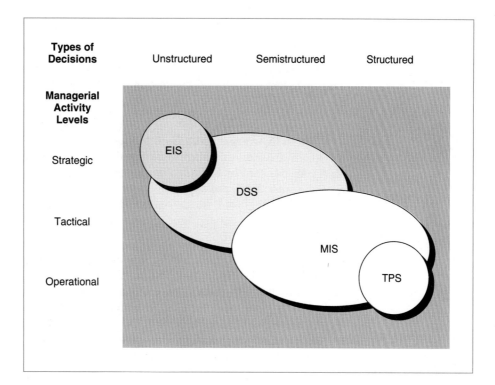

make the final decisions. On the other hand, an EIS is normally used by only one person—a top-level executive—to view information in a format specifically designed for his or her needs. Based on this information, an executive may detect a problem or a competitive opportunity that requires investigation.

A DSS has been used in many different situations, including the following:

- At Texaco, to determine the most profitable blend of petroleum products

- By the San Francisco police department, to analyze various scenarios regarding shift length and patrol car staffing

- At Popeye's Famous Fried Chicken, to decide on a takeover of Church's Chicken and Biscuits

On the other hand, EISs have been used in the following situations:

- By Midland Marine Bank, to give executives a better awareness of the bank's earning picture

- At Bank of Boston, to help executives identify problems that cost the bank millions of dollars

- By Lockheed Aircraft Company, to allow executives to monitor the progress of planes on the assembly line or view updates on sales negotiations with foreign governments

Now that we have reviewed the use of DSS and EIS and looked at some examples of their use, we discuss each type of information system in more detail.

10.1 An Overview of Decision Support Systems

DSS was first suggested in the early 1970s by information systems researchers. In particular, G.M. Gorry and M.S. Scott Morton[3] noted the need for an information system that would give decision makers more than the summary results provided by the TPS or the reports provided by MIS. At the same time, researchers concluded that the mathematical models developed by management scientists could not be used in all types of decisions. Finally, Data Base Management Systems (DBMS) were developed to access needed information through user queries. These concurrent developments together formed the concept of DSS.

Recall from Chapter 3 that a DSS is composed of three elements—the data base, the model base, and the dialog base. The data base contains the many files of information generated by the TPS, and the model base comprises management science and other mathematical models that are used to analyze data. The dialog base provides a user friendly interactive front end to the DSS. Often, the dialog base uses graphics to allow the user to choose among data files and models. Graphics are also important for displaying data and the results of using the models.

In addition to these three elements is the all-important human user—whether a single executive, someone who runs the system for the manager, or a staff of analysts. Figure 10–3 shows all four elements of a DSS—data base, model base, dialog base, and human user.

Decision Support System at ProYacht, Inc.

ProYacht, Inc., a manufacturer of sailboats and windsurfers, may expand its operations by purchasing Cool Water Marinas, a marina chain. To make this decision, ProYacht must evaluate the locations of its dealers along with those of Cool Water Marinas, forecast sales with and without the merger, and track the effects of competitors on the merger. Using a DSS, analysts at ProYacht evaluate the reams of demographic and market data that might impinge on the decision. This system uses IBM compatible personal computers based on the Intel 80486 chip that are linked to CD-ROM disk players. The disks store data on population, income, and boat ownership.

Although demographic factors traditionally account for less than 50 percent of dealer decisions, the ProYacht DSS is indispensable to top management during the buyout process. Because ProYacht's staff cannot physically visit each Cool Water Marina location, they plot location models on a screen to measure their proximity to existing ProYacht dealers and retailers. With this information and the market analysis results, ProYacht's management can decide whether the merger will lead to increased total sales and profit. If it decides to purchase Cool Water Marinas, ProYacht's management can use

[3] G.M. Gorry and M.S. Scott Morton, "A Framework for Management Information Systems," *Sloan Management Review,* Fall 1971.

FIGURE 10–3

Decision Support
System

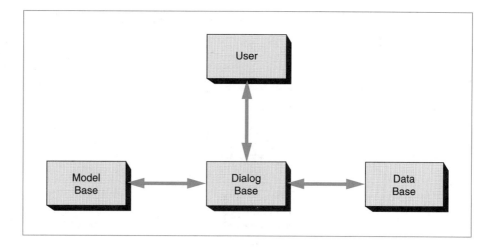

Measuring
Profitability at
McKesson
Corporation

In the wholesale pharmaceutical business, profit margins are razor-thin, with profits reduced to pennies on each sales dollar. At McKesson Corporation, a PC-based DSS is providing a way to increase the company's profitability by concentrating on the details of each sale and each customer. Although the company's 1990 revenues were $7.8 billion, McKesson found that not all sales dollars bring in the same profit. For example, one customer may pay bills faster than another, boosting cash flow. On the other hand, another customer's orders may require inventory increases that stretch working capital to the limit.

To increase its profitability, McKesson uses a spreadsheet on a personal computer to work through variables and calculate profitability on a product-by-product and customer-by-customer basis. By knowing how profitable a par-

ticular customer or product is, McKesson management can decide how to price new business, whether to change a product's price, or whether to pursue new business. The DSS also highlights situations in which one customer "subsidizes" another because of the cost difference of serving the two customers.

Having knowledge on profitability cannot guarantee higher profits in all cases because competitive pressures may keep the company from taking a desirable action. However, the profitability DSS has proved very helpful in other ways. In 1989, for example, it was used to help negotiate a $400 million contract with the Wal-Mart chain of discount stores for drug and beauty products.

SOURCE: A. Richard Immel, "McKesson's Monster 1-2-3 Profitability Models," *Lotus,* September 1990, pp. 13–14.

FIGURE 10–4   *Addition of Cool Water Marinas to ProYacht, Inc.*

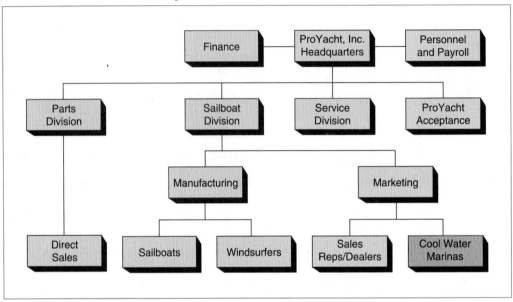

the same DSS to decide whether a Cool Water marina should be closed, continued, or ultimately converted into a ProYacht dealer.

In the ProYacht example, the data base contains a large amount of demographic data about boat registrations and sales that are used in the forecasting and location models to aid management's decision making. If the decision is positive, this information helps management decide the fate of dealer, marina, and retailer locations. The dialog base consists of a graphic display of analysis results, as well as the locations of dealers, marinas, and retailers. Figure 10–4 shows the relationship of the proposed Cool Water Marinas acquisition to the remainder of the existing ProYacht, Inc. organization.

*Features and
Characteristics
of Decision
Support Systems*

Any definition of DSS includes the following four major characteristics:

1. Computer-based system that helps decision makers with semistructured and unstructured problems

2. Supports but does not replace decision maker's intuition and judgment

3. Composed of both data and models

4. Improves the *effectiveness* of decisions

We now consider how these four characteristics figure in the DSS used by ProYacht to decide whether to buy Cool Water Marinas and then to decide which Cool Water locations to close. The buyout decision is a good example of an unstructured problem that occurs only once. The second decision is a semistructured decision in that various location models can be used to compare existing dealerships, but the final "close or convert'' decision must be made by ProYacht's management. Only a computer-based system would allow ProYacht management to analyze the huge amount of sales and demographic data and to compare the hundreds of combined ProYacht and Cool Water locations.

In this case, the second characteristic is apparent in that both decisions—the buyout and the close-or-convert decisions—must still be made by management. The mathematical models and data in the DSS can suggest the result of making one decision over another, but the DSS cannot make the final decision.

The third characteristic of a DSS—being composed of data and models—is also obvious in the ProYacht case. Although billions of characters of demographic registration and sales data are available to analysts, these data are not very helpful until used in the models that evaluate locations and forecast sales. Even though DSS has both data and model components, one component may be more evident to the user than the other. For example, when marina and dealership locations are plotted and compared, the data component is more evident. However, data or models alone cannot provide the needed information to management.

Finally, ProYacht's DSS improved decision-making effectiveness by providing management with information in a usable form. For example, by plotting existing sales locations, decision makers could see clearly that many Cool Water marinas are in the same vicinity as ProYacht dealers. This last point highlights the importance in DSS of using graphics to demonstrate the results of data queries or model solutions. By clearly displaying results in a graphic form, a DSS improves the effectiveness of managerial decision making.

Benefits of Using Decision Support Systems

In addition to the obvious benefits from using DSS (such as solving complex problems in a short amount of time), several other advantages are associated with the use of a DSS. These benefits include the following:

1. Capability to test different scenarios or to respond quickly to unexpected situations

2. Improvement in communication and gain of new insights about a particular situation

3. Cost savings and improved management control

4. Structured decision-making process results in decisions that are more defensible

For ProYacht, Inc., management benefits from the use of a DSS in all of these ways. For example, analysts can compare the effects of merging versus not merging, examine the size of the combined company and the proximity of sites, and test the effects of closing or converting Cool Water Marinas on ProYacht's overall marketing plan.

In the second case, ProYacht's management benefits from the use of the DSS for improving communication and gaining insights. For example, managers must communicate with one another about the results of the forecasting and location analyses. The graphical display of the combined dealerships also shows them something new—that both companies had followed a similar location strategy.

For the third benefit, ProYacht's management should be able to reduce costs after seeing the dealership locations and the sales forecast. Finally, in the fourth case, through the use of a DSS, management can more easily defend the decision concerning Cool Water Marinas because the logic and analyses that contribute to the final decision are documented.

10.2 Types of Decision Support Systems

Decision Support System Generators

The ProYacht DSS is an example of one type of DSS — a specific DSS. The other types are the DSS generator and DSS tools. A **specific DSS** supports a specific application and is ready for use by decision makers. A specific DSS can be used, for example, to blend gasoline or determine the optimal police force distribution.

To develop a specific DSS, a DSS generator is often used. A **DSS generator** is computer software that provides the capability to quickly and easily develop a specific DSS. Rather than using a computer language to develop a specific DSS, developers use the various modules and tools in the DSS generator. One of the first such DSS generators was the Geodata Analysis and Display System (GADS) developed by IBM in the early 1970s. The GADS DSS generator was first used to develop a police force allocation specific DSS for San Jose, CA. Using this DSS, an officer could display a map of the city and request data by zone on service, response time, and activity level. This same DSS generator was used to build other specific DSSs for various situations, including setting school attendance boundaries, establishing sales territories, and routing copier repair personnel. IBM used the GADS DSS generator to quickly (in less than a month) build a specific DSS that would support the assignment of its customer service engineers.

Numerous other DSS generators have been developed for both mainframes and personal computers. In fact, by 1985, over 60 mainframe DSS generators existed. Many mainframe DSS generators also have PC versions. A good example of a DSS generator that has both mainframe and PC versions is IFPS (Interactive Financial Planning Systems) from Execucom Systems, Inc. Originally developed in the 1970s for use on mainframes, IFPS has since been modified to run on personal computers.

Spreadsheets, data base management packages, and integrated packages are also used as DSS generators. Spreadsheets such as Lotus 1-2-3, Excel from Microsoft, and Quattro from Borland are often used as DSS generators. Spreadsheet packages have various features that make them excellent DSS generators, including the following:

- The commonly used spreadsheet–user interface

- Inclusion of financial and mathematical functions that can make complex computations

- Availability of macro languages that can be used to write programs for the modeling logic

- Capability to input data base files from commonly used data base management packages

PC-based data base management packages such as dBase IV and RBase are also used as DSS generators because of built-in data base manipulation capabilities and user friendly interface. These data base management packages also have powerful programming

FIGURE 10–5

*Relationship
Among Types of
Decision Support
Systems*

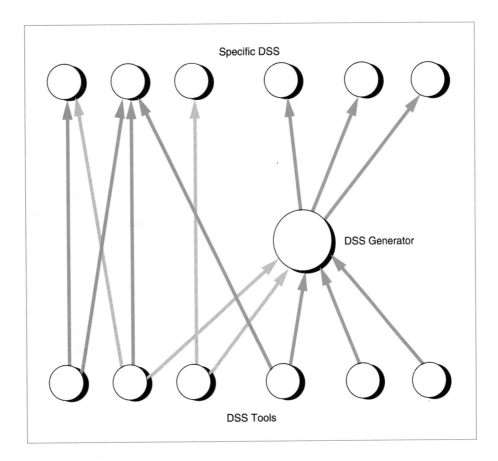

languages that allow developers to handle the modeling logic. When combined with operating system batch commands, these packages become even more useful as DSS generators. With spreadsheet, data base, graphics, and word processing functions combined in a single package, a PC-based integrated software package offers developers another option as a DSS generator.

*Decision
Support System
Tools*

Just as DSS generators are used to build specific DSSs, **DSS tools** facilitate the creation of DSS generators. These tools include programming languages, financial and mathematical functions, optimization, simulation, and forecasting model procedures, hardware and software graphics, and data base query systems. DSS tools are generally used to create the DSS generators that then create specific DSSs. These same DSS tools can also be used to create specific DSSs directly. The relationship between a specific DSS, DSS generators, and DSS tools is shown in Figure 10–5.

FIGURE 10–6

***Expanded View of
Decision Support
Systems***

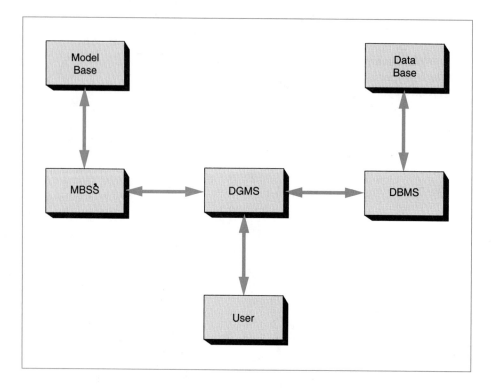

10.3 Elements of Decision Support Systems

As shown in Figure 10–3, the DSS is composed of three computer-based elements—the data base, the model base, and the dialog base—plus the human user. This section examines in detail each of the three elements plus the interaction with the human user. We also consider how the four parts of the DSS work together to support managerial decision making.

The interactions among the three DSS elements must be managed by software systems —the **Data Base Management System (DBMS), the Model Base Software System (MBSS),** and the **Dialog Generation and Management System (DGMS).** These systems are shown in the conceptual DSS in Figure 10–6. As with the use of DBMS, discussed in Chapters 5 and 6, these three software systems must be in place for the overall DSS to work. We now consider the important aspects of each system.

Data Base Management System

The DBMS supplies the data that models use in their analyses and allows managers to make direct queries. Where does the DSS data base obtain the needed data? These data basically have three sources—the organization's primary data base, external data, and data entered interactively by the user. The DBMS must be able to extract the proper data from the primary data base, capture needed data from external sources, and allow interactive entry of other data. The data are then stored in the DSS data base, which is managed by a DBMS. The DBMS must execute various functions, including management of data storage, retrieval of required data, and generation of reports. Figure 10–7 shows the operation of the DBMS. The DBMS must combine, condense, and filter data;

FIGURE 10–7   *Operation of Data Base Management Systems*

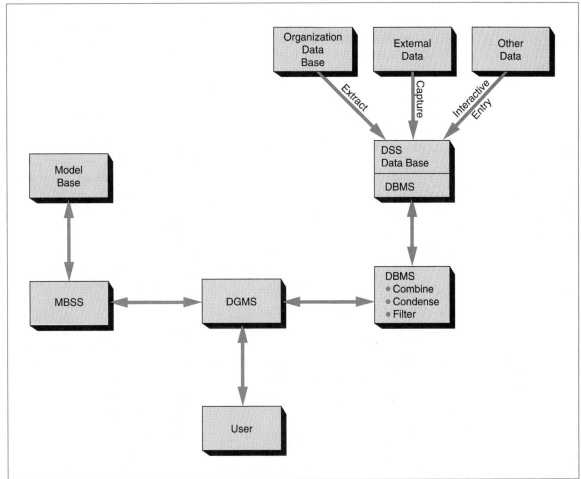

add or delete data sources; and allow for restructuring of the data base by the user as needed for decision making.

Model Base Software System

Like the DSS data base, the DSS model base requires a software system that can handle the following three very important operations:

1. Interaction with the dialog system, so the user can view the possible models, request data that are not available from the data base, and see the results of a model's analyses

2. Management of various models, so a model that is requested by the user is available in a form that is consistent with other models and with the data available from the DBMS

3. Interaction with the DBMS, to obtain the data needed by the chosen model

For a DSS to be used by managers, the first MBSS operation must work extremely well. If managers cannot easily view the available models, choose one that meets their needs, integrate them as needed, and then view the output from the model in an understandable form, they will quickly look for some other tool to help them with their decision making. In fact, one reason often given for the failure to use the tools of management science is that the models are hard to use and do not provide output in a usable form.

The MBSS must manage the various models the way a DBMS manages the data base. The functions include adding, deleting, and modifying models; cataloging, linking, and accessing models; and creating new models by using predefined modules and subroutines.

The last MBSS operation—obtaining data from the data base needed by the chosen model—requires that the MBSS interact with the data base to obtain internal data. The overall operation of the MBSS within the DSS is shown in Figure 10–8.

Types of Models

In Chapter 2, we briefly discussed three types of models commonly used in a DSS—forecasting, optimization, and simulation. In a **forecasting model,** historical data, managerial assumptions, and a forecasting formula are combined to produce a "guess" at future activities. For example, a university would like to predict the number of incoming freshmen in order to plan dormitory space. As applications begin to arrive in the fall, predictions can be made on how many students will actually matriculate the following year. This prediction report would be based on the number and quality of applications compared with previous years, the acceptance rate, and the attendance rate for students accepted. Although the predicted number of students probably becomes more accurate as the actual beginning of school approaches, even the earliest prediction reports help the administration to make plans. Early plans are refined as the forecasts improve each month.

In an **optimization model,** the user implements a mathematical technique that determines the best possible solution to the model. The most common forms of optimization are unconstrained methods using calculus and constrained methods such as linear and integer programming. With constrained methods, the range of possible solutions is somehow restricted. For example, we may wish to find the maximum profit associated with production of a particular product, which is constrained by the availability of raw materials and labor hours.

With a **simulation model,** the decision maker uses a series of values to simulate a particular situation. Simulation is often performed when the model that is developed is too complex for optimization techniques or more information on a model is needed than just the best solution. Using a computer, several years of operations can be simulated in just a few seconds. After the results are compiled and analyzed, they can be used to determine the effect of any change on the model. For example, the effect on profit of several promotional schemes and quality levels can be simulated for several years to test their long-term effects. Simulation models are often used for **"what if" analysis.**

FIGURE 10–8   *Operation of Model Base Software Systems*

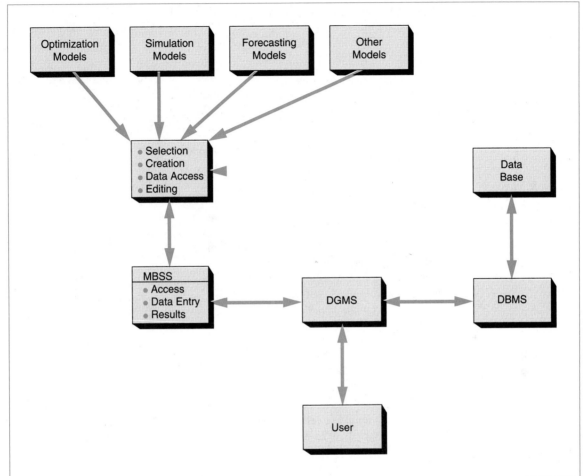

Another way of classifying the models in the model base is by the level of management that uses them—that is, operational models, tactical models, and strategic models. Operational models are used predominately by operational managers to manage the day-to-day activities of an organization, often including small loan approval, inventory analysis, quality control, and production scheduling. These models depend heavily on the organization's data base for needed data. Tactical models are used by middle-level managers who must allocate resources and control costs while carrying out the policies of the organization. Tactical models include defining sales or service regions, oil blending, and short-term capital budgeting. Optimization models for determining the best solution are often used for this type of decision. Finally, strategic models are used by executives to make long-term decisions that affect the organization. The time frame for this type of

A Gasoline Blending DSS at Texaco

Crucial to the effective operation of any oil refinery is the gasoline blending operation. If too much of one type of gasoline is produced, a surplus of that type of gasoline and a shortage of another type may exist, resulting in lower profits for the refinery. Various types of computerized optimization models have been used for several decades to determine the highest profit blend of gasolines. However, these models were not always up-to-date and did not always incorporate data available from refinery data bases and online data acquisition.

To address these problems, Texaco began work in 1980 on a DSS for planning and scheduling its blending operations. Texaco's DSS, called OMEGA, has a data acquisition and query module as well as provisions for using linear and nonlinear equations that predict output blend qualities and volumes. The system allows the user to retrieve a variety of data from refinery data bases and, by selecting from a menu, to construct and solve nonlinear optimization models to arrive at an acceptable blend.

By 1989, OMEGA was installed at all nine Texaco refineries. Use of this DSS has resulted in an estimated $30 million annual increase in profits, improved quality control, supplied better planning and marketing information, and helped managers conduct "What if?" studies.

SOURCE: Calvin W. Dewitt and others, "OMEGA: An Improved Gasoline Blending System for Texaco," *Interfaces,* Jan.–Feb., 1989, pp. 85–101.

decision is usually in years and simulation modeling is often used to handle extremely complex constraints and relationships among variables. The ProYacht decision to buy Cool Water Marinas is an example of the use of strategic models to support decision making.

Dialog Generation and Management System

The two elements of the DSS discussed so far — the DBMS and the MBSS — can be useful on their own. However, for the DSS to support managerial decision making, it *must* have an effective DGMS. In a sense, the DGMS makes the DSS different from a traditional data base or set of management science models by its ease of use and flexibility in manipulating the data and models.

The DGMS has three elements — action language, display language, and user's knowledge. The action language is how the user communicates with the DSS. This communication occurs through keyboard commands, selections from a menu, use of a mouse or trackball to select icons on the screen, or even voice or handwritten commands.

The DSS presents output through the display language. In other words, display language creates what the user sees on the screen or reads on the printed page. The use of graphics is growing as more DSSs use bar and pie graphs, or combinations of various types of graphs, to show the relationships among the variables in a model.

FIGURE 10–9

Operations of Dialog Generation and Management System

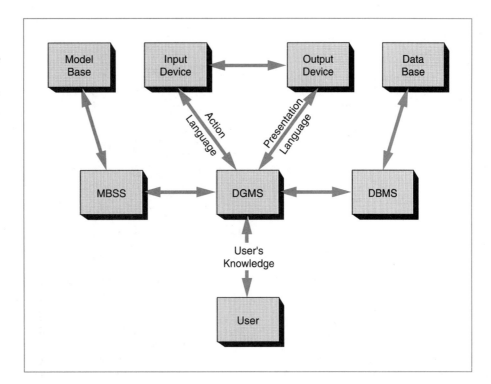

Finally, the user's knowledge is what the user brings to the interface with the DSS. This knowledge may be in the user's head, in a user's manual, or in reference materials. This part of the DGMS is shared with the user element, discussed in the next section. Figure 10–9 shows the operations of the DGMS.

DSS User The ideal user of the DSS is the manager who makes the decision. However, two other types of users may also access the DSS—staff analysts and "DSS chauffeurs." Staff analysts are specialists in a particular decision area (for example, finance, marketing, or production). As members of the support staff, this group of users is very familiar with the DSS, spending as much time as necessary to develop alternative solutions to a problem.

On the other hand, the "DSS chauffeur" is an assistant to the decision maker who handles the actual interface with the DSS. In this role, he or she becomes very familiar with the DSS action language and interprets the display language for the decision maker.

Any user(s)—decision maker, staff analyst, or "DSS chauffeur"—must be sufficiently familiar with the problem to understand the interaction between the data base and model base. The user must also ask the right questions and then understand the alternative solutions presented. Because the decision-making executive may not have enough time to learn the action language and interpret the display, staff analysts and "DSS chauffeurs" are often the actual users of the system.

FIGURE 10–10

***Iterative
Development
Process***

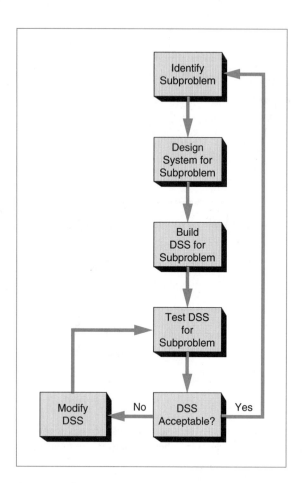

10.4

**Developing a
Decision
Support
System**

Before a DSS can be used, it must be developed. Decision makers must be involved in any development approach to ensure that the final product meets their needs. Because of the unstructured nature of the problems often addressed by a DSS, the structured systems analysis and design approach discussed briefly in Chapter 3 (and in detail in Chapters 12 and 13) may be inappropriate for developing a DSS. This unstructured nature makes it difficult, if not impossible, to determine the components of the final system.

To handle the uncertainty that exists in the development of DSS for unstructured problems, the system must be developed in an iterative manner so that end users can learn from the system as it is developed. In the **iterative design approach,** one small but important part of a problem is selected for development. After this subproblem is satisfactorily solved, it is tested by the DSS user for a short period (say, a few weeks) and modified if necessary. Other subproblems are handled in a similar manner. These subproblems are then combined in a similar interactive manner to form a complete system.

FIGURE 10–11

Positioning of Decision Support System Roles

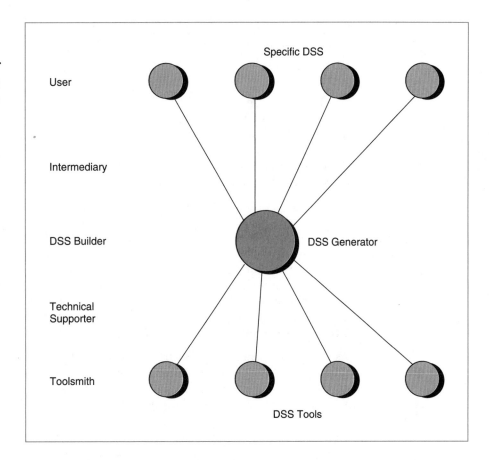

Specific DSS

User

Intermediary

DSS Builder — DSS Generator

Technical Supporter

Toolsmith

DSS Tools

This process, often termed **prototyping,** is repeated until a *relatively* stable DSS is developed. A DSS is only relatively stable, because any DSS changes and is adapted as necessary to meet the changing needs of decision makers. A DSS may also change to include better solution methodologies in the model base or improved computer technology in the model and dialog bases. The iterative design process is shown in Figure 10–10.

Decision Support System Roles

In the iterative development of a DSS, various roles are ideally played by managers and technicians in the project team. Ralph Sprague[4] lists five such roles in the development process—manager or user, intermediary, DSS builder, technical supporter, and toolsmith. The manager or user is the ultimate decision maker who uses the specific DSS, and the intermediary is actually the ''DSS chauffeur'' mentioned earlier. The DSS builder uses a DSS generator to develop a specific DSS. This person must not only understand how the DSS generator is used to develop a specific DSS, but also the problems to be solved by the decision maker.

[4] Ralph H. Sprague, Jr., ''A Framework for the Development of Decision Support Systems,'' *MIS Quarterly,* 4, 4 (1980).

The technical supporter must be familiar enough with the DSS generator to add new solution methodologies, data bases, and display technologies to the DSS generator as required by the DSS builder. The toolsmith works directly with DSS tools to include new languages, hardware, and other new technology in the DSS. Figure 10–11 shows the positioning of these roles relative to the types of DSS.

In Figure 10–11, note that a one-to-one correspondence between roles and individuals does *not* exist. The manager and the intermediary may be the same person, or the "manager" may actually be a group of decision makers. Similarly, the DSS builder may be a group of analysts who develop the DSS. In any case, the manager role is supported by all other roles for better decision making.

10.5 Group Decision Support Systems

The discussion so far has assumed that, in most cases, the decision maker is a single person, and the DSS is designed to support this decision maker. However, evidence does not support the single decision maker concept except for relatively minor decisions. In most large public or private international organizations, major decisions are made collectively. Even if a single executive makes the final decision, he or she usually gives strong consideration to the consensus opinion of his or her advisors. Because of this collective nature of decision making, various researchers have suggested the need for **Group Decision Support Systems (GDSS).**

As defined by Geraldine DeSanctis and Brent Gallupe, a GDSS is an "interactive computer-based system that facilitates the solution of unstructured problems by a set of decision makers working together as a group." [5] The key word in this decision is "facilitates," because the emphasis of a GDSS is not on providing alternatives from which the group chooses, but on improving the group decision-making process. As any organization manager can attest, group decision making occurs during meetings. At these meetings, typically 5–20 individuals from different functional units and hierarchical levels meet face-to-face to discuss issues of mutual concern. Differences of opinion are usually handled by compromise.

A GDSS usually has a DSS imbedded within it providing data and alternative solutions to members of the group. However, the GDSS is more than just a DSS used by a group. In addition to the data base and model base in the DSS, the GDSS must have the necessary hardware—display screens, individual workstations, and telecommunications network—that allows easy communication within the group. The GDSS also requires special applications software that allows the group to work on solutions as well as private work. This software must also allow for free communications among individuals of the group and between group members and a special person not unlike the DSS chauffeur. However, this "GDSS facilitator" has the role of helping the group use the GDSS hardware and software to reach a decision. If a group member requests a specific analysis, the facilitator can run an imbedded DSS and use the display screen to show the results of various analyses. Figure 10–12 shows a model of a GDSS.

---

[5] Geraldine DeSanctis and Brent Gallupe, "Group Decision Support Systems: A New Frontier," *Database,* Winter 1985.

FIGURE 10–12

*Model of a Group
Decision Support
System*

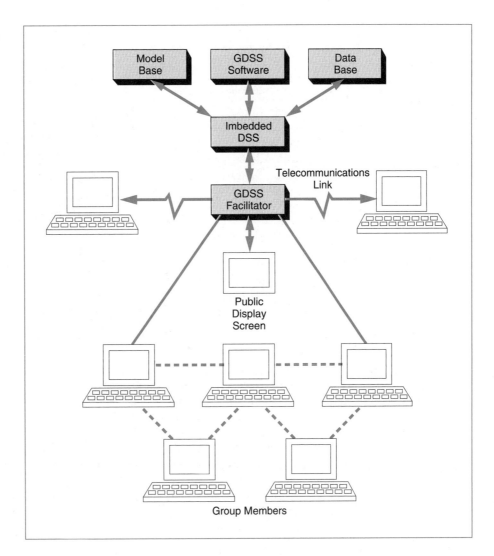

*Group Decision
Support System
Scenarios*

According to DeSanctis and Gallupe, four possible scenarios exist for using a GDSS—decision room, local decision network, teleconferencing, and remote decision making. In the **decision room** scenario, group members are all physically located in a special room equipped with individual workstations and a display screen. Group members can communicate verbally or by sending messages between workstations. The facilitator can display desired analyses, or members can show the results of a private analysis. After various alternatives are tested, the group can move toward a consensus on the appropriate decision.

In the **local decision network,** group members remain at their individual locations and send messages among workstations through a network. This scenario loses the face-to-face component but increases flexibility by not requiring members to attend an actual

Companies Use
Groupware to
Share
Information

A new type of software that allows computer users to share information is groupware. One of the early products in this class of software is Notes from Lotus Development Corporation. Notes is a communications tool that allows users to see and share different views of the same information. Although still not a widely used product, Notes has helped some companies find ways to allow their employees to work together better.

- The Progressive Corporation, an insurance company, uses Notes extensively for tracking projects and resolving problems. At Progressive, any member of a support team at company headquarters can take a call about a support topic and enter that topic in the Notes data base accessed by other members of the team.

- At the Minnesota Department of Revenue, a Notes workstation is used by a vendor supplying the department with a new type of data base system. By using Notes, the normal contractual relationship between user and vendor turned into a partnership, and questions from the department were answered with corrections to the data base system code.

SOURCE: Robert L. Scheier, ''IS Staffs Put Lotus Notes to Work—and Reap the Benefits,'' *PC Week,* June 3, 1991, p. 14.

meeting. In the **teleconferencing** scenario, members are divided into subgroups that are physically distant from one another. Each subgroup is in a special room (similar to that used for the decision room scenario), and each subgroup sees the same display. Using telecommunications, members of the subgroups can communicate with one another. Finally, the **remote decision making** alternative uses wide area networks to allow the same type of communications between member workstations as in the local decision network scenario. This system may often use the fax mode to communicate about complex issues. By using fax machines, decision makers can send sophisticated diagrams and figures. GDSS is now a small part of the overall information system, but as telecommunications systems grow in use, so too will the use of GDSS.

10.6 Executive Information Systems

When the concept of DSS was first suggested in the 1970s, it was aimed at the decision makers in an organization who needed better information than that provided by MIS-generated reports. Early researchers hoped that DSS would be used by top-level executives in their decision making. Unfortunately, to make a DSS powerful enough to solve complex problems using the available data required that the user be knowledgeable about the models being used and proficient in the use of the computer–user interface. Although some top-level executives have taken the time and made the effort to learn how to use DSS or the ''DSS chauffeur'' discussed earlier, researchers found that the actual use of the DSS was pushed down the managerial hierarchy to middle-level managers or staff analysts. These individuals would respond to questions from executives by working with the DSS.

A Control Room EIS

A major problem in the banking industry during the last decade has been a lack of control over problems. Rather than let superiors know about problem loans or late accounts receivable, managers have often covered up problems until they could be solved. At the Bank of Boston, an EIS "control room" ensures that problems are brought to the surface and solved immediately.

The control room idea originated with a group of information systems employees, who concluded that bank paperwork was no different from the production flow in a factory. Taking this analogy a step further, the group decided that an EIS control room could alert managers to problem areas just like the control room at a nuclear plant warns managers of problems. This unique EIS even used colors to designate the current status of a problem—green for no problem, yellow for a potential problem, and red for a full-blown problem.

Individual managers call into the "control room" software group each day to give the current status of their departments. The software group then updates the EIS. Executives access the EIS and can immediately see the status of all departments from the identifiable colors. An executive can then "drill down" into the data base of the problem department to determine the cause of the problem. Bank of Boston executives feel that, at a cost of only $300,000, the EIS is a big success, catching errors that could have cost the bank millions of dollars.

SOURCE: Robert L. Scheier, "Bank Enlists EIS in Battle to Boost Control," *PC Week,* February 5, 1990, pp. 129, 131.

When researchers investigated why executives were not using DSS, they discovered that executives were usually short of time and needed information in a very specific form. Based on these time restrictions and information needs, the use of executive information systems (EIS) was proposed. As defined by D.W. Delong and J.F. Rockart,[6] an EIS is a user friendly, graphically oriented, computer-based information system that provides rapid access to timely information and direct access to management reports. To understand EIS, we first need to look at what makes top-level executives unique in any organization.

Who Needs an Executive Information System?

The top executives of any organization often carry titles of Chief Executive Officer (CEO), Chief Operating Officer (COO), and Chief Financial Officer (CFO). All members of the "executive suite" are responsible for the long-term well-being of an organization. Such executives are not just middle-level managers who make more money, they must have a vision of the organization beyond just their department or a budgeting period. Executives also have a wider range of responsibilities and interests than lower-level managers. Figure 10–13 shows a typical organization chart with the positions that would normally be classified as executive in the shaded box.

[6] D.W. DeLong and J.F. Rockart, "Identifying the Attributes of Successful Executive Support System Implementation," in *DSS 86 Transactions,* 7th Annual Conference on DSS (San Francisco: The Institute of Management Sciences, June 1987).

FIGURE 10–13

*Executives in an
Organization*

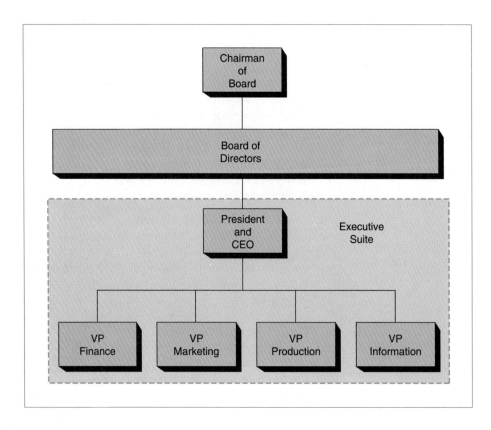

Executives also do different types of work from lower-level managers. Researchers have tried to determine the various roles that executives have in an organization. Classical management theory describes five managerial functions—plan, organize, staff, direct, and control. However, this says little about what managers actually do. In 1968, Henry Mintzberg[7] observed five executives for a sufficient period to develop three types of roles—interpersonal, informational, and decisional. These three types and the actual executive roles that are included in each type are shown in Figure 10–14.

Mintzberg's roles show that an executive must do many different things in a finite amount of time each day. For this reason, time is an executive's most precious commodity. One role requires information of all types—the monitoring role. In this role, the manager is constantly vigilant for problems that must be solved. Although much of this information is generated in meetings, information also comes from other sources, including computer data bases. However, unless that information is current and easy to obtain, it is of no use to the executive. The need for current information precludes the use of traditional MIS reports, which are often too old for the executive to use. Similarly, the

---

[7] Henry Mintzberg, *The Nature of Managerial Work* (New York: Harper & Row, 1973).

FIGURE 10–14

Mintzberg's
Executive Roles

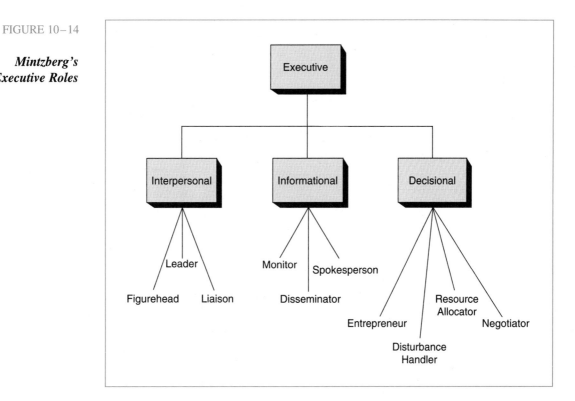

need for ease of access often eliminates the use of a DSS. For this reason, executives are using an EIS to provide the needed information.

Executives want information in a specific form, which may vary from person to person. One executive may want to see the price of the firm's stock or that of competitors, customers, or suppliers on a real-time basis, while another may want to see a daily production schedule report. Each executive may use a different indicator to monitor activities, and any EIS must comply with this information requirement. For this reason, the EIS is often called a ''personalized presentation system'' that shows the data the executive wants in the desired form.

EIS often features personal computers linked directly to an organization's mainframe. In this arrangement, mainframes are the repositories of up-to-date information drawn from the organization's data base and extracted from external data bases. The mainframe also filters and compresses the information.

Personal computers provide the ease-of-use and graphic output required by the EIS. Menu-driven or icon-based selection systems are used so that an executive can select the type and form of information to be displayed. Some executives have no problem using a keyboard to make these selections, but alternative forms of input, such as a mouse, touchscreen, trackball, or voice recognition system, may be used to find the needed data.

FIGURE 10–15

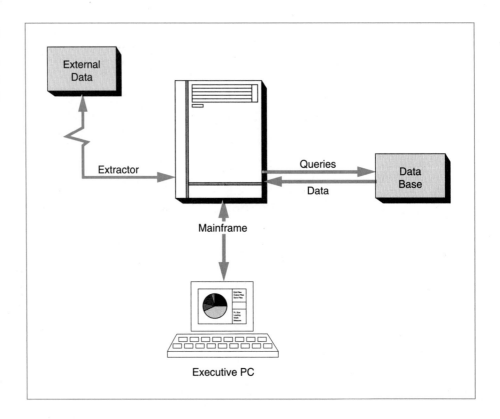

The data are often displayed as colorful and informative graphics on high resolution screens. Figure 10–15 shows the structure of a typical EIS.

Executive Information System at ProYacht, Inc.

Like virtually all manufacturers across the country, ProYacht, Inc. is always looking for ways to improve its profitability. ProYacht's EIS provides information that executives would not otherwise have. The ProYacht EIS consists of a personal computer with a custom-designed graphic interface that is linked to ProYacht's mainframe and gives executives access to a variety of applications and standard reports. The executives use personal computers because of their user friendliness, but the data and programs actually reside on the mainframe.

Widely used applications on ProYacht's EIS include the competitor group analysis, the financial report, the contribution margin report, and the human resources report. The competitor group analysis enables an executive to judge ProYacht's performance compared with that of a group of competing sailboat and windsurfer manufacturers. The financial report displays as many as eight different reports on profitability, sales trends, and manufacturing costs. The contribution margin report allows executives to look at standard reports on division profitability or even to see data for a specific product. Finally, the human resources report provides information on the number of employees, expenses, and turnovers. After the first year of operation for the ProYacht EIS, senior executives were far more knowledgeable about ProYacht's earnings performance than in past years. This increased awareness allowed them to take timely action, for example, to counter a competitor's promotional campaign or to reduce costs.

Characteristics of Executive Information Systems

An EIS must have the following five characteristics to provide needed information:

1. Provide timely information in a form that the executive can use. Only the needed information should be supplied.

2. Contain extensive graphics capabilities so information is presented in an easy-to-understand form; for example, exceptions to expected results should be highlighted.

3. Allow the manager to "drill down" to reach the information behind the graphics on the screen. This function requires a sophisticated DBMS that responds to executives' questions.

4. Be easy to use, with minimal learning time required.

5. Have access to internal data and data on an organization's environment, for example, customers, competitors, and government.

In addition to these five characteristics, the EIS must include data other than traditional accounting values that indicate the health of the company. These **key performance indicators** show executives where the company stands relative to its competition and company objectives.

The ProYacht EIS fits these characteristics in various ways. First, the combined personal computer and mainframe system uses an easy custom-designed graphical interface. Mainframe data are compressed and filtered into needed reports concerning the internal performance of the company and that of the competition.

"Drill-down," an important feature of any EIS, allows an executive to pinpoint the underlying cause of a problem in the data being displayed. For example, an executive may want to view the data behind a graph, and the EIS must make this type of investigation possible. In the ProYacht EIS, if the human resources report shows an abnormal turnover level in a particular division, the executive may want to look at other data on that particular department to determine if a personnel problem exists.

Executives probably do not make any major decisions based on just the data provided by an EIS. Instead, they may bring the problem they have discovered through monitoring to the attention of a lower-level manager or analyst, who then uses a DSS to find the cause of the problem and suggest possible solutions. Recalling Mintzberg's roles, the EIS can enhance the monitoring role. The decisional roles—entrepreneur, disturbance handler, resource allocator, and negotiator—can be enhanced through a DSS.

10.7 Summary

Any organization's long-term survival depends on the quality of decisions made by its managers. When decisions tend to be unstructured, sophisticated information systems are needed to provide the required information and answers to managers' questions. Depending on the level of the decision makers involved and the types of queries, either DSS or EIS is needed. In the decision-making process, EIS is useful for identifying problems, gathering data, and monitoring the results of a decision. On the other hand, DSS is needed for identifying and evaluating alternatives and selecting the best course of action. DSS is most often used at middle levels of management, and EIS is used by executives.

DSS is made up of a data base, model base, dialog base, and user. The data base contains the data used by the models in the DSS. The dialog base provides a ''user friendly'' front-end for the system. The user who interfaces with the dialog base may be the decision maker, but more often the user is a group of staff analysts or a middle-level tactical manager. DSS characteristics include helping decision makers with semistructured and unstructured problems; supporting, but not replacing, the decision maker's judgment; being composed of both data and models; and improving the effectiveness of decisions. Benefits of using DSS include the capability to test scenarios, better communication and learning, cost savings and improved control, and more defensible decisions. The three types of DSS are the specific DSS, DSS generators, and DSS tools. Composed of DSS tools, DSS generators are used to create a specific DSS. An effective DSS must have software that allows the interaction among the data base, model base, and dialog base. This software is the DBMS, the MBSS, and the DGMS. A DSS is developed using an iterative approach. GDSS is used to facilitate the group decision-making process.

EIS provides needed information for executives in their monitoring role. These systems are graphically oriented and often feature personal computers linked to mainframe computers. An EIS must rapidly provide timely information in an easy-to-understand graphical form, provide access to the information behind the graphs, be easy to use, and have access to internal and external data. An EIS is commonly used to identify problems for which alternative solutions are found using DSS.

Key Terms

ad hoc decisions
Data Base Management System (DBMS)
decision making
decision room
Decision Support System (DSS)
Dialog Generation and Management System (DGMS)
DSS generator
DSS tools
Executive Information System (EIS)
forecasting model
Group Decision Support Systems (GDSS)
iterative design approach

key performance indicators
local decision network
Model Base Software System (MBSS)
optimization model
programmed decisions
prototyping
remote decision making
simulation model
specific DSS
structured decisions
teleconferencing
unprogrammed decisions
unstructured decisions
''what if'' analysis

Review Questions

1. Discuss briefly the differences among structured, semistructured, and unstructured decisions.

2. What is the role of information systems in decision making?

3. Briefly compare DSS and EIS in terms of how they are used.

4. What developments led to the concept of DSS?

5. What are the three parts of a DSS? Which one does the user interact with?

6. List the four major characteristics of DSS.

7. Apply the four characteristics in Question 6 to the ProYacht DSS discussed in this chapter.

8. List the benefits of using a DSS. Discuss how ProYacht benefited from the use of a DSS.

9. Discuss the types of DSS in use today. Which of these types of DSS is a spreadsheet?

10. What is the purpose of a DBMS in a DSS? What is the purpose of an MBSS?

11. What are the three types of models used in DSS? How can models be matched with managerial levels?

12. How is a DSS usually developed? What are the five DSS roles in the development of a DSS?

13. What are the four GDSS scenarios? Which scenario allows users to remain at their individual locations and send messages between their workstations?

14. What is the purpose of an EIS, and who needs one?

15. List the five characteristics of an EIS. What is the ''drill down'' characteristic of an EIS?

Discussion Questions

1. TPSs were developed to process day-to-day transactions and collect data, DBMS was developed so that users could access data for a variety of applications, and management science models were developed to analyze data. How are all these developments combined to help managers cope with uncertain environments that have numerous economic and operational constraints on activities?

2. For each step in the decision-making process, explain how a DSS can assist management in making a decision.

3. DSS is not used extensively by top management. Considering top management's role, why not? What characteristics of EISs fill top management's information requirements?

4. In the structured approach to systems development, a user's needs are defined, the specifications of the systems are developed, and the system is implemented. Why does this approach not work well for DSS development? What development procedure is needed to overcome this problem? How can end users develop their own DSS? In many cases, decisions are made by groups; what new developments can facilitate this process?

Case 10–1

Christian Brothers Vineyards

The craft of wine making traditionally has depended on time, quality grapes, and the wine maker's expertise. Today, the Christian Brothers Napa Valley vineyards add a new ingredient to the ancient process. "Almost everyone in the company uses a PC [personal computer]," says Tom Eddy, director of wine making for the St. Helena, CA vintner. Indeed, sales forecasts, crop estimates, blend formulas—virtually all aspects of the wine-making process from harvest through bottling—are tracked, analyzed, and recorded using personal computers. "The PC gives me the tool to stay one step ahead of my competitors because I understand the business better," Eddy explains. "I know when to make the right moves in terms of changing a blend formula or in terms of buying or selling grapes and wine. Because the PC keeps me appraised of changes in the marketplace, I always have the first shot at getting the best quality."

Because it can grow most of the grapes used in its premium wines, Christian Brothers can better control and maintain the quality of its products, a significant advantage over other vintners who covet Napa grapes but who are not blessed with Napa acreage. Christian Brothers hopes to use this advantage to establish greater market share in premium varietal wines. To leverage this advantage, the company makes extensive use of its more that 80 IBM and Compaq Computer Corporation personal computers; the predominant software tool deployed in the quest to make better wine is Lotus Development Corporation's Lotus 1-2-3. But Christian Brothers managers who use the spreadsheet program have stretched its use far beyond simply calculating budgets. "I do the same thing with wine making that an accountant does with a cost analysis," Eddy says. "The accountant may want to know what effect the purchase of $1 million worth of equipment will have on the company five years from now. That's the same kind of question I ask, only it concerns wine making."

The personal computer is crucial to Christian Brothers because wine making is an enormously complex business. Although five-year sales forecasts are moving targets for most businesses, Christian Brothers must treat the numbers as gospel, because a forecast five years in the future requires action today. Vineyards must be planted years in advance in order to make the types and quantities of wine called for in the sales forecast. Marketing forecasts may be etched in stone, but even the best-laid plans can run afoul of the weather or unforeseen characteristics of a vintage that may force the vintner to downgrade the chardonnay to a blend wine, such as chablis. The 1987 harvest, for example, was down 15 percent from what had been predicted in June because of a prolonged drought. With the Master Allocation Report, a customized Lotus spreadsheet designed by Christian Brothers, Eddy can determine exactly how many grapes he needs for next year's crush. The report is fed by numbers generated from other Lotus spreadsheets used by managers throughout the company. The vineyard manager supplies Eddy with a crop forecast by grape variety for each of the company's approximately 1,250 Napa Valley acres. Eddy then correlates the crop forecast with the sales forecast for each variety as well as with the inventories, the aging time required for each wine, and the tons of grapes needed to meet projected demand. A ton of chardonnay grapes, for example, produces approximately 145 gallons of wine that is then fermented, aged, and bottled. The permutations in this spreadsheet are immense. Each variety of wine requires a different aging time, and the quantity of grapes needed to produce a bottle of wine varies by variety. "The report tells me exactly how many grapes by variety I'll need for next year's harvest," Eddy says. "If the report tells me that I'll need 200 tons of chardonnay grapes, for example, but the crop forecast is for only 175 tons, then I know that I'll have to buy 25 tons of Chardonnay grapes. But because I know that today [a year in advance], I can contract for the best grapes at the best price. If I had to wait until next summer, I'd get lousy grapes and pay top price for them."

The personal computer can take Eddy one step beyond knowing the number of grapes to buy; it can direct him to the grower and the vineyard that produced the best grapes in the past. As 1-2-3 provides an electronic audit trail for the accountant, it also gives Eddy a precise history of each Christian Brothers wine. The process begins each fall, after the grapes are crushed and fermentation is completed. "When the wine is in a raw state, I get a handle on the quality immediately by tasting it," Eddy explains. "I record my tasting notes on the personal computer, along with the volume of each tank, the lot number, and other particulars, such as where the grapes came from."

Data concerning the volume, location, variety, and characteristics of each wine are kept on the company's minicomputer. Eddy sends and retrieves his tasting notes and other information using IBM's sophisticated hardware and software. About one-half of the company's 80 personal computers are linked to the minicomputer. If Eddy discovers a particularly good wine, he can easily check the history of the tank to determine where the grape originated by accessing the minicomputer. Should he wish to purchase more grapes in the future from the same grower or use one of Christian Brothers' own vineyards as a possible source for future premium estate wines, he can quickly access the information on his personal computer. "Not only can I find where the grape came from but what type of soil they were grown in," he says. "Before we had the PCs, it would take two people three to four days to come up with the information. Now I can do it in five minutes."

The personal computer may help track the wine from harvest to bottling, but the wine's flavor has the most direct bearing on marketing and inventory. Eddy constantly updates minicomputer data based on the tasting notes gathered on his personal computer. "Let's say I taste a chardonnay today that's developed an off-character," he says. "I'd probably downgrade that to a chablis." The result is a reshuffling of the bulk wine inventory with a direct bearing on how much wine is available to meet sales projections. The move means the inventory of chardonnay has been cut, with a corresponding increase in that available for chablis. However, because the system is updated constantly and inventory is correlated with sales forecasts, Eddy knows exactly when and how much wine to bottle in order to meet projected demand.

"The PC is a tremendous wine-making tool. By keeping a running inventory by wine types, I can call up a report and know when to have wine ready for bottling three months in advance," he explains. This three-month lead time is vital to the wine maker, because wine must age briefly in the bottle before it is shipped. The personal computer tells him three months in advance how much wine to bottle, so he is rarely caught without enough wine ready to meet sales forecasts, despite the fickle nature of the wine-making business.

The personal computer can further help the wine-making process by taking the mystery out of making blended wines, such as chablis. Eddy uses his personal computer to run a blend report that lists specifications for a blend wine, such as the desired amount of alcohol, sugar, and acid. If Eddy encounters a problem with the wine, he can use the personal computer to determine why the blend went wrong and how to fix it. "If, for example, the alcoholic content of the wine is too high," Eddy explains, "we can go back and check the composition of all wines used to make the blend. If we find one tank of wine with a high alcohol content, all we have to do is substitute that tank for one with less alcohol to get the desired results."

For Christian Brothers, the personal computer and its linkages to a minicomputer are essential to timely decision making and keeping up with the competition in the art of wine making.

SOURCE: Adapted with permission from Zarley, Graig, "From Grape to Bottle: PCs Plot Vintner's Art," *PC Week,* November 10, 1987, pp. 59, 71, and 73. Copyright © 1987, Ziff Communications Company.

Case Questions

1. List the decisions that are supported by Christian Brothers' computer system.

2. How are the various components of a DSS used to support these decisions?

3. How does Christian Brothers use a network to provide its operational and managerial personnel with the information they need for operations and decision making?

Case 10–2
Avon Products

Avon's corporate MIS department was set up just a few years ago to better manage the company's continuing metamorphosis into a multifaceted corporation.

With the luxury of new corporate computing architecture, the MIS vice president urged top management to deliver some of this information electronically in an EIS. The idea caught on. "People really understood the need for this system," the MIS VP explained. The entire development process went quickly. They "interviewed in April and May, presented the concept in June, got the OK and set up the first prototype in September." The prototype met with instant approval. "The CEO saw it and immediately said, 'Let's implement it,'" according to the MIS vice president.

To develop an EIS, the MIS vice president and others in the MIS group conducted interviews to uncover the information that would help executives run the business better. They interviewed executives and staff, and gathered information needs from both the top down and the bottom up. Based on the interviews, the group identified over 70 applications of importance, from human resource information to business indicators. These applications were then classified into four basic groups: financial, human resource, competitive, and administrative.

An unexpected setback in the health care division helped seal the project. "Our COO said that if he had the EIS in place prior to that, it would have been possible to see the problem and act to head it off before it developed into anything serious," noted the MIS vice president.

The programming team was a unique aspect of the project. Rather than recruit programmers who understood business, they looked for M.B.A.s who knew or wanted to learn programming. About 12 M.B.A.s were hired as programmers, on the theory that they would really understand the needs of the business. "I think the quality of our product is better because we hired business people, and what we have today reflects that," the MIS vice president explained. "If you bring in good people, they will challenge the functional departments to think differently, and I think it helped us add a lot of value to the project."

The EIS resulting from this effort is a marvel of conciseness, extreme ease of use, and usefulness. The system resides on the company's IBM mainframes, but service is delivered to executives via personal computers. All selections from the menu-driven product are made by using a mouse. When executives log onto the system, they see a menu divided in half; the left side contains internal Avon information, such as financial indicators, and the right side contains external information, such as news and competitive analyses.

Under the theory that less is more, the Avon EIS is heavily graphics oriented, presenting more information concisely. Using a mouse, the user simply moves the cursor over a menu choice, and if another level of information exists behind that selection, the cursor changes color. Clicking the mouse brings up the next level of detail. For example, under financial indicators, an executive could check the net sales of any company within Avon. Immediately, a chart showing net sales appears on the screen. Dropping down to the next level of detail, a user can examine the profit-and-loss statements for each division, then the line items, and so on.

Individuals who want to take further action based on the information presented can choose a utility icon on the screen. They can then lay out a report, using Notes (a group DSS product from Lotus Development Corporation), download the figures to Lotus 1-2-3, or print a hard copy. An electronic mail function allows users to transmit the entire document to other users.

From the beginning, one objective of the plan was presenting information graphically and in full color. Consistent with that intent, all hard copy is delivered in color. Using color graphics ''allows the executives to see the trends and see what has happened from a business point of view much faster than they would by just looking at numbers,'' according to the MIS vice president.

Unlike some systems that are totally preformatted, analysis on the Avon EIS is done dynamically. Users can customize important views, or set upper and lower limits or variances they want to examine. Other main menu choices include 30 days' worth of business and financial news from Dow Jones News Service and competitive analyses that let users compare the performance of any Avon division against that of selected competitors. Executives can also customize which ratios or companies they want to compare with Avon based on quarterly statements, sales growth, inventory turnover, or a number of other measures. Up to 15 companies can be compared at one time, letting an executive see instantly how Avon stacks up against the competition.

Perhaps the most concise indicators on the system are the Hot Buttons that identify major business trends. Hot Buttons are colored flags on the screen; the top part of the flag represents the current month, and the bottom represents the trend for the last two months. If the top part of the flag is green, then the month (or trend) is above plan. If the color is blue, the trend is flat. If it is red, the trend or month is below plan. Therefore, the comparison of the actual month to the business plan and to the two-month trend is very simple. Executives can point and click on individual flags to see the detailed information behind them. Response to the system has been extremely positive, and training time is virtually nonexistent. The CEO simply said, ''Let me try it,'' and worked through the system. Help screens are also provided. In one example, the system let Avon executives quickly see a business downturn in the Avon division so they could make the appropriate corrections the next Christmas season.

Despite examples of how the system has affected profits, there was never a demand to cost-justify it, because upper management believed it would help executives make better decisions. This trend is emerging as corporate computing evolves, according to the MIS vice president. He believes that the first computers were installed for direct cost savings, such as cutting payroll costs. The next stage saw the use of computers in the production, marketing, and distribution of products. Now, businesses in the service sector are looking to differentiate themselves more. ''The higher you get in this movement, the less you can cost-justify things,'' according to the MIS vice president. ''It's no longer a case of cranking up inventory level, but more in the area of highlighting opportunities or problems in the organization.''

Clearly, Avon is counting on EIS. For in the aggressive world of beauty and health care products, simply looking good is not enough.

SOURCE: Adapted with permission from Pepper, Jon, ''Executive Info System: Easy, Easier, Easiest,'' *PC Week,* February 9, 1988, pp. 48–49. Copyright © 1988, Ziff Communications Company.

Case Questions

1. How did Avon develop its EIS? Why was this development process important?

2. What characteristics of Avon's EIS make it easier to use than a DSS?

3. Why do you think the EIS is not cost-justified?

4. How did Avon get management's support for the system?

5. If a product manager wants to compare Avon's sales performance with a competitor's, what does the manager do? What comparative statistics are available? What level of detail is provided, and what reports are available from the EIS to help manage product decisions?

Artificial Intelligence and Expert Systems

11

Introduction   One of today's computer applications with an exciting future is the use of artificial intelligence in managing an organization. This field of study is defined various ways, but for our purposes, **Artificial Intelligence (AI)** refers to ''. . . a broad range of computer applications that resemble human intelligence and behavior.''[1] Because this definition is so general, the term *AI* is applied to many different types of computer systems and applications, including creation of ''natural'' languages (rather than computer languages) for giving the computer instructions, use of robots, alternative forms of input (handwriting and voice), computers ''learning'' to solve problems, machine vision that allows the inspection and measure of manufactured items, and the expert systems discussed briefly in Chapter 2. This list is by no means all the applications of AI, but these applications have a direct effect on computer users and managers.

AI is considered so important that it is one of the fastest growing high-tech areas. Many companies spend large amounts of money either to develop AI systems or to purchase systems developed by other companies. A great deal of research is concentrating on AI, but apparently no plans exist for developing a real-life version of HAL from the movie *2001: A Space Odyssey.* In that story, HAL could reason and eventually took over the spaceship. The sequel, *2010: The Year We Make Contact,* reveals the problem—humans.

---

[1] Alan Freedman, *The Computer Glossary,* 4th Ed. (Point Pleasant, PA: The Computer Language Company, 1989), p. 33.

To appreciate the directions in which AI is moving, consider the following list of applications developed by the Stanford Research Institute (SRI) for the 1990s:

- Expert parenting systems that monitor children's activities and alert parents when problems are brewing
- Intelligent games that automatically adjust to the skill of the players and that change over time to avoid player boredom
- Story generators and animation packages for creating personalized entertainment
- Expert systems for helping do-it-yourselfers
- Intelligent control of appliances through voice commands
- Advice on issues ranging from nutrition to taxes
- Improved systems for working with physically challenged individuals
- Expert information request systems

Since this list was created in 1982, some applications have been developed, especially in the area of expert systems, that can provide advice or information on various issues. The use of voice control of appliances is also becoming a reality.

AI is applied in many exciting areas, but it is also very controversial. To many people, AI is the most important area of computer research today. However, other writers feel AI cannot exist, because intelligence is a strictly human quality. In fact, H.L. Dreyfus and S.E. Dreyfus argue in their book *Mind over Machine* that "human intelligence can never be replaced by machine intelligence because we are not ourselves 'thinking machines.' . . . Each of us has, and uses every day, a power of intuitive intelligence that enables us to understand, to speak, and to cope skillfully with our everyday environment."[2] We do not propose to become involved in the semantics of this argument, but rather to discuss the applications of AI as they are used in the world around us. In particular, we consider in some detail a commonly used application of AI known as an expert system. In an expert system, a computer becomes an "expert" on a subject by combining knowledge and rules to aid users in decision-making tasks that require a fair amount of expertise, yet are fairly routine in occurrence. We also briefly consider a topic closely related to AI called neural networks.

Historical Perspective The idea of an intelligent machine has intrigued philosophers since the time of the Greeks, but not until the digital computer came into wide use in the 1950s did researchers actually try to create such a machine. In 1956, a conference of researchers was held at Dartmouth College, at which the name "artificial intelligence" was suggested by John McCarthy. The next year, McCarthy developed a computer language specifically designed for AI. This language—LISP (for LISt Processor)—treats everything from sentences to mathematical formulas as lists of symbols. This approach allows LISP to work with flexible systems that can handle ambiguous situations involving complex problems.

[2] H.L. Dreyfus and S.E. Dreyfus, *Mind over Machine* (New York: The Free Press, 1986), p. xx.

After an initial period of naive enthusiasm during which much was written about the potential of AI, researchers realized that building true intelligent machines was extremely difficult. The first useful product was an expert system called DENDRAL, developed in the mid-1960s at Stanford University for interpreting test data to determine the structure of an organic molecule. Over the last 25 years, dramatic improvements in hardware coupled with a tremendous decrease in cost has led to the application of AI in many other areas. However, we still cannot say that we have developed intelligent machines like those written about in science fiction literature. Such machines are often called the "fifth generation" of computers, because current computers are the fourth generation.

Japan and the Fifth Generation

During the 1980s, Japan became a global leader in the manufacture of automobiles and electronics. However, the United States held its lead in computer technology. Japan makes many of the chips used in U.S. machines, but with the exception of laptop personal computers, Japanese machines have made few inroads into the computer market. Rather than attempt to just equal what U.S. companies are doing, Japan has worked for almost 10 years on a program to "leap-frog" U.S. companies by working on the next generation of machines—the so-called "fifth generation" computers. To oversee this project, the Japanese government has pooled its resources with eight of the country's largest electronic companies to form the Institute for New Generation Computer Technology. This institute is committed to the development of the necessary hardware and software for the fifth generation machine by the end of this century. This computer may be much faster and smarter than anything available today and may incorporate many AI concepts to handle the following tasks:

- Listen when the user talks and then respond to the user's request
- Help program itself and other computers
- Make logical inferences from information it receives from the user
- Translate among various human languages
- Treat graphics like symbols or numbers
- Learn from its own experience

11.1 Applications of Artificial Intelligence

As we noted earlier, AI has been applied to numerous areas including natural languages, robotics, nonkeyboard forms of input, and expert systems. In the rest of this section, we consider a few of these applications. The remainder of the chapter covers expert systems in detail and also briefly considers neural networks.

Natural Languages

One area of AI research that is of great interest to computer scientists is the capability for a computer to understand **natural languages**—for example, everyday English—rather than a sometimes cryptic computer language. With a natural language AI system, a user need not learn a special computer language to give the computer instructions. Using such a system, a manager could access a data base by simply entering questions in "plain" English. For example, the instruction, "How many female employees have been hired since January first?'' would be answered with the appropriate number. This question could then be followed up by the question, ''How many are paid more than $30,000?'' with no ambiguity about the group being referred to.

Two approaches are being used to develop natural language systems. In one approach, each letter and word is analyzed to determine the meaning of the sentence. This analytic approach for mainframe computers is used by several large corporations. The second approach is an intuitive approach that compares the sentence being input to other sentences stored in the computer. If an exact comparison cannot be found, then the closest match is used. One shortcoming of this natural language system involves the similarity of many English words. For example, the question about number of females ''hired'' can be confused with a question about the number ''fired,'' because the two words sound and look alike.

Several recent packages for use on personal computers have some natural language characteristics. Data base packages like *Clout* and *Q & A* allow the user to retrieve information from a data base in a natural language form. One interesting feature of *Q & A* is the Teach facility. If, in the process of interpreting a user's request, *Q & A* finds a word that is not part of its 450-word vocabulary, it prompts the user to teach it the meaning of the new word. When *Q & A* determines what it believes is the meaning of the command, it asks *Shall I do the following?,* which is followed by the list of procedures it has determined the user wants accomplished. Another interesting natural language product is PC-IQ from A.I. Solutions which allows the user to enter DOS commands in ''plain English.'' For example, instead of entering ''COPY A:*.DBF C:\DBASE\'' as a DOS command, with PC-IQ the user enters the command ''Copy all files ending in DBF from drive A to my dBASE directory.'' The package responds with the appropriate DOS command and an explanation of what it is going to do. If the package cannot figure out the user command, it requests more information. PC-IQ can be personalized as either conversational or formal depending on the user's needs.

Although these packages offer some hope of making a user's job easier, most experts agree that the development of a true natural language system that works at even a third-grade level is still in the future. Problems involve the need for such a system to understand the world around it and determine the context of a command.

Robotics   Another application of AI is the field of **robotics**—that is, the use of machines to perform work. Currently, robots are used extensively by the automobile industry to handle heavy, dirty, or dangerous tasks such as spot welding the body of an automobile or materials handling. They are also helpful in the electronics industry because robots can perform the same precision task time after time. These robots are not nearly as sophisticated as the walking, talking C3PO of *Star Wars* fame. An industrial robot is little more than a mechanical arm controlled by a microprocessor chip. The robot performs a specified set of tasks from instructions built into the chip. Although not very cute, these robots have had a big impact on the automobile industry, in which the use of robots has given Japanese companies an advantage over labor intensive U.S. companies.

Help for Nurses from HelpMate

If you have ever been in the hospital, you know that nurses and other health professionals can use all of the help they can get. In the future, help may be in the form of a HelpMate android built by Transitions Research Incorporated to perform many tasks that often take nurses away from their primary health-care duties. For example, ordering and delivering dinner trays for patients who miss mealtime can use valuable nursing time. At Danbury Hospital in Connecticut, a four and one-half foot tall HelpMate prototype named "Rosco" has delivered dinner trays for the dietary department since 1987. Rosco does not require a fixed robot guidance system. Instead, the floor plan of the hospital is stored in its memory, so the robot actually looks for the distance between the wall and intersections to guide its way. This type of navigation is combined with vision, sonar, and infrared sensors. Rosco controls elevators by infrared remote control similar to that used with TV and VCR remote controls. When Rosco senses a nonmoving obstacle, it stops and computes a course around the obstacle; for moving obstacles such as patients or staff, Rosco simply stops and allows the person to move before continuing on its way.

Future uses of HelpMate androids in a hospital setting may include transporting medical records or lab specimens. The builder of HelpMate also hopes to sell it for home use, including a companion robot for outdoor work.

SOURCE: "HelpMate Is on the Way," *Electronic House,* April 3, 1989, p. 4.

The use of robots for industrial tasks grew quickly during the early part of the 1980s, but this growth has slowed during the second half of the decade. In fact, the future of robotics may actually be in the service industry, where 75 percent of the work exists. Robots may be used in hospitals, security, commercial cleaning, and the support of elderly people. These tasks require the use of "smart" robots that can see where they are going, note obstacles, and avoid them. Another name for smart robots that can move and have a built-in microprocessor is **android.** A key problem that must be solved before androids are widely used is that of three-dimensional sight. Without this, robots cannot move around in a crowded hospital hallway or a small apartment.

Nonkeyboard Forms of Input

Although the keyboard is the predominate method of data input, many people are put off by it. "Keyboardphobia" may be part of the reason for the success of the Apple Macintosh mouse, which is used to select from among icons and pull-down menus. This problem may sound like a hardware issue, but the input hardware device is useless without the appropriate software. Besides the mouse, nonkeyboard forms of input may involve **voice input** and **handwritten input.** Both voice input and handwritten input require the computer to display some degree of intelligence to decipher the input. Some new **personal digital assistants (PDAs)** have no keyboard at all. All data is entered using a pen by printing or drawing on a screen.

Several problems are involved in building a computer that accepts voice input—words run together, similar sounding words that mean different things (*to*, *too*, and *two*), and different voices from multiple speakers. Yet, voice input is a key breakthrough in computer technology that can create a friendlier environment for the novice user. Similarly, the use of handwritten input—using a stylus to actually write on the screen—has its own set of problems, including deciphering different or hard-to-read handwriting.

11.2 Expert Systems in Business

In almost every organization, one or more individuals are key to the successful operation of the organization because of their problem solving skills and knowledge about the business and its environment. These people are experts in their field and, without them, very little would be accomplished. Experts can cut through superfluous, unimportant details and get to the heart of a problem. Whether their expertise is used to decide when a commercial soup is ready to be canned or to diagnose a pulmonary disease, experts use a body of knowledge and "rules of thumb" to decide or make recommendations to others who make decisions. Experts can also be expected to "degrade gracefully"—that is, they inform their clients when they are moving out of their field of expertise so problems are avoided.

Such experts are obviously important to any organization, but they can also be very scarce and expensive. One 1986 study showed that with benefits, recruitment and turnover, profit sharing, bonuses, travel, training, and administrative support, the yearly cost of an engineering expert with a base salary of $54,000 was actually over $122,000.[3] In 1993 dollars, this is equivalent to over $150,000! In addition, when an expert retires, dies, or otherwise leaves the company, his or her expertise and years of experience can be difficult to replace.

Because of the importance of experts to all types of organizations, researchers wanted to store an experts' years of knowledge in a computer. Early attempts to do this using data bases proved unworkable, because the reasoning that an expert uses to reach a decision could not be stored in a data base. The first expert systems developed in the mid-1960s have been expanded and applied to many commercial situations, including engineering, law, medicine, tax planning, education, finance, manufacturing, and sales.

An **expert system** can be defined as "a computer-based system that uses knowledge, facts, and reasoning techniques to solve problems that normally require the abilities of human experts."[4] Expert systems are an application of AI that has enjoyed wide use in

---

[3] Leilani Allen, "The Cost of an Expert," *Computerworld*, July 21, 1986, pp. 64–68.

[4] James Martin and Steven Oxman, *Building Expert Systems—A Tutorial* (Englewood Cliffs, NJ: Prentice-Hall, 1988), p. 14.

FIGURE 11–1

Expert System Elements

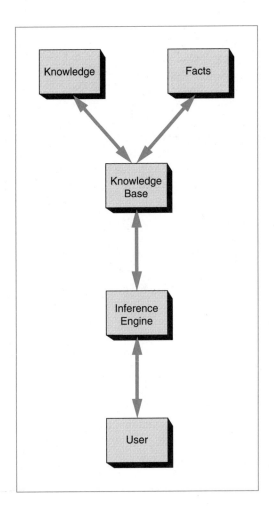

business, government, and industry. Expert systems are different from Decision Support Systems (DSS). Although DSS provides solutions to problems that the manager can incorporate into his or her decision making, expert systems actually suggest courses of action.

Our definition of an expert system emphasizes problem solving using three elements — knowledge, facts, and reasoning techniques. The knowledge and facts are stored in an expert system's **knowledge base,** and the reasoning capabilities are handled by its **inference engine.** These elements are shown in Figure 11–1.

Examples of productivity gains resulting from using expert systems include a ten-fold decrease in the time required to design a camera lens and a 300-fold decrease in the time needed to organize a computer system for a customer. Every user may not benefit to this extent, but expert systems are used in many different types of organizations.

When a Data Base Didn't Work

A common problem among many large manufacturers is that of lost, defective, or damaged parts. General Dynamics Electric Boat Division, a manufacturer of nuclear submarines, wanted to store and retrieve information on such "nonconformance" situations, but found that a Data Base Management System (DBMS) could store the data, but could not evaluate results.

To solve this problem, the IS staff used an AI approach. A rule-based expert system did not work, because a change in a rule meant starting all over again. So, they tried a different approach and designed a system around similarities. This system asks users for information about a nonconformance and then searches its knowledge base for a documented case similar to this one. "Case-based reasoning" allows General Dynamics to find a previous nonconformance that represents the best potential resolution to the current problem. If the system finds too many similar cases, it requests more information to narrow down the choices.

SOURCE: Alan Radding, "Choosing the Application: General Dynamics Electric Boat Division," *Computerworld*, July 29, 1991, p. 61.

Applications of Expert Systems

Expert systems are used in numerous situations, including the following:

1. Desire to reduce the cost of developing a solution to a problem

2. Unavailability of experts at the work site

3. Desire to have a computer system that uses the knowledge of the organization's experts

4. Need to reach a decision that requires several human experts

5. Desire to retain business expertise while allowing the human expert to return to other tasks

6. Need to amortize the cost of expertise over a large number of difficult decision-making tasks

7. Expected loss (retirement) of key personnel with years of experience

Before we look further into types of expert systems and how they work, we mention several examples of expert systems:

- The first working expert system, called DENDRAL, was developed in 1965 at Stanford University. Descendants of this system are still used in laboratories all over the world.

- Using techniques learned from DENDRAL, computer scientists and doctors at Stanford Medical Center created MYCIN to diagnose diseases of the blood by incorporating knowledge and rules used by the doctors.

- Prospector, developed at Stanford Research Institute, aids geologists in exploring for minerals. This system led to the discovery of a $100 million deposit of molybdenum in Washington state.

- To preserve the knowledge and experience of the man who controlled the huge cooker ovens at Campbell Soup Co. for 44 years, an expert system named COOKER was developed. COOKER not only contains much of this man's factual knowledge, but also his rules of thumb for reasoning through problems with the ovens.

- To aid companies in making important financial decisions, the Financial Advisor expert system incorporates the analytical abilities of numerous experts in finance, taxation, and other areas of business. One user of Financial Advisor claims the system even answers questions that he does not think to ask.

- To design its VAX computer systems to meet customers' needs, the XCON expert system was developed by Digital Equipment Corporation (DEC). XCON ensures that ordered components are matched with the requisite facilities. DEC saves between $70 million and $100 million per year using XCON.

TABLE 11–1

Expert System Applications

Expert System	Area	Purpose
AALPS	Defense	Advises on the loading of cargo on military transport aircraft
XCON	Computer	Designs computer systems
GCA	Education	Advises graduate students on which courses to take
AIR-CYL	Engineering	Designs air cylinders according to user requirements
TAXADVISOR	Finance	Recommends tax and estate plans to maximize the wealth transferred at death
GREASE	Manufacturing	Aids in the selection or design of parts that should extend the life of manufacturing machinery
PUFF	Medicine	Analyzes patient data to identify possible lung disorders
REAL ESTATE AGENT	Sales	Consults on the selection of an apartment
WILLARD	Science	Forecasts the likelihood of severe thunderstorms in the midwestern United States

SOURCE: James Martin and Steven Oxman, *Building Expert Systems—A Tutorial* (Englewood Cliffs, NJ: Prentice-Hall, 1988), pp. 39–42.

Beating the Competition with an Expert System

A very competitive part of the airline industry is each airline's frequent flyer program. Traditionally, these plans have rewarded flyers with free trips based on the miles traveled on a specific airline. Recently, airlines have begun to look at rewarding flyers for taking a specific number of round trips. In 1990, United Airlines offered its frequent flyers a free trip for every three round trips taken from the *same* "hub" city. In an effort to better this offer, American Airlines offered a free trip for taking three round trips *anywhere* on its network.

Before American came out with this offer, the airline had to develop an expert system that would automate the process of verifying the who, when, and where of frequent flying. American had to consider all types of round trips, not simply the variety in which the passenger leaves point A for point B and then returns to point A. Actually, seven or eight types of round trips are possible, due to the hub-and-spoke system used by major airlines. A round trip can even involve a missing leg if the flyer uses a different airline or drives from one airport to another. The expert system had to recognize all types of round trips with an error rate of less than 2 percent.

The expert system required for this frequent flyer plan was developed on an IBM PS/2 Model 80 in just 12 weeks at a cost of $212,000. The system was then transferred to a mainframe that would process the records of the 1 million American Airlines frequent flyers. The expert system could identify round trips from among 10 million flight segments. Revenue implications for American are impossible to calculate, but the airline feels very good about its plan.

SOURCE: Michael Alexander, "American's Expert System Takes Off," *Computerworld,* July 8, 1991, p. 20.

Several thousand expert systems are used in commercial applications, education, or research all over the world. Table 11–1 shows some of these expert systems along with their purpose and area of application.

Expert Systems at ProYacht, Inc. Acceptance Division

One of the most important decisions that many companies face involves the extension of credit to individuals and other companies. Extending credit to the wrong customers can lead to a large number of bad loans for even the most astute company. Recall that ProYacht, Inc. has a financing division called ProYacht Acceptance, which makes loans to individual customers to finance their purchase of sailboats from ProYacht dealers. Currently, ProYacht uses a fairly simple computerized decision model to decide whether to extend credit to a customer. In the past, this division had been profitable for ProYacht. However, because of the large number of personal bankruptcies over the past few years, an increasing number of sailboat purchasers have defaulted on their loans. In light of this recent development, ProYacht may use an expert system to assist its loan managers in deciding which customers are eligible for a boat loan. In such an expert system, the knowledge base contains information on boat sizes and purchase prices and a list of rules for determining the customer's eligibility for a loan. Management feels that such a

FIGURE 11–2   *ProYacht, Inc. Organization Chart*

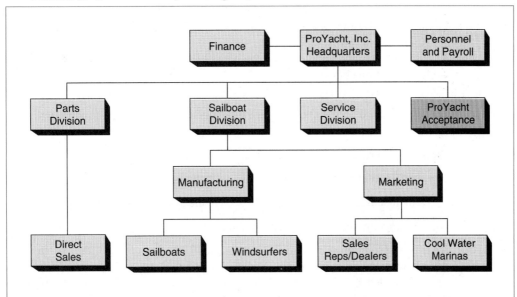

system can manipulate more variables in a logical way than the currently used decision methodology. Figure 11–2 shows the relationship of the ProYacht Acceptance division to the remainder of the ProYacht, Inc. organization.

At ProYacht, credit is extended to boat buyers on the basis of loan amount, annual income, net assets, years of employment, and number of dependents. Assume that ProYacht's loan-granting policies include the following rule: IF purchaser's income is greater than $90,000 AND purchaser has assets more than 3 times the loan amount AND purchaser has worked for at least 9 years AND purchaser has no more than 2 dependents, THEN approve the loan. If the facts about a particular loan are as follows:

Loan Amount: $25,000
Annual Income: $100,000
Net Assets: $60,000
Years of Employment: 10
Number of dependents: 2

then the loan will be denied. Three out of four conditions are met, but net assets are not more than three times the loan amount.

A series of facts and rules like the IF–THEN statement for the ProYacht example would be used to create a complete expert system. An **IF–THEN rule** states that if a particular condition is true, a specified conclusion should also be true. This expert system would provide questions for the ProYacht Acceptance employee to ask of the borrower. However, rather than asking the same questions of every borrower, the expert system changes the questions to match previous answers, as a human expert would. The inference engine would then combine the borrower's information with the system's facts and rules to determine if the borrower should receive a loan. If the information meets all conditions, the expert system recommends that the individual be extended credit. On the other hand, if the borrower's answers fail to meet the criteria, the expert system recommends that the individual be turned down for the loan.

11.3 Characteristics of Expert Systems

James Martin and Steven Oxman[5] have suggested that the following four characteristics further define expert systems:

1. Should perform at an expert's level of competence

2. Uses an inference engine to make its deductions

3. Expertise based on the special knowledge the system has acquired

4. No programming is needed to use the acquired knowledge

An expert system must be able to deduce conclusions from special knowledge that is gained from one or more human experts. In the ProYacht Acceptance example, this special knowledge is the criteria for extending credit to a boat buyer. The expert system would use any "rules of thumb" developed by human experts for determining eligibility. For example, if the customer's ratio of loan size to net assets is a crucial deciding point, then the expert (and the expert system) would ask this question first, because the answer may limit the extension of credit. In this way, an expert system is far more than a knowledge system, because it involves reasoning as well as facts.

Characteristics 2 and 3 in the list are direct consequences of the first characteristic. An expert system cannot carry out the reasoning function without the inference engine. The rules and facts would be of little use without the inference engine to combine them with information it gleans from the user. Remember that the knowledge base and inference engine are separate entities and that the same inference engine can be used with numerous knowledge bases. The user need only develop an individual knowledge base, because the inference engine remains constant from system to system. In the ProYacht Acceptance example, the inference engine works with the rules and facts in the knowledge base for granting credit. The same inference engine could be used with an expert system that would advise applicants how to change their application to be eligible for a loan—for example, increase the down payment to reduce the loan size.

An inference engine is useless without the facts and rules it uses to develop new questions or suggestions. This knowledge must be acquired from human experts. Note that although the knowledge base can exist in many different forms, it stores experts' knowledge as individual packets of information. This independence means the knowledge base is easy to view, expand, or change. For the ProYacht Acceptance example, the knowledge base contains all the facts and rules concerning boats, purchase prices, current interest rates, repayment plans, and the financial data for the prospective buyer. Because

---

[5] Martin and Oxman, p. 31.

these facts are stored individually, it is easy to look at the list of rules and facts, to add the rules and facts for new economic or financial conditions, or to change them based on more recent history. For example, the amount of available credit can be increased if an optimistic economic forecast is seen for a particular region.

The final characteristic clearly differentiates expert systems from conventional information systems. In conventional systems, the knowledge and processing components are combined into a computer program, which executes instructions sequentially based on an algorithm. Although output from an expert system depends to some extent on the programming of the inference engine, it depends to a much larger extent on the knowledge base derived from human experts and on the information input by the user.

Uncertain and Incomplete Information

In addition to the previously listed characteristics, an important feature of expert systems is their capability to handle uncertain or incomplete information. A mathematical field known as **fuzzy logic** is used to analyze these problems. In many situations, the result of a particular IF–THEN rule may not be known, or users may not supply complete answers to a query. In these cases, a human expert can only make educated guesses about the result of a certain set of conditions. Although managers want to be *sure* about the result of some actions, they must often make decisions based on uncertain or incomplete information.

In the ProYacht Acceptance example, assume that loan-granting procedures include a rule asking for an individual customer's assets, such as home equity, automobiles owned, and checking or savings account balance. The customer may not supply a complete answer to this question, resulting in a request for other information or even denial of the loan.

Most expert systems can handle uncertain and incomplete information. Uncertain information from a customer is often assigned a confidence factor. **Confidence Factors (CNF)** are an informal scale measure (for example, 0–100) of the extent to which an expert believes information to be true. For example, assume an expert believes that a customer with assets at least twice the value of the boat loan has a 70 percent chance of a repaying the loan. This rule might be stated as follows:

IF Assets > Twice Loan Size THEN Repayment CNF 70

Similarly, if the expert believes that a customer with assets at least three times the value of the boat loan has a 95 percent chance of repaying the loan, the rule might be stated as follows:

IF Assets > Three Times Loan Size THEN Repayment CNF 95

Incomplete information is handled in various ways by expert systems, but usually the expert system requests the missing information from the user. If the information is unavailable, the system may *backtrack* from its current line of reasoning and attempt to follow another line to reach a different conclusion. If too much information is missing, the expert system displays a message to this effect and requests more information to proceed.

TABLE 11–2

*Expert System
Problem-Solving
Activities*

Problem Area	Example
Interpretation	Interpreting oil well logs
Prediction	Predicting the occurrence of severe weather
Diagnosis	Diagnosing lung conditions
Design	Designing computer systems
Planning	Planning a large construction project
Monitoring	Monitoring radiation levels in a nuclear power plant
Debugging	Suggesting solutions to problems with a computer network
Repairing	Leading a technician through the step-by-step process of repairing a large piece of construction equipment
Instruction	Teaching programmers new languages
Control	Controlling a blast furnace

*Classification
of Expert
Systems*

Expert systems can be classified in many ways; in Table 11–1, systems were classified by field of use. Expert systems can also be classified by their purpose. Efraim Turban[6] suggests that expert systems can be classified according to the problem area that they address, including interpretation, prediction, diagnosis, design, planning, monitoring, debugging, repairing, instruction, and control. In some of these roles, the expert system can actually be considered more of an assistant, colleague, or teacher. For example, the expert system may suggest a diagnosis for an illness or problem, but the human user actually makes the final decision. Table 11–2 shows these 10 problem areas and examples of expert system use.

These classifications are meant to illustrate generally how expert systems are used. An actual expert system may address two or more problems simultaneously.

Expert systems can also be classified in terms of how the reasoning capabilities of the inference engine are developed. In terms of development, expert systems are rule-based or example-based. A **rule-based system** is built by entering a list of IF–THEN rules. On the other hand, an **example-based system** generates rules or conclusions from past cases or histories, often entered into the system as tables. The system then uses inductive reasoning to create its decision-making rules from these tables. Rule-based systems are more difficult to create than example-based systems, because the developer must write the rules in the form required by the expert system. On the other hand, rule-based systems tend to be more reliable, because the rules developed by an example-based system can be incorrect if the examples are wrong or misleading. Table 11–3 shows an example-based table for the ProYacht Acceptance division expert system for deciding whether or not to extend credit to customers.

---

[6] Efraim Turban, *Decision Support and Expert Systems* (New York: Macmillian, 1990), p. 437.

TABLE 11–3

***Example-Based
System Table***

Loan Size	Income	Net Assets	Years Employed	Number of Dependents	Loan Approved
$25,000	$100,000	$60,000	10	2	No
15,000	150,000	0	1	0	Yes
30,000	70,000	95,000	11	2	Yes
15,000	25,000	65,000	15	0	Yes

Based on these examples, the following IF–THEN rules can be deduced for ProYacht, as well as the IF–THEN rule illustrated earlier:

- IF income is more than nine times the loan amount, THEN approve the loan.

- IF income is at least $25,000 AND net assets are more than four times the loan amount AND employee has worked at least 15 years, THEN approve the loan.

11.4 Expert System Components

Most expert systems are written so that the user simply inputs data and answers questions to receive various recommendations. To understand how this occurs, we need to examine the components of an expert system. Experts use a body of knowledge and a combination of experience, intuition, hunches, good guesses, and creative decision-making ability; an expert system must include many of these same features.

Recall that an expert system is made up of two main parts—a knowledge base and an inference engine. The knowledge base includes all the facts and rules surrounding a problem, and the inference engine works with the facts and rules in the knowledge base to make recommendations. In addition to the knowledge base and inference engine, two other expert system components must be considered—the knowledge acquisition facility and the explanation facility. The **Knowledge Acquisition Facility (KAF)** facilitates the acquisition of knowledge from human experts. The **explanation facility** is a part of the inference engine that can explain why or how a recommendation is reached. We discuss each of these four elements in the following paragraphs and show how they interact. These four components are shown in Figure 11–3, along with the human user and human expert.

The Knowledge Base

The knowledge base of an expert system, where the facts and rules are stored, actually has two parts—the domain data base and the rule data base. The **domain data base,** like the data bases discussed in Chapter 6, contains the facts about the subject considered by the expert system. The domain data base management system manages the facts efficiently so they are available to the inference engine as needed. The ProYacht domain data base contains the fact that a 22-foot sailboat retails for $9,985.

The **rule data base** contains the rules used in the reasoning element of the expert system. As with the domain data base, the rules are stored and managed. They are combined with the facts as needed by the inference engine. These facts and rules should include as much of an expert's experience and intuition as possible in the form of IF–THEN rules. We

FIGURE 11–3

***Expert System
Components***

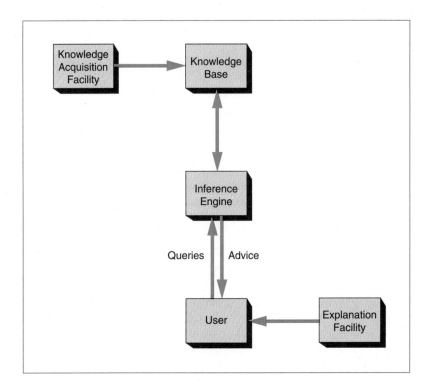

have already seen three such IF–THEN rules for ProYacht Acceptance. Another rule might be: IF boat purchased is a 22-foot sailboat, THEN loan should not exceed $7,988. The inference engine implements this rule via the facts that the 22-foot sailboat costs $9,985 and that ProYacht does not loan more than 80 percent of the retail price of a boat. Figure 11–4 shows the domain data base and the rule data base in an expert system.

*The Inference
Engine*

The reasoning component of the expert system is the inference engine, which comprises one or more problem-solving procedures. The approach used for this problem solving is called symbolic reasoning. In **symbolic reasoning,** symbols are used to represent the problem concepts. Various strategies and rules are then applied to manipulate these symbols for decision-making purposes.

Inference engines use one of two methods to arrive at a final decision—backward chaining and forward chaining. In **backward chaining,** the inference engine seeks a path to a specific goal, for example, the loan amount for which a customer is eligible. It assumes the goal is true, collects all rules that support it, and tests these rules to determine if they are true. If the rules are true, then the original assumption is true. The term "chaining" comes from the fact that one rule being tested true "fires" another rule, leading to a chain of rules.

In **forward chaining,** the inference engine starts with the facts of the case. The facts are applied to the IF part of the rules. Rules that do not apply are eliminated until a conclusion that fits the facts is found.

FIGURE 11–4

***Expert System
with Knowledge
Base Components***

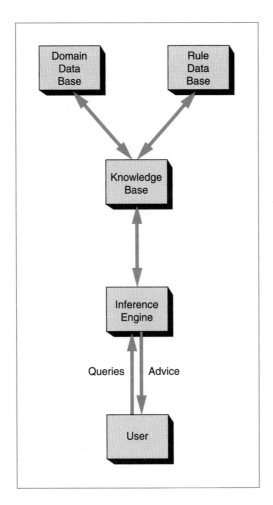

Because the inference engine is a "black box" that the user does not see, the choice of backward chaining or forward chaining is closely associated with the choice of an expert system. In general, if the user must choose one alternative from a range of choices to achieve an objective, then backward chaining is best. However, if the user is not looking for a particular solution or many solutions exist, then forward chaining may be best. Some systems even use characteristics of both systems in their inference engines.

Associated with the inference engine is the user interface. The **user interface** is the front end of the system, which the user sees. The user interface includes the questions that are asked of the user and the displayed results based on the user's responses. Obviously, the user interface should be easy to use, but still retain the capability to ask questions and display responses. Figure 11–5 shows the expert system with a user interface between the user and the inference engine.

FIGURE 11–5

Expert System Showing User Interface

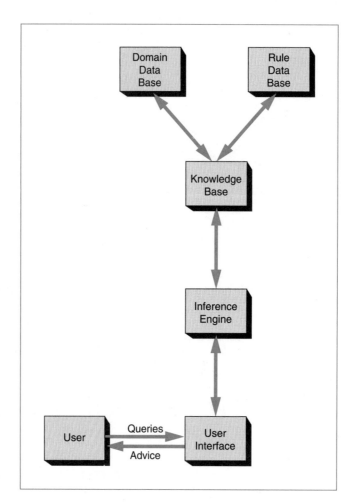

ProYacht Acceptance should have a user interface that asks specific questions regarding a loan applicant's income, net assets, number of years worked, and number of dependents. The interface should then provide exact information on whether the applicant is eligible for a loan or why the applicant is not eligible.

The Knowledge Acquisition Facility

As previously stated, the knowledge in the expert system truly sets it apart from conventional information systems. Getting the rules and facts into the knowledge base is easier said than done, for several reasons. First, many experts do not really know exactly how they reason through a problem to reach a solution. Second, even if they have a good idea what facts and rules they use, they may not be able to put this information into a form that can be input into a knowledge base. Finally, experts may not have the time or knowledge to enter and test their facts and rules in an expert system. For these reasons, most expert systems have a KAF that resolves many problems.

If experts can formulate their knowledge in the form of rules and facts, the KAF provides a user friendly front end to the knowledge base that sets up a dialogue with the expert to acquire information. If an expert cannot formulate knowledge in this form or have the time or interest to work with the KAF, someone else may handle the interface between the expert and the KAF. This specialist, known as a **knowledge engineer,** is trained in extracting the facts and rules used by experts for input to an expert system. In addition to working with human experts to extract their expertise, knowledge engineers must also be able to work with textbooks, data bases, spreadsheets, research reports, and photographs or drawings to extract information to be placed in the knowledge base. Figure 11–6 shows how the KAF and knowledge engineer interact in the expert system.

For ProYacht Acceptance, the knowledge engineer would work with the list of policies that ProYacht has developed for granting credit to arrive at the rules and facts for the knowledge base. The knowledge engineer would also work with the human loan administrator to derive the special rules of thumb used to speed the loan eligibility decision. These rules may involve the order in which questions are asked or other special considerations. For example, if the loan administrator knows that a person with income below $20,000 cannot qualify for a loan, the income question may be asked first. The process can be stopped and a great deal of time saved if the customer's income is less than $20,000. This type of information can be incorporated in the expert system to speed its search.

The
Explanation
Facility

A unique aspect of expert systems is the ability to answer queries from the user as to ''why'' a particular question is asked and ''how'' a specific recommendation is made. This *justification* aspect of expert systems further sets them apart from conventional information systems. To provide these explanations to the user, the expert system uses the explanation facility, as shown in Figure 11–7.

The explanation facility of the expert system can provide the answers to ''why'' and ''how'' questions by keeping track of the rules implemented to reach the current point in the process. When a ''why'' question is asked, the explanation facility provides the rule that is being tested and the reason the information is needed to test this rule. Similarly, when a ''how'' question is asked, the explanation facility shows the line of reasoning, or **logic trace,** that is used to arrive at the current conclusion. Figure 11–8 shows the result of a query to a popular expert system, VP-Expert, for the ProYacht Acceptance example.

11.5
Developing
Expert
Systems

The first expert systems—such as DENDRAL, XCON, and MYCIN—were large-scale computer systems developed on mainframe computers using such standard computer languages as FORTRAN or COBOL or special AI languages like LISP or PROLOG. These systems were extremely expensive to develop, but they led to today's many expert systems. One extremely important insight came from this early work: The power of an expert system is derived from the facts and rules in the knowledge base and not from the specific inference engine in use. In other words, the knowledge base for an existing expert system can be ''stripped'' of the facts and rules to yield the shell of an expert system. This shell has the mechanisms for using knowledge to make inferences, but it contains no knowledge. The first **expert system shell** was created by removing the

FIGURE 11–6

***Use of Knowledge
Acquisition
Facility and
Knowledge
Engineer in an
Expert System***

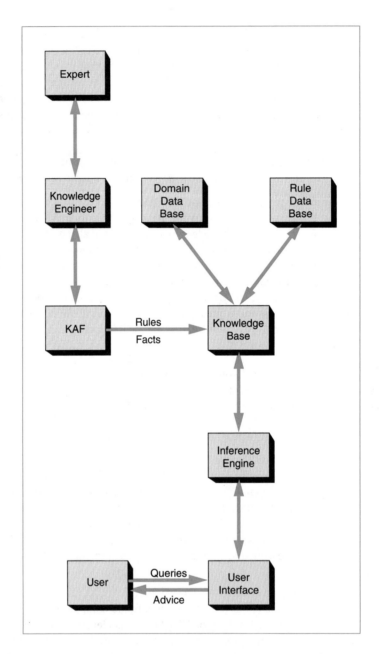

knowledge from MYCIN, an early expert system. MYCIN was created to diagnose diseases of the blood, but after the blood disease knowledge was replaced by information on lung conditions, the resulting expert system was PUFF.

FIGURE 11–7

Expert System
with Explanation
Facility

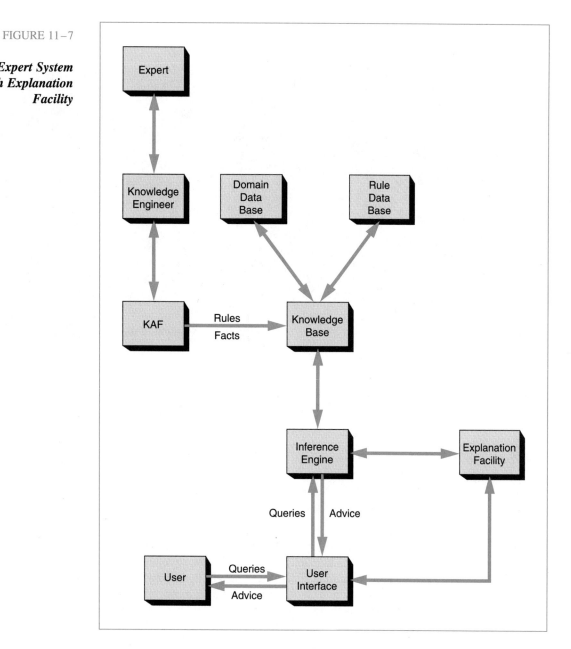

Because inference engines can be used for many different situations, developing expert systems using expert system shells can be relatively easy. Many companies also find that small expert systems can help in many situations. For example, Du Pont has used expert

FIGURE 11–8   *Use of Explanation Facility*

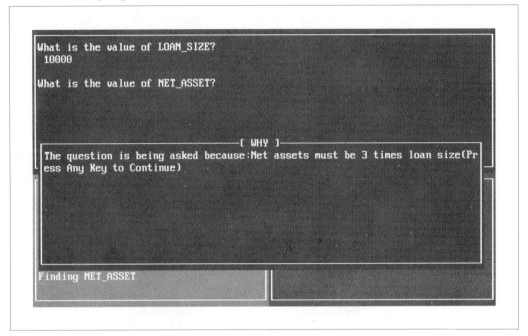

system shells to develop over 1,000 small expert systems (40–500 rules) for many different applications throughout the company.

Expert System Shells

Most expert system shells can be classified as either rule-based or hybrid systems. Rule-based systems are the oldest and simplest shells, commonly based on the original MYCIN shell. Hybrid systems are sophisticated shells that can support several different ways of representing data and handling the logic in the inference engine.

Construction of expert systems using shells can be closely compared with the use of data base management systems (DBMS) to create a data base. In constructing a data base, the DBMS provides functions that determine the structure of the data base; enter, delete, or edit data; and rearrange or retrieve data from the data base. Similarly, the expert system shells allow users who are not proficient with expert systems or AI languages to create expert systems. In fact, Martin and Oxman[7] have stated:

Most future expert systems will be developed using an expert system shell. The system developers will not hand-code the basic system components. [They] will rely on the expert system shell vendors to develop, enhance, and maintain these shell products.

They further suggest the following three steps for developing an expert system using an expert system shell:

---

[7] Martin and Oxman, p. 50.

FIGURE 11–9 **Sample Interaction with VP-Expert**

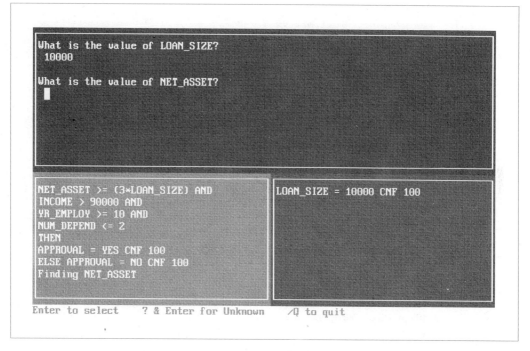

```
What is the value of LOAN_SIZE?
  10000

What is the value of NET_ASSET?
  █


NET_ASSET >= (3*LOAN_SIZE) AND        LOAN_SIZE = 10000 CNF 100
INCOME > 90000 AND
YR_EMPLOY >= 10 AND
NUM_DEPEND <= 2
THEN
APPROVAL = YES CNF 100
ELSE APPROVAL = NO CNF 100
Finding NET_ASSET

Enter to select     ? & Enter for Unknown    /Q to quit
```

1. Study the domain (area of knowledge) to be supported by the expert system.

2. Determine which expert system shell is best for the domain being replicated.

3. Develop the expert system by filling the shell with knowledge.

Developing an expert system using a shell is similar to the iterative process used in the prototype development of Decision Support Systems (DSS). This approach involves selecting a small but important part of the problem and designing a system to solve that problem. Once this prototype for the subproblem is solved, the system is tested by the user for a short time period and, if necessary, modified.

After the expert system for the initial subproblem is deemed satisfactory by the user, other subproblems are handled in a similar manner, until an expert system for the entire problem is developed. Because the key to the expert system is the knowledge base, which is easily changed, the expert system itself can be changed by editing existing facts and rules or by adding new ones as they are available.

Using VP-Expert to Create an Expert System

A popular expert system shell for creating small expert systems (fewer than 500 rules) is VP-Expert from Paperback Software. Although VP-Expert is actually a rule-based system, it can also use an example-based table to deduce rules. This capability can make the job of creating the rules much easier. VP-Expert also allows the developer to assign confidence factors (CNF) to the outcomes from rules. The inference engine then considers the CNF when it develops its line of reasoning.

FIGURE 11–10   ***Results for a Loan Applicant***

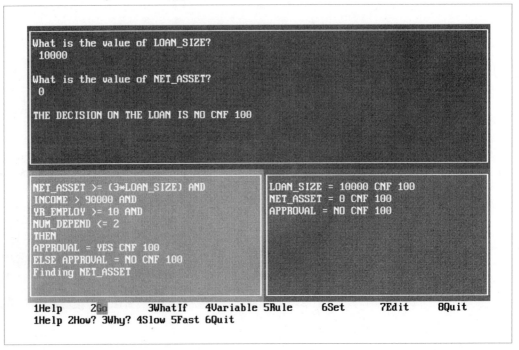

FIGURE 11–11   ***Rules Used to Determine Loan Eligibility***

For the ProYacht example, we use the four rules given earlier to create an expert system. Figure 11–9 shows a sample interaction between a user and VP-Expert. Figure 11–10 shows the results for an applicant who is seeking a $10,000 loan and who has an income of $24,500, has no net assets, has worked for 3 years, and has no dependents. Note that the applicant is turned down because of insufficient income.

A VP-Expert user can see the rules currently in effect through various commands. Figure 11–11 shows the rules used to make a loan decision for the applicant discussed above.

11.6 Expert System Implications for Managers

Although still in their infancy compared with other parts of an organization's information system, expert systems will be used by an increasing number of managers searching for ways to make tough decisions. Another impetus to the growth of expert system use is the increased availability of people with academic backgrounds in AI and expert systems. More PC-based expert system shells should also increase the use of expert systems for problem solving.

Integration of Expert and Decision Support Systems

Managers who want to improve their decision making may find a natural combination in expert systems and DSS. DSS provides a manager with more information about decisions and alternative solutions to problems using data and a model selected by the user. One natural integration of expert systems into DSS is their use to select the model to be used in DSS analysis. Currently, the user must be familiar with the models in the model base, but with expert systems, the user need not choose the model. The expert system can make the choice.

11.7 Neural Networks

Since John Von Neumann first developed the stored program concept, most computers have been **serial machines**—that is, they work on only one instruction at a time. A needed instruction or piece of data is retrieved from memory. Most computers must be given explicit instructions by the human user to process instructions or data. The serial nature of computers and the need to be programmed to solve many problems are two restrictions that seriously hamper computer speed and applicability to numerous problems.

Current technology is aimed at circumventing these restrictions by using an area of research that is similar to AI in its objectives but different in the methods used to reach those objectives. These neural networks seek to somehow replicate the neuron-synapse processing that occurs in the human brain. A **neural network** is a program or algorithm that is "trained" to handle some task. As with training animals or educating humans, this learning process depends on repetition. Neural networks are not programmed with explicit instructions like expert systems and other problem-solving systems. Instead, neural networks simulate a system of interconnected units—the **neurons**—sending messages to one another at a high rate of speed. The neural network receives input and then responds in a manner similar to human thought. Neural networks are currently being developed for various pattern-matching tasks like handwriting or speech recognition, fingerprint evaluation, and credit risk evaluation. A goal of defense researchers is a

FIGURE 11-12   *Example of a Neural Network*

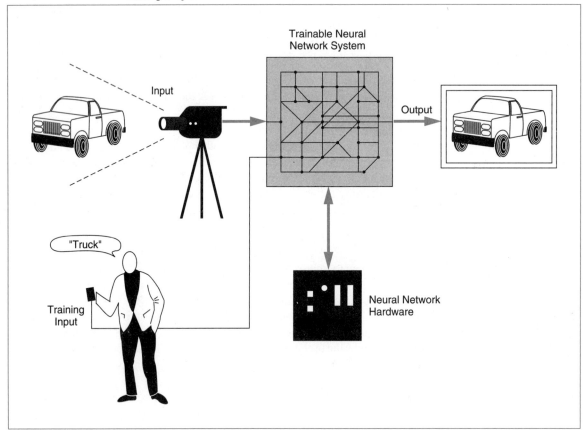

neural network that can recognize an enemy missile in real time—that is, fast enough to respond before the missile reaches its target.

As an example, assume that a neural network is taught to recognize a truck. With a serial computer, a human would write a program giving the computer instructions on how to recognize a truck. On the other hand, with the neural network shown in Figure 11–12, the computer would be shown a truck and simultaneously informed that the object is a truck. After a sufficient number of repetitions, the computer would recognize a truck on its own.

The original concept of neural networks involved imitating the brain's interconnected web of neurons with thousands of processors operating simultaneously in a massively parallel computer. However, this approach to neural networks was found to be extremely difficult and expensive to develop. In its place, simulated neural networks are created with single processors by using a technique called **backward propagation.** This methodology compares inputs and decides which incoming signal is strongest or best matches

Applications of Neural Networks

Although the application of neural networks is still in its infancy, an increasing number of organizations have experienced some success with them. Among these organizations are the following:

- Chase Manhattan Bank uses neural networks to make initial assessments of loan applications. The quality of the bank's assessments has improved almost 5 percent.

- Sumitomo Heavy Industries in Japan has developed a neural network system that inspects apples on a conveyor belt at the rate of 40 apples per second. The system counts and evaluates defects as a part of the grading process.

- Ford Motor Company is working on a neural network that "listens" to data input from a car's microprocessor just as a mechanic would listen to a car engine. Ford hopes to use this system as a diagnostic tool at the end of the production line or at the dealer.

- A Connecticut currency trader has developed a neural network that uses historical data on inflation, money supply, interest rates, and currency prices, as well as current economic indicators. The currency trader follows the network's advice religiously for his investment portfolios.

SOURCE: Andrew Maykuth, "Add a Few Points to Your PC's IQ," *Lotus*, July 1991, pp. 11–13.

a previously recognized pattern. After this comparison, the processor triggers an output that reinforces the pattern being matched.

Problems with Neural Networks

Although neural networks hold great promise for solving many problems, they also have definite drawbacks. For example, neural networks are not well-suited for making precise calculations, and they do not make logical deductions well. In general, they cannot recognize anything that does not contain some sort of pattern. Another drawback of neural networks is that determining how the network arrives at a conclusion is impossible. Its logic contains no "audit trail."

11.8 Summary

AI is any combination of computer hardware and software systems that exhibits some level of human intelligence. The term *AI* can refer to many different types of computer systems and applications, including natural languages, robots, alternative forms of input, computers "learning" to solve problems, and expert systems. With a natural language AI system, a user would not need to learn a special computer language to give the computer instructions. In the field of robotics, machines are used to perform work. Using AI, alternative forms of input such as voice and handwritten input can be used.

An expert system is an application of AI that uses knowledge, facts, and reasoning techniques to solve problems that normally require the abilities of human experts. The knowledge and facts are stored in the knowledge base, and the reasoning capabilities are handled by the inference engine of the expert system.

An expert system should perform at an expert's level of competence, use an inference engine to produce its deductions, use special knowledge acquired from experts, and not include programming for how the system uses its knowledge base. Ten problem areas commonly addressed by expert systems are interpretation, prediction, diagnosis, design, planning, monitoring, debugging, repairing, instruction, and control.

Two types of expert system development are commonly used—rule-based systems or example-based systems. In addition to the knowledge base and inference engine, two other components of an expert system are the KAF and the explanation facility. Inference engines use one of two methods to arrive at a final decision—backward chaining or forward chaining. An expert system shell has the mechanisms for using knowledge to make inferences, but it contains no knowledge.

Although still very new, expert systems are expected to grow in use as more managers discover how an expert system can help them to make their tough business decisions.

Neural networks are information systems that can be ''taught'' to recognize patterns in a manner similar to that used by the human brain. They are not programmed like other types of software.

Key Terms

android	knowledge base
Artificial Intelligence (AI)	knowledge engineer
backward chaining	knowledge system
backward propagation	logic trace
Confidence Factors (CNF)	natural languages
domain data base	neural network
example-based system	neurons
expert system	personal digital assistants
expert system shell	robotics
explanation facility	rule-based system
forward chaining	rule data base
fuzzy logic	serial machines
handwritten input	symbolic reasoning
IF-THEN rule	user interface
inference engine	voice input
Knowledge Acquisition Facility (KAF)	

Review Questions

1. Define AI. List some areas to which AI has been applied.

2. What is meant by the term ''fifth generation'' when applied to computers? What is expected from fifth generation computers?

3. Discuss the differences between industrial robots and androids.

4. Name some nonkeyboard forms of input. Discuss the current development of this form of input.

5. What is an expert system? Why are expert systems being applied in business?

6. What are the three elements of an expert system? Which element actually handles the reasoning part of the expert system?

7. List some situations in which expert systems can be useful. Discuss one situation in detail.

8. Name the four characteristics of an expert system. Apply these four characteristics to the ProYacht Acceptance case.

9. How do expert systems handle uncertain and incomplete knowledge? What is a CNF? Define fuzzy logic.

10. What is the difference between rule-based and example-based systems? Show how one of the rules in the text was developed from Table 11–3.

11. What are the components of an expert system? What is the difference between the domain data base and the rule data base?

12. What are the two methods used by the inference engine to arrive at a final decision? Discuss the differences between the two methods.

13. What is the KAF? Why is it important to an expert system?

14. Discuss the methods used in developing an expert system. What is an expert system shell?

15. Discuss how neural networks differ from traditional software packages. What is backward propagation? For what kinds of problems are neural networks best suited?

Discussion Questions

1. An engineering firm that specializes in road construction believes that it can use an expert system to design overpasses, plan the most effective routes for new highways, estimate costs, and suggest alternative bridge designs for complex intersections. Is an expert system or a DSS more appropriate for each of these tasks? How would the firm develop an expert system for one of the appropriate uses? What steps are involved in this development?

2. Discuss the characteristics of a problem for which an expert system could be developed. Be sure to distinguish the characteristics from those that lead to the use of a DSS.

3. For each of the following situations, briefly describe the knowledge base, the type of inference engine, the KAF, and the need to use an explanation facility:
   a. Retirement planning by a bank's financial advisor
   b. Designing of a personal computer system that suggests software and hardware based on clients' needs and business environment
   c. Forecasting clothing trends in the garment industry
   d. Training wildlife management personnel for the park service
   e. Buying grain for processing into flour products, such as cereal and bread

Case 11–1

Western
University

Western University is a large public university located in the western part of the United States. Like all public and private colleges and universities, Western has a financial aid office that oversees the distribution of loans, scholarships, and fellowships to students. Such offices often award scholarships based on a student's hometown, major, and grade point average and SAT or ACT score. Scholarships may also be available to children of employees of a specific company. A financial aid office at such a university commonly has hundreds of scholarships, each with a particular array of conditions the student must meet before the award is made. For example, a scholarship might have the following criteria: Student must be a resident of Washington County, major in agriculture, and have either a GPA of at least 3.0 or an SAT score of at least 1000. A student who meets these conditions is eligible for a $1,000 scholarship.

All the scholarships for which a student might qualify are usually listed in a book. However, searching this book for a particular scholarship that matches a student's qualifications can be difficult for a person who is not familiar with scholarship criteria. For this reason, most financial aid offices employ at least one person as an "expert counselor" to help students who are interested in scholarship possibilities. Unfortunately, this counselor may need quite a long time to become a true expert on the scholarship program, and the counselor quite often leaves after a few years to take a different job or to pursue other interests.

To make it easier for students to determine if they qualify for financial aid, Western University is considering implementing an expert system to help the financial aid counselor. In such an expert system, the knowledge base should contain information on scholarship facts and a list of rules to determine a student's eligibility. For the previous example, the facts would be as follows:

County of Residence: Washington
Major: Agriculture
SAT Score: 1000
GPA: 3.0

For this example, the rule would be:

IF   Student is from Washington County AND
          Student is Agriculture major AND
          Student has at least a 3.0 grade point average OR
          Student has SAT score of at least 1000
THEN   Student is eligible for $1,000 scholarship

Case Questions

1. What type of inference engine and reasoning capability are used in this situation?

2. How would the university develop its information on the availability of scholarships?

3. Would such an expert system be useful to counselors? Why? Would it make the university more competitive in attracting good students?

Case 11-2

Texaco

Texaco is developing a pilot project to integrate AI into its manufacturing process at its refineries in an effort to save utility costs and improve environmental controls. At the company's Port Arthur chemical plant in Texas, a Local Area Network (LAN) links an expert system machine with the plant's computerized process control system to give operators advice on correcting problems in the plant's operation. The system also monitors the plant's devices for equipment failures. Texaco officials hope the ability to monitor the manufacturing process will help them save money and minimize the plant's negative effect on the environment.

The pilot site is a chemical plant. The plant is a large complex of reactors and distillation towers where petroleum feedstock, or refined crude oil, is refined into various chemicals. Throughout the processing, the ambient temperature, the chemical properties of the feedstock, and the flow of materials may vary. Operators try to keep the yield of the product at an optimum level while conducting safe operations. They must carefully watch the temperature and pressure of the materials and be ready to adjust the process if necessary. If the project is successful, Texaco could expand it to the 25 other units at the Port Arthur plant and to the company's 10 other refineries in the United States, Canada, and Europe.

The Port Arthur test is an example of integrated AI. "Most other expert systems are stand-alone units, which require someone to go to a special terminal or printer," said a knowledge engineer in Texaco's Computer and Information Systems Department (CISD). "By linking the AI computers to the company's other computers, AI programs and development tools can be operating in the background but still be fully accessible and useful." The expert system is needed because of the complex nature of Port Arthur's operations. An expert system knows only what you tell it. Texaco knowledge engineers spent several months talking to process control engineers and plant operators to write the series of rules that the expert system uses to consider a problem. Texaco's expert system uses the Prototype Intelligence Control (PICON) software system written in LISP, a common AI language.

Texaco uses a minicomputer process control system called TDACS. The PICON system is integrated into the TDACS system using a LAN. The PICON system monitors the process control system data at all times. As it senses a problem, the system sends alert messages recommending specific actions to the operators logged on the TDACS system. PICON can also send longer, more complete explanations to an expert bulletin file, which operators can read later. "There are some 900 process variables," said one of the staff at CISD. "People may have a hard time monitoring all of that data every few seconds, but the PICON system doesn't. It can evaluate the sensor data in real time and send back messages to plant operators at an average of 40 packets per second."

Monitoring faulty equipment is another PICON function that has an impact on utility cost reduction. PICON monitors the data from each sensor constantly and compares it with prior readings. PICON uses what AI engineers refer to as "deep knowledge" to interpret the meaning of deviations from standard expected readings. Deep knowledge is information that a human accumulates from experience. Sometimes this interpretation indicates an equipment failure. If a sensor failure occurs, PICON could send a message to the

TDACS system to tag the sensor as faulty and provide a suggested reason for the fault. PICON is also expected to reduce the amount of down time for the plant due to failed sensors.

Controlling the effect of the plant on the environment is an important concern. To safely run the plant, refining operations may often have to burn off some chemicals and gas. Without balancing the manufacturing process by this flaring, an accident could occur, because a chemical refinery is really a controlled explosion. Because flaring can be costly and harmful to the environment, Texaco wants to reduce the amount of flaring from its plants. The PICON system can help control the manufacturing process by suggesting that operators lower the temperature of some process or adjust a particular pump or heater to reduce the flaring.

Adapted from Guengerich, Steven, "AI System Cuts Plant's Power Costs," *PC Week,* July 7, 1977, p. C10–C11. Copyright © 1977, Ziff Communications Company.

Case Questions

1. What monitoring problem led to the development of the PICON expert system?

2. What is in PICON's knowledge base? How was it developed?

3. How does it tie into operations to reduce power costs?

IV

Developing and Acquiring Information System Resources

Section IV discusses developing and acquiring the information system resources described in Section III. Chapters 12 and 13 describe structured systems development. Chapter 12 focuses on defining the project, assessing its feasibility, and analyzing the information requirements. Chapter 13 focuses on designing and implementing a new information system. Chapter 14 discusses procedures for acquiring the hardware and software to implement a new information system. Finally, Chapter 15 considers prototype and end user development procedures as alternatives to the traditional systems development life cycle.

Structured Systems Development: Definition and Analysis

C H A P T E R

12

Introduction   As we have discussed throughout this text, information systems are invaluable to any organization. Information systems can be used to process transactions quickly, accumulate data for further processing, provide management with operational reports, provide information for tactical decision making, and support strategic decision making. However, information systems are almost never "ready made"—they must be carefully designed and built to accomplish these important tasks. In designing and building an information system, the requirements of management must be carefully analyzed; the information system should provide management with the information it needs to accomplish its goals. The process of analyzing information requirements, designing systems to meet these requirements, and building these systems is called **systems development.** Systems development is not a simple task. A well-designed information system requires careful planning, organizing, staffing, coordinating, directing, controlling, and integrating all system elements—including personnel, hardware, software, data, and procedures—into an effective system.

The process of systems development can take place when a new system is needed or when an old system must be revised. Either situation can occur when management's information requirements change or when new technology enables management to acquire more or better information than before. Consider again ProYacht, Inc.'s acquisition of Cool Water Marinas, as discussed in Chapter 10 on decision support systems. This change in the business would probably require the development of a new information system that could account for dock space rental as well as normal retail business at each marina. Information for this type of business would be quite different from that for the sailboat manufacturing and sales business.

FIGURE 12–1

Information System Life Cycle

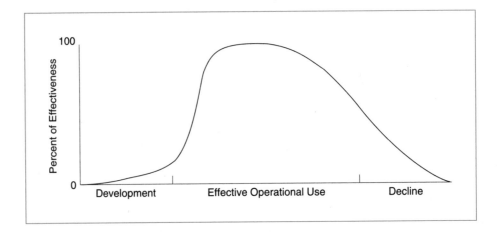

On the other hand, assume that ProYacht gives each of its sales representatives a portable personal computer, thereby placing tremendous communications capability in the hands of its sales personnel. With this new technology, sales representatives could serve their customers better by communicating directly with the company data base stored on a centralized computer to determine the stock status and production schedules for each line of boats. In this example, the information system must be modified to make this information available to the sales representatives.

An organization might consider developing a new information system when the existing system has been modified repeatedly to meet changing business conditions and technology. After several modifications, a system may begin to resemble a "patchwork" of subsystems that do not work well together. This process results in **system degradation,** in which the performance of the system drops off markedly and the quality of information provided by the system suffers.

Information System Life Cycle

As a result of changing business conditions and changing technology, no information system lasts forever. All systems go through an **information system life cycle,** as shown in Figure 12–1. Systems are developed, used and maintained, and modified; then they decline. At some point in the life cycle, an established system must be modified for continued use, or a new system must be developed to replace the declining system. The rate at which this process of development, use, and decline progresses depends on the nature of the business environment, changing business conditions, and technological advances. Rapid changes in any of these can accelerate the life cycle dramatically.

For this reason, all systems must be continually monitored to ensure that they satisfy business needs and to determine when they must be upgraded, maintained, or scrapped in favor of a new system.

System Development Life Cycle

The process used to modify an existing system or develop a new system is called the **system development life cycle.** This continual process is also called systems development, or simply, systems analysis and design. It consists of seven phases: project definition, feasibility study, requirements analysis, high-level systems design, detailed design,

FIGURE 12–2 *Systems Development Life Cycle*

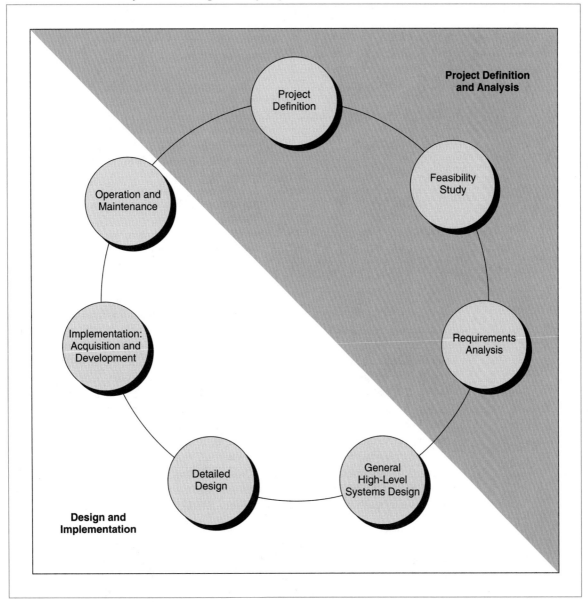

implementation (acquisition and program development), and operation. Project definition is required to identify the problem or opportunity. Once a project is identified, a feasible solution must be determined. Next, a careful analysis of management's information requirements is necessary in order to specify the nature of the system needed to help management deal with a problem or opportunity. Once these requirements are deter-

TABLE 12–1

**Objectives of the
Systems
Development Life
Cycle Phases**

Phases	Objective
Project Definition	Identify the problem or opportunity
Feasibility Study	Determine whether a feasible solution exists given economic, technological, and operational constraints
Requirements Analysis	Develop a logical description of information requirements
General High-Level Systems Designs	Develop a high-level design for several alternatives and recommend one for detailed design
Detailed Design	Develop software specifications for development or acquisition, and develop hardware specifications for acquisition
Implementation: Acquisition and Software Development	Request proposals, develop or acquire software, acquire hardware, install hardware and software, test and convert to new system
Operation and Maintenance	Ensure the system continues to work properly and meets management information requirements

mined, a general high-level design of a system that meets these specifications is prepared. The detailed design of the system, including hardware and software specifications, should comply with the general design selected. Once an information system is designed and the hardware and software requirements are specified in detail, the needed software and hardware are acquired, the software is written if necessary, and the system is installed. Finally, the information system must be operated and maintained to provide management with the information it needs to accomplish the objectives of the organization. The development of an information system involves much more than the physical aspects of design; it involves careful and logical consideration of management and operating personnel's information requirements. The person who performs these tasks or oversees a project team that performs these activities is called a **systems analyst.** The seven phases of the systems development life cycle are shown in Figure 12–2, and the objectives of each phase are shown in Table 12–1.

The key idea behind the seven-phases systems development life cycle is that the process moves from a broad, logical understanding of information needs to a detailed solution of the problem. This process can be compared with the construction process for a building. This process goes from an idea to a set of preliminary sketches and plans to blueprints to the actual construction. In both the construction of a building and the systems development process, the movement is from a logical concept to a physical entity.

Note in Figure 12–2 that the systems development life cycle is divided into two broad phases — project definition and analysis and design and implementation. A key distinction exists between these two phases. The objective of the definition and analysis phase is to define the scope of the project and decide what must be done to resolve it. Often, the definition of the project and the study of feasible solutions is called the planning phase of systems development. The second phase involves deciding how to solve the problem and then implementing the solution.

All seven phases are summarized in the following paragraphs, with detailed discussions in this and the next two chapters. This chapter covers the project definition, feasibility study, and analysis phases, and Chapter 13 covers the general design, detailed design, implementation, and operation phases. These discussions concentrate on the internal development of information systems. The acquisition of information systems is covered in Chapter 14. Alternative approaches to systems development are presented in Chapter 15.

Project Definition   The need for a new or revised system can be the result of several events, including a change in management objectives, new technology, or an old system that is too expensive to maintain even though it performs adequately. Two approaches can be used to define a project before the systems analysis and design process begins. First, a problem with the current system may be identified. Second, a project may be defined based on the information processing objectives of the system. Changes in technology and business may change these objectives and create the need for a systems development project. Once management knows that a problem exists or that information objectives are no longer being met, the project definition process begins.

When management and system users agree that a problem or opportunity exists, the first step in project definition is to assign an analyst to investigate the problem, the need for new information, or the need to use new technology. The analyst obtains a broad understanding of the project from management and users — why they need new information or the benefits of using new technology. Based on these meetings, the analyst prepares a written declaration of the users' objectives and the scope of the project. The analyst also prepares a preliminary cost-benefit estimate. When users and management agree on the objectives and scope of the project, the analyst can move to the next step. In summary, the analyst must determine why a new or revised system is needed and what its objectives are.

Feasibility Study   After users and management agree with the analyst's definition of the project, the analyst can investigate the nature of the problem or the new information requirements. A feasibility study answers the following two questions:

1. Is the project worth pursuing?

2. Does a possible solution to the problem exist or can the new information be delivered?

If the answer to either question is no, then the systems development process is terminated.

In a feasibility study, the analyst does not attempt to find a way to actually implement the project. The objective of this step is to obtain a better understanding of the information requirements and possible ways to meet these requirements. The analyst must assess the economic, technological, and operational feasibility of each of these possible ways to meet these information requirements. The declaration of objectives and scope of the project prepared in the first step is refined here, and the cost-benefit estimate is also revised. Based on the analyst's report, management decides whether to continue with the process. In summary, the analyst determines if a feasible solution exists.

Analysis   After the feasibility study shows that the project is worth pursuing and that an acceptable solution probably exists, the analysis stage of the process is initiated. In this phase, the analyst works closely with users to develop a logical model of management's information requirements. This requires a determination of the information needed by management and operating personnel to carry out their responsibilities. The model is a simplified version of reality that does not attempt to capture every detail of management's needs. Instead, the model is useful for conceptualizing what new information is needed or for determining what must be done to solve an information problem. After the analyst develops a logical model of the system, users and management must determine if the new model will solve the problem, satisfy management's information needs, or achieve the benefits of new technology.

General High-Level Design   After the analysis phase of the process, the analyst knows what must be done to meet management's information needs but not how to do it. In this phase, the analyst develops an outline of how these needs might be satisfied. This high-level design does not include detailed specifications. In the general design process, the systems analyst develops several alternatives for a new system and recommends one for further detailed design. These recommendations are then presented to users and management for approval and comments.

Detailed Design   If the solution suggested by the analyst is selected by users and management, then the process of detailed design can begin with this alternative as the general strategy. This process should determine exactly how the system should be implemented. The detailed design includes specifications on computer hardware and software needed for the system. If the software can be purchased from a commercial vendor, then the specifications should provide all the information necessary to select a package. On the other hand, if the software must be developed, the specifications should be detailed enough for programmers to understand program requirements. These specifications are analogous to an engineer's blueprints in that they should show the user what the finished product will look like. They should be sufficient to guide the actions of programmers and vendors.

Implementation   In this phase, the detailed plans developed in the previous phase are put into action. Any needed hardware is purchased and installed. The acquisition of commercial software must also occur in this phase. Program development must also occur at this stage. Both hardware and software products should be tested to ensure that specifications are met. Software testing is extremely important to ensure that the programs are bug-free and perform to users' expectations. After the testing and installation, the organization actually begins using the new system.

Operations and Maintenance   Any system, no matter how well it is designed, must be continually modified to handle changes in input, output, or logic requirements. Maintenance is an ongoing process that keeps a system operating and up to date by facilitating necessary changes. Although it may seem like a minor part of the analysis, design, and implementation process, maintenance of existing systems occupies about 70% of a professional programmer's time. If the systems analysis and design process has followed the structured approach suggested in this text, operations and maintenance should be much easier.

Computer-Aided Software Engineering

All of the systems development life cycle phases can be expedited via **Computer-Aided Software Engineering (CASE)** software packages. CASE tools can be integrated and designed so that each phase or step in the development process can be integrated with the others. An analyst can start with the project definition, analyze the problem, design a new system, and specify the programming or acquisition needs. Each development tool described in this and the next chapter can be automated via CASE software. CASE tools can even write programming code from an analyst's specifications. The result is a more rapid development of information systems.

12.1 Approaches to Systems Development

Several approaches to systems development are used today by organizations—"traditional" programming methods, a formal structured systems analysis and design, prototyping, end user development, and acquisition of systems from outside vendors. These approaches share similarities, but also have many important differences. In addition, many development projects use a combination of these approaches.

"Traditional" Programming Methods

Although computerized information systems have been used for many years, some organizations still do not go through each step outlined in the systems development life cycle. Instead, the user and the person developing the information system meet and decide what should be done. Once this decision is made, the programmer works on the various computer programs that make up the information system, meeting with the user when questions arise. This approach can result in a usable information system for the initial user, but it also results in an information system that is poorly documented, poorly planned, not integrated into the overall organization information plan, and difficult to maintain and modify. Because these systems just evolve, organizations that use the "traditional" programming approach usually have an uncoordinated "hodgepodge" information system that cannot deliver the information needed for the organization to operate in today's competitive economy.

Structured Approach

Because of the problems with "traditional" programming, structured systems analysis and design was developed. This approach closely follows the seven phases of the systems development life cycle shown in Figure 12–2. It is called **structured systems analysis and design** because each phase must be completed in order after certain objectives are achieved. A report to management is prepared at the end of each phase, and management approval must be obtained before the next phase is initiated. This approach is useful when information requirements and the necessary data for these requirements can be specified by users, particularly for large Transaction Processing Systems (TPS) and Management Information Systems (MIS). This approach is also appropriate when the major components of the system must be integrated into a comprehensive system. The major disadvantage to the structured approach is that it takes a significant amount of time to develop a new system.

Prototyping   Often management cannot specify its needs ahead of time because technology is so new, a change in business conditions requires vastly different information, or a new system is needed quickly. Moreover, the user may recognize what he or she needs yet not be able to articulate these needs during the analysis stages. The development process must be expedited, but the risk of developing a system that does not meet users' needs is high. In such cases, a **prototype** system that contains the bare essentials can be developed and used on a trial basis. After some experience with the prototype, users can further define their requirements or try a completely different approach to solving the problem. A revised or new prototype is then designed for use. In this manner, prototyping is an iterative process. An information system is briefly analyzed, designed, used, reanalyzed, redesigned, used some more, reanalyzed, and so on, until management has a system that meets its needs. Usually, the system becomes more comprehensive with each iteration. When the user is satisfied, the prototype is implemented.

The prototyping approach is best used for Decision Support Systems (DSS), because managers may not be able to specify their needs or the models and technology are new. Unfortunately, many of the safeguards built into the structured approach do not exist with prototyping, and large-scale systems such as those used in transaction processing are difficult to develop. Prototyping is useful when needs change rapidly, requirements are difficult for management to articulate without seeing the system first, the risk of developing the wrong system is high, or several alternative systems must be viewed prior to actual acceptance. Prototype development procedures are discussed at length in Chapter 15.

End User   With **end user development,** users develop their own software via a personal computer
Development   using a PC-based data base, spreadsheet, word processing, and communication software or on a larger computer system using a Data Base Management System (DBMS) or high-level languages. This approach is especially useful for DSS if the system must be built very quickly to accommodate a pressing need or if management needs only a simple model or access to certain data. Users of large data base systems and mainframe modeling systems such as Interactive Financial Planning Systems (IFPS) can also develop software using the report generating and modeling capabilities of these systems. Moreover, new fourth generation languages may be used for end user development. To support less technically sophisticated users, many organizations have in-house consultants to assist in the development process.

This approach expedites the development process, because the user controls the development process and can proceed rapidly without the need for formal reports and approvals at each stage of development. Management can obtain its information quickly by simply developing its own systems. On the negative side, these systems tend to be small in scope, be simple in design, and lack the controls and integration with other systems required in the structured approach.

Acquisition   A final method used to develop a new system is to simply acquire it from hardware and software vendors. Methods of acquisition are discussed in detail in Chapter 14. Another approach would be to hire a third party consultant to develop the system using any of the methods above. This procedure is called **out-sourcing.** Sometimes third parties do all the

FIGURE 12–3

Comparison of Approaches to Systems Development

Traditional Programming	Advantages
	Evolutionary development
	Disadvantages
	Not planned
	Not documented
	Not integrated or coordinated
Structured Approach	Advantages
	Well planned and coordinated
	Meets objectives and requirements
	Leads to well-integrated systems
	Better for complex TPSs and MISs
	Disadvantages
	Time consuming
	May not be appropriate when requirements cannot be specified
Prototyping	Advantages
	Fast development of prototype
	Good when management cannot easily specify requirements
	Iterative process
	Better for DSS
	Disadvantages
	Not as well coordinated or controlled
	May lead to inefficient and incomplete systems
End User Development	Advantages
	Fast
	Good for rapid development of personal DSS
	Uses data base and other end user development tools
	Used effectively for less complex systems
	Disadvantages
	Uncontrolled and poorly documented
	Data and programs are not integrated
	Not appropriate for large complex systems
Acquisition (Out Sourcing)	Advantages
	Acquire outside expertise that organization may not have
	Can be cost effective if commercially available software is used
	Disadvantages
	Costly for custom development
	May not meet user needs as well as custom software

work and deliver it to the organization when the system is ready to use. For such a **turnkey system,** the organization just "turns the key" to operate it. An organization may also use a **service bureau** to do all its computing for a fee.

In each case, the entire system can be developed at one time or it can be developed in phases. A phased approach is useful when the technology and final system configuration are uncertain at the beginning of the development process or when the entire project is so big that it must be developed one module at a time. Figure 12–3 compares these five approaches to developing information systems showing how each approach uses the seven phases discussed earlier.

This chapter and Chapter 13 discuss a structured approach to systems analysis and design. Chapter 14 focuses on the acquisition of information systems, and Chapter 15 is devoted to a substantive discussion of prototyping and end user development.

12.2 Planning, Personnel, and Organizational Change

Top management and senior executives are responsible for developing a strategic plan for an organization's information system. This plan should outline the major informational requirements of the organization and set basic guidelines on how to implement information projects. All new projects should fall within these general guidelines. Senior management must approve and actively support all systems projects for their ultimate success. A major reason for system failure is the lack of management support. In summary, the systems development process should be guided by the organization's strategic plan that defines the overall goals of the organization and its information needs.

Management and Information System Personnel Involvement

To ensure that systems in development are in agreement with the strategic plan, a top-level **steering committee** guides the planning, development, and implementation of systems. Members of this committee should include division managers for whom systems are being developed and senior information officers. The committee must have knowledge of strategic, tactical, and operational plans in order to assess a systems development project's compliance with these plans. The committee also must possess objectivity in assessing corporate priorities as well as considerable experience in using information systems. In practice, this committee acts for management in guiding and approving the activities involved in an information systems project.

The **project team** is the group of information system professionals and users who actually build a specific application. This project team may include systems analysts, programmers, and data base specialists, as well as representatives of the managers who will eventually use the information. The team leader overseeing the entire project reports to the steering committee.

Systems analysts are actively involved in many phases of systems development. Their knowledge of the business and of information systems is invaluable in bridging the gap between management and the information technology specialists of vendors and the organization's own programmers who must implement the detailed design.

Sociotechnical Environment and System Change

In the development of information systems, changes in technology and systems must be understood in terms of impact on people and on the organization. An organization does not merely change from a batch to an online system, for example. A new system may change an employee's responsibilities, the types of decisions made, organizational structure, and the basic way of doing business. In general, a person's responsibilities and the information available to him or her may change. In summary, changes may alter both the social and technological elements in an organization.

As a result, the design and implementation of information systems must consider the factors that affect an organization's social environment. Organizational, behavioral, and decision-making concepts are extremely important. Careful attention must be given to decision-making needs and the flow of transaction information in the new as well as in the old organization. Analysts must design user interfaces that are easy to use. Finally, they must anticipate and plan for organizational differences that accompany the change in the information system.

For these reasons, participation in system design should be solicited at every level of the organization, especially the managerial level. Management must communicate fully with all parties involved, explaining the reasons for the changes, the expected informational results, and the anticipated organizational changes. The need for new personnel or training should be fully disclosed to reduce apprehension and lead to a smoother change.

Because of the sociotechnical nature of information systems and their potential impact on an organization, changes must be well planned and controlled. It is often infeasible to modify or change an entire system at one time because the project could become unmanageable. For large projects, analysts may decide to change one segment of the system at a time rather than the entire system at once. In this **phased** or **modular approach,** clear objectives for each module are set, and the design and implementation for each module should proceed in an orderly fashion under the direction of the project team and steering committee. The design and implementation of subsystems or modules has the advantages of better control and immediate completion targets. In addition, the necessary training and organizational changes can proceed in a controlled manner. As a result, management and users may see more rapid progress, use portions of the new system, and be more satisfied with the development process.

The phased approach to systems development requires special attention to system interfaces. Old and new systems must interface in order to carry out the daily activities of the organization. Furthermore, new systems must be designed to anticipate interfaces with modules that may be developed at a later date. Systems with a loose interface are easier to develop, but they do not evolve into tight integrated systems. To obtain a "tightly coupled" integrated system in the future, management must consider system boundaries and future interfaces with other systems. For example, a manufacturing firm may some-day want to tie its new system to a supplier's system to order and receive materials just in time for production.

The essential planning and control activities occur in the project definition and feasibility study steps in the system development life cycle. Plans are updated and refined with more and more detail as the development phases are completed. Network analysis, such as the **Program Evaluation Review Technique (PERT)** described in Chapter 16, is useful in this overall planning and control process. This procedure can be extended beyond the simple scheduling of time, to the management of such resources as the analysts, programmers, accountants, and engineers who comprise a project team. Even the budgetary consequences of the resources used in analysis, design, and implementation, as well as the acquisition of hardware and software, can be assessed using this software.

In addition to the scheduling and resource management control provided by effective use of PERT or Critical Path Method (CPM), the development process can benefit by an independent review at the end of each phase in the development cycle. A **structured walk through** can accomplish this by using another team or analyst to review the recommendations, analysis, or design. The analyst must ensure that all plans meet the objectives, selection criteria, information requirements, constraints, or specifications of the preceeding phase in the development cycle. A structured walk through should determine that nothing major is overlooked in the system development process.

12.3 The Sun Products Case

We return again to ProYacht, Inc., a successful builder of quality sailboats. To take advantage of its distribution channels and positive financial position, ProYacht decides to expand its business into the aluminum fishing and pontoon boat areas. To facilitate the expansion, ProYacht management decides to acquire the Sun Products Company, an old and respected manufacturer of quality aluminum and pontoon boats whose plant is located outside of Green Bay, Wisconsin. Currently, Sun's annual sales are approximately $5 million, but with ProYacht's national distribution and marketing system, that figure could double in the next few years. After the acquisition, Sun Products will be a separate division with its own manufacturing and marketing, as shown in the revised organization chart in Figure 12–4.

ProYacht management is extremely enthusiastic about the quality of Sun's products but not with the company's financial performance and reputation for slow delivery. These problems are due to an antiquated system of processing sales orders, scheduling production to meet these orders, shipping the boats, and billing customers. The file processing

FIGURE 12–4   ***ProYacht, Inc. Organization Chart***

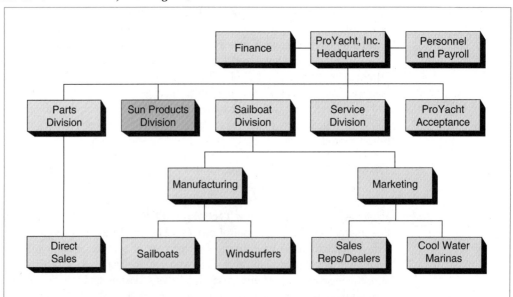

system runs on an old minicomputer. Boat orders are keyed into the system, and production work orders based on these sales orders are prepared. As the boats are built, they are added to finished goods inventory. When boats are shipped, customers are billed and inventory is reduced by the number and type of boat shipped. Because these systems are not integrated, when a sale is made to a dealer, the salesperson can never be sure that the boat is in stock or if it can be produced for delivery in time for the season. Moreover, once a boat is ordered, the progress of the order cannot be tracked as it is scheduled and manufactured. As a result, large inventories are carried so that the company can satisfy customer needs.

After examining Sun's operations, ProYacht determines that the system includes no way to indicate that an order is complete. Orders could be processed more than once or never shipped at all if components did not arrive in a timely manner. Sometimes customers were billed for boats that were never shipped, and other times boats were shipped with incorrect bills or no bills at all. In several cases, when boats were not shipped on time, Sun lost the business of these retail dealers. Many boats from those who refused deliveries are still sitting in the field behind the plant as obsolete inventory.

ProYacht concludes that these problems have contributed to Sun's poor profit performance over the last few years. Correcting these problems is made a high priority project by ProYacht management, and a systems analyst is assigned to study the problems and report back to ProYacht.

12.4 Project Definition

As discussed earlier, the first phase in the structured systems development process is the careful definition of a project. This phase involves the recognition and subsequent definition of the problem to be resolved or the information needs that are required due to changing business conditions or technology. At the end of this phase, the systems analyst or project team must determine why the project must be undertaken and what its objectives are. The key activities involved in a formal definition of the project are outlined in Figure 12–5. These activities are as follows:

1. Recognize the need to solve a problem or to improve the information management receives from the system.

2. Identify the project or the reason for the new or revised system.

3. Identify the project's objectives and constraints.

4. Identify possible alternatives, the scope of the project, and a rough estimate of costs and benefits.

5. Prepare a scope and objective statement to summarize these activities and to outline a feasibility study to continue the project planning.

Based on these activities, management determines whether to continue with the development of the project.

Recognize Need

The need to develop a new system or modify an existing system must first be recognized. This situation often occurs when management does not receive the information needed to

FIGURE 12–5

Project Definition

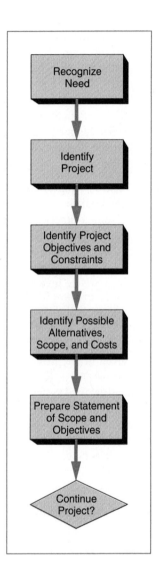

carry out responsibilities. Technological changes may also render the current system obsolete, or problems may exist in the operation of the current system. In general, a need must be recognized.

Project Identification

A project must be carefully identified. Problems and new information needs must be investigated, identified, and brought to the attention of management or the steering committee. Such an investigation is not easy, because the systems analyst must sort through many symptoms to determine the underlying problems. For example, customers not receiving shipments on a timely basis is a symptom. The real cause of this problem may be an inadequate inventory and production information system or an outdated scheduling procedure in manufacturing.

Identification of Objectives and Constraints

The analyst must then identify the objectives of the project. Objectives may range from a simple extension or modification of an existing system to the development of a completely new information system. In a perfect situation, only the objectives are considered in the development of an information system. In the real world, however, organizations are constrained by numerous economic, technological, operational, and organizational constraints. For example, management may want a sophisticated financial planning system, but the cost may be prohibitive. As another example, management may want specific hardware, but the organization does not have personnel trained to operate it. As an example of a technical constraint, the proposed system for Sun Products must support intensive interaction for 200 sales representatives. To determine the objectives in light of the constraints imposed on the organization, the analyst outlines possible options for a new system so that management can see how the proposed system would fit into the organization's strategic plan.

Preliminary Identification of Alternatives and Project Scope and Costs

At this stage, some preliminary identification of alternative ways to solve the problem, deliver the needed information, or incorporate new technology should be outlined. Alternatives should be founded on the objectives and constraints placed on the project. These alternatives indicate the size and scope of the project, including cost and magnitude of the organizational changes involved in the project. In addition, a preliminary cost-benefit analysis should be prepared. This analysis includes a rough estimate of the various costs involved in developing and operating the system compared with the benefits expected from the system.

Preparation of a Statement of Scope and Objectives

After considering the results of all previous steps, the analyst can prepare a statement of scope and objectives summarizing these findings. This statement includes the description of the project; why it is being undertaken; what it expects to accomplish; its development and operational constraints; some preliminary options for solving the problem or providing needed information; and a preliminary estimate of the project's scope, costs, and benefits. Finally, it should outline the scope of the feasibility study to follow if the project is approved by management or the steering committee. Project definition completes the first part of the planning process an organization must undergo before actually beginning the formal analysis, design, and implementation of an information system.

Project Definition for Sun Products

To illustrate project definition, we return to ProYacht, Inc., which has assigned Jennifer Santos to the task of analyzing the problem with Sun Products' information system. To do this, she first reviews existing complaints to be sure they are authentic. An analyst must determine if complaints are significant enough to proceed with the project, or if they are just isolated instances. Santos' review of the complaints includes an analysis of dates and quantities of sales orders, production schedules, shipping documents, and invoices. The review convinces her that a major problem does indeed exist.

Santos spends a significant amount of time interviewing sales and production personnel to get a better idea of the magnitude of the problem and the potential source of the difficulty. There is no substitute for these interviews, because they reveal more than just a review of documents. For example, in Santos' discussion with Sun's sales manager Ray Horne, she discovers that his sales personnel never know what is in stock. They just take orders, promise customers a reasonable delivery date based on ''gut'' feelings from past experience, and hope for the best. They receive a monthly printout of inventory from the current accounting system, but it is out of date the day it arrives. In critical situations, sales personnel call a friend at the warehouse or someone in production to check inventory or production status.

In Santos' interview with Fred Broadway, manufacturing superintendent at Sun, she learns that his department cannot start some work orders until parts are ordered and received. Unfortunately, this process can take several weeks.

In her interviews with Sun's managers, Santos discusses the nature of the boat business. Because the business is seasonal, timely product delivery is critical. She also finds that brand substitution is common among dealers, so if Sun does not serve its customers, someone else will. In other words, customer service is the key to a firm's success.

From these interviews, Santos concludes that the problem with Sun Products is an inventory system that cannot be accessed by sales personnel who must intelligently process sales orders. In addition, the raw materials inventory system is not responsive to changes in production. The current system uses a decision model that allows stock to run low before orders are placed. From her analysis, Santos estimates that lost sales total about $250,000 per year due to various inventory problems, and that with a normal profit margin of 10 percent, Sun loses $25,000 in profits each year. This estimate does not count the ill will that the current system creates, resulting in future lost sales. She further concludes that this problem will get worse if sales increase.

The objective of the project is an inventory system that is up to date for work in process, including work orders pending scheduling, finished goods, and raw materials. A second objective is to make inventory information available to sales personnel for better customer relations.

According to all the personnel involved, the major constraints on the system include training employees to carefully enter the needed information and a requirement for sufficient savings to justify the new system.

Santos' preliminary proposal is a computerized inventory system that starts with a sales order or forecast, indicates the orders waiting on components, tracks work in process for each order through the production process, and indicates the boats ready for shipment. Using this system, Sun can produce boats for specific orders as well as standard models for inventory based on a sales forecast. Because this system is online, sales personnel can enter an order number to determine the status of an order or enter a boat stock number to determine the availability of a particular model. These data would be entered via personal computers in a sales office or via portable personal computers carried by Sun Products sales representatives to customer offices.

Santos proposes a 1-month feasibility study to determine if an information system to serve Sun's customers better can be created. The estimated cost of this feasibility study is $7,500, including one-half of her salary, her assistant's salary, and some travel and

FIGURE 12–6

Statement of Scope and Objectives

Statement of Scope and Objectives:	March 21, 1992
The Project:	Finished Goods and Work-in-Process Inventory
The Problem:	Inadequate inventory information to process a sales order and to follow up on orders in the manufacturing process
Project Objectives:	Provide better information to sales personnel
Project Scope:	The new system will be used by all Sun Products sales representatives. The cost should not exceed the cost savings in inventory and lost sales over a 3-year period; this is $75,000.
Preliminary Ideas:	An online order entry system with perpetual finished goods and work-in-process inventory and a provision for expediting orders
Feasibility Study:	One-month feasibility study using a systems analyst, an assistant, the sales manager, and the resident industrial engineer will cost $7,500.

incidental expenses for the month. The proposed project team consists of Santos, her assistant, sales manager Horne, and Sun's resident industrial engineer, Shirley Moore. From these discussions, and reviews of the documented evidence and the business environment, Santos prepares a statement of scope and objectives summarizing the problem definition phase. This statement is shown in Figure 12–6.

12.5 Feasibility Study

The next major step in the planning process is the completion of a feasibility study or project study proposal. Given the initial description of the nature of the project, management or the steering committee authorizes a feasibility study. The objective of a feasibility study is to determine whether there is a solution to the problem or information need, given technological, economic, and operational constraints. **Technical feasibility** means that the technology exists to pursue the project. **Operational feasibility** means that the project can be implemented within the organization's constraints, including organizational, behavioral, personnel, and day-to-day operational activities. Finally, **economic feasibility** means that a solution's expected benefits exceed the costs. These benefits and costs may not all be tangible, and they may extend over several years. If a project is technically infeasible, then it cannot be implemented and further investigation should be discontinued. Only if the project is technically feasible will it be checked for operational feasibility. Finally, if the project is both technically and operationally feasible, is it tested for economic feasibility.

The feasibility study is a brief overview of the analysis and design process outlined in Figure 12–2 consisting of the eight steps shown in Figure 12–7.

In the Sun Products case, ProYacht's management wants to know if a feasible solution exists and if that solution is cost beneficial. This assessment is absolutely essential, because not every problem is solvable given technological, operational, and economic constraints.

FIGURE 12–7

Feasibility Study

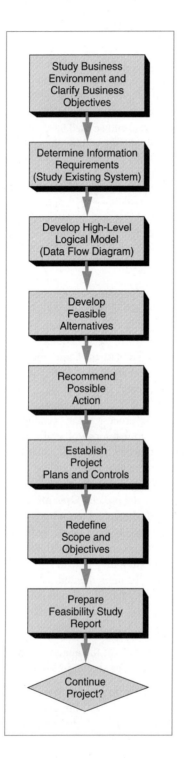

Understanding the Business Environment

The project team must acquire an understanding of the firm's objectives, policies, and resources and the nature of the business in which the firm is operating. An understanding of the business environment is absolutely essential to an assessment of project feasibility. This step is most important if the feasibility study is conducted by an outside consulting firm such as a software house or a CPA firm. Various methods for accomplishing this task are discussed in the analysis section of this chapter.

Determine Information Requirements

Given the study of the business environment, the analysts must then examine the nature of the problem and the information needed by management in more depth. Gaining this understanding means investigating the expressed need for a system revision. Sometimes the existing system can be studied to obtain an understanding of the overall information flow requirements.

For Sun Products, the project team must clearly understand the manufacturing and marketing organization and how these departments interface during order processing, because communication at this interface is essential for the firm to compete effectively. Sales personnel must know inventory levels and order status to serve their customers. Manufacturing must have good feedback from sales in order to purchase the appropriate materials in the right quantity to meet all sales orders.

Developing a High-Level Model

Next, analysts must develop a high-level model of the system to describe what must be accomplished by the new or revised system. A model is a simplified version of the system that allows analysts to understand the important parts of the system. They must determine the major transaction processing activities, key data requirements, major data flows, and sources and destinations of data flows. Typically, analysts use a **data flow diagram** like the one for Sun Products shown in Figure 12–8. This model enables management and the project team to better discuss the problem and refine the possible solutions to the problem.

The essential activities shown in Figure 12–8 are needed to process a Sun Products sales order and ultimately deliver products to customers. These activities are enter sales order; manufacture boats, if necessary; ship boats; and bill customer.

Both the source and the destination for key information are the customer. The essential files are open sales orders not filled because boats are in the manufacturing process, finished boat inventory, and customer and accounts receivable data.

The overall flow of data through the major processing steps, its storage, and its ultimate destination are outlined in the high-level data flow diagram in Figure 12–8.

Feasible Alternatives

The analyst or project team must develop some alternative ways to provide management or operating personnel with the information needed to achieve the objectives of the project. These objectives may be the resolution of a problem, supplying of more or different information because of changing business conditions, or the adoption of more advanced technology. Usually these proposals include a low-cost alternative that just meets the objectives of the project, an intermediate system that meets the basic objectives and enhances the decision making and competitive position of the firm for the

FIGURE 12–8

**Data Flow
Diagram**

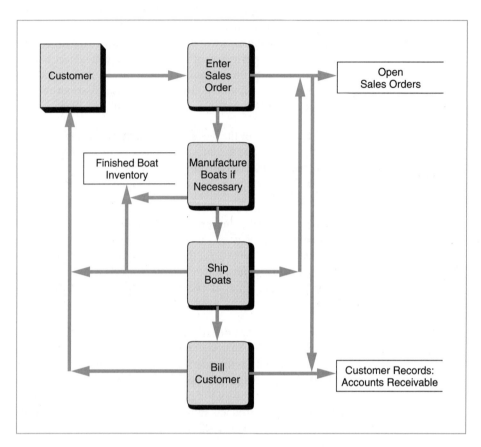

foreseeable future, and a more comprehensive solution that uses current technology to maximize future potential. The default solution is, of course, doing nothing at all. The three types of alternatives give management a perspective on the cost and benefits of a "bare bones" system at one end of the spectrum and the potential available with the most advanced systems. These alternatives also provide an intermediate system that goes slightly beyond the minimum requirements.

At ProYacht, Inc., Jennifer Santos proposes three alternative solutions to Sun Products' problem. The alternatives are developed more completely in the general high-level design phase presented in Chapter 13. The least expensive alternative is a simple perpetual inventory system that generates daily reports on the status of finished goods, open sales orders, work in process (with no indication of the degree of completion), the next day's production schedule, and raw material and component inventory. This simple data base system would keep up with sales orders, work orders, and inventory. The system could use a personal computer with a large data base and reporting package.

The second alternative is an online system of personal computers equipped with modems. Sun Products sales personnel would communicate with an online data base containing dealer (marina) information, finished stock information, and production scheduling information. A salesperson could process a sales order immediately if credit is good and boats are in stock. If the boats are not in stock, the salesperson could inquire about entering the sales order into production or even revising the production schedule. If the boats could be manufactured in time, sales personnel could then proceed with the sales order.

The third and most comprehensive option is an Electronic Data Interchange (EDI) system that uses a Just-in-Time (JIT) approach to ordering raw materials and to servicing dealers rapidly. It contains the online query features in the second alternative, in which a salesperson can access inventory, sales order, and work order files to process an order and to respond to customer requests. Provision is also made for large dealers (or marinas) to link their computers to Sun's computer to automatically enter a sales order when the dealer's stock is low on certain models or when a retail customer wishes to make a purchase that is not in stock at the dealer.

Evaluating Feasible Alternatives

The project team may recommend one of these alternatives as a feasible solution. Such a choice is never clear cut, because each option usually has its pluses and minuses. A rough cost-benefit analysis can be performed at this juncture to ascertain the economic feasibility of each alternative. The basis of this choice is an estimate of the costs and benefits for each option. In most cases, the costs are easier to estimate than the benefits, because benefits are often not tangible.

Costs may be broken down into the cost of developing the system and the cost of operating the system. About one-fourth of development costs are spent in the definition through analysis steps, in which management is trying to determine requirements and feasible options. One-half is usually expended during the actual design phase, and the remaining one-fourth is spent during the implementation phase. Although it is not the case here with the use of personal computers, operating costs can sometimes far exceed development costs, because operating expenses usually involve personnel expenses. Net present value is often used as a criterion for an initial comparison, because it is an estimate of the system's economic contribution to the well being of the organization.

For the three options in the Sun Products example, a cost-benefit analysis is shown in Figure 12–9. The estimated cost of a complete analysis, design, and implementation ranges from $48,000 to $160,000, depending on the option selected for software acquisition or development. Operating costs range from $10,000 to $30,000 for the next 5 years, depending on the option selected. Expected benefits range from $25,000 to $78,000 from increased sales and the reduction of obsolete inventory, yielding a net present value ranging from $8,862 to $21,958 for the options shown.

The selection process involves more than this analysis, however. For example, sales manager Ray Horne really likes the intermediate system, because each salesperson has

FIGURE 12–9

Rough Cost-
Benefit Analysis
for Sun Products

	Batch	Online	EDI
Initial Investment			
Development	$20,000	$30,000	$ 55,000
Hardware	20,000	50,000	75,000
Software	5,000	10,000	20,000
Installation	3,000	5,000	10,000
Total	$48,000	$95,000	$160,000
Annual Operating Costs	$10,000	$20,000	$ 30,000
Annual Benefits	$25,000	$50,000	$ 78,000
Net Present Value at 10% Interest for 5 years	$ 8,862	$18,724	$ 21,958

access to current information, an essential element in today's competitive market. Horne is wary of the completely automatic system, because of the absence of human interaction. He worries about a customer making a mistake that disrupts Sun's production schedule and, ultimately, Sun's ability to deliver products on time. In his mind, this lack of control is serious, even though the cost-benefit analysis indicates that this has the greatest net present value (that is, the best investment) because of the reduction in sales personnel.

Project controls, such as the time estimates shown in Figure 12–10, must be developed for each alternative. A list of tasks to be completed, projected personnel assignments, and the nature of project status reports to help manage the project must be developed. These controls and plans are incorporated into an **implementation schedule** for each alternative, which includes an estimate of the resources and time needed to implement the proposed alternative. These plans are useful for checking compliance with design schedules, assigning staff, and determining project progress. Based on Sun's feasibility study, Jennifer Santos estimates that option 2, for example, can be fully implemented in 6–9 months using readily available personal computer hardware and either purchasing or writing programs in-house. The latter software development option should take 9 months. All of these plans need to be revised as the development of the information system continues.

Preliminary
Recommendation
and
Management
Report

The project team recommends the intermediate system as the most promising option based on an analysis of the project's economic, operational, and technical feasibility and the recommendations of potential users. A report is prepared for management, which should include the proposed alternative and the rationale for its selection, a cost-benefit analysis, an implementation schedule, and a revised statement of scope and objectives. The revised statement of scope and objectives, along with the implementation schedule, should show management the magnitude of the project and the resources (time, money, and personnel) needed to implement the system. Finally, the project's objectives must be

FIGURE 12–10

Implementation Schedule for Sun Products

Activities	Resources	Time (Weeks)	Status Reports and Output
High-Level Design (Several Alternatives): Information Flow Identify Hardware Identify Software Cost Benefit Analysis Implementation Schedules	Project Team	4	Alternative Descriptions Systems Flowcharts
Comparative Analysis	Project Team	1	Design Recommendation
Detailed Design: Output Input Programming Modules	Project Team and Programmers	9	Specifications: Screens and Reports Data Entry Formats Structured Charts Structured English (Pseudo code)
Data/File Structure Communication Operating Organizational Changes			Data File Layouts Procedures Responsibilities
Implementation Software Development: Writing Code Program Testing	Programmers	10	Software Code
Training	Project Team	4	
File Conversion	Project Team	4	New Files/Data Base
System Conversion	Project Team	4	Operating System
Total Time (Weeks)		36	

reconciled with the long-range objectives of the organization, which may require help from the steering committee. Authorization to continue the project is then obtained.

Based on this report, management can proceed with a thorough analysis if it deems the project to be well defined and it recognizes that a feasible alternative to the current system has a high probability of success. Alternatively, management may wish to examine the project more by extending the feasibility study or cancel the project because viable options do not exist.

12.6 Analysis

The objective of analysis is to determine the information requirements of the system. The project team (analysts for small projects) must determine what must be done to solve the information problem or take advantage of a new situation or technology. The result of the analysis is a set of information requirements for systems design. Basic analysis steps are shown in Figure 12–11.

FIGURE 12–11

Systems Analysis

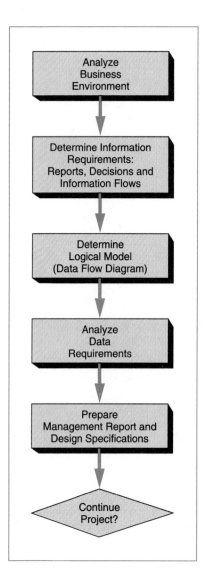

Analysis of Business Environment

First, the project team must study the nature of the business environment and information requirements in more depth. This study is important but can be extremely difficult for the following reasons:

1. Personnel may change during the development life cycle.

2. Technology used to provide the information is changing rapidly.

3. Personnel may have hidden political agendas.

4. Managers often cannot express their information needs clearly.

5. Totally new systems can deliver information to support decisions in ways never considered feasible before.

The project team or analyst must spend time in the shop, sales office, warehouse, and management offices to gain a thorough understanding of the physical aspects of the business. This physical distribution system is the area that management wants to monitor, control, operate, and even change, as economic conditions dictate, with its new information system.

The project team must ask questions about the organization's objectives and management policies. The team must gain an understanding of the organization's market, products, and customer characteristics. The team must also learn what reports, decisions, and transactions are essential to the success and daily activity of the organization. Questions about the firm's resources, such as capital, personnel, customer good will, research capability, and financial assets, must also be asked.

Questions like these must be asked whether the project is an Executive Information System (EIS), Decision Support System (DSS), Management Information System (MIS), or operational Transaction Processing System (TPS). Sun Products is an example of a TPS.

Determine Information Requirements

The analysis phase of structured analysis and design involves an examination of the requirements for management decision making, transaction processing, and reporting activities. Each potential application must be studied in depth to determine these needs.

This analysis requires a major commitment of personnel (usually an expanded project team), time, and financial resources. In general, output requirements are determined first, followed by the process needed to provide these outputs. Finally, the project team determines the input needed to obtain the desired output. All requirements must fit within the constraints imposed on the system. For example, the application may need to operate in a particular data base environment. All decision-making processes must be identified, information requirements in terms of transactions and reports must be specified, and the characteristics of each type of information must be spelled out. A study of the existing system may provide a general understanding of the decisions made, the transactions involved, and the reports generated. Processing steps needed to generate this output then must be identified. Inputs such as documents, records, files, and data, as well as the volume, media, origin, and location of this input, should be identified. Data necessary to support information and reporting requirements must be identified. Finally, communications requirements may need to be identified.

This analysis determines not only the information requirements of the information system, but also a minimum set of requirements for the proposed or modified system. Any proposed design must meet these minimum requirements, whether the system is developed by the organization or purchased from outside vendors.

Curing a High-Tech Hangover

It's the morning after for Corporate America—following a decade-long binge on information technology. Sobering up after spending nearly $900 billion in the service sector alone, companies are wondering what happened to the promised payoff. White collar productivity, although rebounding a bit lately, is still below its late 1970s level, before all that treasure was spent on fancy computers and systems. Feeling betrayed by info-gurus who promised "killer apps"—computer applications that would give them strategic competitive advantages—CEOs are holding down budgets for information technology. Frustrated at the lack of progress and by the high cost of the computer systems, a few are even turning over the management of their information systems to outsiders.

What's needed? A corporate "12-step" program for technology sobriety. Companies are realizing that it's people who improve productivity; computers are merely powerful tools. The first step is to define and analyze the actual work being done. Without going back to the basics of corporate strategy and good management, the addition of new technology can actually bollix things up, making them more complex, confusing, and expensive. But once corporate goals are understood and the flow of work is clear, ap-

plying information technology can boost productivity. Wal-Mart Stores, Inc., for example, uses computerized cash registers and satellite dishes on store roofs to monitor sales and order new goods. Its choice of information technology is appropriate to its strategy of selling products that consumers want as cheaply as possible.

All the other steps involve matching technology with the way people work. The temptation by corporate information managers to buy the most powerful technology often results in bells and whistles that white collar workers don't understand and don't use. By buying much simpler, tried-and-true products, companies not only can raise productivity but also save money. Bringing white collar workers into decisions about what technology to buy makes a lot of sense, too. Employees can tell managers what they need and then test it out to see if it works in real world situations. This allows them to "buy into" the introduction of new information systems. Instead of technology busters, employees become technology boosters.

Reprinted from June 15, 1992 issue of *Business Week* by special permission, copyright © 1992 by McGraw-Hill, Inc.

Approaches to Analyzing Information Requirements

The following approaches may be used to gain an understanding of system information requirements:

1. Byproduct of transaction processing approach

2. Bottom-up approach

3. Analysis of key success factors

4. Complete enterprise analysis of an organization's information requirements

Sometimes the first two are classified as a bottom-up approach and the last two may be called a top-down approach.

Byproduct Approach   Historically many organizations have used the **byproduct approach** to determine information requirements. In this approach, management uses byproduct information generated by the organization's TPS to satisfy its decision-making needs. In many cases, the byproduct information is simple accounting information. The advantage to this approach is that it provides the TPS the information needed for operational control. The major disadvantage is that it does not necessarily give management the type of information needed for decision making or reporting. In general, summarized transaction information does not support the information needs of middle and upper management who require much more externally generated data for their decision making. A TPS is a poor basis upon which to determine MIS, DSS, or EIS information requirements.

Bottom-Up Approach   In the **bottom-up approach,** the development process is driven by the response to current problems. Systems analysts respond to user requests and management demands for more or different information. This conservative method of developing information system requirements is not likely to disrupt the sociotechnical structure of the organization. Users do not willingly disrupt their organizational behavioral patterns. The problem with this method is that it does not factor in the strategic information plan, nor does it easily respond to real changes in technology or the business environment. Moreover, it can often lead to information overload as managers continually ask for more information.

Key Success Factors   Another way to determine the information requirements of an organization is to determine its **key success factors,** which are a function of the industry and the objectives of the organization. The project team or systems analysts must understand the nature of the business, what makes an organization succeed, and how management plans to achieve success in that business. This knowledge can be obtained through careful research of the industry and extended interviews with top management. Analysts can then determine the key decisions and information flows that are necessary to achieve success. This top-down approach is founded on the environment, the business strategy, and the organization used to implement this strategy.

The major advantage of this method of determining information needs is that it concentrates the search for these needs on the elements important to the success of the organization. This approach generates a much smaller information set than that developed using the byproduct or bottom-up approach, but it provides more relevant information for middle and top managers who use MIS, DSS, and EIS. This approach is especially useful when changes in technology, competitive environment, and organization structure are frequent, because success factors change with environmental changes. The negative side of this approach is that it does not assess transactional and operational needs as well as the bottom-up approach.

Enterprise Analysis Approach   A comprehensive approach to the assessment of an organization's information requirements involves systematically analyzing the entire enterprise. **Enterprise analysis** is a top-down method. Using this method, analysts study the organization, its functions, its processes, and the data it needs to support these functions. The objective is to pull all these needs into an information system that can support all levels of management from operational to strategic. Its strength is that it considers all the information needs of management and operational personnel and attempts to integrate these needs. It is especially useful for a large organization that must completely overhaul its information system. The need for an overhaul may be the result of relying on the bottom-up approach for many years. The resulting hodgepodge of individual unintegrated systems does not effectively support managerial decision making. This method's disadvantage is that it does not focus development efforts on the information that is really important to the success of the organization. As a result, the system may generate too much information that no one can use, especially operational personnel. This top-down approach is founded on the environment, the business strategy, and the organization needed to implement this strategy.

Each approach to determining information needs has its advantages and disadvantages. An organization should use the one that best suits the type and scope of the proposed system. For example, the byproduct and bottom-up approaches definitely favor the development of a system that satisfies the needs of a TPS in a relatively stable environment. On the other hand, the top-down success factors analysis or the enterprise analysis are more advantageous in the development of MIS, DSS, and EIS.

We focus on top-down approaches because information requirements should be viewed from an organizational perspective to fully support an organization's decision-making and transaction processing needs. The other approaches are useful for minor revisions to existing systems that basically comply with an organization's master or strategic information plan. The problem with the byproduct or the bottom-up approach is that new technology or changing business conditions often require totally different ways of accessing and processing data into information.

Regardless of the approach, analysts must do some serious fact finding to follow up on the expressed need for a system revision. Interviews must be conducted with the top, middle, and operational managers who initiate the request. The fact-finding interviews should clarify the problems, the information needs, the affected organizational units, the current procedures used to provide information, and the relationship between the proposed project and the long-range goals of the organization.

At this stage, analysts may study the existing system to determine what is currently done to meet management and operating personnel information needs. Systems flowcharts and data flow diagrams are generally helpful in describing how the current system works. The extent to which a study of the existing system is needed depends on the magnitude of the system change. If the expected change is marginal—such as the addition of a few applications to an existing DBMS—a study of the existing system is very important. If the expected change is major, the old system may bear so little resemblance to the new system that studying the old system may only define some reporting needs. This situation often exists when new technology vastly improves the access to information and the analysis of data, as in DSS and AI systems.

Analysis Techniques and Tools

Several sources may be used by the project team to solicit the information needed to determine a system's information requirements. These sources include existing documents, questionnaires, interviews, observations, and hierarchy charts of activities. **Documents** include procedure manuals, reports and other output, input forms and screens, flowcharts of the current system, and model input requirements. The analyst must be sure that these documents are up to date.

Questionnaires enable the analyst to solicit a large amount of data from several users. Although questionnaires are a relatively efficient way to collect large amounts of data from a large sample, they are often superficial and subject to misinterpretation and bias from leading questions. They are most useful in obtaining a broad perspective of information needs.

Interviews overcome some of the problems of questionnaires, because the analyst can probe in depth the nature of a problem and what information is needed to resolve it. On the other hand, only a few key people can usually be interviewed, and proper interviews are difficult to conduct. Interviews are most important in the assessment of key success factors and determining the needs of DSS and EIS.

An analyst should use **personal observations** when investigating system information needs. For example, during the analysis of the Sun Products sales order system, Jennifer Santos observed that salespersons seldom wasted time calling to check inventory status from month-old inventory listings. A salesperson simply placed the order, guessed at a delivery date, and hoped Sun could ship it on time.

Most decision-making and reporting activities are part of a hierarchy of activities. **Hierarchy charts** like Figure 12–12 are often used to outline this hierarchy. Hierarchy charts show the important relationships that must be considered in specifying the information requirements of an organization. These charts can ultimately be subdivided into detailed activities and can serve as a basis for top-down modular programming, discussed in Chapter 13. Hierarchy charts are automated in contemporary CASE packages to assist analysts in describing decision-making networks.

During the analysis of the order entry system, Jennifer Santos concludes that the major decision-making and transaction activities for Sun Products are those displayed in the hierarchy chart shown in Figure 12–12. These activities are organized in the hierarchy chart under three major categories. These are sales order processing, production scheduling, and shipping and billing.

Data Flow Diagram

From an analysis of information system requirements, the analyst devises a logical model of the new or revised system for use in the subsequent design. At this point, the most important processes, reports, data, and information flows are determined. The following reports and queries are needed by management and sales personnel for a typical sales order processing system:

1. Sales

2. Gross Profit (Sales − Manufacturing Costs)

FIGURE 12–12   *Hierarchy Chart*

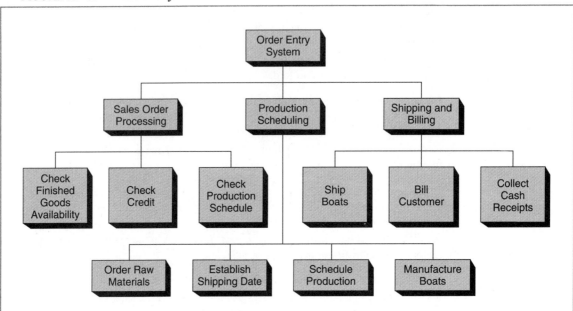

3. Contribution to Profit and Fixed Costs (Sales − All Variable Costs)

4. Commissions

5. Inventory and Product Availability Reports

6. Production Schedule

7. Shipping Schedule

8. Billing and Cash Collections

9. Late Delivery

10. Returns

11. All Reports by Product Line, Region, Sales Representative, and Dealer

Other reports, decisions, and transactions the system must support are likewise determined at this time.

A logical information flow from sources to destinations, via decision-making, reporting, and transaction processing steps, must be determined using data flow diagrams. Each process in the data flow diagram may be exploded (described in more detail) for system designers to develop controls, refine data requirements, and possibly write programs for various processes.

Data flow diagrams, introduced in Chapter 2, add considerable structure to systems analysis and design. They help the analyst define the data stores needed and, consequently, to formulate the files or data base structure needed. Data flow diagrams can lead to the development of modules software development and programming. They also form the basis for system flowcharting and actual physical designs, as illustrated in the next chapter. Preparing a data flow diagram can be time consuming and tedious. Today, CASE software packages can automate some flowcharting tasks as well as develop prototype programs directly from data flow diagrams. CASE packages contain provisions that can link data flow diagrams and hierarchy charts, which describe information requirements, to programming modules.

For a better understanding of Sun Product's activities, consider the sales order processing network in the data flow diagram in Figure 12–13. The key activity is the sale of the product. Generating information to enable a salesperson to accomplish a sale is the major objective of the system. These activities are related to the transactions and decisions shown in the hierarchy chart in Figure 12–12.

From Jennifer Santos' analysis she determines that the major activities are those shown as squares with rounded corners in the data flow diagram in Figure 12–13. These activities are those found in the second alternative (intermediate proposal).

The content of work orders and various inventory documents is described in Chapter 9. The key data needed for this intermediate proposal are also shown in the open rectangles in the data flow diagrams in Figure 12–13.

Sources and destinations for information are shown as squares in Figure 12–13. The sources of information for this processing network consist of customer orders, economic information for forecasting customer demand, inventory of finished goods, inventory of raw materials, and planning specifications of each boat manufactured. Output generally consists of feedback to salespersons on the availability of products, status of open sales orders and work orders, a report to the production department on the manufacturing schedule, orders for raw materials to be sent to suppliers, customer shipping information, and an update of inventory status records. Note that the information output from one process can be the input to the next decision, report, or transaction.

Analysis of Data Base Requirements

In most cases, a decision or transaction processing network needs a data base or set of data files. The requirements of this data base or file management system must be analyzed in addition to information flow requirements.

For a data base environment in which many applications share a common data base, the analysis involves the data and the DBMS for the entire organization. The DBMS must be designed to accommodate the data required for many current and future applications. The project team must carefully analyze the data requirements of the entire operation that ultimately uses the data base. A top-down approach with an analysis of key success factors or a complete enterprise analysis is usually necessary to set the guidelines for the

FIGURE 12–13   *Detailed Data Flow Diagram*

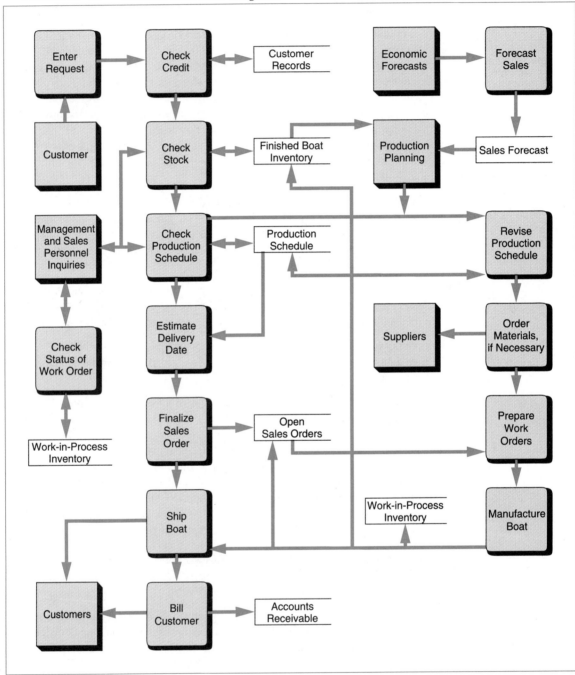

FIGURE 12–14   *Data Dictionary*

Field Name	Aliases	Size	Type	Data Location	Source	Processes			
Transaction Number	Sales Number	4	N	Sales	Sales	Sales	Billing	Inventory	Production
Dealer Name		25	N	Dealer/Rep	Marketing	Sales	Billing		Production
Dealer Number		5	A	Dealer/Rep	Marketing	Sales	Billing		Production
Customer Name		25	A	Customer	Marketing	Sales	Billing		Production
Customer Number		6	N	Customer	Marketing	Sales	Billing		Production
Date		6	D	Sales	Sales	Sales	Billing		Production
Product Number	Model Number	6	A	Product	Production	Sales	Billing	Inventory	Production
Boat Name		10	A	Product	Production	Sales	Billing	Inventory	Production
Number Ordered	Quantity	10	N	Sales	Sales	Sales	Billing	Inventory	Production
Delivery Date		6	D	Sales	Sales	Sales	Billing		Production
Sales Amount	Price	7	N	Sales	Sales	Sales	Billing		
Salesperson	Sales Rep	2	N	Personnel	Personnel	Sales			
Terms	Discount	2	N	Sales	Sales	Sales	Billing		

entire system. Once these guidelines are set, new applications are easily added to the data base because data and applications are independent, as pointed out in Chapters 5 and 6.

A data dictionary can help perform an analysis of data requirements. A **data dictionary** is a list of data elements that make up each data store needed by the information system. Figure 12–14 illustrates an example of a data dictionary that describes the characteristics of the data stored in the open sales order file for Sun Products. The data structure, which is a key component of a data dictionary, includes the sales transaction number, dealer name and number, customer name and number, date, product number and boat product name, the number of each (boat model) ordered, expected delivery date for each product, sales amount or price of each model, salesperson, and terms. Salespeople can use the product (model) number to reference the inventory file, the work order and production schedule file, and the manufacturing specification file to fully process a sales order. These references are also called relations, as described in Chapter 6. They are commonly used in integrated systems, such as the one recommended by systems analysts for Sun Products. Note that each item listed in the structure is followed by a description, form (such as field size and data type), file or relational table locations, data sources, processes that use the data element, and other names (called aliases) used for the data element.

*Management
Report and
Design
Specifications*

The project team uses the description of the activities, data stores, and flows from the data flow diagram; the description of input, processing procedures, and output; and the description of data needed to accomplish these activities to prepare information system specifications for the design phase. At this point, a structured walk through by an independent person or group ensures that the analysis of management's needs is complete. The final product of the analysis phase should be clear information, data and processing requirements that can be used to design a system.

Management reviews this analysis of system requirements and determines whether to continue the project. If it decides to continue, this analysis is then used as the basis for the general and detailed system design and acquisition.

**12.7 Computer-
Aided
Software
Engineering**

CASE software packages can be used to expedite the planning and analysis steps in the project definition, feasibility study, and the analysis phases. CASE software can help organize, model, and analyze such knowledge about a business as goals, problems, success factors, physical processes, business functions, business entities, and organization structure. For example, the association between physical processes and their data

FIGURE 12–15   ***Computer-Aided Software Engineering Decomposition (Hierarchy) Chart***

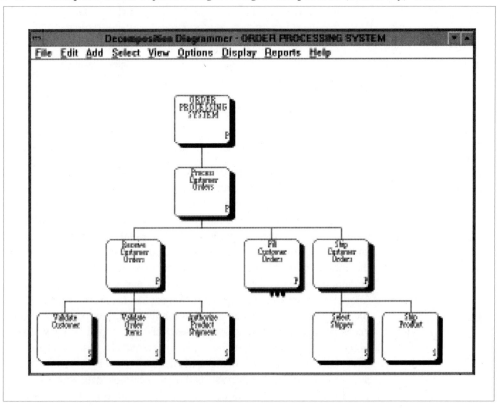

FIGURE 12–16   *Computer-Aided Software Engineering Entity Relationship Diagram*

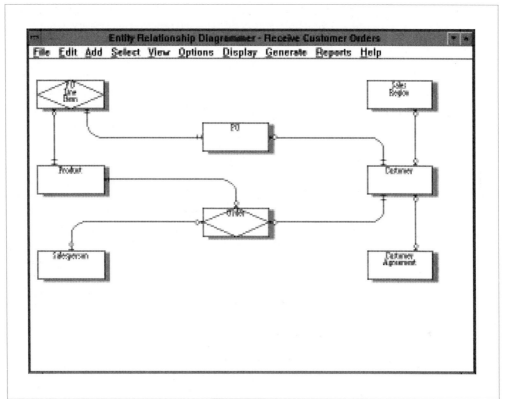

requirements or between data sources and uses can be developed via CASE software, as shown in Figure 12–15. Using CASE decomposition tools, which resemble hierarchy charts, analysts can separate processes, goals, and functions into modules for further analysis. Most CASE packages have provisions for drawing data flow diagrams and **entity relationship diagrams** that outline all the relationships among the various entities (functions and organizational units) in a business organization. These relationships are expressed in terms of processes, data flows, and data requirements. Entity relationship diagrams, illustrated in Figure 12–16, are invaluable for the construction of data bases during the design stages of systems development. More sophisticated CASE packages ensure that all diagrams are interrelated and founded on a common knowledge base. The result is a logically consistent set of diagrams that flag missing elements or caution users on the addition of new requirements that are not part of other previously developed analysis.

CASE is a valuable tool for systems analysis. With it, analysts can understand the activities of a particular business entity and how information is exchanged, created, and used. CASE helps identify the data and processes necessary to meet users' requirements and demonstrates how these processes interrelate.

12.8 Summary

In the information system life cycle, systems are developed, used, maintained, and modified. After time, or as technology and requirements change, they decline. Then new systems need to be developed. The system's development life cycle consists of seven phases.

The sequence of phases and of the various steps within each phase are important when an organization takes a structured approach to information systems development. First, the project must be defined. The project may be the resolution of a problem, the need to provide management with new or different information, or the use of new technology. These projects are often the result of business environment changes or new uses of information technology. Second, the feasibility of implementing the project must be determined with respect to technology, operations, and economics. After a feasible alternative is identified, a thorough analysis of information requirements can begin. During the analysis, the problem or opportunity is studied in depth, and information requirements are specified in terms of output, processing, input, data, and information flows. Information requirements may be determined using a bottom-up, key success factor or an enterprise analysis approach. Sometimes the information provided to management is just the by-product of the TPS. Numerous techniques can help the project team or systems analysts in their analysis of information requirements. These are: hierarchy charts, questionnaires, interviews, observations, and data flow diagrams. CASE tools may also be used to automate the analysis. The results of the analysis are reported to management, which decides whether to begin the design of a new or revised system to meet these requirements.

Once a decision is made to continue a high-level systems design, detailed design, implementation, and operation phases are undertaken. These last four phases are discussed in detail in the next chapter.

Key Terms

bottom-up approach	entity relationship diagram
byproduct approach	hierarchy charts
Computer-Aided Software Engineering (CASE)	implementation schedule
	information system life cycle
data dictionary	interviews
data flow diagram	key success factors
documents	modular approach
economic feasibility	operational feasibility
end user development	out-sourcing
enterprise analysis	personal observations

phased approach
Program Evaluation Review
    Technique (PERT)
project controls
project team
prototype
questionnaires
service bureau
steering committee

structured systems analysis and design
structured walk through
system development life cycle
system degradation
systems analyst
systems development
technical feasibility
turnkey system

**Review
Questions**

1. List at least six situations that may prompt management to review its information system.

2. Contrast several different ways to develop an information system. Specify conditions under which each is appropriate.

3. What is the basic philosophy behind the structured approach to analysis and design?

4. List the structured systems development phases. Which are used to indicate what must be done? Which are used to indicate how a project can be ultimately implemented?

5. What is a steering committee? What members of a management team typically make up a steering committee?

6. What is a project team, and who typically participates on a project team?

7. Briefly note the major tasks in the analysis phase of structured systems development.

8. Should a systems analyst develop an entire system at one time? If not, how should the analyst structure the development process?

9. Why are organizational and behavioral considerations important in the development of new information systems?

10. What pitfall may be involved in starting the system definition phase with an analysis of the current system?

11. What is a feasibility study? What three types of feasibility are considered when identifying potential solutions to a problem?

12. What is the major objective of the analysis phase of systems development?

13. Give several examples of environmental considerations for systems definition and analysis. Why is each important in the context of a management information system and a decision support system?

14. Contrast the four ways of determining information requirements. When is each most appropriate?

15. What problems can arise from an inappropriate use of the evolutionary bottom-up or system byproduct approach to systems development?

16. Why are data flow diagrams used in the analysis phase to define user requirements?

17. Why is it important to consider other applications in the determination of information requirements in a data base system?

18. How can CASE be used to expedite systems analysis?

Discussion Questions

1. A systems analyst is in a hurry to begin the programming of a new sales analysis and advertising productivity program. She decides to save time by skipping the problem definition and analysis systems development phases. Comment on her approach and the problems she may encounter.

2. Given the following situations, select the most appropriate method of information requirements analysis and systems development. Briefly state the reason for each choice.
   a. A bank is installing a DSS for the management of its trust fund investments.
   b. A manufacturing firm is revising its payroll system to accommodate at least 1,000 employees.
   c. A retail department store is developing a totally new sales processing, inventory, purchasing, and marketing system.
   d. A computer chip manufacturer is developing a new system to schedule and control the manufacture of its products.
   e. A manager is developing a travel budget for her department to determine her department's travel needs for next year.

3. The structured development process is time consuming and expensive. To shorten and tightly control the process, a software developer purchases CASE software. Discuss how this makes the software company more competitive and increases the quality of its product.

4. Discuss the role of the steering committee and the project team in a development project. Why is it important to consider the organizational impact of system change? How is this impact controlled?

Case 12–1
Audio Visual Corporation

Audio Visual Corporation of Worcester, MA, manufactures and sells visual display equipment. Most sales are made through seven sales offices located in Los Angeles, Seattle, Minneapolis, Cleveland, Dallas, Boston, and Atlanta. Each sales office has a warehouse located nearby to carry an inventory of new equipment and replacement parts. The remaining sales are made through manufacturers' representatives. Audio Visual's manufacturing operations are conducted in a single plant, which is highly departmentalized. In addition to the assembly department, several departments are responsible for the various components used in the visual display equipment. The plant also has maintenance, engineering, scheduling, and cost accounting departments.

During its early years, Audio Visual had a centralized decision-making organization. Top management formulated all plans and directed all operations. As the company expanded, some decision making was decentralized, although information processing was still highly centralized. Departments coordinated their plans with the corporate office but were free to develop individual sales programs. As the company expanded, information processing problems developed. The newly hired MIS department employees are responsible for improving the company's information processing system.

Early in 1991, management decided that its MIS needed upgrading. As a result, the company ordered a technologically advanced computer that was installed in July 1992. The main processing equipment is still located at corporate headquarters, and each sales office is connected with the main processing unit by remote terminals.

The integration of the new computer into the Audio Visual information system was carried out by an MIS staff of a manager and four systems analysts, who were hired in the spring of 1990. The department's other employees—programmers, machine operators, and data entry personnel—have been with the company for several years.

The MIS analysts identified the weaknesses of the information system in existence prior to the acquisition of the new computer. During the 12 months since the acquisition of the new equipment, the following applications have been redesigned or developed and are now operational: payroll, production scheduling, financial statement preparation, customer billing, raw material usage, and finished goods inventory. The operating departments of Audio Visual that were affected by the system changes were rarely consulted or contacted until the system was operational and the new reports were distributed.

The president of Audio Visual is very pleased with the work of the MIS department. During a recent conversation, the president stated: "The MIS people are doing a good job, and I have full confidence in their work. We paid a lot of money for the new equipment and the MIS people certainly cost enough, but the combination of the new equipment and new MIS staff should solve all of our problems."

Recently, other conversations regarding the computer and information system have taken place. One was between Jerry Adama, plant manager, and Bill Taylor, the MIS manager; the other was between Adama and Terri Williams, the new personnel manager.

Taylor–Adama Conversation:
Adama: Bill, you're trying to run my plant for me. I'm supposed to be the manager, yet you keep interfering. I wish you would mind your own business.
Taylor: You've got a job to do, but so does my department. As we analyzed the information needed for production scheduling and top management, we saw where improvements could be made in the work flow. Now that the system is operational, you can't reroute work and change procedures, because that would destroy the value of the information we're processing. And while I'm on that subject, it's getting to the point where we can't trust the information we're getting from production. The mark sense

cards we receive from production indicating what was produced in a department contain a lot of errors.

Adama: I'm responsible for the efficient operation of production. Quite frankly, I think I'm the best judge of production efficiency. The system you installed has reduced my work force and increased the work load of the remaining employees, but I don't see that this has improved anything. In fact, it might explain the high error rate in the cards.

Taylor: This new computer cost a lot of money, and I'm trying to be sure that the company gets its money's worth.

Adama–Williams Conversation:

Adama: My best production assistant, the one I'm grooming to be a supervisor when the next opening occurs, said he was thinking of quitting. When I asked him why, he said he didn't enjoy the work anymore. He's not the only one who is unhappy. Supervisors and department heads no longer have a voice in establishing production schedules. This new computer system has taken away the contribution we used to make to company planning and control. We seem to be going back to the days when top management made all the decisions. I have more production problems now than I used to. I think it boils down to a lack of interest on the part of my management team. I know the problem is within my area, but I think you might be able to help me.

Williams: I have no recommendations for you now, but I've had similar complaints from purchasing and shipping. I think we should get your concerns on the agenda for our next plant management meeting.

SOURCE: Adapted from the CMA Examination.

Case Questions

1. Apparently the development and transition of the new computer-based system has created problems among the personnel of Audio Visual Corporation. Identify and briefly discuss the apparent causes of these problems.

2. How could the company have avoided the problems? What steps should be taken to avoid such problems in the future?

Case 12–2
Channel 17

Channel 17 in River City, an affiliate of a national television network, broadcasts both local and national shows. The primary source of Channel 17's revenue is spot advertising and promotion, and the station's inventory consists of 10-, 20-, and 30-second advertising time slots. Management has two primary objectives—to maximize profits and to provide community service.

It is industry practice to place different values on different time slots. A 30-second commercial, for example, costs less at 2:00 A.M. than during prime time. Shows with high ratings command a higher price for their associated commercial time slots than do less popular programs. Moreover, the industry typically has a priority system for guaranteeing time slots. A higher price is paid for a 10-second guaranteed slot during the 6:00 P.M. news than for a 10-second slot at the same time that is not guaranteed and may be bumped by another commercial. A commercial may be bumped for one that costs more or by a public service announcement. Because of the diversity in time slot changes, the station salespeople are constantly trying to obtain the greatest amount of revenue for the array of time slots available.

Currently, the station does all scheduling of commercials and public service announcements using a large spreadsheet, which eventually becomes a report for the Federal Communications Commission (FCC). The spreadsheet was created using a popular spreadsheet software package. Records of each time slot's usage must be filed with the FCC, and each customer must have a record of actual commercial time and cost.

Channel 17 must cut off sales 2 days prior to broadcast time in order to prepare the programming constraints, such as scheduling the same time each night for some spots and allowing sufficient time duration between conflicting spots. Due to this time delay, sales that could increase the station's profits are lost. Moreover, prior to the cutoff, salespeople are often not aware of available time.

SOURCE: Adapted with permission from Case 12–10 in R.A. Leitch and K. Roscoe Davis, *Accounting Information Systems* (Englewood Cliffs, NJ: Prentice-Hall, Inc., 1991), pp. 375–76.

Case Questions   Your systems development company has been engaged for a problem definition and feasibility study to assess the problems at Channel 17.

1. Prepare a statement of scope and objectives.

2. As part of the feasibility study, describe the reporting requirements, major decision-making activities, information processing modes, and general hardware and software requirements that may be necessary. (Hint: Consider the use of portable personal computers by the sales staff.)

3. To expedite the systems development process, explain how you would use CASE to prepare a feasibility study and an analysis of Channel 17's information requirements.

4. (Optional) Prepare a data flow diagram of activities required to prepare an advertising and commercial schedule.

Structured Systems Development: Design and Implementation

C   H   A   P   T   E   R

13

Introduction

In Chapter 12, the major phases required to develop an information system were outlined. They are shown in Figure 13–1. The first three phases were discussed in the last chapter. In this chapter, we review the remaining four phases. In the structured approach to systems development, the project definition, feasibility study, and analysis phases of this process must be completed prior to beginning the design phases. Prototype development and end user development, discussed in detail in Chapter 15, are iterative procedures.

The objective of systems design is to specify an alternative that integrates all the components of a system to provide management and operating personnel with the information they need to accomplish their objectives. The goal of the implementation phase is to acquire or to develop the software, acquire the necessary hardware, and convert to the new or revised information system specified in the design phases. The overall objective of the design and implementation of information systems is the ultimate satisfaction of decision, transaction processing, and reporting needs of management. To accomplish this, the systems analyst or the project team must carefully review the findings of the systems analysis phase.

13.1 General High-Level Systems Design

Given authorization by management to continue, systems analysts can begin the general high-level design phase. After a thorough analysis of information requirements, the project team or the systems analysts must develop several high-level design alternatives. One alternative is selected for detailed design in the next stage in the development cycle.

FIGURE 13–1   *System Development Life Cycle*

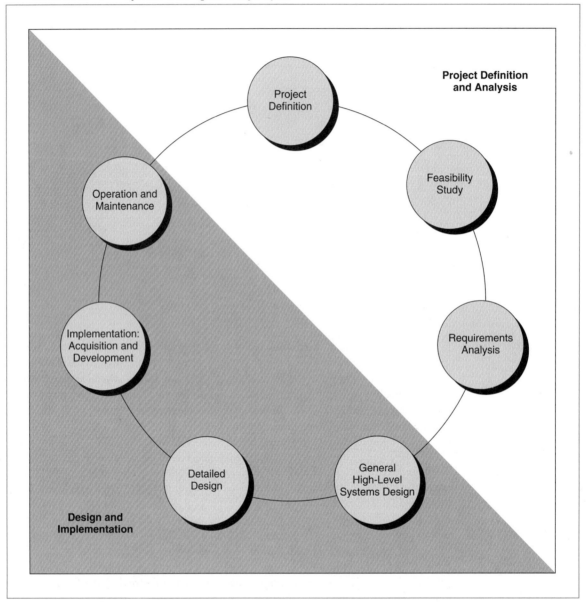

In a high-level design, the project team or analysts only lay out possible configurations of the various system components.

The beginning of this general, or conceptual, design phase is a creative process, and many concepts should be pursued. In this phase, the project team moves from a logical to a physical model of the information system. At the end of this phase, one alternative is selected and recommended to management for a detailed design of the components necessary to implement the system. The general high-level systems design follows the steps outlined in Figure 13–2.

At this stage in the development process, all the components of the information system must be incorporated into a general high-level design. These components include the following:

1. Required outputs (reports, data stored for future use, or online query) stated in the systems analysis

2. Input needed to generate these outputs

3. Processing steps to transform inputs into outputs

4. Data (files or data base elements) to support the information processing requirements of the system

5. Procedures to manage the input, processing, storage, and output activities in the organization

6. Controls to manage and ensure the reliability and security of these activities

As with any step in the development cycle, the general design phase must be well planned and organized. System users such as managers and operations personnel should be included as part of the project team during the general design process to ensure that alternatives are feasible and basic information requirements are met.

Operational constraints related to operations, decision making, subsystem coordination, and interfaces with other systems must be considered prior to general design. Operational and behavioral constraints related to the implementation of change and the organization structure must also be considered. Hardware and software technological constraints should be given careful thought in terms of the hardware available, the characteristics of available software, and feasibility with respect to existing files and data base structures. A cost-benefit analysis should be performed for each alternative.

Several general alternative designs, or **models,** should be developed. The systems requirements for each model should be spelled out in more detail than in the feasibility study. Particular attention should be given to information output, data input, data storage methods and organization, processing procedures, communication procedures, and system operations. Moreover, the staffing of the system and its operations must be considered.

Alternatives for Sun Products

During the feasibility study for Sun Products, three alternatives were proposed. Assume that these alternatives are still valid. After a thorough analysis of Sun's information processing needs, each plan can now be expressed in more detail. The least expensive alternative is a simple perpetual inventory system that generates reports at the end of each day on the status of finished goods, open sales orders, work in process (with no indication of degree of completion), the next day's production schedule, and raw material and component inventory. This simple data base system would keep track of sales orders, work orders, and inventory through a personal computer with a large data base and

FIGURE 13–2

General High-Level Design

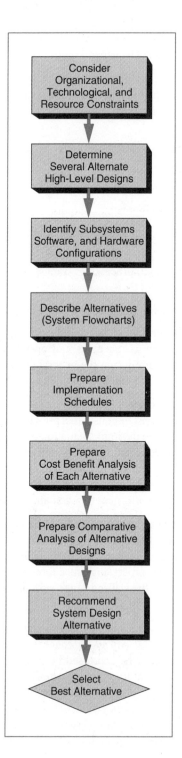

reporting package. Data would be entered in an online mode as orders are initiated, boats are sold, work orders are completed, and so on, and output would be in a batch mode at the end of the day. Communication with salespersons would occur via telephone, and a marketing clerk would indicate the latest inventory and sales order status, which would be no more than one day old.

The second alternative is an online system, in which sales personnel use personal computers equipped with modems. Sun Products sales personnel would communicate with an online data base containing information on customers, finished stock, and production schedules. They could process a sales order immediately and ship the boats if credit is good and boats are in stock. If the boats are not in stock, the production schedule is checked to see if a sufficient number are in the manufacturing process. If this is the case, they are then sold to the customer and shipped when finished. The sales order remains in an open order file until the boats are shipped. The customer is billed when the boats are shipped, and the sales order is no longer open. If the boats are not in production, the production schedule is revised to manufacture the ordered boats. The production schedule may also be revised according to sales forecasts in anticipation of sales orders, given the boats in finished goods inventory. Before any boat can be manufactured, personnel must have sufficient materials on hand. Once the manufacture of more boats is scheduled, the sales order is completed and a work order is prepared for the factory. This sales order remains in an open order file until the boats are shipped.

Throughout the manufacture of the boats, the progress of work orders and sales orders is monitored. Workers in the plant enter the progress made on each order by keying into the system the number of boats completed and labor and materials used. Sales personnel can access the data to check the status of any order. Finally, the customer is billed when the boats are shipped, and the open sales order is closed.

The third and most comprehensive option is an Electronic Data Interchange (EDI) system that uses a Just-in-Time (JIT) approach to ordering raw materials and servicing customers rapidly. It contains all the online query features of the second option. In addition, large dealers could link their computers to Sun's computer to automatically enter a sales order when the dealer's stock is low on certain models or when a retail customer wishes to make a purchase and the marina or dealer is out of stock. Dealer and Sun computers would each be equipped with a program and a modem so that an order can be entered, stock checked, production rescheduled if necessary, and a reply sent to the dealer concerning the likelihood of complying with the order by a specific delivery date. When the shipment is made, an invoice would automatically be forwarded to the dealer through the interconnected computers. Finally, the dealer could transfer funds to Sun's bank to pay for the shipment of boats.

Identification of Subsystem, Software, and Equipment Configurations

Analysts must now plan the subsystems needed for each alternative, the software needed to support information processing requirements, and the equipment needed to run the software. Based on the requirements outlined in the analysis phase, the project team then determines how to accomplish each alternative using systems flowcharts, described in Chapter 3. **Systems flowcharts** are used in the design stage because they specify how processing is accomplished, how the data are stored, how data and information are

FIGURE 13–3   *Systems Flowchart*

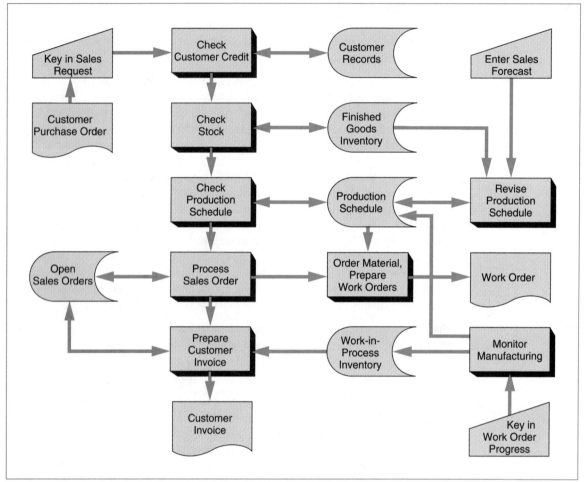

transmitted, how information is output, and how data are input into the information system. The proposed system flowchart for the second alternative, which is described in the previous section, is shown in Figure 13–3. These general system flowcharts are used to communicate the aspects of each alternative to management or the steering committee for final approval and authorization to continue the detailed design of the alternative selected.

Some analysts still prefer to use data flow diagrams in the general design phase; these diagrams are effective in describing the essential flows, data stores, and processing steps for each possible alternative. These analysts describe their general design at a higher level, not at the level of detail shown in a systems flowchart.

FIGURE 13–4

*Revised Cost-
Benefit Analysis
for Sun Products*

	Batch	Online	EDI
Initial Investment			
Development	$20,000	$30,000	$ 65,000
Hardware	20,000	50,000	100,000
Software	5,000	10,000	30,000
Installation	3,000	5,000	10,000
Total	$48,000	$95,000	$205,000
Annual Operating Costs	$15,000	$28,000	$ 45,000
Recovery of Lost Sales	$22,000	$45,000	$ 70,000
Reduction in Inventory	8,000	15,000	35,000
Annual Benefits	$30,000	$60,000	$105,000
Net Present Value	$ 8,862	$26,305	$ 22,447
10% Interest, 5 years			

Technical support for each alternative should be specified. For large, complex systems, technical support involves data management and updating requirements. The mode of processing, such as the online mode required by the second alternative, also suggests hardware and software requirements. For systems like Sun's, in which salespeople must interact with the inventory and production system, communication requirements must be specified in greater detail. In some cases, an alternative may be the purchase of a commercially available application package that meets the minimum specifications of the system. The acquisition of commercial systems is discussed in Chapter 14. Attention should also be directed to the control features of the proposed alternatives so that errors and fraudulent activities are minimized, as discussed in Chapter 17.

*Implementation
Schedules and
Cost-Benefit
Analysis*

Schedules for detailed design, implementation (acquisition or software development and conversion), and operation and maintenance of the system should be estimated for each alternative. One alternative may be operational in one month using commercially available software for production scheduling. Another alternative that meets the information requirements better must be programmed and may take six months to implement. These timing differences could be very important in selecting the best alternative.

Costs and benefits should be estimated for each alternative so that management can make an intelligent decision on how to proceed. Current and future, tangible and intangible costs and benefits should be included, because intangible benefits often comprise the major reason to change to a new system. Information that enables management to make timely and accurate decisions often gives the organization a critical competitive edge. Figure 13–4 illustrates a revised cost-benefit analysis for the three alternatives considered for improving Sun Products sales order processing. It is different from the rough cost-benefit analysis that was prepared during the feasibility study because the system analyst knows much more after a thorough analysis and assessment of several design alternatives in the high-level design phase. For example, the anticipated benefits for the on-line alternatives are greater than previously estimated.

FIGURE 13–5

Comparative Analysis

Important Attributes	Weights Assigned to Scores	Scores		
		Batch	Online	EDI
Net Present Value	10	5	10	6
Time to Develop	6	10	7	4
Ease of Use	8	2	8	6
Training Required	6	10	7	5
Volume of Transactions	10	2	7	10
Quality of Information	10	2	9	10
Size of Investment	5	10	8	5
Speed	5	1	7	10
Weighted Score		281	483	437

Comparison and Recommendation of an Alternative

A comparative analysis, illustrated in Figure 13–5, is prepared for each general design. This is simply the sum of the weights which reflect the relative importance of each attribute times the score for each attribute. Based on this comparative analysis and a careful assessment of the organization's environmental, organizational, and behavioral factors, a final recommendation is prepared and presented to management or the steering committee for approval. This recommendation is that the on-line (intermediate) alternative be selected for Sun Products. The culmination of the project team's creative effort, this report should include sufficient specifications for each alternative to initiate the detailed design of the alternative that management selects. The project team should not give management only one alternative. A clear and unambiguous recommendation is necessary, but all viable alternatives should be presented to permit easy comparison by management. A structured walk through may be performed by another team or analyst to review how each alternative meets the information requirements determined during the analysis phase of the development life cycle. This procedure ensures that nothing major is overlooked in the general design phase and that suggested alternatives are representative of the possible solutions to the problem or the information needs.

13.2 Detailed Systems Design

In this phase of structured systems analysis and design, the project team states specifically how the system selected in the general design will operate. The detailed systems design should include the specifications to be used either to acquire or to develop software and to acquire the necessary hardware for the new system. The detailed steps of this phase in the structured approach are outlined in Figure 13–6. The principal objectives of this phase are as follows:

1. Design a network of information flows and decision-making activities, and specify interfaces with other systems.

2. Establish the specifications for output, input, storage, processing, and communication operations and controls.

FIGURE 13–6

*Detailed Systems
Design*

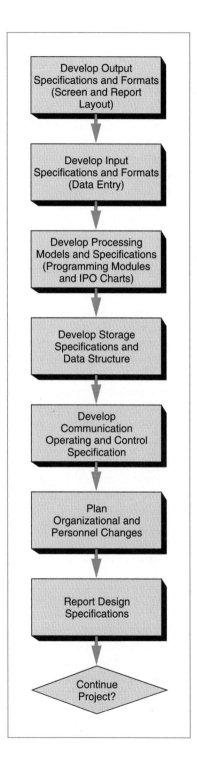

3. Plan organizational and personnel changes, including actual details on programming activities.

4. Plan the actual system implementation (programming, conversion, and training).

Decision-making model, reporting, and transaction processing requirements must be defined more precisely than they were in the general high-level design phase. Each decision model, report, and transaction must be thoroughly described to ensure that alternative technical approaches are evaluated adequately. Output, input, processing, storage, and operating specifications must be prepared. **Hierarchy charts** may be used to identify separate activities and the components of these activities that can be developed as separate modules as shown in Chapter 12. **Input, Processing, and Output (IPO) charts** may then be used to describe the output, processing, input, and storage requirements of each activity, as described later in this chapter. Both tools can be useful in structuring the design process so that information requirements are accurately transformed into specifications for programmers or specifications used in the system acquisition process.

Output Specifications

The starting point in any design sequence is the determination of output specifications. Output from a system may be in terms of periodic reports, online queries, or data stored for future use, as discussed in earlier chapters. Screen and report layout provisions are present in most comprehensive **Computer-Aided Software Engineering (CASE)** packages. With CASE, a systems analyst or project team can design output that is consistent with the system, its processing steps, programs, and data. In general, the content, form, volume, timing, media, and format of output must be specified for each alternative.

In the Sun Products detailed design stage, **output content** is stated in terms of the information needed for each Sun Products activity outlined in the systems flowchart. For example, salespersons would receive output on portable personal computers consisting of the number and models (product number) of boats on hand and scheduled for production. Other output would be the prices, discounts available to the customer, and expected shipping dates, all displayed in a screen like that in Figure 13–7. Estimates of the frequency (volume) of such salesperson requests are needed to specify the software and hardware for the system.

In general, the **output form** refers to how information is presented. Output form could be tabular, graphic, written, or even voice. The **media** refers to the physical characteristic of the output such as a display monitor, a printed report, magnetic tapes, and disks for storage of input data. Perhaps the most widely used media in Management Information Systems (MIS) is a printed report. **Output timing** indicates when information is output, for example, instantaneous online output or periodic reports on a daily or monthly basis. A tabular form displayed on a portable PC screen is recommended in the Sun Products sales order case. In a system that provides the latest inventory figures in daily printed reports, the form is also tabular but the media is a combination of printout and telephone communication.

FIGURE 13–7

Output Display

```
SALESPERSON  11

INQUIRY DATE   3/22/92

MODEL NUMBER   SB2200

NUMBER ON HAND  25

SCHEDULED FOR PRODUCTION  20

SUGGESTED WHOLESALE PRICE  $8,000

SUGGESTED RETAIL PRICE  $9,985

DISCOUNT AVAILABLE   10%

SHIPPING DATE FOR PRODUCTION  5/18/92
```

Output format refers to the text, graphic, and tabular **layout** used to display the output. The layout is the particular arrangement of columns and rows, location of data, and type of graph, for example. This display must be easy for the user to understand and manipulate for controlling operations or making decisions.

Input Specifications

Input may originate from terminals, personal computers, machine-readable documents, optically scanned data, keyed data, tape, and magnetic disk, as discussed in Chapter 5. Input forms, data structure, and reports must be designed to capture and store this input. Input methods and procedures must also be designed in detail, given the preliminary hardware and software specifications. As with output, the content, timing, form, media, format, and volume of input must be specified for each alternative. Data entry timing may be very important when information is needed quickly. Input speed may be important when the volume of input is large.

Sometimes input specifications must comply with data base or file specifications, including necessary input content for the records, fields, and field characteristics for each data element. The input format must also be designed so that data entry is accomplished with minimal errors.

For Sun's proposed order entry system, the input content includes the name and number of the customer (usually a marina or boat dealer), billing address, address to which the boats are shipped, product model (number) and boat description, quantity ordered, data of the order and expected delivery date, price charged the dealer, discounts that apply to

FIGURE 13–8

Input Screen

```
SALESPERSON  11

DATE  3/25/92
EXPECTED DELIVERY DATE _____

CUSTOMER/DEALER NAME _____

CUSTOMER/DEALER NUMBER _____

BILLING ADDRESS _____
     _____

SHIPPING ADDRESS _____
     _____

PRODUCT (MODEL) NUMBER _____  QUANTITY _____.
PRODUCT (MODEL) NUMBER _____  QUANTITY _____.
PRODUCT (MODEL) NUMBER _____  QUANTITY _____.

DISCOUNT AVAILABLE  10%
```

the dealer, and salesperson's number. The salesperson's number is an example of data that are collected at the time of sale for Sun's data base even though it is not necessary for the sales transaction. Such data may be necessary for the calculation of bonuses and commissions.

In Sun's online example, data should be entered on the manufacturing work order number and the boats completed for each work order at each stage in the production process. These data are necessary so that salespersons can respond to customers on the progress of sales orders and let them know when boats may be available.

Because Sun's sales orders must be entered and immediate responses must be received to process a sales order, the input media must be a terminal. In Sun's case the terminal is a portable microcomputer. A sample input screen for Sun Products' proposed online sales order input is shown in Figure 13–8.

Processing Specifications

Each processing activity may be analyzed using an IPO chart to describe what is done at each step in the decision-making, reporting, and transaction processing network. These steps represent separate identifiable activities in the processing of information. Often these steps are identified in hierarchy charts and data flow diagrams. IPO charts are useful for detailing the management decision-making process (logic or model) and the necessary input to and output from this process. These charts can also help describe the nature, frequency, and volume of information that must flow through the system for storage in the data base. From this, data elements can be determined and organized into files,

FIGURE 13–9   *Input, Processing, and Output Chart*

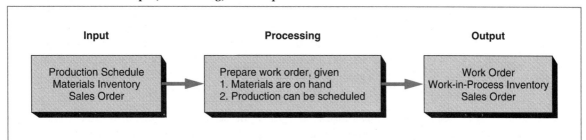

records, and data bases depending on their characteristics (described in Chapters 5 and 6). IPO charts are also very useful in top-down modular programming approaches used to develop software, as described later in this chapter. Using an IPO chart, a project team can describe the processing activities, input, and output for each decision-making or reporting activity in the information system. The IPO chart shown in Figure 13–9 for Sun Products shows the processing needed to prepare a work order from a pending sales order when materials are on hand and the production schedule can accommodate a new work order. From this description, a set of specifications can be prepared for the acquisition or the development of software and the acquisition of hardware.

Processing timing, speed, and volume must be specified because they have a tremendous impact on the nature of the system's software, hardware, storage, and communication requirements. Hardware specifications must be developed at this time to accommodate the new system requirements for hardware.

Sun's processing system must be able to handle the volume of input transactions from 100 salespersons who make an average of 10 inquiries per day. Some salespeople may require online interaction with the production schedule to expedite a sales order. The system should have sufficient communication and processing speed so that it does not bog down at peak times. A salesperson should always be able to access the system to make a sale.

Storage Specifications

At this stage, specifications for the data to be stored must be finalized. **Data dictionaries** can outline the various data elements that are needed, their sources, their uses, and other key characteristics. These elements can be organized in files or in a data base for use in current and future applications. **Data models** discussed in Chapters 5 and 6 include the sequential, indexed sequential, and direct methods of file organizations, as well as the hierarchical, network, and relational data base structures. Contemporary CASE packages may be used to define these data structures to be consistent with information processing needs, data input, and information output. These structures may be easily displayed graphically to help the analyst design the data base needed by the system. These structures may be developed by CASE methods from the information flows portrayed via hierarchy charts, data flow diagrams, and entity relationship diagrams.

The volume of data to be stored, the frequency with which data are accessed, and the storage media must be considered in the specifications of data structure and storage requirements. For example, when very large volumes of data must be processed in a batch mode, then a sequential file structure is most appropriate. A payroll system for a large company would be a good example of such a need. A disk must be used for random access processing requirements. If batch processing is required for a large volume of data organized in a sequential way, magnetic tape may be specified.

As an example of storage specifications, the second alternative in the Sun Products sales entry problem requires an online direct access method because of the need for immediate response to requests. A report at the end of the day is not enough. For Sun Products, data must be stored on disk because of the random access requirements.

Communication, Operating, and Control Procedures

Systems analysts must develop specifications for communication procedures, including the characteristics of the communication network, the protocol, and the hardware. All aspects of the communication system for wide area networks and local area networks were discussed in Chapter 7. The communication links between suppliers and customers must also be specified.

Operating procedures must be specified to process transactions in accordance with the desires of management. Operating procedures must also be developed for effective use of the new system by employees. The operating procedures should be documented in user and computer operator manuals, so that transactions are processed accordingly, reports are distributed to the appropriate parties, input is checked, authorization is given when necessary, and errors are properly corrected. For example, a user manual item might state that customer credit should be checked prior to processing a sales order.

This phase should include the assignment of operating procedure responsibilities to individuals and to parts of the organization. Assignments help to establish responsibility and authority for information processing. For example, a major change to the production schedule may require the approval of both the sales manager and the production manager before an order can be expedited.

Control procedures ensure that the system operates as designed with maximum protection against errors, breakdowns, and fraud. These must be specified. Procedures for the maintenance of data base and data file integrity, including backup procedures, must also be specified. Control procedures are outlined in Chapter 17.

Plan Organizational and Personnel Changes

The project team should prepare for any organizational changes. The project team should quickly and accurately communicate the nature of these changes, along with the compelling reasons for the changes, to all affected personnel. System changes can often alter individual responsibilities and interpersonal relationships and, as a result, cause a great deal of frustration and anxiety. Therefore, careful consideration must be given to the communication of these changes, which may include hiring of new personnel or training of current personnel.

At this point, an assessment of personnel requirements should be made, and qualifications needed to run the system must to be outlined. Personnel may need to be hired, transferred, fired, or retrained. Every effort should be made to retain existing personnel through transfers or retraining. A good track record in fair treatment of personnel makes this change and all future changes much easier.

After software, hardware, data files, personnel and organizational changes are specified, site planning and preparation is a major consideration, especially if more space, different air conditioning, fire protection, or special security are required. An implementation (acquisition, development, and conversion) plan and schedule must also be specified. This plan may require a preliminary assessment on whether to acquire or develop software. Program Evaluation Review Technique (PERT), which is discussed in Chapter 16, may be used extensively to develop this plan.

Report to
Management

The project team delivers to management a report that describes in detail the specifications for the proposed system. This description includes revised systems flowcharts to indicate the proposed flow of transactions and information through the transaction processing, reporting, and decision-making network of the organization. All specifications for hardware and software are described, including the tools needed to program the software, the system, and its interfaces with management and other systems. In addition, the cost-benefit analysis must be revised, because the system must ultimately be justified on a cost-benefit basis. Finally, the report should indicate an implementation plan. A **structured walk through** may be performed here to ensure that the specifications for the new or revised system follow logically from the alternative selected during the general high-level design phase.

13.3
Implementation

Following the approval of management or the steering committee, implementation of the information system should commence. In the Sun Products example the on-line (intermediate/second) alternative is approved. Implementation involves the development or acquisition of software, the acquisition of hardware, and the integration of all system components into a working information system. Specifically, implementation includes the development/acquisition, installation, testing, conversion, documentation, and training activities shown in Figure 13–10. The alternate implementation paths shown in Figure 13–10 are based on management's decision to either develop or acquire its software. Software development is discussed in this chapter, and acquisition of software and hardware is discussed in Chapter 14. All implementation steps must be carefully scheduled. For a large project, project management techniques are useful in scheduling the necessary activities and resources.

Software
Development
versus
Acquisition

At some point in the detailed design and implementation process, management must decide to either acquire software or develop its own. This decision may be made at the beginning of the detailed design where the specifications from the general high-level design are forwarded to potential vendors. On the other hand, this decision may be made at the beginning of the implementation process when all specifications are completed. This decision may also be made at any juncture in this process as specifications become more detailed. At the point this decision is made, the project team or analyst should study

FIGURE 13–10

*Implementation
Alternatives:
Software
Development
versus Acquisition*

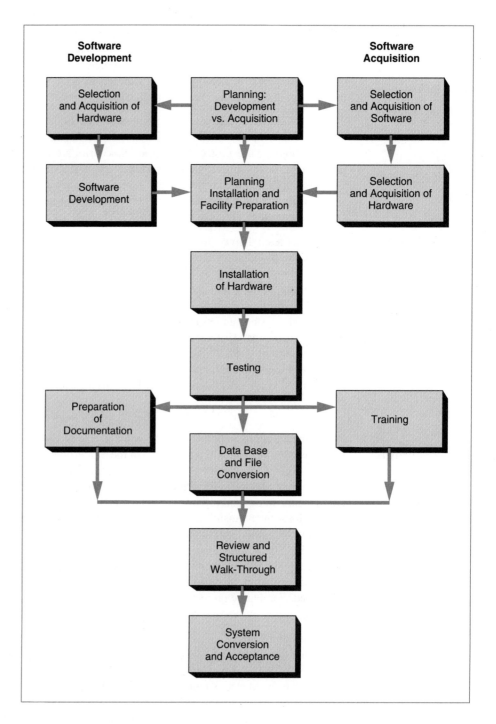

various software approaches, with supporting hardware, and specify system needs with respect to hardware, software, telecommunications, and data base organization. After this decision, system implementation branches as shown in Figure 13–10 to systems acquisition or development.

One of the major differences between the two approaches is timing. If an organization elects to write its own software, it is probably done after hardware is selected or already in place. In these cases, the software is constrained by the hardware. When the decision to acquire software is made, hardware decisions are often deferred until the software is selected because not all software will run on all hardware. After software is developed or acquired, implementation proceeds as shown in Figure 13–10.

The decision to develop or purchase commercial software should be based on the relative advantages of acquisition versus development of software, which are discussed in detail in Chapter 14. In general, the decision is based on the trade-off between the unique requirements of each business and the reliability and lower cost of acquired software.

Top-Down Software Development

Software development is the analysis, design, and implementation of computer programs. Software development spans the detailed design, implementation, and maintenance phases of structured analysis and design. From the specifications developed during the detailed design phase of the systems development life cycle, software development includes the steps shown in Figure 13–11.

Each step is discussed as part of the software (program) development life cycle. In the development process, it is useful to separate the definition of software requirements and the software design from the actual software coding. This separation adds structure to the top-down development of programs, enhancing their understandability, maintenance, and reliability. In fact, CASE systems lead directly to the development of information system software modules and programs for these modules.

An effective approach to software development is the top-down approach, which follows from the specifications spelled out in the detailed design phase. These specifications describe the requirements of the application programs needed to implement the system design. **Top-down development** (also called top-down design) is accomplished by first viewing the program as a whole and deciding how it can be divided into small programming blocks or modules. This "top-level" stage of the design process emphasizes the overall design of the program. The programmer should simply try to state the program as a sequence of steps that need to be carried out. No attention to detail is given as this "big picture" is developed, much like the general design phase described earlier in this chapter.

A program module is then developed for each specific task. A module that is too complicated to perform a specific task is broken up into another, lower level of modules. These tasks often follow from the activities outlined in a hierarchy chart or the structured chart described in the next section. This process of subdividing tasks continues until no more modules are needed. Figure 13–12 shows what a top-down design of a program can look like.

FIGURE 13–11

Software Development Life Cycle

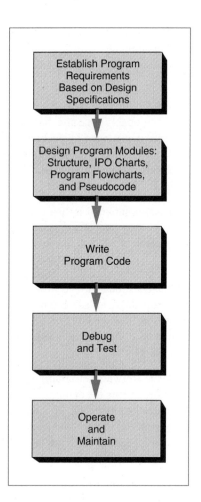

In Figure 13–12, the main program, or module, links all other modules — input, computational, and output. These general modules are common for most programs. The computational module is further broken down into individual modules, each handling a particular computation. Because each module performs a recognizable activity, each should be designed and written as a separate unit. Modules must also be able to communicate with the remainder of the program through linkages with the main program or with other modules. In a complex program, analysts may write and test each module separately before trying to test the program as a whole. If each module is correct and the main program handles the linkages properly, then the entire program should run smoothly.

Program requirements for each module should be specified, and plans should be made to schedule all programming tasks for each module in the system. The following program requirements are needed:

FIGURE 13–12

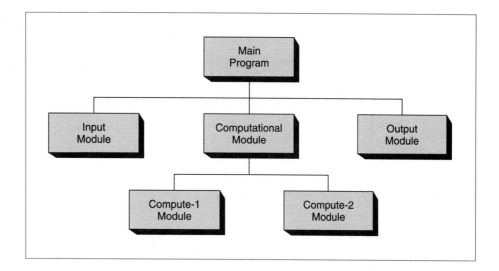

1. Description and purpose

2. Input specifications

3. Output specifications

4. Files to be used

5. Processing logic, including decision tables and algorithms

6. Coding language and standards

7. Testing specifications

8. Criteria and conversion specifications

9. Systems environment in which the program will operate

10. Documentation needed to operate the program

Given these requirements, program logic can be developed for each separate task.

Some confusion may exist about the difference between structured programming and top-down design. Remember that top-down design is an approach to the design of efficient and easily maintained programs, and **structured programming** is a method of implementing this design using a particular programming language. Structured programming is a technical aspect of programming and will not be covered in this text. In both concepts, however, the use of blocks or modules is extremely important.

In summary, a top-down modular approach makes it easy to design, program, test, modify, and maintain a program because it is composed of well-defined integrated modules. Each module represents a particular activity that can be designed, programmed, tested, and run separately.

FIGURE 13–13   *Structured Chart Using Computer-Aided Software Engineering*

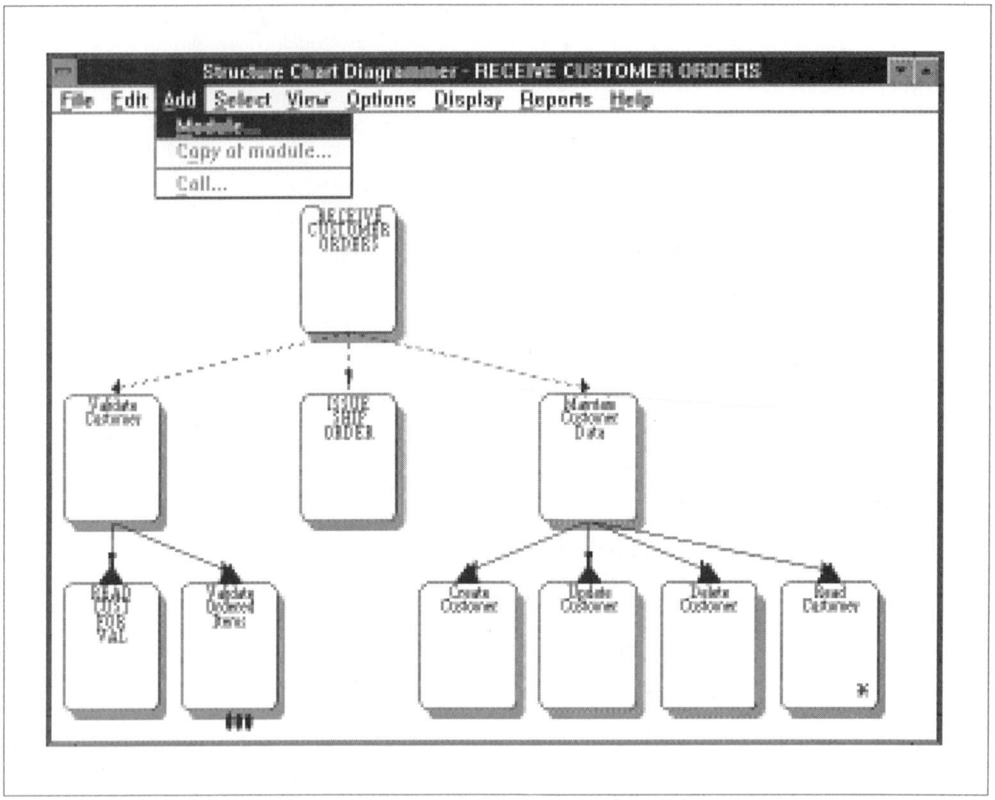

Top-Down Design Techniques and Tools

In implementing a top-down design, various techniques and tools are available. These include structured charts (which are like hierarchy charts), IPO charts, pseudocode, program flowcharts, and action diagrams.

A **structured chart** has various levels, like a company's organization chart. Its top level represents controlling activities for various detailed tasks, and the flow of information between these controlling activities and the detailed tasks is shown. In general, a structured chart shows how each task fits into the overall program organization. It does not contain program logic. The structured chart does show the subdivision of an application into smaller modules to facilitate programming. These modules may be further subdivided so a programmer can write program code in a structured manner. Figure 13–13 shows a structured chart using CASE that shows each submodule as an identifiable activity needed to process a customer order.

IPO charts may be developed for each module in the hierarchy or structured chart. Sometimes called IPO tables, they are used to describe what is done in each processing task in the program module. IPO charts show the input to the module, the processing that takes place in the module, the output from the module, and the data input from and to a

FIGURE 13–14

*Example of
Pseudocode
for Checking
Inventory and
Processing
a Sales Order*

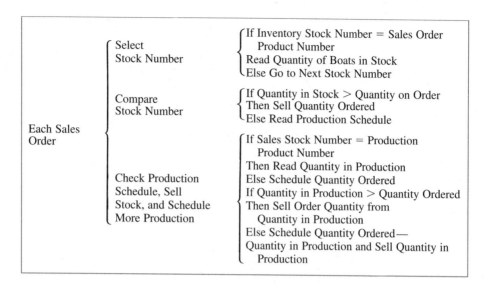

Each Sales Order

Select Stock Number
{ If Inventory Stock Number = Sales Order
   Product Number
Read Quantity of Boats in Stock
Else Go to Next Stock Number

Compare Stock Number
{ If Quantity in Stock > Quantity on Order
Then Sell Quantity Ordered
Else Read Production Schedule

Check Production Schedule, Sell Stock, and Schedule More Production
{ If Sales Stock Number = Production
   Product Number
Then Read Quantity in Production
Else Schedule Quantity Ordered
If Quantity in Production > Quantity Ordered
Then Sell Order Quantity from
   Quantity in Production
Else Schedule Quantity Ordered—
Quantity in Production and Sell Quantity in
   Production

data base for each processing task. This breakdown helps programmers structure their programming logic to include the necessary interfaces with input and output data to other modules or to controlling modules in the hierarchy.

The logic of each processing activity represented in a structured or IPO chart can be described in several ways. System designers may use pseudocode, program flowcharts, or action diagrams.

More detail can be provided for each module in the IPO or structured chart through pseudocode. CASE software can also generate pseudocode from these charts. **Pseudocode,** sometimes called structured English, represents program logic in English terms. The analyst simply concentrates on the input, processing logic, and output without worrying about specific coding syntax and terminology. Pseudocode is very useful in the design of Transaction Processing Systems (TPS) and Management Information Systems (MIS) in which activities are well structured. An example of pseudocode is presented in Figure 13–14. In general, pseudocode bridges the gap between the logic of a processing activity and the actual program coding.

In contrast to pseudocode, **program flowcharts** graphically describe the processing logic, along with its input and output. Program flowcharts use a combination of well-known symbols and mathematical expressions to depict a processing activity. Program flowcharts are better than pseudocode for describing the abstract logic found in Decision Support Systems (DSS) and Executive Information Systems (EIS). Flowcharts are not particularly useful for portraying large complex programs, because they are so time consuming and tedious to develop. Program flowcharts describe the logic of a processing step, whereas systems flowcharts simply note the presence of the step in context with other processing steps, storage, inputs, outputs, and data flows. Program flowcharts and pseudocode can be easily translated into program code by an experienced programmer.

FIGURE 13–15   *Action Diagram Using Computer-Aided Software Engineering*

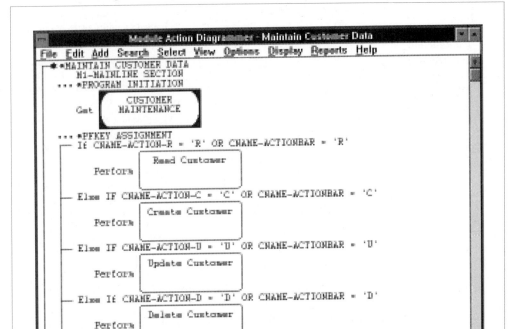

In fact, some fourth generation languages can translate pseudocode directly into programming code.

These development tools can be automated using CASE software. **Action diagrams** that represent data flow and processing activities can be sketched on a computer using CASE and then converted into computer code. An example of an action diagram is presented in Figure 13–15. Program flowcharts can also be translated into prototype programs via CASE.

Programming   With the top-down approach to program design, the programming logic and a modular structure are completed and documented using the appropriate tools such as structured charts, IPO charts, pseudocode or program flowcharts, and action diagrams. Now, programmers begin to translate these documents into program modules that can be executed by the computer. A program written in modular fashion is very easy to follow and understand. In the future, a modular program is also much easier to test and modify. With this approach, each module can be developed by a different programmer and easily integrated into a complete software application.

FIGURE 13–16   *Interpretation and Compilation in Translating Code into Machine Language*

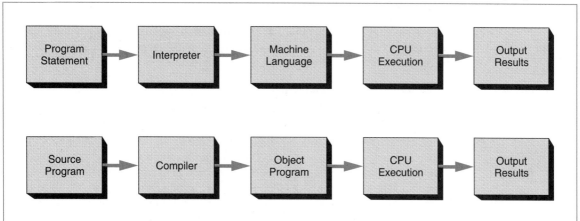

During the actual writing of the program, the programmer is allowed considerable latitude. However, he or she must make the program easy to follow and ensure that it complies with the logic outlined in the program specifications. Each program must also comply with programming language syntactic (grammatical) form. Programmers usually write code in a high-level language and then translate it into a machine language program, as shown in Figure 13–16. Depending on the language and application, two methods can be used for this translation—interpretation and compilation. With **interpretation,** each statement is converted during the execution of the program. During program debug, errors are generated for each statement that does not comply with the syntactic form of the language. On the other hand, with **compilation,** a program is translated as a whole into machine language and then executed. At this time, logic errors in programming may appear and must be corrected. For example, in some languages, statements are executed in order. Therefore, a product number used in a statement must be defined in a statement that precedes it in logical sequence. Otherwise the programmer sees a syntax error during the interpretation of the code into machine language. Prior to compilation, the code is called **source code;** after compilation, it is **object code.** Interpretation and compilation are compared in Figure 13–16.

Another approach to programming is called Object-Oriented Programming Systems (OOPS). With OOPS, a programmer uses previously developed standardized generic modules to develop a program. For example, the programmers for Sun Products order entry system may use an off-the-shelf module to program the access to finished goods inventory.

Implementation of a top-down modular design depends to a large extent on the programming language. All languages have some means to allow the programmer to modularize the program. Languages take different approaches and are better suited for some applications than others. In any language, the programmer should put as much detailed logic as possible in the modules referred to by the main program or by other modules. This modular approach to coding is often called structured programming.

Program coding is a long, labor intensive process. However, the programmer may use such techniques as fourth generation language application generators and CASE prototype methods to improve programming productivity.

Environmental Factors

Input, processing logic, and output are not the only factors that must be considered in software design. The volume of input and output, the data structure that may already exist, the computational environment, storage capacity, communication possibilities, required throughput (or turnaround) of information are all very important considerations in the design of computer software. For example, a program may perform quite differently in an interactive personal computer data base environment than it does in a mainframe batch processing environment. Sun Products' business environment, for example, may require immediate information turnaround for salespersons who access the finished goods inventory file in order to determine if needed boats are ready for immediate delivery or if a work order for more boats should be processed.

Software Development with CASE

CASE can expedite the specification of software requirements and the programming of software to meet these specifications. Specifications are spelled out in the design phases using hierarchy charts, data flow diagrams, and entity relationship diagrams. From these graphically displayed specifications and the information requirements they represent, data bases can be designed and programs can be designed and written using CASE software. Structured charts can be used by programmers to further specify the modules needed to meet the information requirements of the system. These modules can be programmed separately yet be tightly integrated into a complete application program that smoothly interfaces with the data base and other application programs.

The creation of the data base structure and the programs follows from the CASE knowledge base developed during the design phases. The **knowledge base** contains all the specifications that were developed graphically. It enforces consistency among the graphical diagrams used to design and implement the system.

Planning, Preparation, and Installation of Physical Facilities

After financial arrangements are made, hardware, software, communication equipment, and forms should be ordered. Operating and control procedures should be planned, and arrangements should be made for training. Programming and testing should be organized and scheduled. Details on user's manuals and other documentation should be given to vendors, programmers, and systems analysts. Conversion should be scheduled. If required, new personnel should be selected and trained.

While all these activities are progressing, the physical site should be prepared and the hardware and software should be installed. If the software is developed, these development activities could parallel the planning and preparation activities. The amount of physical preparation depends on the amount of computing equipment to be installed. If new equipment is replacing old equipment, then site preparation could be minimal. Other development projects may require the construction of new facilities with sufficient power, communication, and climate control to house more or a different type of equipment. After the hardware is installed, it should be tested to ensure that all maintenance, operating, utility, and other routines provided by the vendor are functioning as specified.

Testing   All programs, application systems, and hardware must be tested thoroughly to ensure that they meet the specifications outlined during the design phases and that they operate properly. Moreover, they must be tested to ensure that they meet the information requirements outlined by management during the analysis phase of the project. Several levels of tests are performed for an application. First, each module is tested. Then, testing involves the program, the program in conjunction with other programs, the entire system, and finally, the program under actual operating conditions.

Program Testing and Debugging After all programs are coded, the program and the application are tested, as shown in Figure 13–11. Problems found during the testing must be corrected. This process is called **debugging.** In a **logical check,** programmers should verify that the program complies with the objectives of each module and that the modules are compatible with other modules, data bases or files, and procedures.

Next, the program must be tested with test data. **Test data** can be a set of random transactions, an actual group of transactions, or a set of controlled transactions, which may be fictitious, good, or bad. Using controlled test data, the tester already knows which transactions should be rejected by the program and which ones are legitimate. Bogus transactions should cover every possible problem to make sure the program does not process bad transactions. Examples of bad transactions are those with incomplete data or incorrect account numbers, those out of sequence, and those that do not balance or satisfy some other numerical control. Good transactions should cover every conceivable type of transaction to be sure the program accurately processes each one. When the number of different types of transactions is enormous, test data generators can be used to create a large number of good and bad transactions.

When the results of this test are compared with expected results, differences must be carefully reconciled and the program corrected. The debugging should begin with the program logic as expressed in pseudocode or the program flowchart. Test data should find both coding and logic problems. If differences are not due to logic errors, the code should be checked next. Documents such as IPO charts, structured charts, or pseudocode must be corrected along with the program. Testing should be performed using the hardware, operating system, and, if applicable, the data base of the new system so that programmers can ensure that the logic, coding, and syntax all work on the system.

Remember that no amount of testing can guarantee the complete elimination of bugs. Extensive testing only reduces the possibility of bugs and the cost and possible embarrassment associated with their discovery after the program is fully implemented. These test results are an important part of the system's documentation.

Systems Testing All programs, groups of programs (strings), data files, and operating procedures must be tested as a complete system to ensure compliance with management's expectations. This procedure is called a **systems test.** The emphasis of a systems test is on the interfaces among strings of programs, the operating system, data base systems, controls, operating procedures, and other systems of the organization.

Testing
Failures at Sun
Microsystems

As a leader in the fast-growing workstation market, Sun Microsystems decided several years ago that its existing minicomputer-based production/inventory system was inadequate. To rectify this problem, the company started a three-year structured systems analysis and design process to create a new information system that would accept orders for workstations, break the orders down into parts, and schedule inventory ordering and production. As a part of this process, the company conducted months of testing and parallel implementation.

However, when Sun "pulled the plug" on the old system, management quickly discovered that even with the extensive analysis, design, and testing efforts, the new system was too unstable to handle the huge volume of orders. Sun tried to go back to the old system, but it could not keep up with the flood of orders either. A Sun spokesperson said, "We were sitting with a stack of paper orders 3 feet high waiting to be entered into the system." As a result, Sun could not plan its production, leading to a drop in revenue in the fourth quarter of that year.

SOURCE: Robert L. Schier, "Taking the Quick Path to Systems Design," *PC Week,* June 19, 1989, pp. 65, 69.

The systems test is a fairly complex undertaking. The system operations manual and documentation must be reviewed with computer operators and control personnel to ensure that utility program support, operating instructions, restart procedures, and systems controls are clear. Procedures and assignment of responsibility for obtaining data must be clear. The data base or master files must be tested for the handling of input, processing, and output. Transaction data representing a full range of valid and invalid operational possibilities must again be prepared and run using the entire system. The limits of the system must be determined, including the following:

1. Processing capacity, such as throughput, turnaround, and access time

2. The system's ability to handle the typical volume of transactions

3. The system's ability to restart and recover when it crashes

In the Sun Products example, the system must be able to handle normal sales orders, rush orders, out-of-stock conditions, and production breakdowns.

After all procedures are working well, the data are available, and the programs are tested, the systems test is performed. The results of this test are thoroughly reviewed by systems personnel and management to ensure that the system is functioning in accordance with design specifications. Problems are reconciled, and corrections to programs and procedures are made. The system is retested as often as necessary, for it must satisfy the requirements of management for effectiveness, efficiency, and data integrity through good controls.

*Data Base and
File Conversion*

After the software is acquired and the equipment is installed, the data base must be prepared. This task can be difficult if the organization is converting from a manual system to a computer system, if the files are large, and if the files are old and not up to date. Manual files may have numerous errors and omissions that must be resolved. Large files take a long time to convert. Old files may contain inconsistent, missing, and incompatible data when they are not maintained. Missing data must be reconstructed to bring old files or data bases up to date. Often, the old data must be entered into the system, often involving tedious keying operations or optical scanning. In many cases, data can be converted from one storage medium to another using some special programs. The conversion process must be carefully controlled so that valuable data are not lost, misclassified, or destroyed. The final step prior to the actual conversion of the system should be a structured walk through to ensure that all the systems and programs are working as they should.

In summary, file conversion is often time consuming because large numbers of records need to be converted from an old medium to a new medium. Throughout this process careful attention must be given to the integrity of the old and new files. Controls must be in place to ensure accurate conversion and that no data are lost.

*System
Conversion*

System conversion is the transition stage between the old and new information systems, in which the old system is switched to the new. To accomplish this, time tables for file and program conversion must be prepared. The actual system conversion approach may vary depending on the situation. In a **direct approach,** the old system is stopped and the new system is started immediately. This method may be suitable when the differences between the old and the new information systems are so great that any comparison is meaningless. This approach is fast and often inexpensive. In most cases, however, this approach is very risky, because the old system cannot be used as backup if the new one fails or has serious bugs.

For example, Sun Products may not want to convert directly to a new system, even though this procedure is fast and cheap. If the new system does not work, the company has no way to transact a sales order and may lose sales.

With **parallel conversion,** both old and new systems are operated simultaneously. The results are compared and reconciled, and the new system is corrected for differences, if necessary. If the old and new systems are quite different, this approach is not appropriate, because any reconciliation is impossible. For example, an online inventory system cannot be compared with monthly printouts. Parallel conversion does offer considerable protection for the company and its records. However, it is very costly in terms of the personnel used to operate two systems at once. To alleviate this problem, old data may be processed on the new system in a more compressed time frame. For example, Sun Products could process its spring sales figures again on the new system during the first week in July and reconcile any differences with the spring sales figures processed on the old system.

Another approach is to implement the new system as a **pilot** in a branch or small subset of the organization. Using this method, risk is localized and problems can be corrected in the pilot situation prior to an organization-wide implementation. For example, Sun Products may decide to use the new system in its Florida sales offices first, then gradually expand it to other offices as the bugs are corrected.

Phase-in conversion can be used when small subsystems are implemented one at a time. One piece of a system is implemented, and the bugs are ironed out prior to the implementation of the next phase. This method has the major disadvantage of too many subsystem interfaces and the perception that the implementation will never be complete. Sometimes the job may never be finished, and a piecemeal system may result.

Documentation
Concurrently with data base and file conversion, computer operations documentation must be completed with specific instructions for operating the system. **Documentation** includes data base and file requirements, hardware and software operations, restart procedures, program documentation, file labeling, and retention requirements.

The user's manual should be completed at this stage in systems development and contain the following:

1. A system flowchart describing all flows, documents, and procedures

2. Operating instructions for each system, including input, processing, and output reports

3. Schedules for input submission, processing, and output generation

4. Control and security procedures

5. Assignment of responsibility

6. Description of all files and data to be used by each system

7. Instruction for completion of operating forms

8. Complete documentation of each program

Good documentation is essential for the smooth operation of any information system. System users must know how it works and how to use the information they receive from the system. Good documentation is also important in training new personnel.

Training
Training is important to the ultimate success of the information system. All users—including management and operations personnel who use the information as well as computer operators and MIS personnel who provide the information—must be trained on the system. Without training, management may misuse information, operations personnel may key in the wrong data, or systems personnel may use the wrong data set in processing data. The result can be chaos, lost data, and disruption of business.

User training can begin in parallel with the data conversion process, but it must be completed prior to the actual conversion to the new system. This training may consist of group seminars, individual study of procedure manuals, tutorials, and on-the-job training.

**13.4
Operations
and
Maintenance**

The operation of the new information system should start and the use of the old system should cease according to schedule. The early results should be evaluated with users who no longer rely on the old system. Any adjustments and corrections to the system should be made at this point. After these modifications, the system should be turned over to users.

The system should be maintained on a regular basis. Usually a considerable amount of routine maintenance activity occurs for any system. Minor problems do arise and some modules may require reprogramming or modification. This activity may seem unimportant, but for many organizations, maintenance comprises 70% of the programming budget. Management of the information system is the subject of Chapter 16.

The system should be evaluated to ensure that it complies with the requirements in the original project definition. Operations must be monitored to ensure that management receives what it needs. The system may need to be revised to accommodate these needs. As noted in Chapter 12, major changes in business or new technology may render a system inadequate or obsolete. In such cases, a major revision or even a new system may be needed. In the case discussed here, ProYacht needed a new system to process sales orders for its new Sun Products division.

13.5 Summary

After the information requirements are specified through an analysis of transaction processing, decision-making, and reporting needs, the new system can be designed and implemented. This chapter presents the various steps that lead to a structured high-level system design, detailed design, implementation, and operation. The project definition, feasibility, and analysis phases were presented in Chapter 12. Particular emphasis is given in this chapter to software development, which is often a major component of the implementation phase of information systems development.

The design phase begins with a general high-level design of a system that can satisfy the company's information needs. The objective of this phase is to evaluate several alternatives and select a particular course of action. A detailed design can then commence, and specifications for input, output, storage, communication, and operating procedures are prepared. Implementation can involve the development or the acquisition of software and the acquisition of hardware to meet the specifications outlined in the detailed design phase. An organization that decides to develop its software should use a top-down modular approach for designing and coding new programs. Once written, programs require substantial testing to ensure they comply with design specifications and reliability standards. When system conversion occurs, management and operations personnel should be ready to use the new system. All these structured approach phases should be performed in order. Further, if the structured approach to systems development is used, the development proceeds in a very logical way from a conceptual view of the system to the actual implementation. All charts, diagrams, coding, corrections, testing, and conversion steps fit into this structured approach and lead to well-organized and maintained information systems. As the system is used and the business environment and technology change, the systems development life cycle begins again with a new project definition, feasibility study, and analysis of information needs.

CASE packages can expedite this development process and link all the steps together via integrated software and a knowledge base of specifications. As a result, CASE can be used effectively to develop a well-integrated information system.

Key Terms

action diagrams
compilation
Computer Aided Software
   Engineering (CASE)
data dictionaries
data models
debugging
direct approach
documentation
hierarchy charts
interpretation
Input, Processing, and Output (IPO)
   charts
knowledge base
layout
logical check
media
models
object code

output content
output form
output format
output timing
parallel conversion
phase-in conversion
pilot
program flowcharts
pseudocode
software development
source code
structured chart
structured programming
structured walk through
system conversion
systems flowcharts
systems test
test data
top-down development

Review Questions

1. What is the major difference between the analysis phase and design phase?

2. Describe in sequential order the major tasks in a general high-level information system design. What major information processing activities must be specified?

3. What is the general sequence of activities in the detailed design phase?

4. What is the desired output of the general high-level systems design phase? What is the desired output of the detailed systems design phase?

5. What is the general philosophy behind top-down software development?

6. What tools are useful for defining program modules? What tools are useful in describing the specifications for each program module?

7. How can hierarchy and IPO charts assist analysts in the design phases?

8. What are the advantages of pseudocode over program flowcharting?

9. Compare program testing with systems testing.

10. Why is data conversion such a difficult task in the process of changing to a new information system?

11. List the advantages and disadvantages of the various systems conversion procedures.

12. List the tasks in the implementation phase, assuming an organization develops its own software.

13. How can CASE be used to expedite the design and implementation process?

14. Why is it important to follow the structured approach outlined in this chapter for the design and implementation of an information system? What can go wrong if steps or phases are skipped?

15. What provisions are present in comprehensive CASE packages that are useful to the software development effort?

Discussion Questions

1. Athens Products has analyzed its information needs for a new sales, marketing, and distribution system. The new system should speed Athens' product delivery and cut its costs. Athens is considering two alternatives for the new system. One plan involves the development of its own marketing and distribution software, and the other alternative involves the use of commercially available software. The second alternative has a higher net present value over a 5-year period. Athens management selects the first alternative instead. Explain why management may have made this choice.

2. In the development of a new system for monitoring production at a plant, management wanted to cut development costs as much as possible. Therefore, the project team skipped the use of hierarchy charts (structured charts), IPO charts, pseudocode, and program flowcharts, even though the company's unique situation would require the development of original software. The programmers developed the programs from general design specifications they were given, but discovered during testing that many subroutines were missing. Why do you think this happened? Could the use of CASE, with its supporting software and knowledge base, have eliminated this problem? Why?

3. It can be argued that a system designer should start with output, determine processing and input specifications, and then determine data and communication procedures needed to support these activities. Why is this order important? Can CASE be used to coordinate these design steps? How?

4. The conversion of one system to another must be carefully controlled so that data are not lost or compromised and the organization can continue to operate. The use of parallel conversion is often recommended when both systems are operated concurrently and differences are reconciled before the new system operates on its own. A friend of yours who manages several travel agencies throughout the state used a new system for one week in one office and then converted the entire operation to the new system without running any office

in parallel. How big a risk did she take? Explain why she may have taken this approach.

Lockheed Missile & Space Company, Inc., Austin Division (LAD) implemented an advanced Material Requirement Planning (MRP) system as the key component of Computer-Integrated Manufacturing (CIM). The system took more than four years to develop and required a $5 million investment in software and hardware. Although the process seemed overwhelming, Lockheed says its business would have been doomed without it.

The previous systems used in Austin were based in Sunnyvale, CA, so Austin could not control changes, nor could it operate if the Sunnyvale computers were down. With the two-hour time difference, Sunnyvale had to bring its systems up two hours early to match Austin's operating schedule. Because of its computer problems, Austin could not predict when it could deliver its products, it had problems meeting schedules and budgets, and it was about to lose its competitive position in the marketplace.

LAD management formed a team to study the situation. That team's project led to a computer-integrated Operations Support System (OSS) in which all areas of LAD could communicate electronically. Major processes were exploded to lower detailed levels to discover, document, and review information needs. The results of the analysis were captured on a PC-based CASE tool. Analyses were developed for all functions within and interfacing with manufacturing. Transaction volumes were accumulated for data entry and output points; this information served as the foundation for subsequent analysis and design.

In the project team, the major responsibility for defining detailed system specifications, developing user manuals, and designing training programs was given to representatives from manufacturing, materials, and product assurance. The data processing representative was responsible for developing acceptance test procedures, writing the user manuals, providing data processing training, creating requirement specifications, and interfacing with vendors. The data input functional area provided general administrative support, as well as word processing, scheduling, and data entry services. Program controls personnel monitored the project activity and developed project reviews. Representatives from logistics, finance, engineering, human resources, and management controls met with the project team and provided timely inputs on system requirements. LAD could have shortened the process by using consultants; but the extra time taken was valuable, because the participants developed a common vision of their needs.

LAD developed its cost-benefit analysis from preliminary discussions with vendors, information system personnel, and consultants. The project team prepared a list of specifications, which included vendor tasks, an installation schedule estimate, and details on manufacturing and system interface requirements.

After visiting 15 other companies and examining approximately 30 software packages, LAD management selected hardware first, contrary to the suggestions of the professionals. Tandem hardware was currently used for factory floor data collection, and IBM hardware was used for the operations systems. The project team wanted to continue with the Tandem equipment for the factory floor, which narrowed the software selection process considerably. Any software had to interface with the Tandem and IBM hardware. The external systems provided inputs to LAD's new operating systems, and outputs of the OSS fed existing corporate external systems. LAD's interfacing requirements were developed after the team compared the financial systems function and data requirements with the manufacturing function and requirements.

LAD's team prepared selection criteria, evaluation criteria, and summary evaluation sheets for software packages to be evaluated by the selection committee. Considering the potential for biased decision making, LAD developed a complex blind scoring system, so no team member could be influenced by a vendor name.

The implementation procedure was scheduled to span 30 months. The features of the plan were as follows:

1. Installation of software—LAD planned to prepare detailed specifications for the software package immediately after the software contract was awarded, so LAD could determine how existing modules could be modified and pinpoint where new modules must be developed. At the same time, LAD information personnel created the necessary interfaces.

2. Pilot test—As pieces of the software system were delivered, the project team conducted a conference room pilot test. A list of all possible activities was generated and evaluated to see if any system modifications were needed.

3. Live pilot test—After the project team completed the conference room pilot, it conducted a hands-on pilot test on a small project in one work center. The team gathered factory floor data, performed tests, and evaluated the results to ascertain if any system modifications were necessary.

4. Initialization and loading of master files—Prior to cutting away from the old system entirely, the team initialized and loaded into the OSS the master files needed to check stop orders. The old and new systems then ran concurrently.

5. System (volume) test—After all master files and existing data were loaded, extensive tests were run employing large numbers of transactions to evaluate system performance under stress. Shop floor control, time and attendance, and material inventory control system results were studied in detail. Potential problems were alleviated before LAD converted to the new system.

6. Training—During system implementation and testing, training sessions were developed and conducted for all employees affected by the new system. Training included an overview of the entire package followed by in-depth, hands-on instruction, so that all personnel obtained explicit knowledge about the module with which they would be dealing and how the different modules were tied together.

7. Conversion (phase-in/cutover)—Alternative conversion plans were evaluated, from an abrupt cutover of the entire system to a phase-in of each module indi-

vidually. After the system was implemented, system responsibility was turned over to the operating staff.

The expertise of the project manager and commitment of the project team compensated for such early problems as incomplete software modules and differences in interpretation of requirements. Management involvement and good education and training for the duration of the project were major attributes to its success. About 500 people were trained on the system. All hardware and software vendors provided resources in the form of on-site support and development, which greatly enhanced the team's responsiveness to problems.

In addition, weekly status reports and meetings for active participants increased communication. Updates of the project plan were prompt, and monthly briefings and/or reports —including accomplishments and the schedule of upcoming meetings—for top executives helped raise crucial issues at the right time.

When the implementation process was completed on time and under budget, the system performed the functions as shown in Figure 13–17. The new system helped LAD in the following ways:

- Employees accessing information on computer terminals and preparing documentation electronically

- Government approvals to use electronic sign-off for payroll processing and payment

- Ability to meet delivery schedules 95% to 100% of the time, compared with an earlier 50% to 60% rate

- Cutting costs by 22% in manufacturing coordination and support area by not replacing attrition losses

- Increased productivity

Although significant time and resources must be devoted to satisfy corporate financial reporting requirements, the system provided management with more information, including cost data, than was available before. LAD's real-time integrated system provided opportunities for better operating controls. Anyone could check project or employee data any time during the process, and LAD could react immediately to any situation.

SOURCE: Adapted with permission from C. Kenneth Howery, Earl D. Bennett, and Sarah Reed, ''How Lockheed Implemented CIM,'' *Management Accounting,* December 1991, pp. 22–28.

Case Questions

1. Who comprised LAD's project team?

2. What constraints did LAD face in selecting a system?

3. What functions does the new CIM system perform?

4. Name the key steps in LAD's implementation of the new system.

5. How was CASE used in the development process?

6. In retrospect, was the implementation successful?

FIGURE 13–17 **Lockheed Missile & Space Company, Inc. Operations Support Systems**

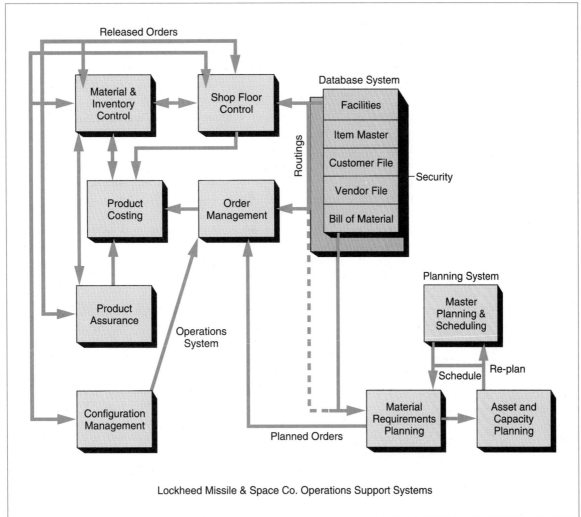

Lockheed Missile & Space Co. Operations Support Systems

Case 13–2
Capital Rental Car, Inc.

Capital Rental Car, Inc. is relatively new to the national rental car business. They are present in many of the busiest airports and vacation destinations. They have a fleet of 25,000 vehicles and must maintain a million rental rates on these vehicles. Cars may be rented in a tremendous number of ways. There are different prices, specials, and discounts for each model and for each location. Approximately a thousand of these rate variations change each day. This is a complex task for market analysts.

Analysts at Capital decided to build an expert system to help manage these rental rates. First, analysts outlined the various modules that described the various decision-making activities involved in determining various rates. These modules served as the basis for programming the expert system. Then they used a popular microcomputer systems shell to aid in the development of the programs. These programs were then embedded into the rate-management system that runs on the company's mainframe. The rate-management program interfaces with the customer information control data base system on the mainframe.

To develop the knowledge base for the expert system, Capital used an example-based system to determine how past rental rates were set. They used relevant information on the mainframe, such as purchase price, maintenance records, operating costs, frequency of use, location, and customer characteristics, to help develop the domain data base. It was decided to use a forward chaining inference engine. Because all users were familiar with the business, little attention was devoted to the user interface; simple rate tables were sufficient.

The programing went well. Rules were developed, and, with the aid of the expert shell, an expert system was quickly developed and tested. Testing was accomplished by comparing the rates determined by the system with those set by experts in the organization. The program worked amazingly well.

It was then embedded into the mainframe system and Capital converted to the new system after a two-month period of running the new expert system and the old manual system simultaneously. Very few problems were found during the parallel runs, and those that were discovered were quickly fixed.

After the system had run for several months, competitors became very aggressive and cut rates in certain areas to drive out the new competition. The focus of much of this aggressive activity was towards Capital Rental Car. However, the new system failed to help management respond to the competitors' predatory pricing strategy and Capital lost much of its hard earned market shares. Capital tried to modify its system to incorporate competitor activity, but it could not figure out the logical decision-making paths used by the expert system. It could not trace the logic so that it could be modified. After six months of this nightmare, Capital scrapped its new expert system because it could not deal with actions of competitors and reverted to manual systems based on MIS reports. They wished that they had opted for a decision support system rather than an expert system so that management could use it as a decision aide. It may have been easier to incorporate competitor information into a decision-supported system.

Case Questions   1. What software development techniques may have helped Capital avoid the lack of decision modules related to competitive actions?

2. What provision should have been included in the expert system that would have enabled programmers to trace the logic of the program in order to modify it to accommodate additional modules?

3. Should any additional testing have been done to prevent this type of problem? If so, describe the nature of such a test.

4. Was anything overlooked in terms of data requirements? What?

5. From the description above, what general design step appears to have been eliminated? Would the inclusion of this step have helped Capital develop a more appropriate system? Why?

Acquisition of Information Systems

C H A P T E R

14

Introduction   The objective of the information systems development process is to provide management with the information needed to operate an organization's day-to-day activities, manage an organization's various functions, set a strategic course for the organization, and report on operations. Having determined the requirements for such a system, management must either build its own system, as outlined in Chapters 13 and 15, or acquire a system from an outside vendor, as described in this chapter. This **make or buy decision** must be carefully analyzed.

In many situations, acquiring a software system is better than developing one using the organization's resources. In most cases, an organization acquires its hardware from external sources. Thus, management must understand what is involved in the acquisition of hardware and software. Like software development, software and hardware acquisition follows the systems development life cycle. Recall that this process begins with project definition, followed by a feasibility study, an analysis of the information needs, and design of the information system. In the design steps, a set of specifications is developed for a new or revised information system. These specifications provide the basis for a make (develop) or buy (acquire) decision. In Chapter 13, the specifications were used to develop application software that could input, process, and output the information specified by the detailed design. In this chapter, we consider the option of acquiring this software from outside vendors rather than writing the programs using organization personnel. Recall that this phase in the development life cycle was called the **implementation: acquisition and development** phase.

FIGURE 14–1

Hardware and Software Acquisition

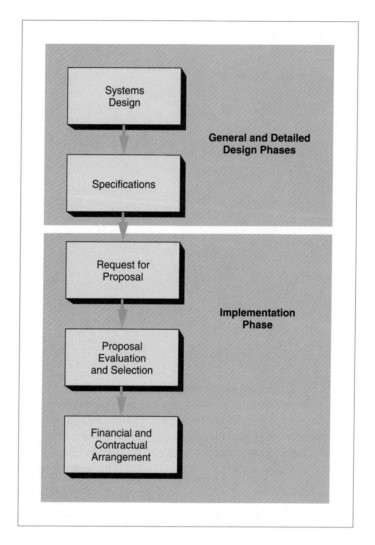

General and Detailed Design Phases

Systems Design

Specifications

Implementation Phase

Request for Proposal

Proposal Evaluation and Selection

Financial and Contractual Arrangement

Based on the specifications, a **request for proposal (RFP)** is prepared and sent to prospective vendors, whose responses are evaluated. Vendors are then selected based on the criteria that are important to the organization. Sometimes this involves a cost-benefit analysis and an analysis of financing alternatives.

Finally the system is implemented and maintained using the steps outlined in the previous chapter. In addition to discussing the acquisition steps in this chapter, we review the various types of hardware and software vendors and focus on the acquisition of a personal computer. The steps involved in the hardware and software acquisition process are shown in Figure 14–1.

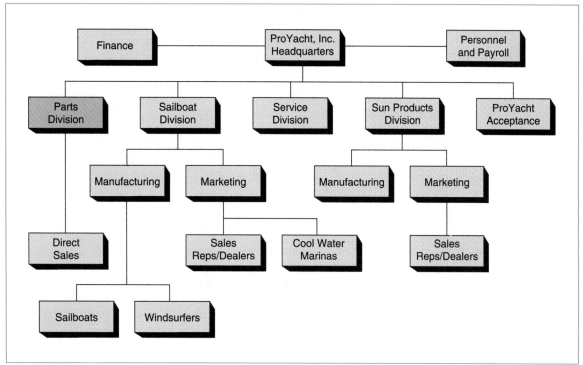

FIGURE 14-2　　*ProYacht, Inc. Parts Division and Organization Chart*

The basic acquisition process—determining needs and preparing specifications through the design process, sending out RFPs, and evaluating and selecting vendors—is the same for software and hardware. Ideally, software selection should precede the selection of hardware, because hardware specifications are contingent on the software selected, unless the organization already has hardware. In the latter case, software selection may be constrained by hardware.

The ProYacht, Inc. Parts Division

As an example of the hardware and software acquisition process, consider the ProYacht, Inc. parts division shown in Figure 14–2. This division purchases various types of boat and marine parts from manufacturers and resells them to its dealers and other marine retailers. This division currently uses a batch processing system on an old minicomputer that updates its inventory of approximately 500 items supplied by over 100 vendors. When ProYacht was primarily a sailboat manufacturing company, this system could handle transactions with approximately 100 dealers and marinas.

However, with ProYacht's acquisition of Cool Water Marinas (Chapter 10) and Sun Products Company (Chapter 12), the inventory system must now deal with over 1,000 items from approximately 200 vendors. The number of dealers and marinas could increase to over 200, and the number of transactions per day from the initiation of the order to the ultimate collection of cash is projected to grow to 1200.

Due to this increase in the size of the parts inventory system, ProYacht management decides to upgrade the information system to be more like the one used by the sailboat manufacturing division. To ensure that more information is available for managerial decision making, management requires an integrated system with less paperwork. Better inventory information would help sales representatives determine the items available, as well as assist ProYacht buyers in procurement activities.

As a first step in system acquisition, ProYacht management adopts a policy of allowing vendors to suggest appropriate software for the inventory system and a hardware configuration to run the selected software. This system should require either a small minicomputer with terminals or a Local Area Network (LAN) composed of personal computers with a high-speed personal computer as the file server. Moreover, management wants software that is flexible enough to run on PC-based Disk Operating Systems (DOS), UNIX operating systems, or leading minicomputer operating systems to enable growth without a change of software.

14.1 The Make or Buy Decision

As described earlier, an information system takes data from a variety of sources, then stores and processes these data into useful information for operational control, reporting needs, and decision-making models. Management can use software developed by the organization or it can acquire software. In other words, management must decide whether to make or to buy the software components of the information system. Because few companies have the capability to develop their own hardware, we consider only the software development decision.

Various criteria can be used in making the decision to develop (make) or to acquire (buy) software. One such criterion is the net present value of the cash flows associated with the development of software compared with the acquisition of software. **Net present value** is an economic concept used to discount cash flows (in and out) to current dollars so that economic comparisons can be made. An application of the use of net present value to the development of ProYacht's inventory accounting software system is shown in Figure 14-3.

In Figure 14-3, the net present value of the costs associated with developing and operating a software system are significantly higher than those associated with buying and operating a similar system. A large portion of these higher costs are associated with developing and testing software rather than buying software. For purchased software packages, the cost of designing and programming is spread out among all users of a software package rather being borne by a single user.

Advantages of Purchasing Software

In addition to economic reasons for purchasing rather than developing software, other advantages to purchasing packaged software are as follows:

1. Errors in the software have already been corrected (hopefully) by the software company.

2. The time between purchasing a software package and using it is much shorter than the time between the decision to write a program and having it ready to use.

FIGURE 14–3

**Costs Associated
with a Make or
Buy Decision**

	Make	Buy
Development/Acquisition Costs		
Develop Specifications	$ 2,000	$2,000
Prepare RFP		500
Evaluate Proposals		1,000
Contractual and Financial Arrangements		200
Software Price		6,200
Develop Programs	10,000	
Test Programs	2,000	500
Implementation	3,000	2,000
Total Development/Acquisition Cost	$17,000	$12,400
Annual Operating Costs and Maintenance	2,000	200
Net Present Value for 5 Years Interest at 10%	$24,582	$13,158

3. Cost is usually a known factor with a purchased package, but costs can often escalate when a program is being written.

4. Software companies often provide technical support to users and also upgrade the software for current users at a reduced cost.

*Disadvantages
of Purchasing
Software*

Several disadvantages to purchasing software may lead to a decision to develop software even though that development takes longer and probably costs more. These disadvantages include the following:

1. A mismatch may exist between the software attributes and user information needs. Necessary information may not be available in the format or at the time needed for the business, or far too much information may be available for managers to use, for employees to input, or for the company to maintain in a data base.

2. The vendor may discontinue the particular package or even go out of business.

3. Because the development expertise is outside the organization, maintaining or modifying the software may be difficult.

Once the advantages and disadvantages of buying or developing software are thoroughly considered, management must then undertake the make or buy decision. Often, an organization may seek the assistance of systems analysis and design experts in this difficult decision.

Hints for Acquiring Data Base Software

As discussed in Chapters 5 and 6, virtually every organization needs data base management software. Users should carefully consider the following hints on acquiring this software:

- Know how data base management software differs from other types of software.

- Understand the differences between flat file and relational data bases and the best applications for each type of data base system.

- Define the needed data base applications and their scope.

- Identify all required data elements, regardless of whether they are input directly or derived from other fields.

- Identify all data, record, and file-manipulation functions required.

- Identify all physical data base requirements, including the number of record-selection rules and sort parameters.

SOURCE: Nancy S. Mueller, "Teaching Users to Assess Their Software Needs," *PC Week,* July 22, 1991, p. 69.

14.2 Acquisition Options and Vendors

Today, a large number of options are available to an organization that seeks to acquire either hardware or software. Matching these options to the requirements of the organization is not an easy task. This process must be performed methodically using the steps outlined in Figure 14–1, with the selection of software preceding that of hardware. The acquisition market can be divided into hardware, software, and services.

Hardware includes all the mainframe, minicomputer, personal computer, storage, communication, input, and output equipment noted throughout this text. Mainframe and minicomputer hardware vendors include such manufacturers as International Business Machines Corporation (IBM), Amdahl, Bull, Digital Equipment Corporation (DEC), Cray Research, Sun, Unisys, Fujitsu Ltd., NEC Corporation, Siemens AG, and National Cash Register (NCR). Some companies specialize in certain market segments, for example, NCR in retailing, Cray in science, and DEC and Sun in minicomputers. Most of these companies also sell Data Base Management Systems (DBMS), operating systems, and application software that run on their hardware.

The PC hardware market is dominated by firms such as IBM, Apple, Compaq, Dell, and Tandy. Because personal computers can be assembled with readily available components, many small manufacturers have captured a reasonable share of mail order markets. Most hardware companies also sell software for their hardware.

Many other companies supply the software that runs on the hardware sold by previously mentioned firms. For example, some firms specialize in business software for mainframes, and others specialize in data base products for mainframes. Companies like Microsoft, Apple, Lotus, WordPerfect Corporation, Borland, and Novell specialize in PC applications software. Many very small vendors offer useful products for certain seg-

Who Needs a Minicomputer?

Dudley Cook, president of the systems consulting firm Executive Insight Group, suggests that most minicomputer buyers fall into one of the following five categories:

- Small firms in which a minicomputer is the only system in use

- Departments of large firms that use a single minicomputer as a general department processor; this minicomputer is also part of a distributed data processing system

- Companies that use a minicomputer as a specialized processor for a particular application, for example, a data base processor; again, this minicomputer is usually part of a distributed data processing system

- Companies that move from a mainframe to a minicomputer environment, often using one or more minicomputers with a PC-based LAN

- Companies that use the minicomputer as a specialized file server for a LAN

SOURCE: Alan Radding, ''Minicomputers: For Each Buyer, a Different Perspective,'' *Computerworld,* September 24, 1990, pp. 75–76.

ments of the hardware or software market. Some large corporations such as Boeing Aerospace also sell the products developed by their own Management Information System (MIS) staffs, thus spreading development costs over a larger user base.

Value-Added Vendors and Original Equipment Manufacturers

Instead of acquiring hardware from one vendor and perhaps software from another, or writing its own software, a firm may wish to acquire a ready-to-operate system from a single vendor. With such **turn-key systems,** the user simply ''turns the key'' to implement the system. Vendors may secure software and hardware from several other vendors and assemble the components into a specialized system for a particular industry need, such as an office management system for attorneys. These **value-added vendors** add value to a system beyond that of the original suppliers by combining the various hardware and software components into a useful combination.

Alternatives for Systems Development and Acquisition

In addition to the make or buy decision, an organization can look at other alternatives. Basically three such alternatives are available—timesharing, service bureaus, and outsourcing. In the first case, processing time is rented on someone else's computer system, and in the second case, another organization is paid to process the data. In the last case, an organization may contract for someone else to operate its system.

Timesharing **Timesharing** provides access to mainframe hardware via terminals located at the user's place of business and offers the user the power of a mainframe computer for file storage and problem solving at a fraction of the cost associated with renting, leasing, or purchasing equipment. These services are usually provided by such large organizations as universities and financial institutions that have time to sell on their fast mainframe systems. Users are often small organizations that need mainframe power to do large, complex analyses, yet cannot afford to purchase and operate a mainframe.

The mainframe hardware and software in timesharing systems must be capable of processing many programs at one time so that many users can operate the system concurrently with little or no degradation in processing time. Users simply purchase time and run their programs in a multiprocessing environment as if each is the sole user of the system.

The advantages of timesharing systems include the following:

1. Users have immediate access to tremendous computing power at a fraction of what it would cost to own and operate similar equipment.

2. The multiprocessing or multiprogramming environment gives the user the appearance of being the sole user of the system.

3. Each user's files are stored online for immediate access, which is restricted via user passwords.

4. Users can access private applications as well as packages provided by the timesharing vendor.

The disadvantages of timesharing are as follows:

1. The potential exists for loss of key data and programs that reside in another organization's computer system. In other words, the control of a firm's data assets can be questionable.

2. The cost of communicating large amounts of data in an online mode with a timesharing system is high compared with batch-oriented service bureaus. Timesharing is simply not designed to process large amounts of data due to the limited input, communication, and output capabilities.

In general, timesharing is cost effective for complex problem-solving analyses that require little input and output but a great deal of computing time. A company that might consider the use of timesharing is an aerospace subcontractor that needs tremendous computing power to solve complex problems yet does not have the resources for its own computer.

Service Bureaus   An organization that has large amounts of data to be processed but does not have its own processing capabilities may use a service bureau. A **service bureau** specializes in providing data processing capabilities to its customers. Like timesharing, this processing occurs at the vendor's site and not at the user's place of business. However, with service bureaus, the processing is done in batches. These batches may be submitted in handwritten form for keying into the computer, or they may be submitted in an electronic or machine readable form, such as documents that can be optically scanned.

Service bureaus are primarily used by small businesses that do not have the resources to invest in and operate an information processing system. Service bureaus usually develop or purchase one or more batch processing packages and spread the cost of the development or purchase over a large number of users. The service bureau prescribes the form of user input and the reports that are available from the data.

The advantages to the user of service bureaus include the following:

1. Little or no investment in information processing equipment and personnel is needed.

2. A minimum commitment to a processing environment is required.

3. A service bureau is a low-cost alternative to having a full-scale information system.

4. Through a service bureau, an organization that did not use computers may begin to move toward computerization.

The disadvantages are as follows:

1. The organization loses control of its data.

2. Little or no control over cost increases exists.

3. Because of the lack of flexibility in input, processing, and output form, the service bureau cannot tailor the system to a user's particular needs.

In general, service bureaus are excellent for standardized batch processing jobs in which the user does not want to invest in a computerized information system. Some examples of jobs suited to a service bureau are payroll systems for small companies, billing systems for small medical practices, and tax preparation programs for small Certified Public Accountant (CPA) firms.

Outsourcing   For companies with very little information processing experience whose processing needs cannot be handled via timesharing or a service bureau, the third option is outsourcing. With **outsourcing,** a company contracts with an outside organization to staff, manage, and operate its entire information system. The disadvantage to this approach is that a third party controls and operates one of the company's key resources — its information.

14.3 Hardware and Software Acquisition

As indicated in Figure 14–1, basic information specifications or requirements need to be developed first in the systems development process. These specifications are derived from the design stages in which several alternatives are outlined and the most appropriate one is selected for development or acquisition. The specifications or requirements may also evolve from an iterative prototype analysis. Based on these specifications, an RFP is prepared and sent to prospective vendors. RFPs should be sent to software vendors first,

When to Lease Hardware

When the Internal Revenue Service (IRS) automated its auditing operations, it decided to equip its agents with Zenith laptop personal computers. However, rather than buying the 18,000 machines it would need, the IRS chose to lease them. In so doing, the IRS could have the equipment it needed immediately without up-front capital investment and without fear of being "stuck" a few years down the road with out-of-date equipment.

Leasing personal computers provides the following advantages:

- The use of state-of-the-art machines without incurring debt

- A hedge against obsolescence

- Favorable treatment under federal tax laws.

Leasing can be favorable for companies that:

- Plan to upgrade to newer personal computers frequently

- Cannot or do not want to dispose of older personal computers

- Earn more on their money by investing in the business rather than in personal computers

A key to the best leasing deal for a company is close attention to lease negotiations. A small business may have to accept the leasing terms as offered, but larger firms that lease thousands of personal computers can negotiate on price as well as on maintenance. A good leasing contract should specify that the equipment will work when it arrives, who will fix it if it does not work, and that the customer will have sufficient time to test the equipment. The company should also demand that the equipment leasing and financing agreement be linked in a single contract, so that if the equipment fails, the financing agreement is also nullified.

SOURCE: Robert L. Scheier, "PC Leasing Can Be Cost-Effective," *PC Week*, July 17, 1989, p. 85.

because the software actually provides the user with needed information, and a specific software package may not run on all hardware. After software is selected or developed, hardware requirements are specified, and if new hardware is required, RFPs are sent to hardware vendors. It can be disastrous to select hardware first and then discover it cannot support the best software for the project. Vendors' responses to hardware RFPs are evaluated based on the criteria that are important to the organization. If the organization already has appropriate hardware, then the software selection is constrained by the organization's hardware. This process is shown in Figure 14–4.

The discussion that follows focuses on the RFPs and the selection of software. Essentially the same procedure is used for the selection of hardware after the software is selected. Some examples of hardware selection are illustrated as the acquisition sequence is discussed.

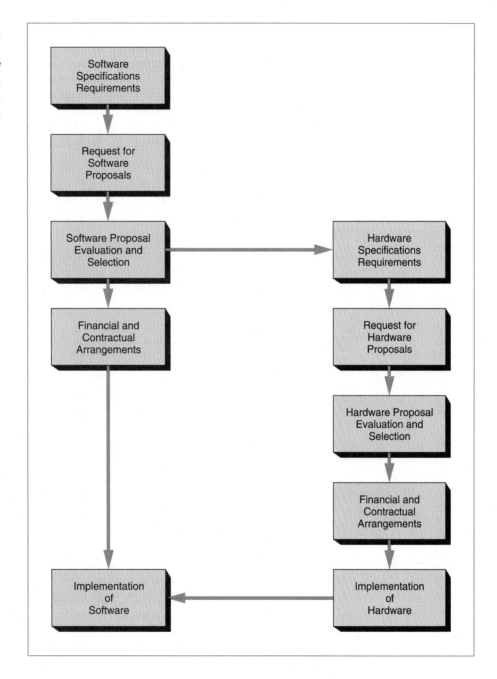

FIGURE 14–4

Hardware and Software Acquisition Sequence

Specification of Information System Requirements

The first step in system acquisition requires that **information system requirements** be specified. The structured approach to systems development assumes that the client or organization has sufficient expertise to propose specific software characteristics to vendors and to request bids from these vendors. This assumption may not be correct, depending on the expertise of the project team or management who develop the specifications and on the nature of the system that is developed. If the software has already been selected, requirements are stated in terms of the hardware configurations needed to run the software.

Vendors can be approached in several ways at different points in the systems development and implementation sequence. In one scenario, the organization requests vendors to supply proposals that satisfy the company's specific systems design. Detailed bids can be made for the computer, software, and telecommunication resources required for the system.

Advice from prospective vendors may be helpful if a firm does not have a great deal of technical expertise. A company with little in-house expertise and no access to the expertise of a consultant may choose to work closely with one vendor from the outset of the general design process.

If management does not know what technology is available or if user needs are ill defined, then system requirements may not be specified for vendors in detail. In this case, system performance objectives and constraints may be outlined for vendors, who have considerable experience, to offer suggestions about the system. This scenario may be started earlier in the general design stage, following the completion of the systems requirements. Performance objectives should be accompanied by all data flow diagrams and other analysis detail to aid vendors in proposing a solution to the problem. Likewise, after software is selected, vendors can suggest the equipment configuration that runs the software most effectively and efficiently for the organization's particular environment.

Request for Proposal

Objectives and specifications are formulated into a formal RFP, which communicates the objectives and constraints of the system. A detailed RFP specifies the exact characteristics of the software needed by management. With a detailed set of specifications, each vendor bids on exactly the same basis, and an evaluation is more easily accomplished. On the other hand, with a more flexible approach, the user can learn from the vendor's proposals and use the vendor's expertise in solving similar problems. For example, a small bank may need to interface with an Electronic Data Interchange (EDI) system, yet not know what is involved. So the bank can only express its objectives with expected operating activities at expected volumes.

A typical RFP includes the following specifications that proposals are expected to meet or exceed:

1. A complete description of the project, including all available documentation such as data flow diagrams and system flowcharts of the alternative selected; a description of user interfaces and financial constraints

2. Performance objectives, such as number of transactions that can be entered, data access speed, processing speed, reliability, and the maximum number of system users at one time; organizational and behavioral constraints, such as the need to distribute data and system ease of use

3. Required data and software backup systems at the user's place of business and at a remote location, in case some disaster strikes the user

4. Vendor service requirements, such as a hot line for software problems and 24-hour equipment replacement

5. Any technical specifications related to hardware, such as storage capacity of disks, modem speed, or the type of personal computers to be used as workstations; these specifications include compatibility with existing and planned systems, as well as requirements for software or hardware demonstrations

6. The expected criteria for comparing proposals, including benchmark and proposed simulation tests

7. Implementation plans, including delivery, installation, and system conversion dates

8. Policy constraints based on a user's strategic information plan, such as a preference for a specific operating system or the need to operate in a particular data base environment or to interface with other systems

These specifications should indicate what is absolutely essential for a proposed system and what is desirable over and above the essential set of specifications. Remember that specifications apply to software first; only after software is selected do they apply to the acquisition of hardware.

Potential vendors should be prescreened if possible to determine those most likely to meet the specifications. For large systems, the vendor list tends to be short; for PC-based accounting systems, the list can be enormous. The RFP should be sent only to viable vendors, with a required proposal return date. For large, well-defined systems, RFPs are usually submitted to a variety of vendors to generate competitive bids. However, for small systems in an organization that does not have much computer expertise, the organization may prefer to deal with one vendor for software and hardware components. This is especially true for value-added systems designed for specific applications. The RFP for ProYacht's parts inventory system is shown in Figure 14–5.

Evaluation of Proposals

All vendors' proposals meeting the essential systems requirements should be evaluated. This evaluation of the proposals should be based on the organization's strategic and master plans for information systems. Only if the proposal agrees with the strategic and master plans for information systems is it considered in terms of other criteria.

If a proposal fits the company's information plans, then various key aspects of the proposal are examined. Proposal evaluation methods include priority weighting,

FIGURE 14–5

*Request for
Proposal for
ProYacht, Inc.
Parts Inventory
System Software*

Description of System Requirements
1. Systems flowchart of general system requirements attached
2. Expected volume of activity
   a. Inventory items   1,000
   b. Vendors   200
   c. Orders per day   120
   d. Number of customers   500
   e. General ledger items   4,600
   f. Number of salespersons communicating with data base   100
   g. Number of reporting workstations   10
3. All applications must be integrated
4. All data must be online for instantaneous access
5. Must be able to double the volume in five years
6. Expandability to 200 salespersons in five years
7. Easy access to accounting, inventory, and customer data
8. Flexible reporting formats
9. Capability of handling 10 concurrent transactions
10. Compatability with current MS-DOS hardware
11. Easy for nonaccounting marketing and sales personnel to use
12. On-site training of personnel
13. Local back-up software site
14. 24-hour vendor hot-line service
15. Reasonable upgrade policy
16. Approximate budget   6,200
17. Multiuser network capabilities
18. Selection criteria
    a. Cost
    b. Service and maintenance arrangements
    c. Vendor reputation and financial viability
    d. Software features
    e. Ease of use
    f. Initial and continued training
    g. Upgrade policy
    h. Network capabilities
    i. RAM and secondary storage requirements
    j. Clarity of user documentation
    k. Test results
    l. Size of installed user base
    m. Size and quality of development staff
    n. References from current users
    o. Assistance in installation and conversion
    p. Demonstration of ability to handle expected work load
    q. Reliability and error statistics
    r. Multiuser capability and degradation
    s. Backup and recovery features
    t. Compatibility and transferability of data with other systems
19. Proposals due 1/31/93
20. Implementation to begin 3/30/93

performance benchmarks, or simulation of the proposed system. Like any decision involving multiple criteria, no clear-cut winner of these comparisons is usually obvious, and many tradeoffs must be made.

Priority Weighting Method   A common set of criteria must be used for a weighted comparison of software or hardware. These criteria may be broken down into software, hardware, and general criteria.

From a software perspective, the criteria often include the following:

1. Compliance with specifications

2. Compatibility with existing software programs

3. Software support and update policies

4. Utility and file management features

5. Operating system and data base environment

Hardware selection criteria often include:

1. Capability to run selected software

2. Computer processing speed and number of terminals or personal computers that can be supported

3. Access speed and storage capacity

4. Compatibility with other manufacturer's hardware

5. Modularity to enable the addition of components and peripheral support

6. Reliability statistics on down time

Even the compatibility of mainframes is important, because information processing environments are often integrated. Mainframes must work well with data bases, input/output devices, storage devices, and software.

In addition to these specific criteria for software and hardware, some general criteria apply to both hardware and software, including the following:

1. Financial arrangements, including price, lease, or rent payments and maintenance contracts

2. Vendor support with technical assistance and training

3. Implementation support

4. Testing and conversion support

5. Documentation, flowcharts, and operation manuals

6. Reputation of vendor

FIGURE 14–6

Weighted Comparison of Software Vendor Proposals

Selection Criteria	Priority Weight	Scores		
		Vendor A	Ideal World	Vendor C
a. Cost	10	9	7	6
b. Service and maintenance arrangements	5	3	6	5
c. Vendor reputation and financial viability	5	2	10	8
d. Software features	10	8	9	7
e. Ease of use	8	10	9	4
f. Initial and continued training	5	2	10	4
g. Upgrade policy	3	7	8	3
h. Network capabilities	10	7	10	4
i. RAM and secondary storage requirements	7	6	4	8
j. Clarity of user documentation	5	8	9	3
k. Test results	8	9	9	8
l. Size of installed user base	3	2	10	8
m. Size and quality of development staff	3	6	8	3
n. References from current users	7	1	8	6
o. Assistance in installation and conversion	3	8	4	3
p. Demonstration of ability to handle expected work load	8	5	9	6
q. Reliability and error statistics	3	9	9	10
r. Multiuser capability and degradation	7	4	9	3
s. Backup and recovery features	4	3	2	5
t. Compatibility and transferability of data with other systems	3	6	4	8
Total Score		710	935	658

Some key items to consider in assessing the reputation of a vendor include its installed base, size of its major customers, financial viability, and references of current users. A site visit is most desirable to see the software in use firsthand.

For example, consider the RFP shown in Figure 14–5 for a new multiuser accounting and inventory system for ProYacht's parts division management. The RFP was sent to accounting software vendors, and ProYacht received three proposals. A weighted comparison of these three proposals is shown in Figure 14–6. The weight 1–10 attached to each criterion is multiplied by the score each package receives for each criterion and then summed over all the criteria to arrive at a composite score for each software package.

The analysis in Figure 14–6 shows that World accounting network software is preferable to the others. ProYacht then uses the characteristics of this software as well as the general operating characteristics presented earlier in the RFP for software to generate an RFP for several hardware vendors. They receive four responses from hardware vendors for the following configurations, each of which meets the hardware requirements listed in the RFP, including running a 10-workstation network with the selected software.[1]

---

[1] SOURCE: Adapted from Thé, Lee, "Can LANs Beat Minis?" *PC Magazine,* May 29, 1990, pp. 195–222.

1. A LAN with an i486 IBM compatible file server running an MS-DOS compatible network operating system

2. A LAN with an i486 IBM compatible server running the UNIX operating system

3. A LAN with an IBM PS/2 Model 95 file server running an MS-DOS compatible network operating system

4. A minicomputer equipped with terminals

Each proposal runs World accounting software. Based on a weighting scheme similar to that used for the selection of software, the PS/2-based LAN is a slight favorite. ProYacht management decides to run the software on each system to see which system works the best.

Benchmark Tests   One of the best ways to evaluate software or hardware is to test it using programs and data typical of the actual conditions under which the proposed system will operate. In a **benchmark test,** problems and sets of transactions can be run on the vendor's proposed systems configuration to test the entire system for the handling of transaction volume and anticipated problems. For example, in a transaction intensive situation with a tremendous amount of online input and output, access time is a significant benchmark for comparing disk storage configurations. On the other hand, in a decision support modeling situation that involves the solution of numerous optimization problems with hundreds of constraints, computer processing time is important. These comparisons are not always sufficient, because they do not represent a real business environment in which the throughput, mix, and volume of transactions are more important than just speed.

As an example, in an attempt to approximate the operating environment of the new parts accounting system, ProYacht, Inc. uses benchmark tests to determine the best hardware system from among the four proposed. Recall that ProYacht has already selected World accounting and inventory software. To simulate operating conditions, management proposes a benchmark test using 10 workstations at which orders for parts are entered one at a time and then concurrently. Special software is used to enter these data automatically, enabling each workstation to approximate 10 actual users for a total of 100 simulated users. This test is designed to simulate 100 salespersons, each entering 12 orders of 5 lines each into the system. The current information system commonly has 10 requests at one time for information on parts. For testing sequential and concurrent reporting, 10 reports are requested from 10 workstations. Mixed processing is also simulated combining both data entry and reporting at each workstation. Finally, the World accounting system is tested for the type of activity typical for such a parts inventory system. A comparison of these benchmark tests for the four hardware configurations shows that the minicomputer system degrades between 50 and 70 users when they are added incrementally. Overall, the IBM PS/2 LAN is the clear performance winner of this benchmark test.

Performance alone is not enough to make a clear decision, because price must also be considered. In the final analysis, given the most promising benchmark test results, a

Con Ed Saves Money by Upgrading

Rather than replace its nearly 500 out-of-date personal computers, Consolidated Edison opted to replace the motherboard on each computer, retaining the existing video system, monitor, and disk drives. An upgrade to new personal computers would have cost Con Ed an average of $4,000 for each new Intel 80386-based computer with high-density drives and a high-resolution color monitor. Replacing only the motherboard—the electronic circuit board that contains the Central Processing Unit (CPU), internal memory, and related circuitry—cost $900 per machine. The new motherboards, containing 386 CPU chips, 4 Mbytes of Random Access Memory (RAM), and new power supplies, provided Con Ed with increased computing power and allowed the company to keep its existing hard disks—often packed with important corporate data. This decision saved Con Ed almost $1,500,000 over acquiring new computers.

SOURCE: Robert L. Scheier, ''Motherboard Upgrades Save Con Ed Money,'' *PC Week*, May 14, 1990, pp. 139–40.

reasonable price performance ratio, the importance of equipment compatibility, and the need to run other software at individual workstations, the PS/2 LAN is selected to run the World accounting software.

Simulation   Using another computer system, a **simulation model** can be constructed from the input, processing, and output characteristics of the hardware; the access speed of the data base hardware and software; the number and characteristics of input/output devices; the frequency distributions of typical workloads; and the unique characteristics of the workloads. Simulation need not be done on the equipment being tested; only the ability to model the proposed system's computing environment and user demands is necessary. In general, simulation may be used to predict response time, transaction processing time, and turnaround time for an online system.

Financial Arrangements

The organization must now determine whether to buy, lease, or rent the equipment or the software and how to finance this decision. First, the organization must assess its needs with respect to current hardware and software, expected future requirements due to changing business conditions, current expertise in information systems, and rate of technology change. Consideration must also be given to such hardware and software variables as the ability to upgrade equipment, expected value of the equipment at the end of the rental or payment period, risk of obsolescence, life of hardware and software relative to the company's needs, nature of lease and rental contracts (such as the cancelability of leases and maintenance provided), and cost. A capital budgeting approach to this decision using net present value may be used to assess cash flows for hardware, software, maintenance, installation, training, conversion, implementation, programming, testing, personnel, and the overall development and implementation process.

Some general guidelines are helpful when determining financial arrangements for system acquisition. Purchase arrangements are superior if equipment is kept for several years, the company's business environment remains relatively stable in the foreseeable future, or an upgrade path exists. Cancelable leases, on the other hand, can accommodate changes in business conditions and technology. Often, purchase clauses are included at the end of the lease period to enable a company to purchase the leased system. Cash outflows may be higher for leasing than for a purchase, because the lessee assumes the risk of obsolescence and often maintains the equipment. The most flexible arrangement is a short-term rental. However, this situation results in the highest cash outflow and may be unsatisfactory if the equipment and software used change frequently. Users in a constant state of flux cannot reap the benefits of a stable information system. Another alternative is to rent, lease, and purchase various components based on their expected life and flexibility attributes.

Cost-Benefit Analysis

Financial arrangements must be incorporated into a revised **cost-benefit analysis.** Recall that an initial cost-benefit analysis is made during the feasibility study at the beginning of systems development. Now, better estimates of the costs and benefits of the new system must be developed, including costs for the hardware, software, development, training, support, data, and communication. Initial system costs are only the beginning; operating costs can also be substantial. Figure 14–7 shows a cost-benefit analysis of financial options for the PS/2-based LAN selected by ProYacht, Inc. The purchase option has the greatest net present value, which is the discounted cash flow (benefits less costs) less the initial investment in hardware, software, and implementation.

In this analysis, the purchase of a PS/2 LAN is clearly superior to the leasing option. Although the leasing option is more flexible because upgrading the system is easier, ProYacht still opts to purchase the LAN because that option costs less and the company does not foresee changing its system in the near future. Also, management wants to acquire a good system and use it for several years before considering any change that could be disruptive to daily business activities.

When an organization decides what system it wants to purchase or lease, the company should secure a good **vendor contract.** This contract should include the following items:

1. The name and description of the hardware or software

2. Terms related to the cost, rental, or lease agreements

3. Continuing expectations regarding training, updates, maintenance arrangements, and technical support for the hardware or software

4. Delivery dates, testing arrangements, and implementation schedule, if applicable

5. Performance expectations, such as throughput volume and storage capacity

6. Provisions for any breach of contract

7. License arrangements for multiple users, such as in the ProYacht situation

FIGURE 14–7

**Revised Cost-
Benefit Analysis**

Ten-Workstation Network		
	Purchase	Lease Hardware
Hardware and Software Costs		
Hardware*	$56,000	
Software	6,200	$ 6,200
Network Operating	5,000	
Implementation Costs		
Installation	2,000	2,000
Testing	1,000	1,000
Training	1,000	1,000
Data Conversion	1,000	1,000
Total Installation Price	$72,200	$11,200
Annual Operating Expenses		
Hardware	$ 800	$20,000
Software	400	400
Development and Training	1,000	1,000
Support	1,000	500
Data	500	500
Communication	2,000	2,000
Total Annual Operating Expenses	$ 5,700	$24,400
Estimated Annual Benefits**	$28,000	$28,000
Annual Benefits − Annual Operating Expenses	$22,300	$ 3,600
Net Present Value Interest Rate at 10%	$12,335	$ 2,447

* PS/2 Model 95/486 Server and PC Terminals
  MSA repeat box per five servers and wiring

** Added contribution of increased parts sales and reduction in carrying costs of inventory

This contract should be clear and allow no misunderstandings between the parties at a future date. The objective is a good working relationship between the user and the vendor and not an adversarial relationship. The organization should include in the contract everything that could possibly go wrong. For example, should the equipment be delivered late, the organization would be late in implementing the new system and therefore may need to use a timesharing service for another year. An agreed-upon penalty should be established in the contract for this late delivery. An organization may want to obtain legal advise from an attorney specializing in information technology purchase or leasing arrangements. The contract for the software or hardware purchased or leased should be approved by management or the steering committee.

Implementation

Following the selection of software and hardware vendors and the consummation of the financial and contractual arrangements, implementation should commence. **Implementation** is the process of installing hardware and software, testing each component, testing the entire system, and converting the current system to the new system. Details regarding each step are discussed in Chapter 13. Operating procedures should be planned, and arrangements should be made with the vendor and within the organization for staff training. If new employees are required, well-qualified personnel should be selected.

The site should be prepared for new hardware, if necessary. On completion of new facilities, hardware can be installed and tested to ensure that all maintenance, operating, utility, and other routines provided by the vendor are functioning as specified. After hardware is tested, software can be tested to ensure that it runs on the hardware.

Finally, the entire system (software and hardware) should be tested prior to conversion. **Conversion** is the process of changing from the old to the new system. As discussed in Chapter 13, great care should be taken in converting data to the new system. For example, ProYacht does not want to delete or misclassify some inventory during the conversion of its inventory data to its new system.

A suitable conversion procedure must be determined. To convert directly would entail great risk, because the new system might not work when the sales and inventory personnel begin to use it. A pilot approach is not feasible, because the installation is company-wide and therefore not amenable to an approach that installs the system in only one division at a time. Thus, ProYacht decides to run the old and new systems in parallel for several months and reconcile any differences before converting completely to the new system.

14.4 Acquiring Personal Computer Systems

Since the early 1980s and the introduction of the original IBM PC, acquiring a personal computer and its associated software has become a subject of great interest. More individuals are deciding to obtain a computer for the office, business, or home. In this text, we concentrate on the acquisition of a personal computer for individual productivity needs at the office. Companies are finding that personal computers can save money and increase profits, and individuals are discovering that they can increase their personal productivity. The prospective user must research many makes and models of personal computers and types of business and personal productivity software. To complicate things, personal computers are not equally effective in handling different tasks. For example, one machine might be great for graphics and desktop publishing software, but not have the speed or memory to handle business-related tasks like data base analysis or financial modeling using large spreadsheets. Thus, the most important criteria in the selection of a computer and associated software are the individual's personal productivity needs. For example, a marketing manager for ProYacht may need a personal computer that can communicate with the company's marketing, distribution, and inventory data base and download key information for decision making.

The decision to acquire a personal computer should follow the same basic development phases outlined in Chapters 12 and 13, as well as the suggestions for the acquisition of hardware set forth in this chapter. However, for this individual decision, the steps can be expedited and can be less formal. Organizations may have an information center or consultants to aid individuals with this decision, but otherwise, an individual has very little assistance.

Because of the importance of this topic, we present a helpful guide to prospective PC hardware and software users. This guide is also a practical application of the structured acquisition approach outlined earlier in this chapter. Each individual's needs are unique, and the computer that suits one person may not work for another, and vice versa. For that reason, suggesting the acquisition of a particular brand of computer over another is not a sound approach. Instead, we suggest a five-step process that follows the acquisition sequence presented in Figure 14–4. The system selected depends on the results of this procedure.

The following five steps can be used for acquiring a PC system:

1. Define the information and personal productivity needs that the personal computer should meet.

2. Determine which software package meets these needs.

3. Determine which hardware systems support the software selected in Step 2.

4. Find vendors that can provide the hardware and software selected in previous steps.

5. Acquire the software and hardware system.

The user should already have learned what computers can and cannot do. The user should also have some idea of the computer's current and future tasks. Tasks may include financial analysis, correspondence or paper writing, data base management, small business management, or special applications programming. Because of the variety of software available today, determining the software that satisfies user needs requires much time and research. After the software that meets user needs is selected, the choice of computers is narrowed, because all computers do not run all software. The vendors that carry compatible software and hardware can also be selected.

Because individuals often find additional uses for personal computers requiring more hardware devices and software, expandability and flexibility are very important considerations in the final decision. Moreover, software vendors constantly upgrade their product lines, including more features to enhance user productivity. For example, a buyer who plans to use the computer for financial analysis may add a data base management package or a laser printer to the system at a later date. By planning ahead, the individual acquiring the computer avoids being locked out of the future.

Define
Information
and Personal
Productivity
Needs

This first step is analogous to the problem definition, feasibility study, and analysis of information requirements for systems development presented in Chapter 12. Too many times, a computer is acquired without a clear definition of user needs. The computer may be acquired because such a purchase is trendy rather than for its use as a business tool. Because the personal computer is a tool, its use must be defined before the prospective user investigates the personal computer market. Needs should be ranked to help the buyer determine the most appropriate computer to buy. Otherwise, acquired software may not actually meet the user's needs, or the computer may be too slow or have insufficient disk capacity or graphics capability.

Tradeoffs may make the decision more complicated. For example, easy-to-use software may be desirable, but it may not be sophisticated enough to handle a complex financial model. On the other hand, a sophisticated accounting package may be desirable for the information generated, but it may be too difficult for the company's staff to use.

Determine
Software
that Meets
Requirements

The next step is to look for software that meets the requirements defined in the previous step. The software should be selected first, because the software actually provides the user with the information he or she needs. The software also defines the hardware requirements. A user courts disaster by acquiring hardware first and then trying to find software. For example, a small building contractor acquires a used brand X computer, only to find that the memory intensive construction scheduling and Computer-Aided Design (CAD) software does not run because the computer's memory cannot be expanded sufficiently.

In software selection, user needs and level of computer experience should be matched with the software. Simply buying the most popular package on the market is not always appropriate. For example, a well-known accounting package may require the input of 10 data fields per sales transaction and print out 10 different sales analysis reports. However, if the business needs only a simple cash receipts and disbursements program, then this package may be more than is needed.

An individual can select software in several ways, including reading articles or reviews about the software, visiting a computer store, and actually trying out the software. Occasionally, a computer magazine reviews an entire class of software, comparing the available packages feature-by-feature and offering benchmark comparisons that may be helpful to the prospective user.

Visiting a computer store can be helpful if the prospective user talks with a knowledge-able salesperson. The user's needs must be clearly expressed to the salesperson; this explanation of needs is similar to the RFP discussed earlier in the chapter. The prospective user should see a demonstration of the software and its features. Bringing sample data enables the user to approximate the use of the software under simulated conditions. Ease of use and applicability to the task are only two of many criteria for selecting a software package. The **software demonstration** should also include a review of the

TABLE 14–1

*Operating Systems
and Types of
Personal
Computer*

Operating System	Examples
MS-DOS	Compaq Deskpro, Dell
OS/2	IBM PS/2 Model 80
Macintosh	Mac Classic, Mac II, Power Books
UNIX	NeXT

user's manual and any other documentation for the software. Poor documentation is a warning signal that the system itself may be difficult to use.

The actual use of software is, without a doubt, the best way to decide which software package to acquire. Therefore, the user should look for a money-back guarantee or permission to try the software out for a prescribed period of time. By so doing, the user has a better opportunity to choose the best package.

A crucial question in selecting software is the degree of available support from the vendor or software developer. At the high end of the spectrum are companies that offer unlimited free **software support** for their products over toll-free telephone lines. At the other extreme are companies that offer no support at all. Some companies may require payment for each minute of help they provide or use 900 numbers to charge the caller. In addition, some software is supported by trained employees at local computer stores. Buying software that does not have any type of technical support is a risky proposition, at best.

Even after this research, evaluation, and testing of software, a buyer may not be able to make an objective choice between two or more packages. The choice may be complicated by price versus ease of use versus the reputation of the vendor. All these criteria are important, and some tradeoffs among them may be necessary.

*Determine
Acceptable
Hardware*

After choosing the software that meets the needs defined in Step 1, the user selects hardware that runs the software. Because all computers do not run all software, this matching process is important. Recall that computers have different **operating systems,** which direct computer operations (MS-DOS, OS/2, UNIX, or Macintosh). The operating system also controls the software that can be run on the computer. Some typical examples of operating systems and corresponding types of computers are shown in Table 14–1.

Hardware for a personal computer was discussed originally in Chapter 4. PC components include the **Central Processing Unit (CPU),** keyboard, video screen, secondary storage, printer, modem, and possibly a mouse. Because the keyboard and CPU come with the computer, the decisions facing the buyer usually involve the characteristics of the operating system, amount of internal and secondary storage, type of video system, type of modem, type of printer, and expandability of the system. Many decisions may be determined by the software selected.

As software is more sophisticated and users have more reasons to process and store data on a computer, the requirement for faster CPUs and more RAM and disk storage has grown. Current users need fast CPUs, large amounts of RAM, at least one floppy drive, and a hard disk drive. Likewise, the amount of internal memory and secondary storage that is needed depends on the software and the projected uses of the computer. Few personal computers are sold today with less than 1 Mbyte of RAM and many have at least 5 Mbyte. The capability to add more memory is important, because each succeeding upgrade of software that is easier and has more features seems to require more memory.

If the projected use of the computer involves large amounts of secondary storage, such as the large data bases required by ProYacht's parts system, then a large-capacity (at least 100 Mbyte) hard disk drive should be included. In addition to a large-capacity hard disk drive, some form of tape backup should be used to protect against loss of precious software and data.

The user must decide what type of monitor and printer is needed for the software selected. The user can generally choose between a monochrome (one-color) monitor or a color monitor, although some portable computers and Macintosh computers have built-in monitors. A user who works with text or numbers only might consider using a monochrome monitor, because of the high quality of the text displayed. On the other hand, a text and color graphics user needs a color monitor that can display high-resolution graphics and crisp text.

Dot matrix, ink jet, or laser printers are used in most businesses. A dot matrix printer, which uses tiny dots to form characters on paper, is usually sufficient for draft documents or some types of personnel work. However, dot matrix printer output is almost never acceptable for business correspondence or reports. Ink jet printers form dots on paper by spraying ink from a row of tiny nozzles. These printers are quieter than dot matrix printers and provide professional letter quality output. A laser printer uses a laser light beam to "write" dots on a drum coated with light-sensitive material. The dot pattern is then transferred to paper using a toner similar to that used in a copier. These printers produce very high-quality print, using at least 300 dots per inch to form the letters. They can also create different type sizes and fonts to produce output on standard size paper. A laser printer is required for most business output that is used by others in the organization, that contains graphic or tabular information, and that is distributed to users outside the organization. An organization might consider networking when acquiring a laser printer, so that the expense of a laser printer can be shared by many users on a network.

Most modems sold today typically range from 1200 to 9600 bits per second (bps), and are either external or internal. Many people even buy modems that double as fax machines. In any case, because the communication software is the important factor, the modem should be selected to complement that software.

With the exception of the modem, all of the components listed above are necessary to make full use of a computer. The exception to this is the Macintosh, which also requires a mouse. Thus, the acquisition of a complete package system, possibly including software, should be considered. A careful, structured approach to system acquisition should be followed.

In addition to classification by operating system, personal computers can be classified into the following four major categories of business computers:

1. IBM XT and AT compatible

2. IBM PS/2

3. Apple Macintosh

4. Others (such as SUN and NeXT)

IBM XT and AT compatible computers are compatible with the original IBM XT and AT personal computers; these computers run any software written for the XT and AT. IBM no longer markets the original PC, XT, or AT, but many other companies market compatible computers that run the large amount of software written for MS-DOS. Many companies also sell AT compatible computers based on the newer and faster Intel 80386 and 80486 CPU chips. This type of computer is popular with business and industry.

IBM developed PS/2 computers to replace the original PC, XT, and AT computers. Depending on the model, PS/2 computers feature high-resolution video systems, a different internal communications system, $3\frac{1}{2}$-inch disk drives, and the capability to run the OS/2 operating system. Like AT compatible computers, all these machines can run the software written for MS-DOS and are based on Intel chips, but they are engineered to be difficult for other companies to replicate.

The Apple Macintosh, first available in 1984, is an extremely innovative computer. Macintosh combines text and graphics on a high-resolution white screen or color monitor. For creating newsletters, forms, and business graphics, the Macintosh has no peer. The entire field of desktop publishing is the result of the Macintosh's unique abilities. Because of its increasing popularity, more software is written for use by the Macintosh for traditional business applications.

The SUN and NeXT computers are UNIX-based personal computers. NeXT was developed by Steven Jobs, who was a founder of Apple Computers, and incorporates many innovative hardware and software features. SUN is popular as an engineering workstation.

In many situations, an individual may want a portable personal computer to carry to work or home and use while traveling or visiting customers' offices. Portable computers are available in four sizes—luggables, laptops, notebooks, and what manufacturers call "hand-held computers" or "personal digital assistants (PDAs)." These four sizes are distinguished by weight and computing power. A computer that is easily carried around is a laptop or notebook; heavier computers are luggables, usually weighing over 20 pounds. Laptops are full-featured computers weighing between 10 and 20 pounds, and notebooks are smaller—weighing less than 10 pounds—and often fit into a standard

*Using Laptops
as a Strategic
Tool*

After an insurance agent sells a life insurance policy, various forms associated with the health and financial status of the buyer must be completed. These forms are then sent to the home office for underwriting, a process that can take several weeks, during which the prospective client might cancel the policy. A company that shortens this time lag between the sale of a policy and the completion of the underwriting process has a significant advantage over its competitors.

At New York Life, laptops are combined with an expert system to enable the company's agents to do just that—shorten the process so that the agent and buyer immediately know if the policy is accepted. Laptops enable the agent to complete several day's paperwork in a matter of minutes and generate payment schedules or provide a graphical display of a family's financial picture. In addition, for policies valued less than $250,000, after the agent types in data about the person's age, health habits, and medical condition, the expert system (or the ''underwriter in a box'') can immediately determine whether the prospective client is a good insurance risk.

Using laptops also allows an agent to dial into the regional office minicomputer for security checks on potential clients. Agents can also dial into New York Life's mainframe to download existing client files. Agents particularly like this system because their commission checks arrive faster, fewer mistakes occur, and the entire process is reduced to a few days.

SOURCE: Maryfran Johnson, ''New York Life Sold on Laptops,'' *Computerworld,* August 6, 1990, p. 39.

briefcase. Hand-held computers and PDAs can be held in the palm of the hand, but they do not offer the computational power and full-sized keyboard of the larger machines. Some PDAs are the size of paperback books and weigh less than a pound. They are designed for specialized computational needs. Some have no keyboard; data is simply printed on a screen with a stylus, and the computer converts it to text or graphics. All four types of portable computers use some type of flat screen display—Liquid Crystal Diode (LCD) or gas plasma technology. Macintosh has a new Power Book laptop line that runs any software designed for desktop Macintosh computers.

In summary, the personal computer selected must meet a particular user's needs, including running the selected software. Because all software does not run on all personal computers, the software must be selected first.

Select a Vendor

After software and hardware are selected, the user must choose a vendor(s) from which to acquire the software and hardware. Three choices are available to most people for buying computer hardware and software:

1. Retail computer software store

2. Hardware or software manufacturer

3. Mail order

Each option has good points and bad points. A retail computer store stocks a range of computer hardware and software and usually has a knowledgeable staff. Retail salespeople can often help with problems, and for a computer novice, a computer store can be a good place to learn about the various types of hardware and software. Specialty retail computer stores may sell one particular type of equipment—for example, printers.

Large organizations may have special arrangements that allow them to acquire PC hardware and software through the computer software manufacturer. The manufacturer may even have a service department with skilled technicians who service personal computers. Substantial discounts can be obtained on hardware and software, but this process is not recommended if the hardware or software does not accomplish the defined task. For example, acquiring a laptop at a low price through an organization's contract with the manufacturer is counterproductive if the computer's memory is insufficient to run needed spreadsheet programs.

Often, the least expensive way to buy computer software and hardware is through the mail. A buyer can save a great deal of money by using a mail order company, but the prospective user must be well informed and experienced enough to set up the equipment or install the software without help. Another point to consider about software acquired from a mail order house is that it usually cannot be tested before it is acquired and, once opened, may not be returned for a cash refund. This situation is slowly changing as mail order houses are now establishing return policies.

A key point to consider in selecting a hardware supplier is service. Although a computer is usually a trouble-free machine with few moving parts, sooner or later, service is needed. A disk drive might be out of alignment or a key stuck, but some type repair is necessary. Most retail computer stores have repair services to handle such problems. Most equipment has at least a 1-year warranty that is honored by a retail store on equipment it sells. However, equipment that is acquired from another source—for example, through a mail order house—may need to be returned to the factory at the buyer's expense. The user may acquire a service contract from either the seller or from a third-party service company. In general, businesses with a large number of machines should probably acquire such an agreement.

Make the
Acquisition

After the selections of software, hardware, and the supplier, making the acquisition is the final step. This step generally does not involve the financing and contract considerations noted earlier in this chapter. Before the acquisition, a user might consider the following checklist to ensure that his or her system does not need extra items:

1. Are all printer and monitor cables included in the system or are they acquired separately?

2. Are any additional network or interface cards needed?

3. Is communications software included with the modem? If not, what is the cost of software that is compatible with the computer?

4. Is the system expandable for additional memory or disk drives?

5. Does the cost include initial acquisition of blank floppy disks, printer paper, and, for a tape backup system, tape cartridges?

6. If a laser printer is acquired, is the toner cartridge included in the acquisition price?

After the questions in this checklist are answered satisfactorily, the acquisition can be made with the knowledge that the system will run immediately. If any answers imply that additional equipment or software is needed for the desired system, then more research might be necessary before the final acquisition.

A new personal computer should be immediately "burned in" by running it for a day or so, because components usually fail during the first 50–100 hours of operation or not at all. The user can improve the chance of catching a problem at the start, while the computer is still within the warranty period. After this process, the software should be tested to detect any problems. Testing should be fairly comprehensive and include those activities for which the system is acquired. After this "burn-in" phase is completed and the software is tested, the personal computer can be used for business needs or personal productivity.

14.5 Summary

The acquisition of hardware and software follows the specification of the information needs and the development of a general design to accommodate these needs. Software should be selected before hardware is specified and selected. The specification of information needs may be specific or it may be stated in terms of general objectives and constraints. These specifications are submitted to prospective vendors in an RFP. If the specifications are detailed, vendors can respond easily with bids. If they are general in nature, vendors must use their creative talents to propose a solution to the customer's needs. These proposals are evaluated based on the criteria that are important to the business or organization that requested the proposals. Prospective users must then make the necessary financial and contractual arrangements to acquire the hardware or software. The site for hardware is prepared and the process of implementation begun.

For personal computers, an individual user must assess his or her own needs and research the acquisition of hardware and software. Assessment of needs is just as important here as in the acquisition of a large system. The most important criterion in the selection of hardware and software is that they meet the information processing needs of the intended users.

Key Terms

acquisition and development
benchmark test
conversion
cost-benefit analysis

Central Processing Unit (CPU)
implementation
information system requirements
make or buy decision

net present value
operating systems
outsourcing
Personal Digital Assistant (PDA)
Request for Proposal (RFP)
service bureau
simulation model

software demonstration
software support
timesharing
turn-key systems
value-added vendors
vendor contract

**Review
Questions**

1. Why is the system acquisition decision called a "make or buy decision"? At what point in the structured systems analysis process is this decision made?

2. List the advantages of purchasing software. List the disadvantages of purchasing software.

3. Discuss the use of net present value as a criterion for deciding whether to develop or acquire software.

4. What are value-added vendors? What service do they provide?

5. List three alternatives to developing or acquiring an information system. Briefly discuss the differences among the three.

6. List the advantages and disadvantages of timesharing and of service bureaus.

7. List the steps in the hardware and software acquisition process. Which steps are the same for hardware and software?

8. What is an RFP? What do information requirements have to do with an RFP? What specifications are included in an RFP?

9. List three ways of evaluating a proposal.

10. List various criteria that apply to both hardware and software acquisition that should be included in a priority weighting scheme.

11. What is the difference between benchmark testing and simulation?

12. List the items that should be included in a vendor contract.

13. What steps should be included in the implementation of a new information system?

14. What steps are suggested for acquiring a PC system? How can an individual user determine software requirements?

15. What types of PC systems are commonly used in organizations today?

**Discussion
Questions**

1. Consider the acquisition of software for a regional savings and loan with 80,000 savings customers and 35,000 mortgages to service. The organization is growing at a rate of 10 percent per year. Currently, a mid-size mainframe

computer is used to process all savings and loan transactions and reports. Multiple users must be on the system at the same time to serve many customers at three branches. What software requirements would you include in an RFP?

2. A local florist needs to computerize her inventory and sales activities to accommodate a growing volume of business and to obtain the necessary managerial information to stay competitive. A restaurant owner in the same shopping center recently purchased a Model Z personal computer and had great success with its use in controlling costs. The restaurant owner convinces the florist to buy a Model Z personal computer. Now, she is looking for appropriate software. Is this the way to acquire a personal computer system? If not, why not? What steps should the florist have followed?

3. A glass company that supplies glass to local businesses decides to put its accounting system on a computer. The company has no experience with computers, and the bookkeeper is terrified of them. Management has no idea what information a computer can provide for decision making. How should the company proceed with its acquisition process and why?

Case 14–1
Crystal Landscape and Pool Construction Company

Crystal Landscape and Pool Construction Company (CLPCC) is considering computerizing its transaction processing, cost estimation, construction management, engineering, and design activities. Accounting, management, engineers, and architects will all use the new system. The company is considering two alternative networks. One option would use a minicomputer with terminal interfaces. All processing would be done by the minicomputer, which could use sophisticated engineering and drafting software. Cost of the system includes $50,000 for equipment, $15,000 for software, $5,000 for the operating system, $2,000 for installation, $1,000 for testing, $3,000 for training CLPCC employees, and $2,500 for conversion of all the transaction and engineering data. The other alternative is a LAN, which would cost $35,000 for all the personal computers that function as servers and terminals. Processing would be performed at each workstation, so less sophisticated engineering and drafting software would be employed. Its software and operating system would cost $5,000 and $2,000, respectively. Annual operating costs would include the following for each configuration:

	Minicomputer	LAN
Operating Personnel	$60,000	$20,000
Maintenance	2,000	1,000
Software Updates	0	2,000
Development and Training	5,000	2,000
Technical Support	5,000	2,000
Data Input Personnel	20,000	20,000
Communication Lines	2,000	2,000

The minicomputer is much more expensive to operate, except that new versions of the software are often available for microcomputer use. In general, the minicomputer would offer users powerful but expensive programs, resulting in annual benefits over the current system of around $130,000. The disadvantage of the minicomputer is that users would not have personal computers at their disposal for individual work. The advantage of the LAN is that each user would have a personal computer, but the personal computer's processing power is considerably less, resulting in an estimated annual saving of only $75,000.

Case Questions

1. Evaluate these two alternatives with the information given and your knowledge of these types of systems and select the best one. Assume a 5-year life and a cost of capital of 10 percent.

2. Explain why you made your selection.

3. What other factors would you like to consider in your evaluation of these two proposals? What would you like to examine for each system before you finalize your choice?

Case 14–2
Great Western Railroad

Great Western Railroad serves the western, Rocky Mountain, and Great Plains states. With its successful freight business, the company has expanded rapidly, even buying out several smaller rail lines. Its increasing track mileage and rolling stock have become difficult to maintain, route effectively, and schedule. To relieve the scheduling problems and to get a handle on costs, management has engaged a systems consultant to develop a new scheduling and cost system. The consultant recommended Super Scheduler III and Profit Analyzer (a cost management system) to solve Great Western's problems. Both systems are widely used in the transportation industry, and Great Western's management feels they are adequate. Minor modifications were needed because of the magnitude and complexity of Great Western's routes and large amount of equipment. The programs were quickly modified, implemented, and successfully tested. Systems testing was skipped, and the new programs were implemented as written. No parallel run was performed because the systems were reliable for other companies. The following disasters have now occurred:

1. The scheduling algorithm ran well until a large snowstorm hit Denver and virtually stopped rail service in the Rockies.

2. The schedule failed when too many engines were in the repair yard because the linear programming optimization model could not find the ''best'' alternative when no feasible alternative existed.

3. The cost system did not interface with the new scheduling system or with the current accounting system.

4. The current maintenance system did not interface with the cost system or the scheduling system, so maintenance costs were always recorded late and the scheduling system had no information on the equipment in maintenance.

5. Data had to be keyed into the new system by hand, which caused late scheduling for dispatching trains from many terminals. No train ran on schedule.

6. Customers started to use a competitor who could deliver goods on time.

Case Questions   What went wrong? What should the consultant and Great Western have done to avoid these costly blunders?

Alternative Systems Development Methodologies

15

Introduction   As discussed in Chapters 12 and 13, the accepted method of developing a computer-based information system is a process known as **structured systems development.** This process involves an analysis of needs, designing specifications, and implementing a system to meet an organization's needs. If the new information system involves creating custom software, then the software must be designed and programmed. On the other hand, if the software can be purchased, the analyst must know enough about commercial software to make a recommendation to management. Finally, if the new information system requires hardware, then its purchase is also part of this process.

The process of systems development can be thought of as a sequence of seven phases, with each phase depending on the successful completion of the previous phases. These seven phases, also called the **structured systems analysis and design cycle,** are shown in Figure 15–1.

The systems development cycle begins at project definition, when the user becomes aware that either an existing system is not working correctly or a new system is needed. The movement from project definition through the feasibility study to the final implementation and operation phases takes the analyst from a general, logical understanding of the problem to a detailed solution of the problem.

In the first three phases — project definition, feasibility study, and requirements analysis — the systems analyst gathers data, decides what problem should be solved, determines if a problem solution is feasible, generates a set of requirements for the resolution of the problem, and moves toward a detailed understanding of the system. In the general design phase, the analyst builds on the requirements developed by the systems analyst and

FIGURE 15–1   *The Systems Development Cycle*

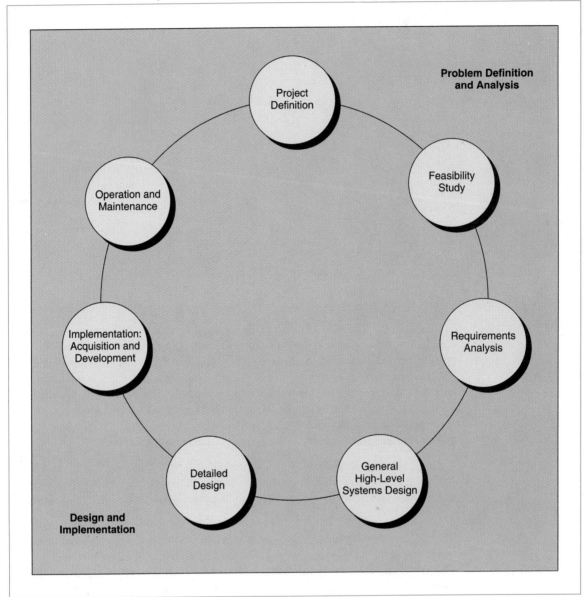

begins the physical design for the system. In this phase, several alternatives are developed and assessed and one is selected. In the detailed design phase, specifications are
developed for the alternative selected. This may involve specifications for writing the
needed software as outlined in Chapter 13, or acquiring a new system as outlined in
Chapter 14.

In the implementation: acquisition or development phase, software is acquired or developed and installed. Software may be programmed in this phase to meet design specifications. In the operation and maintenance phase, the system is in place, and users must monitor system performance, iron out any day-to-day problems, and keep the system running.

Problems with the Structured Approach

The structured systems analysis and design approach to developing information systems has evolved over the past four decades in response to the increasing cost and complexity of large-scale systems. All very large projects, whether information systems or space shuttles, require effective management, and structured techniques are the only way to carry out this management process. However, two trends in computing had led to other systems development methodologies. First, individuals had increased access to the computer during the late 1970s and early 1980s, through either terminals tied into mainframes or personal computers. These users found many new ways for the computer to help them perform their jobs more efficiently. Second, at the same time that users were finding computers more accessible, the Information System (IS) departments in many organizations were overwhelmed by user demands for additional services.

These two trends in computing are not unrelated, because as workers discovered the power of the computer, they also expected more from their IS department. These increased expectations often included developing software for specific applications, making needed information available from a mainframe data base, and maintaining or upgrading existing software systems. The many jobs submitted to the IS department created a backlog of unfinished work, so an IS professional might take well over one year to complete a user's project. By then, the project was often out of date and of no use. Many users may not have submitted jobs to the IS department because of this delay, creating an invisible backlog of unsubmitted jobs.

In addition to the problems of slow development of new systems, structured systems analysis and design methods may not be adequate for creating Decision Support Systems (DSS) and Executive Information Systems (EIS). Recall that structured methodology requires users to define their needs clearly before the design process begins. This may not always be possible in the development of DSS or EIS. End users are managers or executives who may not be able to state their needs, because they are not accustomed to using new information technology or accessing the vast amount of information that is available. Analysts may need to provide end users with intermediate versions of DSS and EIS, which they can use to better define their actual needs.

Alternative Approaches to Systems Development

Users' frustrations with the long delays in systems development and the need to work with intermediate versions of a system have led to the use of two new approaches to system development—prototyping and end user computing. In **prototyping,** after consultation with the user, the IS professional develops a "quick and dirty" prototype version of the desired system for testing by the user. Based on the user's comments, the IS professional modifies the prototype. This process continues until an acceptable version is completed. The iterative aspect of prototyping enables users to define their needs in more specific terms as they work with each new version of the prototype. Although the prototype may be used as a production system, more likely it is the model for the production version or leads to a better definition of user's needs.

The key to prototyping is the use of so-called "fourth generation languages"—very high-level computer languages that can be used to develop IS applications quickly. Data Base Management Systems (DBMS) that include similar languages are also often used for prototyping information systems.

In end user computing, the user takes over some of the roles of system developer and creates a working information system to meet his or her own needs. These applications are often created with end user tools that make the system development easier. PC-based spreadsheets and DBMSs are examples of end user tools.

15.1
Prototyping

Prototyping can be defined as the interactive creation of an information system on a trial basis for testing and approval. First, the process must be interactive; that is, the system user must be willing to work closely with an IS professional to explain the problem, test each version of the prototype as it is developed, and then discuss the modifications that must be made. The prototype is a "trial" product; it may end up being the production system, but this is not its initial purpose. Its primary purpose is to serve as the foundation for the final system.

In prototyping, the developer "short circuits" the lengthy systems analysis and design process to create a usable system quickly. The key word here is "quickly," and in the best case, the development of the first version of the prototype should take only a few

Developing Software in a Hurry at Kodak

When the sales and marketing department at Kodak Company in Rochester, NY, decided to create a huge data base of its domestic and international users, the idea was immediately popular with all concerned groups except one—the IS department. No one bothered to tell the department about this project—called Propassport—until the 20,000 names needed to be entered in the multifaceted data base. When finally informed of Propassport, the IS department estimated that, with traditional approaches to systems development, the project would require at least a year to complete. However, the sales and marketing department wanted it done in six weeks.

This confrontation between the needs of the sales and marketing department and the way in which the IS department handled projects led to a shortened development cycle for Propassport. With much gnashing of teeth, the IS development team met the sales and marketing department's schedule. However, the experience caused repercussions at Kodak, including the creation of a new IS department group to handle future problems like this. The Rapid Deployment Group evaluates new technology and implements it without the formal evaluation process.

SOURCE: James Daly, "Cooking Up Short-order Software," *Computerworld*, December 16, 1991, p. 75.

FIGURE 15–2   ***Organization Chart for ProYacht, Inc.***

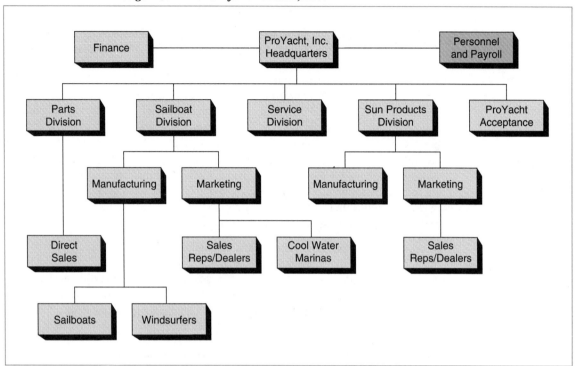

days using tools that speed up the process. The final system may evolve through a series of iterations.

ProYacht Personnel and Payroll Systems

As discussed in earlier chapters, ProYacht, Inc. manufactures and markets a line of sailboats. Recently, the company has added a line of marinas (Cool Water Marinas) and a line of aluminum boats (Sun Products). These new acquisitions are putting additional pressure on ProYacht's personnel and payroll system. This system is used to query its personnel files, to track production hours and sales commissions, and to process weekly and monthly payroll. Currently, the outside service bureau that is handling ProYacht's payroll uses an old batch processing system. The organization chart for ProYacht is shown in Figure 15–2, with the personnel division highlighted.

As a result of increased processing requirements, ProYacht's management wants the IS department to develop an online personnel and payroll management system that would allow managers to control personnel-related activities in all divisions. However, a two-year project backlog in the IS department has prevented analysts from developing such a system. So when the service bureau informed ProYacht that at the end of the current contract period—only a few weeks away—it would not continue to run the company's payroll, panic set in. A new system must be developed by the time the service bureau terminates its services. However, the IS department manager estimates that a team of three programmers would need a *minimum* of five months to develop a new payroll system.

At this point, the IS manager's superior reassigns an outside consultant working on other projects to the payroll system project in an attempt to "get something up and running." Because the consultant knows that traditional development methods cannot work in this situation, he decides to use prototyping. First, he interviews the payroll manager to determine what had to be done to develop an online payroll system. No attempt is made to develop detailed specifications as in the structured approach; instead, a working model is developed. The consultant, working with a special high-level computer language, creates prototype screens and processes over the next two days. The prototype is shown to the payroll manager, who points out several mistakes for the consultant to correct. This process continues for a week, during which the payroll manager becomes enthusiastic about the prospects of actually having a system running before the end of the service bureau's contract. In fact, she and her staff have several valuable ideas for the consultant about better ways to handle various problems.

When the service bureau's contract actually ends, the consultant has developed a production version of the prototype, a version heartily accepted by the payroll department. A working information system is produced in a fraction of the time estimated by the IS department. Other ProYacht managers are so impressed with the working prototype and the speed with which it was developed that the same approach is taken for replacing the batch system used for processing personnel records.

Features of Prototyping

As defined by Efraim Turban,[1] prototyping has the following five key features:

1. Users learning about information requirements is built into the design process.

2. Development is an iterative process with short intervals between system versions and rapid feedback from the user. The emphasis is on speed.

3. The user is closely involved in the development process.

4. The initial prototype has a low cost that does not require special justification.

5. With the iterative nature of prototyping and the feedback it provides, management develops information requirements while seeing what a new system can do.

In ProYacht's payroll system example, all these features are present. The consultant starts learning when he meets with the payroll manager and continues this process in subsequent meetings. The payroll manager also learns more about her department's information requirements and can make useful suggestions during the development process.

This project definitely has short intervals, often less than a day, between system versions. Feedback is almost immediate as the payroll staff reviews screens and processes. The payroll department is involved in the project from the beginning and participates in all

---

[1] Efraim Turban, *Decision Support and Expert Systems* (New York: Macmillan, 1990), p. 197.

aspects of the systems analysis and design process. The initial prototype is completed in only two days and can be considered "low cost" compared with the minimum five-month development process estimated by the IS department. Finally, no detailed specifications are produced—they evolve during the development process from interaction with the staff.

Note the similarity between the prototyping methodology discussed here and the iterative approach to development for decision support and expert systems. This similarity should not be surprising, because the need to develop a useful DSS or EIS quickly was a driving force behind prototyping. A prototype DSS or EIS is useful in understanding a problem; it may be developed into a production version of the system through a series of iterations.

Types of Prototypes

Various types of prototypes are used for systems development today. A prototype may be a mock-up prototype, an interactive prototype, a working model, or a production model. A **mock-up prototype** is like a clay model of an automobile—it looks like the final product, but does not actually do anything. For an information system, the mock-up demonstrates the display screens for input, output, queries, and user interaction. This prototype helps the user quickly determine what the final system should have. This expedited design process is also called a **demo system,** because the process should demonstrate what the system looks like.

An **interactive prototype** is like the mock-up, but it allows the prospective user to interact with the screens. No actual processing takes place, but a simulated dialogue can be executed for a specific set of inputs and outputs. As with the mock-up, the interactive prototype quickly creates a system design and gives the user the "look and feel" of the final product.

A **working model prototype** is like the first hand-built version of a new automobile—it actually works, but it is not as efficient as the final product. The important difference between the prototype information system and the prototype automobile is that the automobile is more expensive than the production line version, but the information system must be less expensive than the final version. A working model prototype can also help a user understand the problem at hand. This prototype is also called a **disposable system.** A "quick and dirty" system is rushed into operation without extensive documentation, backup plans, or the guarantee that the system complies with all standards and information requirements. The key to using a disposable system is picking the right application (for example, a one-time analysis of a new plant) and not making the system permanent simply because it works for a short while.

The **production model prototype** is like ProYacht's payroll system; the prototype is the starting point for the development of the complete production version. In this process, a small prototype of the most important part of the system is developed. When that part meets users' needs, it is expanded iteratively until a final production version is completed. Tasks performed sequentially in the structured design approach should be overlapped. For example, testing begins when users define their requirements for the system.

TABLE 15–1

*Comparison of
Prototyping and
Structured
Approaches*

Structured	Prototyping
1. Project Identification 2. Feasibility Study	1. Identify project and check feasibility
3. Analysis 4. General Design 5. Detailed Design	2. Develop prototype 3. Trial use of prototype and refinement or enhancement of prototype
6. Implementation	4. Prototype is implemented or used as model for implementation
7. Maintenance	5. Maintenance

As one developer said, ''We can't wait nine months to have a baby anymore, we have to do it in two. And it has to come out perfect and it has to run when it's two weeks old.'' [2]

*The Prototype
Development
Process*

The first three types of prototypes discussed above could be considered a *throwaway* variety—they are used to learn more about the problem, the user's needs, or the required design. On the other hand, the last type of prototype—the production model prototype—is an *evolutionary* variety used to develop a production system. The production model is actually a methodology for developing an information system. Like the structured systems analysis and design process, a step-by-step development process in prototyping is used to develop an information system. Authors have suggested different names for the steps of this process, but most agree that the five steps are as follows:

1. Developer identifies user's problem through discussions with user and determines if a system that solves the problem is feasible.

2. Working prototype is developed for a key element of the system.

3. User works with prototype, learns more about information requirements, and provides feedback to developer, who refines and enhances the prototype until it meets user's information requirements.

4. The prototype is either implemented or used as a model for the implementation phase of structured process.

5. Information system is maintained.

The prototype design process is shown in Figure 15–3. Note that Step 3 is repeated as often as necessary for the prototype to be accepted by the user. This iterative prototyping process is clearly distinguished from the sequential structured method, which has no provision for the repetition of phases. The prototyping process is compared with the structured design process in Table 15–1. In the table, the problem identification and

---

[2] Robert L. Schier, ''Taking the Quick Path to Systems Design,'' and ''In a Development Jam? Try a Disposable System,'' *PC Week,* June 19, 1989, pp. 65, 69. Copyright © 1989, Ziff Communications Company.

FIGURE 15–3

The Prototyping Process

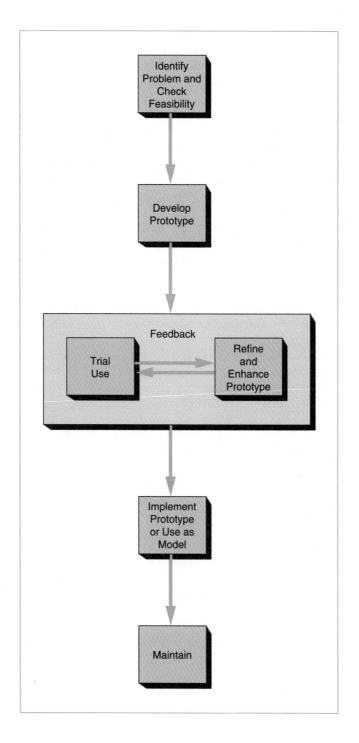

feasibility study phases of the structured process are combined into the first prototyping step. The analysis, general design, and detailed design phases are compressed into the second and third prototyping steps. Both development methods have compatible implementation and maintenance steps. The key differences are the iterative nature of prototyping and its compression of the often complicated analysis, general design, and detailed design phases.

From our discussions, it is easy to see how prototyping has advantages over the structured approach. Prototyping can be much quicker than the structured approach, because it compresses the analysis, general design, and detailed design phases. A project may be completed using prototyping in as little as 10–20 percent of the time required by traditional methods. A reduction in time leads to a corresponding reduction in cost. Prototyping also involves greater interaction between the user and the developer; this situation is especially helpful when users' requirements are not clear. The developer may not be sure about hardware or software requirements, and prototyping allows different scenarios to be considered.

Problems with prototyping can occur when it is used for the wrong type of problem or not used correctly. These problems can include inadequate documentation and testing and an unwillingness to ''throw away'' a prototype and develop the final product. The need for a speedy development can lead to the use of a prototype that is not complete, debugged, or documented. Problems may not be evident until a later time, when the new system is found to be incompatible with an existing system that was not considered in the prototype process. Even if no bugs are apparent in the prototype, inadequate documentation in the form of user's manuals and software descriptions can be a problem, especially if the original developer and user have moved on to new projects. In this case, no one can explain the rationale behind the prototype or the underlying computer programs. This problem can be avoided by reverting to the structured approach for testing and implementation after the prototype is used for the analysis, general design, and detailed design phases.

Although prototyping can be a useful method for developing some types of information systems, notably DSS and expert systems, it may not be appropriate for other types of information systems. Large-scale systems involving batch processing or systems with sophisticated algorithms are probably not appropriate for prototyping. The resulting system probably will not work well. In addition, a prototype may not fit in with existing information systems, or it may be incompatible with the organization's data base.

Users may be so happy with a prototype that they are unwilling to work with the developer to create the final product. The tools used to create a prototype are not aimed at efficiency (see the next section for a discussion of these tools), but at enabling the developer to create the prototype quickly. The user that stays with the prototype may find that its inefficiency slows down needed processing. On the other hand, if the prototype is a model for a production system that is written in a more efficient computer language using the structured approach, such problems are less likely to occur.

**15.2
Prototyping
Tools**

Most prototyping is done using integrated data base environments, program generators, or fourth generation programming languages. **Data base environments,** discussed in detail in Chapters 5 and 6, include query languages, report writers, and applications generators. **Query languages** like IBM's SQL allow the user to build a series of queries into the data base that result in the retrieval of needed data. With **report writers,** a user can generate a needed report in a desired format. **Applications generators** like MANTIS from Cincom allow the user to create entire applications based on the data base. Applications include creating files, input screens, and report screens.

Program generators are software packages that enable a developer to create multiple instructions, or **code,** in a high-level language. The program generator converts one or two commands from the developer into the equivalent high-level language code, for example, COBOL. The program generator may not develop code that is as efficient as code created by human programmers, but the time to generate the program is reduced. Besides speeding up the coding process, use of a program generator can result in the development of standardized segments of code. This standardized code may then be used in other projects, reducing the development time for those projects.

The other tool often used for prototyping is a **fourth generation language.** These languages were developed after such high-level languages as COBOL, BASIC, and FORTRAN. A fourth generation language enables the user to develop programs in a fraction of the time needed for a typical high-level language. Programs written in a fourth generation language tend to be less efficient than those written in a high-level language or even with a program generator, but the increasing power and speed of computers and their decreasing cost reduce the effects of this problem.

*Historical
Perspective*

Since the first computers, programmers have wanted the computer to execute as many instructions as possible using the least amount of code. With most computer languages, one instruction from the programmer causes the computer to execute more than one internal command. The first computer languages were just the binary instruction codes to the computer, so the programmer entered one instruction for each command to be carried out.

The next step was the use of assembler languages, which allowed the programmer to use mnemonic commands instead of binary instruction codes. Assembler languages were a great improvement, but they still required the user to know exactly how the computer worked. If binary instruction codes are "first generation language" and assembler languages are "second generation," then high-level languages such as COBOL, BASIC, and FORTRAN are "third generation languages." Third generation language instructions are a step further removed from the computer's machine code than assembler languages, because their English-like instructions are turned into machine code by interpreters or compilers. A single statement in one of these languages results in many machine code commands.

The first three generations of languages are considered to be procedural languages. A **procedural language** requires the user to specify *what* is to be done—that is, the task to be accomplished—as well as to specify *how* the task is be accomplished by providing all

Prototyping at Coca-Cola with R:Base

Coca-Cola Foods Division must consider hundreds of variables for promotional sales opportunities for dozens of brands, sizes, and flavors of food in all regions of the country. Each sales variable is linked with different promotion opportunities, causing a logistical nightmare for marketing. To organize this information, the Sales Systems, Planning, and Information Department turned to a PC-based data base management software package —R:Base—to prototype the required information system. This information system would also direct manufacturing to produce various amount of each product, handle deductions and allowances, inform brand managers of upcoming promotions, and enable all company divisions to communicate with one another.

The R:Base prototype was created in one six-hour working session. The department manager estimated that 2,000 worker-hours of time were saved by not designing the information system in COBOL. The prototype was never meant to be a finished system, but the IS people could ask the sales force about the prototype, thereby ensuring that the final system was correct. Using the prototype as a design, programmers coded the actual mainframe system in COBOL. As the department manager said, "You could never do that on the mainframe—six months later you'd have a system up and running, but by then business problems would have changed."

SOURCE: Jeffrey S. Young, "Building Monster Databases," *Business Software*, July 1986, pp. 12–17.

the necessary logic. On the other hand, a **nonprocedural language** requires that the user specify only what is to be done, and the computer provides the majority of the logic necessary to accomplish the task.

Beyond these third generation languages are at least two more generations. A range of fourth generation languages exist, and fifth generation languages based on research in the area of artificial intelligence appear to be right beyond the horizon.

The first fourth generation languages—such as NOMAD and RAMIS—were developed for use on mainframe computers. Most fourth generation languages were developed by time-sharing firms to meet the demand from aggressive managers who felt the IS department was taking too long to develop the information system needed. With the ever-increasing power and memory of personal computers, many mainframe fourth generation languages are being moved onto the smaller computers. There is even a PC version of NOMAD.

Fourth Generation Languages

Whereas high-level or third generation languages use computer power to convert user's instructions into machine code, fourth generation languages use this same computer power to move even farther away from the machine code level. With fourth generation languages, the programmer can develop applications software without specifying all the details. The fourth generation language supplies much of the information that a programmer normally provides in a third generation language. An increase in productivity often results when persons program in a fourth generation language. In fact, James Martin declared, ''A language should not be called fourth generation unless users can obtain results in one-tenth the time with COBOL, or less.'' [3]

For example, consider again ProYacht's payroll system development project. In that situation, the developer first used a fourth generation language to create the screens that the user would see. If he used COBOL, then he would have had to write specific instructions for moving the cursor to various points on the screen, accepting input characters one at a time, checking for terminators, and so on. On the other hand, with a fourth generation language, he could simply ''paint'' the screen and let the fourth generation language generate the machine code that displays the screen when the program is run.

An example of a PC-based DBMS that has many fourth generation language characteristics is dBASE. In dBASE, the single command LIST displays data base records from beginning to end. With a traditional third generation language, the programmer must give the computer all the instructions required to access each record, test for the end of the file, display the record on the screen, and then repeat this operation until all records are displayed.

Another primary difference between third and fourth generation languages is that most third generation languages are procedural, and many fourth generation languages are nonprocedural. As a result, with fourth generation languages, a programmer can concentrate on the task at hand without worrying so much about how it is going to be done. The user specifies what a program should do and lets the system decide how to do it. The number of instructions necessary to carry out an operation is significantly reduced. For example, a third generation language program requiring 1,000 instructions might be accomplished by a fourth generation language with fewer than 50 instructions.

The reduction in the number of instructions required to accomplish a task means a corresponding reduction in the training time required for someone to become proficient in the use of a fourth generation language. A COBOL programmer may be proficient after several weeks of training and at least six months of experience, but a typical fourth generation language can be taught in one or two days and requires a few weeks of experience. A fourth generation language program is also easy to change. The dBASE LIST command could quickly be changed to LIST FOR SALARY > 50000 to list only those records of employees with a salary greater than $50,000.

Typical situations for which a fourth generation language might be used for developing prototypes include the following:[4]

- Project tracking and planning

- Market research

- Sales analysis

---

[3] James Martin, *System Development without Programmers* (Englewood Cliffs, NJ: Prentice-Hall, 1982).

[4] Nicholas Rawlings, ''4GLs Improve Analysis Features of an MIS,'' *Data Management,* August 1987, pp. 19–21.

- Financial modeling
- Production scheduling and control
- Quality control
- Scientific research

These areas are often considered low priority by IS departments, so they are prime targets for prototyping with a fourth generation language.

As an example of the use of a fourth generation language, consider a PC-based product called the Clarion Developer. This program allows the user to create customized application programs with pop-up windows, point-and-shoot menus, online help, and high-quality reports without writing a single line of program code. Clarion allows the developer to build applications in the following three simple steps:

1. Design application files
2. Paint screens and design reports
3. Link screens and reports together with the files to create a whole program

With Clarion, a simple on-screen monthly calendar can be built in just a few hours. The calendar shows the days of the month and can "pop-up" an appointment calendar for any given day. Creating this calendar using a traditional programming language would take a great deal more time. This calendar is shown in Figure 15–4.

FIGURE 15–4   *Use of Clarion Developer*

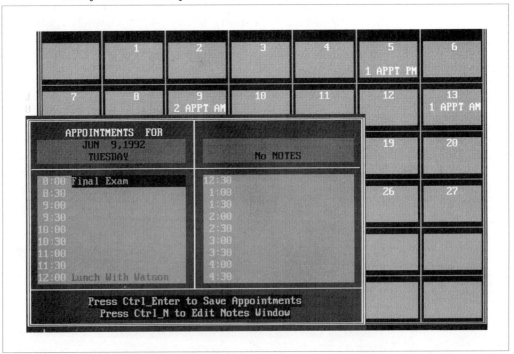

Fast Action with a Fourth Generation Language Puts Casino on a Roll

When the Foxwoods Casino opened in February 1992 in Ledyard, CT, it had already undergone dramatic growth. Built on virgin forest land in less than two years by the Mashantucket Pequot Indians, the casino is expected to gross $100 million per year. Less than a year before it opened, casino managers had no computers and no IS plan. However, by using a fourth generation language called Progress, the IS staff created the needed software applications for less than one-fourth the cost of comparable software developed for a casino in Atlantic City.

The system development process involved several rewrites of the software during the year before the opening, mostly the result of management's frantic pace of getting the casino built and organized. The Progress language was flexible enough to let the IS staff easily make needed changes. The final design was not decided upon until five months before the opening date, so the final programming was a pressure-packed operation, with many elements finished just in time for user training to begin.

Once the casino was open, an IS staff member was assigned to write a job applicant tracking module for the human resources package. With the fourth generation language, the needed software was created in less than a week. This module has since swollen to a data base with over 200,000 records with no problems.

SOURCE: Paul Gillin, "Fast Action, Not Luck, Puts Casino on a Roll," *Computerworld,* June 8, 1992, p. 50.

Why does anyone continue to use a traditional third generation language when a fourth generation language can be used? With all their benefits, fourth generation languages do have some serious shortcomings. The primary disadvantages of fourth generation languages when compared with a third generation language are that they are inefficient and slow. Because a fourth generation language is primarily oriented toward speed of development, it does not have the efficiencies of file manipulation that are an intimate part of such languages as COBOL. Similarly, users of fourth generation languages find that they process data more slowly than with a traditional language. For this reason, fourth generation languages are not recommended for applications involving large amounts of transaction processing or repetitive calculations. A fourth generation language can be used for the design stage of these applications, as long as the user realizes that the prototype is only for design purposes.

15.3 End User Computing

Because IS departments took so long to complete projects, some frustrated but conscientious users tried to find ways to complete projects on their own. In some cases, they had to learn a programming language to create software, or they found new ways to use an applications software package. This group of users is referred to as "power users," "level three users," or most commonly "end users."

An **end user** is a non-IS professional who uses the computer to solve problems associated with his or her job. This definition has two key aspects. First, the end user is *not* an IS professional and, therefore, does not routinely design or develop software for other members of his or her organization. Although the result of an end user's computer work may be used by other employees, this is not the original intent of the job. Second, an end user's primary purpose in using the computer is to solve his or her job-related problems and to work more efficiently. End users often teach themselves how to use new software or learn new computing techniques, then pass along their knowledge to new employees.

Since the late 1970s, the work of end users on the computer, or **End User Computing (EUC),** has become an important part of computing in organizations. According to some estimates, EUC utilizes 40–50 percent of an organization's computer resources. Other studies show that EUC is growing at a rate of 50–90 percent per year. The primary reason for this increase in the importance of EUC is that end users can cut development time from months and years down to days and weeks and get the information they need to support decision making. The applications developed by end users can actually solve a problem while it is *still* a problem.

The systems analysis and design process is a carefully thought out procedure for solving user's problems, but it creates a backlog of uncompleted user jobs. In EUC, the end user short-circuits this process by going directly to the analysis and design steps. He or she knows what the problem is and does not worry about the feasibility of solving the problem. A problem that is not easily solvable is evident soon enough. The end user then combines the analysis and design steps into a single problem-solving step. After an idea for solving the problem is developed, the user selects the appropriate applications software package or writes a computer program. The end user also combines the software design and programming steps using highly interactive software packages and languages. After the application is developed, the end user seldom worries about the maintenance step, other than to solve any problems in the application as they occur. Unfortunately, this end user attitude can lead to problems for co-workers or later system users.

Types of End Users

In theory, anyone who uses a computer, directly or indirectly, is an "end user." The person who makes an airline reservation through a computerized service is an indirect end user, but for purposes of discussion, we consider only direct end users. Direct end users can be further classified as IS professionals and non-IS professionals. From our previous definition of end user, we are only interested in the latter group. J.R. Rockart and L. Flannery[5] have developed finer classifications of this group of end users, as follows:

1. Nonprogramming end users

2. Command level end users

[5] J.R. Rockart and L. Flannery, "The Management of End User Computing," *Communications of the ACM,* 26:10 (October 1983), 776–884.

3. End user programmers

4. Functional support end users

Nonprogramming end users tend to use applications software at its lowest level and do not extend their knowledge of the software beyond what is needed to solve basic problems. They typically use menu-driven software. For example, a beginning end user might use Lotus 1-2-3 to set up a small spreadsheet for a budgeting or forecasting problem. However, this user probably might not attempt to use the graphics or data base facilities of 1-2-3 to further analyze the data.

Command level end users can solve more job-related problems by increasing their knowledge of the software and exploring its limits. In our Lotus 1-2-3 example, the command level end user would use the data base and graphics facilities, build much bigger spreadsheets, and research **software add-ins**—software that can expand a spreadsheet's use.

End user programmers push the software to the limit and write their own procedures for solving complicated problems. They may even write computer programs to solve problems that cannot be handled by commercial applications software. In the Lotus 1-2-3 example, an end user programmer actually writes programs using spreadsheet macros. Often these macros are used to develop skeleton spreadsheets called templates containing labels and formulas. The user solves a problem by entering data in these templates.

Functional support end users are ''local experts.'' Their knowledge of a particular software package or computer language makes them informal centers of computer use in their functional areas. Often, they develop software applications for fellow workers. However, they do not view themselves as IS professionals, but rather as financial analysts or marketing researchers whose primary job is to provide tools and procedures for applications software to solve problems. In the context of the Lotus 1-2-3 example, a functional support end user would be the person other workers approached for help in using 1-2-3.

In the remainder of this discussion, we consider only command level end users, end user programmers, and functional support end users. Nonprogramming end users usually do not develop their own applications.

End Users and Systems Analysis and Design

Earlier in the chapter, we stated that a primary problem with structured systems analysis and design is the tremendous project backlog—both visible and invisible—that occurs. One reason for the evolution of the end user was the time it took for the IS department to solve problems. End users can avoid these delays by developing their own applications. Recall from our earlier discussions that the structured systems analysis and design process tries to account for every possible requirement, problem, and concern, so nothing is left to chance. ''Structure'' exists in every element of this process—from the development of data flow diagrams that describe system requirements to system flowcharts that describe the operation of alternative systems to the program code itself. Because the product may have multiple users, the result is often a compromise between the exact needs of end users and the economic and technical realities of the IS department. Another element of the structured approach is its use for large, expensive projects requiring many months of development time. Finally, structured systems analysis and design offers tremendous advantages over the approach taken by some systems developers in which the programming process is started without prior design work.

The end user expedites the structured process by taking on many roles. He or she is the end user, systems analyst, programmer, computer operator, and data input clerk, all in one person. The user is more interested in the application than in the technical aspects of systems design. As a result, the user may employ a trial-and-error method with ready-made end user tools. This flexibility allows the user to interact with the computer and determine which of a series of formulas provides the needed answers. In the process, the user quite often arrives at a better understanding of the problem. Because the end user may also be the sole user of the system, he or she need not compromise on the resulting application. Figure 15–5 shows the end user approach to developing applications, and Table 15–2 compares the end user development approach to the structured approach.

Risks and Problems with End User Development

Although end users can certainly solve problems much faster than analysts using the classical approach, certain risks must be considered in this approach to developing applications. Because end users tend to jump right into the analysis and design steps, there are numerous risks in using this approach. For example, the user may spend his or her time ineffectively, solve the wrong problem, solve the problem incorrectly, use the incorrect end user tool to solve the problem, fail to develop necessary documentation, or fail to test the application thoroughly. An end user may become so involved with using the computer that the primary job is forgotten. A user may also end up ''re-inventing the wheel'' by not using available applications.

Because end users are usually solving problems for their own needs, they may not create any documentation about their applications. If no one else uses the application, this situation is not a problem. If, on the other hand, another user needs the application or the end user who developed the application leaves the organization, the lack of documentation can be a big problem. End users are notorious for assuming that their system works as planned without completely testing it. Unfortunately, bugs must then be corrected as they are found after the implementation of the system. One study shows that over 40 percent of spreadsheets contain some type of logic errors.

Many risks of EUC could be avoided if the end user would discuss his or her problem solution with a fellow worker, use an appropriate end user tool, and develop adequate documentation for his or her application. Many companies require end users to employ standardized procedures for testing and writing documentation for their applications. For example, spreadsheets should be designed with specific input, documentation, and computation areas. Doing this allows the end user's co-workers or successors to understand what has been done in the application.

15.4 End User Software Tools

As fourth generation languages make a programmer's job easier in creating prototypes, end user tools do the same for EUC. **End user tools** include PC-based third and fourth generation languages, data base query languages, spreadsheet macros, desktop organiz-

FIGURE 15–5

***End User
Applications
Development***

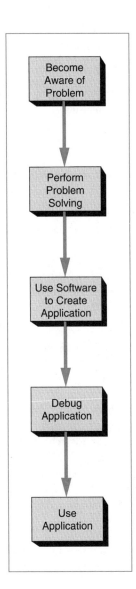

ers and keyboard macro instructions, and various nonprocedural software packages. In
each case, the end user tool allows the end user to do his or her job better.

*Personal
Computer-
Based
Languages*

Virtually all third generation mainframe languages have PC versions, including COBOL,
Pascal, and FORTRAN. Many fourth generation languages have also been converted for
PC use. In addition, some languages are unique to personal computers, including GW-
BASIC from Microsoft, Turbo Pascal from Borland, and the various versions of C. For
users of MS-DOS computers, the capability to group DOS commands into a batch file is

TABLE 15-2

*Comparison of
End User and
Structured
Development*

End User Development	*Structured Development*
Spontaneous	Planned
Inefficient	Efficient
Uncompromising	Compromising
Quick	Certain
Dominated by application experts	Dominated by technical experts
Debugged as problems are found	Thoroughly tested before use

an important asset. With **batch files,** it is possible to create loops and make decisions using special **batch commands.**

*Data Base
Query
Languages*

We have already discussed the power of a data base query language to retrieve with a single command the same information that would require numerous instructions in a third generation language. For both mainframe and PC-based relational data bases, sequential query language is extremely powerful and is being used in more and more situations.

Many DBMSs can have the package run through an entire series of commands for the data base file. These file processing programs, often called **command files,** extend the power of these packages.

*Spreadsheet
Macros*

A popular spreadsheet-based end user tool is the **spreadsheet macro,** which is a series of commands listed one after the other, so each command is executed in order. Macro commands can cause program looping or decide which command is executed next. Spreadsheet macros are actually another programming language that gives the user more control over the spreadsheet. Macros can be used to generate menus or to retrieve, execute, and then save multiple spreadsheet files without any commands from the user. Figure 15-6 shows a spreadsheet macro that is used to move the cursor to various locations for users to enter data.

*Desktop
Organizers and
Keyboard
Macros*

Two useful end user tools are desktop organizers and keyboard macros. A **desktop organizer** is a utility program that usually "hides" in an unused portion of memory and can be accessed while the user is in another application program. When the desktop organizer is accessed, the user can choose such actions as viewing a calendar, using a

FIGURE 15-6

*Spreadsheet
Macro*

```
{GOTO}A5~
{GETLABEL "Input employee's name", @CELLPOINTER("ADDRESS")}{RIGHT}
{GETLABEL "Input employee's SS Number", @CELLPOINTER("ADDRESS")}{RIGHT}
{GETNUMBER "Input employee's pay rate", @CELLPOINTER("ADDRESS")}{RIGHT}
{DOWN}{END}{LEFT}
{GETLABEL "Do you wish to continue—Y or N?",YESNO}
{IF YESNO="Y"}{BRANCH LOOP}
{QUIT}
```

notepad or calculator, or accessing a dialer to dial a phone. Two or more of these activities can be performed simultaneously to "organize" the user's on-screen "desktop."

A **keyboard macro** is a way of recording a series of keystrokes that can be replayed at a later time by pressing a single set of keys. This tool is useful when the same word or phrase is used repeatedly in a word processing package or the same series of keystroke commands is needed.

Nonprocedural Software Packages

Many software packages are available to the end user that do not require any programming knowledge. These **nonprocedural software packages** allow users to work with text, graphics, and numbers by simply answering questions and entering data. Business and personal accounting packages and graphics packages are good examples of this type of software.

Information Centers

As a result of end user development, managers and workers have found that instead of waiting for the IS department to meet all their information needs, they can solve many problems themselves with a personal computer. Moreover, due to increased use of prototyping and end user development, the need for a large staff of IS analysts to analyze and design information systems has not grown as rapidly as the development of information systems. In some organizations, this need may have actually decreased. The IS department has consequently lost some control over the flow of information and the quality of applications development. Various approaches to coordinating the use of personal computers with the IS department are aimed at keeping the information system under control. One answer is the concept of the **Information Center (IC),** which combines the processing power of the organization's mainframe with PC software that is easy to develop and use. The IC is discussed in more detail in Chapter 16.

15.5 Summary

The structured systems analysis and design approach is used for developing and acquiring hardware and software systems. This approach involves the system development cycle—project definition, feasibility study, analysis, general design, detailed design, implementation: acquisition or development, and operation. This approach is used in many cases, but problems include slow development of new systems and inability to create DSS and EIS. In response to these problems, alternative methods are used for carrying out the systems development process, including prototyping and end user programming.

Prototyping is the interactive creation of an information system on a trial basis for testing and approval. The resulting prototype is a "trial" product that eventually may be a production system. In prototyping, the developer shortens the often lengthy systems analysis and design process to quickly create a usable system. The features of prototyping include learning built into the design process, repetitive development and rapid feedback from user, close involvement of user, low cost of initial prototype, and dynamic managerial development of information requirements. The types of prototypes include mock-up, interactive, working model, and production model prototypes. Prototyping is a five-step process—identify user's problem, create working prototype, user works with prototype and provides feedback, implement prototype or use as a model, and maintain information system. Problems with prototyping include inadequate documentation and testing, use of prototyping for the wrong type of problem, and an unwillingness to "throw away" a prototype and develop the final product. Prototyping tools include integrated data base environments, program generators, or fourth generation programming languages.

Users' frustration with long development times caused conscientious workers—end users—to find ways to complete projects on their own. An end user is a non-IS professional who uses the computer to solve job-related problems. The four types of end users are nonprogramming end users, command level end users, end user programmers, and functional support end users. End-user development procedures allow these users to compress the system development phases to quickly develop a usable system for their own use without the need for IS staff. Problems with end user programming include the user not solving the correct problem, solving it incorrectly, not using the appropriate tool, and not providing adequate documentation of work. End user tools include PC-based third and fourth generation languages, data base query languages, spreadsheets, desktop organizers and keyboard macros, and various nonprocedural software packages. To meet the needs of end users, ICs are being created.

Key Terms

applications generator
batch command
batch file
code
command file
command level end user
data base environment
demo system
desktop organizer
disposable system
end user
end user computing (EUC)
end user programmer
end user tool
fourth generation language
functional support end user
Information Center (IC)
interactive prototype

keyboard macro
mock-up prototype
nonprocedural language
nonprocedural software package
nonprogramming end user
procedural language
production model prototype
program generator
prototyping
query languages
report writer
software add-in
spreadsheet macro
structured systems analysis and design
   cycle
structured systems development
working model prototype

Review Questions

1. Name some shortcomings of the structured systems development process.

2. Name two possible alternatives to the structured systems development (analysis and design) process. What is invisible backlog?

3. What is the difference between prototyping and EUC?

4. List five features of prototyping. What is the emphasis of prototyping?

5. List the various types of prototyping. Which type is also called a demo system?

6. Which types of prototype could actually be used in a production environment?

7. Outline the prototype development process. What phases of the systems development process are compressed in prototyping?

8. Discuss some potential problems of prototyping.

9. List and discuss briefly three prototyping tools. What is the difference between a fourth generation language and CASE?

10. What is an end user? What is EUC?

11. List the various types of end users. Which ones actually write programs?

12. Compare the end user development and structured development processes.

13. What are some potential risks and problems with EUC?

14. List and discuss three end user programming tools.

15. How does an IC relate to EUC?

Discussion Questions

1. How and why did technology lead to the advent of EUC and prototype development? What is the difference between these?

2. For each situation below, indicate which systems development procedure would be preferable and why:
   a. A manager needs to plan next month's travel expenses.
   b. The accounts receivable system for a large utility company must be revised to accommodate rapid growth and new technology.
   c. Management needs a new system to support its capital investments, but cannot specify exactly what information it needs from the system.
   d. Management needs to access the data stored in the company data base for a variety of needs that change often.
   e. An oil company needs a new production management system to manage its refineries.
   f. Executives need a system to trace trends in style and sales in the fashion business.
   g. Management needs a new budgeting system and the IS department is backed up with new requests for systems.

3. How have fourth generation languages enhanced end user development? Why are these languages not used universally for all system development?

4. A traffic manager for a freight company needs a new system to schedule the company's fleet of trucks, yet he does not quite know how to express all the variables that affect scheduling decisions. He believes some new optimization algorithms may help, but he is not sure how. The IS manager suggests using prototype development. Why?

Case 15–1
Fiber Products

A new manager for Fiber Products uses a spreadsheet developed by her predecessor. After entering some figures, the manager feels the spreadsheet does not look right; in fact, she believes the spreadsheet has several errors. Actual sales, expenses and net income are compared with planned amounts and expressed as variances.

Fiber Products Budget and Quarterly Income Statement Comparison

	Actual			Actual Total	Budgeted Total	Variance from Budget
Revenues						
Sales	13000	15000	17000	45000	50000	5000
Other	1000	1200	500	2700	3000	– 500
Total	14000	14200	17500	45700	53000	7300
Cost of goods sold	5000	7500	10000	22500	25000	2500
Contribution	9000	6700	7500	30000	28000	– 2000
Contribution %	64.29%	47.18%	42.86%	65.65%	52.83%	
Fixed expenses						
Selling	3000	5000	6000	14000	12000	– 2000
Administration	2000	2500	2000	6500	5000	– 1500
Total	5000	7500	8000	20500	17000	– 3500
Net income	4000	– 800	15500	18700	11000	– 7700

Case Questions

Required:

1. Find the errors in the spreadsheet. Describe the most likely cause of the errors.

2. What user development procedures, policies, and practices would have reduced the potential for these errors?

Case 15–2
Agritech, Inc.

Agritech, Inc. is a new company in the fast growing fields of agriculture biotechnology and genetic engineering. Its research in genetically engineered plant varieties is beginning to pay huge dividends. Agritech has been using a series of spreadsheets to manage its financial affairs and to plan its research efforts, but now it must shift from a small research company to a manufacturing company to produce and sell its new products. It currently needs a decision support model to do its marketing, production, distribution and financial planning; in the long run it will need to develop a corporate planning model to help management guide its growth and future research efforts.

Agritech has asked you and several other software vendors to bid on the development of such a financial planning system. You have asked Agritech what kind of information it needs and its response was, "I'm not sure, but I will know what I need when I see it." The marketing manager explains, "I don't have the foggiest idea how to price our products, because we have no marketing or manufacturing data. All we have in our data base is scientific data." Moreover, management indicated that the corporate planning model should run on its advanced personal computer network and accommodate multiple users. The president, moreover, says, "We need something fast. Customers are clamoring for prices, and we need to construct a manufacturing facility as fast as we can to accommodate the demand for our products."

Case Questions

1. What information systems development approach would you recommend in this case? How would you explain your approach to the president of Agritech?

2. What must you learn from them to develop a fully functional corporate planning model? Will the recommended approach help? How?

3. What are the drawbacks of your recommended approach to developing an information system?

V

Managing the Information Resource

Section V discusses important issues in managing the information resource. Chapter 16 describes the problems of managing information systems and includes a discussion of career opportunities for information system personnel. Chapter 17 explores issues about controlling and monitoring information systems and includes a section on computer crime. Finally, Chapter 18 focuses on the exciting future of information systems.

Management of Information Systems

16

Introduction

Throughout this text, we have emphasized that information is a key asset for any organization. The Information System (IS) is crucial for the delivery of information to the individuals who must make the decisions that determine the future well-being of the organization. These decision makers are usually **managers** who supervise other workers in the organization. In most organizations, managers ensure that objectives are met and that the business operates within budget or makes a profit. In Chapter 3, Henri Fayol defined managerial roles as planning, organizing, staffing, directing, and controlling the activities of the organization.[1] In another study, Henry Mintzberg[2] observed five executives for a sufficient period to develop three types of roles — interpersonal, informational, and decisional. Under the interpersonal type, he included figurehead, leader, and liaison roles. For the informational type, he included monitor, disseminator, and spokesperson roles. Finally, under the decisional type, he included entrepreneur, disturbance handler, resource allocator, and negotiator roles. Regardless of how the roles are classified, the manager must handle many different tasks in the organization and is a key person in its success or failure.

Just as the organization as a whole must be managed so that it survives and prospers, so too must the individual units of the organization be managed. For example, the production department or division must be managed so that products or services of an acceptable quality are produced efficiently. The IS must also be properly managed to provide the needed information to the managers in the organization. All five elements of the IS —

---

[1] Henri Fayol, *Administration industrielle et generale* (Paris: Dunods, 1950 [first published 1916]).

[2] Henry Mintzberg, *The Nature of Managerial Work* (New York: Harper & Row, 1973).

FIGURE 16–1

***Location of Data
Processing
Manager***

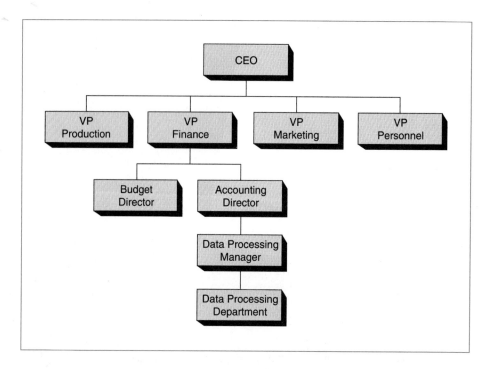

FIGURE 16–1

***Location of Data
Processing
Manager***

hardware, software, data, procedures, and personnel—must be managed effectively to make this happen. Therefore, the **Management of Information Systems (MoIS)** is an important topic that must be given appropriate attention. This chapter discusses the various managerial issues involved in MoIS.

*Historical
Perspective*

We first discuss some changes in the organization of IS that have taken place over the last 30 years. During the 1960s, computers were first introduced into organizations as tools that could be used to process raw facts (data) into information, and the information system was highly **centralized.** A clearly definable **data processing department** commonly consisted of a mainframe computer, its accompanying input/output devices, support personnel, and other IS professionals. The IS was, to a large extent, isolated from other functional areas, and many workers' only contact with the IS was through the information created by the data processing department. Managing the IS consisted primarily of overseeing the operations of the data processing department, so the highest IS executive was typically the manager of that department. Because much of the processing involved financial or accounting data, the data processing manager often reported to the budget or accounting director, as seen in the organization chart shown in Figure 16–1. The accounting director is often called the controller.

To reduce the isolation of the data processing department, separate Management Information System (MIS) departments were developed so that the use of information could be more widespread. In the 1970s, functional departments or geographically remote areas of an organization obtained minicomputers to perform local processing. If these mini-

FIGURE 16–2

*Location of
Information
System Director*

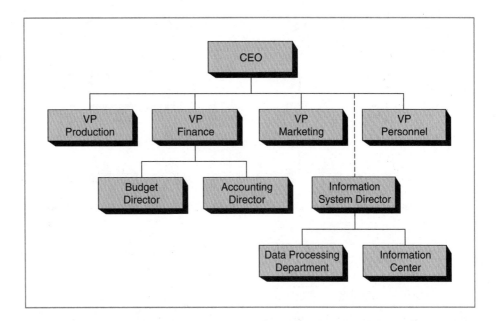

computers were linked to the organization's mainframe, then **distributed data processing** was possible. Eventually, users were impatient with the slow pace of systems development that was often associated with the centralized data processing environment. These users started doing some of their own systems development, as discussed in Chapter 15. They also wanted more control over data processing activities. As a result, there was a move toward a **decentralized information system,** which required that IS management be more aware of users' needs. In response to these needs, the first **Information Centers (ICs)** were established. Recall from Chapter 15 that an IC helps users combine the processing power of the organization's mainframe with easy-to-use computer software. IS managers still retained the bulk of the purchasing power and carried out the majority of processing for the organization. Because the IS had grown in its importance of the overall organization, the position of the highest IS executive was often directly below the vice presidential level, as seen in Figure 16–2. In Figure 16–2, the IS director is concerned with the IC and the data processing department.

*The
Introduction of
the Chief
Information
Officer*

In the 1980s and early 1990s, the PC revolution fueled the trend toward decentralized ISs. Not only did functional departments have computers, but individuals had powerful personal computers sitting on their desks. Control of the IS was moving from the organization to individuals who were making their own hardware and software purchasing decisions. Local Area Networks (LANs) linked end users and provided needed software. At the same time, centralized mainframe operations were integrated with the demands of the minicomputer-based departments and the PC-oriented end users.

These developments, along with the recognition of the value of having an effective IS, have led to a different approach to IS management. Many companies now realize that a **Chief Information Officer (CIO)** is needed just as much as a Chief Executive Officer

FIGURE 16-3   *Position of Chief Information Officer*

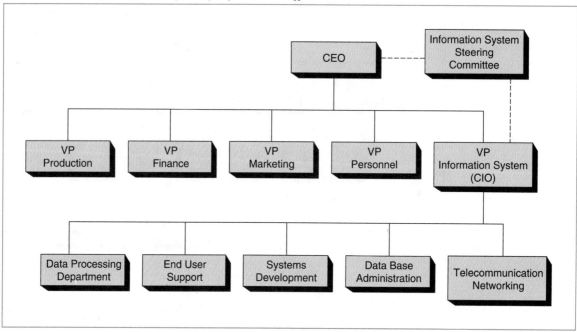

(CEO) and a Chief Financial Officer (CFO). CIO may not be the actual title, but the responsibilities are clear—strategically managing and using the corporate information resources. The CIO is a member of top management and performs much the same role for company data as the CFO does for the company budget, including planning new programs, ensuring that corporate data are used appropriately, and educating management about the use of information. At ProYacht, Inc., the head of the IS is called the Director of Corporate Information Systems rather than the CIO.

The first reference to the CIO was by William Synnott and William Gruber in 1981,[3] when they noted that properly used information can be a priceless strategic tool. When used with a thorough understanding of a company's needs and direction, information can give the company a clear competitive edge. From those authors' point of view, a CIO would ensure that the greatest competitive advantage was gained from corporate information. The organization chart in Figure 16-3 shows the position of the CIO in relation to other corporate officers.

In Figure 16-3, note that the CIO is responsible for many elements of the IS, including the end user support area (including the IC), data processing department, systems development department, data base administration, and the telecommunications/networking department. In the figure, the **IS steering committee** is composed of high-level managers

[3] William Synnott and William Gruber, *Information Resource Management: Opportunities and Strategies for the 1980's* (New York: Wiley, 1981).

from each functional area (marketing, production, finance, and personnel) who provide direction to the CIO as to their information needs. At ProYacht, representatives of each division make up the steering committee. The key role of the steering committee in the system analysis and design process is outlined in Chapters 12 and 13.

By 1987, surveys showed that as many as one-half of the *Fortune* 500 companies had created a CIO position. More than just upgraded data processing managers, these individuals examine the big information–management picture and involve the various divisions of the company in harnessing information technology to gain the needed competitive edge. By the mid-1990s, most successful corporations should have a CIO.

16.1 Information System Planning

A key activity in MoIS is that of planning to ensure that the IS provides the support needed by all levels of management. Planning is the first of Fayol's managerial roles, and it must be carried out before any other role. Planning involves determining objectives and then defining ways to achieve those objectives. In addition, IS planning requires that the IS match the overall objectives of the organization. Failure to carry out IS planning or the development of an IS plan that does not match the organization's overall objectives can have severe negative consequences. Every IS professional has ''war stories'' of decisions made in the absence of an IS plan or decisions that did not match the IS plan.

IS planning can be carried out at several levels. At the top level of IS management is the development of an **IS strategic plan,** which sets forth long-term IS objectives. Implementing the IS strategic plan requires the development of an **IS operational plan** at the lower levels of IS management. This plan identifies and carries out the day-to-day tasks necessary to implement the IS strategic plan. In addition to strategic and operational plans, an organization must develop contingency plans. An **IS contingency plan** details the organization's reaction to an event that has a large-scale negative impact, for example, a fire or earthquake.

IS strategic planning involves determining a long-term plan for IS development. This plan must support the corporate strategic plan. If it does not, the IS will not support the organization's information needs to achieve the desired competitive advantage.

Developing an IS strategic plan is an iterative, multistep process that involves the CEO, CIO, IS steering committee, and IS planning committee. The planning committee is made up of various IS department heads (IC and systems development, for example) who advise the CIO on the planning process. Large companies also have an IS planner, who develops and refines the IS strategic plan. In most cases, however, the CIO or an assistant is primarily responsible for this task.

The steps in developing an IS strategic plan are as follows:

1. Analyze corporate strategic plan and determine how the IS can aid in reaching the objectives enumerated in that plan.

2. Develop a set of objectives for the IS strategic plan.

3. Develop a list of steps, or the **master plan,** which leads to the accomplishment of the stated IS objectives.

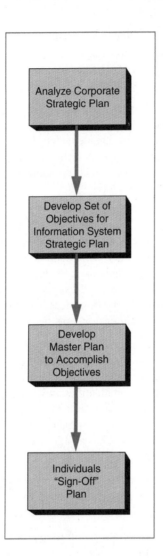

FIGURE 16–4

Development of Information System Strategic Plan

All individuals involved in the planning process must ''sign off'' the plan before it is accepted and implemented. This process is demonstrated in Figure 16–4.

Once the IS strategic plan is accepted by the CEO and IS steering committee, it is implemented through a series of long- and short-term plans. A long-term plan involves the required hardware and software acquisitions and system developments that extend beyond three years. On the other hand, short-term plans last for less than three years.

16.2 Hardware Management

As we noted earlier, the IS composed of hardware, software, data, procedures, and personnel must be managed effectively as a part of the MoIS. The elements of the IS are shown in Figure 16–5. In this section, we discuss some issues involved in the management of hardware. Managing the other IS elements is considered in subsequent sections.

FIGURE 16–5

Information System Elements

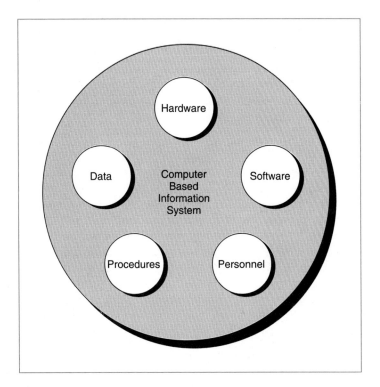

In managing hardware, four issues must be considered—acquisition, cost allocation, control, and security. Hardware acquisition refers to the process that is used to choose and obtain the desired hardware items that meet the needs of long- and short-term plans. Cost allocation issues involve developing policies for charging the costs of operating the IS to users. Hardware control refers to the policies and procedures for restricting the use of hardware to processing that furthers the objectives in the IS strategic plan. Finally, hardware security refers to the protection of hardware from human and natural threats. We have already discussed the acquisition of hardware in Chapter 14, and control and security issues are discussed in detail in the next chapter. The development of contingency plans to deal with the security issues are also discussed in Chapter 17. Therefore, we concentrate on cost allocation issues in the next section.

Cost Allocation

Although the cost of hardware today is plummeting, mainframe hardware still costs millions of dollars and minicomputers can cost well over $100,000. Additional costs of software purchase or development, human support, supplies, and system operation make developing and operating an IS a significant cost to any organization.

Although most cost allocation questions involve the use of mainframes and/or minicomputers, even the use of personal computers can require the allocation of IS costs if an IC or LAN is involved. For an IC, the organization may want to allocate the cost of personnel and software. Because the cost of installing a LAN can easily exceed $100,000 without counting the cost of personal computers and required software, these costs may also need to be allocated. Regardless of the type of IS used, a question that most IS system managers face sooner or later is: How are the costs of the IS allocated to its users?

In many situations, multiple objectives are simultaneously at work in determining cost allocation policies. On one hand, these costs must be allocated somewhere in the organization to arrive at a "bottom line" profit value. At the same time, the IS should be available to as many people as possible to make them more effective in their work. Depending on how costs are allocated, one objective may be favored over the other; they may also conflict.

Various approaches have been suggested for the allocation of these costs. At one extreme is the idea of making IS use "free," similar to the corporate library. At the other end of the cost allocation spectrum is the policy of charging all costs of running the IS directly to users depending on the amount of use. Problems exist with both extremes. The former approach ignores the fact that users may need to share the computer resources. With a mainframe or minicomputer, use can be limited by the processing power of the computer and number of workstations. Even a PC LAN may have only a limited number of copies of a software package that must be shared among users. On the other hand, workers are encouraged to use the available resources without worrying about the company's "bottom line."

Charging users a cost based on the amount of their use allocates the resources on an economic basis. This allocation policy encourages responsible use and not the excess usage often found when computer time is "free." However, this approach can penalize heavy IS users who may produce the greatest competitive advantage for the company. A disastrous side effect of this policy is the central computer sitting inactive because the heavy users are out of funds to "purchase" processing time.

User Chargeback Policies

To handle the problem of allocating IS costs to users, **chargeback policies** are often instituted. Four types of chargeback policies are generally used. We have already mentioned two of these policies—the "free" use policy and cost allocation based on use. Two other chargeback policies are variations on these two extremes. In one case, users are allocated a set amount of time on the mainframe. This time is often computed in terms of dollars—so-called "funny money"—which the user can spend in processing time and disk storage. This type of system is common in many academic environments.

Although the "funny money" chargeback system lets users know how much processing time they are using, it does not actually restrict computer use unless "real" dollar penalties are assessed for exceeding the budget allocation. Some organizations find this policy a useful way to shift from the "free" use policy to one that involves actual charges for IS use. This policy helps managers plan and budget the magnitude of information resources needed and keeps users within budgetary bounds.

Another chargeback system divides costs associated with the IS into fixed and variable components. The fixed components associated with permanent hardware, software, and personnel are budgeted as a fixed charge to the organization segment that requests the resource capacity. This allocation encourages use of the equipment. Variable operating costs are allocated based on actual use to control the usage.

The selection of a particular chargeback policy should be made in the same way as other decisions involving the IS — in line with the IS strategic plan. For example, the organization should not develop an IS strategic plan that emphasizes widespread IS use and then select a chargeback policy that discourages IS use.

16.3 Managing Systems Development

We have discussed in previous chapters that software can be either developed or purchased. If the decision is made to purchase software, then the procurement procedures discussed in Chapter 14 should be used. Management's involvement in this process is primarily ensuring that the standard selection and purchasing procedures are followed and that the system does what the managers want it to do. If software is developed using the systems analysis and design procedures discussed in Chapters 12 and 13, then management must pay careful attention to the complexities of the development process. Otherwise, the organization may be faced with a software development project that is late, over budget, does not work as designed, or all three. Regardless of how much analysis and design work occurs prior to the actual writing of computer software, the process still involves a large degree of programmers' creativity and experience. In addition, most development projects need multiple workers, thereby requiring a high degree of cooperation and communication among individual programmers.

Problems in the Development Process

The major problems that lead to systems failures in the development process include the tendency to shorten some development steps in the structured approach, use a prototype in lieu of a final fully developed system, or engage in shoddy end user development procedures. Table 16–1 outlines the problems that can occur if a particular phase of the structured systems development cycle is not properly completed.

Frederick P. Brooks on System Design

Frederick Brooks was the manager of the team of systems programmers that developed the operating system for the IBM System/360, which was the industry standard from the mid-1960s to the early 1970s. Before that, he was the project manager for the hardware team for the same system. This operating system, known as OS/360, was the result of many people working for several years to arrive at a workable system. In his book on the problems with managing software development, Brooks makes the following comments:

In most projects, the first system built is barely usable. It may be too slow, too big, too awkward to use, or all three. There is no alternative but to start again, smarting but smarter, and build a redesigned version in which these problems are solved. The discard and redesign may be done in one lump, or it may be done piece-by-piece. But all large-system experience shows that it will be done. Where a new system concept or new technology is used, one has to build a system to throw away, for even the best planning is not so omniscient as to get it right the first time.

SOURCE: Frederick P. Brooks, *The Mythical Man Month: Essays on Software Engineering* (Reading, MA: Addison-Wesley, 1975), p. 116.

Phase	Result of Noncompletion of Phase
1. Problem Definition	Solutions for the wrong problem
2. Feasibility Study	Overestimation of effects of technology Underestimation of costs Attempting a project beyond the capability of the organization
3. Analysis	Inadequate definition of information requirements Distribution to management of the wrong information at the wrong time
4. General Design	Incomplete consideration of alternatives Failure to specify complete system requirements for alternatives
5. Detailed Design	No common set of criteria for preparation or evaluation of proposals Incomplete design specifications
6. Implementation: Acquisition and Development	No program testing No training Lost data at conversion Poorly written programs with many errors
7. Operations and Maintenance	No follow up on compliance with objectives Poorly run system Controls not functioning System degradation

TABLE 16–1

Problems in the Structured Systems Development Cycle

These problems are often the result of unreasonable demands by functional managers, unrealistic estimates by IS managers, changing priorities, and a lack of understanding of the development process. In the first case, functional managers may suffer from the ''I want it yesterday!'' syndrome. For example, a manager reads about a competitor's new IS and immediately decides that his or her department needs a similar one *now*. Unaware of the time needed to develop a new IS, the functional manager, and possibly top management, places unreasonable demands on the IS manager to come up with such a system immediately.

When this scenario occurs, the second type of problem naturally follows—the IS manager attempts to meet the demands for a new IS by providing overly optimistic estimates of the time required to develop the project. Then, as the project is developed, the IS manager may use the ''90 percent'' solution to deflect continuing demands for the completion of the project. As the estimated time of completion nears, the IS manager invariably reports that the project is ''90 percent complete,'' regardless of the true status of the project.

Another rationale for the IS manager's overly optimistic response is the fear of being criticized or possibly fired. This response mechanism is not limited to the software development industry; it occurs in the development of any type of large-scale project in which top management pressures a department for acceptable results. NASA has experienced this problem in at least two instances. Because top management was not notified that O-rings on the *Challenger* space shuttle might not work in near-freezing weather, the launch proceeded and the *Challenger* exploded. In the second instance, managers were not informed that the mirrors on the Hubble Space Telescope were ground incorrectly, so defective equipment was launched. Such problems follow from a poor analysis of information requirements and of the time needed to develop a system to satisfy those requirements.

When a project is underway for several months without immediate results, the original enthusiasm for it may be lost and functional managers may think about other projects or concerns. This situation can lead to a shift of priorities to new, more exciting projects and a corresponding reduction in resources for existing projects. For systems development personnel, this change in priorities can cause frustration, reduced productivity level, and problems with meeting project deadlines.

As a result of these three problem areas, projects may be developed more slowly than expected. If the schedule for a systems development starts to slip, IS managers may be pressured to complete the project on time. Because non-IS managers do not understand the systems development process, they may suggest that additional people be assigned to the project to speed up the process. Unfortunately, adding people to a systems development project often just slows it down. This situation is an example of Brooks' Law. Named after Frederick P. Brooks, who was the project manager for the development of the first large-scale mainframe operating system in the 1960s, Brooks' Law states that *adding people to a late software project will make it later!* Brooks noted that this occurs because systems development is not the type of task for which people and time are

*Baxter
Underestimates
the Cost of
Developing
Software*

As discussed in Chapter 1, Baxter Healthcare Corporation has successfully used information strategically to gain a competitive advantage. Its ASAP product ordering system electronically links hospital purchasing departments with Baxter's home office to speed product shipment. However, this experience in systems development failed to help Baxter turn a profit on software developed for sale to other companies. Baxter apparently underestimated the cost of developing and supporting new software, and at the same time, overestimated the value of the Baxter name in this market. As a result of this combination of errors, Baxter was forced to split off two of its software divisions as part of a joint venture with IBM.

Baxter's software divisions had estimated software sales of between $150 million and $250 million, but the costs of support and upgrades kept the software from being as profitable as Baxter had hoped. Experts note that a software firm typically must spend 25% of its revenues in basic support and another 15% on research and development of software upgrades. The need for support was especially crucial for the minicomputer systems Baxter was installing. Although the company could install 15 or 20 systems in six months, it could not support them and develop software upgrades at the same time.

SOURCE: Robert L. Scheier, ''IS Leader Baxter Healthcare Falters in Software Market,'' *PC Week,* October 9, 1989, pp. 95, 101.

interchangeable resources.[4] Worse, the task requires a great deal of communication among co-workers, so adding people to a project after the planning stage causes delays because new people must be brought up to speed.

*Managing
Systems
Development
Problems*

In the preceding discussion, we noted three types of systems development problems that often face IS managers. Although the use of prototyping and other alternative system development methodologies can result in shorter turnaround times between the initiation of a project and usable results, these methodologies are not always appropriate for developing a large-scale IS. In these cases, managers must find other ways to solve these problems. One solution is simply to follow the IS strategic plan. The IS strategic plan must be dynamic and account for changes in the marketplace. With a well-designed IS strategic plan, many problems do not occur. Functional managers' requests for project development would be considered *only* if they fit into the IS strategic plan. Similarly, an IS manager would not need to make overly optimistic estimates about the time required to complete a project. Once a project that is part of the IS strategic plan is begun, development priorities do not change.

To manage the development process efficiently and to avoid rushing through various phases of the process, many organizations resort to project management techniques. **Project management** refers to a wide range of techniques and procedures used to

[4] Frederick P. Brooks, *The Mythical Man Month: Essays on Software Engineering* (Reading, MA: Addison-Wesley, 1975).

manage any type of large-scale project, including construction projects, military systems, space exploration projects, and software systems. These techniques help to schedule project steps, control activities from time and budget perspectives, and allocate resources to ensure timely completion of various steps in the development process.

In general, project management involves managing the people working on a project, determining the scope and quality of the final product, controlling the budget, and scheduling the parts of the project. Virtually all large-scale projects are carried out by a team of people — the **project team** — as discussed in Chapters 12 and 13. A **team leader** manages the day-to-day work of the team and ensures that overall objectives of the project are met. For many years, organizations assumed that an IS professional should lead a team of the information professionals developing the system. However, with the ever-increasing importance given to the eventual user of the system, team leaders are often selected from the management of the user department. As a result, users are more involved in the system development, so the final product more closely meets their needs.

The team leader must ensure that the scope and quality of the project are acceptable within management's budgetary controls and the user department's time demands. A common problem involving the scope and quality of a project is the user requesting software system features beyond those in the original plan. As indicated in Chapter 12, this may happen when users elaborate on their information needs in the analysis phase of systems development or identify their needs in the iterative prototyping process. Decisions must be made as to whether the features can be added to the project without affecting the original quality requirements, budget constraints, and schedule. Team management must be willing to make these tough decisions, because quality, costs, and schedules can all slip, resulting in a poorly developed system that is over budget and late. In several well-known cases, commercial software products were announced, but poor project management resulted in a product with many errors (''bugs'') or no product at all (often referred to as ''vaporware'').

Various techniques can help team management with the budgeting and scheduling of a project. Bar and line graphs that are updated periodically can keep managers aware of the current status of actual costs compared with the planned level of spending. For scheduling control, two commonly used tools are the Gantt chart and network models. These models can be used to manage such human resources as programmers and analysts as well as the financial resources needed to develop and implement the project. A **Gantt chart** is a series of horizontal bars showing the proposed schedule and the actual start and finish times for each project element. Conceptually simple, Gantt charts are powerful tools for evaluating the current status of a project. For example, Figure 16–6 shows a sample Gantt chart for a software development project. In this example, task A was begun on time but finished late, and task B was begun late but finished on time. Task C was begun on time and is still in progress.

Gantt charts are powerful tools for project scheduling, but they do not show precedence relationships — that is, what activities must precede other activities. These relationships can be shown through the use of such network models as **Critical Path Method/Project Evaluation Review Technique (CPM/PERT).** In CPM/PERT, tasks are shown as

FIGURE 16–6   *Example of Gantt Chart*

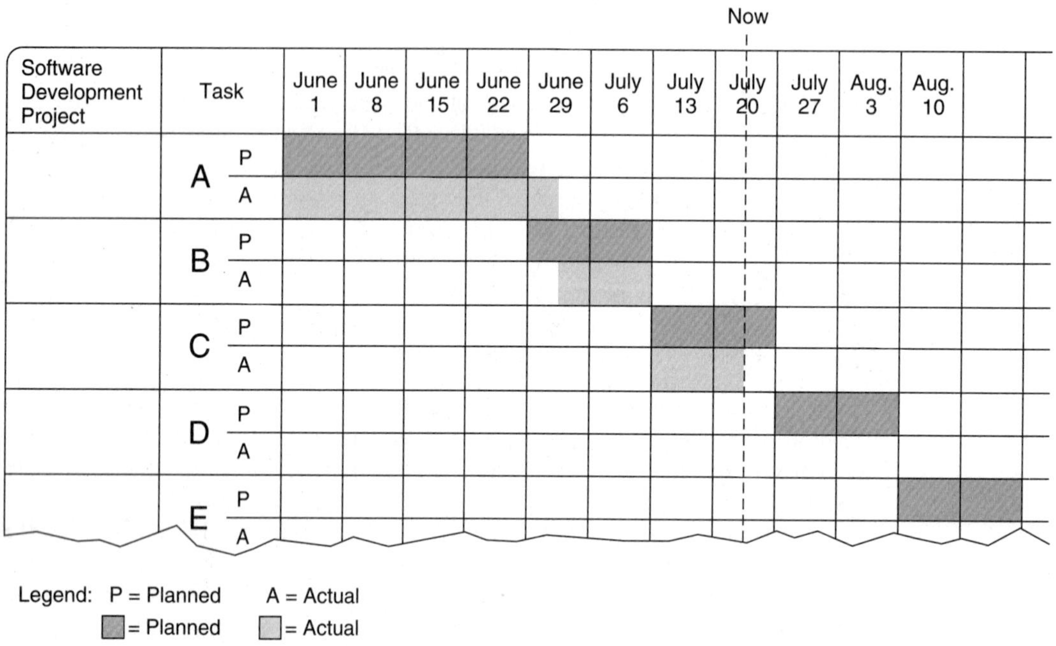

Software Development Project	Task		June 1	June 8	June 15	June 22	June 29	July 6	July 13	July 20 (Now)	July 27	Aug. 3	Aug. 10		
	A	P	▓	▓	▓	▓									
		A	░	░	░										
	B	P					▓	▓							
		A					░	░							
	C	P							▓	▓					
		A								░					
	D	P									▓	▓			
		A													
	E	P											▓	▓	
		A													

Legend: P = Planned   A = Actual
        ▓ = Planned   ░ = Actual

arrows on a network, and the minimum possible time required to complete a project can be computed. Figure 16–7 shows the list of activities for the same sample software development project that was used earlier to demonstrate a Gantt chart.

CPM/PERT is especially useful with a large network of activities, as with any large development project. The network for the activities listed in Figure 16–7 is presented in Figure 16–8; the figure shows many nodes and activities, as well as estimated times of completion. A numbered node indicates the beginning and end of an activity, such as programming, and letters designate activities. For each activity to commence, another activity or set of activities must be completed. For example, in Figure 16–8, before beginning Activity O (test and debug programs), N and F must be complete.

As activities are completed, comparisons can be made between planned schedule times and actual times. These times and their network can be used to compute the critical path, which is the heavy solid line in Figure 16–8. The **critical path** is the path through the network with the longest estimated time for completion. Any delay along this path delays implementation of the system. In this example, the critical path consists of Activities A, B, C, D, E, H, I, K, L, N, O, P, R, U, and W. On the critical path, the project takes a total of 49 weeks to complete. Any activity not on this path has some slack time, so the start of that activity can be delayed or that activity can take longer to complete if the need arises.

FIGURE 16–7

Activities and Expected Time of Completion

Description	Activity	Time (Weeks)	Preceding Activity
Determine output requirements	A	4	
Determine processing activities	B	2	A
Determine data requirements	C	2	B
Determine input	D	2	C
Establish control procedures	E	2	D
Select and install hardware	F	10	E
Plan conversion and backup	G	1	E
Detail processing activities	H	3	E
Identify programming modules	I	1	H
Determine data structure	J	1	E
Plan programming	K	2	I&J
Specify programming details	L	4	K
Outline user, operations, and program manuals	M	1	L
Write programs	N	3	L
Test and debug programs	O	8	F&N
Structured walk through of programs	P	1	O
Complete documentation and manuals	Q	1	M
Test the system	R	2	P&Q
Collect data for conversion	S	1	C,G,I&J
Convert data files	T	2	S,F,N
Conversion volume test (parallel runs)	U	12	R,T
Complete user training	V	8	M
Convert to the new system	W	1	V,U

However, if all slack time is used, then that activity becomes critical. The network may be revised throughout the project as actual times replace estimated times.

Through the use of Gantt charts and CPM/PERT network techniques, team management can monitor the progress of a project and determine if additional resources or time are needed to complete the project as originally planned. Brooks' Law holds for projects that are behind schedule during the end-stages of the development process. However, problems found early in the development process can often be corrected by adding people in the initial stages.

These management techniques were originally used to manage a project's budget and schedule manually. Now, many project management software packages can do the same thing faster and with much less effort. Such packages for the personal computer include Harvard Project Manager, Microsoft Project for Windows, Mac Project, and TimeLine

FIGURE 16–8   *Critical Path Method/Project Evaluation Review Technique Network*

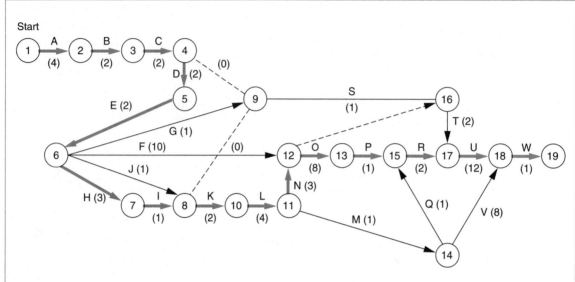

SOURCE: Adapted with permission from Robert A. Leitch and K. Roscoe Davis, *Accounting Information Systems* (Englewood Cliffs, NJ: Prentice-Hall, 1992), p. 406.

4.0. Many packages now also offer high-quality presentation graphics for use in displaying the Gantt charts and network models in multiple colors. Figure 16–9 shows the use of one such project management software package.

16.4 Data Management

We emphasize throughout this text that data and information are the lifeblood of most organizations and integral parts of the IS. Data and information must also be effectively managed to be available to individuals and departments within the organization. **Data management** is the function of controlling the acquisition, analysis, storage, retrieval, and distribution of data. Data management encompasses the **data base administrator** position discussed in Chapter 6, but it goes beyond this single position to provide the overall management of data as an organizational resource. These operations were discussed in detail in Chapters 5 and 6, so this area is not discussed in any further detail here.

16.5 Personnel Management

The management of IS personnel is among the most important functions of MoIS. Without people, the IS would not operate at all. What complicates the management of IS personnel is that they tend to view their jobs differently from most other professions. Instead of considering themselves employees of an organization, IS professionals view themselves as members of the "IS profession" who happen to be working for that organization. This attitude results in high turnover levels as IS professionals look for higher pay and better benefits with another organization. A shortage of qualified IS

FIGURE 16–9   *Output from Project Management Software Package*

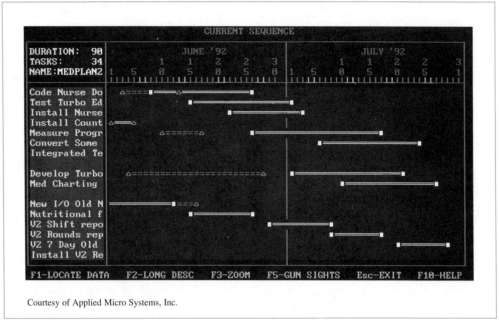

Courtesy of Applied Micro Systems, Inc.

people and average salaries higher than other white collar workers compound this problem.

IS professionals are usually very dedicated to their projects and pay little attention to a 40-hour work week or ''normal'' working hours. IS professionals may work all night or weekends to solve a problem. During the development of the Apple Macintosh computer, members of the development team wore shirts that said, ''Working 90 hours a week and loving it!''

These characteristics of IS professionals—loyalty to the IS profession and tendency to work flexible hours—can cause problems for managers who try to treat them like other employees. A continuing shortage of experienced programmers and analysts means these IS professionals can always move to another organization if they are unhappy with their pay or benefits. Management must be sensitive to the level of pay and benefits in the industry and ensure that their employees are compensated at that level.

IS compensation is growing at a rapid rate. A survey of 31 major U.S. corporations showed an average increase in IS compensation of almost 15 percent for the 1989–1990 period.[5] Table 16–2 shows the growth in salaries of selected IS professionals from 1989 to 1990.

---

[5] Alan J. Ryan, ''Salaries of IS Jobs Skyrocket,'' *Computerworld,* June 18, 1990, p. 8.

TABLE 16–2

Increase in
Information
System
Professionals
Compensation,
1989–1990

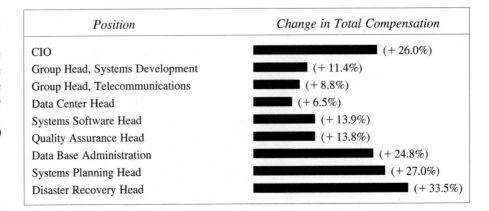

Position	Change in Total Compensation
CIO	(+ 26.0%)
Group Head, Systems Development	(+ 11.4%)
Group Head, Telecommunications	(+ 8.8%)
Data Center Head	(+ 6.5%)
Systems Software Head	(+ 13.9%)
Quality Assurance Head	(+ 13.8%)
Data Base Administration	(+ 24.8%)
Systems Planning Head	(+ 27.0%)
Disaster Recovery Head	(+ 33.5%)

Any attempt to force IS professionals to work so-called "normal" office hours can quickly lead to a reduction in productivity or a loss of personnel, or both. Because IS professionals tend to be task oriented, they should be judged on the results of their work, not the hours they work. On the other hand, IS professionals should be available to discuss project status with users and other members of the team. The team leader must handle the trade-off between the task and career orientation of IS professionals and the needs and goals of the organization.

Information
System Careers

The managers of IS personnel should be aware of career paths that are available in that field. In the IS profession, career fields can be categorized as IS management, end user support, communications, systems and programming, technical services and operations, and data base administration. Table 16–3 shows these six areas, selected job titles for each area, and the average compensation for these positions for large corporations.[6]

IS management refers to individuals like the CIO who have responsibility for the overall IS, including all other areas listed in the table. End user support involves the support of PC-based end users through the IC. Management of the LAN may be part of end user support or communications. The PC specialist provides technical support to end users who are acquiring and using PC hardware and software.

The communications area is rapidly growing as organizations rely more on networks to handle their information needs. A position in this area can involve managing an organization's LAN or wide area network, as well as overseeing voice and data communications, including Electronic Data Interchange (EDI) with outside firms. Analysts and programmers design and write the software that is used with the IS. Many IS professionals start their careers as programmers and then branch out into other areas as they gain IS experience and knowledge.

---

[6] David A. Ludlum, "The Envelope Please . . . ," *Computerworld,* September 3, 1990, pp. 57, 59.

TABLE 16–3

Information System Job Titles and Compensation

Area	Job Titles	Compensation
IS Management	CIO	$104,801
	IS Manager/Supervisor	75,110
End User Support	Manager, End User Computing	$56,139
	IC Manager	55,452
	LAN Manager	45,868
	PC Specialist	35,827
Communications	Network Manager	$58,610
	Telecommunications Manager	55,555
	Communications Specialist	40,971
Systems and Programming	Systems/Programming Manager	$64,457
	Project Leader	52,579
	Senior Systems Analyst	47,967
	Senior Programmer/Analyst	42,841
	Programmer	29,880
Technical Services and Operations	Technical Services Manager	$62,836
	Senior Operating Systems Programmer	51,271
	Operations Manager	50,893
	Operations Shift Supervisor	35,402
Data Base Administration	Data Base Manager/Administrator	$57,270
	Data Base Analyst	45,275

SOURCE: David A. Ludlum, ''The Envelope Please . . . ,'' *Computerworld,* September 3, 1990, pp. 57, 59.

Technical services and operations handle much of the data processing that is carried out on a mainframe. Operating system programmers must be available to solve any problems that arise in the mainframe operating system. Also included in this area are machine operators who run the computer, load jobs, and file output. Finally, the data base administration group oversees the design and maintenance of the organization's data base to ensure its integrity and stability.

Information System Personnel Management Problems

In addition to the problems already noted in the management of IS personnel, three other problems exist. These problems include the bias in the pay scale toward managerial roles, the assignment of system maintenance tasks, and the management of telecommuters. As seen in Table 16–3, the highest paid individual in each IS career area is the department manager. Therefore, a person must move into a managerial role to reach the highest pay level in his or her field. This situation is not unique to the IS field; it is a common trend in most areas of business, industry, and government, with the possible exception of higher education. Unfortunately, a person who is very good at a staff role such as programming may not be good at managing other people. In Table 16–3, the difference in pay between the highest paid nonmanagement person in the system and programming areas (the Senior Systems Analyst) and the department manager is almost $17,000. This failure to reward a person for an outstanding job in a nonmanagerial role can lead to unhappiness and turnover.

Previous discussions of systems development emphasized development of new software systems. However, as much as 70 percent of system development time is actually devoted to maintaining existing systems. This work involves finding and correcting bugs in a system, upgrading a system for new hardware, or converting a system to run on a different type or size of computer. For example, a program that is written in COBOL may need to be converted to run on a personal computer.

The problem with system maintenance work is that it is often considered the most boring and tedious type of systems development work, and few IS professionals want to be assigned to this job. Managers wonder who should be assigned to perform the maintenance job—experienced employees who may be familiar with the system or new employees who can gain experience from the task. Each approach has pros and cons. Experienced employees may feel that they should work on developing new systems due to their experience and seniority. On the other hand, recently hired employees may bring with them more recent systems development techniques that should be used in developing new systems.

Obviously, no one answer is right. The systems development manager must take advantage of each employee's skills for the good of the organization and attempt to honor each employee's interests. Otherwise, the employee turnover problem can be exacerbated when more mobile employees find other positions, leaving the organization with less mobile (often embittered) employees.

The third issue is facing more IS managers every day—how to handle telecommuters. Recall from Chapter 7 that a telecommuter works at home some or all of the time and uses telecommunications to interact with the office. The management of telecommuters must deal with the loss of contact with the office and the measurement of productivity.

With the increased availability of personal computers and high-speed communications with the organization's mainframe, telecommuting is expected to increase significantly from the 38 million people who telecommuted in 1991. One negative way to handle this problem is to simply not allow the practice. Unfortunately, the organization may lose good people to a company that allows employees to work at home. To handle the problem of loss of office contact, an organization may use the concept of "flex time," requiring telecommuters to spend some "core time" in the office each week. Productivity measures should be worked out in advance and discussed regularly with each telecommuter. If these issues are met, telecommuting can work well for both the organization and the worker.

Telecommuting at J.C. Penney

In addition to its many outlets around the country, retailing giant J.C. Penney operates an extensive telemarketing branch that handles calls for catalog orders. In 1981, to handle surges of incoming calls at its telephone sales outlets, the company allowed a few sales associates to work at home. In 1990, this program had grown so large that one-half of J.C. Penney's 16 telemarketing centers had over 200 telecommuters. To be part of this program, workers must have at least one year of experience at the in-house telephone center. Each telecommuter is equipped with a terminal and two telephone lines for voice and data. When sudden surges in demand occur, a centralized call-forwarding system routes calls to a telecommuter. With this system, an overflow call can be handled in as little as five minutes, compared with the several hours required for a phone center employee to handle the call.

Company representatives visit each telecommuter to ensure that sufficient work space is available—at least 35 square feet—in a remote area of the home. Telecommuters are treated like in-store employees in terms of salary, benefits, and promotions. In addition, productivity and morale of the telecommuters have remained the same or even increased compared with those of in-house workers.

SOURCE: Kathleen Christensen, ''Remote Control,'' *PC Computing,* February 1990, pp. 90–94.

16.6 Managing Procedures

The final element of an IS that must be managed is the set of procedures used to run IS operations. This area is also referred to as **operations management.** In this key area, much of the actual IS planning and controlling of operations is executed. Operations management comprises several issues that we have already discussed, including user chargeback procedures, operations personnel management, and systems maintenance. Also included are such issues as system documentation, data processing management, and operational planning.

System Documentation

A key job of operations management is the preparation, maintenance, and distribution of system documentation. **System documentation** consists of all written documents that describe the IS and the procedures for carrying out data processing tasks. It serves several important roles in the IS. First, system documentation is the primary means of communicating essential elements of the IS to its users. Second, system documentation provides the policies and procedures that should be followed in the operation of IS computers and software. Third, system documentation can be used for training new employees in IS operations. Finally, it serves as the basis for changes in the IS.

Although the preparation and maintenance of system documentation are often viewed as onerous tasks to be avoided if possible, they are still very important to IS operations. The absence of appropriate documentation can be a sign of weakness within the management of the IS. An organization without a technical writing staff may need to employ professional writers for this task to ensure that it is done correctly.

A special type of documentation is program documentation. Recall that computer software is made up of one or more computer programs that are written by one or more individuals. **Program documentation** describes the logic behind the programs for the software user and other programmers who work with or maintain the software. Software should be adequately documented both in the programs themselves and with written documents that describe program operations. Without documentation, the software may not be used after the original programmer leaves the organization.

Data Processing Management

The data processing operation of the IS carries on much of an organization's day-to-day processing of data into information. Such operations as payroll, accounting, inventory control, and transaction processing and MIS tasks (discussed in Chapters 8 and 9) fall under the general heading of data processing. The effective management of the data processing operation is crucial to the well-being of an organization and involves the following tasks:

- Defining procedures for the operation of the computer system and ensuring that these procedures are carried out

- Scheduling operating personnel

- Scheduling processing jobs on the computer system

- Monitoring the operation of the computer system in terms of utilization, performance, and costs

- Ensuring that routine maintenance and software backup operations are performed as scheduled

- Providing controls and security for the computer system

- Maintaining a data base

- Maintaining a tape, disk pack, and program library to control access to data and programs

- Overseeing IC activities

Data processing management is more like the management of production facilities rather than like any other type of IS management. It requires constant attention to the implementation of procedures and the meeting of processing (production) schedules.

Operational Planning

The third element of managing operations is operational planning. **Operational planning** involves implementing the objectives set forth in the IS strategic plan. The goal of operational planning is to plan for future hardware, software, and personnel needs. For example, if the strategic plan calls for a 25 percent increase in mainframe processing capability within the next five years, operational planning considers the various hardware and software options that will make this additional capability available when needed.

A detailed form of operational planning is production planning, which provides short-term plans for the existing processing system. This type of planning schedules jobs to run at specific times over the next period—often in terms of weeks or months.

Because both operational and production planning are essential for fulfilling the IS strategic plan, they should not be ignored in favor of long-range plans. IS management must ensure that both types of plans are taken seriously and performed in a timely manner.

16.7 Information Centers

Before the introduction of the personal computer into the workplace, the IS manager was responsible only for one department and the interaction between users and a mainframe. With the advent of personal computers, much has changed. The managers and workers in an organization do not need to wait for the IS department to meet all their information needs. An employee can purchase a personal computer for less than $3,000 and solve some of those problems without the IS department. In the process, the following new group of problems has arisen:

- What type of personal computer should be purchased?

- Should everybody have the same type of personal computer?

- How can errors be avoided in PC data entry?

- How should software be selected?

- How can conflicting analyses from different departments be compared?

- How can the computers be hooked together or into the organization's mainframe?

When these problems are combined with the IS department's loss of control over the organization's flow of information, personal computers initially may cause more problems than they solve. Various approaches for coordinating the use of personal computers with the IS department have been suggested, but no single solution exists for all situations. Each organization must solve this problem according to its own needs.

One answer to the increased emphasis on personal computers is the concept of the information center, which combines the advantages of personal computers and an IS department. The IC is not a computer center. It is an organization that helps users combine the processing power of the organization's mainframe with easy-to-use PC programming languages and limited support of the IS department. The IC provides expanded information processing power while avoiding the problems of information processing complexity and the power struggles that often occur when computing power is decentralized. The IS department guarantees adequate processing power and helps clients (individuals or departments) within the organization to choose software. The software is then installed and tested by IS personnel, and required client training is carried out. The client provides the time and effort to use and manage this particular system through individual personal computers.

Generally, the IC helps with consulting and training activities, so that users can develop their own software. Clearly, a successful IC must have the following characteristics:

- Adequate support from senior management to provide the necessary funding

- Sufficient software packages to allow the client to cover a broad spectrum of work

- Individual clients willing to do the required work

- An IS department committed to the IC concept

- A comprehensive plan to develop, install, and maintain the IC

If these conditions hold, then an IC can do many things for end users, including the following:

1. Developing standards for end user applications development, testing, and documentation

2. Training end users to develop applications

3. Acting as a consultant to end users on purchase and use of hardware and software

The IC is a very important aspect of data processing management activities in many organizations. It has reduced the duplication of effort, expedited system development, and enhanced the control of end user development.

Developing Standards

To avoid some of the problems discussed earlier in the chapter that can occur when end user programmers develop software systems, the IC can set standards for designing, testing, and documenting the systems they create. These standards can require that end users discuss their work with co-workers, follow standardized formats for their projects, and extensively test their systems. In addition to setting standards for software development, the IC can be involved creating policies for users that ensure data and software security, avoid software piracy problems, and keep computers virus-free.

Training

A key role of the IC can be in training novice users and existing end users. New computer users can be trained in the use of computers to perform their jobs better. Similarly, current end users can be helped to increase their abilities with advanced software development techniques. The IC can provide various types of training including classroom, one-on-one training, computer-based training, and interactive video systems. Members of the IC can also provide information to users in brochures or periodic seminars on the availability and use of new software packages. This type of training can greatly reduce the number of users' questions.

Consulting

Because end users often have many questions about software and hardware acquisitions, the use of an existing software package, or about the software development and maintenance standards mentioned earlier, the IC often acts as a consultant. The IC can provide information for users to make hardware and software acquisition decisions. For example, the IC can answer users' questions about the type of secondary storage, video system, and amount of internal memory needed in a personal computer. Similarly, the IC can provide comparisons or reviews of software packages that a user is considering. IC members can also provide users with information on "quirks" in new releases of existing software packages or answer questions about how to use the advanced features of a software package. The IC can answer questions about the organization's hardware and software standards. In effect, the IC enforces these standards by ensuring that the user considers them only in the acquisition process.

16.8 Summary

The management and control of an organization's information resource (MoIS) is important. An IS must be well planned and operated. IS strategic plans ensure that resources are expended on the projects that fit into the overall information strategy of the organization. In many organizations, a CIO oversees all information processing and development activities.

Hardware and software cost an enormous amount of money that must be allocated to users and ultimately to the products or services the organization produces. As a result, users may need to be charged for their use of the system. This allocation must be done so that employees use, but do not waste, system resources and are not penalized for that use for the benefit of the organization.

Another important aspect of MoIS is the management of the systems development process. Many problems occur when a manager promises too much and hurries the development process. The process must be well managed and controlled. Steering committees and project teams can oversee the development from a management perspective. Gantt charts and CPM/PERT networks can effectively schedule and manage the development process and the allocation of resources to this process. Furthermore, to assist end users in the development of an IS, organizations may adopt the IC concept.

Not only does system development need to be managed, but hardware and software, data resources and those who operate the IS must also be managed. The data base administrator is often responsible for managing the data base. Personnel management poses real problems due to the many career opportunities for systems personnel. Innovative job structures are needed to utilize the technology available and harness the energies of those who work in the IS.

Finally, a well-managed system has adequate documentation, controls its data processing activities, and plans IS activities. To manage the proliferation of end users and personal computers in the organization, the IC sets standards and consults with and trains users.

Key Terms

centralized
chargeback policy
Chief Information Officer (CIO)

critical path
Critical Path Method/Project Evaluation Review Technique (CPM/PERT)

data base administrator
data management
data processing department
decentralized information system
distributed data processing
Gantt chart
Information Center (IC)
IS contingency plan
IS operational plan
IS steering committee
IS strategic plan

Management of Information Systems
 (MoIS)
manager
master plan
operational planning
operations management
program documentation
project management
project team
system documentation
team leader

**Review
Questions**

1. List the five elements of the IS that must be managed. What name is given to this type of management?

2. What name is commonly used to describe the executive in charge of an organization's IS? What other names are used to describe this position?

3. What plan outlines the long-term objectives of an IS? What plan helps identify the tasks necessary to carry out the previously named plan?

4. What plan details an organization's response to an event that has a large-scale negative impact on the organization?

5. What four issues must be considered in hardware management?

6. Why must hardware costs be allocated? List four chargeback policies.

7. What major problems lead to failures in the systems development process? What causes these problems?

8. What does Brooks' Law say about systems development?

9. How is project management related to systems development? What two tools are often used in project management?

10. Name some characteristics of IS professionals. How do these characteristics affect the management of an IS?

11. What three problems affect the management of IS personnel?

12. What type of management is involved with planning and controlling IS operations? What is the name for the written documents that describe the IS?

13. List four tasks involved in managing the data processing operation.

14. List three problems that have arisen due to the availability of personal computers in an organization.

15. What conditions must exist for a successful IC? List three IC functions.

Discussion Questions

1. Most organizations have scarce resources, and IS departments are no exception. What techniques can an IS use to schedule programmers and systems analysts and assign them to various tasks? Explain how these techniques can help in the following situations:
   a. When one project has slack time
   b. When three analysts are needed to do the job of five
   c. When one project falls behind schedule

2. In the last several years, ICs have evolved into an important activity, and CIOs have emerged as key figures in the information processing activities of organizations. Why? What essential roles do ICs and CIOs perform?

3. Midwestern Products manufactures a wide variety of consumer products. The company must continually research new ideas, explore new markets, manufacture new products, distribute these products to a changing population, promote its products effectively, and sell its products to a demanding public at a profit. It uses a large mainframe to support analyses of these trends and research for each product. Products are all considered profit centers. Midwestern has allowed each consumer product division to use the main computing facilities without charge. However, because management believes that the divisions are abusing the privilege, it is considering establishing a chargeback policy in which all costs for computer use are allocated on a usage time basis. Is this a good idea? Why or why not?

4. Assuming that you would someday like to manage a computer center, trace an appropriate career path. Suppose that you love the challenge of solving very difficult programming problems. What might your career path look like? What tasks are involved in most day-to-day software development? Do you see any potential problems in terms of career paths and development tasks for the future of the software industry? Referring back to earlier chapters, how can CASE help solve some of these problems?

Case 16–1
St. Anne's Hospital

St. Anne's Hospital of Ottawa, Ontario, Canada has decided to develop and implement a computer-based IS as soon as possible. St. Anne's MIS manager has identified the following activities, with their expected durations and precedence relationships, that would be involved in the undertaking:

Activity Code	Description of Activity	Expected Duration (Days)	Codes of Predecessor Activities[a]
A	Prepare system requirements	10	
B	Plan design phase	3	A
C	Design system	20	B, F
D	Verify feasibility	2	C
E	Organize project	5	A
F	Establish plans and controls	3	E
G	Prepare design specifications	2	C
H	Prepare audit and control specifications	4	G
I	Prepare job description for new employees	3	H
J	Prepare training guides	3	I
K	Prepare logic diagrams and programs	20	D
L	Prepare test data	4	K
M	Perform program testing and debugging	5	L
N	Select and order system resources	20	D
O	Install computer system	12	N
P	Perform system testing and debugging	5	M, O
Q	Prepare program documentation	5	M, O
R	Prepare system documentation	3	J, Q
S	Plan for system support	2	R
T	Perform final system check out and cutover	3	Q

[a] Activities that must be completed *prior* to starting the listed activity.

SOURCE: Adapted with permission from Society of Management Accountants of Canada (SMAC), May 1976, Information Systems Section, No. 1.

Case Question

Prepare a PERT network diagram and specify the activities on the critical path.

Case 16–2
Virginia Forest Products

The IS at Virginia Forest Products has evolved from a simple accounting IS to one that uses a large mainframe to support transaction processing, management information, decision support, and executive information systems. The IS is housed in the accounting department where it originated. All development requests must be approved and scheduled by the controller.

This arrangement has generated some problems, as characterized by the following excepts from several conversations:

"I can never get IS personnel to pay attention to my marketing problems. I need to track sales and assess the impact of housing trends on sales and the distribution of wood products," said the marketing vice president.

"I have had several staff members purchase personal computers that just sit on their desks. I wish I could get someone to help train my staff to use those things," said a personnel manager.

"I cannot seem to coordinate my activities with the production of pulp wood; our systems cannot communicate effectively. They involve an extraordinary amount of paperwork," said the head of paper products.

"I need some help developing spreadsheet macros for my budget planning model," said a finance staff person.

"Systems development around here seems to have no common objective. No policies are in place, and no one seems to know where we are going with our IS. I sense no rationale for how projects get priority, except perhaps first come, first served, or the project involves some critical financial area," said a disgruntled production manager.

Case Questions

1. What are the underlying causes of these problems?

2. What should the company do to correct these problems and better serve its information needs?

Controls in Information Systems

17

Introduction   Many **risks** are associated with managing an organization. Risk can be defined as the potential for some type of loss. Risk is an accepted part of business, and in many cases, the greater the risk, the greater the opportunity for profit. However, management usually wants to reduce the risks that have nothing to do with helping the organization reach its goals. A key area in which management can reduce risk is the organization's Information System (IS). Risks associated with the IS vary with the organization, the nature of the decision, and the type of transaction. An organization's exposure to risk can be reduced through an effective control and security system. Such a system can improve IS's security, data integrity, and information delivery.

Information System Risks   Although unauthorized access from outside parties is often the most publicized risk involving an IS, it is not considered by experts to be the most important. Research has shown that the greatest risk to the IS is from accidental errors made by employees. Outside access is actually ranked somewhere near the bottom of risks. Internal concerns involve unintentional errors or omissions during the input, processing, or output of data; the theft of computers and peripheral devices (printers or monitors); intentional damage by disgruntled or dishonest employees; and damage from fire, water, or natural disasters. We include natural forces because destruction by fire, water, wind, or earthquake can be as devastating as the criminal who seeks personal gain. The magnitude of these risks is huge, considering that over 100,000 commercial and government computer installations across the country exchange all types of information hourly. Add to this the daily electronic transfer of over one trillion dollars among banks and financial institutions in the United States, Europe, and Japan, and the potential for loss is enormous.

Many problems lead to erroneous data. In turn, bad data can lead to bad decisions, resulting in enormous losses to the organization. These losses may be much larger than the simple loss of data. Bad data can also lead to a lack of confidence in the IS, rendering the system useless. User confidence in the integrity of data is very important for decision making.

Another risk to the IS is **computer crime,** which is the theft of money, merchandise, or data using a computer or the unauthorized incursion into computer data files. Computer crime includes the following:

- Theft of funds by manipulating the company's financial records

- Theft of merchandise by manipulating inventory records to hide the loss or by charging the merchandise to a fake account or to a customer's account

- Theft of company data, including company consumer data, customer lists, or computer programs

- Damage to the computer or data storage by an angry employee or ex-employee, including physical damage to the hardware, destruction of such mass storage devices as disks or tape, or damage to computer programs

- Incursions into the computer programs or files or unauthorized use of the computer by individuals for the ''fun of it'' or for the challenge of breaking into a computer

17.1 Control of Information Systems

Risks to the IS are reduced through the use of controls. These controls are frequently called internal controls. **Controls** can be defined as managerial plans and policies adopted to safeguard information assets, ensure integrity of data and information, and deliver appropriate information to decision makers. Control has long been considered one of management's roles, along with planning, organizing, staffing, and directing the organization. However, control of the IS is much different from control of manual systems because of the invisibility and speed of processing, undetected input errors, concentration of responsibility, and susceptibility of the equipment to a wide range of physical threats.

Aspects of Information System Control

There are three important aspects of control in the IS—security, data integrity, and information delivery. **Security** is the protection of the IS from unauthorized access and outside forces, including computer criminals. **Data integrity** involves safeguarding the data and information that are crucial to the IS, and **information delivery** involves ensuring that the appropriate information reaches the decision makers who need it. It is impossible to control the IS without considering all three aspects. Without security, the IS is open for attack from outside and inside forces. Without data integrity, the processing function of the IS is worthless, because decision makers cannot rely on either the data or resulting information. Finally, without appropriate information delivery, the IS will not fulfill its stated purpose of providing the organization's decision makers with the information they need. Figure 17-1 shows the three aspects of control applied to the IS, and Table 17-1 shows types of security, integrity, and delivery problems that can lead to loss

FIGURE 17-1   *Aspects of Information System Control*

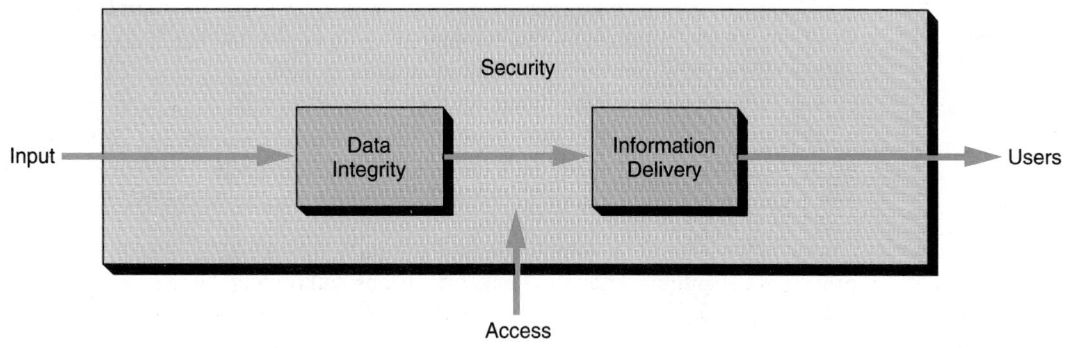

of valuable data resources as well as loss of confidence in the data that are used for decision making. We discuss each aspect of IS control in this chapter.

Control Points   To guard against the loss of hardware, software, or data, management must establish control procedures at critical points within the IS. These critical points differ according to the nature of the organization and its IS requirements. Obviously, the control structure for

TABLE 17-1

Types of Control Problems

Security Problems
• Fire, water, or other natural destructive forces • Fraud or other use of computer for illegal activities • Inappropriate access to computer facilities • Use of data base for illegal or inappropriate activities • Compromised data sent over communication links • Collusion between workers leading to fraudulent activities
Data Integrity Problems
• Processing errors that repeat themselves due to software or hardware problems • Cascading errors due to the speed of processing and lack of human intervention • Incorrect data entry due to human errors, failure of hardware, or ineffective entry control procedures • Data loss during file transfers, wrong or old data files, or inadvertent erasure of disk or tape • Inability to trace the processing of a transaction
Information Delivery Problems
• Mismatch between user requirements and information generated by the IS • Inappropriate selection of hardware and/or software • Improperly processed data due to errors in hardware or software

a Computer-Based Information System (CBIS) is quite different from that used for a manual system, because the risks are different and arise from different kinds of activities. For example, in manual transaction processing, critical points of control are the initial recording of the transaction, the transfer of an asset to another individual, and the authorization for payment. Each point is an area in the process in which the system is exposed to errors and possible fraudulent activities, often where a separation of responsibilities among various individuals occurs. In the manual system, the focus of control involves traditional custodial, authoritative, and recording activities. The control structure includes authorization, organizational independence, and close supervision.

On the other hand, in a computer-based transaction processing system, the computer processes the entire transaction, makes decisions authorizing the transfer of assets, and reviews such transactions and decisions. This type of system can cause a number of security, data integrity, and information delivery problems, including the following:

1. Many files affected by one transaction

2. Files readable only by machine

3. Information generated automatically with little human intervention

4. Errors not easily observable and easily undetected

5. Program changes erased without a trace

6. Transactions difficult to trace

7. Control procedures not always visible

To avoid the problems listed above, it is necessary to set up computerized control procedures in the information system. The control structure, which includes these procedures, must replace the control structure found in manual processing systems.

17.2 Control Structure

The methodology used to protect the IS from the security, data integrity, and information delivery problems shown in Table 17–1 is referred to as the control structure. The **control structure** is composed of the control environment and the combination of the IS and the control procedures used to protect the IS from the risks that surround it. As shown in Figure 17–2, the IS and control procedures are embedded within the control environment. The control structure helps provide IS users with accurate and reliable information for their decision making. It also helps secure the system from unauthorized access.

We have already discussed the risks involved in maintaining an IS. In the next sections, we cover the control environment and the IS and control procedures.

The Control Environment

The **control environment** shown in Figure 17–2 consists of managerial philosophy, organization structure, steering committee, and management control. **Managerial philosophy** includes management's attitudes and actions toward controlling risk. If management emphasizes the control of IS risk, employees' attitudes on this topic should be

When Design
and Testing
Controls Fail

It started innocently enough. At 2:25 PM on January 12, 1990, the software on an AT&T computer located in New York City decided that the computer was overloaded and began to reject telephone calls. Other computers in the AT&T long distance network automatically picked up the calls rejected by the New York City computer. Soon these computers exhibited the same symptoms and also rejected calls. Eventually, all 114 computers on the network were affected, and users of the AT&T long distance system received a busy signal or the "All circuits are busy" message. For over nine hours, AT&T users could not make long distance calls, causing AT&T to lose between $60 and $75 million in revenues.

After the system was back in operation, engineers found that a single logic error or "bug" caused all the problems. This bug was in all of AT&T's computers because they all had the same software. The bug was probably introduced when the existing software system was upgraded, and the design and testing controls did not detect it. Although software designers constantly strive to ensure that bug-free software is implemented, this ideal situation is not always possible in a program like AT&T's, which contains over 1 million lines of code. Even when so-called "fault-tolerant" computer systems attempt to reduce a runaway system failure like AT&T's, the entire system can go down if all modules simultaneously suffer from the same malady.

SOURCE: Thomas McCarroll and Paul A. Witteman, "Ghost in the Machine," *Time,* January 29, 1990, pp. 58–59.

significantly affected. Without a positive managerial attitude toward the control of risk, IS risks cannot be controlled.

The **organization structure** provides the overall framework for planning, directing, and controlling an organization and has a significant influence on the control environment. It specifies reporting, transaction processing, and decision-making relationships. Inherent

FIGURE 17–2

Control Structure

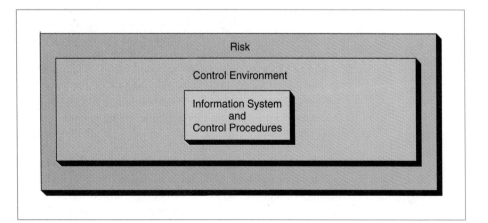

in the organization structure are the lines of authority and responsibility among individuals in the organization. These lines are crucial for ensuring that responsibility for IS control is clearly defined.

The **steering committee** develops plans and determines policies for the organization's IS. The composition of the steering committee was presented in Chapter 16. Its attitude toward the control of IS risks is also important to the control structure.

Management control methods describe how management keeps track of the authority delegated to others and supervises company activities effectively. Management controls are essential for transaction processing, reporting, and decision making. In theory, owners and managers must be able to monitor the performance and effort of employees and departments to assess their compliance with managerial policies, procedures, and objectives, often outlined in plans and budgets. These monitoring activities are a major component of what is generally known as a feedback control system.

Control Procedures

To avoid the types of problems discussed earlier, control procedures must be implemented. **Control procedures** are the policies and procedures applied by management to provide reasonable assurance that its objectives will be achieved and that information obtained during the accomplishment of these objectives is accurate. Effective procedures are also necessary to ensure compliance with the contracts between management and employees that spell out budgetary expectations, standards, and employee compensation. **General controls** apply to the IS in general, and **application controls** apply to specific applications or combinations of applications.

In general, control procedures ensure proper authorization of transactions and activities, clear separation of duties (such as separating computer programming from computer operations), adequate documents and records, effective safeguards for secured facilities, and independent checks on performance.

The Information System

From the perspective of management, an effective **Information System** (IS) must be designed to support the transaction processing, reporting, and decision-making requirements of the organization's management system. The nature and type of the IS is influenced by the requirements for managerial reporting and decision making. The presence of a well-designed IS and the complete coordination of its elements enhances the control structure. The IS department establishes policies and procedures for the processing of transactions, inquiries, and reports. Because every transaction, inquiry, or report is processed the same way each time, effective control over these activities is established. This control is especially important for small businesses, in which manual systems may be sloppy. The presence of a well-designed PC accounting system with good commercial software brings order to the processing and reporting activities of the small business.

Elements of the Control Structure

The implementation of computerized control structures in the IS is shown in Figure 17–3. These control structures consist of the CBIS and its elements shown by the rectangles and the various controls represented by the circles. Note that the types of controls are divided into general controls and application controls.

FIGURE 17–3   *Control Structures in Computer-Based Information System*

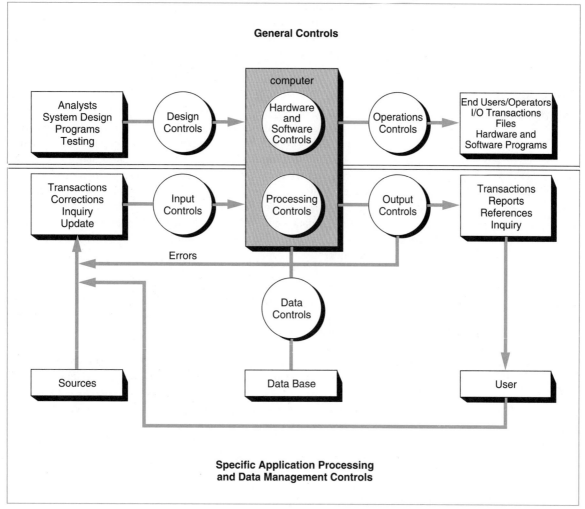

In Figure 17–3, the IS is composed of systems development, data input, the computer system, operations, information output, and the data base. The general controls consist of design controls that monitor the systems development process, hardware and software controls that monitor hardware and software operation, and operations controls that monitor the IS operation by personnel. Application controls include input controls that check the validity of the data input, processing controls that ensure the data are processed correctly, output controls that monitor the correctness of the information output, and data controls that monitor the organization's data base. Many of these controls are discussed in detail in later sections.

The control procedures shown in Figure 17–3 should be integrated to act as a network of controls. The probability of an error getting through an effective network (sequence) of controls is significantly reduced. Management should strive for controls that are *synergistic*—that is, the controls together have a greater effect than the sum of their individual contributions to the control structure.

Control Points at ProYacht

As an example of the use of control points in a CBIS, consider ProYacht, which makes sailboats, windsurfers, and, through its Sun Products subsidiary, aluminum boats. To improve the ordering process for its customers, ProYacht has a telecommunications system that allows a dealer or representative using a personal computer and modem to access its computer system. To control the potential for errors and fraud, ProYacht has created the input editing and screening control procedures shown in Figure 17–4. In this system, data are entered into the dealer's or representative's personal computer, transmitted to ProYacht's data processing center, and stored on magnetic disk storage, awaiting processing. Before the data are stored, the customer's personal computer is checked for access authorization. Access is allowed through the use of a password and a special PC hardware attachment.

Data leaving the storage area are edited using some of the procedures discussed in Chapter 5, including checks for completeness, reasonableness, and accuracy. Errors in input data are displayed and relayed to a correction process, which may entail feedback to the customer's personal computer for correction.

This data input editing and screening system has several control procedures for detecting and correcting unauthorized, incomplete, unreasonable, and inaccurate input data. For example, an unauthorized user may have an acceptable password but may not be using a personal computer with the appropriate hardware attachment. A user who gets through these controls may not have all the information necessary to enter a complete transaction. Similarly, a transposition error may seem complete, but the system will detect it as unreasonable.

Organizing for Control

For IS control, a well-planned and properly functioning IS organization is critical. The key to this control is the segregation of functions between the IS department and the user. The major functions within the IS department—operations, systems development (analysis, design, and implementation), data entry, and data supervision—should also be segregated. A typical organization chart showing these responsibilities separated appears in Figure 17–5. Under this organization plan, systems analysts and programmers are responsible for the development and maintenance of programs. These systems development personnel should be separated from the operators who have access to computer processing equipment. Similarly, the documentation, data files, and programs fall under data supervision (the librarian), so that operators cannot access documentation they do not need, and only authorized users can access certain data. In large organizations, disk and tape libraries control data files when not in use by authorized personnel. Finally, the actual input of data into the system is controlled by a data entry group. In all cases, the

FIGURE 17–4   *Data Editing and Screening Process at ProYacht, Inc.*

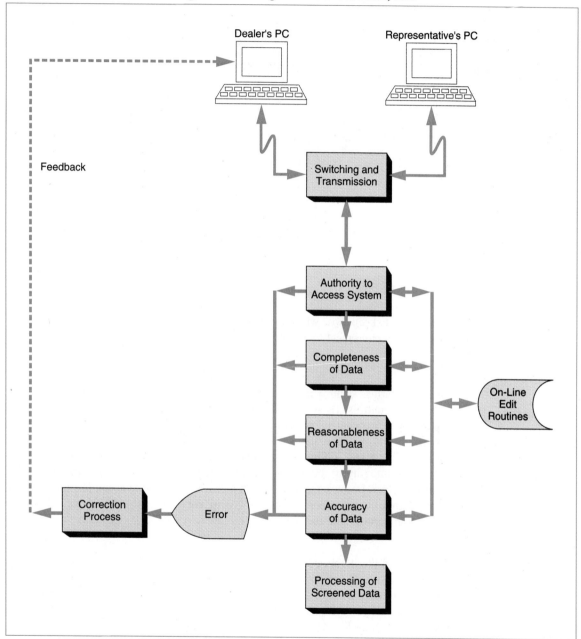

FIGURE 17–5

Information
System
Organization

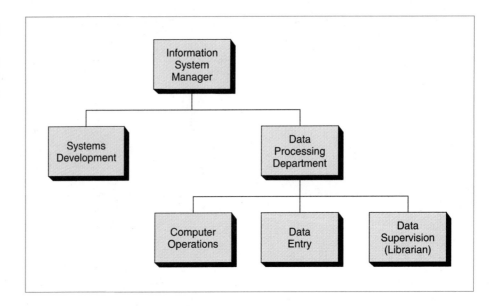

objective is to keep those who may wish to perpetrate fraud from accessing the information, data, or equipment they need to do so.

17.3 Types of Controls

As noted earlier, control procedures may be classified as either general controls or application controls. These controls can also be classified as access control procedures, input control procedures, processing control procedures, output control procedures, and procedural and documentation controls. This classification scheme may be displayed as the matrix illustrated in Figure 17–6. Each type of control procedure ensures either data security or integrity or the ultimate delivery of needed information to the appropriate decision maker. Because the definition of a general control and an application control is often blurred in contemporary CBISs, we discuss these controls in terms of their use rather than according to their classification.

Access Control Procedures

To safeguard the IS, access control procedures must be used. **Access controls** restrict user access to hardware, software, or data. These controls help to prevent accidental errors, unauthorized use of a program or a data file, improper use of a system's resources (such as computer time and storage space), and unauthorized breach of communication within the system. In particular, access controls include the following provisions:

- Access to program documentation should be allowed only to persons who require it

- Access to computer hardware should be limited to authorized individuals

FIGURE 17–6

General and
Application
Control Matrix

| | Control Procedures | |
	General	Application
Access	Control Computer Access	Password
Input	Screen Design	Batch Total
Processing	Good System Development Procedures	Program Testing
Output	Distribution Log (Record)	Reconcile Output
Procedures	Training	Program Documentation (Manual)

- Access to data and programs should be limited to individuals authorized to process or maintain particular systems

Access control can be accomplished in part by physical security of the hardware, software, and data, discussed in detail later in this chapter. Good organization, specifically the use of a librarian in the data supervision group, is also an important factor in access control. In addition, a system of passwords, screen-blanking software, and key-locks can control access to PC-based systems and networks. Some access control methods may be unique to a particular application. Passwords and control problems unique to online, distributed, integrated, and data base systems are discussed later.

Input Control
Procedures

Accurate data input can be ensured through **input controls.** Input control procedures primarily help to provide data integrity and to avoid the problem of *garbage in, garbage out* (GIGO). Such procedures check that data are authorized and correctly converted into machine readable form, and that no data (including data transmitted over communication lines) are lost, suppressed, duplicated, or otherwise improperly changed. Usually these input controls apply to specific applications.

The input process has five basic situations in which data are either entered, checked, or changed:

1. Transaction entry
2. Transaction update
3. File and data base maintenance
4. Inquiries
5. Error correction

The systems designer must select the appropriate input method for each situation based on the organization's processing needs, the control features, and the attributes associated with each input method.

For data entry and updating, a series of **data entry controls** ensure more accurate data input. As discussed in Chapter 5, validation of input data is necessary for accurate transaction processing. Such validation can include system logs or checks on a field, a record, batches of entries, and a file. **Field checks** attempt to check the validity of a single field independent of other fields, and **record checks** ensure that the logical relationships among fields are valid. **Batch checks** control the accuracy and completeness of fields and records and ensure that all records are input into the processing cycle. **File checks** are useful for making sure the correct files are processed.

Two types of logs should be maintained on all input. A **transaction log** is a list of all transactions entered into the system. **Error logs,** which are generated by the computer when an error occurs, include such details as time, data, and type of error. Corrections are also logged.

Processing
Control
Procedures

Processing controls should provide reasonable assurance that data processing complies with management's specifications. Controls that ensure data integrity are also useful when processing data into information. Four types of processing controls are processing and logic controls, file and data base controls, software controls, and hardware controls.

Processing and logic controls primarily ensure that the IS satisfies the objectives in the structured analysis and design phases discussed in Chapters 12 and 13. In other words, a well-designed and thoroughly tested system delivers useful and accurate information to decision makers. These controls are usually unique to each application.

General programming controls are included in this control category. Sequence checks match master and transaction files, and end-of-file procedures ensure that entire files are processed. Processing sequences ensure that master files are changed prior to updating, and run-to-run totals confirm that each program processes all data at each stage in the processing cycle. A redundancy check compares details with control totals. Concurrency controls for data base systems prevent a deadlock when several users attempt to access the same set of data.

File and data base controls ensure that the correct files are processed and that files and data bases are protected from compromise. File and data base controls are usually general controls, used in many applications. External and internal file labels must match, and file totals are checked to verify that all records are accounted for. A record of use is maintained for each file. Other file and data base controls are generally provided through the system hardware and software and the access controls noted earlier in this chapter. Finally, file and data base maintenance procedures are established for changes to records.

The most important processing **software control** ensures that transactions and information for reporting and decision-making needs are processed in accordance with management's objectives. For this result, an organization must follow a well-planned system of software development and implementation. Other general software controls restrict access to the operating and data base system and provide for backup, recovery, and restart procedures. Code comparison can detect a compromise in software or in the operating or data base system. In this control process, programs are periodically compared with a backup copy for differences, run against a test data base and compared with previously generated reports, and reviewed for size changes to detect evidence of a software change.

For **hardware controls,** hardware manufacturers provide overflow and read/write checks to ensure that data are not lost and that input and output are accurate and free of transcription errors. Another important type of hardware control is the parity check. In parity checking, a bit is added to each byte and set to one or zero, depending on the number of one-bits in the byte. Each time the byte is moved, this parity bit is checked to ensure that the byte of information is not corrupted in any way. Hardware controls are usually classified as general controls.

Output Control Procedures

Output controls ensure the accuracy of such output as reports, data updates, or inquiries. With these controls, only authorized personnel receive the results of the output. Output controls are mostly general controls used in a variety of applications. Output should be reconciled with input and processing control totals to ensure that all transactions are accounted for and processed in compliance with managerial objectives. Often this reconciliation involves some type of procedure for error correction, for example, displaying a list of errors. Output should also be scanned and tested to ensure that it has been properly processed. A sample of the output is examined to determine if it meets management's objectives. The extent of this testing is a function of input and processing controls. Finally, output should be distributed only to authorized users. This last objective is not difficult to achieve if results are displayed on a terminal in an online system with appropriate access controls. However, this objective can be very difficult when printed reports are generated. In this case, controls must be maintained over the storage of such output media as payroll checks, the report generating program, the report printing program, the actual printing operation, the distribution of multiple copies, the review for errors, and the storage and retention of output.

Procedural and Documentation Controls

Documentation controls include the up-to-date maintenance of source documents, including reports, audit trails, procedures, and the data base controls that document data structure and job responsibilities. **Procedural controls** are found in written manuals that provide step-by-step procedures to be followed by computer operators, data entry personnel, and users for the smooth flow of information and the implementation of appropriate control features. For example, all routing processing activities should follow a schedule. Documentation controls are usually general, whereas procedural controls can be unique to specific applications.

The separation of IS functions shown in Figure 17–5 is essential to ensuring compliance with control procedures. In data base systems, the data base administrator plays an important role in IS control and would report to the IS manager.

17.4 Security Issues

In the majority of situations, the computer that is the heart of a CBIS is used for ethical and legal purposes. With two objectives of control—data integrity and the delivery of appropriate information to users—it is assumed that the control is needed to avoid errors in input, processing, and output. However, we have also noted that security is needed to protect the computer from illegal access and intentional damage. This illegal or unethical use of computers has received quite a bit of notoriety recently, with heavy media coverage of computer viruses and break-ins. High school- and college-age individuals who use the computer for unethical or illegal purposes are often pranksters, but many other cases involve the theft of large sums of money or the destruction of computer data or software. There are two types of security—physical security and data security. **Physical security** safeguards the hardware component of the IS, and **data security** protects the data and software elements.

Physical Security

To provide physical security for hardware requires safeguards that can protect the hardware (which includes the data processing center, terminals, and data or tape library) from unauthorized persons, theft, fire, water, and other natural disasters. A new physical threat to the computer is the increase in terrorist activities. A car or truck bomb can easily render a computer and data or tape library unusable.

Methods of physical security include locating the facility where it can effectively be protected from terrorist activities, controlling entry to the computer facility through finger, eye, or voice prints to identify individuals, and, as simple as it sounds, locking doors. Figure 17–7 shows a schematic of a physical security process.

Damage from fire or water is an obvious danger, but these threats are often ignored when an organization plans a computer facility. As with any electronic machinery, a short circuit can cause an electrical fire in the hardware. Nonelectrical fires extinguished with water can also result in great damage, because water can destroy delicate computer circuits. For this reason, the danger from water must be considered when planning the computer security system. Sprinkler systems are a common protection against fire, but they can cause more damage to a computer than the fire itself. Several years ago, a government agency's sprinklers went off by accident, soaking the computers and causing many problems. Newer sprinkler systems limit the damage. Halogen gas is often used to deprive a fire of oxygen; but it poses a danger to the ozone layer.

To avoid a complete loss of data in any disaster, organizations should establish a regular policy of backing up system files and storing these backups in a physically separate facility. Recall that a backup is a second (or even a third) copy of a data file on a secondary storage device other than the primary disk secondary storage.

FIGURE 17–7   *Physical Security Procedures*

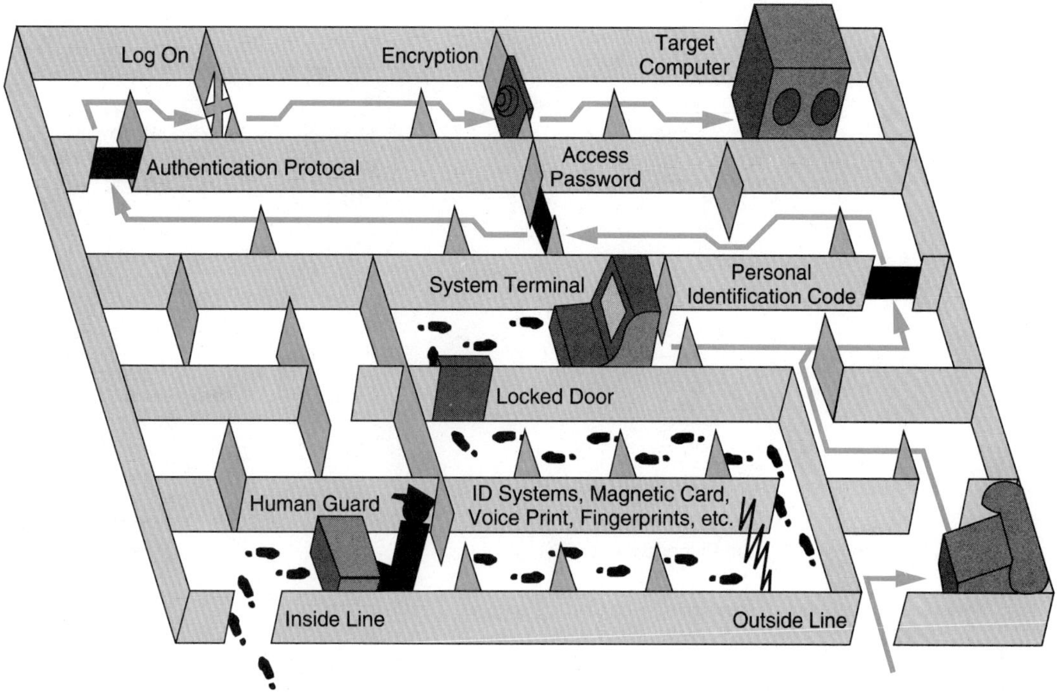

Data Security

Protecting software and data is entirely different from protecting hardware. Computer hardware can almost always be replaced, but an organization's data are irreplaceable; data may be its most important asset. Even if not destroyed, data can fall into a competitor's hands, a situation with disastrous implications for private companies or national governments. For this reason, data and software must be protected from unauthorized use.

Conflicting with the issue of protection is the fact that the computer should be readily available and as easy to use as possible. In general, this objective has precedence, as organizations emphasize user friendly systems. When this movement toward easy-to-use systems is combined with recent technological and software advancements, the growing need for users to access larger amounts of data, and the decentralization of computer systems, the result is a massive data security problem.

The popularity of the personal computer has compounded this problem by vastly expanding the number of people who have access to the equipment necessary to carry out computer crimes. Either a personal computer or a mainframe terminal can be combined

FIGURE 17–8

Unauthorized Access Methods

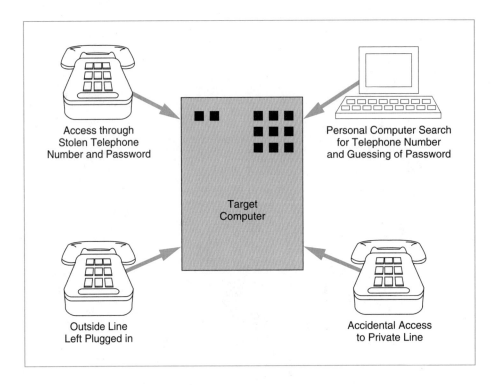

with a modem to break into computer systems; usually, buying a personal computer and modem is easier than gaining access to a mainframe terminal.

The primary method of protecting a computer and its files is the password. A **password** is a sequence of letters and/or digits supposedly known only to the user that must be entered before the computer system can be accessed. Most people are accustomed to using a type of password called a **Personal Identification Number (PIN)** to access a bank account from an Automatic Teller Machine (ATM). Unfortunately, many passwords are common, such as a birthdate or the name of the user's child or pet. With such easily guessed passwords, any computer system that has a phone line can be broken into. Figure 17–8 shows some methods used to gain unauthorized access to dial-up computer systems.

Any solution to the computer security problem must include methods of physically protecting the data and information stored on the computer. Unauthorized release or modification of this data and information must also be prevented. Although new hardware and software have an important role in solving this problem, a change in people's attitudes is even more important. People may feel that using multiple passwords to protect the computer is too much trouble. Too often, a password is short and has been chosen by the user to be easily remembered. For security purposes, passwords should be combinations of unrelated letters and digits and should be changed every 30 days. Until top management realizes that risking data security can be costly and users are forced to take more care with passwords, the computer security problem will not be solved.

Data Protection
Methods

Some methods currently used to protect computer software and data include password policies, systems audit software, security software packages, call-back systems, port protection devices, data encryption systems, and anti-virus policies and software. **Password policies** should not allow users to choose their own passwords, require that passwords be longer than four letters or digits, and require that all passwords be changed periodically. A user should also change a password immediately if any evidence exists that security has been breached. Finally, if an employee is fired or leaves under less than pleasant circumstances, *all* passwords should be changed. Failure to change all passwords can leave the system open for intrusion.

Systems audit software keeps track of all attempts to log on the computer, with particular attention to unsuccessful attempts. This tracking system can be part of the transaction log noted earlier. This systems log indicates who has used the system at any given time, including unauthorized users. In one criminal case, the systems log indicated the time of entry and the terminal from which a series of rogue programs was entered, enabling authorities to determine the probable culprit immediately.

Security software packages protect the computer system by various means. A package may require a user to wait at least five seconds between attempts to enter a password. A user may also have to hang up the phone and redial after three unsuccessful attempts to log on. In either case, the objective is to prevent unauthorized users from repeatedly guessing passwords. ATMs often ''eat'' the user's card after three unsuccessful tries.

A similar type of security system is a **call-back system,** which accepts calls and passwords from users, looks up the phone number associated with the user, and then calls the user back at that number. If the password is stolen and the unauthorized user is not at the correct number, he or she cannot access the computer.

Port protection devices are an extra level of security that separates the user from the computer. A port protection device requires the user to enter a second password to access a port, an entry line coming into the computer. Some devices also camouflage the computer by answering with a simulated voice rather than the high-pitched carrier signal commonly used for computer communications. As a result, recognition of the system by an unauthorized computer search is avoided.

Data encryption systems are combinations of software and hardware that convert data output into an unreadable form for transmittal over a network. The process transforms cleartext (a readable form) into ciphertext (an unreadable form) at the source computer and performs the reverse process at the destination. The American National Standards Institute (ANSI) has developed the Data Encryption Standard (DES), which is the most widely used standard encryption method. Figure 17–9 shows the use of an encryption system.

A problem for many computer systems is vulnerability to a virus attack. **Computer viruses** are small computer programs that can replicate themselves, causing either benign or destructive results. In the Cornell Virus case, a Cornell University graduate student sent a program through a nationwide academic research network—InterNet—just to prove that it could be done. Unfortunately, the program contained an error that caused

FIGURE 17–9   *Encryption Process*

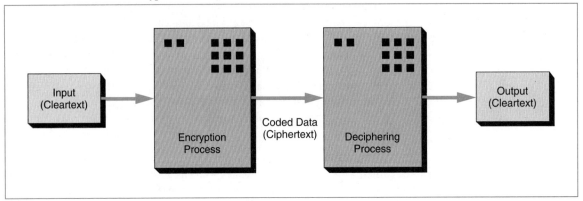

repeated replications of the program, which eventually took over available memory in over 6,000 computers. Many viruses threaten today's computer systems. In fact, an official of the Electronic Data Processing Auditors Association testified before Congress that hundreds of thousands of virus attacks have occurred in recent years. **Anti-virus policies and software** include directives on avoiding the use of software of unknown origin that has not been thoroughly tested, software that limits the replication of a program received over a network, and software that prevents a virus from attaching itself to the systems software.

17.5 Personnel Aspects of Information System Control

The personnel management component of the control environment is the most important aspect of the control structure. Clearly defined control and security procedures are necessary, but personnel are needed to execute those procedures. Employees must be trained to use information effectively. System designers must develop procedures to ensure the integrity and security of the system and its data. They must also prepare adequate procedures manuals for system users. The data base administrator must manage the operation and modification of the data base. Finally, computer operators must comply with the instructions in operator's manuals to produce information on a timely basis.

The first element in changing people's attitudes toward control and security is education. People must understand that unauthorized intrusion, no matter how innocent it seems, is a crime punishable by a fine or imprisonment, or both. Management must be willing to run a complete background check on every prospective employee to determine if any security issues were present with previous positions. The offender in a Texas computer virus case (see box on page 546) was fired from one position and charged with a crime but was still able to obtain a similar position at another company. Only after his picture appeared in the media did the second company check his background.

Another way to encourage users' awareness of the importance of control and security procedures is to involve them in the design of the control system. Failure to involve users can result in a system that is secure and has excellent controls on paper but is worthless

Password Rules

Password systems are only as secure as the passwords themselves. A recent survey of a government agency showed that 43% of over 1,500 employees used two-character passwords and over 25% used one-character passwords. Obviously, because these passwords are easy to guess, they provide only minimal security to the system. To combat this problem, organizations should encourage their members to use the following rules in designating passwords:

- Words from another (non-English) language

- Female family names at least two generations back

- Obscure cities and towns from other countries, as long as the original (non-Americanized) spelling is used

- Existing words with letters replaced, added, or switched (for example, OBBSCURE)

- Two words together separated by a control character (for example, GO&CRAZY)

SOURCE: Harold Highland, ''Password Puzzlers,'' *Computerworld*, June 11, 1990, p. 89.

because users cannot operate the prescribed controls. A very complex password system is a good example of this problem. In other cases, users may spend more time devising ways to circumvent the security measures than doing their work because the security system is so difficult to use. System users must recognize that people, not machines, can give or accept responsibility for computer security, data integrity, and the delivery of useful information. The study of this aspect of computer ethics is growing in importance as the use of computers grows.

17.6 Contingency Planning

So far in this chapter, we have discussed the use of control and security procedures to avoid the loss of hardware, software, and data and to ensure data integrity and the delivery of appropriate information to decision makers. What happens when the controls and the security fail and hardware, software, and/or data are lost? To answer this question, we must assume the worse and then plan for it. **Contingency planning** involves making plans that cover all possible situations and events. Our discussion covers two contingencies for which most large information systems must plan—loss of data on secondary storage and loss of the data processing center. In the first case, if a mainframe disk pack or a PC hard disk ''crashed,'' a contingency plan should indicate the backup from which the information could be transferred to another disk pack or hard disk. The lack of a contingency plan can be catastrophic due to the loss of data that cannot be recovered.

In the second case, consider one consequence of the 1992 hurricane in Miami. Numerous data processing centers were shut down for several days due to the loss of power and services. A contingency plan for this situation would outline how an organization could continue operations. In this section, we cover the types of contingency plans for both of these disasters.

*The Texas
Virus Trial*

On Saturday, September 21, 1985, a computer programmer at USPA & IRA, Inc. discovered he could not log on to the company's computer. His unhappiness at this difficulty soon magnified when accounting personnel found that 168,000 sales commission records had been deleted. Operators who examined the log of operations noticed that the system had been used during the night when no one should have been in the building. The police were notified of a possible break-in, and the sales commissions data were painfully restored from backup tapes.

On the following Monday morning, the system crashed within ten minutes of the first use of the computer. When systems programmers studied the situation, they realized the problem involved more than just lost data. They found a small control language program composed of a single command that would take the system down whenever a certain file was accessed. Using the day this program was created—September 3, 1985—as their guide, the systems programmers found that other programs created on the same day were also designed to disrupt the company's computer operations. These programs, often referred to as "trip wires" and "time bombs," were set to

go off when certain parts of computer memory were activated. One program was designed to wipe out two sections of memory, duplicate itself, change its name, and execute itself again one month later. To resolve the problem of the rogue programs, the entire system was restored from scratch to "decontaminate" it.

Once the system was repaired, attention was turned to the source of the damaging programs. The leading suspect was a senior programmer who had been fired recently due to his inability to get along with other employees. System logs showed that the programs had been entered from that ex-employee's office on September 3 using his personal identification code. The ex-employee was arrested and charged under a "harmful access to computer" Texas statute. At his trial in 1988, the ex-employee claimed that someone else had entered the programs, but he was found guilty, sentenced to seven years of probation, and ordered to repay the system repair costs incurred by the company—some $12,000.

SOURCE: Edward J. Joyce, "Time Bomb—Inside the Texas Virus Trial," *Computer Decisions,* December 1988, pp. 38–43.

*Backup and
Restart
Procedures*

An important IS hardware component is secondary storage—that is, permanent storage outside of the computer's internal memory. Because internal memory is both limited and volatile, secondary storage must hold data and information that are not being processed at any particular moment. Magnetic tape or disk can be used as secondary storage, and an organization would be wise to have a backup to this primary secondary storage. **Backup** is an alternate form of storage that contains a current copy of the material in primary secondary storage. In a mainframe environment, operators commonly make a daily tape backup of the disk packs that are used for secondary storage. If a tape drive is not available, then a second disk pack may be used. If a backup is not available and the system disk pack crashes, all the data on the disk pack may be lost. Backups on magnetic tapes are often stored in a different building from the primary tape library. Although a tape does not "crash," it can become unreadable due to everyday use. Without sufficient controls, a file can be accidentally written over, resulting in a loss of the original data. A backup helps a user avoid the pain and suffering of trying to read individual files from a worn-out tape or trying to find enough data to reconstruct the files inadvertently written over.

In a business, a definite policy on backups is needed, including a **backup hierarchy** in which three or four backup units are rotated, with the oldest unit becoming the new master disk in each backup. This policy is similar to the use of a second backup, except that the third and fourth backups do not always contain the most recent copy of the material. However, these backups do provide a margin of safety if both the working copy and the backup copy are lost. In critical cases, a hard (printed) copy of the latest version of the data or program should be kept against the possibility that backup units fail to preserve data electronically. In this case, the information on the printed copy can still be entered from the keyboard.

For personal computers, the individual user is responsible for backing up his or her hard disk to disk or tape. Users who are lax about this chore lose data when a PC hard disk fails (which it does, sooner or later.) For this reason, many IS professionals are unwilling to let PC users safeguard important organizational data.

Even when data are not lost from secondary storage, a method of restarting a mainframe computer must be available when it goes "down" unexpectedly due to power failure or other problems. Such a procedure, called **checkpoint/restart,** involves the use of a checkpoint copy of the computer's current memory that is periodically saved to disk. When the computer is restarted, a restart program copies the last checkpoint into memory and begins processing from that point. Although not foolproof, the checkpoint/restart procedure can save an operator the effort of redoing some processing, effort that can then be used to recover what was in the computer's memory.

For a data base system, these checkpoint copies are created by "dumping" a copy of the data base at periodic intervals to a disk or tape. Between these dumps, all transactions and other data base activities are logged on to a file or disk. If the system crashes, the data base can be reconstructed by backing up to the last dump and reconstructing the data base at the time of the crash.

Preparing for Loss of Data Processing Center

An aspect of contingency planning that is every bit as important as secondary storage backups or checkpoint/restart procedures is providing an alternate data processing site in case the primary center is inoperable. In 1989, this happened to numerous organizations in San Francisco and Charleston, SC when these cities were hit by natural calamities (earthquake and hurricane, respectively). With their heavy reliance on the organization's computer, many managers admit they could not operate for more than a few days without some type of computer support.

TABLE 17–2

Contingency Plans

Plan	Advantages	Disadvantages
Hot Site Agreement	Immediate availability	High cost of processing ($> \$250,000$ per year) capability; possible conflict with other firms needing the same site
Cold Site Agreement	Low cost and immediate availability	Firm must quickly find and install a computer at the site
Reciprocal Agreement	Low cost	Both firms may be affected by disaster; operations of both firms must be reduced
Backup Data Processing Site	Immediate availability	High cost

To provide for alternate sites, four types of contingency plans are possible—hot site agreement, cold site agreement, reciprocal agreement, and backup data processing site. In a **hot site agreement,** a disaster recovery firm agrees to set up a comparable mainframe computer center (the "hot site") that will be available to the organization if needed. On the other hand, in a **cold site agreement,** a disaster recovery firm agrees to have ready a site in which a mainframe computer can be installed, if necessary. In a **reciprocal agreement,** two firms agree to provide data processing for each other in case of a disaster. Finally, with a **backup data processing site,** an organization creates an alternate computer center that is virtually identical to the primary data processing center. Each plan has its advantages and disadvantages, as shown in Table 17–2.

In making contingency plans, an organization must decide how crucial the immediate availability of an alternate site is to operations. If the operation stops immediately when the computer is down, as in a travel service, then establishing a backup computer center or paying the cost of a hot site is a small price to pay for continued operation. On the other hand, some insurance companies estimate that they can continue operations for as long as six days without a computer. In this case, a cold site agreement may be acceptable. If two companies have surplus computing capacity and are not located in the same geographical area, then a reciprocal agreement contingency plan may be acceptable. The worst decision is no decision at all. In that case, an organization flirts with permanent closure in the event of a natural disaster.

17.7 Security and the Personal Computer

In general, the PC control environment is different from that for larger business computer systems. Procedures tend to be more casual, with many people having easy access to personal computers. The personal computer has had a major impact on computer security because it allows unauthorized users with modems to break into other computer systems. A new group of PC security problems involves the use of the personal computer in the office and the security of personal computers in a network. As with mainframe computers, both physical and data security must be considered in the use of a personal

When a Backup System Went Wrong

Because information continues to be the lifeblood of the modern organization, the computer systems that provide this information are extremely important to the management of the organization. Computer systems must have support systems to keep them running. These power supplies, cooling systems, communication networks, building structures, and their emergency backups are just as important as the computer system itself. When the support system fails, the computer system can no longer function, and emergency backups must be ready to operate instantaneously. If the backup fails to work or does not work correctly, the computer system suffers.

An example of this occurred when the Securities Industry Automation Corporation (SIAC) computer was shut down by an electrical fire that did not occur in the computer system. SIAC provides data processing services to both the New York and American stock exchanges (NYEX and AMEX). The fire was in the basement of SIAC's Manhattan data center, and the computer center was on the fourteenth floor. Unfortunately, the company's fire safety system had been incorrectly wired, and the basement fire was mistaken for one in the computer center. As a result, the computer center was erroneously shut down for three hours, and both stock exchanges failed to open, putting billions of dollars of transactions on hold.

SOURCE: Elliot M. Kass, ''Playing with Fire,'' *Information Week,* April 2, 1990, pp. 48–54.

computer. In this section, we briefly cover both issues as they pertain to the use of a personal computer.

Personal computers are small and easily stolen unless they are secured to a heavy object, such as a desk or table. Even then, the covers of computers can be removed and disk drives and other internal devices stolen, leaving the computer useless. Although the cost of replacing a personal computer is quite small compared with the cost of replacing mainframe equipment, a small hard disk can contain valuable data and information. For example, the 3M Corporation calculates that the loss of a hard disk with 20 Mbytes of sales and marketing data would require 17 days to recreate at a cost of $17,000.[1] Floppy disks are even easier to steal when they are left on a desk or stored in an unlocked drawer or cabinet. A locked door may be more important for PC security than it is with larger, less portable computers.

Care must be taken to protect the personal computer from environmental harm. In protecting the computer from damage, the normal precautions for any piece of office equipment against fire, water, dust, and other physical damage should be taken. The user must also protect the computer and its data against, of all things, electricity. Too much electricity or too little and the wrong kind or the right kind applied in the wrong manner can all cause problems. If a computer is hit by a **voltage surge** or **spike** like lightning or

[1] Mikkel Aaland, ''Preventing Computer Disaster,'' *Working Woman,* November 1988, p. 88–92.

other electrical disturbances, the sudden increase in the electrical supply can destroy delicate chips and other electrical parts. For this reason, **surge protectors** that plug into a normal wall outlet are recommended to protect the computer. The computer and peripherals are then plugged into the surge protector in the outlet. When a surge hits the outlet, a circuit breaker is thrown in the surge protector, and the PC system is protected.

Too little electricity, as in a brown- or black-out, can cause the loss of all data from internal memory. Because internal memory is usually volatile and depends on a constant power source to retain information, loss of power means loss of memory. Devices that continue to provide power to a computer can be expensive, so the best defense against a power outage is frequent saving of information in Random Access Memory (RAM) to disk. The problem of static electricity must be considered in the use of a personal computer. In a dry climate, walking across a rug can generate enough static electricity to damage data or electrical parts. Protection against static electricity can be provided by anti-static spray, touch-pads, or special floor covers.

Data Security for the Personal Computer

Data security for a personal computer is similar in many ways to that for a mainframe, except that normally only a single user is involved. Data are protected when a user locks disks up when they are not in use. With a hard disk model, lockup mechanisms can be on the computer itself. With some operating systems, passwords can be used to protect files from unauthorized use or damage. Information can be made to disappear from the screen at the pressing of a single key if an unauthorized person is present.

Backing up data on personal computers frequently is just as important as on mainframe computers. Unfortunately, PC users sometimes delay this task as long as possible. To avoid the potentially expensive problems of hard disk crashes or an errant command that destroys the data on a disk, PC users should perform frequent backups using disks or tape.

Network Security

The ever-increasing number of PC networks has made network security an important consideration. With networks, security procedures are a combination of those used on mainframes and personal computers. As with mainframes, passwords are often used to control network access, and the user has only restricted file access. As with personal computers, physical security involves locking up the workstation when not in use. Encryption packages for networks are similar to those for mainframes. Data sent to another terminal in the network are protected from unauthorized access. Network operating systems must also ensure that users cannot copy software from the file server and that only the licensed number of users can access a given software package. For example, if a college has purchased only 10 copies of a certain package to be used on 100 network workstations, the network operating system must ensure that only 10 users access the package at a time.

Personal Computer Software Controls

PC software packages are increasingly offering many built-in controls for the security of the PC IS. These controls can check input data, control the location of input in spreadsheets, require passwords, and separate user from programmer. An accounting package can check that all data on a screen are complete, that input account numbers match actual account numbers in the data base, and that all transactions add up to a predetermined batch total before transactions are processed. Similarly, spreadsheet templates can designate only a select number of fields for data entry, thereby preventing the alteration of other fields by unauthorized personnel. Password protection is available for user-written and commercial programs. Finally, because commercial software is acquired from outside parties, users and programmers are separate. As a result, most users do not know the inner working of the software and cannot modify it. In general, components of the IS itself can add a great deal to IS control structure. The simple fact that transactions are processed the same way every day adds tremendous control over data processing operations that may have been manual in the past.

17.8 Summary

IS controls must be designed to reduce the risks of unauthorized access by outsiders; accidental errors in the input, processing, and output operations; theft; criminal activities by employees; and natural forces. Computer crime is the theft of money, merchandise, or data using a computer. IS controls seek to protect the IS from unauthorized access, ensure the integrity of data, and make sure accurate information is delivered to IS users. Computer security is defined as the protection of the IS from unauthorized access and outside forces. Types of security include physical security and data security. Data integrity and data delivery problems must also be controlled. Various procedures must be implemented at control points to maintain IS controls.

The control structure, or methodology used to protect the IS, considers the IS risks, and is composed of the control environment, the IS, and the control procedures. The control environment consists of the managerial philosophy, organization structure, steering committee, and management control.

Control procedures are the policies and procedures applied by management to ensure that its objectives are achieved and the information obtained from the IS is reasonably accurate. Two types of procedures are general controls and application controls. A well-planned and properly functioning IS organization is critical to control the IS. Control procedures can also be classified as access control procedures, input control procedures, processing control procedures, output control procedures, and procedural and documentation controls. Access controls govern hardware, software, or data access, and input control procedures ensure that the data being processed are properly input. Processing control procedures should provide reasonable assurance that processing complies with management's specifications. Output control procedures ensure the accuracy of the output, such as reports, data updates, or inquiries and that only authorized personnel receive the output. Documentation controls include the maintenance of up-to-date source documents, and procedural controls are written manuals of step-by-step IS procedures.

Physical security for hardware (which includes the data processing center, terminals, and data/tape library) includes safeguards that protect equipment from unauthorized persons, theft, fire, water, natural disasters, and terrorist activities. Data security involves protecting the computer data and software, often with passwords.

In the process of implementing, operating, and using the control structure and in ensuring the security of a computer system, the personnel management component of the control environment is a most important aspect. Employees should know the risks that face an IS and their roles in protecting that IS.

Contingency planning covers all possible negative situations for an organization, including loss of data on secondary storage and loss of the data processing center. Backup policies for secondary storage and checkpoint/restart procedures are important elements of contingency planning.

Control and security of personal computers is different from that of mainframe computers. Personal computers must be protected from theft and environmental harm, and PC data must be backed up and protected from theft. Network security is a new security problem that often uses mainframe solutions.

Key Terms

access control
anti-virus policies and software
application control
backup
backup data processing site
backup hierarchy
batch check
call-back system
checkpoint/restart
cold site agreement
computer crime
computer virus
contingency planning
control
control environment
control procedure
control structure
data encryption system
data entry control
data integrity
data security
documentation control
error log
field check
file and data base controls
file check
general control
hardware control

hot site agreement
information delivery
Information System (IS)
input control
management control
managerial philosophy
organization structure
output control
password
password policy
Personal Identification Number (PIN)
physical security
port protection device
procedural control
processing and logic control
processing control
reciprocal agreement
record check
risk
security
security software package
software control
spike
steering committee
surge protector
systems audit software
transaction log
voltage surge

Review Questions

1. Why are controls needed in an information system? Why is security also an important concern?

2. What is the difference between controls and security? Give an example of each.

3. List three types of computer crime.

4. What are the two types of security? Name two aspects of control.

5. What problems are caused by computerized transactions?

6. Name the elements of the control structure. What elements constitute the control environment?

7. In what two ways are control procedures classified? List the elements of these two classifications.

8. List the various types of access controls. What are the five data entry situations that require input controls?

9. What are control totals and what are they used for? What types of transaction logs should be kept?

10. List three methods other than passwords used to protect data on a computer. Explain how one of these methods works.

11. Discuss the use of passwords to discourage unauthorized access.

12. Why are backup policies so important to a computer system? What is the backup hierarchy?

13. List various approaches to preparing for the loss of the data processing center.

14. How is PC security different from mainframe security?

15. Why is the importance of network security increasing? What are examples of network security procedures?

Discussion Questions

1. Computer system controls and security measures cost money to install and operate. What should determine the set of controls that is most appropriate for an organization and why?

2. With an increasing number of organizations using personal computers, managers and office personnel have greater access to data. Personal computers can process information as stand-alone workstations, are networked with other personal computers on local area and wide area networks, and are used for distributed data storage and processing. What risks does this explosion in personal computers pose for organizations today?

3. Discuss the positive control features of personal computers and their associated software for small business.

4. Consider a network of computers that uses hundreds of personal computers as terminals. Describe how security and control procedures can be used to manage the data access of these personal computers.

5. Consider a supermarket chain that ties each store's cash registers into a computer in that store. Each store, in turn, is linked to a central computing facility. Cash registers read bar codes electronically. Because prices are not marked on each product, registers cannot be operated in a manual mode. All pricing, sales, and inventory information is stored at each store. Describe the backup and recovery provisions and procedures you would recommend for this supermarket chain.

6. Design and development progress in computer-based information systems (CBIS) has been impressive in the past two decades. Traditionally, computer-based data processing systems were arranged by departments and applications. Computers were applied to single, large-volume applications, such as inventory control or customer billing. Large files were built for each application. As more applications were added, data management problems developed. Many files contained redundant data. Businesses tried to integrate the data processing systems to support management needs for decision making and online inquiry. As a consequence, the data base system was developed. It is composed of the data base itself, the data base management system, and the individual application programs. Moreover, in distributed processing and local area network systems, managers can interact with individual data bases or the corporate data base via communication lines or network software.

    a. Identify special control features a company should consider incorporating into its data base system.

    b. Identify special control features a company should consider to prevent access to its telecommunications and network data transmissions.
    (CMA adapted with permission)

Case 17–1
Simmons
Corporation

Simmons Corporation, a retailing concern with stores and warehouses located throughout the United States, is designing a new integrated computer-based IS. In conjunction with the design of the new system, the company's management is reviewing IS security to determine if new control features should be incorporated. Two specific areas of concern are the confidentiality of company and customer records and the safekeeping of computer equipment, files, and IS facilities.

The new IS will process all company records, including sales, purchase, financial, budget, customer, creditor, and personnel information. The stores and warehouses will be linked to the main computer at corporate headquarters by a system of remote terminals. Data will be communicated directly to corporate headquarters or to another location from each terminal in the network.

Currently, certain reports have restricted distribution because not all levels of management need to receive them or because they contain confidential information. The remote terminals in the new system may provide access to this restricted data by unauthorized personnel. Top management is concerned that confidential information may be used improperly.

The company is also concerned about potential physical threats to the system, such as sabotage, fire damage, water damage, power failure, or magnetic radiation. Should such an event cause a shutdown of the present system, adequate backup records would allow the company to reconstruct necessary information at a reasonable cost on a timely basis. With the new system, however, a computer shutdown would severely limit company activities until the system could become operational again.

SOURCE: CMA adapted with permission

Case Questions

1. Identify and briefly explain the problems Simmons Corporation could experience with respect to the confidentiality of information and records in the new system.

2. Recommend control procedures for the new system that would ensure the confidentiality of information and records.

3. What safeguards can Simmons Corporation develop to provide physical security for its computer equipment, files, and IS facilities?

Case 17–2
Aidbart
Company

Aidbart Company has recently installed a new online data base computer system. Remote terminals are located throughout the company, at least one in each department. Jane Lanta, Vice President of Finance, has overall responsibility for the company's IS, but she relies heavily on Ivan West, Director of IS, for technical assistance and direction.

Lanta was a primary supporter of the new system because she knew it would provide labor savings. However, she is concerned about security of the new system. In the Purchasing Department, Lanta observed an Aidbart buyer using a terminal to inquire about the current price of a specific part used by Aidbart. The new system displayed the data regarding the part, each Aidbart product that used the part, and the total manufacturing cost of the products using the part. The buyer told Lanta that he could also change the cost of parts with the new system.

Lanta met with West to review her concerns regarding the new system. Lanta stated, ''Ivan, I am concerned about the type and amount of data that can be accessed through the terminals. How can we protect ourselves against unauthorized access to data in our computer file? Also, what happens if we have a natural disaster like a fire, a passive threat like a power outage, or some active threat resulting in malicious damage? Could we continue to operate? We need to show management that we are on top of these things. Please outline the procedures we now have, or need to have, to protect ourselves.''

West responded, "Jane, areas of vulnerability exist in the design and implementation of any IS. Some of these problems are more prevalent in online systems such as ours, especially with respect to privacy, integrity, and confidentiality of data. The four major points of vulnerability with which we should be concerned are the hardware, the software, the people, and the network."

SOURCE: CMA adapted with permission

Case Questions

1. For each major point of vulnerability identified by West,
   a. Give one potential threat to the system.
   b. Identify appropriate action to protect the system from that threat.

2. West must develop a contingency plan for Aidbart Company's new system to be prepared for a natural disaster, passive threat, or active threat to the system.
   a. Discuss why Aidbart should have a contingency plan.
   b. Outline and briefly describe the major components of a contingency plan that could be implemented in the case of a natural disaster, passive threat, or active threat to the system.

Case 17–3
National
Commercial
Bank

National Commercial Bank has 15 branches and maintains a mainframe computer system at its corporate headquarters. National was recently visited by the state banking examiners, who have some concerns about National's computer operations.

During the last few years, each branch has purchased a number of microcomputers for communicating with the mainframe in the simulation mode. The branch also uses these microcomputers to download information from the mainframe and, in the local mode, manipulate customer data to make banking decisions at the branch level. Each microcomputer is initially supplied with a word processing application package to formulate correspondence to customers, a spreadsheet package to perform credit and loan analyses beyond the basic credit analysis package on the mainframe, and a data base management package to formulate customer market and sensitivity information. National's centralized data processing department is responsible only for mainframe operations; microcomputer security is the responsibility of each branch.

Because the bank examiners believe National's computer system is at risk, they have advised National to review the recommendations in a recent regulatory agency letter. This informative letter emphasizes the risks associated with end user operations and encourages banking management to establish sound control policies. More specifically, microcomputer end user operations have outpaced the implementation of adequate controls and have taken processing control out of the centralized environment, leaving areas of the bank's IS vulnerable.

The letter also emphasizes that the responsibility for corporate policies identifying management control practices for all areas of information processing activities resides with the board of directors. The existence, adequacy, and compliance with these policies and practices will be part of the regular banking examiners' review. The following three types of controls are required for adequate IS control and security:

1. Processing controls

2. Physical and environmental controls

3. Spreadsheet program development controls

SOURCE: CMA adapted with permission

Case Questions   Recommend specific control procedures that National Commercial Bank should implement for each type of control identified above.

The Future of Information Systems

18

Introduction

In Chapter 1, we discussed the effect of information technology on today's organizations. It is useful in managing the organization and in achieving competitive advantages. Throughout this text, we have reiterated this point, showing how the information system works within an organization to provide accurate and relevant information to the individuals who need it. Although the use of information technology has had a dramatic effect on organizations of all sizes and types, we should keep in mind that we have only scratched the surface. The dramatic advances in all parts of information technology are just now beginning to take off, and organizations that fail to take advantage of them may soon fail to be competitive.

In this chapter, we first look at the predicted effects of information systems on organizations. This introduction is followed by discussions of future changes in the five elements of information systems—hardware, software, data, procedures, and personnel.

Changing the Organization

Information technology in the twenty-first century will dramatically change the way an organization is set up to carry out its primary mission. Peter Drucker[1] has suggested that information technology will transform how an organization makes decisions, structures management, and even performs its work. In the first case, analyses that would have once taken worker-years to perform manually can now be performed in a matter of hours with a personal computer and spreadsheet. These analyses will provide information that will change decision making from a "hit-and-miss" proposition to a process resulting from a thorough analysis of the organization's business strategy.

---

[1] Peter F. Drucker, "The Coming of the New Organization," *Harvard Business Review,* January/February 1988, pp. 45–53.

In the second case, according to Drucker, the widespread use of information in an organization will cause a sharp reduction in the number of management levels and managers, resulting in a "flattening" of the organization. Middle managers currently serve as "relays" between the specialists who actually carry out the work and the top-level managers who make the policy decisions. In an information-based organization, this intervening management level will no longer be needed.

Finally, the way an organization actually performs its work will be modified by the organization-wide availability of information. The production process has normally been considered a *sequence* of activities, each separate and independent from the other. According to Drucker, the research, development, manufacturing, and marketing activities will be combined, and a team of specialists will work together in *synchrony* from the first research efforts to the placement of the product on the market. This trend was discussed in Chapter 9 on Management Information Systems (MIS), in which the extensive use of a large data base enhanced cooperation among various functional groups in a firm.

Drucker states two requirements for the organization of the future to take full advantage of available information technology. First, the organization must be structured around clearly stated goals that define what is expected of each element in the organization. Just as an orchestra is composed of many musicians performing a single piece of music, so too a future organization should be composed of many specialists working toward one, or at most a few, goals. Drucker's other requirement is that each individual must be responsible for the information at his or her disposal. In other words, each worker should constantly evaluate the information needed to carry out his or her responsibilities, as well as information generated for other uses.

Challenges to Information Systems

Drucker foresees great changes in future organizations. However, to make these changes possible, the field of Information Systems (IS) faces serious challenges. These challenges, as stated by Donald Marchand, are "to develop technology architectures that can support the sharing and value added that come from using information in the right place at the right time." [2] We can say that we want information to be in the hands of those who need it, but actually making this happen is the challenge facing information systems. According to Marchand, ideally, competitive organizations will build networks and systems to ensure that information is available to those who need it, including employees, customers, dealers, and suppliers.

For Marchand, factors that complicate this challenge include the almost unbelievably fast pace of change in technology and the resistance to change from within an organization. Today, many IS professionals joke that by the time hardware is selected, purchased, and delivered, it is already out of date. At the same time, other functional area users, impatient with IS professionals, are purchasing personal computers and software on their own rather than waiting for the mainframe shop to complete needed projects.

---

[2] Donald A. Marchand as quoted in "Information Systems: Tying It All Together," *Industry Week,* August 20, 1990, p. 20.

Any change brings about resistance, and the organization's structural changes suggested by Drucker will almost certainly result in massive resistance from those affected. Middle-level managers who have provided much-needed information to top-level management are not about to disappear just because the IS makes them unnecessary. Similarly, the functional areas that are accustomed to the sequential product development process are going to fight to retain their current role. All members of the organization who are uncomfortable with the role of the IS will resist these changes. These people and functional areas must be convinced of the necessity of integrating information into their jobs and, ultimately, accepting the modifications the IS brings. This may be the biggest challenge to developing the future organization that uses information for a competitive advantage.

Downsizing and Outsourcing

Two somewhat controversial IS trends are downsizing and outsourcing. **Downsizing** is the process of either moving processing applications from a mainframe to personal computers or replacing a mainframe with a PC network, or both. Several reasons exist for considering downsizing, including reduced costs, increased flexibility, and ease of use. Mainframe systems are extremely expensive to purchase and operate compared with a PC network. In terms of flexibility, because of the cost of a mainframe system, management may be unwilling to change to another system, even if the current system is obsolete. Personal computers are often much easier to use than mainframes, especially now with the advent of such graphics-based systems as the Macintosh and Windows for IBM compatible PCs.

However, downsizing causes problems, especially when the wrong application is moved to a PC system. Transaction Processing Systems (TPS) involving many transactions are not usually amenable to running on a PC system, so a downsized system may not be able to handle the organization's data processing demands. Cultural differences also occur between mainframe systems programmers and many PC-based end users. They simply do not speak the same language, resulting in massive miscommunication during down-sizing.

To make downsizing work in the future will require careful planning and the education of both the mainframe staff and end users. The resulting IS design should be one that really meets the strategic needs of the organization.

Outsourcing involves turning over some or all of the responsibility for the IS to an outside group. An example of outsourcing is Kodak's decision to turn over its IS department to IBM. Kodak evaluated its IS department and decided that no strategic value existed for performing these operations internally. IBM was brought in to consolidate five Kodak facilities and to provide the necessary IS services. This decision is expected to save Kodak over $1 billion by the end of this decade.

The future of outsourcing appears to be bright as more companies take a hard look at what really makes them competitive. If organizations ascertain that they can ''buy'' an IS more effectively than they can ''make'' it, then outsourcing is a feasible alternative. Andersen Consulting predicts that by the mid-1990s, more than 50 percent of major multinational corporations and government agencies will be using outsourcing to some degree.

The ability to electronically transfer data from one user to another or from one mainframe to another or to a personal computer is a strategic weapon in the arsenal of today's organizations. This growth in telecommunications has significantly changed the communications industry. As evidence of this, we need only look at the blending of computers and communications at the industrial level. Many companies are combining their communications and data processing departments.

Currently, telecommunications involve transferring data between computers through Electronic Data Interchange (EDI); accessing external data bases; transferring money through Electronic Funds Transfer (EFT); and communicating with other users with voice, data, and graphics. Many individuals can also **telecommute**—that is, perform their work at home through communications with the office computer(s). In 1990, almost 60 percent of personal computers in homes were used for work-related purposes.

The trend in telecommunications is toward the use of digital rather than analog signals to transmit data, voice, and graphics. The use of digital signals for communication through the Integrated Service Digital Network (ISDN) will dramatically transform telecommunications by increasing transmission capabilities. ISDN users will have almost instantaneous access to worldwide data bases at speeds beyond current telephone networks and will be able to transfer voice, data, images, and text at high speeds over the same lines. Additional ISDN uses will likely include an increase in PC networks and videotex, or the use of a computer and telephone to order goods and services without leaving the home or office. ISDN will probably contribute to the continued growth of EDI as companies discover ways to eliminate the large amount of paper that flows between organizations.

Although stand-alone personal computers have had a tremendous effect on how people work and access information, networked personal computers on Local Area Networks (LANs) will have an even greater effect. The percentage of personal computers that are networked has increased from only 5 percent in 1985 to 40 percent in 1990, a growth rate that is expected to continue. In the future, individuals working with networked personal computers will be able to access, exchange, and manipulate information in ways that we cannot even imagine now. Multiple employees will be able to work simultaneously with a body of information over a LAN, leading to enhanced productivity through such group-oriented activities as group decision support systems.

Completing this information resource picture is the concept of integrating networked personal computers with mainframes to access the huge volumes of information residing on the larger machines. The integration of personal computers and mainframe data bases should theoretically lead to the long-awaited productivity increases for PC users.

In looking at the future of the IS, we must consider how each of the five elements—hardware, software, data, procedures, and personnel—will change over time. Predicting the future of hardware is easier than for the other elements, because everyone agrees that computer hardware will continue to get smaller, faster, and cheaper. In the rest of this chapter, we suggest how each IS element will change over time.

*Bill Gates'
View of the
Future*

One person who stands out as a leader in the computer industry is Bill Gates, cofounder and CEO of Microsoft, the world's largest PC software company. Named the wealthiest man in America in 1992, Gates started as a teen-age computer hacker who, with Paul Allen, wrote the first version of BASIC for a personal computer. In 1980, his company was asked by IBM to create an operating system for its forthcoming IBM PC, and the rest is history. Currently employing close to 10,000 people, Microsoft is still blazing new trails with products like Windows that redefine the way people use IBM compatible personal computers.

Gates' view of the future can be summarized in one sentence: Give users the tools to create their own revolution. In his version of the future, users could filter through mountains of data to retrieve needed information in many forms—print, sound, and video—and then, by pressing a key, manipulate this information into a truly usable form. Gates would de-emphasize the machine, making it less noticeable as it goes about its job. The keyboard will disappear, replaced by handwritten input. In essence, the computer will become a consumer appliance as common in the future as the VCR and telephone are today.

SOURCE: William F. Allman, ''Evolutionary Revolutionary,'' *U.S. News & World Report*, December 24, 1990, pp. 49–50.

18.1 The Future of Hardware

As computer chip technology continues to improve, computers will simultaneously become smaller, faster, and cheaper. Modern computer technology began in 1947 with the invention of the transistor. In the late 1960s, chips with 1,000 transistors could be made, and this number has increased dramatically over the past 20 years. Today, chips like the Intel i486 contain over one million transistors. Experts predict the appearance of chips with 100 million transistors by the end of the century. The miniaturization of computer components has led to the availability of laptop computers weighing less than 5 pounds that have all the power of many desktop personal computers. Handheld computers and **personal digital assistants (PDA)** weighing less than 1 pound can be used for special purpose computing.

*The Future of
Mainframes*

A common conception is that eventually all systems will be downsized, a trend discussed earlier in this chapter. However, mainframes will probably remain in use, at least for the foreseeable future. The International Data Corporation (IDC) has noted the following reasons for this:[3]

- Mainframes cannot be matched by small processors for high-volume transaction processing applications.

- Mainframes have sophisticated security mechanisms that control both access to

---

[3] ''IDC White Paper—Information Systems: The Next 10 Years,'' *Computerworld*, December 1990.

and transmission of sensitive, valuable data. These types of security mechanisms are just now being considered for networked personal computers.

- Mainframes commonly have formal, standardized backup and recovery procedures. PC users are notorious for not backing up data.

- Mainframes help provide the control and resources needed to carry on a global business.

- Mainframes provide controls and auditing facilities needed to maintain data, applications, and operating system integrity.

Trends in Chip Design

Researchers who think 100 million transistors on a chip may be the limit of current technology are seeking other ways to increase chip capacity. These new architectures may include chips that are physically larger than the current ½ cm square surface or three-dimensional designs. Research is also ongoing into **nanotechnology,** which is the ability to build complex objects on a molecular scale using atom-by-atom precision. Current microtechnology operates on a scale of a micrometer (one-millionth of a meter), but nanotechnology will work on a scale of a nanometer—one-billionth of a meter. One objective of nanotechnology is a memory chip 1 mm on a side capable of storing *trillions* of bytes of information.

The speed of computers is measured in MIPS (millions of instructions per second) and BIPS (billions of instructions per second). The original IBM PC ran at approximately one-third MIPS, but today's low-priced personal computers run at around 1 MIPS, mainframes run at 100 MIPS, and supercomputers run between 1 and 10 BIPS. These speeds should grow dramatically over the next 25 years. Figure 18–1 shows one expert's prediction of the increase in speeds of various type of computers.

Even this expert's predictions may be conservative. For example, consider the Intel i486 chip that was introduced in 1989. The i486 runs at 15 MIPS, twice as fast as the Intel 80386 chip that has recently come into wide use. Intel also plans to produce a version of the i486 chip using a new type of technology called **Emitter-Coupled Logic (ECL)** that will run at 120 MIPS. The ECL chips may be available by the mid-1990s. Successors to the i486—the i586 and i686—are also being designed and tested.

As chips contain more transistors and run faster, their cost has been reduced dramatically. Richard Shaffer, editor of *Technology Computer Letter,* has noted that computers are decreasing in price at a rate of 20–35 percent per year. Shaffer thinks that today's $2 million mainframe may cost $10,000 in 12 years. To understand his conclusion, consider the fact that in 1976, an IBM System 370 mainframe cost over $1 million. Today, the same computing power is available on a personal computer.[4]

The Future of Personal Computers

One dramatic change during the 1980s was the increase in the use of personal computers in the office. In fact, in 1990, sales of personal computers exceeded those of mainframe hardware for the first time. From all indications, this growth will continue, and possibly

[4] Robert Moskowitz, "A Typical Desktop System in the Year 2001," *Lotus,* December 1988, p. 10.

FIGURE 18–1

Prediction of Computer Speeds

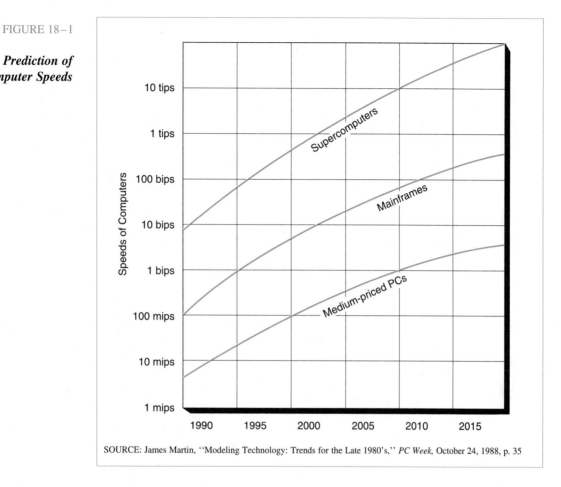

SOURCE: James Martin, ''Modeling Technology: Trends for the Late 1980's,'' *PC Week,* October 24, 1988, p. 35

accelerate, as more uses are found for the personal computer in the office and manufacturing plant.

We have already noted that with the increasing speed of chips, personal computers can handle computing requirements once reserved for mainframes. Although the mainframe can still process data at a faster speed, the cost per million instructions processed is much less for a personal computer. In fact, by 1995, the cost will be $472/MIPS on a personal computer compared with over $25,000/MIPS for a mainframe.[5] The stand-alone personal computer may soon be a thing of the past as personal computers are increasingly networked. Networks allow users to access data banks of all types and at widely separated locations, as well as to communicate with other users. Mainframes will likely become managers of information and networks.

---

[5] William F. Allman, ''Desktop Dilemma,'' *U.S. News & World Report,* December 24, 1990, pp. 46–48.

For PC data storage, the near future will see increased memory capacity for both Random Access Memory (RAM) and Read-Only Memory (ROM) chips within the computer, as well as increased storage on hard, floppy, microfloppy disks, and CD and optical drives. RAM capacity of over one million characters is standard on most personal computers, and memory in the 4–8 Mbyte range has become common as more multitasking operating systems are used. Microfloppy disks that hold almost 1½ million characters are already available; capacities of over 10 Mbytes will soon be on the market. The use of 3½ inch microfloppies has overtaken the once popular 5¼ inch floppy as most new systems provide this size drive.

In 1988, the NeXT computer was introduced with read *and* write optical disk secondary storage. As improvements are made in the access speed for this type of storage, optical disks will make Gbytes (one billion characters) of external memory available to the PC user. The use of CD-ROM for disseminating information such as that normally found in an encyclopedia will increase as more applications are found.

The resolution of PC video systems will also increase as newer and more powerful graphics systems are developed. IBM has already introduced a video system with resolution higher than that available with the VGA system for its PS/2 line of computers.

Personal Computer Productivity

As of the early 1990s, the use of computers has not caused the expected increase in service industry productivity. This situation is shown in Figure 18–2, which compares the rate of white collar high-tech investment and the output per worker for the period 1980–1990.

This failure of the increase in service industry productivity to keep pace with increased computer use is blamed on several factors. The first reason is a lack of communication and integration among mainframe users and users of various types of personal computers. Employees have simply been given computers with little or no thought given to how the computers would be used. Second, PC applications have focused on the individual personal computer. As manufacturing firms have discovered, there is no such thing as an increase in "individual productivity." Employees must work together for the organization to realize an increase in productivity. Finally, because many PC applications simply replicate existing manual activities, many users have yet to discover the real power of computing and data accessibility.

The lack of communication and integration and the focus on the individual personal computer should fade with the explosive growth of networking and new software designed to foster communication and integration of individual workers. The last problem —PC applications replacing manual activities—parallels the introduction of electric motors in manufacturing industries in the first quarter of this century; productivity increases were realized slowly. Managers had to learn what to do with their *new* potential. The same situation faces today's managers, who are still learning about the power of the personal computer.

Multimedia

Just a decade after the personal computer revolutionized the computer industry, working with a personal computer means more than just crunching numbers and processing

FIGURE 18–2 *White Collar Investment and Output*

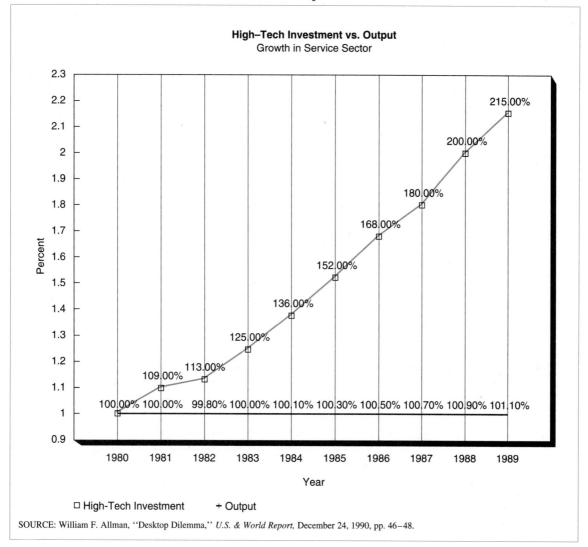

High–Tech Investment vs. Output
Growth in Service Sector

SOURCE: William F. Allman, "Desktop Dilemma," *U.S. & World Report,* December 24, 1990, pp. 46–48.

words. If the predictions of major computer companies — Apple, IBM, Intel, and Microsoft, to name a few — are correct, the personal computer will soon be combined with video and audio equipment to produce a **multimedia** tool. This combination of video cassette recorders, laser disks, and high-fidelity stereo with personal computers that can work with full motion video is predicted to change the way people work, learn, and play. Companies may not agree about what multimedia means, but they do agree that it is the next PC frontier, with a predicted market of over $11 billion by 1993.

One example of this concept is the experimental multimedia recruitment program developed by the New York Life Insurance Company. This application allows a prospective employee to navigate a series of menus with information describing the company in general as well as the Boston home office. When the user finds a topic of interest, he or she can use a mouse to select the corresponding box to see video clips of agents and managers talking about themselves, their jobs, and NY Life in general. The company feels that this multimedia application is worth hundreds of thousands of dollars in time and labor savings. The company also gives the impression of being on the cutting edge, resulting in better recruiting.[6]

Other applications are expected in business, education, and the home. In business, multimedia is already being used for sales demonstrations and training, and it is expected to become an even more important part of the over $4 billion worldwide market for presentations. For example, using multimedia, an employee being transferred to a new city can preview houses and narrow choices without leaving his or her office. In education, a multimedia system could teach employees to perform their current jobs better or to handle new jobs. For example, Tandem Computer developed a multimedia simulation that instructs employees on repairing computer equipment. This application saves Tandem thousands of dollars each day in instruction costs.[7] Many industry leaders feel that multimedia may be the system that makes the personal computer as widespread in the home as the television and VCR are today. However, most analysts feel this will not happen until multimedia systems cost less than $1,000, something that may happen by the mid-1990s.

Experimental Approaches to Chip Design

Most experts feel that the theoretical limit of silicon chip miniaturization will not arrive for 5–10 years, but researchers are already working on new substances superior to silicon for chips. One of these substances is another semiconductor material called **gallium arsenide.** Gallium arsenide is five times as fast as silicon in transmitting electrons, resulting in more computing speed. In 1989, IBM announced that it had developed a gallium arsenide chip that uses **optoelectronic technology,** in which laser light is used to transmit data at 1 billion bits per second. IBM believes this technology could be used to create detailed images for economic forecasts, hypersonic aircraft simulations, or demographic studies. These images could require billions or even trillions of data bits.

Recent developments in the area of superconductivity have renewed interest in an alternative to the transistor—the Josephson Junction. **Superconductivity** is the property of certain materials at low temperatures to conduct electricity without resistance, and a **Josephson Junction** is a very fast type of switch that works with superconductors. Until recently, superconductivity was possible only at extremely low temperatures—near absolute zero. Because of the problems involved in achieving superconductivity, research by IBM on the Josephson Junction was terminated in 1983. However, over the last few years, researchers have found materials that exhibit superconductivity at dramatically increased temperatures. In 1989, two Japanese firms, Hitachi and Fujitsu, an-

---

[6] Richard Pastore, "NY Life Gives Recruits a Multimedia Look Inside," *Computerworld,* March 18, 1991, p. 39.

[7] Don Steinberg, "Multimedia Is the Message," *PC Computing,* September 1990, pp. 135–51.

FIGURE 18–3   ***Comparison of Serial and Parallel Processing***

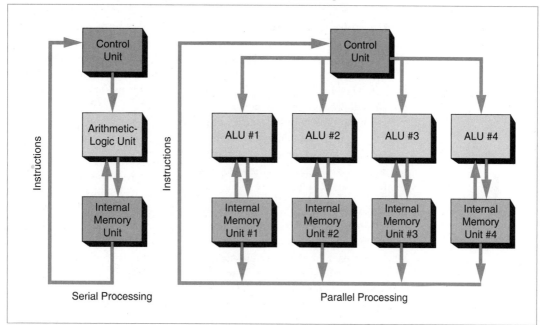

nounced that they had successfully tested superconducting microprocessor units that use the Josephson Junction technology to process over 250 million instructions per second. This speed is five times faster than the speed of today's fastest microprocessor units.

Parallel Processing

Since John von Neumann's stored program, most computers have been **serial machines;** that is, they work on only one instruction at a time. When a new instruction or piece of data is needed, it is fetched from memory before being processed. The serial nature of computers seriously restricts their speed and applicability to some types of problems. Current research is aimed at circumventing these restrictions via parallel processing.

Parallel processing involves using multiple Central Processing Units (CPUs) to execute several instructions simultaneously. Obviously, parallel processing is much faster than serial processing, because multiple instructions are executed in the time required to execute one instruction. Figure 18–3 shows the difference between serial and parallel processing.

Currently, many supercomputers use a type of parallel processing known as **array processing,** in which the computer executes the same operation on a list of values. For example, instead of adding two lists of numbers together one pair at a time to arrive at a third list, one instruction causes all pairs on the two lists to be summed at one time. Future computers will use more advanced types of parallel processing, including multiple processors that execute multiple executions in parallel or the actual division of a task into parts that are processed simultaneously.

The Fastest Computer

Parallel data processing is one way to carry out parallel processing, and one company has been working on parallel-process supercomputers since 1984. Led by MIT graduate Danny Hillis, the Thinking Machines Corporation developed a multiprocessing computer and entered it in a competition to determine the fastest computer. Running at an almost unbelievable *5.2 billion* instructions per second, this computer won the independently sponsored contest.

The parallel-process supercomputer from Thinking Machines is similar to the human brain in that it has up to 16,000 processors, each of which communicates with another processor like a telephone network. To accomplish this, Thinking Machines uses individual computer processing chips. In addition, specially designed software ensures that the proces-

sors can communicate with one another and send billions of messages back and forth. Newer versions of Thinking Machines computers are claimed to run at one *trillion* instructions per second, far faster than any supercomputer previously available.

Examples of problems for which the parallel-process approach to supercomputing would be appropriate include image processing, document retrieval, and fluid dynamics. American Express has ordered two of Thinking Machine's supercomputers to enhance customer service by speeding the collection-billing data process for both merchants and cardholders.

SOURCE: Michael Alexander, "Parallel Computer Wins FLOPS Race," *Computerworld,* March 25, 1991, p. 20, and "Thinking Machines Thinks Big," *Computerworld,* November 4, 1991, p. 12.

18.2 The Software of the Future

The fact that computers become faster every day does not ensure more use by the public. The key to increasing computer use is making computers easier to use. Truly user friendly operating systems and applications programs must be introduced, and the applicability of the computer to home and business problems not previously solved must be expanded. Even current users constantly expect more from their computers. As one person said, "The more we use computers, the more we expect from them."

Software is expected to change in the future to allow easy movement of information between different software packages and between different types of computers; integration of text, numbers, image, and voice; visual rather than textual data representations; the use of nonkeyboard forms of input; and the continued application of artificial intelligence to software. All these changes should aid in resolving productivity problems.

Integration of Software

As users more frequently combine information from multiple packages and from different types of computers, they are demanding that the process be easier. As a result, software developers are now creating packages that work with a small number of "standard" file types—like Lotus 1-2-3 .WK1 files or dBASE .DBF files—and creating linkages to these files. In addition, operating environments like the Macintosh and Microsoft Windows for IBM compatible personal computers are allowing users to access different packages for different parts of a job, cutting and pasting results as needed. All

Macintosh applications work the same general way, making it easier to use a large variety of software with limited training or startup costs. This trend is expected to continue with IBM compatible users creating a graph in one package, using a window to enter a word processing package, and bringing the graph directly into the word processing document without ever leaving the original graphics package. Users will also find it very easy to use a statistics package because it looks and operates like the spreadsheet that he or she uses every day.

Integration of Different Types of Data

People who are comfortable with computers will demand that the computer handle all forms of data, not just text or numbers. Some new software systems can now combine pictures and voice with the text and numbers. This capability will become more widespread as several companies work on systems that integrate these different forms of data. The concept of the **compound document** that incorporates all four data forms is already a reality, as users send these data over telephone lines. For example, a picture can be scanned and transmitted over a computer network accompanied by a written explanation. A voice message can also be saved and output along with the document to explain its features. Finally, a spreadsheet with calculations pertinent to the picture might also be transmitted over the same network.

Some ''future'' concepts are already available to some extent on the Macintosh with appropriate software. For example, a Mac user can record graphic images and digital voice messages that are saved along with the software. With these features, a manager can verbally ''tell'' and show a clerk what to do with a spreadsheet without writing lengthy instructions or providing instructions personally.

Visual Forms of Data

Without a doubt, graphics will be very important in future computer use. Most people are more comfortable with pictures than with text or numbers, and graphical messages tend to communicate more quickly than textual ones. For example, output from a data base package may show a picture of a tractor rather than a field entry of ''farm equipment.'' This move to visual forms is evident in the Presentation Manager front end of the OS/2 operating system and in the Microsoft Windows operating environment. The use of a mouse and icons to make selections from a menu was pioneered by Apple. This easy-to-use method of operating a computer will soon be the rule rather than the exception on all types of computers.

Nonkeyboard Forms of Input

Just as graphical data are easier to understand than textual forms, many users are more comfortable with an input device other than a keyboard. We noted earlier that many people are put off by having to communicate via the keyboard. This ''keyboardphobia'' may be part of the reason for the success of the Apple Macintosh, which uses a **mouse** to select from among icons and pull-down menus. This problem sounds like a hardware issue, but a hardware device used for input is useless without appropriate software. Two other nonkeyboard forms of input are **voice input** and **handwritten input.** Many problems are involved in building a computer that can accept voice input—words run together, similar sounding words that mean different things (for example, *to, too,* and *two*), and different voices from multiple speakers. Yet, voice input is a key breakthrough in computer technology that would create a friendlier environment for the novice user.

Views of the Future

At the Association of Computing Machinery's 1991 annual Computer Science Conference, the following four keynote speakers provided their views of the twenty-first century:

- Craig Fields, president of Microelectrics and Computer Technology Corporation, foresees a global explosion of digital networking and distributed computing that will include user friendly interfaces and the common use of AI.

- Phil D. Hester, director of IBM's Advanced Workstation Division Engineering Center, predicts workstations running at 100 plus MIPS as well as photorealistic, three-dimensional visualization capability and interfaces to create "virtual reality."

- H.T. Kung, professor of computer science at Carnegie-Mellon University, thinks that parallel computing will be common if certain conditions are met—easy development of software for parallel machines, improved interprocessor support, and a networking arrangement that pairs parallel machines with general purpose computers.

- John McCarthy, professor of computer science at Stanford University and a pioneer in the study of AI, looks for a new type of computer language that communicates with people or other computer programs by understanding sentences involving assertions, questions, requests, and permissions.

SOURCE: Michael Alexander, "Looking Ahead to the Next Century," *Computerworld*, March 4, 1991, p. 18.

Similarly, handwritten input from a stylus that writes on the screen has its own set of problems, particularly the deciphering of each individual's handwriting.

Both voice input and handwritten input are applications of **Artificial Intelligence** (AI) that require the computer to display some degree of intelligence to decipher what is input or written. The computer may never be able to display human-like intelligence, but software can help the computer handle problems involving voice and handwritten input.

18.3 Trends in Data Management

Currently, an organization's data management usually involves a large relational Data Base Management System (DBMS) located on the central mainframe. For security reasons, these data are often unavailable to the end users who may need the information for analyses. However, the proliferation of personal computers attached to networks is changing this situation. Users will be made responsible for their own data within guidelines set by management. This policy can occasionally lead to accidents and lost, incomplete, or duplicate data, but many IS managers feel the risk is worth the result, because end users can perform needed analyses more easily. Currently, researchers are investigating how to partition data among distributed users, so all users can access needed data that may be scattered throughout the organization.

Text
Management

A form of data that is extremely important in all organizations is text, or the written word. The personal computer was supposed to bring about the paperless office, but today only 1 percent of all business information is retained in electronic form. Data on paper will never be eliminated, but great opportunities exist for the reduction of paper transferred and stored in offices. More documents are stored electronically as word processing documents on individual or networked personal computers. Incoming and non-word processing documents are frequently converted to electronic forms and stored by using scanners and stored by using **imaging systems.**

Two problems areas are evident with these documents — storage requirements and capability to find needed text. In the first case, text and graphics can use large amounts of magnetic disk storage. In the second case, users often cannot find needed information. For example, it may be difficult to locate and include all the documents that refer to a particular topic in an analysis. A solution to both problems is a **text management system** that uses CD-ROM. Recall that CD-ROM is a form of optical storage similar to an audio compact disk (CD) that can store large amounts of text and graphics — up to 250,000 pages of text. The CD-ROM text management system allows a user to retrieve text based on certain words or phrases in the document.

Another trend for the future is the use of hierarchical referencing (hypertext) systems, such as the Apple Hypercard. These systems can search through text and other data base material to locate information in the form of text, data, and graphics that relate to a particular topic. As more organizations begin storing their documents electronically, the use of text management systems should also grow dramatically.

18.4 The Future of Information System Personnel

As an organization becomes more information based, the personnel component of the IS must also change. Downsizing and outsourcing can negatively affect experienced IS professionals who find themselves working in a changing environment. Some experienced mainframe programmers may find the move to PC software development a welcome change, but not all IS professionals feel that way. Outsourcing can eliminate the entire IS area and lead to uncertainty about jobs. However, existing IS professionals are often the first people hired by the organization assuming IS responsibilities.

Another major change predicted for IS professionals is an increasing role as consultants to end users rather than creators of new information systems. Individuals who have worked for 10–20 years as part of systems development teams will now be required to answer all types of hardware and software questions in different functional departments.

Another trend is a continued demand for professionals who are trained in both business functions and systems development. Most system failures occur because analysts and programmers do not understand user requirements, and users do not articulate their information needs clearly to analysts and programmers. Individuals who can bridge the gap between these two areas can ensure that systems do not fail because of misunderstandings.

The United States creates more software than any other country, but the supply of programmers in this country is not growing to meet the demand. Because more software code is written in COBOL than in all other computer languages combined, the demand for COBOL programmers will probably continue unabated in the future. The programmer shortage must be met by increasing the salary of programmers, hiring programmers from other countries, or sending software projects overseas to be created.

End User Programmers

In previous chapters, we defined the end user as a non-data processing professional who uses the computer to solve job-related problems. End users who are familiar with various PC-based software packages are demanding more ready-made applications developed on such packages as Lotus 1-2-3 or dBASE IV. This demand has resulted in the need for a new type of programmer—the **end user programmer**—who creates specific applications in a popular package. For example, an end user may need a business analysis application on Lotus 1-2-3. Rather than taking the time and effort to create such an application, the end user interacts with an end user programmer who is an expert on 1-2-3. The end user programmer then creates the spreadsheet template to meet the end user's specific needs.

Because end users and their application software packages did not exist 10 years ago, the position of end user programmer did not exist until quite recently. However, the demand for persons with expertise in various PC-based software packages should grow dramatically in the near future. End user programmers must have training and experience in creating applications in various software packages, or they may choose to specialize in one package. Many community colleges and technical schools now offer advanced courses in popular packages to prepare a person trained in business, engineering, sciences, or the arts to work as an end user programmer.

18.5 Trends in Operations Management

As a result of hardware trends, the field of operations management is changing in the areas of system documentation and data processing management. Much of the system documentation needed for training and the day-to-day management of computer operations will be stored on a CD-ROM using the text management systems discussed earlier in this chapter. Operators will no longer waste time trying to find the loose-leaf binder that contains the information on a particular part of the computer system. Instead, via text management and CD-ROM, the needed information will be quickly found and displayed on the screen. This trend is also expected to affect the distribution of computer software documentation, as purchasers will receive a CD-ROM disk rather than a thick binder of information. Replacing the 1,000 pages of documentation for WordPerfect 5.1 with a single CD-ROM disk, for example, would be much more efficient for the user. Moreover, voice documentation that is saved along with the software is expected to replace application software manuals. End users can also add their own verbal notes to remind their colleagues or other users how to use a program.

In the operation of mainframe computers, several trends are being predicted by IDC, a firm that specializes in collected data about information systems. First, the mainframes of the future will be huge providers of data for a distributed network of computers. Second, the era of the "self-managed system"—that is, a computer system that, for the most part, manages itself and all peripherals—is not far away. Future systems will require so much technical sophistication that they will control the master console with little or no human input. Obviously, this is another example of the use of AI and expert systems. Although mainframe operations may be moving toward a level of self-control, the need for human operators of PC networks will increase as more personal computers are networked.

18.6 Summary

One of the most dramatic effects of information technology on future organizations will be the way an organization is set up to carry out its primary mission. The availability of information will result in more and better analyses, a flatter organization, and a difference in the way organizations do their work. The fast pace of change in technology itself and the resistance to change from within the organization will be problems for the IS. Two IS trends that are becoming more evident today are downsizing and outsourcing. The ability to transfer data from one user to another or from a mainframe to another mainframe or to a personal computer will continue to be an important strategic weapon for today's organizations. The implementation of digital communication signals on the ISDN is predicted to transform telecommunications dramatically by increasing transmission capabilities. The stand-alone personal computer will become a rarity in most competitive organizations.

Most experts agree that computers will simultaneously become smaller, faster, and cheaper. They also agree that although the use of personal computers will continue to grow, only a mainframe can handle some applications. The processing speed of computer chips is predicted to grow dramatically in the near future, and the cost of processing will drop. The way data and information are stored and displayed will be improved. Finally, the future should bring a hoped-for increase in productivity through the use of computers. Multimedia is expected to have a revolutionary effect on how computers are used in organizations. Experimental chip designs include optoelectronic chips and chips that use superconductivity to process data faster. Parallel processing is also expected to become a widespread technique.

Software will become easier to use and more integrated, and the use of graphical user interfaces will increase. Other future areas of change for software include easy movement of information between different software packages and between different types of computers; integration of text, numbers, images, and voice; visual rather than textual data representations; the use of nonkeyboard forms of input; and the continued application of AI to software. The trend in data management appears to be toward making users responsible for their own data within guidelines set forth by the organization's IS department. Text management will be used to oversee this important form of data.

As the organization becomes more information based, the personnel component of the IS must respond to such trends as downsizing and outsourcing. IS professionals will act as consultants to end users rather than create new information systems. However, demand will continue for programmers and for professionals who are trained in business functions and systems development. The end user programmer will also be in demand as more applications packages are used. Operations management is also changing in the areas of system documentation and data processing management. The use of CD-ROM and verbal documentation will become more important in system documentation. The era of the ''self-managed system'' — that is, a computer system that manages itself — is not far away.

Key Terms

array processing
Artificial Intelligence (AI)
compound document
downsizing
Emitter-Coupled Logic (ECL)
end user programmer
gallium arsenide
handwritten input
imaging system
Josephson Junction
mouse

multimedia
nanotechnology
optoelectronic technology
outsourcing
parallel processing
personal digital assistant (PDA)
serial machine
superconductivity
telecommute
text management system
voice input

Review Questions

1. In what ways does Peter Drucker believe that information technology will change an organization? How does Drucker believe an organization should take advantage of information technology?

2. What is the difference between downsizing and outsourcing?

3. What is the predicted effect of the increased use of ISDN on EDI in the future? What status of networked personal computers is predicted for the future?

4. What reasons are given for the continued use of mainframes?

5. What reasons are given for the failure of personal computers to produce dramatic increases in white collar productivity?

6. What are the components of multimedia?

7. Why is the prediction of the future of hardware easier to make than with other computer areas?

8. What is the difference between serial and parallel processing?

9. Why is gallium arsenide being considered as the replacement for silicon in chip manufacturing? What is a Josephson Junction?

10. How will superconductivity speed computer processing?

11. In what areas is software expected to change in the future?

12. What is a compound document? How does it relate to the software of the future?

13. Name three trends in text management.

14. What trends are foreseen in personnel management? What is an end user programmer?

15. What trends are foreseen in the management of mainframe computers?

Discussion Questions

1. The consensus is that the widespread use of personal computers over the last several years in the service industry has not materially improved productivity. State why you believe that major productivity improvements will occur in the next ten years.

2. Discuss the effects that you believe will transpire in decision making in the future. Who will make the decisions, on what basis, and with what assistance from new technological developments?

3. How will compound documents enable managers to perform their jobs better? Give an example of how compound documents might improve the management of the financial affairs of your university.

4. If your university used hypertext and CD-ROM for its catalog and course schedule, how might such systems improve registration procedures, develop an effective course of study for students, and control the use of faculty and classroom resources?

Case 18–1
Global Enterprises

Global Enterprises is an import and export business that buys merchandise from numerous vendors throughout the world and sells to customers on a worldwide basis. The company also schedules the shipment of merchandise from country to country; to and from distribution centers (ports, airports, and rail and trucking terminals); and to and from manufacturers, resellers, and wholesalers. Personal computers are used for distribution problem analysis, planning, determining duties and tariffs, calculating charges using various exchange rates, communication among vendors and clients, and other office management problems. Office and sales representatives have personal computers with communication capability. Offices are located in every major city, shipping terminal, or port, and sales representatives call on vendors and customers regularly to offer their import and export services. Sales representatives' microcomputers are linked via a worldwide telecommunication network into a large data base located in San Francisco. Sophisticated models are used to schedule shipments and manage the financing of these transactions. All accounting is done in the home office. Current exchange rates; shipping rates, regulations, and schedules; tax laws and duties; import and export restrictions; and vendor and customer data are maintained on the large data base in San Francisco. Global Enterprises handles millions of transactions, and billions of dollars flow through its accounts each year.

Case Questions

1. What changes in communication technology will affect Global Enterprises' operations? How?

2. In the future, will there be a need for firms that are organized like this one with local representatives and offices? What impact may information technology have on the organization?

3. Will it be feasible to transfer the data that reside in the home office to the local offices and sales representatives? How can this be accomplished? How will this affect the organization?

4. How could Global Enterprises use compound documents and multimedia to market its services?

Glossary

A

absolute address The actual location of a record in secondary storage. (Chapter 5)

access controls Controls that restrict user access to hardware, software, and data and help to prevent accidental errors, unauthorized use of a program or a data file, improper use of a system's resources, and unauthorized breach of communication within the system. (Chapter 17)

accounts receivable Money owed to a firm and when payments are due. Often, a module of a business accounting software package. (Chapter 8)

acquisition and development Stage in the development life cycle that outlines the option of acquiring software from outside vendors or writing the programs using organization personnel. (Chapter 14)

action diagrams Development tools that represent data flow and processing activities and can be sketched on a computer using CASE and then converted into computer code. (Chapter 13)

activity ratio The number of records updated compared with the total number of records in the file. (Chapter 5)

activity-based cost (ABC) systems Accounting costing system based on many cost drivers, resulting in more accurate product costing and cost estimation. (Chapter 9)

ad hoc decisions Decisions requiring judgment and insight, are nonroutine, where no agreed upon procedure exists for making the decision. (Chapter 10)

address The location of data or instructions in internal memory; the location of a record in direct access secondary storage. (Chapter 5)

administrative cycle A summarization and posting process in which the general ledger accounts for sales, expenses related to sales, inventory, accounts payable, accounts receivable, cash, payroll, and fixed assets are posted in batch form from various journals where they are recorded. (Chapter 8)

aging schedule A list of receivables for all customers indicating the portion of each customer's account that is past due and by how long. (Chapter 8)

analysis The third phase in the system development process in which the analyst determines the information requirements of management for the new system. (Chapters 3 and 12)

android Robots with a built in microprocessor that can move around. (Chapter 11)

anti-virus policies Organizational policies that help prevent the entry of a computer virus into computers. (Chapter 17)

anti-virus software Software that limits or prevents the entry of a virus into a computer system. (Chapter 17)

application controls Control procedures that apply to specific applications or combinations of applications. (Chapter 17)

applications generators Prototyping tools that allow the user to create entire applications based on the data base. (Chapter 15)

application software Software which constitutes the greatest proportion of software used on computers and performs very-specialized tasks including all the computer's processing and problem-solving tasks. (Chapters 2 and 4)

array processing A type of parallel processing that allows supercomputers to perform the same operation on a list of values simultaneously. (Chapter 18)

artificial intelligence (AI) Hardware and software systems that exhibit the same type of intelligence-related activities as humans, such as listening, reading, speaking, solving problems, and making inferences. (Chapters 2, 11, and 18)

asynchronous communication A form of communication between computers that does not require that the computers be synchronized in the rate at which they process data. (Chapter 7)

attributes Data items or fields within a table or flat file. (Chapter 6)

avoidance of uncertainty Adding more certainty in decision making. Often accomplished by shortening the time horizons of

B

the decision-making process. (Chapter 3)

back order   A note to the customer and to the vendor indicating that the order will be shipped as soon as the merchandise is received in inventory. (Chapter 8)

backup   A policy of storing all information on some form of secondary storage in case the information on the original disk is lost. (Chapters 4 and 17)

backup data processing site   A location created by an organization where an alternate computer center that is virtually identical to the primary data processing center is kept to prepare for loss of information. (Chapter 17)

backup hierarchy   A policy of backing up information on floppy disks that rotates the use of three or four disks as the most recent backup disk. (Chapter 17)

backward chaining   Method used to arrive at a final decision in which the inference engine seeks a specific goal, assumes the goal is true, collects all rules that support it, and tests these rules to determine if they are true. (Chapter 11)

backward propagation   Technique used to simulate neural networks with single processors. (Chapter 11)

batch checks   Data entry controls for the accuracy and completeness of fields and records. Totaling values in particular fields to ensure that all records are input and processed. (Chapter 17)

batch commands   Especially in MS-DOS-based personal computers, commands that cause batch files to execute. (Chapter 15)

batch files   A file containing multiple DOS commands for execution at the same time. (Chapter 15)

batch mode   A processing mode in which similar transactions are accumulated in a batch, or single group, and periodically processed. (Chapter 8)

batch processing system   Combining data from multiple users or time periods and submitting to the computer for processing in a batch. (Chapter 2)

benchmark test   Software evaluation technique in which problems and sets of transactions can be run on the vendor's proposed configuration to test the entire system for the handling of transaction volume and anticipated problems. (Chapter 14)

bill of lading   A record that accompanies a merchandise shipment, so that the carrier is aware of the nature and destination of the shipment and who will compensate the carrier. (Chapter 8)

bill of materials   A data sheet which describes the components and materials and their quantities for each product. (Chapters 8 and 9)

binary number system   Base 2 number system based on zero and one which is used to perform all processing on a computer because the transistors are on/off switches. (Chapter 4)

bit   The basic unit of measure in a computer; contraction of BInary and digiT. (Chapters 4, 5, and 7)

block code   A classification system that characterizes transactions via blocks, either numbers or letters, that have some meaning. (Chapter 8)

booting process   The process of starting up a computer before the user gives the computer any instructions. (Chapter 4)

bottom-up approach   Approach to determining IS requirements in which the development process is driven by the response to current problems. (Chapter 12)

boundary   The delineation between the system and its environment. (Chapter 3)

bounded rationality   The bounds on the search process in decision making. (Chapter 3)

bridge   A combination of hardware and software that connects two similar networks. (Chapter 7)

bulletin board service   A telecommunications service that enables users to interact with each other. (Chapter 7)

bus network   A computer network in which computers are tied into a main cable or bus without a central computer. (Chapter 7)

bus   The main cable in a bus network that links the central computers with all other computers in the network. (Chapter 7)

business plan   A plan supporting a request for additional capital that outlines the future revenues and expenses for new ventures. (Chapter 9)

byproduct approach   Historical approach used in many organizations for determining IS requirements in which management uses byproduct information generated by the organization's TPS to satisfy its-decision-making needs. (Chapter 12)

byte A group of eight bits—equivalent to a single character. (Chapters 4 and 5)

C

call-back system A type of computer security system that accepts calls and passwords from a user, looks up the phone numbers associated with the user, and calls the user back at that number. An unauthorized user would not be at the correct number, so access would be denied. (Chapter 17)

central processing unit (CPU) The part of the computer that handles the actual processing of data into information. (Chapters 4 and 14)

centralized organization structure Structure of an organization in which all the control and decision-making authority are vested in a few individuals at the home office. (Chapter 3)

chargeback policies Policies instituted to handle the problem of allocating IS costs to users. (Chapter 16)

checkpoint/restart Process ensuring that a method of restarting a mainframe computer is available when it goes ''down'' unexpectedly due to power failure or other problems. (Chapter 17)

Chief Information Officer (CIO) The top information manager in an organization; ensures that the greatest possible competitive ad-

vantage is gained from corporate information. (Chapter 16)

classification system Processing system involving coding data so that it can be stored for effective use by managers. (Chapter 8)

client server A computer in a network that is often dedicated to a single purpose; all of the processing burden is on the central computer. (Chapter 7)

clock card A record of the times an employee enters or leaves the plant. (Chapter 8)

coaxial cable A type of LAN cable similar to that used to transmit cable television signals into your home. (Chapter 7)

code (computer) Multiple instructions for the computer that are joined to form a program. (Chapter 15)

cognitive style Style by which an individual assesses information and evaluates various alternatives. (Chapter 3)

cold site agreement An agreement in which a disaster recovery firm agrees to have ready a site in which a mainframe computer can be installed, if necessary. (Chapter 17)

color monitor A video screen that displays multiple colors. (Chapter 4)

command file A file that will execute a program when the filename is entered. (Chapter 15)

command level end users An end user who can solve more job-related problems by increasing their knowledge of the software and exploring its limits. (Chapter 15)

command-driven package A package that does not prompt

the user for a command, but rather requires the user to know and enter the needed commands and data at the appropriate time. (Chapter 4)

communications software A type of software package that enables the computer and modem to communicate with other computers including uploading and downloading files. (Chapter 4)

competitive advantage An advantage gained over one's competitors through the use of information. (Chapter 1)

competitive forces The five major forces of competition in an industry include rivalry among existing competitors, threat of new entrants into the market, pressure from substitute products, bargaining power of suppliers, and bargaining power of customers. (Chapter 1)

compilation The process of converting the entire source program into machine language before executing any of the program. (Chapter 13)

compound document A form of telecommunications combining written, voice, and computer communications to express an idea clearly. (Chapter 18)

computer An electronic, automatic machine that manipulates and stores symbols based on instructions from the user. (Chapters 1 and 4)

computer crime The unauthorized invasion of a computer data file or theft of money, merchandise, data, or computer time using a computer. (Chapter 17)

computer hardware The electronic part of the computer that stores and manipulates symbols under the direction of the computer software. (Chapter 2)

computer networks Two or more computers linked together using telecommunications; the computers can share data, spread out processing chores, or serve as huge repositories of information for users. (Chapter 7)

computer software The set of programs used to operate the hardware and to process data into information. (Chapter 2)

computer virus A self-replicating, potentially damaging computer program sent over a computer network by mischievous or malicious persons. (Chapter 17)

computer word The number of bytes with which a computer works. (Chapter 4)

computer-aided design (CAD) A graphics software package that assists the user in developing engineering and architectural designs. (Chapters 1 and 9)

computer-aided manufacturing (CAM) System composed of any combination of computer assistance in the manufacturing environment. (Chapters 8 and 9)

computer-aided software engineering (CASE) Advanced software designed to help in all phases of system development, including analysis and design and writing the programs for the system. (Chapters 12 and 13)

computer-based information system (CBIS) The concept of the information system in general that has assumed increasing amounts of manual data processing. (Chapter 2)

computer-integrated manufacturing (CIM) System that computerizes the whole product conversion operation. (Chapters 8 and 9)

confidence factors An informal scale measure (for example 0–100) of the extent to which an expert believes information to be true. (Chapter 11)

contingency planning Control procedure that involves making plans that cover all possible situations and events. (Chapter 17)

control environment Environment that consists of managerial philosophy, organization structure, steering committee, and management control. (Chapter 17)

control function A function in a DBMS that actually controls the data base access and monitors storage. (Chapter 6)

control procedures The policies and procedures applied by management to provide reasonable assurance that its objectives will be achieved and that information obtained during the accomplishment of these objectives is accurate. (Chapter 17)

control structure The methodology used to protect the IS from the security, data integrity, and information delivery problems that can occur; structure composed of the risks, the control environment, and the combination of the IS and the control procedures. (Chapter 17)

conversion cycle Steps used by a manufacturing organization to convert labor, material, and capital into goods and services. (Chapter 8)

conversion The process of changing from the old to the new system. (Chapters 13 and 14)

cost-benefit analysis A comparison of two proposed systems in terms of their relative costs to their projected benefits. (Chapters 12, 13, and 14)

critical path The path through the network with the longest estimated time for completion. (Chapter 16)

Critical Path Method/Project Evaluation Review Technique (CPM/PERT) Network model in which tasks are shown as arrows on a network, and the minimum possible time required to complete a project can be computed. (Chapter 16)

cursor A blinking rectangle or underscore of light on the screen that designates the current position on the screen. (Chapter 4)

cylinder A storage scheme on disk packs where all tracks with the same track number make up a vertical cylinder. (Chapter 4)

D

data All of the raw facts that are processed by the computer to supply management with the information needed to engage in its various activities. (Chapters 1, 2, and 3)

data base A collection of information that is arranged for easy manipulation and retrieval. (Chapters 2, 4, 5, and 6)

data base administrator The person who controls the overall operations of the data base and acts as the custodian of the data base. (Chapter 6 and 16)

data base concept The logical integration of data, as compared with a file processing system in which each application uses a separate file. (Chapter 6)

data base environments DBMS that includes query languages, report writers, and applications generators. (Chapters 6 and 15)

data base management system (DBMS) A software system that bridges the gap between data and applications so that it is possible to find data that fit some criteria from the data base. (Chapters 2, 4, 5, 6, and 10)

data base manager (DBM) A function in a DBMS that actually controls the data base access and monitors storage. (Chapter 6)

data (base) models Logical model of the data base used to structure data in a DBMS including relational, hierarchical, and network data models. (Chapters 5, 6, and 15)

data base structure The data base fields defined in terms of their names, widths, and types. (Chapter 6)

data base users People who may place many demands on the data base for transaction processing (TPS), management information (MIS), decision support (DSS), and executive information (EIS) requirements. (Chapter 6)

data communication Any communication between two computers that involves a transfer of data. (Chapter 7)

data definition language (DDL) A component of DBMSs that links the logical and the physical representations of data and helps describe the logical structure of the data base. (Chapter 6)

data dependence Problem occurring when different departments in an organization collect, process, and store information using different software; the files are dependent upon their original version of software. (Chapter 5)

data dictionary A list of data elements along with information regarding name, source, description, and use. (Chapters 6, 12, and 13)

data encryption system Combinations of software and hardware that convert data output into an unreadable form for transmittal over a network. (Chapter 17)

data entry controls Controls in a series that ensure more accurate data input. (Chapter 17)

data entry problem The processing of data into information is restricted by the slow rate at which input occurs and errors made during input. (Chapter 5)

data entry screen A set of requests to the user for data that are displayed on the screen of a monitor. (Chapter 5)

data files A file containing records with the same type of information, which may be data, text, or programs. (Chapter 2)

data flow diagramming A method of systems design that shows the sources, flows, and storage of data and information in a system. (Chapter 3)

data flow diagrams A logical information flow from sources to destinations, via decision-making, reporting, and transaction processing steps. (Chapter 12)

data hierarchy The order in which data or information is organized in the computer. (Chapter 5)

data independence The separation of applications and data that allows a significant degree of flexibility and accessibility that does not exist in single-file systems. (Chapter 6)

data integration Individual data items form traditional files are integrated to form the data base, and a DBMS separates the data from the applications programs. (Chapter 6)

data integrity Problem occurring when the same information is stored in multiple files throughout an organization and any change in one file must be changed in all files. (Chapters 5 and 17)

data integrity rules Rules followed by relational data bases which provide a more fundamental degree of data integrity than other data base structures, including single-file systems. (Chapter 6)

data management The function of controlling the acquisition, analysis, storage, retrieval, and distribution of data. (Chapter 16)

data manipulation language (DML) A component of DBMSs that describes how applications and end users may process data; provides the ability to carry out a variety of actions through manipulation verbs and associated operands. (Chapter 6)

data processing (DP) The process of converting raw data into information. (Chapter 2)

data processing department   A department consisting of a mainframe computer, its accompanying input/output devices, support personnel, and other IS professionals. (Chapter 16)

data redundancy   Problem occurring when there is a repetition of the same data on different files; therefore, the system is more costly to the organization than necessary. (Chapter 5)

data security   Security that protects the data and software elements. (Chapter 17)

data structure   The data base fields defined in terms of their names, widths, and types. (Chapter 6)

debugging   The process of tracking down and correcting execution errors in a program. (Chapter 13)

decentralized information system   System which stores and processes information for decentralized organizations. (Chapter 16)

decentralized organization structure   Structure of an organization that gives functional or product managers more control and responsibility to make decisions. (Chapter 3)

decision making   Recognizing problems, generating alternative solutions to the problem, choosing among the alternatives, and implementing the chosen alternative. (Chapters 3 and 10)

decision room   Scenario for using a GDSS in which group members are all physically located in a special room equipped with individual workstations and a display screen. (Chapter 10)

decision support system (DSS)   An information system that combines data with models and graphics to answer a decision maker's questions about the data. (Chapters 2 and 10)

decision-making models   Mathematical and behavioral models that may be used to handle the decision-making process. (Chapter 3)

delayed conference   A form of teleconferencing in which the participant's comments are stored sequentially as they are entered; these comments are read and replied to over a long period of time by other participants. (Chapter 7)

demand reports   Reports requested by a manager on a particular subject. (Chapter 2)

demo system   Process that demonstrates an information system through a mock-up with display screens for input, output queries, and user interaction. (Chapter 15)

deposit slip   A listing of all cash and checks received from customers that is prepared and deposited in the bank. (Chapter 8)

descendant node   In the hierarchical data base, the next generation (sons/daughters) of records, each individual record is linked via a pointer. (Chapter 6)

desktop organizer   A utility program that usually ''hides'' in an unused portion of memory and can be accessed while the user is in another application program. (Chapter 15)

detailed systems design   The fifth phase in the system development process, in which the specifications are spelled out for the

development of computer software or purchase of various elements of the proposed information system. (Chapters 3 and 12)

dialog generation and management system (DGMS)   An element of the DSS that makes the DSS different from a traditional data base or set of management science models by its ease of use and flexibility in manipulating the data models; its three elements are action language, display language, and user's knowledge. (Chapter 10)

direct access file organization   Files organized so that each record may accessed directly regardless of its relative position on the file or the order in which the records were placed on the file. (Chapter 5)

direct access storage   Storage method providing the computer the capability of going directly to any character on a disk. (Chapter 4)

direct access storage device (DASD)   A secondary storage device on which information can be accessed in any desired order. (Chapter 5)

direct conversion   System conversion method in which the old system is stopped and the new system is started immediately. (Chapter 13)

disk drive   A device which writes information onto or reads information from magnetic disk. (Chapter 4)

disk operating system (DOS)   An operating system for a personal computer that depends on disk for secondary storage. (Chapter 4)

disk packs A collection of magnetic disks about the size of a record album used on mainframe. (Chapter 4)

diskless workstations In a LAN, a personal computer that does not have a disk drive and is dependent on the file server for disk access. (Chapter 7)

disposable system A working model prototype that can help a user understand the problem at hand without extensive documentation, backup plans, or the guarantee that the system complies with all standards and information requirements. (Chapter 15)

distributed data bases Small and specialized data bases which are separate from a primary data base; usually associated with minicomputers in a distributed data processing arrangement. (Chapters 6 and 7)

distributed data processing (DDP) A processing system which uses a mainframe computer for storage of data bases and for large-scale processing combined with minicomputers or personal computers for local processing. (Chapters 7 and 16)

distributed system An information system in which the components are spread over a wide area. (Chapters 3 and 9)

division/remainder procedure Procedure in which the primary key number is divided by the prime number closest to but less than the number of storage positions on the disk, and the remainder is used as the relative address. (Chapter 5)

documentation A written description of a software package and the tasks it can perform; in a program, the explanation of the logic and program statements. (Chapter 13)

documentation controls Procedure that includes the up-to-date maintenance of source documents, including reports, audit trails, procedures, and the data base controls that document data structure and job responsibilities. (Chapter 17)

domain data base Part of the knowledge base of an expert system that contains the facts about the subject considered by the expert system. (Chapter 11)

downsizing The process of replacing a mainframe or a minicomputer system with a local area network (LAN). (Chapter 18)

DSS generator A general purpose decision support package that contains many models which the user can combine to solve his or her problems and provides the capability to quickly and easily develop a specific DSS. (Chapter 10)

DSS tools Instruments to facilitate the creation of DSS generators including programming languages, financial and mathematical functions, optimization, simulation, and forecasting model procedures, hardware and software graphics, and data base query systems. (Chapter 10)

dumb terminal A device with keyboard and screen but no CPU or secondary storage. Its sole purpose is as an input/output device for a mainframe or minicomputer. (Chapter 7)

E

economic feasibility Element of a feasibility study that determines if a solution's expected benefits exceed costs. (Chapter 12)

editing Checking computer data for reasonableness or discrepancies; also, the process of changing a statement without having to reenter it entirely. (Chapter 5)

electronic cash registers Cash register equipped with a light pen (or holographic light) that reads the bar code present on every product. (Chapter 8)

electronic data interchange (EDI) Allows computers to exchange electronic transmissions of data and information and, therefore, automate much routine business between retail stores, distributors, and manufacturers. (Chapters 2, 7, and 8)

electronic filing Storage of a document on some form of secondary storage for later retrieval. (Chapter 2)

electronic funds transfer (EFT) EDI that links retailers and distributors to banks or other financial institutions to allow automatic payments for orders received from suppliers. (Chapter 7)

electronic mail The process of sending letters, documents, and messages between computers. (Chapters 2 and 7)

Emitter-Coupled Logic (ECL) A new chip technology that will allow computers to process at incredible speeds. (Chapter 18)

end user A non-data processing professional who uses existing software to its fullest extent to do a job better. (Chapters 4, 6, and 15)

end user computing (EUC) Systems development approach in which the user takes over some of the roles of system developer and creates a working information system to meet his or her own needs. (Chapter 15)

end user development Approach to systems development in which users develop their own software via a personal computer and PC-based data base, spreadsheet, word processing, and communication software or via a Data Base Management System (DBMS). (Chapter 12)

end user programmer A programmer who creates specific applications for a popular software package. (Chapters 15 and 18)

end user tools Non-procedural packages oriented toward allowing the average computer user to solve problems without having to learn a programming language. (Chapter 15)

enterprise analysis A top-down method of determining IS requirements in which analysts study the organization, its functions, its processes, and the data it needs to support these functions. (Chapter 12)

entity relationship diagram Capability provided by many CASE packages to outline all the relationships among the various entities (functions and organizational units) in a business organization. (Chapter 12)

environment All elements outside of a system which constrain the activities of the system from an organizational perspective, provide input into the system in the form of resources and information, and monitors the output from the system in terms of products, services, and information. (Chapter 3)

error logs Logs that are generated by the computer when an error occurs, including such details as time, data, and type of error. (Chapter 17)

evaluation, operation, and maintenance The seventh phase in the system development process, in which the system is monitored for continued compliance with management needs and maintained for efficient operation. (Chapters 3 and 12)

example-based system Specific development of an expert system that generates rules or conclusions from past cases or histories, often entered into the system as tables. (Chapter 11)

exception reports Report that is generated by the management information system only when an abnormal event occurs. (Chapter 2)

executive information system (EIS) A personalized, easy-to-use system for executives, providing data on the daily operations of an organization. (Chapter 10)

expenditure cycle Transaction cycle in which an organization purchases merchandise for inventory, receives these components, updates accounts payable, disburses cash, adds the merchandise to inventory, reduces inventory due to sales or production, and issues a new pur-

chase order when stock gets low. (Chapter 8)

expert system A computer-based system that uses knowledge, facts, and reasoning techniques to solve problems that normally require the abilities of human experts. (Chapter 11)

expert system shell A software system that contains an expert system inference mechanism but not the knowledge base; the user adds the rules and facts to create a expert system. (Chapter 11)

explanation facility A part of the inference engine that can explain why or how a recommendation is reached. (Chapter 11)

external data Data that are gathered via various industry, market, and economic studies and services to which an organization may subscribe. (Chapter 1)

F

facsimile machine A telecommunications machine to send a reproduction of any document over phone lines to any place in the world. (Chapter 2)

feasibility study The second phase in the system development process, in which the analyst determines whether or not an acceptable solution to the problem exists. (Chapters 3 and 12)

feedback A form of output that is sent back to a system's input or processing function enabling a system to change its operation if necessary. (Chapter 3)

field checks Data entry controls that attempt to check the validity of a single field independent of other fields. (Chapter 17)

field name   An identifier given to a field in a data base file. (Chapter 5)

field   One or more bytes that form a single fact or data item. (Chapter 5)

field type   The type of information (character, numeric, date, or logical) that will be stored in a field. (Chapter 5)

field width   The number of positions set aside for data in a particular field. (Chapter 5)

file and data base controls   Procedures that ensure that the correct files are processed and that files and data bases are protected from compromise. (Chapter 17)

file checks   Data entry controls that are useful for making sure the correct files are processed. (Chapter 17)

file manager   A part of a data base management package that controls the actual creation of the file and various utility functions associated with the use of the file. (Chapter 5)

file processing system   A data management system that can work with only one file at a time to produce various types of reports. (Chapters 5 and 6)

file server   A PC with a hard disk that is used to provide access to files for users of a network. (Chapter 7)

file structure   The type of information needed for each field in terms of field names, widths, and types. (Chapter 5)

financial audit   Audit which attests to the fairness of financial statements. (Chapter 9)

financial statements   Documents prepared on a periodic basis from the general ledger accounts that are used by such outside parties as bankers and regulatory authorities as well as by owners to assess the financial well-being of the organization. (Chapter 8)

flat files   Another name for a table in a relational data model. (Chapter 5)

flexible manufacturing systems (FMS)   System that allows production workstations and machinery to be switched from one operation to another or from one product to another, with a minimum of interruption due to setup time. (Chapter 9)

floppy disks   Disks made of Mylar plastic and covered with iron oxide particles for use of secondary storage with the personal computer. (Chapter 4)

forecasting model   Model combining historical data, managerial assumptions, and a forecasting formula to produce a ''guess'' at future activities. (Chapter 10)

formal information system   System that represents a set of responsibilities and procedures for data input, processing, output, and utilization of information. (Chapter 3)

forward chaining   Method used to arrive at a final decision in which the inference engine starts with the facts of the case, applies the facts to the IF part of the rules, and rules that do not apply are eliminated until a conclusion that fits the facts is found. (Chapter 11)

fourth generation language (4GLs)   Advanced computer languages that make prototyping possible by not requiring the user to develop a complete logical plan before solving a problem on the computer. (Chapter 15)

functional support end users   Local experts with knowledge of a particular software package or computer language that makes them informal centers of computer use in their functional areas. (Chapter 15)

G

gallium arsenide   A semiconductor material that may soon replace silicon in chips because of its higher speed. (Chapter 18)

Gantt chart   A series of horizontal bars showing the proposed schedule and the actual start and finish times for each project element. (Chapter 16)

gateway   A combination of hardware and software that connects two dissimilar computer networks. It allows a LAN user to access a mainframe network without leaving his or her PC. (Chapter 7)

Gbyte   The largest commonly used measure of computer storage, equal to 2^{30} bytes of storage. (Chapter 4)

general controls   Control procedures that apply to the IS in general. (Chapter 17)

general ledger system   The core of the administrative cycle which summarizes the organizations activities in financial terms. (Chapter 8)

general systems design The fourth phase in the system development process, in which an outline is developed of feasible alternatives of how the problem could be solved. (Chapter 3)

graphical user interface (GUI) A GUI uses icons to represent commands and data and uses a mouse to position the cursor over the desired function. (Chapter 4)

graphics software A group of programs for visual presentation of information or for creation of new and different art forms. (Chapter 4)

group code A classification system similar to a block code, except that every number or letter in the code represents something different. (Chapter 8)

group decision support systems (GDSS) An interactive computer-based system that facilitates the solution of unstructured problems by a set of decision makers working together as a group. (Chapter 10)

H

handwritten input A nonkeyboard form of input in which the user can write the input and the computer can decipher the individual characters and accept the information. (Chapters 11 and 18)

hard disk A scaled down version of a mainframe disk pack with metal disks that is used for storing information from a personal computer. (Chapter 4)

hardware controls Procedure in which hardware manufacturers provide overflow and read/write

checks to ensure that data are not lost and that input and output are accurate and free of transcription errors. (Chapter 17)

hardware The electronic part of the computer that stores and manipulates symbols under the direction of the computer software. (Chapter 4)

hashing The process of converting the primary key on a record into a relative address. (Chapter 5)

hierarchical data model A data model in which each element has only one parent or owner. (Chapters 5 and 6)

hierarchy charts A chart that breaks the software program down into smaller modules so that it can be coded and still be coordinated. (Chapters 12 and 13)

hot site agreement Agreement in which a disaster recovery firm agrees to set up a comparable mainframe computer center (the ''hot site'') that will be available to the organization if needed. (Chapter 17)

I

IBM compatible Pcs Computers with the ability to run software written for the original IBM PC or one of its successors. (Chapter 4)

icons Pictures which represent various operations on the computer. (Chapter 4)

IF-THEN rule Rules used in an expert system that together with the facts create the knowledge base. (Chapter 11)

imaging systems Input device that converts paper and non-word processing documents to electronic forms. (Chapter 18)

implementation schedule Document that combines controls and plans for each structured system development alternative and includes an estimate of the resources and time needed to implement the proposed alternative. (Chapter 12)

implementation The sixth phase in the system development process, which involves solving the problem via acquisition, software development, installation of the information system, and the training of personnel on the new elements of the system. (Chapters 3, 13, and 14)

incremental model Decision making model that involves not setting forth any selection criteria or a set of alternatives, resulting in an alternative which appears only marginally different from the current mode of operation. (Chapter 3)

indexed file A second file containing one or more fields from the original flat file arranged in order of some value (the index). (Chapter 5)

indexed sequential access method (ISAM) Method which combines direct and sequential access methods using disk storage in a way similar to the method used in telephone books for storing names, addresses, and phone numbers. (Chapter 5)

inference engine Element of an expert system emphasizing problem solving that handles the reasoning capabilities. (Chapter 11)

informal information system System that is not as well organized as a formal system. The most common informal information system is the "grapevine" which informally passes information around an organization. (Chapter 3)

informated factory A workplace where computers perform operations and supply workers with information on the processing operations. (Chapter 1)

information center (IC) An organization that enables users to combine the processing power of the organization's mainframe with easy-to-use PC software. (Chapters 15 and 16)

information Data that has been processed into a form that is useful to the user. (Chapter 1)

information delivery Control that involves ensuring that the appropriate information reaches the decision makers that need it. (Chapter 17)

information revolution A change in society in which an organization's success is a function of its information resources and how effectively it uses these resources to compete in todays dynamic environment. (Chapter 1)

information society A society in which the majority of the workers are involved in the transmittal of information. (Chapters 1)

information system A system within an organization which converts raw data into information that is useful to managers and other interested parties. (Chapters 3 and 17)

information system life cycle Phases of the life of an information system including development, use and maintenance, modification, and the declination of use. (Chapter 12)

information system requirements The first step in system acquisition that defines the software characteristics to vendors. (Chapter 14)

information technology The use of computers for information and productivity. (Chapters 1 and 2)

information-based organization An organization in which power resides with those who have the information and the strength of the organization comes from the tremendous explosion in the availability of computing power. (Chapter 1)

input controls Specific controls that ensure accurate data input; procedures that primarily help to provide data integrity and to avoid the problem of garbage in, garbage out (GIGO). (Chapter 17)

input, processing, and output (IPO) chart A chart for each module of a software package showing the input to the module, the processing that takes place in the module, and the output from the module. (Chapter 13)

integrated accounting system System that requires an entry in only one part of the system and updates automatically all other applications in the system. (Chapter 8)

integrated circuit The combination of transistors and circuits on a chip. (Chapter 4)

integrated system A computer system with all of its activities coordinated through effective management and information systems. (Chapter 3)

interactive prototype A type of prototype that allows the prospective user to interact with the screens. (Chapter 15)

internal data base A data base that contains data of the organizations daily activities. (Chapter 2)

internal data Data that are generated by the daily activities of the organization as it produces its goods and services and interacts with vendors and the customers. (Chapter 1)

internal memory The part of the computer used to internally store instructions and data. (Chapter 4)

interpretation The conversion of a high-level language into machine language. (Chapter 13)

inverted file A second file containing one or more fields from the original flat file arranged in order of some value (the index). (Chapter 5)

invoice A bill sent to a customer for services rendered or merchandise purchased. (Chapter 8)

IS contingency plan Plan that details the organization's reaction to an event that has a large-scale negative impact. (Chapter 16)

IS operational plan Lower level IS management plan that identifies and carries out the day-to-day tasks necessary to implement the IS strategic plan. (Chapter 16)

IS steering committee Committee composed of high-level managers from each functional area who provide direction to the CIO as to their information needs. (Chapter 16)

IS strategic plan Top level of IS management plan which sets forth long-term IS objectives. (Chapter 16)

iterative design approach DSS development approach in which one small but important part of a problem is selected for development. (Chapters 10 and 11)

J

job cost sheet Document that provides detailed and summarized costs of specific products. (Chapter 8)

job social structure Organizational structure that includes individual employees' jobs and career paths and the nature and responsibilities of individual employees' jobs. (Chapter 3)

join operation Relational operation that combines all the data from two or more relations using the primary keys of each relation to create one large combined relation. (Chapter 6)

Josephson Junction A super-fast electronic switch that works at temperatures close to absolute zero. (Chapter 18)

journal A list of the financial aspects of each transaction of an organization. (Chapter 8)

just-in-time (JIT) manufacturing A manufacturing process that pulls a product through the manufacturing system as it is needed by the next workstation, sales, or the distribution system. (Chapter 9)

just-in-time (JIT) system A system that informs vendors when supplies are needed so that they are shipped and arrive ''just in time'' for utilization in the production process. (Chapter 1)

K

Kanban ticket A move ticket that is used to signal the need for a workstation to provide needed components for the next station in sequence. (Chapter 9)

Kbytes 1 Kbyte equals 1,024 bytes. (Chapter 4)

key performance indicators Data other than accounting values that indicate the health of the company and show executives where the company stands relative to its competition and company objectives. (Chapter 10)

key success factors Approach to determining IS requirements in which functions of the industry and the objectives of the organization are determined. (Chapter 12)

key-to-disk machine Machine that enables the user to input data for storage on a magnetic disk from a keyboard like that used on a computer. (Chapter 5)

keyboard An input device made up of keys which allow input of the alphanumeric and punctuation characters. (Chapter 4)

keyboard buffer A temporary storage area within a computer to speed the slow data input rate. (Chapter 5)

keyboard macro End user software tool that is a way of recording a series of keystrokes that can be replayed at a later time by pressing a single set of keys. (Chapter 15)

knowledge acquisition facility (KAF) Component of the expert system that facilitates the acquisition of knowledge from human experts. (Chapter 11)

knowledge base In an expert system, the facts, judgements, rules intuition, and experience provided by the group of experts. (Chapters 11 and 13)

knowledge engineer A specialist in expert systems that can convert an expert's knowledge into the rules and facts in an expert system. (Chapter 11)

L

labor distribution A record of the time spent on various work orders and other plant activities. (Chapter 8)

leased line Special high-speed telephone lines that are leased from the telephone company for the express purpose of carrying data between computers. (Chapter 7)

linked list A group of records, each of which points to the next record in a sequential order. (Chapter 5)

local area network (LAN) Office information systems that are comprised of a variety of electronic and computerized office equipment that are connected within an organization. (Chapters 2 and 7)

local decision network Scenario for using a GDSS in which group members remain at their individual locations and send messages among workstations through a network. (Chapter 10)

logic trace The line of reasoning that is used to arrive at the current conclusion and is shown by the explanation facility. (Chapter 11)

logical check Debugging process in which programmers should verify that the program complies with the objectives of each module and that the modules are compatible with other modules, data base or files, and procedures. (Chapter 13)

logical integration Logical association among data base files that can be either established explicitly using a structural model like the hierarchy or the network data models or implicitly using the relational data model. (Chapter 6)

logical view View of the data that defines how data are organized and accessed for applications and the end user interface. (Chapter 6)

M

mainframe A very large and fast computer that requires a special support staff and a special physical environment. (Chapter 4)

make or buy decision The decision of an organization to either build its own system or acquire a system from an outside vendor after management has determined the requirements for the system. (Chapter 14)

management control Methods that describe how management keeps track of the authority delegated to others and supervises company activities effectively. (Chapter 17)

management information system (MIS) An integrated information system which generates reports to support operations, management, and decision-making functions in an organization. (Chapters 2 and 9)

management of information systems (MoIS) The management of all five elements of the IS

(hardware, software, data, procedures, and personnel) to provide the needed information to the managers in the organization. (Chapter 16)

management system The system in an organization that monitors the physical system and makes decisions regarding the input, transformation process, and the nature of the output. (Chapter 3)

managerial philosophy Control environment that includes management's attitudes and actions toward controlling risk. (Chapter 17)

many-to-many model A data model characterized by a network, because each data element can have numerous roots or parents. (Chapter 5)

market intelligence Data collection activity when competitor's information is involved. (Chapter 9)

market research Data collection activity when consumers and retailers are involved. (Chapter 9)

master file update A file process in which an existing file is updated with the additions of new records to the file, deletions of records from the file, or changes of records on the file. (Chapter 5)

master plan for information systems The overall information strategy developed from decisions and evaluations on the vendors' proposals. (Chapters 14 and 16)

material requirements planning (MRP) Procedures to accomplish the scheduling and material requisition task that often uses software to handle these

decision-making activities and eliminate some reports found in a traditional system. (Chapters 8 and 9)

matrix organization A combination of structure in an organization in which employees are organized both by function and by project. (Chapter 3)

Mbytes Measure of computer memory equal to 2^{20} bytes of storage. (Chapter 4)

menu A list of commands or requests for data. (Chapter 4)

menu-driven package A software package that uses a menu to allow the user to make selections of commands or to enter data. (Chapter 4)

microfloppy A floppy disk that is $3\frac{1}{2}$ inches in diameter and is contained within a hard plastic cartridge. (Chapter 4)

midsize computer Another name for a minicomputer. (Chapter 4)

minicomputer The computer size between a mainframe and a personal computer which is used by many organizations that need more processing power than that available with personal computers, but at less cost than that for a mainframe. (Chapter 4)

mnemonic code A classification system that is similar to a group code, except that each aspect of the code has a readily identifiable meaning. (Chapter 8)

mock-up prototype Type of prototype that looks like the final product, but does not actually do anything. (Chapter 15)

model A simplified version of the system that allows the analyst to understand the system's important parts. (Chapters 2 and 13)

model base   A collection of models that are used and solved as needed to arrive at a solution in a decision support system. (Chapter 2)

model base software system (MBSS)   System that manages various models similar to the way a DBMS manages the data base; its functions include adding, deleting, and modifying models; cataloging, linking, and accessing models; and creating new models by using predefined modules and subroutines. (Chapter 10)

modem   A communications device that modulates computer signals into outgoing audio signals and demodulates incoming audio signals into computer signals. (Chapters 4 and 7)

modular approach   IS development approach in which clear objectives for each module are set, and the design and implementation for each module proceed in an orderly fashion under the direction of the project team and steering committee. (Chapter 12)

monitor   A cathode ray tube output device that shows the output on a video screen. (Chapter 4)

monochrome monitor   A video screen that displays a single-color light symbols on a contrasting background. (Chapter 4)

mouse   An input device that allows input through movement over a flat surface--about the size of a mouse and connected to the computer via long cord. (Chapters 4 and 18)

multimedia   Multimedia is a combination of the traditional PC with a VCR, optical storage disk, compact disks, and high fidelity stereo which will provide interactive full motion video. (Chapter 18)

multiple access network   A local area network in which all users can transmit at any time, but collision-detecting software is necessary to control transmissions. (Chapter 7)

N

nanotechnology   The ability to build complex objects on a molecular scale using atom-by-atom precision. (Chapter 18)

natural languages   Languages that use everyday terminology and grammar to communicate with the computer. (Chapter 11)

net present value   An economic concept used to discount cash flows (in and out) to current dollars so that economic comparisons can be made. (Chapter 14)

network administrator   Individual who manages the network and controls which users have access to the various software programs and data files. (Chapter 7)

network data model   A data model in which each element may have more than one parent or owner. (Chapters 5 and 6)

network operating system   Operating system designed to manage the interaction between various local personal computers and the central file server. (Chapter 7)

neural network   Computer processing using multiple processors that are "trained," through repetition, to handle some task without an extensive, highly specific program. (Chapter 11)

neurons   The interconnected units in a neural network that send messages to one another at a high rate of speed. (Chapter 11)

node   The location of a computer or terminal in a network or electronic mail system that allows a user to access the main system from the terminal and send mail to any other user on the network, as long as the other user's address is known. (Chapter 7)

nonprocedural language   A computer language that does not require the user to develop a logical procedure but only to answer questions or make choices from a menu. (Chapter 15)

nonprocedural software packages   Software packages that allow users to work with text, graphics, and numbers by simply answering questions and entering data. (Chapter 15)

nonprogramming end users   End users who tend to use applications software at its lowest level and do not extend their knowledge of the software beyond what is needed to solve basic problems. (Chapter 15)

normalization rules   Rules followed by relational data bases which provide a more fundamental degree of data integrity than other data base structures, including single-file systems. (Chapter 6)

O

object code Program code after compilation to a machine language program that is actually executed by the computer. (Chapter 13)

office information system (OIS) A machine or machines combined with a communication system and users to efficiently handle the job of obtaining, organizing, storing, retrieving, and preparing needed information within an organization; also called office automation. (Chapter 2)

one-to-many model The situation in a data model where one field is related to multiple other fields. (Chapter 5)

online mode A transaction processing mode in which all transactions are processed as they occur. (Chapter 8)

online processing system A system in which all transactions are processed as they occur. (Chapters 2 and 3)

open order file Revenue cycle document that is used to keep track of the order, especially useful when orders may be in process for a long time. (Chapter 8)

operating system The primary component of systems software; manages the many tasks which are going on concurrently within a computer. (Chapters 2, 4, and 14)

operational audit Audit which monitors a company's compliance with plans, policies, and budgets. (Chapter 9)

operational feasibility Element of a feasibility study that determines that the project can be implemented within the organization's constraints, including organizational, behavioral, personnel, and day-to-day operational activities. (Chapter 12)

operational management The lowest level supervisors who need detailed information on the day-to-day operation of a company's production process. (Chapter 1)

operational planning The third element of managing operations that involves implementing the objectives set forth in the IS strategic plan. (Chapter 16)

operations management The final element of an IS that must be managed which consists of a set of procedures used to run IS operations. (Chapter 16)

optical character recognition (OCR) A process which reads characters into the computer. (Chapter 9)

optical disk A form of secondary storage that uses lasers and pits in a reflective surface to store information. (Chapter 4)

optimization model Model in which the user implements a mathematical technique that determines the best possible solution to the model. (Chapter 10)

optoelectronic technology Laser light used to transmit data at the rate of 1 billion bits per second. (Chapter 18)

order entry The initial transaction processing activity on the revenue cycle, also referred to as a sale of merchandise. (Chapter 8)

organization structure The method of organizing individuals within an organization by differing responsibilities and functions. (Chapters 3 and 17)

organizational constraints Areas within an organization that affect the speed of decision making and the boundaries within which individuals and organizations may search for solutions. (Chapter 3)

organizational learning A concept that states that all organizations learn and adapt with time to changes in the environment. (Chapter 3)

organizational objectives A set of short and long term goals of an organization. (Chapter 3)

output content The information needed for each activity outlined in the systems flowchart. (Chapter 13)

output controls Procedure that ensures the accuracy of such output as reports, data updates, or inquiries. (Chapter 17)

output form The presentation of the information output from the system. (Chapter 13)

output format The text, graphic, and tabular layout used to display the output. (Chapter 13)

output timing An indication of when information is output, such as instantaneous online output or periodic reports on a daily or monthly basis. (Chapter 13)

outsourcing An acquisition approach in which an organization hires a third party consultant to develop the system. (Chapters 12, 14, and 18)

overflow area   In the use of ISAM, an area of storage to which new records are added when the original storage area is filled. (Chapter 5)

overhead   The total of all the costs associated with plant assets and administration that is allocated to each work order and posted to the job cost sheet. (Chapter 8)

P

packet switching   In a wide area network, dividing long messages into smaller data units to be transmitted more easily through a network. (Chapter 7)

packets   The smaller data units into which long messages from the host computer are divided for transmission using packet switching. (Chapter 7)

packing slip   Shipping document made up of the data on the sales order and the record of the actual number of parts picked for shipping of merchandise. (Chapter 8)

page printer   A high-speed printer capable of printing an entire page in one motion. (Chapter 4)

parallel conversion   The conversion of one system to another which has both systems running in parallel before completing the conversion. (Chapter 13)

parallel form   The processing of data 16, 32, or 64 bits at a time. (Chapter 7)

parallel processing   A form of computer processing that allows multiple instructions to be processed simultaneously. (Chapter 18)

parent node   The first record entered while using the hierarchical data base. (Chapter 6)

password   A sequence of letters and/or digits supposedly known only to the user that must be entered before the computer system can be accessed. (Chapter 17)

password policies   Rules that should include not allowing users to choose their own passwords, requiring that passwords be longer than four letters or digits, and changing all passwords periodically. (Chapter 17)

peer-to-peer   A LAN configuration in smaller networks in which the emphasis is on users sharing files. Each computer can function as both a server and a workstation, instead of as a single dedicated file server. (Chapter 7)

perpetual inventory system   Inventory system that is continually updated with each transaction. Personnel need only enter a stock number to determine the current status of an inventory item. (Chapter 8)

personal computers   Small, one user computers that are relatively inexpensive to own and do not require a special environment or special knowledge to use them. (Chapter 4)

personal identification number (PIN)   A password used to access a bank account from an Automatic Teller Machine (ATM). (Chapter 17)

personal productivity software   PC applications software, so called because it allows individuals to increase their productivity. (Chapter 4)

phase-in conversion   System conversion that can be used when small subsystems are implemented one at a time and de-

bugged before the next subsystem is implemented. (Chapter 13)

phased approach   IS development approach in which clear objectives for each module are set, and the design and implementation for each module proceed in an orderly fashion under the direction of the project team and steering committee. (Chapter 12)

physical security   Security for the hardware component of the IS. (Chapter 17)

physical system   A part of an organizational system that transforms such input resources as personnel, financial capital, raw materials or components, equipment, and information into products and services. (Chapter 3)

physical view   View of the data that describes how they are physically stored on some type of magnetic media. (Chapter 6)

point-of-sale (POS) systems   Special systems that have been developed to process sales transactions in an organization in which the volume of transactions is so high that the formal preparation of sales orders would be impractical. (Chapter 8)

pointer system   A linking system in which a field in one record in a list points to the next record in the list. (Chapter 5)

port protection devices   An extra level of security that separates the user from the computer. (Chapter 17)

ports   An entry line to the computer. (Chapter 7)

primary key   The one field or combination of fields that uniquely identifies a record among all records on a data base. (Chapters 5 and 6)

problem avoiders Individual decision makers who seek every method to avoid any sort of problem. (Chapter 3)

problem seekers Individual decision makers who relish the challenge of tackling interesting problems. (Chapter 3)

problem solvers Individual decision makers who deal with problems as they arise. (Chapter 3)

problematic search Concept that implies that the search for alternative solutions to a problem starts with the problem itself and then moves to the next most likely problem location. (Chapter 3)

procedural controls Controls that are found in written manuals that provide step-by-step procedures to be followed by computer operators, data entry personnel, and users for the smooth flow of information and the implementation of appropriate control features. (Chapter 17)

procedural language A computer language that requires the programmer to develop a logical procedure to perform some task. (Chapter 15)

processing and logic controls Procedure that primarily ensures that the IS satisfies the objectives in the structured analysis and design phases. (Chapter 17)

processing controls Procedures that should provide reasonable assurances that data processing complies with management's specifications. (Chapter 17)

processing/internal memory Unit that handles the actual processing of data into information, as well as the necessary internal

storage of data and information. (Chapter 2)

production model prototype Prototype that is the starting point for the development of the complete production version. (Chapter 15)

production schedule Work order, stored in the computer, that provides production operations with the basic information it needs to assemble its products. (Chapter 8)

program documentation A description of the logic behind the programs for the software user and other programmers who work with or maintain the software. (Chapter 16)

program evaluation review technique (PERT) Network analysis procedure that can be extended beyond the simple scheduling of time, to the management of such resources as the analysts, programmers, accountants, and engineers of a project team. (Chapter 12)

program flowcharts Graphical description that is developed from a combination of well-known symbols and mathematical expressions to depict a processing activity. (Chapter 13)

program generators A prototyping tool that allows the user to generate computer code in a high-level language without having to actually write the code. (Chapter 15)

programmed decision Decisions which can be made by following a set of rules, are usually made frequently, and are especially amendable to solution by computerized techniques. (Chapters 3 and 10)

programs A series of instructions or rules for the computer to perform manipulation and storage of symbols. (Chapter 4)

project controls Specific criteria and tasks to be completed and followed in the process of developing a system. (Chapter 12)

project definition The first phase in the system development process, that may involve determining a new information need or defining an opportunity in the marketplace. (Chapter 3)

project management A wide range of techniques and procedures used to manage any type of large-scale project, including construction projects, military systems, space exploration projects, and software systems. (Chapter 16)

project team The group of information system professionals who actually build a specific application. (Chapters 12 and 16)

projection operation Relational operation that reduces the number of columns in the relations needed by the user or report, thereby reducing the amount of data to those relevant fields. (Chapter 6)

protocol The set of rules two computers follow when communicating with each other. (Chapter 7)

prototype A system that contains the bare essentials that can be developed and used on a trial basis to help users to further define their requirements or develop a completely different approach to solving the problem. (Chapter 12)

prototyping Creating a "quick and dirty" version of software to get around the lengthy systems analysis and design process. (Chapter 15)

pseudocode A written form of an algorithm that can be easily converted into a computer program. (Chapter 13)

pull-down menu A submenu that uses icons to represent various commands or operations and which appears as needed. (Chapter 4)

purchase order Purchase document that is prepared from a sales forecast outlining the acquisition of merchandise for resale or the manufacture of a company's products. (Chapter 8)

purchase requisition Purchase document that is sent to the purchasing department, which specifies what needs to be purchased. (Chapter 8)

Q

quasi-resolution of conflict Concept that conflicts occurring naturally in an organization may be resolved by allowing the organizational segments or individuals to pursue their own goals and make their own decisions within specified bounds. (Chapter 3)

query language A computer language associated with the use of data base management packages that allows a user to request information. (Chapters 6 and 15)

query languages A computer language associated with the use of data base management packages that allows a user to request information. (Chapters 6 and 15)

R

random access File organization method in which any record on the disk may be accessed directly without going through any previous records, as long as the user of the software knows the address of that record. (Chapter 5)

random access memory (RAM) The section of memory that is available for storing the instructions to the computer and the symbols to be manipulated. (Chapter 4)

rational model Decision-making model that assumes that the decision maker has a set goal; the criteria for ranking or evaluating this goal; a weighing or ordering procedure, in the case of multiple objectives; and a finite set of alternative courses of action, each with known outcomes. (Chapter 3)

read only memory (ROM) The section of memory that is placed in the computer during the manufacturing process and remains there even after computer is turned off. (Chapter 4)

read/write head The part of a disk or tape drive that handles the actual transfer of information to or from the disk or tape. (Chapter 4)

real-time conference A form of teleconferencing in which all participants are logged onto the system at the same time. (Chapter 7)

real-time processing Processing system used when several users are competing for the same resource. (Chapters 2 and 8)

receiving report Purchase document prepared by a clerk when the goods are received at the warehouse that indicates the items received how many were received, and the date. (Chapter 8)

reciprocal agreement Agreement in which two firms agree to provide data processing for each other in case of a disaster. (Chapter 17)

record A collection of fields with information that usually pertains to only one subject (person, place, event, and so on). (Chapter 5)

record checks Data entry controls that ensure that the logical relationships among fields are valid. (Chapter 17)

record number The physical position of a record in a list. (Chapter 5)

relational data model A data model in which elements are represented as being parts of tables which are then related through common elements. (Chapters 5 and 6)

relational operations Operations on relational tables to generate information like that found in a single large transaction file using a relation including projection, join, and selection operations. (Chapters 5 and 6)

relations Tables in a relational data model that are simply flat files in which the rows correspond to records and the columns are fields. (Chapter 6)

relative address The location of a record in secondary storage relative to all other records. (Chapter 5)

remote decision making   Scenario for using a GDSS that uses wide area networks to allow the same type of communications between member workstations as in the local decision network scenario. (Chapter 10)

report generator   The part of a data base management package that handles the reporting of information in whatever order is desired by the user. (Chapter 5)

report writers   Prototyping tool that allows users to generate a needed report in a desired format. (Chapter 15)

Request for Proposal (RFP)   Notification of an organization's need for software that is prepared and sent to prospective vendors with detailed specifications. (Chapter 14)

revenue cycle   Transaction cycle that typically consists of an order entry process, a shipping and inventory process, a billing process, an accounts receivable process, and a collection process. (Chapter 8)

ring network   A computer network that links multiple computers in a circle or ring with no host computer. (Chapter 7)

robotics   The use of machines to perform physical tasks in place of humans. (Chapter 11)

root node   The first record entered while using the hierarchical data base. (Chapter 6)

rule data base   Part of the knowledge base of an expert system that contains the rules used in the reasoning element of the expert system. (Chapter 11)

rule-based system   Specific development of an expert system that is built by entering a list of IF-THEN rules. (Chapter 11)

S

sales forecast   Future sales prediction requiring input from field sales personnel who have firsthand information about current and future trends. (Chapter 9)

sales order processing systems   System that automates the entire process of documenting production, shipment, and billings for each particular product. (Chapter 8)

sales strategy   A specific plan for advertising and promotion that depends on the product involved and the company's overall goals. (Chapter 9)

satisficing   The use of satisfactory, rather than optimal selection criteria in the decision making process. (Chapter 3)

scheduled reports   Report generated by the MIS on a regular basis containing summary reports of the results of the data processing operation. (Chapter 2)

schema   A logical plan for determining the data elements in a data base and the relationships among these elements. (Chapters 5 and 6)

secondary keys   Fields or combinations of fields that are not necessarily unique to a record but that can be used to find a group of records. (Chapter 5)

secondary storage units   Storage area outside of the computer used to hold an overflow of information or to save information

when the computer is turned off. (Chapters 2 and 4)

security software packages   Special software package that protects the computer system by various means. (Chapter 17)

selection operation   Relational operation that is used to identify the records (rows) that satisfy the user or the report criteria. (Chapter 6)

semantic data modeling   An advanced relational model in which management may want its data base to reflect the organization's natural business transactions and entities; relational data base that may not comply totally with all the normalization rules. (Chapter 6)

semistructured decisions   Decisions that fall somewhere between unstructured decisions and structured decisions for which both human intuition and mathematical methods might be used. (Chapter 3)

separate application packages   Individual software packages that will not automatically update other application packages when one transaction is entered into a specific package. (Chapter 8)

sequential access   A form of access in which the records are physically stored in the same order in which they are accessed. (Chapters 4 and 5)

sequential access storage device   A secondary storage device that stores information in such a way that information must be read in the same order that it is written onto the device. (Chapter 5)

sequential code Coding scheme in which every record is given a sequential numeric code; a useful method for controlling and referencing transactions by number. (Chapter 8)

sequential file organization A file organization system used for records that need to be accessed in the order in which they were physically stored. (Chapter 5)

serial form The processing of data one bit at a time. (Chapter 7)

serial machines A computer that can process only one instruction at a time. (Chapters 11 and 18)

serial port The connection between the computer and the modem cable. (Chapter 7)

service bureau An organization that provides all data processing and computations required for another organization for a fee. (Chapters 12 and 14)

simulation model Model in which the decision-maker uses a series of values to simulate a particular situation. (Chapters 10 and 14)

smart machine Computer-based machine that can make decisions and provide information. (Chapter 1)

software control The most important processing control that ensures that transactions and information for reporting and decision-making needs are processed in accordance with management's objectives. (Chapter 17)

software demonstration A demonstration of software and its features shown to a prospective user that includes a review of the user's manual and any other documentation for the software. (Chapter 14)

software development Method of producing software including the detailed design, implementation, and maintenance phases of structured analysis and design of the computer programs. (Chapter 13)

software Human-provided logic without which the computer can do nothing. (Chapters 4 and 13)

software package One or more programs that are combined with a set of directions, or user's manual. (Chapters 4 and 14)

software support The available support and instruction available from the vendor or software developer. (Chapter 14)

sort Concept used in reference to a flat file which involves arranging information in a file in some specific order. (Chapter 5)

sort/merge operation Approach to accessing information on separate files that requires the user to combine information from two files into one. (Chapter 5)

source code Program code prior to compilation into machine language. (Chapter 13)

specific DSS A decision support system that has been developed to solve a specific problem; it is usually written in a high-level language. (Chapter 10)

spike An electrical disturbance, such as lightening, that causes a sudden increase in electrical supply and can destroy delicate chips and other electrical parts. (Chapter 17)

spreadsheet A table having rows and columns of values labels and formulas that can be used to make calculations, plan budgets, make forecasts, and ask ''What if?'' questions about the data. (Chapter 4)

spreadsheet macros A sequential series of spreadsheet keyboard commands that the user determines and thereafter can put into play by pressing the few keys that represent the particular macro. (Chapter 15)

standard operating procedures (SOP) The specific rules and regulations that large bureaucracies have to specify how decisions are to be made, what policies must be followed, and what resources are at the disposal of the decision maker. (Chapter 3)

star network A computer network with one host computer to which many smaller computers or terminals are linked. (Chapter 7)

steering committee A top-level group that guides the planning, development, and implementation of systems. (Chapters 12 and 17)

strategic information Information that can be used in many ways to help a company obtain an advantage over its competition. (Chapter 2)

strategic information system (SIS) An information system used by top management to support a company's competitive strategy. (Chapters 2 and 11)

strategic management Level of management that involves the determination of the organization's objectives, the strategy required to accomplish these objectives, and the organizational structure needed to implement the strategy. (Chapter 1)

strategic planning Objectives defined by the organization's executives must be defined, actions to accomplish the objectives are selected, and the resources necessary to implement the actions are determined. (Chapters 1 and 3)

structured chart Top-down tool that has various levels where its top level represents controlling activates for various detailed tasks, and the flow of information between these controlling activities and the detailed tasks is shown. (Chapter 13)

structured decisions Decisions which can be made by following a set of rules, are usually made frequently, and are especially amendable to solution by computerized techniques. (Chapters 2, 3, and 10)

structured programming A method of implementing a top-down design using a particular programming language in which the use of blocks or modules is very important. (Chapter 13)

SQL A data base query language with commands that are concise and work well across a variety of computer platforms. (Chapter 6)

structured systems analysis and design An approach for managing the development of new systems or modifying old systems in the systems life cycle. (Chapters 3, 12, 13, and 15)

structured systems development The process of developing a system to meet a new need or to solve a problem in an existing system. (Chapters 3, 12, and 13)

structured walk through A part of the system analysis and design process in which the analyst presents the current status of

the process to his or her peers. (Chapters 12 and 13)

suboptimization The problem which occurs if each component (input, transformation, and output) is allowed to operate separately. (Chapter 3)

subschema A reduced view of the data base for a particular application. (Chapters 5 and 6)

subsystem A small section of a system which works as a system on its own to handle some detailed task for the larger system. (Chapter 3)

supercomputers A subset of mainframes which are the biggest, fastest computers used today.(Chapter 4)

superconductivity The property of certain materials at low temperatures to conduct electricity without resistance. (Chapter 18)

surge protectors Device that protects the computer and peripherals that are plugged into it from voltage surges and spikes. (Chapter 17)

symbolic reasoning A problem solving approach in which symbols are used to represent the problem concepts. (Chapter 11)

synchronous communication A form of communication between computers that does not require the computers to be synchronized and allows large numbers of characters to be sent as a block. (Chapter 7)

system A set of elements or components organized and integrated for the purpose of achieving a particular goal or objective. (Chapter 3)

system conversion The transition stage between the old and new information systems, in which

the old system is switched to the new system. (Chapter 13)

system development life cycle The seven phases, often called the analysis and design, used to develop an information system to meet a new need or to solve a problem in an existing system. (Chapters 3 and 12)

system flowcharting A standardized graphical method of presentation that demonstrates the interrelationships among the elements of an information system. (Chapter 3)

systems analyst A person who carries out the systems analysis and design process by careful and logical consideration of management and operating personnel's information requirements. (Chapter 12)

systems audit software Special software that keeps track of all attempts to log onto the computer, with particular attention to unsuccessful attempts. (Chapter 17)

systems documentation Documentation provided with a system consisting of all written documents that describe the IS and the procedures for carrying out data processing tasks. (Chapter 16)

systems flowcharts A special type of flowchart used in the design stage because they specify how processing is accomplished, how the data are stored, how data and information are transmitted, how information is output, and how data are input into the information system. (Chapter 13)

systems life cycle A sequence of phases a system goes through, including system development, operations, and decline; sometimes refers only to system development. (Chapter 12)

systems software The programming which manages the operations of the computer, controlling input, processing, and output activities, as well as accessing data from storage media. (Chapters 2 and 4)

systems test A procedure in which all programs, groups of programs, data files, and operating procedures must be tested as a complete system to ensure compliance with management's expectations. (Chapter 13)

T

tables of attributes Tables in a relational data model that are simply flat files in which the rows correspond to records and the columns are fields. (Chapter 6)

tactical decisions Decisions made by middle-level managers using summary reports. These are not easily programmable. (Chapter 1)

tape A form of secondary storage composed on thin Mylar tape coated with ferrous oxide particles on which information is recorded in binary form by selective magnetization of spots on the tape. (Chapter 4)

tape drive An electronic device that uses a read/write head to transfer information to and from magnetic tape. (Chapter 4)

team leader The manager of day-to-day work of the team who ensures that overall objectives of the project are met. (Chapter 16)

technical feasibility Element of a feasibility study that determines that the technology exists to pursue the project. (Chapter 12)

telecommunications The combination of a computer with a communications link a modem and appropriate communications software to become a communications tool. (Chapter 7)

telecommuting The process of working at home using either a personal computer or terminal tied into a mainframe. (Chapters 7 and 18)

teleconferencing Scenario for using a GDSS in which members are divided into subgroups that are physically distant from one another. (Chapter 10)

teleprocessing The process of accessing computing power and computerized data files from a distance, generally using terminals and telecommunications facilities. (Chapter 7)

test data Data that are used in hand calculations to determine in advance the results expected from the program. (Chapter 13)

text management system A system that stores large amounts of text and graphics on CD-ROM so that users can find needed information easily. (Chapter 18)

text preparation The function of word processing on a personal computer, scanner, optical character reader software, or by using an electronic typewriter to produce text. (Chapter 2)

time cards A record of the times an employee enters or leaves the plant. (Chapter 8)

timesharing System providing access to mainframe hardware via terminals located at the user's place of business and offers the user the power of a mainframe computer for file storage and problem solving at a fraction of the cost associated with renting, leasing, or purchasing equipment. (Chapter 14)

token A special bit pattern used in a token sharing local area network to determine which user can transmit information. (Chapter 7)

token sharing network A local area network in which a bit pattern, called a token, is used to determine which user on the network can send information. (Chapter 7)

top-down development An approach to writing structured programs that breaks the program up into blocks or modules to be writtenindividually and then combined into the final program. (Chapter 13)

transaction cycle A series of tactical and operational activities that each require a transaction. (Chapter 8)

transaction log A list of all transactions that have been entered on the system. (Chapter 17)

transaction processing Converting raw data into a usable, electronic form. (Chapters 1 and 2)

transaction processing system (TPS) The type of information system used to convert raw data from operations into a machine readable form, store the transaction details, process the transactions, and if needed, print out the details of the transactions. (Chapters 2 and 8)

transactional data Data that are generated by the daily activities of the organization as it produces its goods and services and interacts with vendors and the customers. (Chapter 1)

transactional processing Processing data in an information system by either an online or batch method. (Chapter 2)

transistors Solid state elements on a chip which carry out the control and logic operations. (Chapter 4)

tree data model A data model in which each element has only one parent or owner. (Chapter 6)

turn-around documents Cards on which a worker enters only the time worked and the number of units processed. (Chapter 8)

turnkey system An acquisition method in which third parties do all the work and deliver it to the organization when the system is easy to use, and the organization just "turns the key" to operate it. (Chapters 12 and 14)

twisted pair wiring Transmission medium like that used in telephone lines. (Chapter 7)

U

universal product code (UPC) A bar code present on every product that allows organizations to store product numbers into the register's internal memory that is matched with the price, sale, and discount information. (Chapter 8)

unprogrammed decision Decisions requiring judgment and insight, are nonroutine, and have no agreed upon procedure for making the decision. (Chapters 2, 3, and 10)

unstructured decisions Another name for unprogrammed decisions. (Chapters 2, 3, and 10)

user friendly A software package that is easy to use. (Chapter 4)

user interface A dialogue base that handles the interaction between the system and the user. (Chapters 2, 4, and 11)

user's manual A set of directions for the use of software packages. (Chapter 4)

user's view The information that the user sees as he or she interfaces with the computer to use information for decision making, reporting, or carrying out day-to-day transactions; the report, output display, and input menu. (Chapter 6)

V

value-added network Public networks available by subscription to provide clients with data communications facilities. (Chapters 7 and 14)

value-added vendors Vendors who add value to a system beyond that of the original suppliers by combining the various hardware and software components into a useful combination. (Chapters 7 and 14)

variance The difference between information that is reported and the actual standards. (Chapter 9)

vendor contract A contract stating which system an organization wants to purchase or lease. (Chapter 14)

verification The data entry process is repeated, and the information being entered is compared with the information already on the disk. (Chapter 5)

video disk A read-only form of secondary storage using a laser or optical disk. (Chapter 4)

videotex The process of shopping, banking, or managing stocks and bonds from the home using a computer and communications link. (Chapter 7)

voice input A form of input to computers that uses the spoken word to enter data and instructions; also called voice recognition. (Chapters 11 and 18)

voice mail Extension of the telephone that allows the sending, receiving, storage, and relaying of the spoken messages, which the recipient can access at his or her discretion. (Chapter 2)

voltage surge An electrical disturbance, such as lightening, that causes a sudden increase in electrical supply and can destroy delicate chips and other electrical parts. (Chapter 17)

W

weighted comparison A method for determining which hardware or software system is desired by management based on characteristics. (Chapter 14)

wide area network A network covering more than a single building. (Chapter 7)

word processing software Software designed to manipulate letters, digits, and punctuation marks to compose letters, papers, and documents. (Chapter 4)

work orders Documents prepared in the beginning of the conversion cycle to replenish finished goods inventory when stock gets below a certain point or to produce a new order when such action is in compliance with the production plan. (Chapter 8)

working model prototype Prototype that actually works, but it is not as efficient as the final product. (Chapter 15)

Index